An Introduction to Project Management, Sixth Edition

With a Brief Guide to Microsoft Project Professional 2016

By

Kathy Schwalbe

Professor Emeritus, Augsburg College

Department of Business Administration

Minneapolis, Minnesota

An Introduction to
Project Management, Sixth Edition

Cover Photo: Dan Schwalbe

©2017 Schwalbe Publishing
ISBN-13: 978-1544701899
ISBN-10: 1544701896

Published by Schwalbe Publishing in Minneapolis, MN, September 2017.

Free companion website at ***www.intropm.com***.

Visit ***www. pmtexts.com*** or ***www.kathyschwalbe.com*** for more information on this and other books by Kathy Schwalbe.

For Dan, Anne, Bobby, and Scott
My husband and children continue to be my inspiration.
My son-in-law, Jeremy, and grandson, Freddie,
are welcome additions to our family!

BRIEF TABLE OF CONTENTS

DETAILED TABLE OF CONTENTS

PREFACE

The rapidly changing world has made organizations appreciate the need for good project, program, and portfolio management skills more than ever. Many organizations, including corporations, government agencies, non-profit organizations, colleges, and universities have responded to this need by establishing courses and programs in project management. Hundreds of books are now available on this topic.

After publishing the first two editions of this book, my publisher, Course Technology, now a branch of Cengage Learning, decided not to update it. They publish other books with higher sales, including my *Information Technology Project Management* book, now in its eighth edition. I personally used this text, *An Introduction to Project Management*, in my project management courses at Augsburg College since 2001 because most of my students were not majoring in information technology (IT) fields. I thank Cengage Learning for giving me the rights to self-publish the third and subsequent editions and permission to use some of the content from my IT book. I am also thankful for learning how to self-publish. I also self-published Healthcare Project Management in 2013 (after several people asked me to do so) with co-author Dan Furlong. I hope to keep writing books for years to come. If you have suggestions, let me know!

What makes this book different from other project management books? First of all, people actually enjoy reading it. I get emails every week from readers like you who appreciate my straight-forward, organized writing style. They like the way that I explain concepts and then provide realistic examples to help them learn to apply those concepts. Since I use this text in my own classes, I get a lot of feedback from students and see first-hand what works and does not work in a classroom setting. Several people have commented that they like the cartoons, Jeopardy games on the companion website, and my honest, sometimes humorous style. Project management can be a boring subject, but I think it's one of the most exciting topics and careers, especially if you want to change the world for the better.

This text addresses the need for people in *all* majors and industries to understand and apply good project, program, and portfolio management. It includes many real-world examples in the "What Went Right," "What Went Wrong," "Media Snapshot," "Best Practice," and "Video Highlights" segments. People like to read about and watch videos about real projects to learn from the successes and failures of others. They also realize that there are projects in all aspects of life, from remodeling a house to running a political campaign to developing a new software application.

I'm most excited about the fact that this book provides comprehensive samples of applying various tools and techniques to a realistic project. Many people learn best by example, so I've provided detailed examples of applying project management to a project everyone can relate to. I have never come across a textbook that presents project management concepts and then brings them to life in a fully developed sample project. I also provide template files for creating the sample documents. I believe this approach helps many people truly understand and apply good project management.

NEW TO THE SIXTH EDITION

Building on the success of the previous editions, *An Introduction to Project Management, Sixth Edition* introduces a uniquely effective combination of features. The main changes include the following:

- The entire text has been updated to align with PMI's *A Guide to the Project Management Body of Knowledge (PMBOK® Guide) – Sixth Edition*.

- Chapter 1 includes a new section on the PMI Talent Triangle and the importance of leadership skills.

- Chapter 2 includes a new section on using an agile approach to project planning

- Updated examples and references are provided throughout the text, and user feedback is incorporated.

- The free book website has been updated. New information will be added to the site as needed, and the Links tab will be continuously updated to provide links to recent articles and sites.

APPROACH

This text provides up-to-date information on how good project, program, and portfolio management can help you achieve organizational as well as individual success. Distinct features of this text include its:

- relationship to the Project Management Body of Knowledge as a derivative work

- instructions on using Microsoft Project 2016 and other resources

- use of MindView software

- comprehensive samples of applying tools and techniques to a realistic project

- inclusion of templates and seamless integration of various software applications

- robust and free companion website

PMBOK® Guide Framework

The Project Management Institute (PMI) created *A Guide to the Project Management Body of Knowledge* (the *PMBOK® Guide*) as a framework for understanding project management. The *PMBOK® Guide* is, however, just that—a guide. This text uses the *PMBOK® Guide – Sixth Edition* as a foundation, but goes beyond it by providing more details, highlighting additional topics, and providing a real-world context for project, program, and portfolio management.

Instructions for using Microsoft Project 2016 and other resources

Appendix A of the text includes basic information on project management software and detailed, step-by-step instructions on using the number one stand-alone product, Microsoft Project 2016. You do not need to buy a separate book to learn how to use Project 2016 effectively. Appendix B provides information on other resources, including companion websites, templates, and other project management tools. Appendix C provides detailed information instructors can use for assigning case studies, real and fictitious, as part of their classes.

Examples of using MindView and Basecamp software

Many people like to create mind maps to perform a SWOT analysis, create a WBS, and perform other creative activities. This text includes examples of using MindView software by MatchWare, Inc. and access to a free trial of this software. It also includes a brief user guide for using Basecamp, a totally online project management tool.

Comprehensive Samples of Applying Tools and Techniques to a Realistic Project

After explaining basic concepts, tools, and techniques, this text shows the reader how an organization selected, initiated, planned, executed, monitored and controlled, and closed a realistic project, called the Just-In-Time Training project. It provides *over 50 sample project management deliverables* such as a business case, stakeholder register, project charter, project management plan, work breakdown structure, Gantt chart, cost baseline, Pareto chart, resource histogram, performance report, risk register, contract, lessons-learned report, and so on for this project. You can also access the template files used to create them from the free companion website for this text or from the author's personal website. As one reviewer stated:

> It comprehensively communicates what it really takes to manage a large project, including required deliverables, work products, and documentation. I haven't seen either a text or documentation in industry which communicates this subject this comprehensively or this accurately. (Gilbert S. Leonard, Adjunct Professor and retired project manager, Exxon Mobil Corporation)

Provides Templates and Seamless Integration of Various Software Applications

You do not have to reinvent the wheel when it comes to much of the documentation required for managing projects. This text uses over 50 free template files for creating various documents, spreadsheets, diagrams, and charts. Various software applications are used throughout the text in a seamless fashion. I purposely created the templates in a simple format. Feel free to modify them to meet your needs.

Includes a Free Companion Website (www.intropm.com)

A companion website provides you with a one-stop location to access informative links and tools to enhance your learning. This site will be a valuable resource as you access links mentioned in the text, take online quizzes, and download templates and files for Project 2016. Instructors can access a protected instructor site, which includes the same information plus copyrighted lecture slides, solution files, sample syllabi, and other information. Instructors can also share information on how they use this text in their classes

ORGANIZATION AND CONTENT

An Introduction to Project Management, Sixth Edition, is organized into ten chapters and three appendices. The first two chapters introduce project, program, and portfolio management and discuss different approaches for their selection. You'll read about Global Construction, Inc. and how they decided to pursue the Just-In-Time Training project. The next seven chapters follow the five process groups of project management: initiating, planning (broken down into three chapters), executing, monitoring and controlling, and closing. These seven chapters apply various tools and techniques in each of these process groups to the Just-In-Time Training project. Chapter ten describes recent information and research on best practices. Appendix A provides general information on project management software and a step-by-step guide to using Microsoft Project Professional 2016. Appendix B includes resource information, and Appendix C provides several running case studies students can use to apply what they have learned to real or fictitious projects.

PEDAGOGICAL FEATURES

Several pedagogical features are included in this text to enhance presentation of the materials so that you can more easily understand the concepts and apply them. Throughout the text, emphasis is placed on applying concepts to up-to-date, real-world project management.

Learning Objectives, Chapter Summaries, Quick Quizzes, Discussion Questions, Exercises, Team Projects, and Case Studies

Learning Objectives, Chapter Summaries, Quick Quizzes, Discussion Questions, Exercises, Team Projects, and Case Studies are designed to function as integrated study tools. Learning Objectives reflect what you should be able to accomplish after completing each chapter. Chapter Summaries highlight key concepts you should master. The Quick Quizzes help reinforce your understanding of important concepts in each chapter. The Discussion Questions help guide critical thinking about those key concepts. Exercises provide opportunities to practice important techniques, as do the Team Projects. The Case Studies in Appendix C provide a robust means to apply what you have learned from the text to realistic case studies, similar to the example used throughout the text.

Opening Case and Case Wrap-Up

To set the stage, each chapter begins with an opening case related to the materials in that chapter. These scenarios spark interest and introduce important concepts in a real-world context. As project management concepts and techniques are discussed, they are applied to the opening case and other similar scenarios. Each chapter then closes with a Case Wrap-Up—some problems are overcome and some problems require more effort—to further illustrate the real world of project management.

What Went Right? and What Went Wrong?

Failures, as much as successes, can be valuable learning experiences. Carl Hixson, a program manager at Oracle and adjunct instructor who uses this text, said he loves the anonymous quote, "We need to learn from people's mistakes because we'll never have time to make them all ourselves." Each chapter of the text includes one or more examples of real projects that went right as well as examples of projects that went wrong. These examples further illustrate the importance of mastering key concepts in each chapter.

Media Snapshots, Best Practice, and Video Highlights

The world is full of projects. Several television shows, movies, newspapers, websites, and other media highlight project results, good and bad. Relating project management concepts to all types of projects, as highlighted in the media, will help you understand and see the importance of this growing field. Why not get people excited about studying project management by showing them how to recognize project management concepts in popular television shows, movies, or other media? It is also important to study best practices so readers can learn how to implement project management in an optimum way. Many students also enjoy watching videos to enhance their understanding of topics, so each chapter includes summaries and links to relevant videos.

Cartoons

Each chapter includes a cartoon used with permission from the popular website xkcd.com. These cartoons use humor to illustrate concepts from the text.

Key Terms

The field of project management includes many unique terms that are vital to creating a common language and understanding of the field. Key terms are displayed in boldface and are defined the first time they appear. Definitions of key terms are provided in alphabetical order at the end of each chapter and in a glossary at the end of the text.

Application Software

Learning becomes much more dynamic with hands-on practice using the top project management software tools in the industry, Microsoft Project 2016, MindView, Basecamp, as well as other tools, such as spreadsheet software. Each chapter offers you many opportunities to get hands-on experience and build new software skills by applying concepts to problems posed for them. In this way, the text accommodates both those who learn by reading and those who learn by doing.

SUPPLEMENTS

The following supplemental materials are available when this text is used in a classroom setting. All of the teaching tools available with this text are provided to the instructor on a secure website. Instructors must contact me at schwalbe@augsburg.edu to gain access.

- **Instructor's Manual:** The Instructor's Manual that accompanies this textbook includes additional instructional material to assist in class preparation, including suggestions for lecture topics and additional discussion questions.

- **PowerPoint Presentations:** The instructor site for this text includes lecture slides for each chapter created with Microsoft PowerPoint. These slides provide a teaching aid for classroom presentation, and they can be made available to students on the organization's secure network for online review. Instructors can modify slides or add their own slides for additional topics they introduce to the class.

- **Solution Files:** Solutions to end-of-chapter questions are on the instructor site.

- **Test Banks:** In addition to the Quick Quiz questions in the text and interactive quizzes available from *www.intropm.com*, the secure instructor site includes hundreds of additional test questions in various formats.

- **Student Online Companion:** As mentioned earlier, the free student site includes links to sites mentioned in the text, template files, interactive quizzes, and other helpful resources, especially from the Links tab.

ACKNOWLEDGEMENTS

I thank my many colleagues and experts in the field who contributed information to this book. I especially thank the main reviewers for this edition: Angela Trego, PhD, PE, PMP® from Utah Valley University; Don R. James, PMP®, Adjunct Professor, Lone Star College in Houston, Texas and Founder/Principal Consultant, PMO To Go, LLC; Peter Monkhouse, P.Eng. MBA, PMP®, University of Toronto School of Continuing Studies, Certificate Advisor, Project Management Program; and my proof reader, Gary Liebert, Ph.D. James Stewart from American University in Maryland, Ray Roche from the Canberra Institute of Technology in Australia, and Cindy LeRouge from St. Louis University provided reviews and edits of prior editions. I also thank Randall Munroe, creator of xkcd.com, for allowing me to use his great comics.

I want to thank my students and colleagues at Augsburg College, the University of Minnesota, and corporate classes for providing input. Special thanks to Janet Phetsamone, Ong Thao, and Kendal Vue for their inputs on using Basecamp. I received many valuable comments from them on ways to improve my materials and courses. I am also grateful for the examples students and instructors around the world provide and the questions they ask in classes or via email. I learn new aspects of project management and teaching by interacting with students, faculty, and staff.

Most of all, I am grateful to my family. Without their support, I never could have written this book. My wonderful husband, Dan, was very patient and supportive, as always. His expertise as a lead software developer for Milner Technologies (formerly ComSquared Systems) comes in handy, too. Our three children, Anne, Bobby, and Scott, continue to be very supportive of their mom's work. Our children all understand the main reason why I write—I have a passion for educating future leaders of the world, including them.

As always, I am eager to receive your feedback on this book. Please send all feedback to me at schwalbe@augsburg.edu

Kathy Schwalbe, Ph.D., PMP®
Professor, Department of Business Administration
Augsburg College

ABOUT THE AUTHOR

Kathy Schwalbe was a Professor in the Department of Business Administration at Augsburg College in Minneapolis, where she taught courses in project management, problem solving for business, systems analysis and design, information systems projects, and electronic commerce. She retired from teaching in May 2015 to focus on writing, traveling, and enjoying life! Kathy was also an adjunct faculty member at the University of Minnesota, where she taught a graduate-level course in project management in the engineering department. She also provides training and consulting services to several organizations and speaks at numerous conferences. Kathy's first job out of college was as a project manager in the Air Force. She worked for 10 years in industry before entering academia in 1991. She was an Air Force officer, project manager, systems analyst, senior engineer, and information technology consultant. Kathy is an active member of PMI, having served as the Student Chapter Liaison for the Minnesota chapter, VP of Education for the Minnesota chapter, Editor of the ISSIG Review, Director of Communications for PMI's Information Systems Specific Interest Group, member of PMI's test-writing team, and writer for the community posts. Kathy earned her Ph.D. in Higher Education at the University of Minnesota, her MBA at Northeastern University's High Technology MBA program, and her B.S. in mathematics at the University of Notre Dame. She was named Educator of the Year in 2011 by the Association of Information Technology Professionals (AITP) Education Special Interest Group (EDSIG). Kathy lives in Minnesota with her husband, Dan. They enjoy being empty-nesters after raising three children. Visit her personal website at www.kathyschwalbe.com and the text site at www.intropm.com.

Other books by Kathy Schwalbe:

Information Technology Project Management, Eighth Edition (Boston: Cengage Learning, 2016).

Appendix A: Brief Guide to Microsoft Project Professional 2016 (Minneapolis: Schwalbe Publishing, 2016).

Healthcare Project Management, co-authored with Dan Furlong, (Minneapolis: Schwalbe Publishing, 2013).

.

Chapter 1

An Introduction to Project, Program, and Portfolio Management

LEARNING OBJECTIVES

After reading this chapter, you will be able to:

- Understand the growing need for better project, program, and portfolio management

- Explain what a project is, provide examples of projects, list various attributes of projects, and describe project constraints

- Describe project management and discuss key elements of the project management framework, including project stakeholders, the project management knowledge areas, common tools and techniques, project success factors, and project benefits measurement

- Discuss the relationship between project, program, and portfolio management and their contributions to enterprise success

- Describe the project management profession, including the role of project managers and suggested skills, the role of professional organizations like the Project Management Institute, the importance of certification and ethics, project management careers, and the growth of project and portfolio management software

OPENING CASE

Doug Milis, the Chief Executive Officer (CEO) of Global Construction, Inc., was summarizing annual corporate highlights to the board of directors. Like many other large construction companies, they had a very difficult year. After having scaled down operations a few years ago, this past year they had trouble finding enough qualified workers to meet the growing demand for new construction. When one of the board members asked what he was most proud of that year, Doug thought for a few seconds, and then replied,

"Excellent question, Gabe. Honestly, I think the main reason we survived this year was because we are truly a project-based organization. We have dramatically improved our ability to quickly select and implement projects that help our company succeed and cancel or redirect other projects. All our projects align with our business strategies, and we have consistent processes in place for getting things done. We can also respond quickly to market changes, unlike many of our competitors. Marie Scott, our Director of the Project Management Office (PMO), has done an outstanding job in making this happen. And believe me, it was not easy. It's never easy to implement changes across an entire company. But with this new capability to manage projects across the organization, I am very confident that we will have continued success in years to come."

INTRODUCTION

Many people and organizations today have a new or renewed interest in project management. In the past, project management primarily focused on providing schedule and resource data to top management in just a few industries, such as the military and construction industries. Today's project management involves much more, and people in every industry and every country manage projects. New technologies have become a significant factor in many businesses, and the use of interdisciplinary and global work teams has radically changed the work environment. The facts below demonstrate the significance of project management:

- Demand for projects continues to increase, with GDP contributions from project-oriented industries forecasted to be US$20.2 trillion by 2017. Employers will need 87.7 million individuals working in project management-oriented roles by 2027. "The talent gap could result in a potential loss of some US$207.9 billion in GDP through 2027."[1]

- "Job Outlook 2017" says the market is good for college graduates who demonstrate the most important attribute employers want: the ability to work as part of a team.[2]

- Organizations waste $97 million for every $1 billion spent on projects, according to Project Management Institute's (PMI's) 2017 Pulse of the Profession® report. That represents a 20% improvement from the previous year. Organizations realize that excelling at project management definitely affects the bottom line.[3]

- The United States (U.S.) signed The Program Management Improvement and Accountability Act (PMIAA) into law in December 2016 to enhance best practices in project and program management throughout the federal government.

- In 2015, the average salary for someone in the project management profession in U.S. dollars was $108,200 per year in the U.S.; $134,000 in Switzerland, (the highest-paid country); and $19,602 in Egypt (the lowest-paid country). These average salaries do not include bonuses. The average total compensation for project management workers in the U.S., for example, was $130,000. Of the 9,677 people from the U.S. who responded to PMI's salary survey, 81% had the Project Management Professional (PMP®) credential, and their salary was over 22% higher than those without it. This data is based on responses from over 26,000 people in 34 countries.[4]

- It is also interesting to note that 38% of the salary survey respondents were women, 11% had a degree in project management, and the project management department or Project Management Office (PMO) was the department most listed at 31%.[5]

- Project management is also a vital skill for personal success. Managing a family budget, planning a wedding, remodeling a house, completing a college degree, and many other personal projects can benefit from good project management.

WHAT WENT WRONG?

In 1995, the Standish Group published an often-quoted study entitled "CHAOS." This prestigious consulting firm surveyed 365 information technology (IT) executive managers in the U.S. who managed more than 8,380 IT application projects. As the title of the study suggests, the projects were in a state of chaos. U.S. companies spent more than $250 billion each year in the early 1990s on approximately 175,000 IT application development projects. Examples of these projects included creating a new database for a state department of motor vehicles, developing a new system for car rental and hotel reservations, and implementing a client-server architecture for the banking industry. Their study reported that the overall success rate of IT projects was only 16.2 percent. The surveyors defined success as meeting project goals on time and on budget.

The study also found that more than 31 percent of IT projects were canceled before completion, costing U.S. companies and government agencies more than $81 billion. The authors of this study were adamant about the need for better project management in the IT industry. They explained, "Software development projects are in chaos, and we can no longer imitate the three monkeys—hear no failures, see no failures, speak no failures."[6]

In a later study, PricewaterhouseCoopers surveyed 200 companies from 30 different countries about their project management maturity and found that over half of all projects failed. They also found that only 2.5 percent of corporations consistently met their targets for scope, schedule, and cost goals for all types of projects. These statistics made people understand the need to improve the practice of project management.[7]

Although several researchers question the methodology of the CHAOS studies, their popularity has prompted organizations throughout the world to examine their practices in managing projects. Managers are recognizing that to be successful, they need to be conversant with and use modern project management techniques. People from all types of disciplines—science, liberal arts, education, business, etc.—can benefit from basic project management principles. Individuals are realizing that to remain competitive, they must develop skills to effectively manage the professional and personal projects they undertake. They also realize that many of the concepts of project management, especially interpersonal skills, will help them as they work with people on a day-to-day basis.

Organizations claim that using project management provides advantages, such as:
- Better control of financial, physical, and human resources
- Improved customer relations
- Shorter development times
- Lower costs
- Higher quality and increased reliability
- Higher profit margins
- Improved productivity
- Better internal coordination
- Higher worker morale

In addition to project management, organizations are embracing program and portfolio management to address enterprise-level needs. This chapter introduces projects and project management, describes the differences between project, program, and portfolio management, discusses the role of the project manager, and provides important background information on this growing profession.

WHAT IS A PROJECT?

To discuss project management, it is important to understand the concept of a project. A **project** is "a temporary endeavor undertaken to create a unique product, service, or result."[8] Operations, on the other hand, is work done in organizations to sustain the business. Projects are different from operations in that they end when their objectives have been reached or the project has been terminated.

Examples of Projects

Projects can be large or small and involve one person or thousands of people. They can be done in one day or take years to complete. Examples of projects include the following:

- A young couple hires a firm to design and build them a new house
- A retail store manager works with employees to display a new clothing line
- A college campus upgrades its technology infrastructure to provide wireless Internet access
- A medical technology firm develops a device that connects to smart phones
- A school implements new government standards for tracking student achievement
- A group of musicians starts a company to help children develop their musical talents
- A pharmaceutical company launches a new drug
- A television network develops a system to allow viewers to vote for contestants and provide other feedback on programs
- The automobile industry develops standards for electric cars
- A government group develops a program to track child immunizations

VIDEO HIGHLIGHTS

PMI recognizes outstanding performance in project management by announcing a Project of the Year award winner. Their website lists winners since 1989, and videos summarize several award-winning projects, such as the following:

- 2016: National Synchrotron Light Source II, New York USA
- 2015: El Segundo Refinery Coke Drum Reliability Project, California USA
- 2014: AP60 Phase 1 Project, Jonquiere, Quebec, Canada

You can also see how project management was used on much older projects. Mark Kozak-Holland wrote a book in 2011 called "The History of Project Management." In describing his book, the author states the following: "Think about the Giza Pyramid, the Parthenon, the Colosseum, the Gothic Cathedrals of Medieval Europe, the great voyages of exploration, the Taj Mahal, and the mega projects of the industrial revolutions. Was project management used on these projects? Were the concepts of project management even understood? Can we connect modern and ancient project management?" A 5-minute video does an excellent job of showing how project management was used in building the Giza Pyramid as viewers listen to music while seeing images and text on the screen. You can find this and other videos on the companion website for this text at www.intropm.com.

Project Attributes

As you can see, projects come in all shapes and sizes. The following attributes help to further define a project:

- *A project has a unique purpose.* Every project should have a well-defined objective. For example, many people hire firms to design and build a new house, but each house, like each person, is unique.

- *A project is temporary.* A project has a definite beginning and a definite end. For a home construction project, owners usually have a date in mind when they'd like to move into their new home.

- *A project drives change and enables value creation.* A project is initiated to bring about a change in order to meet a need or desire. Its purpose is to achieve a specific objective which changes the context (a living situation, in this house project example) from a current state to a more desired or valued future state.

- *A project is developed using progressive elaboration or in an iterative fashion.* Projects are often defined broadly when they begin, and as time passes, the specific details of the project become clearer. For example, there are many decisions that must be made in planning and building a new house. It works best to draft preliminary plans for owners to approve before more detailed plans are developed.

- *A project requires resources, often from various areas.* Resources include people, hardware, software, or other assets. Many different types of people, skill sets, and resources are needed to build a home.

- *A project should have a primary customer or sponsor.* Most projects have many interested parties or stakeholders, but someone must take the primary role of sponsorship. The **project sponsor** usually provides the direction and funding for the project.

- *A project involves uncertainty.* Because every project is unique, it is sometimes difficult to define the project's objectives clearly, estimate exactly how long it will take to complete, or determine how much it will cost. External factors also cause uncertainty, such as a supplier going out of business or a project team member needing unplanned time off. Uncertainty is one of the main reasons project management is so challenging, because uncertainty invokes risk.

A good project manager contributes to a project's success. **Project managers** work with the project sponsors, the project team, and the other people involved in a project to define, communicate, and meet project goals. Unlike the pilot captain in the comic in Figure 1-1, project managers (and real pilots, too) must be professional on the job. You can develop skills to help manage uncertainty and other challenges you will face in managing projects.

Figure 1-1. Captain speaking (www.xkcd.com)

Project Constraints

Every project is constrained in different ways. Some project managers focus on scope, schedule, and cost constraints. These limitations are sometimes referred to in project management as the **triple constraint**. To create a successful project, project managers must consider scope, schedule, and cost and balance these three often-competing goals. They must consider the following:

- *Scope*: What work will be done as part of the project? What unique product, service, or result does the customer or sponsor expect from the project?
- *Schedule*: How long should it take to complete the project? What is the timeline?
- *Cost*: What should it cost to complete the project? What is the project's budget? What resources are needed?

Other people focus on the quadruple constraint, which adds quality as a fourth constraint.

- *Quality*: How good does the quality of the products or services need to be? What do we need to do to satisfy the customer?

The *PMBOK® Guide – Sixth Edition* suggests these four constraints *plus* risk and resources, but states that there may be others as well, depending on the project. Figure 1-2 shows these six constraints. The triple constraint goals—scope, schedule, and cost—often have a specific target at the beginning of the project. For example, a couple might initially plan to move into their new 2,000 square foot home in six months and spend $300,000 on the entire project. The couple will have to make many decisions along the way that may affect meeting those goals. They might need to increase the budget to meet scope and time goals or decrease the scope to meet time and budget goals. The other three constraints—quality, risk, and resources—affect the ability to meet scope, schedule, and cost goals. Projects by definition involve uncertainty and resources, and the customer defines quality. No one can predict with one hundred percent accuracy what risks might occur on a project. Resources (people) working on the house might produce different results at different quality levels, and material resources may vary as well. Customers cannot define their quality expectations in detail for a project on day one. These three constraints often affect each other as well as the scope, schedule, and cost goals of a project.

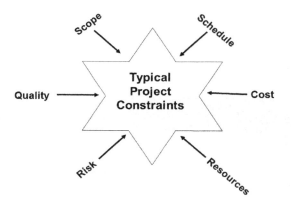

Figure 1-2. Typical project constraints

For example, the couple may have picked out a certain type of flooring for most of their home early in the design process, but that supplier may have run out of stock, forcing them to choose a different flooring to meet the schedule goal. This issue may affect the cost of the project. Projects rarely finish according to the discrete scope, schedule, and cost goals originally planned. Instead of discrete target goals for scope, schedule, and cost, it is often more realistic to set a range of goals that allow for uncertainties, such as spending between $275,000 and $325,000 and having the home completed within five to seven months. These goals allow for inevitable changes due to risk, resources, and quality considerations.

Experienced project managers know that you must decide which constraints are most important on each particular project. If time is most important, you must often change the initial scope and/or cost goals to meet the schedule. You might have to accept more risk and lower quality expectations. If scope goals are most important, you may need to adjust schedule and/or cost goals, decrease risk, and increase quality expectations. If communications is most important, you must focus on that. If there are set procurement goals or constraints, that knowledge might be key to the project. In any case, sponsors must provide some type of target goals for a project's scope, schedule, and cost and define other key constraints for a project. The project manager should be communicating with the sponsor throughout the project to make sure the project meets his or her expectations.

How can you avoid the problems that occur when you meet scope, schedule, and cost goals, but lose sight of customer satisfaction? The answer is *good project management, which includes more than meeting project constraints.*

WHAT IS PROJECT MANAGEMENT?

Project management is "the application of knowledge, skills, tools and techniques to project activities to meet the project requirements."[9] Project managers must not only strive to meet specific scope, schedule, cost, resource, risk, and quality requirements of projects, they must also facilitate the entire process to meet the needs and expectations of the people involved in or affected by project activities.

Figure 1-3 illustrates a framework to help you understand project management. Key elements of this framework include the project stakeholders, project management process groups, knowledge areas, tools and techniques, project success, and the contribution of a portfolio of projects to the success of the entire enterprise. Each of these elements of project management is discussed in more detail in the following sections.

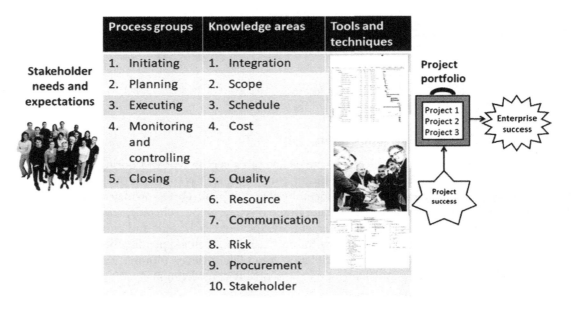

Figure 1-3. Project management framework

Project Stakeholders

Stakeholders are the people involved in or affected by project activities and include the project sponsor, project team, support staff, customers, users, suppliers, and even opponents to the project. These stakeholders often have very different needs and expectations. For example, there are several stakeholders involved in a home construction project.

- The project sponsors would be the potential new homeowners. They would be the people paying for the house and could be on a very tight budget, so they would expect the contractor to provide accurate estimates of the costs involved in building the house. They would also need a realistic idea of when they could move in and what type of home they could afford given their budget constraints. The new homeowners would have to make important decisions to keep the costs of the house within their budget. Can they afford to finish the basement right away? If they can afford to finish the basement, will it affect the projected move-in date? In this example, the project sponsors are also the customers and users for the product, which is the house.

- The project manager in this example would normally be the general contractor responsible for building the house. He or she needs to work with all the project stakeholders to meet their needs and expectations.

- The project team for building the house would include several construction workers, electricians, carpenters, and so on. These stakeholders would need to know exactly what work they must do and when they need to do it. They would need to know if the required materials and equipment will be at the construction site or if they are expected to provide the materials and equipment. Their work would need to be coordinated since there are many interrelated factors involved. For example, the carpenter cannot put in kitchen cabinets until the walls are completed.

- Support staff might include the employers of the homeowners, the general contractor's administrative assistant, and other people who support other stakeholders. The employers of the homeowners might expect their employees to complete their work but allow some flexibility so they can visit the building site or take phone calls related to building the house. The contractor's administrative assistant would support the project by coordinating meetings between the buyers, the contractor, suppliers, and other stakeholders.

- Building a house requires many suppliers. The suppliers would provide the wood, windows, flooring materials, appliances, and other items. Suppliers would expect exact details on what items they need to provide, where and when to deliver those items, and similar information.

- Additional stakeholders would include the city council and mayor, who would be interested in increasing revenues. They might suggest certain guidelines for the minimum value of the homes for providing adequate property taxes. The city may also have regulations to ensure the safety of the public in the area of the construction site. The local housing inspector would also be a stakeholder, concerned with ensuring that everything meets specific codes and regulations.

- There may or may not be opponents to a project. In this example, there might be a neighbor who opposes the project because the workers are making so much noise that she cannot concentrate on her work at home, or the noise might awaken her sleeping children. She might interrupt the workers to voice her complaints or even file a formal complaint. Alternatively, the neighborhood might have association rules concerning new home design and construction. If the homeowners did not follow these rules, they might have to halt construction due to legal issues.

As you can see from this example, there are many different stakeholders on projects, and they all have different interests. Stakeholders' needs and expectations are important in the beginning and throughout the life of a project. Successful project managers develop good relationships with project stakeholders to understand and meet their needs and expectations.

Project Management Process Groups and Knowledge Areas

The five **project management process groups** include initiating, planning, executing, monitoring and controlling, and closing activities. Chapter 3 provides more information on the process groups and how they relate to the ten project management knowledge areas. **Project management knowledge areas** describe the key competencies that project managers must develop. Project managers must have knowledge and skills in all ten of these areas, briefly described as follows:

- Project integration management is an overarching function that coordinates the work of all other knowledge areas. It affects and is affected by all other knowledge areas.
- Project scope management involves working with all appropriate stakeholders to define, gain written agreement for, and manage all the work required to complete the project successfully.
- Project schedule management includes estimating how long it will take to complete the work, developing an acceptable project schedule given cost-effective use of available resources, and ensuring timely completion of the project.
- Project cost management consists of preparing and managing the budget for the project.
- Project quality management ensures that the project will satisfy the stated or implied needs for which it was undertaken.
- Project resource management is concerned with making effective use of the people and physical resources needed for the project.
- Project communications management involves generating, collecting, disseminating, and storing project information.
- Project risk management includes identifying, analyzing, and responding to risks related to the project.
- Project procurement management involves acquiring or procuring goods and services for a project from outside the performing organization.
- Project stakeholder management focuses on identifying project stakeholders, understanding their needs and expectations, and engaging them appropriately throughout the project. Note that PMI renamed project time management to

project schedule management and project human resource management to project resource management in the *PMBOK® Guide – Sixth Edition* in 2017.

Project Management Tools and Techniques

Thomas Carlyle, a famous historian and author, stated, "Man is a tool-using animal. Without tools he is nothing, with tools he is all." As the world continues to become more complex, it is even more important for people to develop and use tools, especially for managing important projects. **Project management tools and techniques** assist project managers and their teams in carrying out work in all ten knowledge areas. For example, some popular schedule-management tools and techniques include Gantt charts, project network diagrams, and critical path analysis. Figure 1-4 lists some commonly used tools and techniques by knowledge area. You will learn more about these and other tools and techniques throughout this text.

Knowledge Area/Category	Tools and Techniques
Integration management	Project selection methods, project management methodologies, project charters, project management plans, **project management software, change requests**, change control boards, project review meetings, **lessons-learned reports**
Scope management	**Scope statements, work breakdown structures**, mind maps, statements of work, **requirements analyses**, scope management plans, scope verification techniques, and scope change controls
Schedule management	**Gantt charts**, project network diagrams, critical-path analyses, crashing, fast tracking, schedule performance measurements
Cost management	Net present value, return on investment, payback analyses, earned value management, project portfolio management, cost estimates, cost management plans, cost baselines
Quality management	Quality metrics, checklists, quality control charts, Pareto diagrams, fishbone diagrams, maturity models, statistical methods
Resource management	Motivation techniques, empathic listening, responsibility assignment matrices, project organizational charts, resource histograms, team building exercises
Communications management	Communications management plans, **kickoff meetings**, conflict management, communications media selection, **status and progress reports**, virtual communications, templates, project websites
Risk management	Risk management plans, risk registers, probability/impact matrices, risk rankings
Procurement management	Make-or-buy analyses, contracts, requests for proposals or quotes, source selections, supplier evaluation matrices
Stakeholder management	Stakeholder registers, stakeholder analyses, issue logs, interpersonal skills, reporting systems

Figure 1-4. Common project management tools and techniques by knowledge area
Note: The bolded items are "super tools."

A survey of 753 project and program managers was conducted to rate several project management tools. Respondents were asked to rate tools on a scale of 1–5 (low to high) based on the extent of their use and the potential of the tools to help improve project success. "Super tools" were defined as those that had high use and high potential for improving project success. These super tools included software for task scheduling (such as project management software), scope statements, requirements analyses, and lessons-learned reports. Tools that were already extensively used and have been found to improve project performance included progress reports, kick-off meetings, Gantt charts, and change requests. These super tools are bolded in Figure 1-4.[10]

The *PMBOK® Guide – Sixth Edition* now lists tools and techniques based on their purpose, as follows:

- *Data gathering*: benchmarking, brainstorming, check sheets, checklists, focus groups, interviews, market research, questionnaires and surveys, statistical sampling

- *Data analysis*: alternatives analysis, assessment of other risk parameters, assumption and constraint analysis, cost of quality, cost-benefit analysis, decision tree analysis, document analysis, earned value analysis, influence diagrams, iteration burndown chart make-or-buy analysis, performance reviews, process analysis, proposal evaluation, regression analysis reserve analysis, risk data quality assessment, risk probability and impact assessment, root cause analysis, sensitivity analysis, simulation stakeholder analysis SWOT analysis, technical performance analysis, trend analysis, variance analysis, and what-if scenario analysis

- *Data representation*: affinity diagrams, cause-and-effect diagrams, control charts, flow charts, hierarchical charts, histograms, logical data models, matrix diagrams, matrix-based charts, mind mapping, probability and impact matrix, scatter diagrams, stakeholder engagement assessment matrix, stakeholder mapping/representation, and text-oriented formats

- *Decision making*: multi-criteria decision analysis and voting

- *Communication*: feedback and presentations

- *Interpersonal and team skills*: active listening, communication styles assessment, conflict management, cultural awareness, decision making, emotional intelligence, facilitation, influencing, leadership, meeting management, motivation, negotiation, networking, nominal group, observation/conversation, political awareness, team building

- *Ungrouped*: advertising, agile release planning, analogous estimating, audits, bidder conferences, bottom-up estimating, change control tools, claims administration, colocation, communication methods, communication models, communication requirements analysis, communication technology, context diagram, contingent response strategies, cost aggregation, critical path method, decomposition, dependency determination and integration, design for X, expert judgment, financing, funding limit reconciliation, ground rules, historical information review, individual and team assessments, information management, inspections, knowledge management, leads and lags, meetings, organization theory, parametric estimating, pre-assignment, precedence diagramming method, problem solving, product analysis, project management information system, project reporting, prompt lists, prototypes, quality improvement methods, recognition and rewards, representations of uncertainty, resource optimization, risk categorization, rolling wave planning, schedule compression, schedule network analysis, source selection analysis, strategies for opportunities strategies for overall project risk, strategies for threats, test and inspection planning, testing/product evaluations, three-point estimating, to-complete performance index, training, virtual teams

These long lists of tools and techniques can be overwhelming. This text will focus on those used most often and with the most potential, providing the context and detailed examples for using them. It is crucial for project managers and their team members to determine which tools will be most useful for their particular projects. Selecting the appropriate tools and techniques (as well the processes, inputs, outputs, and life cycle phases, discussed later in this book) is part of project tailoring. Project management should be tailored to meet the unique needs of projects, organizations, and most importantly, people. After all, projects are done by, and for, people.

Despite its advantages, project management is not a silver bullet that guarantees success on all projects. Some projects, such as those involving new technologies, have a higher degree of uncertainty, so it is more difficult to meet their scope, schedule, and cost goals. Project management is a very broad, often complex discipline. What works on one project may not work on another, so it is essential for project managers to continue to develop their knowledge and skills in managing projects. It is also important to learn from the mistakes and successes of past projects.

Project Success

How do you define the success or failure of a project? There are several ways to define project success. The list that follows outlines a few common criteria for measuring project success as applied to the example project of building a new 2,000 square foot home within six months for $300,000:

- The project met scope, schedule, and cost goals. If the home was 2,000 square feet and met other scope requirements, was completed in six months, and cost $300,000, we could call it a successful project based on these criteria. Note that the CHAOS studies mentioned in the What Went Right? and What Went Wrong? examples used this definition of success.

- The project satisfied the customer/sponsor. Even if the project met initial scope, schedule, and cost goals, the couple paying for the house might not be satisfied. Perhaps the project manager never returned their calls and was rude to them or made important decisions without their approval. Perhaps the quality of some of the construction or materials was not acceptable. If the customers were not happy about important aspects of the project, it would be deemed a failure based on this criterion. Many organizations implement a customer satisfaction rating system for projects to measure project success.

- The results of the project met its main objective, such as making or saving a certain amount of money, providing a good return on investment, or simply making the sponsors happy. If the couple liked their new home and neighborhood after they lived there for a while, even if it cost more or took longer to build or the project manager was rude to them, it would be a successful project based on this criterion. As another example, suppose the owners wanted to keep the house for just a few years and then sell it for a good return. If that happened, the couple would deem the project a success, regardless of other factors involved. Note that for many projects done to meet ROI objectives, financial success cannot be determined until sometime after the project is completed.

Project managers play a vital role in helping projects succeed. Project managers work with the project sponsors, the project team, and the other stakeholders involved in a project to meet project goals. They also work with the sponsor to define success for that particular project. Good project managers do not assume that their definition of success is the same as the sponsors' definition. They take the time to understand their sponsors' expectations. For example, if you are building a home for someone, find out what is most important:

- Meeting scope, schedule, and cost goals of the project to build the home
- Satisfying other needs, such as communicating in a certain way
- Ensuring the project delivers a certain result, such as providing the home of the owners' dreams or a good return on investment.

WHAT WENT RIGHT?

Follow-up studies by the Standish Group (see the previously quoted "CHAOS" study in the What Went Wrong? passage) showed improvement in the statistics for IT projects:

- The number of successful projects (those completed on time, on budget with a satisfactory result) was 29 percent in 2015 based on a sample of over 50,000 software development projects worldwide. The number of failed projects (those canceled or not used after implementation) was 19 percent. That leaves 52% of projects as challenged (over budget, late, and/or poorly implemented). These numbers include projects of all sizes and methodologies.
- The 2015 CHAOS study also summarized the success rates of projects by size, showing that 62% of small projects were successful from 2011-2015 compared to only 2% of grand, 6% of large, 9% of medium, and 21% of moderate size projects. Small projects are obviously easier to complete successfully.
- Agile approaches were also measured across all project sizes from 2011-2015, showing that 39% of all agile projects were successful compared to 11% of waterfall projects. For small projects, 58% of agile projects were successful compared to 44% of waterfall projects. About 10,000 projects were included for these statistics.[11]

The success criteria should help you to develop key performance indicators (KPIs) needed to track project progress. It is important to document this information in enough detail to eliminate ambiguity. A project benefits management plan should be created early in the project life cycle and updated as needed, as described in later chapters.

PROGRAM AND PROJECT PORTFOLIO MANAGEMENT

About one-quarter of the world's gross domestic product is spent on projects. Projects make up a significant portion of work in most business organizations or enterprises, and successfully managing those projects is crucial to enterprise success. Two important concepts that help projects meet enterprise goals are the use of programs and project portfolio management.

Programs

A **program** is "a group of related projects, subsidiary programs, and program activities managed in a coordinated manner to obtain benefits not available from managing them individually." [12] Programs are not large projects; a **megaproject** is a very large project that typically costs over US $1 billion, affects over one million people, and lasts several years.

MEDIA SNAPSHOT

Popular Mechanics provides a list (including photos) of the 25 most impressive megaprojects throughout the world. Several are listed below, showing the time and cost required to complete them (US$):

- Panama Canal Expansion Project, Panama, Central America: 11 years, $5.25 billion. The original canal was built in 1914. The expansion project widened and deepened the canal to allow for larger ships.
- Port Mann Bridge, Vancouver, British Columbia, Canada: 6 years, $1.92 billion. Port Mann Bridge is the second largest bridge in North America, spanning 6,866 feet.
- Three Gorges Dam, China: 17 years, $22 billion. This dam on the Yangtze River is 595 feet tall, 131 feet wide, and over 7,600 feet long, with 32 main turbines producing electricity. [13]

As you can imagine, it is often more economical to group projects together to help streamline management, staffing, purchasing, and other work. The following are examples of programs (Figure 1-5 illustrates the first program in the list).

- A construction firm has programs for building single-family homes, apartment buildings, and office buildings, as shown in Figure 1-5. Each home, apartment building, and office building is a separate project for a specific sponsor, but each type of building is part of a program. There would be several benefits to managing these projects under one program. For example, for the single-family homes, the program manager could try to get planning approvals for all the homes at once, advertise them together, and purchase common materials in bulk to earn discounts.
- A clothing firm has a program to analyze customer-buying patterns. Projects under this program might include one to send out and analyze electronic surveys, one to conduct several focus groups in different geographic locations with different types of buyers, and a project to develop an information system to help collect and analyze current customers' buying patterns.

- A government agency has a program for children's services, which includes a project to provide pre-natal care for expectant mothers, a project to immunize newborns and young children, and a project for developmental testing for pre-school children, to name a few.

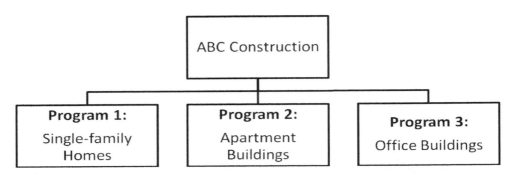

Figure 1-5. Example programs

A **program manager** provides leadership and direction for the project managers heading the projects within the program. Program managers also coordinate the efforts of project teams, functional groups, suppliers, and operations staff supporting the projects to ensure that project products and processes are implemented to maximize benefits. Program managers are responsible for more than the delivery of project results; they are change agents responsible for the success of products and processes produced by those projects.

Program managers often have review meetings with all their project managers to share important information and coordinate important aspects of each project. Many program managers worked as project managers earlier in their careers, and they enjoy sharing their wisdom and expertise with their project managers. Effective program managers recognize that managing a program is much more complex than managing a single project. In addition to skills required for project managers, program managers must also possess strong business knowledge, leadership capability, and communication skills.

Project Portfolio Management

A **portfolio** is defined as "projects, programs, subsidiary portfolios, and operations managed as a group to achieve strategic objectives."[14] Many organizations support an emerging business strategy of project portfolio management (also called just portfolio management) by continuously selecting and managing the optimum set of projects and programs to deliver maximum business value.

Portfolio managers need to understand how projects fit into the bigger picture of the organization, especially in terms of corporate strategy, finances, and business risks. They create portfolios based on meeting specific organizational goals, such as maximizing the value of the portfolio or making effective use of limited resources. Portfolio managers help their organizations make wise investment decisions by helping to select and analyze projects from a strategic perspective. Portfolio managers may or may not have previous experience as project or program managers. It is most important that they have strong financial and analytical skills and understand how projects and programs can contribute to meeting strategic goals.

The main distinction between project or program management and portfolio management is a focus on meeting tactical versus strategic goals. Tactical goals are generally more specific and short-term than strategic goals, which emphasize long-term goals for an organization. Individual projects and programs often address tactical goals, whereas portfolio management addresses strategic goals. Project and program management address questions like:

- Are we carrying out projects well?

- Are projects on time and budget?

- Do project stakeholders know what they should be doing?

Portfolio management addresses questions like:

- Are we working on the right projects?

- Are we investing in the right areas?

- Do we have the right resources to be competitive?

There can be portfolios for all types of projects. For example:

- In a construction firm, strategic goals might include increasing profit margins on large projects, decreasing costs on supplies, and improving skill levels of key workers. Projects could be grouped into these three categories for portfolio management purposes.

- In a clothing firm, strategic goals might include improving the effectiveness of IT, introducing new clothing lines, reducing inventory costs, and increasing customer satisfaction. These might be the main categories for their portfolio of projects.

- A government agency for children's services could group projects into a portfolio based on strategies such as improving health, providing education, and so on to help make optimum decisions on use of available funds and resources.

Figure 1-6 provides a comparative overview of project, program, and portfolio management. **Organizational project management** is a "framework in which portfolio, program, and project management are integrated with organizational enablers in order to achieve strategic objectives." [15]

Organizational Project Management

	Projects	Programs	Portfolios
Definition	A project is a temporary endeavor undertaken to create a unique product, service, or result.	A program is a group of related projects, subsidiary programs and program activities that are managed in a coordinated way to obtain benefits not available from managing them individually.	A portfolio is a collection of projects, programs, subsidiary portfolios, and operations managed as a group to achieve strategic objectives.
Management	Project managers manage the project team to meet the project objectives.	Programs are managed by program managers who ensure that program benefits are delivered as expected, by coordinating the activities of a program's components.	Portfolio managers may manage or coordinate portfolio management staff, or program and project staff that may have reporting responsibilities into the aggregate portfolio.
Monitoring	Project managers monitor and control the work of producing the products, services, or results that the project was undertaken to produce	Program managers monitor the progress of program components to ensure the overall goals, schedules, budget, and benefits of the program will be met.	Portfolio managers monitor strategic changes and aggregate resource allocation, performance results, and risk of the portfolio.
Success	Success is measured by product and project quality, timeliness, budget compliance, and degree of customer satisfaction.	A program's success is measured by the program's ability to deliver its intended benefits to an organization, and by the program' efficiency and effectiveness in delivering those benefits.	Success is measured in terms of the aggregate investment performance and benefit realization of the portfolio.

Figure 1-6. Organizational project management framework (parts of figure)
Source: Project Management Institute, Inc., *A Guide to the Project Management Body of Knowledge (PMBOK® Guide) – Sixth Edition* (2017).

Organizations group projects into portfolios to help them make better investment decisions, such as increasing, decreasing, discontinuing, or changing specific projects or programs based on their financial performance, risks, resource utilization, and similar factors that affect business value. If a construction firm has much higher profit margins on apartment buildings than single-family homes, for example, it might choose to pursue more apartment building projects. The firm might also create a new project to investigate ways to increase profits for single-family home projects. On the other hand, if the company has too many projects focused on financial performance and not enough focused on improving its work force, the portfolio manager might suggest initiating more projects to support that strategic goal. Just like a personal financial portfolio, a business's portfolio should be diversified to account for risk.

By grouping projects into portfolios, organizations can better tie their projects to meeting strategic goals. Portfolio management can also help organizations do a better job of managing its human resources by hiring, training, and retaining workers to support the projects in the organization's portfolio. For example, if the construction firm needs more people with experience in building apartment buildings, they can make necessary adjustments by hiring or training current workers in the necessary skills.

THE PROJECT MANAGEMENT PROFESSION

As you can imagine, good project managers should have a variety of skills. Good program and portfolio managers often need additional skills and experience in managing projects and understanding organizational strategies. This section describes some of the skills that help you manage projects, and you will learn many more throughout this text. If you are serious about considering a career in project management, you should consider becoming a certified Project Management Professional. You should also be familiar with some of the project management software products available on the market today.

Suggested Skills for Project, Program, and Portfolio Managers

Project managers and their teams must develop knowledge and skills in the following areas:

- All ten project management knowledge areas
- The application area (domain, industry, market, etc.)
- The project environment (politics, culture, change management, etc.)
- General business (financial management, strategic planning, etc.)
- Human relations (leadership, motivation, negotiations, etc.)

An earlier section of this chapter introduced the ten project management knowledge areas, as well as some tools and techniques that project managers use. The application area refers to the application to which project management is applied. For example, a project manager responsible for building houses or apartment buildings should understand the construction industry, including standards and regulations important to that industry and those types of construction projects. A project manager leading a large software development project must know a lot about that application area. A project manager in education, entertainment, the government, and other fields must understand those application areas. The application area is defined by the product, service, or result. Many organizations have defined their approach to creating specific products. The project is about applying that approach, i.e., the product defines the project.

The project environment differs from organization to organization and project to project, but there are some skills that will help in most project environments. These skills include understanding change, and understanding how organizations work within their social, political, and physical environments. Project managers must be comfortable leading and handling change, since most projects introduce changes in organizations and involve changes within the projects themselves. Project managers need to understand the organizations they work in and how products are developed and services are provided. For example, it takes different skills and behavior to manage a project for a Fortune 100 company in the U.S. than it does to manage a government project for a new business in Poland or India. It also takes different skills and behaviors to manage a project in the construction industry from one in the entertainment or pharmaceutical industry.

Project managers should also possess general business knowledge and skills. They should understand important topics related to financial management, accounting, procurement, sales, marketing, contracts, manufacturing, distribution, logistics, the supply chain, strategic planning, tactical planning, operations management, organizational structures and behavior, personnel administration, compensation, benefits, career paths, and health and safety practices. On some projects, it will be critical for project managers to have substantial experience in one or several of these general business areas. On other projects, project managers can delegate detailed responsibility for some of these areas to a team member, support staff, or even a supplier. Even so, the project managers must be intelligent and experienced enough to know which of these areas are most important and who is qualified to do the work. They must also make and/or take responsibility for all key project decisions.

Achieving high performance on projects requires human relations skills, also known as *soft skills*. Some of these soft skills include effective communication, influencing the organization to get things done, leadership, motivation, negotiation, conflict management, and problem solving. Project managers must lead their project teams by providing vision, delegating work, creating an energetic and positive environment, and setting an example of appropriate and effective behavior. Project managers must focus on teamwork skills in order to use their people effectively. They need to be able to motivate different types of people and develop *esprit de corps* within the project team and with other project stakeholders.

PMI Talent Triangle and the Importance of Leadership Skills

PMI developed a talent triangle to emphasize the types of skills project managers need to continuously develop. The talent triangle includes:

1. *Technical project management skills:* Understanding the knowledge areas, process groups, and project management tools and techniques fall into this category.

2. *Strategic and business management skills:* Topics include strategic planning (described in more detail in Chapter 2), financial management, accounting, marketing, and other topics listed in the previous section.

3. *Leadership skills:* Leadership and management are terms often used interchangeably, although there are differences. Generally, a **leader** focuses on long-term goals and big-picture objectives, while inspiring people to reach those goals. A **manager** often deals with the day-to-day details of meeting specific goals. Some people say that, "Managers do things right, and leaders do the right things." "Leaders determine the vision, and managers achieve the vision." "You lead people and manage things."

Leadership is a soft skill, and there is no one best way to be a leader. Peter Northouse, author of a popular text called *Leadership: Theory and Practice*, says, "In the past 60 years, as many as 65 different classification systems have been developed to define the dimensions of leadership."[16] Some classification systems focus on group processes, while others focus on personality traits or behaviors. For example, the *PMBOK® Guide – Sixth Edition* briefly describes the following leadership styles:

1. **Laissez-faire**: Meaning "let go," this hands-off approach lets teams determine their own goals and how to achieve them.
2. **Transactional**: This management by exception approach focuses on achieving goals or compliance by offering team members appropriate rewards and punishments.
3. **Servant leader**: People using this approach focus on relationships and community first and leadership is secondary.
4. **Transformational**: By working with others to identify needed changes, these leaders empower others and guide changes through inspiration.
5. **Charismatic**: These people can inspire others based on their enthusiasm and confidence.
6. **Interactional**: This leadership style is a combination of transactional, transformational, and charismatic.

There are many different leadership styles in addition to the six listed above, and the one thing most experts agree on is that the best leaders are able to adapt their style to the needs of the situation.

Daniel Goleman, author of *Emotional Intelligence*, also wrote a book called *Primal Leadership*, which describes six different styles of leadership and situations where they are most appropriate:

1. *Visionary*: Needed when an organization needs a new direction, and the goal is to move people towards a new set of shared dreams. The leader articulates where the group is going, but lets them decide how to get there by being free to innovate, experiment, and take calculated risks.
2. *Coaching*: One-on-one style that focuses on developing individuals, showing them how to improve their performance. This approach works best with workers who show initiative and request assistance.
3. *Affiliative*: Emphasizes the importance of team work and creating harmony by connecting people to each other. This approach is effective when trying to increase morale, improve communication, or repair broken trust.
4. *Democratic*: Focuses on people's knowledge and skills and creates a commitment to reaching shared goals. This leadership style works best when the leader needs the collective wisdom of the group to decide on the best direction to take for the organization.
5. *Pacesetting*: Used to set high standards for performance. The leader wants work to be done better and faster and expects everyone to put forth their best effort.
6. *Commanding*: Most often used, also called autocratic or military style leadership. This style is most effective in a crisis or when a turnaround is needed.

"The goal for leaders should be to develop a solid understanding of the different styles of leadership and their implications, and reach the point where choosing the right one for the situation becomes second nature to them."[17]

Project managers often take on the role of both leader and manager. Good project managers know that people make or break projects, so they must set a good example to lead their team to success. They are aware of the greater needs of their stakeholders and organizations, so they are visionary in guiding their current projects and in suggesting future ones.

As mentioned earlier, program managers need the same skills as project managers. They often rely on their past experience as project managers, strong business knowledge, leadership capability, and communication skills to handle the responsibility of overseeing the multiple projects that make up their programs. It is most important that portfolio managers have strong financial and analytical skills and understand how projects and programs can contribute to meeting strategic goals.

Companies that excel in project, program, and portfolio management grow project leaders, emphasizing development of business and leadership skills. Instead of thinking of leaders and managers as specific people, it is better to think of people as having leadership skills, such as being visionary and inspiring, and management skills, such as being organized and effective. Therefore, the best project, program, and portfolio managers have leadership and management characteristics; they are visionary yet focused on the bottom line. Above all else, they focus on achieving positive results!

See the Resources link on the companion website (www.intropm.com) for additional readings related to leadership as well as other important topics, including project management certification, as discussed in the following section.

MEDIA SNAPSHOT

A **best practice** is "an optimal way recognized by industry to achieve a stated goal or objective."[18] Robert Butrick, author of The Project Workout, wrote an article on best practices in project management for the Ultimate Business Library's Best Practice book. He suggests that organizations need to follow basic principles of project management, including these two mentioned earlier in this chapter:

•   Make sure your projects are driven by your strategy. Demonstrate how each project you undertake fits your business strategy, and screen out unwanted projects as soon as possible.
•   Engage your stakeholders. Ignoring stakeholders often leads to project failure. Be sure to engage stakeholders at all stages of a project, and encourage teamwork and commitment at all times. Use leadership and open communications to make things happen.[19]

Project Management Certification

Professional certification is an important factor in recognizing and ensuring quality in a profession. The **Project Management Institute (PMI)** is a global professional society for project and program managers. PMI provides certification as a **Project Management Professional (PMP®)**—someone who has documented sufficient project experience, agreed to follow the PMI code of professional conduct, and demonstrated knowledge of the field of project management by passing a comprehensive examination.

The number of people earning PMP® certification continues to increase. In 1993, there were about 1,000 certified project management professionals. By the end of December, 2016 there were 745,891 active certified project management professionals. There were also 32,868 CAPM®s (Certified Associates in Project Management).[20]

Figure 1-7 shows the rapid growth in the number of people earning project management professional certification from 1993 through 2016. Although most PMP®s are in the U.S. and Canada, the PMP® credential is growing in popularity in several countries, such as Japan, China, and India. There are also requirements to maintain active certification status by continuing to develop expertise related to the PMI talent triangle of technical project management, strategic and business management, and leadership.

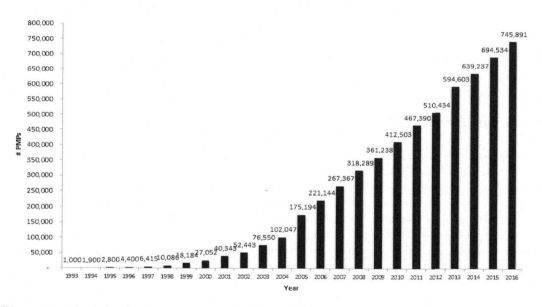

Figure 1-7. Growth in PMP® certification, 1993–2016

Some companies are requiring that all project managers be PMP® certified. Project management certification is also enabling professionals throughout the world to share a common base of knowledge and terminology. For example, any person with PMP® certification can list, describe, and use the ten project management knowledge areas. Sharing a common base of knowledge and set of terminology is important because it helps advance the theory and practice of project management.

Many colleges, universities, and companies around the world now offer courses related to various aspects of project management. You can even earn bachelors, masters, and doctoral degrees in project management. PMI reported in 2008 that of the 280 institutions it has identified that offer degrees in project management, 103 are in mainland China. "When Western companies come into China they are more likely to hire individuals who have PMP®

certification as an additional verification of their skills. In our salary survey, the salary differences in IT, for example, was dramatic. A person with certification could make five to six times as much salary, so there is a terrific incentive to get certified and work for these Western companies." [21] Today, there are even more degree programs in project management. A recent gradschools.com search for "project management" found 370 campus and online accredited graduate, certificate, and doctoral programs from all types of institutions. PMI also manages a Global Accreditation Center (GAC), listing 110 GAC accredited programs in 2017.

PMI Student Membership and Certification Information

As a student, you can join PMI for a reduced fee ($32 vs. $139 in 2017). Consult PMI's website (*www.pmi.org*) for more information. You can network with other students studying project management by joining a local chapter. Many welcome students to attend free events, including job networking. You can volunteer to help develop your skills and serve your community. Students should consider earning the Certified Associate in Project Management (CAPM®) credential from PMI. If you complete a bachelor's degree, you do not need any work experience to earn the CAPM®. However, if you have enough work experience, the PMP® is more marketable. See the companion website (www.intropm.com) section called Links for more information on certification and several other topics.

Ethics in Project Management

Ethics, loosely defined, is a set of principles that guide our decision making based on personal values of what is "right" and "wrong." Making ethical decisions is an important part of our personal and professional lives because it generates trust and respect with other people. Project managers often face ethical dilemmas. For example, several projects involve different payment methods. If a project manager can make more money by doing a job poorly, should he or she do the job poorly? No! If a project manager is personally opposed to the development of nuclear weapons, should he or she refuse to manage a project that helps produce them? Yes! Ethics guide us in making these types of decisions.

PMI approved a new Code of Ethics and Professional Conduct effective January 1, 2007. This code applies not only to PMP®s, but to all PMI members and individuals who hold a PMI certification, apply for a PMI certification, or serve PMI in a volunteer capacity. It is vital for project management practitioners to conduct their work in an ethical manner. Even if you are not affiliated with PMI, these guidelines can help you conduct your work in an ethical manner, which helps the profession earn the confidence of the public, employers, employees, and all project stakeholders. The PMI Code of Ethics and Professional Conduct includes short chapters addressing vision and applicability, responsibility, respect, fairness, and honesty. A few excerpts from this document include the following:

"As <u>practitioners</u> in the global project management community:

2.2.1   We make decisions and take actions based on the best interests of society, public safety, and the environment.

2.2.2   We accept only those assignments that are consistent with our background, experience, skills, and qualifications.

2.2.3.   We fulfill the commitments that we undertake—we do what we say we will do.

3.2.1   We inform ourselves about the norms and customs of others and avoid engaging in behaviors they might consider disrespectful.

3.2.2   We listen to others' points of view, seeking to understand them.

3.2.3   We approach directly those persons with whom we have a conflict or disagreement.

4.2.1   We demonstrate transparency in our decision-making process.

4.2.2   We constantly reexamine our impartiality and objectivity, taking corrective action as appropriate.

4.3.1   We proactively and fully disclose any real or potential conflicts of interest to appropriate stakeholders.

5.2.1   We earnestly seek to understand the truth.

5.2.2   We are truthful in our communications and in our conduct."[22]

In addition, PMI added a new series of questions to the PMP® certification exam in March 2002 and continues to include this topic to emphasize the importance of ethics and professional responsibility.

Project Management Careers

How does one become a project manager? In the past, many people became project managers by accident. They had never heard of the job title, and their organizations did not have a real career path for project managers. They may have led a small project part-time and then been thrown into the role of project manager on a larger project. Today, individuals and organizations often take a more proactive approach. Some people study project management in college and enter the field upon graduation, often as a project coordinator. Others gain expertise in a certain industry and/or application area in a more technical capacity and then move into project management when they believe (or their bosses believe) they can lead a team. Some people earn the CAPM® or PMP® certification to move into project management roles within their own companies or at different ones.

The need for project managers is evident in recent studies and job postings.

- Between 2010 and 2020, 15.7 million new project management roles will be created globally across seven project-intensive industries. Along with job growth, there will be a significant increase in the economic footprint of the profession; the project management profession is slated to grow by USD$6.61 trillion.[23]

- Indeed.com, a popular job search site, listed over 354,000 jobs in the U.S. when searching for project manager in March 2017. Cities with the most openings included New York City, Chicago, Seattle, San Francisco, and Washington, D.C.

- Sixty percent of hiring managers say interest in project management careers among younger job applicants has grown over the past decade. Suggestions for young people interested in breaking into and succeeding in project management include earning a certification (such as the PMP® or CAPM®), volunteering for leadership roles, speaking up for a position, and learning to delegate and empower team members.[24]

What is a typical career path for project managers? Being a project manager is a demanding yet rewarding profession, for the right person. Many people start off leading a small project related to their current job, part-time, to make sure they are cut out for and enjoy the work. Some organizations require their people to have a few years of experience before they let them lead any projects. Others hire entry-level people with the title of project coordinator or project manager.

Many organizations realize that they need to provide a structured career path to develop and maintain their talent pipeline for project managers. After leading a small project, many people go on to lead multiple small projects, larger projects, or become program managers. Some organizations have different levels of project managers, often based on knowledge and experience.

What if you do not want to stay in a project management career path? You can often go back to your former, more technical position, and move along that career path. Or, many ex-project managers move into higher level management positions, such as director, vice president, or even CEO. Some become consultants, educators, or entrepreneurs. Their experience leading projects makes them marketable in several different careers.

Project Management Software

The project management and software development communities have definitely responded to the need to provide more software to assist in managing projects. There are hundreds of tools available, ranging from free online or smart phone apps to enterprise tools costing thousands of dollars to implement and high monthly fees per user. Deciding which project management software to use has become a project in itself. Microsoft Project continues to lead the Project Portfolio Management (PPM) market with 35% of the $874 million market, followed by Oracle (19%), ServiceNow, Inc. (7%), and SAP and Autodesk (5% each).[25]

See Appendix A for details on the various configurations available for Microsoft Project and detailed instructions for using Project Professional 2016, the product available for a free trial. This section provides a summary of the basic types of project management software available and references for finding more information.

Free Trials and Information on Using Project 2016, MindView, Basecamp, and Other Software

A 60-day evaluation copy of Microsoft Project is available from Microsoft's website. Note that the trial is for Project Professional 2016, which requires Windows. You can also access a 30-day trial version of MindView software for PCs, Macs, or an online version at *www.matchware.com*. Basecamp is a totally online project management tool. Educators can request a free Basecamp account without a time restriction from *www.basecamp.com*. See Appendix A for a guide to using Project 2016 and Appendix B for information on MindView and Basecamp. There are many other tools available, and most offer free trials.

Many people still use basic productivity software such as Microsoft Word and Excel to perform many project management functions, including determining project scope, schedule, and cost, assigning resources, and preparing project documentation. People often use productivity software instead of specialized project management software because they already have it and know how to use it. However, there are hundreds of project management software tools that provide specific functionality for managing projects. These project management software tools can be divided into three general categories based on functionality and price:

- *Low-end tools*: These tools provide basic project management features and generally cost less than $200 per user or a low monthly fee for online software. They are often recommended for small projects and single users. Most of these tools allow users to create Gantt charts, which cannot be done easily using current productivity software. Some of these tools are available online while others are stand-alone desktop applications. There are also several smart phone applications, and many online tools include smart phone integration. Examples of popular low-end tools include BaseCamp (described further in Appendix B), Smartsheet, and Trello.

- *Midrange tools*: A step up from low-end tools, midrange tools are designed to handle larger projects, multiple users, and multiple projects. All of these tools can produce Gantt charts and network diagrams, and can assist in critical path analysis, resource allocation, project tracking, status reporting, and other tasks. Prices range from about $200 to $600 per user or require a monthly fee per user. Microsoft Project (Professional, to be specific) is still the most widely used project management software today in this category and in general. Figure 1-8 provides a screen shot from showing a Gantt chart for a project that you can create by following the steps in Appendix A. There is also an enterprise or PPM version of Microsoft Project, as described briefly below and in more detail from Microsoft's website.

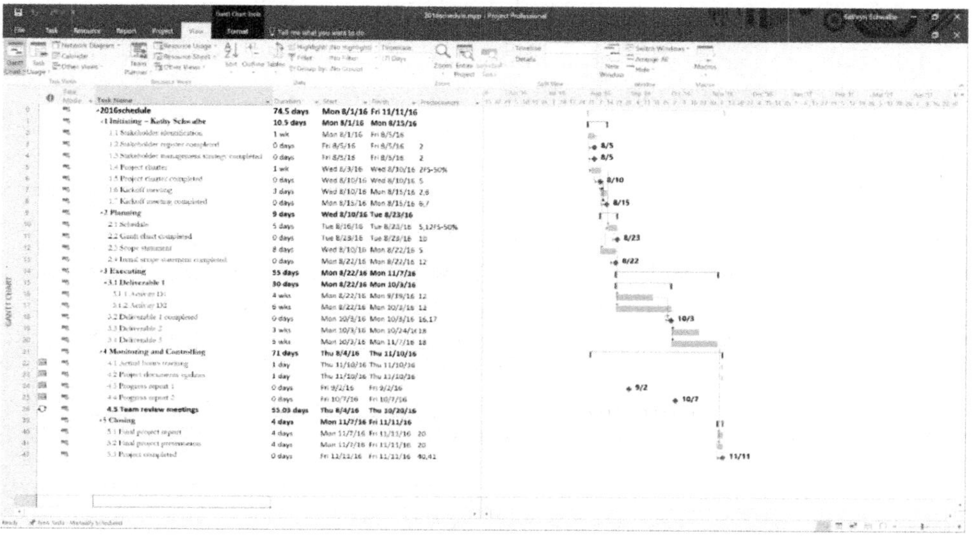

Figure 1-8. Screenshot from Microsoft Project Professional showing a Gantt chart

- *High-end tools*: Another category of project management software is high-end tools, sometimes referred to as PPM or enterprise project management software, as described earlier. These tools provide robust capabilities to handle very large projects, dispersed workgroups, and enterprise and portfolio management functions that summarize and combine individual project information to provide an enterprise view of all projects. These products are generally licensed on a per-user basis, integrate with enterprise database management software, and are accessible via the Internet and smart phones. In mid-2002, Microsoft introduced the first version of their Enterprise Project Management software, and in 2003, they introduced the Microsoft Enterprise Project Management solution, which was updated several times since then. In 2008, Oracle acquired Primavera Software, Inc., another popular tool for project-intensive industries.

Several free or open-source tools are also available. For example, ProjectLibre, LibrePlan, and OpenProject are all free open-source project management tools. Remember, however, that these tools are developed, managed, and maintained by volunteers and may not be well supported. See Appendix B for information on several tools, including Basecamp, which provides free accounts for educators with no time limitation.

By the end of the twentieth century, people in virtually every industry around the globe began to investigate and apply different aspects of project, program, and portfolio management. The sophistication and effectiveness with which organizations use these concepts and tools today is influencing the way companies do business, use resources, and respond to market needs with speed and accuracy. As mentioned earlier, there are many reasons to study project, program, and portfolio management. The number of projects continues to grow, the complexity of these projects continues to increase, and the profession of project management continues to expand and mature. Many colleges, universities, and companies now offer courses related to various aspects of project, program, and portfolio management. The growing number of projects and the evidence that good project management really can make a difference continue to contribute to the growth of this field.

CASE WRAP-UP

Another board member asked Doug Milis, the CEO, to describe more about what the PMO Director did to help the company become more successful at managing projects. He explained how Marie Scott worked with him and all the VPs to reorganize several parts of the company to support their new emphasis on project, program, and project portfolio management. They formed a project team to implement a web-based project management software tool across the enterprise. They formed another team to develop project-based reward systems for all employees. They also authorized funds for a project to educate all employees in project management and to develop a mentoring program for project, program, and project portfolio managers. Doug and Marie had successfully convinced everyone that effectively selecting and managing projects was crucial to their company's future. The board and the company's shareholders were very pleased with the results.

CHAPTER SUMMARY

There is a new or renewed interest in project management today as the number of projects continues to grow and their complexity continues to increase. The majority of projects fail to meet scope, schedule, and cost goals, costing organizations millions of dollars. Using a more disciplined approach to managing all types of projects can help organizations succeed.

A project is a temporary endeavor undertaken to create a unique product, service, or result. Projects are developed incrementally; they require resources, have a sponsor, and involve uncertainty. The triple constraint of project management refers to managing the scope, schedule, and cost dimensions of a project.

Project management is the application of knowledge, skills, tools, and techniques to project activities to meet project requirements. Stakeholders are the people involved in or affected by project activities. A framework for project management includes the project stakeholders, project management knowledge areas, and project management tools and techniques. The ten knowledge areas are project integration management, scope, schedule, cost, quality, human resource, communications, risk, procurement, and stakeholder management.

A program is a group of related projects, subsidiary programs, and program activities managed in a coordinated manner to obtain benefits not available from managing them individually. Project portfolio management involves organizing and managing projects and programs as a portfolio of investments that contribute to the entire enterprise's success. Portfolio management emphasizes meeting strategic goals while project management focuses on tactical goals.

The profession of project management continues to grow and mature. Project, program, and portfolio managers play key roles in helping projects and organizations succeed. They must perform various duties, possess many skills, and continue to develop skills in project management, general management, and their application area, such as IT, healthcare, or construction. Soft skills, especially leadership, are particularly important for project managers. The Project Management Institute (PMI) is an international professional society that provides certification as a Project Management Professional (PMP®) and upholds a code of ethics. The number of people earning PMP® certification continues to grow. Demand for project managers is high, and several organizations provide defined career paths. Hundreds of project management software products are available to assist people in managing projects. Microsoft Project is the most popular.

QUICK QUIZ

Note that you can find additional, interactive quizzes at www.intropm.com

1. Which of the following statements is false?
    A. Demand for project managers continues to increase.
    B. Employers prefer college graduates with the ability to work as part of a team.
    C. Organizations waste $97 million for every $1 billion spent on projects, according to a 2017 PMI report.
    D. According to PMI's salary survey, professionals with a PMP® credential earned 22% more than those without it.

2. Approximately what percentage of global projects fail, according to PricewaterhouseCoopers?
    A. 50%
    B. 30%
    C. 15%
    D. 75%

3. A _____ is a temporary endeavor undertaken to create a unique product, service, or result.
    A. program
    B. process
    C. project
    D. portfolio

4. Which of the following is not an attribute of a project?
    A. projects are unique
    B. projects are developed using progressive elaboration
    C. projects have a primary customer or sponsor
    D. projects involve no uncertainty

5. Which of the following is not part of the triple constraint of project management?
    A. meeting scope goals
    B. meeting schedule goals
    C. meeting communications goals
    D. meeting cost goals

6. _____ is the application of knowledge, skills, tools and techniques to project activities to meet project requirements.
    A. Project management
    B. Program management
    C. Project portfolio management
    D. Requirements management

7.   Project portfolio management addresses _____ goals of an organization, while project management addresses _____ goals.
   A.   strategic, tactical
   B.   tactical, strategic
   C.   internal, external
   D.   external, internal

8.   Several individual housing projects done in the same area by the same firm might best be managed as part of a _____.
   A.   portfolio
   B.   program
   C.   investment
   D.   collaborative

9.   Which of the following skills is not part of PMI's project management talent triangle?
   A.   technical project management
   B.   strategic/business
   C.   application area
   D.   leadership

10.   What is the popular certification program called that the Project Management Institute provides?
   A.   Microsoft Certified Project Manager (MCPM)
   B.   Project Management Professional (PMP®)
   C.   Project Management Expert (PME)
   D.   Project Management Mentor (PMM)

Quick Quiz Answers

1. D, 2. A 3. C, 4. D, 5. C, 6. A, 7. A, 8. B, 9. C, 10. B

DISCUSSION QUESTIONS

1.   Why is there a new or renewed interest in the field of project management? What statistics presented provide the most motivation for you to study project management?
2.   What is a project, and what are its main attributes? How is a project different from what most people do in their day-to-day jobs? What is the triple constraint?
3.   What is project management? Briefly describe the project management framework, providing examples of stakeholders, knowledge areas, tools and techniques, and project success factors.
4.   Discuss the relationship between project, program, and portfolio management and their contribution to enterprise success.
5.   What are suggested skills for project managers? What is the PMI talent triangle? Discuss different leadership styles and your views on leadership.
6.   What role does PMI play in advancing the profession?

7.   What functions can you perform with project management software? What are the main differences between low-end, midrange, and high-end tools?

EXERCISES

Note: These exercises can be done individually or in teams, in-class, as homework, or in a virtual environment. Learners can either write their results in a paper or prepare a short presentation to show their results.

1.   Review PMI's website (www.pmi.org) and read and summarize one article from PM Network (a monthly magazine – under Learning, Publications). Write a one-page paper or prepare a short presentation summarizing key information and your opinion of the article.

2.   Read the latest PMI report called the "Pulse of the Profession." Download the entire report from www.pmi.org – under Learning, Publications. Write a one-page paper or prepare a short presentation summarizing key information and your opinion of the report.

3.   Find an example of a real project with a real project manager. Feel free to use projects in the media (the Olympics, television shows, movies, and so on) or a project from work, if applicable. Write a one-page paper or prepare a short presentation describing the project in terms of its scope, schedule, and cost goals and each of the project's attributes. Try to include information describing what went right and wrong on the project and the role of the project manager and sponsor. Also, describe whether you consider the project to be a success or not and why. Include at least one reference and proper citations.

4.   Go to *www.mastersinprojectmanagement.com* to search for graduate schools that offer courses and programs related to project management. Review schools by location and format. Summarize your findings and opinions in a short paper or presentation.

5.   Review information about various project management software tools. Also, investigate smart phone apps for project management. Write a one-page paper or prepare a short presentation summarizing your findings.

6.   Watch at least three videos of PMI's Project of the Year Award winners from PMI's website. Summarize key points from at least two of the videos. What did the project teams do to ensure success? What challenges did they face, and how did they overcome them? Write a short paper or prepare a presentation summarizing your findings.

7.   Research recent studies about project success, especially those that focus on benefits realization. Write a short paper or prepare a presentation summarizing your findings.

8.   Write a short paper or prepare a presentation summarizing your views of your personal leadership style and experience. How do you think people can improve their leadership skills?

9.   Research information about earning and maintaining PMP® and CAPM® certifications. See the Links section of www.intropm.com for some references. Summarize your findings in a short paper or presentation.

TEAM PROJECTS

1.   Find someone who works as a project manager or is a member of a project team. If possible, find more than one person. Use the interview guidelines below and ask the questions in person, via the phone, or via the Internet. Discuss the results with your team, and then prepare a one- to two-page paper or prepare a short presentation to summarize your findings.

Project Manager Interview Guidelines

Please note that these are guidelines and sample questions only. Use only the questions that seem appropriate, and feel free to add your own. If the interviewee wants to remain anonymous, that's fine. If not, please include his/her name and place of employment as a project manager in your paper. Let him/her know that you are doing this interview for a class assignment and that the information may be shared with others.

The main purpose of these interviews is for students to gain more insight into what project managers really do, what challenges they face, what lessons they've learned, what concepts/tools you're learning about that they really use, and what suggestions they have for you and other students as future team members and project managers. People often like to tell stories or relate particular situations they were in to get their points across. To this end, here are a few sample questions.

1) How did you get into project management?
2) If you had to rate the job of project manager on a scale of 1-10, with 10 being the highest, how would you rate it?
3) Briefly explain the reason for your rating. What do you enjoy most and what do you like least about being a project manager?
4) Did you have any training or special talents or experiences that qualified you to be a project manager? Are you certified or have you thought about becoming certified as a PMP®?
5) What do you feel is the most important thing you do as a project manager? On what task do you spend the most time each day?
6) What are some of the opportunities and risks you have encountered on projects? Please describe any notable successes and failures and what you have learned from them.
7) What are some of the tools, software or otherwise, that you use, and what is your opinion of those tools?
8) What are some steps a project manager can take to improve the effectiveness and efficiency of a team? How does a new project manager gain the respect and loyalty of team members? Can you share any examples of situations you faced related to this topic?
9) What suggestions do you have for working with sponsors and senior managers? Can you share any examples of situations you faced related to this topic?
10) Do you have any suggestions for future project managers, such as any specific preparations they should make, skills they should learn, etc.?

2.   Go to *www.indeed.com* or another job search site and search for jobs as a "project manager" or "program manager" in three geographic regions of your choice. Write a one- to two-page paper or prepare a short presentation summarizing what you found.

3.   As a team, discuss projects that you are currently working on or would like to work on to benefit yourself, your employers, your family, or the broader community. Come up with at least ten projects, and then determine if they could be grouped into programs. Write a one- to two-page paper or prepare a short presentation summarizing your results.

4.   Review information about the exams required for earning PMP® and CAPM® certification. Find and take several sample tests. Document your findings in a one- to two-page paper or short presentation, citing your references.

KEY TERMS

best practice — An optimal way recognized by industry to achieve a stated goal or objective.

Charismatic — These people can inspire others based on their enthusiasm and confidence.

ethics — A set of principles that guide our decision making based on personal values of what is "right" and "wrong."

interactional — This leadership style is a combination of transactional, transformational, and charismatic.

laissez-faire — Meaning "let go," this hands-off approach lets teams determine their own goals and how to achieve them.

leader — A person who focuses on long-term goals and big-picture objectives, while inspiring people to reach those goals.

manager — A person who deals with the day-to-day details of meeting specific goals.

megaproject — A very large project that typically costs over US $1 billion, affects over one million people, and lasts several years.

organizational project management — A framework in which portfolio, program, and project management are integrated with organizational enablers in order to achieve strategic objectives.

portfolio — Projects, programs, subsidiary portfolios, and operations managed as a group to achieve strategic objectives.

program — A group of related projects, subsidiary programs, and program activities managed in a coordinated manner to obtain benefits not available from managing them individually.

program manager — A person who provides leadership and direction for the project managers heading the projects within the program.

project — A temporary endeavor undertaken to create a unique product, service, or result.

project management — The application of knowledge, skills, tools, and techniques to project activities to meet project requirements.

project management process groups — Initiating, planning, executing, monitoring and controlling, and closing.

project manager — The person responsible for working with the project sponsor, the project team, and the other people involved in a project to meet project goals.

Project Management Institute (PMI) — International professional society for project managers.

project management knowledge areas — Project integration management, scope, schedule, cost, quality, human resource, communications, risk, and procurement management.

Project Management Professional (PMP®) — Certification provided by PMI that requires documenting project experience, agreeing to follow the PMI code of ethics, and passing a comprehensive exam.

project management tools and techniques — Methods available to assist project managers and their teams; some popular tools in the time management knowledge area include Gantt charts, network diagrams, critical path analysis, and project management software.

project portfolio management — The grouping and managing of projects and programs as a portfolio of investments.

project sponsor — The person who provides the direction and funding for a project.

servant leader — People using this approach focus on relationships and community first and leadership is secondary.

stakeholders — People involved in or affected by project activities.

transactional — This management by exception approach focuses on achieving goals or compliance by offering team members appropriate rewards and punishments.

transformational — By working with others to identify needed changes, these leaders empower others and guide changes through inspiration.

triple constraint — Balancing scope, schedule, and cost goals.

END NOTES

[1]Project Management Institute, "Project Management Job Growth and Talent Gap 2017-2027," (2017).

[2]National Association of Colleges and Employers, "Job Outlook 2017," (2016).

[3]Project Management Institute, "Pulse of the Profession®: Success Rates Rise: Transforming the High Cost of Low Performance" (2017).

[4]Project Management Institute, Earning Power: Project Management Salary Survey Ninth Edition (2015).

[5]Ibid.

[6]Standish Group, "The CHAOS Report" (*www.standishgroup.com*) (1995).

[7]PriceWaterhouseCoopers, "Boosting Business Performance through Programme and Project Management" (June 2004).

[8]Project Management Institute, Inc., *A Guide to the Project Management Body of Knowledge (PMBOK® Guide) – Sixth Edition* (2017).

[9]Ibid, p. 6.

[10]Claude Besner and Brian Hobbs, "The Perceived Value and Potential Contribution of Project Management Practices to Project Success," PMI Research Conference Proceedings (July 2006).

[11]Shane Hastie and Stéphane Wojewoda, "Standish Group 2015 Chaos Report - Q&A with Jennifer Lynch," InfoQ (October 4, 2015).

[12]Project Management Institute, Inc., *A Guide to the Project Management Body of Knowledge (PMBOK® Guide) – Sixth Edition* (2017).

[13] Tim Newcomb, "The World's 25 Most Impressive Megaprojects," Popular Mechanics (August 11, 2015).

[14] Project Management Institute, Inc., *A Guide to the Project Management Body of Knowledge (PMBOK® Guide) – Sixth Edition* (2017).

[15] Ibid.

[16] Peter Northouse, Leadership: Theory and Practice, Seventh Edition, SAGE Publications, Inc. (2015) p. 5.

[17] Bendelta, "Goleman's 6 leadership styles – and when to use them," Fast Company (December 9, 2014).

[18] Ultimate Business Library, *Best Practice: Ideas and Insights from the World's Foremost Business Thinkers* (New York: Perseus 2003), p. 1.

[19] Ibid., p. 8.

[20] The Project Management Institute, "PMI Today" (February 2017).

[21] Vanessa Wong, "PMI On Specialization and Globalization," Projects@Work (June 23, 2008).

[22] The Project Management Institute, "PMP® Credential Handbook," (August 31, 2011).

[23] The Project Management Institute, "Project Management Talent Gap Report," (March 2013).

[24] Rachel Bertsche, "How to Break Into Project Management—and Succeed," PM Network (March 2015).

[25] Albert Pang, "Top 10 Project Portfolio Management Software Vendors and Market Forecast 2015-2020,"Apps Run The World (June 30, 2016).

Chapter 2

Project, Program, and Portfolio Selection

LEARNING OBJECTIVES

After reading this chapter, you will be able to:

- Describe the importance of aligning projects with business strategy, the strategic planning process, and using a SWOT analysis
- Explain two different approaches to the project planning process—a four-stage traditional approach and an agile approach
- Summarize the various methods for selecting projects and demonstrate how to calculate net present value, return on investment, payback, and the weighted score for a project
- Discuss the program selection process and distinguish the differences between programs and projects
- Describe the project portfolio selection process and the five levels of project portfolio management

---

OPENING CASE

Marie Scott, the director of the Project Management Office for Global Construction, Inc., was facilitating a meeting with several senior managers throughout the company. The purpose of the meeting was to discuss a process for selecting projects, grouping them into programs, and determining how they fit into the organization's portfolio of projects. She had invited an outside consultant to the meeting to provide an objective view of the process.

She could see that several managers were getting bored with the presentation, while others looked concerned that their projects might be cancelled if the company implemented a new approach for project selection. After the consultant's presentation, Marie had each participant write down his or her questions and concerns and hand them in anonymously for her group to review. She was amazed at the obvious lack of understanding of the need for projects to align with business strategy. How should Marie respond?

ALIGNING PROJECTS WITH BUSINESS STRATEGY

Most organizations face hundreds of problems and opportunities for improvement and consider potential projects to address them. These organizations—both large and small—cannot undertake most of the potential projects identified because of resource limitations and other constraints. Therefore, an organization's overall mission and business strategy should guide the project selection process and prioritization of those projects.

WHAT WENT WRONG?

Unfortunately, when deciding to approve projects, many organizations lack a structured process and do not align projects to their mission or key business objectives. Mike Peterson, PMP® and director with PricewaterhouseCoopers' Advisory Services, described an organization that decided it needed to implement a new financial system, which is often a very expensive, challenging project. "With little in the way of analysis, they selected a big-name enterprise resource planning package, and hired a boutique firm to assist with the implementation. At no time did they formally define the benefits the new system was meant to usher in; nor did they decide, exactly, which processes were to be redesigned. Their own assumptions were not articulated, timelines were never devised, nor were the key performance indicators needed to track success ever established."[1]

What was the result of this project? It was completed over budget and behind schedule. Instead of helping the company, it prevented it from closing its books for over 12 months. They could have avoided many problems if they had followed a formal, well-defined process to identify and select projects.

Strategic Planning

Successful leaders look at the big picture or strategic plan of the organization to determine what projects will provide the most value. The same can be said for successful individuals. No one person can do everything, so individuals must pick projects to pursue based on their talents, interests, limitations, and other criteria. **Strategic planning** involves determining long-term objectives by analyzing the strengths and weaknesses of an organization, studying opportunities and threats in the business environment, predicting future trends, and projecting the need for new products and services. Strategic planning provides important information to help organizations identify and select potential projects.

Most organizations have a written strategic plan. This plan usually includes the organization's mission, vision, and goals for the next 3-5 years. For example, the following information is from Nemours Strategic Plan for 2008-2012.[2] U.S. News & World Report ranked Nemours as one of the best children's hospitals in their 2012-2013 edition. Nemours uses its strategic goals along with other tools, such as a SWOT analysis and balanced scorecard, as described in the following sections, to select projects.

Mission: To provide leadership, institutions, and services to restore and improve the health of children through care and programs not readily available, with one high standard of quality and distinction regardless of the recipient's financial status.
Vision: Freedom from disabling conditions.
Goals:
1. Be a leader in improving children's health through our integrated health system; becoming a pre-eminent voice for children
2. Care for each and every child as if they were our own
3. Be a great place to work
4. Be effective stewards of all of our assets, continually improving them to advance our mission

SWOT Analysis

Many people are familiar with **SWOT analysis**—analyzing **S**trengths, **W**eaknesses, **O**pportunities, and **T**hreats—which is used to aid in strategic planning. For a large organization, a SWOT analysis can be very complex. Figure 2-1 provides an example of a SWOT analysis done by Nemours as part of their strategic plan. Notice that they broke down the SWOT into categories for stewardship, customers, process, and people, which are used in their balanced scorecard, described later in this chapter. The company performed a SWOT analysis for each of these categories. The SWOT analysis was then used to identify strategic initiatives, which Nemours defines as one-time projects with a defined beginning, tasks, and conclusion, to which resources are allocated.

Some people like to perform a SWOT analysis by using mind mapping. **Mind mapping** is a technique that uses branches radiating out from a core idea to structure thoughts and ideas. The human brain does not work in a linear fashion. People come up with many unrelated ideas. By putting those ideas down in a visual mind map format, you can often generate more ideas than by just creating lists. You can create mind maps by hand, by using sticky notes, using presentation software like PowerPoint, or by using mind mapping software. Mind mapping can be a more structured, focused, and documented approach to brainstorming individually or in small groups.

	STRENGTHS	WEAKNESSES	OPPORTUNITIES	THREATS
Stewardship	Financial strength	Slowdown in managed care rate increases	External funding of biomedical research	Cost pressures (labor & professional liability)
	Support from the Trust	Declining state revenues	Charitable giving to Nemours	Bad debt particularly related to growing uninsured & underinsured population
	Debt capacity	Declining revenue sources for community organization partners	Approaching 2008 elections to be able to educate candidates	Medicaid reimbursement
	Triple A credit rating & low cost of capital	Office of Development infancy		Significant capital needs
				Change in DE Governor in 2008
Customers	Prevention & Advocacy programs unique among providers	Decline in inpatient admissions	Advocate changes in policies, programs & practices to support child health	Unreimbursed preventative services
	Focus on children's health	Patient and family dissatisfaction as relates to access i.e., phone, scheduling, website navigation	Increase market share in Delaware & Florida	Intense competition in Delaware Valley
	Respected as an expert in child health & health matters		Branding Nemours & other social marketing	Declining birth rate & flat demographics in Delaware
				Litigious environment
Process	Integrated child health system	Infrastructure needs at AIDHC	Distinguishing ourselves in clinical quality, patient safety & child health promotion	Consumer-driven health plans
	Robust electronic environment, commitment to use IS in clinical care		Improve service excellence	Pay-for-performance
	Priority on patient safety & quality			Price transparency
	Special programs: Kidshealth, NHPS & BrightStart!		Address access issues (phone, appointments, bundling)	Inflation on capital projects
	Community & government partnerships to advance policy & practice change in prevention		Integration of clinical treatment and community-based prevention	Technology obsolescence
People	Quality health care professionals & delivery	Competitive pay & benefits package particularly for physicians	Culture change initiatives	Pediatric specialist & nursing shortages
	Low vacancy rates	Organizational culture		Aging workforce
	Below industry turnover rate	Performance management		"Whitewater" change
		Staffing requirements in Orlando		Erosion of trust

Figure 2-1. Sample SWOT analysis (Nemours)

Figure 2-2 shows a sample mind map for part of Nemours' SWOT analysis presented earlier. This diagram was created using MindView software by MatchWare Inc. Notice that this map has four main branches representing strengths, weaknesses, opportunities, and threats. It is simplified to address only items that fall under the "people" perspective. You can then add branches to develop potential project ideas that could address specific items. For example, Nemours identified four strategic initiatives or potential projects for the people perspective as follows:

1. Benefits assessment: Hire an external consultant to conduct a comprehensive benefits and retirement review. Benchmark current benefits and retirement plans to ensure best practices are used and workers are fairly compensated.

2. LeadQuest implementation: Hire an organizational development consultant to assist with the culture change of Nemours. Build high-performing leaders and teams to ensure personal accountability and provide tools for effective feedback, coaching, mentoring, and teambuilding.

3. Values rollout: Develop workshops on each of Nemours core values that will be given every quarter throughout the organization. Ensure that these values are used in recruiting, performance management, delivery of service, etc.

4. Performance management rollout: Develop and rollout a framework for a consistent, objective performance management process. Provide managers with tools to identify clear performance expectations and provide regular development feedback.

By using the SWOT information, you can ensure that project ideas are tied to the organization's strategic plan.

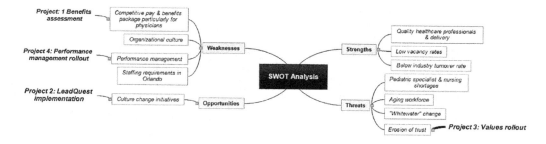

Figure 2-2. Mind map of a SWOT analysis to help identify potential projects (Created with MatchWare's MindView software)

VIDEO HIGHLIGHTS

Many companies and individuals provide video tutorials to teach a new concept or software tool. Mind mapping is no exception. There are several good videos that show you how to create mind maps. For example, youtube.com includes videos by Tony Buzan, author of *The Mind Map Book: How to Use Radiant Thinking to Maximize Your Brain's Untapped Potential*. Other good videos on mind mapping are available by MacGrercy Consultants, ukbraintrainer, and many others.

You can also learn how to use MindView software by watching their online tutorials from *www.matchware.com*. Their videos include a quickstart tutorial of their software and instructions on how to use MindView for project management. For example, you can turn a mind map into a work breakdown structure, as described in Chapter 4 of this text. You can download a 30-day trial of this software for PCs or Macs. An online edition is also available.

TRADITIONAL AND AGILE APPROACHES TO PROJECT PLANNING

One of the most important factors in project success is selecting the best projects to undertake. In addition to using a SWOT analysis, organizations often follow a detailed planning process for project selection. Many organizations follow a traditional approach, often completed in four stages. To make more timely decision, they may also use an agile approach.

Traditional Project Planning Process

Figure 2-3 shows a four-stage planning process for selecting projects. Note the hierarchical structure of this model and the results produced from each stage. Senior executives develop a strategic plan, laying out strategies for the next 3-5 years, as described in the previous section. They usually make slight adjustments to this plan each year and then ask directors and department managers to provide inputs and propose projects. *It is very important to start at the top of the pyramid to select projects that support the organization's business strategy.*

The four stages of this process include:

1. *Strategic planning:* The first step of the project selection process is to determine the organization's strategy, goals, and objectives. This information should come from the strategic plan or strategy planning meetings. For example, if a firm's competitive strategy is cost leadership, it should focus on projects that will help it retain its position as a low-cost producer.

2. *Business area analysis:* The second step is to analyze business processes that are central to achieving strategic goals. For example, could the organization make improvements in sales, manufacturing, engineering, information technology (IT), or other business areas to support the strategic plan?

3. *Project planning:* The next step is to start defining potential projects that address the strategies and business areas identified. Managers should discuss the potential projects' scope, schedule, and cost goals; projected benefits; and constraints as part of this process.

4. *Resource allocation:* The last step in the project planning process is choosing which projects to do and assigning resources for working on them. The amount of resources the organization has available or is willing to acquire will affect decisions on how many projects it can support.

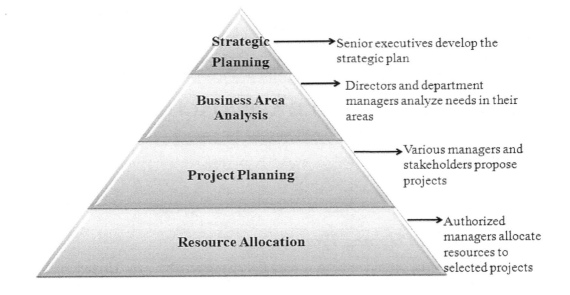

Figure 2-3. Pyramid for a traditional project planning process

While making perfect sense, this four-stage project planning process can be very time-consuming. Organizations must be able to respond to the rapidly changing business environment. They can iterate this traditional process, making updates more frequently. Or they can use an agile approach.

Agile Approach to Project Planning

Much has been written on the topic of "agile" in the past few years. Oxford Dictionaries (July 2017) defines **agile** as "able to move quickly and easily." The same source even includes a definition specific to project management as follows: "Relating to or denoting a method of project management, used especially for software development, that is characterized by the division of tasks into short phases of work and frequent reassessment and adaptation of plans…agile methods replace high-level design with frequent redesign."

The next chapter describes agile project management in more detail, but it is important to note that an agile approach can be used to realize strategic direction. Jamie Barras, SPC4, CSM, PMP®, works for a major retailer in Minneapolis and uses her experience as an agile program manager to promote a more iterative approach to project planning. Jamie believes it is important to first instill an agile mindset where the team values continuous exploration of the customer and market. This exploration helps the team to set direction and define a roadmap of features needed to meet customer expectations. Roadmaps are then reviewed with leaders and aligned with strategy to drive the highest business value. In contrast to the traditional, top-down planning approach, an agile planning approach is much more flexible and allows teams to provide feedback to strategy which can influence a change in direction. It also allows the team freedom to pivot more frequently. Instead of selecting and funding a specific project, the corporation defines the strategic direction, funds teams, and entrusts them to figure out the best approach to define and deliver the greatest business value.

For example, like many large organizations, Jamie's company had a lot of legacy code which makes is difficult to deliver new business features compatible with mobile devices. Some legacy code was written in the 1970s, and it can take many years to convert the code to something more flexible. A team was formed to address this problem. After reviewing the code, the team outlined an approach to replacing the legacy system by defining and prioritizing the key features needed to meet the needs of the users. They provided the new features based on the value they drove for the business, and continuous feedback influenced the next set of features to deliver. By using an agile approach, the business value was realized much faster. Other organizations, including Google, Netflix, and Amazon, are well-known for agile project planning, allowing them to quickly adapt to constant changes.

BEST PRACTICE

Many organizations strive to achieve the speed, flexibility, and customer service of digital companies. In the summer of 2015, the Dutch banking group ING embarked on a journey to shift its traditional organization to an agile model. Bart Schlatmann, former chief operating officer of ING Netherlands, said the company was performing well, but it knew it had to change to meet customer expectations. Their initial focus was on the 3,500 staff members at group headquarters. They spent a lot of time and energy modeling the behavior needed to create an agile culture, focusing on ownership, empowerment, and customer centricity. For example, they implemented a three-week onboarding program, inspired by Zappos, where every employee takes customer calls and moves around key areas of the bank to network and gain a deeper understanding of the business. They also tore down physical walls to create more open spaces, allowing more informal interaction between employees.

When asked to define agility, Schlatmann, provided the following response: "Agility is about flexibility and the ability of an organization to rapidly adapt and steer itself in a new direction. It's about minimizing handovers and bureaucracy, and empowering people. The aim is to build stronger, more rounded professionals out of all our people. Being agile is not just about changing the IT department or any other function on its own. The key has been adhering to the 'end-to-end principle' and working in multidisciplinary teams, or squads, that comprise a mix of marketing specialists, product and commercial specialists, user-experience designers, data analysts, and IT engineers—all focused on solving the client's needs and united by a common definition of success."[3]

METHODS FOR SELECTING PROJECTS

Although people in organizations identify many potential projects as part of their strategic planning process (using a traditional, agile, or combination approach), they also identify projects by working on day-to-day operations. For example, a project manager overseeing an apartment building project might notice that some workers are much more efficient than others are. He or she might suggest a project to provide standardized training on specific skills. A marketing analyst might notice that competitors are using new forms of advertising and suggest a project to respond to this competition. It is important for organizations to encourage workers at all levels, as well as customers, to submit project ideas because they know firsthand what problems they are encountering and what opportunities might be available.

How do senior managers decide which of the many potential projects their organization should pursue? Some projects directly support competitive strategy and are easy choices, but other project ideas require additional thought and analysis. However, organizations need to narrow down the list of potential projects due to resource and time constraints and focus on projects that will be most beneficial. Most large organizations go through a preliminary project prioritization process annually. For example, early each fall Exxon Mobil Corporation's IT organizations work with all their internal client organizations worldwide to identify potential IT projects and resource requirements for the coming year. This process takes about three weeks, followed by meetings to discuss and prioritize potential projects and agree to cut-off lines based on the availability of funds and other resources. Senior management then reviews the prioritized list of potential projects as part of the corporation's fall company planning and budgeting process.

Selecting projects is not an exact science, but it is a critical part of project, program, and project portfolio management. Many methods exist for selecting from among possible projects. Common techniques include:

- Focusing on competitive strategy and broad organizational needs

- Performing net present value analysis or other financial projections

- Using a weighted scoring model

- Implementing a balanced scorecard

- Addressing problems, opportunities, and directives

- Considering project time frame

- Considering project priority

In practice, organizations usually use a combination of these approaches to select projects. Each approach has advantages and disadvantages, and it is up to management to decide the best approach for selecting projects based on their particular organization. In any case, projects should first and foremost address business needs.

Focusing on Competitive Strategy and Broad Organizational Needs

When deciding what projects to undertake, when to undertake them, and to what level, managers must focus on meeting their organizations' many needs. Projects that address competitive strategy are much more likely to be successful because they will be important to the organization's competitive position.

For example, a company might have a competitive strategy of cost leadership, meaning that it attracts customers primarily because its products or services are inexpensive. Wal-Mart (*www.walmart.com*) and Cub Foods (*www.cub.com*) fit into this category; a project to help reduce inventories and, thereby, costs would fit their competitive strategies. Other companies might have a particular focus for their competitive strategies, meaning that they develop products for a particular market niche. Babies"R"Us (*www .babiesrus.com*) and Ron Jon Surf Shop (*www.ronjons.com*) fit into this category; a project to help attract new customers (new parents and grandparents for Babies"R"Us and new surfers for Ron Jon Surf Shop) would fit their competitive strategies.

In addition to projects that directly tie to competitive strategy, organizations might pursue projects that everyone agrees will meet broad organizational needs. These needs might involve minimizing legal or financial risks, improving the firm's IT infrastructure, improving safety or morale, or providing faster customer service. It is often impossible to estimate the financial value of such projects, but everyone agrees that they do have a high value. As the old proverb says,

"It is better to measure gold roughly than to count pennies precisely."

One method for selecting projects based on broad organizational needs is to determine whether they meet three important criteria: need, funding, and will. Do people in the organization agree that the project needs to be done? Does the organization have the capacity to provide adequate funds to perform the project? Is there a strong will to make the project succeed? For example, many visionary chief executive officers (CEOs) can describe a broad need to improve certain aspects of their organizations, such as communications. Although they cannot specifically describe how to improve communications, they might allocate funds to projects that address this need. As projects progress, the organization must reevaluate the need, funding, and will for each project to determine if the projects should be continued, redefined, or terminated.

Another approach to selecting projects based on organizational needs is to focus on factors affecting the organization. These factors can be grouped into four categories, as described in the *PMBOK® Guide – Sixth Edition*:

1. Meeting regulatory, legal, or social requirements

2. Satisfying stakeholders needs or requests

3. Implementing or changing business or technological strategies

4. Creating, improving, or fixing products, processes, or services

Figure 2-4 provides specific examples of factors that lead to creation of a project mapped to these four categories. Note the wide variety of examples. As you can see, there is usually no shortage of potential projects to be done.

Performing Financial Projections

Financial considerations are often an important aspect of the project selection process, especially during tough economic times. As authors Dennis Cohen and Robert Graham put it, "Projects are never ends in themselves. Financially they are always a means to an end, cash."[4] Many organizations require an approved business case before pursuing projects, and financial projections are a critical component of the business case. Three primary methods for determining the projected financial value of projects are net present value analysis, return on investment, and payback analysis. Because project managers often deal with business executives, they must understand how to speak their language, which often boils down to understanding these important financial concepts.

Specific Factor	Examples of Specific Factors	Meet Regulatory, Legal, or Social Requirements	Satisfy Stakeholder Requests or Needs	Create, Improve, or Fix Products, Processes, or Services	Implement or Change Business or Technological Strategies
New technology	An electronics firm authorizes a new project to develop a faster, cheaper, and smaller laptop based on advances in computer memory and electronics technology			X	X
Competitive forces	Lower pricing on products by a competitor results in the need to lower production costs to remain competitive				X
Material issues	A municipal bridge developed cracks in some support members resulting in a project to fix the problems	X		X	
Political changes	A newly elected official instigating project funding changes to a current project				X
Market demand	A car company authorizes a project to build more fuel-efficient cars in response to gasoline shortages		X	X	X
Economic changes	An economic downturn results in a change in the priorities for a current project				X
Customer request	An electric utility authorizes a project to build a substation to serve a new industrial park		X	X	
Stakeholder demands	A stakeholder requires that a new output be produced by the organization		X		
Legal requirement	A chemical manufacturer authorizes a project to establish guidelines for the proper handling of a new toxic material	X			
Business process improvements	An organization implements a project resulting from a Lean Six Sigma value stream mapping exercise			X	
Strategic opportunity or business need	A training company authorizes a project to create a new course to increase its revenues			X	X
Social need	A nongovernmental organization in a developing country authorizes a project to provide potable water systems, latrines, and sanitation education to communities suffering from high rates of infectious diseases		X		
Environmental considerations	A public company authorizes a project to create a new service for electric car sharing to reduce pollution			X	X

Figure 2-4. Examples of factors leading to creation of a project
Source: Project Management Institute, Inc., *A Guide to the Project Management Body of Knowledge (PMBOK® Guide) – Sixth Edition* (2017).

Net Present Value Analysis

Net present value (NPV) analysis is a method of calculating the expected net monetary gain or loss from a project by discounting all expected future cash inflows and outflows to the present point in time. (Detailed steps to walk you through the calculation are outlined in the following paragraphs.) A positive NPV means the return from a project exceeds the **opportunity cost of capital**—the return available by investing the capital elsewhere. For example, is it best to put money into Project A or Project B? Projects with higher NPVs are preferred to projects with lower NPVs if all other criteria are equal. Note that some projects, like those required for regulatory compliance, may have a negative NPV.

Figure 2-5 illustrates the NPV concept for two different projects. Note that this example starts discounting right away in Year 1 and uses a 10% discount rate (located in cell B1 in an Excel spreadsheet). You can use the NPV function in Microsoft Excel to calculate the

NPV quickly. Notice that the sum of the **cash flow**—benefits minus costs, or income minus expenses—is the same for both projects at $2,000,000. The net present values are different, however, because they account for the time value of money. Money earned today is worth more than money earned in the future. Project 1 had a negative cash flow of $4,000,000 in the first year, whereas Project 2 had a negative cash flow of only $2,000,000 in the first year. Although both projects had the same total cash flows without discounting, these cash flows are not of comparable financial value. NPV analysis, therefore, is a method for making equal comparisons between cash flows for multiyear projects. Although this example shows both projects having the same length, NPV also works for projects of different lengths.

				Note that total cash flows are equal, but the NPVs are very different.				
Discount rate		10%						
PROJECT 1		Year 1	Year 2	Year 3	Year 4	Year 5		Total
Benefits	$	-	$ 2,000,000	$ 2,000,000	$ 2,000,000	$ 2,000,000	$	8,000,000
Costs	$	4,000,000	$ 500,000	$ 500,000	$ 500,000	$ 500,000	$	6,000,000
Cash flow	$	(4,000,000)	$ 1,500,000	$ 1,500,000	$ 1,500,000	$ 1,500,000	**$2,000,000**	
NPV		**$686,180**	Formula: =npv(b1,b6:f6)					
PROJECT 2		Year 1	Year 2	Year 3	Year 4	Year 5		Total
Benefits	$	-	$ 3,000,000	$ 3,000,000	$ 3,000,000	$ 3,000,000	$	12,000,000
Costs	$	2,000,000	$ 2,000,000	$ 2,000,000	$ 2,000,000	$ 2,000,000	$	10,000,000
Cash flow	$	(2,000,000)	$ 1,000,000	$ 1,000,000	$ 1,000,000	$ 1,000,000	**$2,000,000**	
NPV		**$1,063,514**	Formula: =npv(b1,b12:f12)					

Figure 2-5. Net present value example

Detailed steps on performing this calculation manually are provided in Figure 2-6.

Discount rate		10%					
				Year			
PROJECT 1		1	2	3	4	5	Total
Benefits	$	-	$ 2,000,000	$ 2,000,000	$ 2,000,000	$2,000,000	$ 8,000,000
Discount factor		0.91	0.83	0.75	0.68	0.62	
Discounted benefits	$	-	$ 1,652,893	$ 1,502,630	$ 1,366,027	$1,241,843	$ 5,763,392
Costs	$ 4,000,000		$ 500,000	$ 500,000	$ 500,000	$ 500,000	$ 6,000,000
Discount factor	0.91		0.83	0.75	0.68	0.62	
Discounted costs	$ 3,636,364		$ 413,223	$ 375,657	$ 341,507	$ 310,461	$ 5,077,212
Total discounted benefits - costs, or NPV						→	$ 686,180

Note: The discount factors are not rounded to two decimal places.
They are calculated using the formula discount factor =1/(1+discount rate)^year.

Figure 2-6. Detailed NPV calculations

There are some items to consider when calculating NPV. Some organizations refer to the investment year for project costs as Year 0 instead of Year 1 and do not discount costs in Year 0. Other organizations start discounting immediately based on their financial procedures;

it is simply a matter of preference for the organization. The discount rate can also vary, based on the prime rate and other economic considerations. Some people consider it to be the rate at which you could borrow money for the project. You can enter costs as negative numbers instead of positive numbers, and you can list costs first and then benefits. For example, Figure 2-7 shows the financial calculations a consulting firm provided in a business case for an intranet project. Note that the discount rate is 8%, costs are not discounted right away (note the Year 0), the discount factors are rounded to two decimal places, costs are listed first, and costs are entered as positive numbers. The NPV and other calculations are still the same; only the format is slightly different. Project managers must be sure to check with financial experts in their organization to find out its guidelines for: when discounting starts, what discount rate to use, and what format the organization prefers. Their finance experts may also perform the calculations for them. Chapter 3 includes a NPV analysis for the Just-In-Time Training Project as part of the business case written to help justify investing in the project.

Discount rate	8%					
Assume the project is completed in Year 0			Year			
	0	1	2	3	Total	
Costs	140,000	40,000	40,000	40,000		
Discount factor	1	0.93	0.86	0.79		
Discounted costs	**140,000**	**37,200**	**34,400**	**31,600**	**243,200**	
Benefits	0	200,000	200,000	200,000		
Discount factor	1	0.93	0.86	0.79		
Discounted benefits	**0**	**186,000**	**172,000**	**158,000**	**516,000**	
Discounted benefits - costs	(140,000)	148,800	137,600	126,400	**272,800**	←NPV
Cumulative benefits - costs	(140,000)	8,800	146,400	272,800		
ROI ──────────→	112%					
	Payback in Year 1					

Figure 2-7. Intranet project NPV example (Schwalbe, Information Technology Project Management, Sixth Edition, 2010)

To determine NPV, follow these steps:

1. Determine the estimated costs and benefits for the life of the project and the products it produces. For example, the intranet project example assumed the project would produce a system in about six months that would be used for three years, so costs are included in Year 0, when the system is developed, and ongoing system costs and projected benefits are included for Years 1, 2, and 3.

2. Determine the discount rate. A **discount rate** is the rate used in discounting future cash flows. It is also called the capitalization rate or opportunity cost of

capital. In Figures 2-5 and 2-6, the discount rate is 10% per year, and in Figure 2-7, the discount rate is 8% per year.

3. Calculate and interpret the net present value. There are several ways to calculate NPV. Most spreadsheet software has a built-in function to calculate NPV. For example, Figure 2-5 shows the formula that Excel uses: =npv(discount rate, range of cash flows), where the discount rate is in cell B1 and the range of cash flows for Project 1 are in cells B6 through F6. To use the NPV function, there must be a row in the spreadsheet (or column, depending on how it is organized) for the cash flow each year, which is the benefit amount for that year minus the cost amount. The result of the formula yields an NPV of $686,180 for Project 1 and an NPV of $1,063,514 for Project 2. Because both projects have positive NPVs, they are both good candidates for selection. However, because Project 2 has a significantly higher NPV than Project 1, it would be the better choice between the two. If the two numbers are close, other methods should be used to help decide which project to select.

The mathematical formula for calculating NPV is:

$$\text{NPV} = \sum_{t=0...n} A_t / (1+r)^t$$

where t equals the year of the cash flow, n is the last year of the cash flow, A_t is the amount of cash flow in year t, and r is the discount rate. If you cannot enter the data into spreadsheet software, you can perform the calculations by hand or with a simple calculator. First, determine the annual **discount factor**—a multiplier for each year based on the discount rate and year—and then apply it to the costs and benefits for each year. The formula for the discount factor is $1/(1+r)^t$, where r is the discount rate, such as 8%, and t is the year. For example, the discount factors used in Figure 2-7 are calculated as follows:

Year 0: discount factor $= 1/(1+0.08)^0 = 1$

Year 1: discount factor $= 1/(1+0.08)^1 = .93$

Year 2: discount factor $= 1/(1+0.08)^2 = .86$

Year 3: discount factor $= 1/(1+0.08)^3 = .79$

The discount factor is the future value of one dollar ($1) today in that year. At the end of year 3, for example, a dollar is worth $0.79.

After determining the discount factor for each year, multiply the costs and benefits by the appropriate discount factor. For example, in Figure 2-7, the discounted cost for Year 1 is $40,000 * .93 = $37,200, where the discount factor is rounded to two decimal places. Next, sum all of the discounted costs and benefits each year to get a total. For example, the total discounted costs in Figure 2-7 are $243,200. To calculate the NPV, take the total discounted benefits and subtract the total discounted costs. In this example, the NPV is $516,000 – $243,200 = $272,800.

Return on Investment

Another important financial consideration is return on investment. **Return on investment (ROI)** is the result of subtracting the project costs from the benefits and then dividing by the costs. For example, if you invest $100 today and next year your investment is worth $110, your ROI is ($110 – 100)/100, or 0.10 (10%). Note that the ROI is always a percentage. It can be positive or negative. It is best to consider discounted costs and benefits for multiyear projects when calculating ROI. Figure 2-7 shows an ROI of 112%. You calculate this number as follows:

$$ROI = (total\ discounted\ benefits - total\ discounted\ costs)/discounted\ costs$$

$$ROI = (516,000 - 243,200) / 243,200 = 112\%$$

The higher the ROI, the better; an ROI of 112% is outstanding. Many organizations have a required rate of return for projects. The **required rate of return** is the minimum acceptable rate of return on an investment. For example, an organization might have a required rate of return of at least 10% for projects. The organization bases the required rate of return on what it could expect to receive elsewhere for an investment of comparable risk.

You can also determine a project's **internal rate of return (IRR)** by finding what discount rate results in an NPV of zero for the project. You can use the Goal Seek function in Excel (use Excel's Help function for more information on Goal Seek) to determine the IRR quickly. Simply set the cell containing the NPV calculation to zero while changing the cell containing the discount rate.

Payback Analysis

Payback analysis is another important financial tool to use when selecting projects. **Payback period** is the amount of time it will take to recoup—in the form of net cash inflows—the total dollars invested in a project. In other words, payback analysis determines how much time will lapse before accrued benefits overtake accrued and continuing costs. Payback, if there is one, occurs in the year when the cumulative benefits minus costs reach or exceed zero.

For example, assume a project cost $100,000 up front with no additional costs, and its annual benefits were $50,000 per year. Payback period is calculated by dividing the cost of the project by the annual cash inflows ($100,000/$50,000), resulting in 2 years in this simple example. If costs and benefits vary each year, you need to find where the lines for the cumulative costs and benefits cross, or where the cumulative cash inflow is equal to zero. The data used to create the chart in Figure 2-8 is provided above the chart.

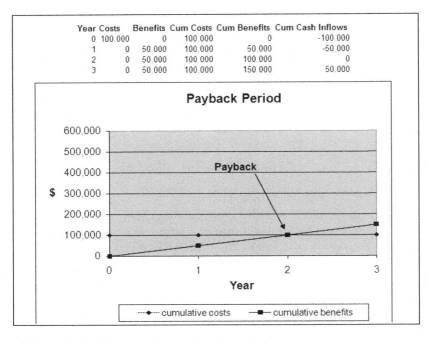

Year	Costs	Benefits	Cum Costs	Cum Benefits	Cum Cash Inflows
0	100.000	0	100.000	0	-100.000
1	0	50.000	100.000	50.000	-50.000
2	0	50.000	100.000	100.000	0
3	0	50.000	100.000	150.000	50.000

Figure 2-8. Charting the payback period

Template Files Available

A template file called *business case financials* is available on the companion website for this text (www.intropm.com) for calculating NPV, ROI, and payback for a project. There is another file called *payback period chart* that you can use to create the chart, if needed. See Appendix B for a list of all template files.

Many organizations have certain recommendations for the length of the payback period of an investment. For example, they might require all IT projects to have a payback period of less than two years or even one year, regardless of the estimated NPV or ROI. However, organizations must also consider long-range goals when making major investments. Many crucial projects, such as drug development or major transportation projects, cannot achieve a payback that quickly or be completed in such a short time period.

To aid in project selection, it is important for project managers to understand the organization's financial expectations for projects. It is also important for management to understand the limitations of financial estimates, because they are just estimates.

Using a Weighted Scoring Model

A **weighted scoring model** is a tool that provides a systematic process for selecting projects based on many criteria. These criteria include such factors as meeting strategic goals or broad organizational needs; addressing specific problems or opportunities; the amount of time it will take to complete the project; the overall priority of the project; and the projected financial performance of the project.

The first step in creating a weighted scoring model is to identify criteria important to the project selection process. It often takes time to develop and reach agreement on these criteria. Holding facilitated brainstorming sessions or using software to exchange ideas can aid in developing these criteria.

For example, suppose your family wants to take a trip. Some possible criteria for selecting which trip to take include the following:

- Total cost of the trip

- Probability of good weather (which you should agree on as being warm and sunny weather for beach activities or cold weather and snow for good skiing conditions)

- Fun activities nearby (which you should agree in advance as being beach activities, snow skiing, etc.)

- Recommendations from other travelers

Next, you assign a weight to each criterion. Once again, determining weights requires consultation and final agreement. These weights indicate how much you value each criterion or how important each criterion is. You can assign weights based on percentage, and the sum of all the criteria's weights must total 100%. You then assign numerical scores to each criterion (for example, 0 to 100) for each project (or trip in this example). The scores indicate how much each project (or trip) meets each criterion. At this point, you can use a spreadsheet application to create a matrix of projects, criteria, weights, and scores. Figure 2-9 provides an example of a weighted scoring model to evaluate four different trips. After assigning weights for the criteria and scores for each trip, you calculate a weighted score for each trip by multiplying the weight for each criterion by its score and adding the resulting values.

For example, you calculate the weighted score for Trip 1 in Figure 2-9 as:

$$25\%*60 + 30\%*80 + 15\%*70 + 30\%*50 = 64.5$$

Criteria	Weight	Trip 1	Trip 2	Trip 3	Trip 4
Total cost of the trip	25%	60	80	90	20
Probability of good weather	30%	80	60	90	70
Fun activities nearby	15%	70	30	50	90
Recommendations	30%	50	50	60	90
Weighted Project Scores	**100%**	**64.5**	**57.5**	**75**	**66.5**

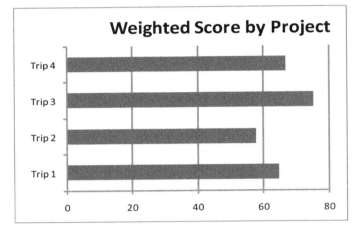

Figure 2-9. Sample weighted scoring model for project selection

Note that in this example, Trip 3 is the obvious choice for selection because it has the highest weighted score. Creating a bar chart to graph the weighted scores for each project allows you to see the results at a glance. If you create the weighted scoring model in a spreadsheet, you can enter the data, create and copy formulas, and perform a "what-if" analysis. For example, suppose you change the weights for the criteria. By having the weighted scoring model in a spreadsheet, you can easily change the weights to update the weighted scores and charts automatically. This capability allows you to investigate various options for different stakeholders quickly. Ideally, the result should be reflective of the group's consensus, and any major disagreements should be documented. A template file called *weighted scoring model* is provided on the companion website for this text.

Many readers of this text are probably familiar with a weighted scoring model because teachers often use them to determine grades. Suppose grades for a class are based on two homework assignments and two exams. To calculate final grades, the teacher would assign a weight to each of these items. Suppose Homework One is worth 10% of the grade, Homework Two is worth 20% of the grade, Test One is worth 20% of the grade, and Test Two is worth 50% of the grade. Students would want to do well on each of these items, but they would focus on performing well on Test Two because it is 50% of the grade.

You can also establish weights by assigning points. For example, a project might receive 100 points if it definitely supports key business objectives, 50 points if it somewhat supports them, and 0 points if it is totally unrelated to key business objectives. With a point model, you can simply add all the points to determine the best projects for selection without having to multiply weights and scores and sum the results.

You can also determine minimum scores or thresholds for specific criteria in a weighted scoring model. For example, suppose an organization decided that it should not consider a project if it does not score at least 50 out of 100 on every criterion. The organization can build this type of threshold into the weighted scoring model to automatically reject projects that do not meet these minimum standards. As you can see, weighted scoring models can aid in project selection decisions.

Implementing a Balanced Scorecard

Dr. Robert Kaplan and Dr. David Norton developed another approach to help select and manage projects that align with business strategy. A **balanced scorecard** is a methodology that converts an organization's value drivers—such as customer service, innovation, operational efficiency, and financial performance—to a series of defined metrics. Organizations record and analyze these metrics to determine how well projects help them achieve strategic goals.

The Balanced Scorecard Institute, which provides training and guidance to organizations using this methodology, quotes Kaplan and Norton's description of the balanced scorecard as follows:

"The balanced scorecard retains traditional financial measures. But financial measures tell the story of past events, an adequate story for industrial age companies for which investments in long-term capabilities and customer relationships were not critical for success. These financial measures are inadequate, however, for guiding and evaluating the journey that information age companies must make to create future value through investment in customers, suppliers, employees, processes, technology, and innovation."[5]

The balanced scorecard approach is often a good fit for organizations because they must address additional factors beyond financial measures in order to fulfill their missions and goals. For example, the following quote and example of a balanced scorecard is from Nemours, a large healthcare company described earlier in this chapter: "The Nemours Strategy Management System (SMS) uses the Balanced Scorecard architecture to articulate the strategy and link key processes, behaviors, and personal accountability, enabling Nemours to close the gap between where it currently is and where it wishes to be."[6] Figure 2-10 shows Nemours' highest order strategy map.

Nemours uses four perspectives in their balanced scorecard approach:

1. *People and Learning*: What resources, skills, training and support must staff have to work effectively? What organizational culture is conducive to strong people performance?
2. *Process Perspective*: What must we excel at in order to satisfy our customers? How do we meet their needs consistently?
3. *Customer Perspective*: How do we meet customer needs and exceed expectations? What do we want the community to say about us?
4. *Stewardship Perspective*: What resources are required to achieve the mission? How are revenue generating strategies balanced with expense management?

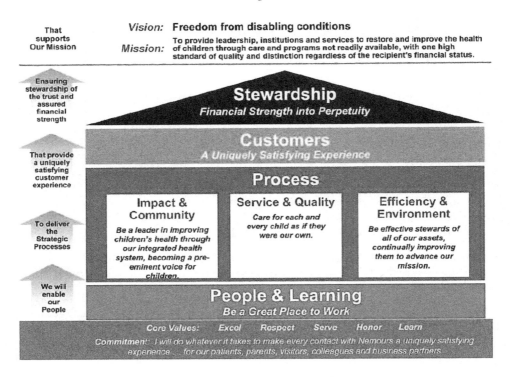

Figure 2-10. Sample balanced scorecard strategy map (Nemours)

Addressing Problems, Opportunities, and Directives

Another method for selecting projects is based on their response to a problem, an opportunity, or a directive, as described in the following list:

- *Problems* are undesirable situations that prevent an organization from achieving its goals. These problems can be current or anticipated. For example, if a bridge in a major city collapses, that problem must be addressed as soon as possible.

- *Opportunities* are chances to improve the organization. For example, a company might want to revamp its website or provide a booth at a conference to attract more customers.

- **Directives** are new requirements imposed by management, government, or some external influence. For example, a college or university may have to meet a requirement to discontinue the use of students' social security numbers for data privacy.

Organizations select projects for any of these reasons. It is often easier to get approval and funding for projects that address problems or directives because the organization must respond to these categories of projects to avoid hurting the business. For example, several years ago Exxon Mobil Corporation realized that it was losing $200,000 each minute its motor fuel store point-of-sale system was down. Getting approval for a $7 million project to re-engineer this critical system was approved and given high priority. Many projects resulting from natural disasters, such as hurricanes and earthquakes, get quick approvals due to their serious nature. Many problems and directives must be resolved quickly, but managers must also consider projects that seek opportunities for improving the organization. Similarly, individuals must consider opportunities to improve themselves by doing things like taking classes in project management.

Project Time Frame

Another approach to project selection is based on the time it will take to complete a project or the date by which it must be done. For example, some potential projects must be finished within a specific time period, such as projects that were done to meet Year 2000 issues. If they cannot be finished by this set date, there may be serious consequences. Likewise, if there is a potential project that is only valid if it can be done by a certain time and there is no way your organization can meet the deadline, it should not be considered. Some projects can be completed very quickly—within a few weeks, days, or even minutes. However, even though many projects can be completed quickly, it is still important to prioritize them while keeping in mind strategy, financials, and resources.

Project Priority

Another method for project selection is the overall priority of the project. Many organizations prioritize projects as being high, medium, or low priority based on the current business environment. For example, if it were crucial to cut operating costs quickly, projects that have the most potential to do so would be given a high priority. The organization should always complete high-priority projects first, even if a lower priority project could be finished in less time. Usually, there are many more potential projects than an organization can undertake at any one time, so it is very important to work on the most important ones first.

As you can see, organizations of all types and sizes can use many approaches to select projects. Many project managers have some say in which projects their organizations select for implementation. Even if they do not, they need to understand the motive and overall business strategy for the projects they are managing. Project managers and team members are often asked to justify their projects, and understanding many of these project selection methods can help them to do so.

PROGRAM SELECTION

After deciding which projects to pursue, organizations need to decide if it is advantageous to manage several projects together as part of a program. There might already be a program that a new project would logically fall under, or the organization might initiate a program and then approve projects for it. Recall that a program is a group of related projects, subsidiary programs, and program activities managed in a coordinated manner to obtain benefits not available from managing them individually.

Focusing on Coordination and Benefits

What does it mean to manage a group of projects in a coordinated way? Project managers focus on managing individual projects. Project managers and their teams have to do many things to achieve individual project success. For example, for projects to build a new house, some of the activities include:

- Working with local government groups to obtain permits

- Finding and managing a land excavation firm to prepare the land

- Coordinating with an architect to understand the house design

- Screening and hiring various construction workers

- Finding appropriate suppliers for the materials

If a construction firm is in charge of developing several houses in the same geographic area, it makes sense to coordinate these common activities for all the housing projects instead of doing them separately.

What benefits and control would be possible by managing projects as part of a program? There are several. For example, potential benefits in the housing program scenario include the following:

- *Saving money*: The construction firm can often save money by using economies of scale. It can purchase materials, obtain services, and hire workers for less money if it is managing the construction of 100 houses instead of just one house.

- *Saving time*: Instead of each project team having to perform similar work, by grouping the projects into a program, one person or group can be responsible for similar work, such as obtaining all the permits for all the houses. This coordination of work usually saves time as well as money.

- *Increasing authority*: A program manager responsible for building 100 houses will have more authority than a project manager responsible for building one house. The program manager can use this authority in multiple situations, such as negotiating better prices with suppliers and obtaining better services in a more timely fashion.

Approaches to Creating Programs

Some new projects naturally fall into existing programs, such as houses being built in a certain geographic area. As another example, many companies use IT, and they usually have a program in place for IT infrastructure projects. Projects might include purchasing new hardware, software, and networking equipment, or determining standards for IT. If a new office opens up in a new location, the project to provide the hardware, software, and networks for that office would logically fall under the infrastructure program.

Other projects might spark the need for developing a new program. For example, Global Construction, Inc., from the opening case, might win a large contract to build an office complex in a foreign country. Instead of viewing the contract as either one huge project or part of an existing program, it would be better to manage the work as its own program that comprises several smaller projects. For example, there might be separate project managers for each building. Grouping related projects into programs helps improve coordination through better communications, planning, management, and control. Organizations must decide when it makes sense to group projects together. When too many projects are part of one program, it might be wise to create a new program to improve their management.

MEDIA SNAPSHOT

Many people enjoy watching the extra features on a DVD that describe the creation of a movie. For example, the extended edition DVD for *Lord of the Rings: The Two Towers* includes detailed descriptions of how the script was created, how huge structures were built, how special effects were made, and how talented professionals overcame numerous obstacles to complete the three movies. Instead of viewing each movie as a separate project, the producer, Peter Jackson, decided to develop all three movies as part of one program.

"By shooting all three films consecutively during one massive production and post-production schedule, New Line Cinema made history. Never before had such a monumental undertaking been contemplated or executed. The commitment of time, resources, and manpower were unheard of as all three films and more than 1,000 effects shots were being produced concurrently with the same director and core cast."[7]

At three years in the making, *The Lord of the Rings* trilogy was the largest production ever to be mounted in the Southern Hemisphere. The production assembled an international cast, employed a crew of 2,500, used over 20,000 days of extras, featured 77 speaking parts, and created 1,200 state-of-the-art computer-generated effects shots. Jackson said that doing detailed planning for all three movies made it much easier than he imagined producing them, and the three movies were completed in less time and for less money by grouping them together. The budget for the three films was reported to be $270 million, and they grossed over $1 billion before the end of 2004. Jackson continued his move making success by directing *The Hobbit* trilogy, with movies released in 2012, 2013, and 2014.

PROJECT PORTFOLIO SELECTION

Projects and programs have existed for a long time, as has some form of project portfolio management. There is no simple process for deciding how to create project portfolios, but the goal of project portfolio management is clear: to help maximize business value to ensure enterprise success. You can measure business value in several ways, such as in market share, profit margins, growth rates, share prices, and customer or employee satisfaction ratings. Many factors are involved in ensuring enterprise success. Organizations cannot pursue only projects that have the best financial value. They must also consider resource availability (including people, equipment, and cash); risks that could affect success; and other concerns, such as potential mergers, public relations, balancing investments, and other factors that affect enterprise success.

Focusing on Enterprise Success

Project managers strive to make their projects successful and naturally focus on doing whatever they can to meet the goals of their particular projects. Likewise, program managers focus on making their programs successful. Project portfolio managers and other senior managers, however, must focus on how all of an organization's projects fit together to help the entire enterprise achieve success. That might mean canceling or putting several projects on hold, reassigning resources from one project to another, suggesting changes in project leadership, or taking other actions that might negatively affect individual projects or programs to help the organization as a whole. For example, a university might have to close a campus to provide quality services at other campuses. Running any large organization is complex, as is project portfolio management.

WHAT WENT RIGHT?

Many companies have seen great returns on investment after implementing basic ideas of project portfolio management. For example, Jane Walton, the project portfolio manager for IT projects at Schlumberger, saved the company $3 million in one year by simply consolidating the organization's 120 IT projects into one portfolio. Before then, all IT projects and their associated programs were managed separately, and no one looked at them as a whole. Manufacturing companies used project portfolio management in the 1960s, and Walton anticipated the need to justify investments in IT projects just as managers have to justify capital investment projects. She found that 80% of the organization's projects overlapped, and 14 separate projects were trying to accomplish the same thing. By looking at all IT projects and programs together, Schlumberger could make better strategic business decisions. The company canceled several projects and merged others to reduce the newly discovered redundancy.[8]

Organizations that excel in project management complete 92 percent of their projects successfully compared to only 33 percent in organizations that do not have good project management processes. Poor project performance, including poor portfolio management, costs over $97 million for every $1 billion invested in projects and programs.[9]

Recall that project portfolio management focuses on strategic issues while individual projects often focus on tactical issues. Portfolios should be formed and continuously updated to help the organization as a whole make better strategic decisions. Organizations normally put all projects into one portfolio, but then often break it down into more detailed sub-portfolios, often set up by major departments or other categories. Several companies create a separate portfolio for IT projects. It is often difficult to measure the financial value of many IT projects, yet these projects are often a large investment and have a strong effect on other business areas. For example, you may have to update your information systems to meet new government regulations based on changes in new healthcare or tax policies. You must comply to stay in business, but you cannot generate a positive return on investment from those particular projects.

Sample Approach for Creating a Project Portfolio

Figure 2-11 illustrates one approach for project portfolio management in which there is one large portfolio for the entire organization. Sections of the portfolio are then broken down to improve the management of projects in each particular sector. For example, Global Construction might have the main portfolio categories shown in the left part of Figure 2-11 (marketing, materials, IT, and HR (human resources)) and divide each of those categories further to address their unique concerns. The right part of this figure shows how the IT projects could be categorized in more detail. For example, there are three basic IT project portfolio categories:

1. *Venture*: Projects in this category would help transform the business. For example, Global Construction might have an IT project to provide Webcams and interactive Web-based reporting on construction sites that would be easily accessible by its customers and suppliers. This project could help transform the business by developing more trusting partnerships with customers and suppliers, who could know exactly what is happening with their construction projects.

2. *Growth*: Projects in this category would help the company grow in terms of revenue. For example, Global Construction might have an IT project to provide information on its corporate website in a new language, such as Chinese or Japanese. This capability could help the company grow its business in those countries.

3. *Core*: Projects in this category must be accomplished to run the business. For example, an IT project to provide computers for new employees would fall under this category.

Note that the *Core* category of IT projects is labeled as **nondiscretionary costs**. This means that the organization has no choice in whether to fund these projects; it must fund them to stay in business. Projects that fall under the *Venture* or *Growth* category would be **discretionary costs** because the organization can use its own discretion in deciding whether to fund them. Also note the arrow in the center of Figure 2-11. This arrow indicates that the risks, value, and timing of projects normally increase as you go from *Core* to *Growth* to *Venture* projects. However, some *Core* projects can also be high risk, have high value, and require good timing.

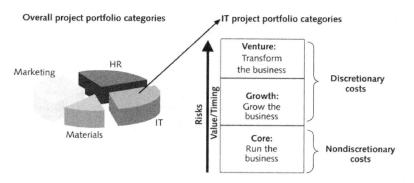

Figure 2-11. Sample project portfolio approach (Schwalbe, Information Technology Project Management, Sixth Edition, 2010)

Five Levels of Project Portfolio Management

As you can imagine, it takes time to understand and apply project portfolio management. You can develop and manage a project portfolio in many ways. Just as projects are unique, so are project portfolios.

An organization can view project portfolio management as having five levels, from simplest to most complex, as follows:

1. Put all of your projects in one list. Many organizations find duplicate or unneeded projects after they identify all the projects on which they are working.

2. Prioritize the projects in your list. It's important to know which projects are most important to an organization so that resources can be applied accordingly.

3. Divide your projects into several categories based on types of investment. Categorizing projects helps you see the big picture, such as how many projects are supporting a growth strategy, how many are helping to increase profit margins, how many relate to marketing, and how many relate to materials. Organizations can create as many categories as they need to help understand and analyze how projects affect business needs and goals.

4. Automate the list. Managers can view project data in many different ways by putting key information into a computerized system. You can enter the project information in spreadsheet software such as Excel. You might have headings for the project name, project manager, project sponsor, business needs addressed, start date, end date, budget, risk, priority, key deliverables, and other items. You can also use more sophisticated tools to help perform project portfolio management, such as enterprise project management software, as described in Chapter 1.

5. Apply modern portfolio theory, including risk-return tools that map project risks. Figure 2-12 provides a sample map to assist in evaluating project risk versus return, or business value. Each bubble represents a project, and the size of the bubble relates to its approved budget (that is, the larger bubbles have larger budgets). Notice that there are not, and should not be, projects in the lower-right quadrant, which is the location of projects that have low relative value and high risk.

As described in Chapter 1, many project portfolio management software products are available on the market today to help analyze portfolios. Consult references on portfolio theory and project portfolio management software for more details on this topic.

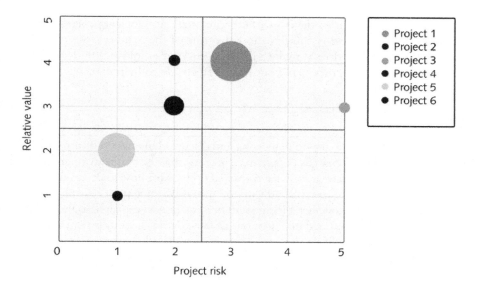

Figure 2-12. Sample project portfolio risk map (Schwalbe, Information Technology Project Management, Sixth Edition, 2010)

Figure 2-13 shows a humorous example of a portfolio management chart listing various fruits, charting them based on their taste and ease of eating. In this example, people would eat a lot more seedless grapes, strawberries, blueberries and peaches and not many grapefruit!

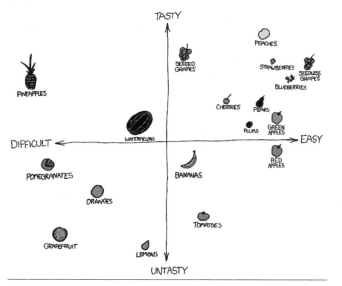

Figure 2-13. Deciding what fruit to eat (www.xkcd.com)

It is important for organizations to develop a fair, consistent, and logical process for selecting projects, programs, and portfolios. Studies show that one of the main reasons people quit their jobs is because they feel they do not make a difference. After employees understand how their work fits into the big picture, they can work more effectively to help themselves and their entire organizations succeed.

CASE WRAP-UP

Marie and her team summarized the inputs from the meeting and discussed them with their CEO, Doug Milis, and other senior managers. They felt people were nervous that the company might not be doing well and that their jobs were in jeopardy. They discussed options for how to proceed and decided that it was important for the CEO to explain the importance of aligning projects with business strategy. Doug and his staff put together a memo and presentation to explain that the company was doing very well, and that they had no intentions of either letting anyone go or cutting major programs. On the contrary, they had far more projects to pursue than they possibly could, and they believed that using project portfolio management would help them select and manage projects better. After everyone heard this information, they were much more open to working with Marie's group to improve their project, program, and portfolio management processes.

CHAPTER SUMMARY

An organization's overall business strategy should guide the project selection process and management of those projects. Many organizations perform a SWOT analysis to help identify potential projects based on their strengths, weaknesses, opportunities, and threats.

Many organizations follow a traditional approach, often completed in four stages. The four stages of this model, from highest to lowest, are strategic planning, business area analysis, project planning, and resource allocation. To make more timely decisions, they can also use an agile approach. Instead of selecting and funding a specific project, you fund a team and entrust them to figure out the best approach to provide the most business value in the shortest amount of time.

Several methods are available for selecting projects. Financial methods include calculating and analyzing the net present value, return on investment, and payback period for projects. You can also use a weighted scoring model; implement a balanced scorecard; address problems, opportunities, and directives; and consider project time frame and project priority to assist in project selection.

After determining what projects to pursue, it is important to decide if projects should be grouped into programs. The main criteria for program selection are the coordination and benefits available by grouping projects together into a program.

There is no simple process for deciding how to create project portfolios, but the goal of project portfolio management is to help maximize business value to ensure enterprise success. There are five levels of complexity for project portfolio management, ranging from simply putting all projects in one list to applying portfolio theory to analyze risks and returns of a project portfolio.

QUICK QUIZ

Note that you can find additional, interactive quizzes at www.intropm.com.

1. Which of the following is not part of a SWOT analysis?

    A. strengths

    B. weaknesses

    C. opportunities

    D. tactics

2. A large company continues to be successful by providing new products and services for its market niche of brides. What is its main competitive strategy?

    A. cost leadership

    B. quality

    C. focus

    D. customer service

3. The last step in the four-stage planning process for projects is _____.

    A. resource allocation

    B. project planning

    C. business area analysis

    D. strategic planning

4. _____ is defined as being able to move quickly and easily.

    A. Flexible

    B. Speed

    C. Customer-centric

    D. Agile

5. Which of the following statements is false concerning the financial analysis of projects?

    A. The higher the net present value the better.

    B. A shorter payback period is better than a longer one.

    C. The required rate of return is the discount rate that results in an NPV of zero for the project.

    D. ROI is the result of subtracting the project costs from the benefits and then dividing by the costs.

6.   A _____ is a methodology that converts an organization's value drivers—such as customer service, innovation, operational efficiency, and financial performance—into a series of defined metrics.

   A.   balanced scorecard

   B.   weighted scoring model

   C.   net present value analysis

   D.   directive

7.   Which of the following is not a major benefit of grouping projects into programs?

   A.   increasing revenues

   B.   increasing authority

   C.   saving money

   D.   saving time

8.   A college approved a project to provide discounts for faculty, students, and staff to use the city's new light-rail system. Under what existing program might this project naturally fit?

   A.   academic enrichment program

   B.   fund-raising program

   C.   entertainment program

   D.   transportation program

9.   The goal of project portfolio management is to help maximize business value to ensure _____.

   A.   profit maximization

   B.   enterprise success

   C.   risk minimization

   D.   competitive advantage

10.   Many organizations find duplicate or unneeded projects after they perform which step in project portfolio management?

   A.   prioritizing the projects in their list

   B.   dividing the projects into several categories based on type of investment

   C.   putting all projects in one list

   D.   applying modern portfolio theory, including risk-return tools that map project risk

Quick Quiz Answers

1. D; 2. C; 3. A; 4. D; 5. C; 6. A; 7. A; 8. D; 9. B; 10. C

DISCUSSION QUESTIONS

1.   Why is it important to align projects to business strategy? What is SWOT analysis? How can you use a mind map to create a SWOT analysis and generate project ideas?

2.   What are the stages called in the four-stage planning process for project selection? How does following this process assist in selecting projects that will provide the most benefit to organizations?

3.   How is an agile approach to project planning different than a traditional approach?

4.   How do you decide which projects to pursue using net present value analysis? How do return on investment and payback period relate to net present value?

5.   What are three main benefits of grouping projects into programs?

6.   What are the five levels of project portfolio management?

EXERCISES

Note: These exercises can be done individually or in teams, in class, as homework, or in a virtual environment. Students can either write their results in a paper or prepare a short presentation to show their results.

1.   Perform a financial analysis for a project using the format provided in Figure 2-5. Assume the projected costs and benefits for this project are spread over four years as follows: Estimated costs are $100,000 in Year 1 and $25,000 each year in Years 2, 3, and 4. (*Hint:* Just change the years in the template file from 0, 1, 2, 3, and 4 to 1, 2, 3, and 4. The discount factors will automatically be recalculated.) Estimated benefits are $0 in Year 1 and $80,000 each year in Years 2, 3, and 4. Use an 8% discount rate. Use the business case financials template provided on the companion website to calculate and clearly display the NPV, ROI, and year in which payback occurs. In addition, write a paragraph explaining whether you would recommend investing in this project based on your financial analysis.

2.   Create a weighted scoring model to determine which project to select. Assume the criteria are cost, strategic value, risk, and financials, with weights of 15%, 40%, 20%, and 25%, respectively. Enter values for Project 1 as 90, 70, 85, and 50; Project 2 as 75, 80, 90, and 70; and Project 3 as 80 for each criterion. Use the weighted scoring model template provided on the companion website to create the model, calculate the weighted score, and graph the results.

3.   Search the Internet to find a real example of how a company or organization uses a structured process to aid in project, program, and/or project portfolio selection. As an alternative, document the process you followed to make a major decision where you had multiple options, such as what college or university to attend, what job to take,

where to live, what car to buy, and so on. Prepare a short paper or presentation summarizing your findings.

4. Research how two different organizations use an agile approach to implementing business strategy. You can use the reference about ING, as described in the Best Practice feature. Prepare a short paper or presentation summarizing your findings.

5. Search the Internet for software that helps organizations perform strategic planning, project selection, or project portfolio management. Summarize at least three different tools and discuss whether or not you think these tools are good investments in a one- to two-page paper. Cite your references.

6. Watch two different videos about creating and using mind maps, as described in the Video Highlights feature in this chapter. You can find your own videos, or use the direct links available from *www.intropm.com*. Summarize key points of the videos in a short paper or presentation.

7. Watch several of the video tutorials for using MindView software from www.matchware.com. Create your own mind map using this software for a project to plan your dream vacation.

TEAM PROJECTS

1. Find someone who has been involved in the project selection process within an organization. Prepare several interview questions, and then ask him or her the questions in person, via the phone, or via the Internet. Be sure to ask if he or she uses any of the project selection tools discussed in this chapter (for example, ROI, weighted scoring models, balanced scorecards, or other methods). Discuss the results with your team, and then prepare a one- to two-page paper or prepare a short presentation summarizing your findings.

2. Search the Internet to find two good examples of how organizations group projects into programs and two examples of how they create project portfolios. Write a one- to two-page paper or prepare a short presentation summarizing your results, being sure to cite your references.

3. Develop criteria that your class could use to help select what projects to pursue for implementation by your class or another group. For example, criteria might include benefits to the organization, interest level of the sponsor, interest level of the class, and fit with class skills and timing. Determine a weight for each criterion, and then enter the criteria and weights into a weighted scoring model, similar to that shown in Figure 2-9. (You can use the template for a weighted scoring model provided on the companion website.) Then review the list of projects you prepared in Chapter 1, Team Project 3, and enter scores for at least five of those projects. Calculate the weighted score for each project. Write a one- to two-page paper or prepare a short presentation summarizing your results.

4.   As a team, discuss other methods you could use to select class projects. Be sure to review the other methods described in this chapter (besides a weighted scoring model). Document your analysis of each approach as it applies to this situation in a two- to three-page paper or 10-minute presentation.

5.   Using your college, university, or an organization your team is familiar with, create a mind map of a SWOT analysis, including at least three branches under each category. Also, add sub-branches with at least four potential project ideas. You can create the mind map by hand, or try using software like MindView (30-day free trial available at www.matchware.com). You can watch video tutorials to learn how to use the software, as described in the Video Highlights feature in this chapter.

KEY TERMS

agile — able to move quickly and easily.

balanced scorecard — A methodology that converts an organization's value drivers to a series of defined metrics.

cash flow — Benefits minus costs, or income minus expenses.

directives — The new requirements imposed by management, government, or some external influence.

discretionary costs — costs that organizations have discretion in deciding whether to fund them

discount factor — A multiplier for each year based on the discount rate and year.

discount rate — The rate used in discounting future cash flows.

internal rate of return (IRR) — The discount rate that results in an NPV of zero for a project.

mind mapping — A technique that uses branches radiating out from a core idea to structure thoughts and ideas.

net present value (NPV) analysis — A method of calculating the expected net monetary gain or loss from a project by discounting all expected future cash inflows and outflows to the present point in time.

nondiscretionary costs — costs that organizations must fund to stay in business

opportunity cost of capital — The return available by investing the capital elsewhere.

payback period — The amount of time it will take to recoup, in the form of net cash inflows, the total dollars invested in a project.

required rate of return — The minimum acceptable rate of return on an investment.

return on investment (ROI) — (Benefits minus costs) divided by costs.

strategic planning — The process of determining long-term objectives by analyzing the strengths and weaknesses of an organization, studying opportunities and threats in the business environment, predicting future trends, and projecting the need for new products and services.

SWOT analysis — Analyzing **S**trengths, **W**eaknesses, **O**pportunities, and **T**hreats.

weighted scoring model — A technique that provides a systematic process for basing project selection on numerous criteria.

END NOTES

[1]Mike Peterson, "Why Are We Doing This Project?" Projects@Work, (*www.projectsatwork.com*) (February 22, 2005).

[2]Nemours, "Blueprint for the Future: Nemours Strategic Plan 2008-2012," Nemours, (2007).

[3]Deepak Mahadevan, "ING's Agile Transformation," McKinsey Quarterly, (January 2017).

[4]Dennis J. Cohen and Robert J. Graham, *The Project Manager's MBA*. San Francisco: Jossey-Bass (2001), p. 31.

[5]The Balanced Scorecard Institute, "What Is a Balanced Scorecard?" (*www.balancedscorecard.org*) (accessed April 2017).

[6]Nemours, "Blueprint for the Future: Nemours Strategic Plan 2008-2012," Nemours, (2007).

[7]The Compleat Sean Bean Website, "Lord of the Rings" (February 23, 2004).

[8]Scott Berinato, "Do the Math," CIO Magazine (October 1, 2001).

[9]Project Management Institute, "Pulse of the Profession®: Success Rates Rise: Transforming the High Cost of Low Performance"" (2017).

Chapter 3
Initiating Projects

LEARNING OBJECTIVES

After reading this chapter, you will be able to:

- Describe the five project management process groups, define a project life cycle, map the process groups to knowledge areas, discuss other project management methodologies, explain the concept of agile project management, and understand the importance of top management commitment and organizational standards
- Discuss the initiating process, including pre-initiating activities
- Prepare a business case to justify the need for a project
- Identify project stakeholders and perform a stakeholder analysis
- Create a project charter and assumption log
- Describe the importance of holding a good project kick-off meeting

OPENING CASE

Marie Scott worked with other managers at Global Construction, Inc. to decide what projects their firm should undertake to meet business needs. Construction is a low-margin, very competitive industry, and productivity improvements are crucial to improving shareholder returns. After participating in several strategic planning and project selection workshops, one of the opportunities the company decided to pursue was just-in-time training. Several managers pointed out that Global Construction was spending more than the industry average on training its employees, especially in its sales, purchasing, engineering, and information technology departments, yet productivity for those workers had not improved much in recent years. They also knew that they needed to transfer knowledge from many of their retiring workers to their younger workers. Global Construction, Inc. still offered most courses during work hours using an instructor-led format, and the course topics had not changed in years.

Several managers knew that their competitors had successfully implemented just-in-time training programs so that their workers could get the type of training they needed when they needed it. For example, much of the training was provided over the Internet, so employees could access it anytime, anywhere. Employees were also able to ask questions of instructors as well as experts within the company at any time via the Internet to help them perform specific job duties. In addition, experts documented important knowledge and let other workers share their suggestions. Management believed that Global Construction could reduce training costs and improve productivity by successfully implementing a project to provide just-in-time training on key topics and promote a more collaborative working environment.

Mike Sundby, the vice president of human resources, was the project's champion. After successfully completing a Phase I Just-In-Time Training study to decide how they should proceed with the overall project, Mike and his directors selected Kristin Maur to lead Phase II of the project. Kristin suggested partnering with an outside firm to help with some of the project's technical aspects. Mike asked Kristin to start forming her project team and to prepare important initiating documents, including a detailed business case, a stakeholder register and engagement strategy, and a project charter for the project. He was also looking forward to participating in the official kick-off meeting.

PROJECT MANAGEMENT PROCESS GROUPS

Recall from Chapter 1 that project management consists of ten project management knowledge areas: project integration, scope, schedule, cost, quality, human resource, communications, risk, procurement, and stakeholder management. Another important concept to understand is that projects involve five project management process groups: initiating, planning, executing, monitoring and controlling, and closing. Applying these process groups in a consistent, structured fashion increases the chance of project success. This chapter briefly describes each project management process group and then describes the initiating process in detail through a case study based on Global Construction's Just-In-Time Training project. Subsequent chapters describe the other process groups and apply them to the same project.

Project management process groups progress from initiating activities to planning activities, executing activities, monitoring and controlling activities, and closing activities. A **process** is a series of actions directed toward a particular result. All projects use the five process groups as outlined in the following list:

- **Initiating processes** include actions to define and authorize new projects and project phases. A project charter and a kick-off meeting are often used during initiation. This chapter will describe initiating processes in detail.

- **Planning processes** include devising and maintaining a workable scheme to ensure that the project meets its scope, schedule, and cost goals as well as organizational needs. There are often many different plans to address various project needs as they relate to each knowledge area. For example, as part of project scope management for the Just-In-Time Training project, the project team will develop a scope statement to plan the work that needs to be done to develop and provide the products and services produced as part of the project. As part of project schedule management, the project team will create a detailed schedule that lets everyone know when specific work will start and end. As part of procurement management, the project team will plan for work that will be done by external organizations to support the project. Chapters 4 through 6 describe the planning processes in detail.

- **Executing processes** include coordinating people and other resources to carry out the project plans and produce the deliverables of the project or phase. A **deliverable** is a product or service produced or provided as part of a project. For example, a project to construct a new office building would include deliverables such as blueprints, cost estimates, progress reports, the building structure, windows, plumbing, and flooring. The Just-In-Time Training project would include deliverables such as a training needs survey, training materials, and classes. Chapter 7 describes executing processes in detail.

- **Monitoring and controlling processes** measure progress toward achieving project goals, monitor deviation from plans, and take corrective action to match progress with plans and customer expectations. For example, the main objective of the Just-In-Time Training project is to provide training to help employees be more productive. If the first training course does not improve productivity or meet other customer expectations, the project team should take corrective action to deliver more suitable training courses. As another example, if the project team continues to miss deadlines in the schedule for the Just-In-Time Training project, the project manager should lead the team in taking corrective action, such as developing a more realistic schedule or securing additional resources to help meet deadlines. Chapter 8 describes monitoring and controlling processes in detail.

- **Closing processes** include formalizing acceptance of the project or phase and bringing it to an orderly end. Administrative activities are often involved in this process group, such as archiving project files, closing out contracts, documenting lessons learned, and receiving formal acceptance of the deliverables. It is also important to plan for a smooth transition of the results of the project to the responsible operational group. For example, after the Just-In-Time Training project is completed, the training department will need to schedule and provide courses developed as part of the project. The planning for this transition should be done as part of the closing process group. Chapter 9 describes closing processes in detail.

The process groups are not isolated events. For example, project managers must perform monitoring and controlling processes throughout the project's life cycle. The level of activity and length of each process group varies for every project. Figure 3-1 shows an example of process group interactions within a project or phase. Normally, executing processes require the most resources and time, followed by planning processes. Initiating and closing processes are usually the shortest (at the beginning and end of a project or phase, respectively), and they require the least amount of resources and time. However, every project is unique, so there can be exceptions.

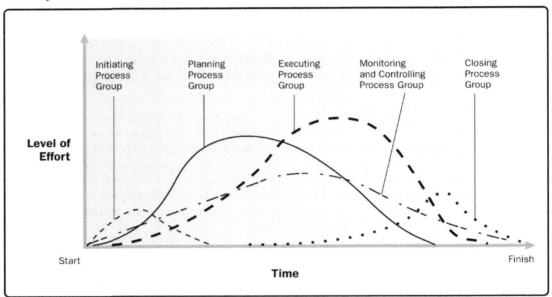

Figure 3-1. Example of process group interactions within a project or phase
Source: Project Management Institute, Inc., *A Guide to the Project Management Body of Knowledge (PMBOK® Guide) – Sixth Edition* (2017).

Many people ask for guidelines on how much time to spend in each process group. In his 2006 book, *Alpha Project Managers: What the Top 2% Know That Everyone Else Does Not*, Andy Crowe collected data from 860 project managers in various companies and industries in the U.S. He found that the best or "alpha" project managers spent more time on every process group than their counterparts except for execution, as shown in Figure 3-2.[1]

Process Group	Alpha PM	Average PM	Alpha Difference (%)
Initiating	2%	1%	100% more
Planning	21%	11%	91% more
Executing	69%	82%	16% less
Monitoring & Controlling	5%	4%	25% more
Closing	3%	2%	50% more
Total	100%	100%	

Figure 3-2. Time spent on each project management process group

This breakdown suggests that the most time should be spent on executing, followed by planning. However, it also suggests, as do several studies since, that most project managers jump in and spend too much time executing the project and not enough time preparing for and then monitoring and controlling the work itself. Because most of project costs are spent during executing, one could conclude that projects that are better planned and controlled will be less costly to complete.

Project Life Cycle

A project life cycle is a series of phases that a project passes through from its start to its finish. The process groups apply to entire projects as well as to project phases. A **phase** is a distinct stage in project development, and most projects have distinct phases as part of their life cycle. The *PMBOK® Guide – Sixth Edition*, suggests four generic names for a project life cycle as shown in Figure 3-3. The first phase, conducted at the start of a project, is simply called starting the project. Before beginning the second phase, organizing and preparing, a review or phase gate meeting should be held to determine if the project should be continued, cancelled, or redirected. Phase gate meetings should also be held before starting the third phase, carrying out the project work, and the fourth and final phase, ending the project.

Also, note the inclusion of pre-project work in Figure 3-3. Organizations often perform a needs assessment, develop a business case, and create a benefits management plan before officially starting a project, often as part of project selection. These documents are discussed in more detail later in this chapter.

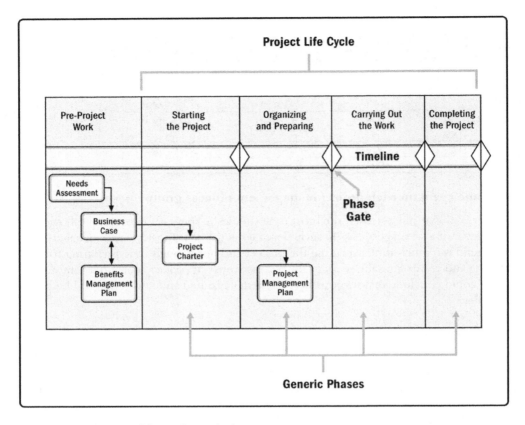

Figure 3-3. Project life cycle and phase gates
Source: Project Management Institute, Inc., *A Guide to the Project Management Body of Knowledge (PMBOK® Guide) – Sixth Edition* (2017).

Project life cycles can be predictive, adaptive, or a hybrid of both approaches. A predictive life cycle, also called plan-driven, is used when the requirements can be well defined at the beginning of a project. For example, if a customer knows they want a particular house built, detailed blueprints can be made and then followed, allowing for minor changes along the way. An adaptive life cycle is used when requirements are not well defined up front. Adaptive approaches can be iterative, incremental, or agile. A hybrid or combination of approaches can be used when the nature of different deliverables calls for different approaches. For example, the customer wanting a particular house might also want smart technology to control lights, music, appliances, etc., but be unsure of what the requirements are at the beginning of the project.

Figure 3-4 shows the continuum of project life cycles, going from plan-driven to agile. In addition to how well requirements are defined, other factors that differ with each approach are how often products are delivered, how change is incorporated, how much key stakeholders are involved, and how risk and cost are controlled. Projects that are highly adaptive often perform all process groups continuously throughout the project life cycle.

Predictive	Iterative	Incremental	Agile
Requirements are defined up-front before development begins	Requirements can be elaborated at periodic intervals during delivery		Requirements are elaborated frequently during delivery
Deliver plans for the eventual deliverable. Then deliver only a single final product at end of project timeline	Delivery can be divided into subsets of the overall product		Delivery occurs frequently with customer-valued subsets of the overall product
Change is constrained as much as possible	Change is incorporated at periodic intervals		Change is incorporated in real-time during delivery
Key stakeholders are involved at specific milestones	Key stakeholders are regularly involved		Key stakeholders are continuously involved
Risk and cost are controlled by detailed planning of mostly knowable considerations	Risk and cost are controlled by progressively elaborating the plans with new information		Risk and cost are controlled as requirements and constraints emerge

Figure 3-4. The continuum of project life cycles
Source: Project Management Institute, Inc., *A Guide to the Project Management Body of Knowledge (PMBOK® Guide) – Sixth Edition* (2017).

Mapping the Process Groups to the Knowledge Areas

You can map the process groups into the ten project management knowledge areas. For example, project integration management includes the following processes:

- Develop project charter (during the initiating process group).

- Develop project management plan (during the planning process group).

- Direct and manage project work (during the executing process group).

- Monitor and control project work and perform integrated change control (during the monitoring and controlling process group).

- Close project or phase (during the closing process group).

Based on the *PMBOK® Guide – Sixth Edition*, there are 49 total processes in project management. Figure 3-5 provides a big-picture view of the relationships among these processes, the process group in which they are typically completed, and the knowledge areas into which they fit. The numbering is based on the chapter and section numbers in the *PMBOK® Guide*. This list of processes by knowledge area is a framework that PMI suggests most projects may require. It's also important to note that project teams should tailor this framework to meet the unique needs of their particular project. Few projects require that all 49 processes be used, for example.

Knowledge Areas	Project Management Process Groups				
	Initiating Process Group	Planning Process Group	Executing Process Group	Monitoring and Controlling Process Group	Closing Process Group
4. Project Integration Management	4.1 Develop Project Charter	4.2 Develop Project Management Plan	4.3 Direct and Manage Project Work 4.4 Manage Project Knowledge	4.5 Monitor and Control Project Work 4.6 Perform Integrated Change Control	4.7 Close Project or Phase
5. Project Scope Management		5.1 Plan Scope Management 5.2 Collect Requirements 5.3 Define Scope 5.4 Create WBS		5.5 Validate Scope 5.6 Control Scope	
6. Project Schedule Management		6.1 Plan Schedule Management 6.2 Define Activities 6.3 Sequence Activities 6.4 Estimate Activity Durations 6.5 Develop Schedule		6.6 Control Schedule	
7. Project Cost Management		7.1 Plan Cost Management 7.2 Estimate Costs 7.3 Determine Budget		7.4 Control Costs	
8. Project Quality Management		8.1 Plan Quality Management	8.2 Manage Quality	8.3 Control Quality	
9. Project Resource Management		9.1 Plan Resource Management 9.2 Estimate Activity Resources	9.3 Acquire Resources 9.4 Develop Team 9.5 Manage Team	9.6 Control Resources	
10. Project Communications Management		10.1 Plan Communications Management	10.2 Manage Communications	10.3 Monitor Communications	
11. Project Risk Management		11.1 Plan Risk Management 11.2 Identify Risks 11.3 Perform Qualitative Risk Analysis 11.4 Perform Quantitative Risk Analysis 11.5 Plan Risk Responses	11.6 Implement Risk Responses	11.7 Monitor Risks	
12. Project Procurement Management		12.1 Plan Procurement Management	12.2 Conduct Procurements	12.3 Control Procurements	
13. Project Stakeholder Management	13.1 Identify Stakeholders	13.2 Plan Stakeholder Engagement	13.3 Manage Stakeholder Engagement	13.4 Monitor Stakeholder Engagement	

Figure 3-5. Project management process group and knowledge area mapping
Source: Project Management Institute, Inc., *A Guide to the Project Management Body of Knowledge (PMBOK® Guide) – Sixth Edition* (2017).

This chapter describes in detail the processes followed and the outputs produced while initiating the Just-In-Time Training project. The *PMBOK® Guide – Sixth Edition*, suggests that the main outputs of initiating include a stakeholder register, a project charter, and an assumptions log. In addition to these outputs, this chapter also includes a kick-off meeting as an initiating output as well as some outputs produced during a pre-initiating process.

You can access templates to help create many of the documents created in project management on the companion website for this text, as summarized in Appendix B. A **template** is a file with a preset format that serves as a starting point for creating various documents so that the format and structure do not have to be re-created. A template can also ensure that critical information is not left out or overlooked. The remaining chapters of this text follow a similar format to describe the processes and outputs used for the Just-In-Time Training project for planning, executing, monitoring and controlling, and closing.

Several organizations use PMI's information as a foundation for developing their own project management methodologies, as described in the next section. Notice in Figure 3-4 that the majority of project management processes occur as part of the planning process group. Because each project is unique, project teams are always trying to do something that has not been done before. To succeed at unique and new activities, project teams must do a fair amount of planning. Recall, however, that the most time and money is normally spent on executing because that is where the project's products and/or services (for example, the buildings for a construction project, the training courses for a training project, etc.) are produced. It is good practice for organizations to determine how project management will work best in their own organizations.

Developing a Project Management Methodology

Some organizations spend a great deal of time and money on training efforts for general project management skills, but after the training, a project manager might still not know how to tailor their project management skills to the organization's particular needs. Because of this problem, some organizations develop their own internal project management methodologies. The *PMBOK® Guide* is a **standard** that describes best practices for *what* should be done to manage a project. A **methodology** describes *how* things should be done.

Besides using the *PMBOK® Guide* as a basis for a project management methodology, many organizations use others, such as the following:

- **PRojects IN Controlled Environments (PRINCE2)**: Originally developed for information technology projects, PRINCE2 was released in 1996 as a generic project management methodology by the U.K. Office of Government Commerce (OCG). It is the de facto standard in the U.K. and is used in over 50 countries. PRINCE2 defines 45 separate sub-processes and organizes these into eight process groups as follows:

    1. Starting Up a Project

    2. Planning

3.   Initiating a Project

4.   Directing a Project

5.   Controlling a Stage

6.   Managing Product Delivery

7.   Managing Stage Boundaries

8.   Closing a Project

- **Rational Unified Process (RUP) framework**: RUP is an iterative software development process that focuses on team productivity and delivers software best practices to all team members. According to RUP expert Bill Cottrell, "RUP embodies industry-standard management and technical methods and techniques to provide a software engineering process particularly suited to creating and maintaining component-based software system solutions."[2] Cottrell explains how you can tailor RUP to include the *PMBOK® Guide* process groups, because several customers asked for that capability.

- **Six Sigma**: Many organizations have projects underway that use Six Sigma methodologies. The work of many project quality experts contributed to the development of today's Six Sigma principles. In their book, The Six Sigma Way, authors Peter Pande, Robert Neuman, and Roland Cavanagh define Six Sigma as "a comprehensive and flexible system for achieving, sustaining and maximizing business success. Six Sigma is uniquely driven by close understanding of customer needs, disciplined use of facts, data, and statistical analysis, and diligent attention to managing, improving, and reinventing business processes."[3] Six Sigma's target for perfection is the achievement of no more than 3.4 defects, errors, or mistakes per million opportunities. The two main methodologies used on Six Sigma projects: DMAIC (Define, Measure, Analyze, Improve, and Control) is used to improve an existing business process, and DMADV (Define, Measure, Analyze, Design, and Verify) is used to create new product or process designs to achieve predictable, defect-free performance. (See websites like *www.isixsigma.com* for more information.)

- **Agile**: Many software development projects use agile methods, meaning they use an iterative workflow and incremental delivery of software in short iterations. Popular agile approaches include Scrum, extreme programming, feature driven development, and lean software development. In 2011, PMI introduced a new certification called Agile Certified Practitioner (ACP) to address the growing interest in agile project management. See the following section for more information on agile project management. Note that agile can also be applied to project planning, as described in Chapter 2, as well as many other areas, including manufacturing and even education.

Many organizations tailor a standard or methodology to meet their unique needs. For example, if organizations use the *PMBOK® Guide* as the basis for their project management methodology, they still have to do a fair amount of work to adapt it to their work environment.

For example, the *PMBOK® Guide – Sixth Edition* lists *what* information a project charter, as described later in this chapter, should address:

- Project purpose

- Measureable project objectives and related success criteria

- High-level requirements

- High-level project description, boundaries, and key deliverables

- Overall project risk

- Summary milestone schedule

- Preapproved financial resources

- Key stakeholder list

- Project approval requirements (i.e., what constitutes project success, who decides the project is successful, and who signs off on the project)

- Project exit criteria (i.e., what are the conditions to be met to close or to cancel the project or phase)

- Assigned project manager, responsibility, and authority level

- Name and authority of the sponsor or other person(s) authorizing the project charter

However, the *PMBOK® Guide* does not provide specific information on *how* the previously listed project charter requirements should be created, when, or by whom. Also, many organizations prefer that project charters be fairly short documents. They might create separate documents with project justification information or approval requirements, if those are lengthy documents. Successful organizations have found that they need to develop and follow a customized, formal project management methodology that describes not only what needs to be done, but also how it should be done in their organizations. They also must involve key stakeholders and ensure that projects are aligned with organizational needs.

Part of creating and following a project management methodology includes the creation and use of templates. Companies that excel in project management know that it does not make sense to reinvent the wheel by having every project manager decide how to create standard documents, such as project charters and business cases. They also know that top management commitment and organizational standards are crucial for project success.

WHAT WENT RIGHT?

William Ibbs and Justin Reginato completed a five-year study to help quantify the value of project management. Among their findings are the following points:

- Organizations with more mature project management practices have better project performance, which result in projects being completed on time and within budget much more often than most projects.
- Project management maturity is strongly correlated with more predictable project schedule and cost performance.
- Organizations that follow good project management methodologies have lower direct costs of project management (6–7 percent) than those that do not (11–20 percent).[4]

A more recent study found that organizations that follow proven project management practices waste *28 times* less money because they successfully complete their strategic initiatives. Only 7 percent of organizations were considered to be champions, meaning 80% or more of their projects were completed on time and budget while meeting original goals and business intent.[5]

Agile Project Management

As described in the previous section on project planning, agile means "able to move quickly and easily." It is also a popular software development methodology. Early software development projects used a waterfall approach, where requirements were defined in detail before any software was written. This approach works when requirements are stable, but as the rate of change of business and technology increased, this approach became unrealistic for many projects. In response to the need to improve the process, a group of 17 people (called the Agile Alliance) developed the Manifesto for Agile Software Development in 2001, as follows:

Manifesto for Agile Software Development

We are uncovering better ways of developing
software by doing it and helping others do it.
Through this work we have come to value:

Individuals and interactions over processes and tools
Working software over comprehensive documentation
Customer collaboration over contract negotiation
Responding to change over following a plan

That is, while there is value in the items on
the right, we value the items on the left more.[6]

Organizations that implement agile are responsible for interpreting and applying these values. Some people associate agile with specific techniques, such as Scrum. **Scrum** is the leading agile development method for completing projects with a complex, innovative scope of work. The term was coined in 1986 in a Harvard Business Review study that compared high-

performing, cross-functional teams to the scrum formation used by rugby teams. The basic
Scrum framework is summarized in the following list and illustrated in Figure 3-6:

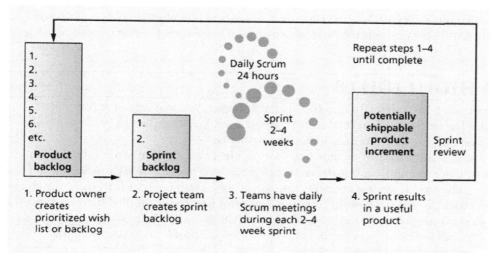

Figure 3-6. Scrum framework (Schwalbe Information Technology Project Management, Revised Seventh Edition, 2014)

A textual description of the Scrum framework follows:

- A product owner creates a prioritized wish list called a product backlog.
- During sprint planning, the team pulls a small chunk from the top of that wish list, a sprint backlog, and decides how to implement those pieces.
- The team has a certain amount of time — a sprint (usually two to four weeks) — to complete its work, but it meets each day to assess its progress (daily Scrum).
- Along the way, the ScrumMaster keeps the team focused on its goal.
- At the end of the sprint, the work should be potentially shippable: ready to hand to a customer, put on a store shelf, or show to a stakeholder.
- The sprint ends with a sprint review and retrospective.
- As the next sprint begins, the team chooses another chunk of the product backlog and begins working again.

The cycle repeats until enough items in the product backlog have been completed, the budget is depleted, or a deadline arrives. Which of these milestones marks the end of the work is entirely specific to the project. No matter which impetus stops work, Scrum ensures that the most valuable work has been completed when the project ends.[7]

Today many types of projects use Scrum to help focus on teamwork, complete the most important work first, and add business value. See the Video Highlights describing work done by Wikispeed volunteers, for example. One could view agile and the Scrum framework as methods that simply break down a big project into several smaller projects, defining the scope for each one. Project teams can have brief meetings each day to decide how to get the most important work done first without calling the meetings "scrums." As stated earlier in this chapter, several different methods are available for managing projects. Because projects are unique, someone must decide what processes are needed and how they should be performed. Project teams can follow one specific process, a hybrid of several, or their own customized approach.

VIDEO HIGHLIGHTS

In the Axosoft video "Scrum in 10 Minutes," Hamid Shojaee, an experienced software developer who has worked with several major corporations, briefly explains key concepts like product backlogs, team roles, sprints, and burndown charts.

Techniques from the just-in-time inventory control method **Kanban** can be used in conjunction with Scrum. Kanban was developed in Japan by Toyota Motor Corporation. It uses visual cues to guide workflow. For example, teams can place cards on boards to show the status of work in the backlog, such as new, in progress, and complete. Cards on the board are moved to the right to show progress in completing work. Kanban also helps limit work in progress by making a bottleneck visible so people can collaborate to solve problems that created the bottleneck. Kanban helps improve day-to-day workflow, while Scrum provides the structure for improving the organization of projects. The term "Scrumban" is also used to describe using a combination of Scrum and Kanban.

You can also see how agile techniques can be applied to manufacturing projects like building cars. Joe Justice, a consultant for Scrum, Inc. gave a TEDx talk called Wikispeed describing this process. He also discusses how agile can be used for social good, such as eradicating Polio and developing low-cost medical centers in developing communities. Joe founded the volunteer organization called Wikispeed to create a platform for people to contribute their talents to solving a variety of problems using an agile approach.

The increased interest in agile is based partly on the hope that it will somehow make project management easier. Many books, courses, and consultants are capitalizing on this "new" approach. Seasoned project managers understand that they have always had the option of customizing how they run projects, but that project management is not easy, even when using agile.

The Importance of Top Management Commitment

Without top management commitment, many projects will fail. Some projects have a senior manager called a **champion** who acts as a key proponent for a project. Projects are part of the larger organizational environment, and many factors that might affect a project are out of the project manager's control. Top management commitment is crucial for the following reasons:

- Project managers need adequate resources. The best way to hurt a project is to withhold the required money, human resources, and/or visibility for the project. If project managers have top management commitment, they will also have adequate resources and can focus on completing their specific projects.

- Project managers often require approval for unique project needs in a timely manner. For example, a project team might encounter unexpected issues and need additional resources halfway through the project, or the project manager might need to offer special pay and benefits to attract and retain key project personnel. With top management commitment, project managers can meet these specific needs in a timely manner.

- Project managers must have cooperation from people in other parts of the organization. Because most projects cut across functional areas, top management must help project managers deal with the political issues that often arise in these types of situations. If certain functional managers are not responding to project managers' requests for necessary information, top management must step in to encourage the functional managers to cooperate.

- Project managers often need someone to mentor them to improve their leadership skills. Many project managers come from technical positions and are inexperienced as leaders. Senior managers should take the time to pass on advice on how to be good leaders. They should encourage new project managers to take classes to develop leadership skills and allocate the time and funds for them to do so.

The Need for Organizational Standards

Another deficiency in most organizations is the lack of standards or guidelines to follow that could help in performing project management functions. These standards or guidelines might be as simple as providing standard forms or templates for common project documents, examples of good project documentation, or guidelines on how the project manager should perform certain activities, such as holding a kick-off meeting or providing status information. Providing status information might seem like common sense to senior managers, but many new project managers have never given a project status report and are not used to communicating with a wide variety of project stakeholders. Top management must support the development of these standards and guidelines and encourage or even enforce their use.

Some organizations invest heavily in project management by creating a project management office or center of excellence. A **project management office (PMO)** is an organizational entity created to assist project managers in achieving project goals. Some organizations develop career paths for project managers. Some require that all project managers have some type of project management certification and that all employees have some type of project management training. The implementation of all of these standards demonstrates an organization's commitment to project management and helps ensure project success.

A 2016 study found that 85 percent of U.S. organizations reported having PMOs. Figure 3-7 shows the percentage based on size. Small organizations were defined as those having revenues less than $100 million; mid-size between $100 million and $1 billion, and large over $1 billion. These percentages have grown from previous surveys, showing the growing importance of using standard project management processes in organizations of all sizes. The study also found that PMOs in high-performing organizations were twice as old, on average, as those in low performers (6 vs. 3 years old). [8]

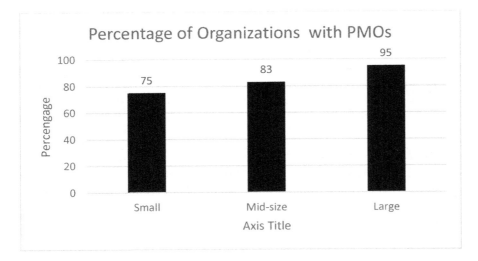

Figure 3-7. Percentage of Organizations with PMOs

Source: PM Solutions, "The State of the Project Management Office (PMO) 2016," 2016.

Below are possible goals of a PMO:

- Collect, organize, and integrate project data for the entire organization

- Research, develop, and share best practices in project management

- Develop and maintain templates, tools, standards, and methodologies

- Develop or coordinate training in various project management topics

- Develop and provide a formal career path for project managers

- Provide project management consulting services

- Provide a structure to house project managers while they are acting in those roles or are between projects

Many people learn best by example. The following section describes an example of how Global Construction applied initiating processes to the Just-In-Time Training project. It uses some of the ideas from the *PMBOK® Guide* and additional ideas to meet the unique needs of this project and organization. Several templates illustrate how project teams prepare various project management documents. You can download these templates from the companion website for this text.

BEST PRACTICE

It is very important to follow best practices while initiating projects, especially to avoid major scope problems. Senior management must take an active role in following these best practices:

- Keep the scope realistic. Don't make projects so large that they can't be completed. Break large projects down into a series of smaller ones.
- Involve users from the start. Assign key users to the project team, invite them to important meetings, and require their signatures on key documents. Assign a manager from the operations group most affected by the project as the project manager. Also, assign a champion to help promote the project.
- Use off-the-shelf hardware, software, or other technology whenever possible. Many people enjoy using the latest and greatest technology, but business needs, not technology trends, must take priority.
- Follow good project management processes. As described in this chapter and others, there are several standards and methodologies for managing projects. Senior managers and project teams should define and use them as appropriate on their projects.

PRE-INITIATING AND INITIATING GLOBAL CONSTRUCTION'S JUST-IN-TIME TRAINING PROJECT

Figure 3-8 illustrates the process that Global Construction will follow for starting the Just-In-Time Training project. Notice that several processes are completed *before* the project initiation starts. First, the project is approved through a formal project selection process and is given the go-ahead. Second, senior managers perform several activities as part of pre-initiating, as described in the following section. Finally, initiating begins as the project manager works with the team and other stakeholders to identify and understand project stakeholders, create the project charter, and hold a kick-off meeting.

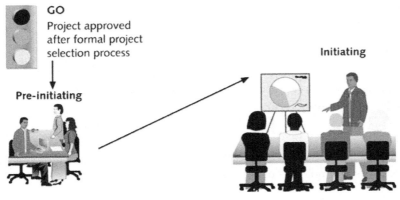

Senior management work together to:

- Determine scope, schedule, and cost constraints

- Identify the project sponsor

- Select the project manager

- Develop a business case for the project

- Review processes/expectations

- Determine if the project should be divided into two or more smaller projects

Project managers lead efforts to:

- Identify and understand project stakeholders

- Create the project charter and assumption log

- Hold a kick-off meeting

Figure 3-8. Initiating process summary

Pre-initiating Processes and Outputs

It is good practice to lay the groundwork for a project before it officially starts. After a project is approved, senior managers should meet to:

- Determine, at a high level, the scope, schedule, and cost constraints for the project

- Identify the project sponsor

- Select the project manager

- Develop a business case for the project, if required

- Meet with the project manager to review the process and expectations for managing the project

- Determine if the project should be divided into two or more smaller projects

The first three activities seem obvious. Of course you need to determine project constraints and decide who will sponsor and manage the project. Many projects require a formal business case before investing a significant amount of money in a project, as described later in this section. But why is it necessary to perform these last two tasks? Many organizations have organizational processes and procedures in place for managing projects. It is very important for project managers to understand them as well as the expectations for the project. For example, will there be formal management reviews for the project, and if so, how often will they be held? Are there any regulations, standards, or guidelines related to the project? Is there historical information or are there reports on lessons learned from past projects that might apply to this project? Senior managers should also share their wisdom with project managers to get the project off to a good start. For example, they might recommend key people who would be good team members for the project or offer suggestions based on past experiences.

Many people know from experience that it is easier to successfully complete a small project than a large one. It often makes sense to break large projects down into two or more smaller projects. For Global Construction's Just-In-Time Training project, senior management decided to use this approach. They knew that when scope, schedule, and cost goals for a large project were unclear, it would help to have a Phase I project to clarify the situation. For a large training project, there is often a study project done first before investing in a larger project.

Lucy Camarena, training director, would sponsor the study project, called the Just-In-Time Training Phase I project. Mike Sundby, the vice president of human resources, would act as the project champion. Lucy assigned one of her senior staff members, Ron Ryan, to manage the project. The scope, schedule, and cost goals and a summary of the approach and assumptions are provided in Figure 3-9.

Senior managers were satisfied with the results of the Phase I project, but they realized that they did not want someone from the HR department to lead the Phase II project. Instead, they wanted a manager from one of their key operating divisions—such as sales, engineering, or purchasing—to lead the project. It was important to have buy-in for this new training program from the operating groups, and a strong project manager from one of those areas would likely have more respect and influence than one from HR. Someone from operations would also know firsthand what type of training people in operations would need. HR posted the position internally, and a selection committee decided that Kristin Maur, a former purchasing specialist and now a sales manager, was the best person to lead the Just-In-Time Training Phase II project.

Scope Goals

- Investigate and document the training taken in the last two years by all internal employees.

- Determine what courses were taken, the cost of all training, the process for approving/assigning training, and the evaluation of the training by participants, if available.

- Survey employees to get their input on what training they believe they'll need in the next two years, how they'd like to take the training (i.e., instructor-led in-house, instructor-led through a local college, university, or training company, Web-based, CD/ROM, etc.). Also, hold focus groups to determine training needs.

- Recommend how to provide the most valuable training for Global Construction employees in the next two years.

- Determine the scope, schedule, and cost goals for the development and implementation of the Just-In-Time Training Phase II project.

Schedule Goal: Three months

Cost Goal: $50,000

Approach/Assumptions:

- All costs would be for internal labor.

- All managers and employees would receive information about this study project.

- A response rate of 30% would be acceptable for the survey.

- The project team would do extensive research to back up their recommendations.

- The team would also provide detailed monthly reports and presentations to a steering committee.

- The final deliverables would include a one-hour final presentation and a comprehensive project report documenting all of the information and recommendations.

Figure 3-9. Summary information for Just-In-Time Training Phase I project

As mentioned earlier, senior managers at Global Construction knew that it was good practice to have experienced managers from operations lead projects that were critical to the operational areas. They also knew that they needed support from several senior managers in the operating divisions as well as other areas, such as IT. So, they asked key managers from several divisions to be on a project steering committee to oversee the project. As its name implies, a project steering committee steers a project in the right direction by overseeing it and providing guidance to the project manager. The people on the steering committee are important stakeholders on the project.

PREPARING A BUSINESS CASE

A key document often produced during the pre-initiation phase of project is a business case. As the name implies, a **business case** is a document that provides financial justification for investing in a project. Some organizations list different project management requirements based on the value of a project. For example, a project estimated to cost less than $50,000 might not require a business case. A project estimated to cost more than $1 million might need an extensive business case signed off by the Chief Financial Officer. Some projects also require a needs assessment before creating a business case, or, as in this example, a detailed needs assessment can be done as part of the project. Some projects also require a project benefits management plan, which can be done during pre-initiation or as part of the project itself, as was done in the Just-In-Time Training project.

Successful organizations initiate projects to meet business needs, and a common business need is to spend money wisely. As described in the opening case, Global Construction believed they could reduce training costs and improve productivity by successfully implementing a project to provide just-in-time training on key business activities. The Phase I project provided a wealth of information to help write a business case for the Phase II project. Kristin and Lucy reviewed this information carefully and worked together to create the business case. They also had one of the company's financial managers review the information for accuracy.

Contents of a Business Case

Like most project documents, the contents of a business case will vary to meet individual project needs. Typical information included in a business case includes the following:

- Introduction/Background
- Business Objective
- Current Situation and Problem/Opportunity Statement
- Critical Assumptions and Constraints
- Analysis of Options and Recommendations
- Preliminary Project Requirements
- Budget Estimate and Financial Analysis
- Schedule Estimate
- Potential Risks
- Exhibits

Because this project is relatively small and is for an internal sponsor, the business case is not as long as many other business cases. The following section shows the initial business case for the Just-In-Time Training project.

Sample Business Case

Kristin reviewed all of the information created from the Phase I project and drafted a business case. She reviewed it with her sponsor, Lucy (the training director) and had Peter from finance review the financial section. Peter told Kristin to be very conservative by not including any benefit projections that were based on productivity improvements. She still estimated that the project would have a 27 percent discounted ROI and payback in the second year after implementation (which is denoted as year 3 in Exhibit A in the Sample business case) after implementing the new training program. The resulting business case, including a detailed financial analysis, is provided in Figure 3-10.

Business Case

1.0 Introduction/ Background

Global Construction employs 10,000 full-time employees in ten different countries and fifteen states in the U.S. They spend an average of $1,000 per employee for training (not including tuition reimbursement), which is higher than the industry average. However, the productivity of workers, especially in the sales, purchasing, engineering, and information technology departments has not improved much in recent years. In the fast-paced, ever-changing construction market, training employees about new products, new technologies, and soft skills across a globally dispersed company with different populations is a challenge. By redesigning training, Global Construction can reduce training costs and improve productivity.

2.0 Business Objective

Global Construction's strategic goals include continuing growth and profitability. They must have a highly skilled workforce to continue to compete in a global environment. Current training programs, however, are expensive and outdated. They can reduce costs by providing more targeted and timely training to their employees and by taking advantage of new technologies and business partnerships. Global Construction can also increase profits by improving productivity, especially by improving supplier management and negotiation skills.

3.0 Current Situation and Problem/Opportunity Statement

Global Construction has not updated its training approach or course offerings in the past five years. Most training is provided on-site during business hours and uses a traditional instructor-led approach with little or no technology involved. Department managers often request slots for various courses, but then they send whoever is available to the course since the department has already paid for it. Therefore, there is often a mismatch between skills needed by employees and the skills taught in a course. The current training is expensive and ineffective. Many employees would like training in key subjects that are currently not provided and that would use more modern approaches and technologies. If the training is directly related to their jobs or interests, employees are willing to take it on their own time, if needed. Survey results indicated that employees are most in need of training in supplier management, negotiating skills, project management, Six Sigma (a quality management methodology) and software applications (i.e., spreadsheet and Web development tools).

4.0 Critical Assumptions and Constraints

This project requires strong participation and cooperation from a wide variety of people. A project steering committee will be formed to provide close oversight and guidance. Some of the requested training will be outsourced, as will development of unique courses. The project will include investigating and taking advantage of new training technologies, such as multimedia and Web-based courses that workers could take on their own time. Employees will also be able to contact instructors and internal experts via the Internet for guidance in performing current work tasks as part of this project.

5.0 Analysis of Options and Recommendation

There are three options for addressing this opportunity:

1. Do nothing. The business is doing well, Global Construction can continue to conduct training as they have done in the past.

2. Instead of providing any internal training, give each employee up to $1,000 to spend on outside training as approved by his/her supervisor. Require employees to stay with the company for one year after using training funds or return the money.

3. Design and implement a new training program as part of this project.

Based on the financial analysis and discussions with key stakeholders, option 3 is the best option.

6.0 Preliminary Project Requirements

The main requirements of this project include the following:

1. Based on survey results, the only current training that does not need to change is the Six Sigma training. No changes will be made in that area. The tuition reimbursement program will continue as is.

2. Training for improving supplier management and negotiating skills, especially international negotiations, have the highest priority since they are most important to the business today and in the next few years. Internal staff will work with outside firms to develop a customized approach to this training that takes advantage of internal experts and new technologies.

3. Demand is also high for training in project management and software applications. The project team will analyze several approaches for this training, including in-house courses, courses offered by local colleges/universities, and computer-based/online courses. They will develop and implement the best combination of approaches for these courses.

4. The project will include updating the corporate Intranet site to explain the new training program, to allow employees to sign up for and evaluate courses, and to track training demand and expenses.

5. The project team will develop an approach for measuring the effect of training on productivity on an annual basis.

7.0 Budget Estimate and Financial Analysis

A preliminary estimate of costs for the entire project is $1,000,000. Half of the cost is for internal labor, $250,000 is for outsourced labor, and $250,000 is for outsourced training programs. These are preliminary estimates that will be revised, as more details become known. Projected benefits are estimated very conservatively. Since the average amount spent on training last year was $1,000/employee, only a 10% or $100/employee reduction was assumed, and no benefits are included for improved productivity. Exhibit A summarizes the projected costs and benefits and shows the estimated net present value (NPV), return on investment (ROI), and the year in which payback occurs. It also lists assumptions made in performing this preliminary financial analysis. All of the financial estimates are very encouraging. The estimated payback is in the second year after implementing the new training program. The NPV is $505,795, and the discounted ROI based on a three-year implementation is 27 percent.

8.0 Schedule Estimate

The sponsor would like to see the entire project completed within one year. Courses will be provided as soon as they are available. The impact of training on productivity will be assessed one year after training is completed and annually thereafter.

9.0 Potential Risks

There are several risks involved with this project. The foremost risk is a lack of interest in the new training program. Employee inputs are crucial for developing the improved training and realizing its potential benefits on improving productivity. There are some technical risks in developing courses using advanced technologies. There are also risks related to outsourcing much of the labor and actual course materials/instruction. The main business risk is investing the time and money into this project and not realizing the projected benefits.

10.0 Exhibits Exhibit A: Financial Analysis

Discount rate	8%				
Assume the project is completed in Year 1					
			Year		
	1	2	3	4	Total
Costs	1,000,000	400,000	400,000	400,000	
Discount factor	0.93	0.86	0.79	0.74	
Discounted costs	925,926	342,936	317,533	294,012	1,880,406
Benefits	-	1,000,000	1,000,000	1,000,000	
Discount factor (rounded to two decimal places)	0.93	0.86	0.79	0.74	
Discounted benefits	-	860,000	790,000	740,000	2,390,000
Discounted benefits - costs	(925,926)	517,064	472,467	445,988	509,594 ◄— NPV
Cumulative benefits - costs	(925,926)	(408,861)	63,606	509,594	

ROI ——————————————►   27%

Payback in Year 3

Assumptions
Costs for the project are based on the following:
  Internal labor costs: $500,000
  Outsourced labor costs: $250,000
  Outsourced training programs: $250,000
After implementation, maintenance costs are estimated at 40% of total development cost
Benefits are estimated based on the following:
  $100/employee/year X 10,000 employees
No benefits are included for increased productivity

Figure 3-10. Sample business case

Now that important pre-initiating activities were completed and the project received the go ahead, Kristin Maur was ready to tackle important processes to initiate the Just-In-Time Training project.

Initiating Processes and Outputs

The main activities normally involved in project initiation include:

- Identifying project stakeholders

- Creating the project charter

- Creating the assumption log

- Holding a kick-off meeting

Key outputs of initiating, as described in the *PMBOK® Guide – Sixth Edition* are shown in Figure 3-11. Even though it is not part of the *PMBOK® Guide*, Kristin's company also requires a formal kick-off meeting as part of the initiating process group. The following sections of this chapter describe most of these outputs in detail for the larger Just-In-Time Training Phase II project, hereafter referred to as the Just-In-Time Training project. Note that change requests and the project management plan are described in later chapters, and project document updates, as its name implies, simply means updating any project documents that need to be updated.

Knowledge area	Initiating process	Outputs
Project integration management	Develop project charter	Project charter
		Assumption log
Project stakeholder management	Identify stakeholders	Stakeholder register
		Change requests
		Project management plan updates
		Project documents updates

Figure 3-11. Initiating processes and outputs

IDENTIFYING STAKEHOLDERS

Recall from Chapter 1 that project stakeholders are the people involved in or affected by project activities. The *PMBOK® Guide – Sixth Edition*, expands on this definition as follows: "Project stakeholders are individuals, groups, or organizations who may affect, be affected by, or perceive themselves to be affected by a decision, activity, or outcome of a project." Stakeholders can be internal to the organization or external.

- Internal project stakeholders generally include the project sponsor, project team, support staff, and internal customers for the project. Other internal stakeholders include top management, other functional managers, and other project managers. Because organizations have limited resources, projects affect top management, other functional managers, and other project managers by using some of the organization's limited resources.

- External project stakeholders include the project's customers (if they are external to the organization), competitors, suppliers, and other external groups that are potentially involved in or affected by the project, such as government officials and concerned citizens.

How does a project manager identify key project stakeholders and find out more about them? The best way is by asking around. There might be formal organizational charts or biographies that can provide some information, but the main goal is to help project managers manage relationships with key stakeholders. Talking to other people who have worked with those stakeholders usually provides the best information. For example, in this case, Kristin Maur knew who some of the key stakeholders were but did not know any of them well. It did not take her long, however, to get the information she needed.

Because the purpose of project management is to meet project requirements and satisfy stakeholders, it is critical that project managers and their teams take adequate time to identify, understand, and manage relationships with all project stakeholders. The main initiating output for this knowledge area is a stakeholder register, and a key technique for understanding stakeholders is a stakeholder analysis.

MEDIA SNAPSHOT

How would you like to have Mick Jagger, Keith Richards, Charlie Watts, and Ronnie Woods (the Rolling Stones) as your product owners? You might think differently about the song, "I can't get no satisfaction" in a different light!

Australia's International Entertainment Consulting (iEC) team executed a three-year, US$5.7 million project to produce a 20,000 square-foot exhibit called "Exhibitionism—The Rolling Stones." The exhibit opened in London in 2016, with stops planned in eleven cities around the world. Project director Ileen Gallagher from ISG Productions focused on making sure the Rolling Stones would get what they wanted and needed. Below are a few quotes from Gallagher and one of her famous stakeholders.

Ms. Gallagher: "When you are working with rock stars, you have to allow time for changes and manage expectations so it does not become a runaway train. There was constant back and forth with the band throughout the project, and we always tried to accommodate their wishes unless it was going to derail the budget or the schedule."

Mick Jagger: "We changed a lot of the ideas that were originally presented and substituted them. So it's been pretty hands-on…To make the decisions about what goes in and what doesn't is really difficult."[9]

Sample Stakeholder Register and Stakeholder Analysis

A **stakeholder register** is a document that includes details related to the identified project stakeholders. It can take various forms and include the following information:

- Identification information: The stakeholders' names, positions, locations, roles in the project, and contact information

- Assessment information: The stakeholders' major requirements and expectations, potential influences, phases of the project where there is the most interest

- Stakeholder classification: Internal/external, supporter/resistor, etc.

Figure 3-12 provides an example of a part of the stakeholder register for Kristin's project. Notice that it includes only basic stakeholder information, such as name, position, if they are internal or external to the organization, role on the project, and contact information. Since this document would be available to other people in their organization, Kristin was careful not to include information that might be sensitive, such as how strongly the stakeholder supported the project or how much power they had. She would keep these and other issues in mind discretely and use them in performing the stakeholder analysis.

Name	Position	Internal/ External	Project Role	Contact Information
Mike Sundby	VP of HR	Internal	Project champion	msundy@globalconstruction.com
Lucy Camerena	Training Director	Internal	Project sponsor	lcamerena@globalconstruction.com
Ron Ryan	Senior HR staff member	Internal	Led the Phase I project	rryan@globalconstruction.com

Figure 3-12. Sample stakeholder register

A **stakeholder analysis** is a technique for analyzing information to determine which stakeholders' interests to focus on and how to increase stakeholder support throughout the project. After identifying key project stakeholders, you can use different classification models to determine an approach for managing relationships with them. For example, you can create a power/interest grid to group stakeholders based on their level of authority (power) and their level of concern (interest) for project outcomes, as shown in Figure 3-13. You should manage relationships with stakeholders 1 and 2, in this example, very closely because they have high interest and high power, especially stakeholder 1. You should keep stakeholders 3 and 4 informed because they have high interest but low power. Stakeholders 5 and 6 should be kept satisfied, perhaps by brief updates on the project, because they have low interest but high power. You should spend the least amount of effort by simply monitoring stakeholders 7 and 8, where both have low interest and low power.

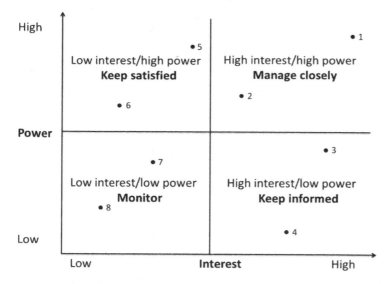

Figure 3-13. Sample stakeholder analysis power/interest grid

It is also important to measure the engagement level of stakeholders throughout the project. You can categorize stakeholders as being one of the following:

- *Unaware:* Unaware of the project and its potential impacts on them

- *Resistant:* Aware of the project yet resistant to change

- *Neutral:* Aware of the project yet neither supportive nor resistant

- *Supportive:* Aware of the project and supportive of change

- *Leading:* Aware of the project and its potential impacts and actively engaged in helping it succeed

The project team should take corrective action as soon as possible if they find that a stakeholder with high interest and high power is also categorized as resistant or unaware. It is very difficult to manage a project under those circumstances. After identifying and analyzing stakeholders, the project manager and team should develop a stakeholder engagement plan, as described in more detail in Chapter 5 on Project Planning.

Figure 3-14 provides a humorous example of analyzing different stakeholders' views of an art project. These characters obviously have different interest levels in the project and interpretations of what's involved.

Figure 3-14. Analyzing stakeholder interests (www.xkcd)

CREATING A PROJECT CHARTER AND ASSUMPTIONS LOG

After top management determines which projects to pursue, it is important to let the rest of the organization know about these projects. Management needs to create and distribute documentation to authorize project initiation. This documentation can take many different forms, but one common form is a project charter. A **project charter** is a document that formally recognizes the existence of a project and provides a summary of the project's objectives and management. It authorizes the project manager to use organizational resources to complete the project. Ideally, the project manager will play a major role in developing the project charter.

Business documents (like the business case, agreements, enterprise environmental factors, and organizational process assets are all inputs used to create a project charter. **Enterprise environmental factors** are conditions, not under immediate control of the project team, that influence, constrain, or direct the project, such as government and industry standards, legal/regulatory requirements, marketplace conditions, and organizational culture. **Organizational process assets** include plans, processes, policies, procedures, and knowledge bases, such as templates and lessons-learned reports.

Instead of project charters, some organizations initiate projects using a simple letter of agreement, whereas others use much longer documents or formal contracts. When Global Construction initiates a building project for an outside organization, it still creates a separate charter and attaches it to the contract, which is usually a much longer, more complex document. (You will see an example of a contract statement of work for outsourced work for this project in Chapter 6.) *A crucial part of the project charter is the sign-off section, where key project stakeholders sign the document to acknowledge their agreement on the need for the project.*

Contents of a Project Charter

Contents of a project charter will also vary to meet individual project needs. Typical information included in a project charter includes the following:

- The project's title and date of authorization

- The project manager's name and contact information

- A summary schedule or timeline, including the planned start and finish dates; if a summary milestone schedule is available, it should also be included or referenced

- A summary of the project's estimated cost and budget allocation

- A brief description of the project objectives, including the business need or other justification for authorizing the project

- Project success criteria or approval requirements, including project approval requirements and who signs off on the project

- A summary of the planned approach for managing the project, which should describe stakeholder needs and expectations, overall project risk, important assumptions and constraints, and should refer to related documents, such as a communications management plan, as available

- A roles and responsibilities matrix

- A sign-off section for signatures of key project stakeholders

- A comments section in which stakeholders can provide important comments related to the project

Project charters are normally short documents. Some are only one-page long, whereas others are much longer. Some charters include signatures of team members, while others do not. The following section shows the project charter for the Just-In-Time Training project. Note the importance of this document because after it is approved, the project manager is authorized to apply organizational resources to project activities.

Sample Project Charter

Kristin drafted a project charter and had the project team members review it before showing it to Lucy. Lucy made a few minor changes, which Kristin incorporated, and then all the key stakeholders who would be working on the project signed the project charter. Figure 3-15 shows the final project charter. Note that Lucy stated her concern about totally changing most training programs and terminating several contracts with local trainers. Also note that Tim Nelson, director of supplier management, wanted to be heavily involved in deciding how to provide the supplier management training. Kristin knew that she would have to consider these concerns address them in detail as part of communications and stakeholder management.

Project Title: Just-In-Time Training Project **Project Start Date:** July 1   **Projected Finish Date:** June 30 (one year later)
Budget Information: The firm has allocated $1,000,000 for this project. Approximately half of these costs will be for internal labor, while the other half will be for outsourced labor and training programs.
Project Manager: Kristin Maur, (610) 752-4896, kmaur@globalconstruction.com
Project Objectives: Develop a new training program that provides just-in-time training to employees on key topics, including supplier management, negotiating skills, project management, and software applications (spreadsheets and Web development). Develop an approach for measuring productivity improvements from this approach to training on an annual basis.
Success Criteria: This project will be successful if it reduces training cost per employee by 10% or $100/employee/year. It should also be completed on time, be run professionally, and meet all of the requirements. The project sponsor will fill out a customer acceptance/project completion form at the end of the project and give the project at least a 7 out of 10 overall rating.
Approach: • Terminate all internal training courses except the Six Sigma training once new courses are developed • Communicate to all employees the plans to improve internal training and let them know that tuition reimbursement will continue as is. • Work closely with internal managers and employees to determine the best approaches for providing training in supplier management, negotiating skills, project management, and software applications. • Research existing training and work with outside experts to develop several alternatives for providing each training topic. • Develop and implement new training. • Take advantage of new training approaches and technologies and encourage employees to take some training during non-work hours.

• Encourage experts within the company to mentor other workers on current job duties.			
• Determine a way to measure the effectiveness of the training and its impact on productivity on an annual basis.			

Roles and Responsibilities:

Name and Signature	*Role*	*Position*	*Contact Information*
Mike Sundby *Mike Sundby*	Project Champion	VP of HR	msundby@ globalconstruction.com
Lucy Camerena *Lucy Camerena*	Project Sponsor	Training Director	lcamerena@ globalconstruction.com
Kristin Maur *Kristin Maur*	Project Manager	Project Manager	kmaur@ globalconstruction.com
Julia Portman *Julia Portman*	Steering Committee Member	VP of IT	jportman@ globalconstruction.com
Tim Nelson *Tim Nelson*	Steering Committee Member	Supplier Management Director	tnelson@ globalconstruction.com
Mohamed Abdul *Mohamed Abdul*	Team Member	Senior programmer/ analyst	mabdul@ globalconstruction.com
Kim Johnson *Kim Johnson*	Team Member	Curriculum designer	kjohnson@ globalconstruction.com

Comments: (Handwritten or typed comments from above stakeholders, if applicable)

"I am concerned about people's reactions to cancelling most internal training and totally changing most training classes. I also hate to terminate some contracts with local training firms we've used for several years. We should try to get some of them involved in this project." Lucy

"I want to review all of the information related to providing the supplier management training. We need to make something available quickly." Tim

Figure 3-15. Sample project charter

Because many projects fail because of unclear requirements and expectations, starting with a project charter makes sense. If project managers are having difficulty obtaining support from project stakeholders, for example, they can refer to what everyone agreed to in the project charter. After the charter is completed, it is good practice to hold an official kick-off meeting for the project.

Contents of an Assumption Log

An assumption log is a document used to record and track assumptions and constraints throughout the project life cycle. It aids in communicating information to key stakeholders and avoids potential confusion. Most projects include several assumptions that affect the scope, time, cost, risk, and other knowledge areas. It is important to document and validate these assumptions.

Sample Assumption Log

For example, Kristin and her team created an initial assumption log, as shown in Figure 3-16. Notice that each assumption should have a unique ID or reference number, description, category, owner or person responsible for following up on and validating the assumption, a due date, status, and actions required as part of the follow-up or validation.

ID	Assumption Description	Category	Owner	Due Date	Status	Actions
108	Supplier management training should be completed first	Time	Kristin	Sep. 1	Closed	Scheduled first
122	Employees will take some of the training during non-work hours	Human resources	Lucy	Nov. 1	Open	Meet with dept. heads to discuss

Figure 3-16. Sample assumption log

HOLDING A PROJECT KICK-OFF MEETING

Experienced project managers know that it is crucial to get projects off to a great start. Holding a good kick-off meeting is an excellent way to do this. A **kick-off meeting** is a meeting held at the beginning of a project so that stakeholders can meet each other, review the goals of the project, and discuss future plans. The kick-off meeting is often held after the business case and project charter are completed, but it could be held sooner, as needed. Note that the *PMBOK® Guide – Sixth Edition*, suggests that the kick-off meeting be held during the end of the planning or start of the executing process group. In the author's experience, it is best hold it earlier.

Project kick-off meetings are often used to get support for a project and clarify roles and responsibilities. If there is a project champion, as there is for this project, he or she should speak first at the kick-off meeting and introduce the project sponsor and project manager. If anyone seems opposed to the project or unwilling to support it, the project champion—an experienced senior manager—should be able to handle the situation.

As discussed earlier in the chapter, there is normally a fair amount of work done before an official kick-off meeting for a project. At a minimum, the project manager and sponsor should have met several times, and other key stakeholders should have been involved in developing the project charter. The project manager should make sure the right people are invited to the kick-off meeting and send out an agenda in advance. For a small project, a kick-off meeting might be an informal meeting of the project team held in a social environment. The main idea is to get the project off to a good start. Ideally the kick-off meeting should be held face-to-face so stakeholders can physically meet each other and be able to pick up on each other's body language. If the meeting has to be held virtually, including video and audio can help to engage and understand participants.

Sample Kick-Off Meeting Agenda

All project meetings with major stakeholders should include an agenda. Figure 3-17 provides the agenda that Kristin provided for the Just-In-Time Training project kick-off meeting. Notice the main topics in an agenda:

- Meeting objective

- Agenda (lists in order the topics to be discussed)

- A section for documenting action items, to whom they are assigned, and when each person will complete the action

- A section to document the date and time of the next meeting

It is good practice to focus on results of meetings, and having sections for documenting action items and deciding on the next meeting date and time on the agenda helps to do so. It is also good practice to document meeting minutes, focusing on key decisions and action items, and to send them to all meeting participants and other appropriate stakeholders within a day or two of a meeting. Meeting minutes are valuable to people who could not attend a meeting since it summarizes key discussions and results of the meeting. If there is a project website or other place for storing project information, the meeting minutes should be stored there.

Just-In-Time Training Project
Kick-off Meeting
July 16

Meeting Objective: Get the project off to an effective start by introducing key stakeholders, reviewing project goals, and discussing future plans

Agenda:

- Introductions of attendees
- Review of the project background
- Review of project-related documents (i.e., business case, project charter, assumptions log)
- Discussion of project organizational structure
- Discussion of project scope, schedule, and cost goals
- Discussion of other important topics
- List of action items from meeting

Action Item	Assigned To	Due Date

Date and time of next meeting:

Figure 3-17. Sample kick-off meeting agenda

CASE WRAP-UP

Kristin was pleased with work completed in initiating the Just-In-Time Training project, as were the project sponsor and other key stakeholders. Kristin met weekly with the project steering committee to review project progress. She found the committee to be very helpful, especially when dealing with several challenges they encountered. For example, it was difficult finding a large enough conference room for the kick-off meeting and setting up the Webcast to allow other stakeholders to participate in the meeting. She was also a bit nervous before running the meeting, but Lucy and Mike, the project sponsor and champion, helped her relax and stepped in when people questioned the need for the project. There were also indications that several key departments would not be represented at the kick-off meeting, but Mike made sure that they were. Kristin could see how important senior management support was on this project, in particular for obtaining buy-in from all parts of the organization.

CHAPTER SUMMARY

The five project management process groups are initiating, planning, executing, monitoring and controlling, and closing. These process groups occur at varying levels of intensity throughout every phase of a project, and specific outputs are produced as a result of each process.

Mapping the main processes of each project management process group into the ten project management knowledge areas provides a big picture of what activities are involved in project management. Some organizations develop their own project management methodologies, often using the standards found in the *PMBOK® Guide* as a foundation. Agile project management is becoming more popular, and Scrum is the leading agile approach. It is important to tailor project management methodologies to meet the organization's particular needs.

Global Construction's Just-In-Time Training project demonstrates the process of initiating a project. After a project is approved, senior managers often meet to perform several pre-initiating activities, as follows:

- Determining the scope, schedule, and cost constraints for the project

- Identifying the project sponsor

- Selecting the project manager

- Developing a business case for the project, if required

- Meeting with the project manager to review the process and expectations for managing the project

- Determining if the project should be divided into two or more smaller projects

The main processes normally involved in project initiation are the following:

- Identifying stakeholders

- Creating the project charter

- Creating an assumptions log

- Holding a kick-off meeting

Descriptions of how each of these processes was accomplished and samples of related outputs are described in the chapter.

QUICK QUIZ

Note that you can find additional, interactive quizzes at www.intropm.com.

1.   In which of the five project management process groups is the most time and money usually spent?

   A. initiating

   B. planning

   C. executing

   D. monitoring and controlling

   E. closing

2.   In which of the five project management process groups are activities performed that relate to each knowledge area?

   A. initiating

   B. planning

   C. executing

   D. monitoring and controlling

   E. closing

3.   The best or "alpha" project managers spend more time on every process group than other project managers except for which one?

   A. initiating

   B. planning

   C. executing

   D. monitoring and controlling

4.   What document provides justification for investing in a project?

   A. project charter

   B. business case

   C. net present value analysis

   D. benefits management plan

5. What document formally recognizes the existence of a project and provides direction on the project's objectives and management?

    A. project charter

    B. business case

    C. stakeholder register

    D. benefits management plan

6. What is a crucial part of the project charter—a section in which key project stakeholders acknowledge their agreement on the need for the project?

    A. project objectives

    B. approach

    C. roles and responsibilities

    D. sign-off

7. Which project document is used to record and track assumptions and constraints throughout the project life cycle?

    A. project charter

    B. constraints log

    C. stakeholder analysis

    D. assumption log

8. All project meetings with major stakeholders should include.

    A. an agenda

    B. food

    C. name tags

    D. all of the above

9. Preparing a stakeholder register and performing a stakeholder analysis are part of which knowledge area?

    A. project integration management

    B. project resource management

    C. project stakeholder management

    D. project communications management

10.   Which of the following is recommended in this text but is not an output of initiating in the *PMBOK® Guide – Sixth Edition*?

        A. project charter

        B. stakeholder register

        C. kick-off meeting

        D. none of the above

Quick Quiz Answers

1. C; 2. B; 3. C; 4. B; 5. A; 6. D; 7. D; 8. A; 9. C; 10. C

DISCUSSION QUESTIONS

1.   Briefly describe what happens in each of the five project management process groups (initiating, planning, executing, monitoring and controlling, and closing). On which process group should team members spend the most time? Why?

2.   Why is it helpful to follow a project management methodology? What do you think about agile project management?

3.   What pre-initiating activities were performed for the Just-In-Time Training project? Does it make sense to do these activities? What are the main initiating activities?

4.   Describe the purpose of a business case and its main contents.

5.   What is the main purpose of performing a stakeholder analysis? What information in it might be sensitive and kept confidential?

6.   Why should projects have a project charter? What is the main information included in a project charter?

7.   Discuss the process for holding a project kick-off meeting. Who should attend? What key topics should be on the agenda?

EXERCISES

1. Find an example of a large project that took more than a year to complete, such as a major construction project. You can ask people at your college, university, or work about a recent project, such as a major fundraising campaign, information systems installation, or building project. You can also find information about projects online such as the Big Dig in Boston (*www.masspike.com/bigdig*), the Patronas Twin Towers in Malaysia, and many other building projects (*www.greatbuildings.com*). Why was the project initiated? Describe some of the pre-initiating and initiating tasks completed for the project. Write a one-page paper or prepare a short presentation summarizing your findings.

2. Review the business case for the Just-In-Time Training project. Do you think there is solid business justification for doing this project? Why or why not? What parts of the business case do you think could be stronger? How? Rewrite a section that you believe can be improved. Write a one-page paper or prepare a short presentation summarizing your findings.

3. Search the Internet for "project charter." Find at least three good references that describe project charters. Write a one-page paper or prepare a short presentation summarizing your findings.

4. Review the project charter for the Just-In-Time Training project. How does this document help clarify what work will be done on the project? Are the success criteria clear for this project? What questions do you have about the scope of the project? Write a one-page paper or prepare a short presentation summarizing your ideas.

5. Watch the videos called "How to Kickoff a Project" and "Starting a New Project" from *www.projectmanager.com*. Also, search for examples of good and bad kickoff meetings. Summarize key points in these videos and your opinion of them in a short paper or presentation.

6. Watch the videos about Scrum, kanban, and Wikispeed described in the Video Highlights feature in this chapter. Summarize your findings in a short paper or presentation.

TEAM PROJECTS

1. Your organization has decided to initiate a project to raise money for an important charity. Assume that there are 1,000 people in your organization. Use the pre-initiating tasks described in this chapter to develop a strategy for how to proceed. Be creative in describing your organization; the charity; the scope, schedule, and cost constraints for the project; and so on. Document your ideas in a one- to two-page paper or a short presentation.

2. You are part of a team in charge of a project to help people in your company (500 people) lose weight. This project is part of a competition, and the top "losers" will be featured in a popular television show. Assume that you have six months to complete

the project and a budget of $10,000. Develop a project charter for this project using the sample provided in this chapter. Be creative in developing detailed information to include in the charter.

3.   Using the information you developed in Team Project 1 or 2, role-play the kick-off meeting for this project. Follow the sample agenda provided in this chapter.

4.   Perform the initiating activities for one of the case studies provided in Appendix C. If you are working on a real team project, perform the applicable pre-initiating and initiating activities for that project. Be sure to work closely with your project sponsor to get the project off to a good start.

5.   As a team, research two different project management methodologies (other than using the *PMBOK® Guide*), such as PRINCE2, RUP, Six Sigma, agile, etc. Summarize your findings in a two- to three-page paper or a short presentation. Try to include examples of projects managed using each methodology.

KEY TERMS

agile — Popular software development method that use an iterative workflow and incremental delivery of software in short iterations.

business case — A document that provides justification for investing in a project.

champion — A senior manager who acts as a key proponent for a project.

closing processes — The actions that involve formalizing acceptance of the project or phase and bringing it to an orderly end.

deliverable — A product or service produced or provided as part of a project.

enterprise environmental factors — conditions, not under immediate control of the project team, that influence, constrain, or direct the project, such as government and industry standards, legal/regulatory requirements, marketplace conditions, and organizational culture.

executing processes — The actions that involve coordinating people and other resources to carry out the project plans and produce the deliverables of the project.

initiating processes — The actions to begin projects and project phases.

kanban — A technique that provides visual cues to guide workflow

kick-off meeting — A meeting held at the beginning of a project so that stakeholders can meet each other, review the goals of the project, and discuss future plans.

methodology — A plan that describes how things should be done to manage a project.

monitoring and controlling processes — The actions taken to measure progress toward achieving project goals, monitor deviation from plans, and take corrective action.

organizational process assets — plans, processes, policies, procedures, and knowledge bases, such as templates and lessons-learned reports.

phase — A distinct stage in project development.

planning processes — The actions that involve devising and maintaining a workable scheme to ensure that the project meets its scope, schedule, and cost goals as well as organizational needs.

process — A series of actions directed toward a particular result.

project charter — A document that formally recognizes the existence of a project and provides a summary of the project's objectives and management.

project management office (PMO) — An organizational entity created to assist project managers in achieving project goals.

PRojects IN Controlled Environments (PRINCE2) — A project management methodology with eight process groups developed in the U.K.

Rational Unified Process (RUP) framework — A project management methodology that uses an iterative software development process that focuses on team productivity and delivers software best practices to all team members.

Scrum — the leading agile development method for completing projects with a complex, innovative scope of work

Six Sigma — A comprehensive and flexible system for achieving, sustaining, and maximizing business success; uniquely driven by close understanding of customer needs, disciplined use of facts, data, and statistical analysis, and diligent attention to managing, improving, and reinventing business processes.

stakeholder register — A document that includes details related to the identified project stakeholders

stakeholder analysis — A technique for analyzing information to determine which stakeholders' interests to focus on and how to increase stakeholder support throughout the project.

standard — A document that describes best practices for what should be done to manage a project.

template — A file with a preset format that serves as a starting point for creating various documents so that the format and structure do not have to be re-created.

END NOTES

[1]Andy Crowe, *Alpha Project Managers: What the Top 2% Know That Everyone Else Does Not*, Velociteach Press (2006).

[2]Bill Cottrell, "Standards, compliance, and Rational Unified Process, Part I: Integrating RUP and the PMBOK®," *IBM Developerworks* (May 10, 2004).

[3]Peter S. Pande, Robert P. Neuman, and Roland R. Cavanagh, *The Six Sigma Way*. New York: McGraw-Hill (2000), p. xi.

[4]William Ibbs and Justin Reginato, *Quantifying the Value of Project Management*, Project Management Institute (2002).

[5]Project Management Institute, "Pulse of the Profession®: Success Rates Rise: Transforming the High Cost of Low Performance" (2017).

[6]Agile Manifesto, www.agilemanifesto.org (accessed April 2017).

[7]Scrum Alliance, "The Scrum Framework in 30 Seconds," www.scrumalliance.org/pages/why-scrum (accessed April 2017).

[8]PM Solutions, "The State of the PMO 2016" (2016).

[9]Novid Parsi, "Musical Influences," PM Network (February 2017).

Chapter 4
Planning Projects, Part 1
(Project Integration and Scope Management)

LEARNING OBJECTIVES

After reading this chapter, you will be able to:

- Describe the importance of creating plans to guide project execution
- List several planning processes and outputs for project integration and scope management
- Discuss the project integration management planning process and explain the purpose and contents of a project management plan
- Describe the project scope management planning processes
- Explain the purpose and contents of a scope management plan and requirements management plan
- Discuss different ways to collect project requirements
- Create a scope statement to define project scope
- Develop a work breakdown structure (WBS) and a WBS dictionary to clearly describe all of the work required for a project

---

OPENING CASE

Kristin Maur continued to work with her project team and other key stakeholders on the Just-In-Time Training project. She knew that it was crucial to do a good job in planning all aspects of the project, and she strongly believed that execution would be much smoother if they had good plans to follow. She also knew that it was important to involve the people who would be doing the work in actually planning the work, and that planning was an iterative process. Involving key people in the planning process and keeping the plans up to date had been her main challenges on past projects, so Kristin focused proactively on those areas. She remembered what her last boss kept telling her about planning: Focus on the 4 Cs: Commit, Communicate, Cooperate, and Collaborate.

Kristin and her team were fortunate to have many templates to use in developing several planning documents, especially for scope management. They could also review examples of planning documents from past and current projects available on Global Construction's intranet site and use project management software to enter key planning data. Kristin also found that the project steering committee that had been set up during project initiation gave her very helpful advice. Several experienced members warned her to be thorough in planning but not to become bogged down in too much detail.

PROJECT PLANNING SHOULD GUIDE PROJECT EXECUTION

Many people have heard the following sayings:

- If you fail to plan, you plan to fail.

- If you don't know where you're going, any road will take you there.

- What gets measured gets managed.

All of these sayings emphasize the fact that planning is crucial to achieving goals. Successful project managers know how important it is to develop, refine, and follow plans to meet project goals, and they know how easy it is to become sidetracked if they do not have good plans to follow. They also know that people are more likely to perform well if they know what they are supposed to do and when.

Planning is often the most difficult and unappreciated process in project management. Often, people do not want to take the time to plan well, but theory and practice show that good planning is crucial to good execution. *The main purpose of project planning is to guide project execution.* To guide execution, plans must be realistic and useful, so a fair amount of effort must go into the project planning process. Recall from Chapter 3 that planning includes processes related to each of the ten project management knowledge areas. This chapter describes the types of planning performed in two of the knowledge areas—project integration and scope management—and summarizes the planning done for Global Construction's Just-In-Time Training project. Chapter 5 focuses on planning for schedule and cost management, and Chapter 6 discusses planning in the other six knowledge areas—quality, resource, communications, stakeholder, risk, and procurement management.

WHAT WENT WRONG?

Based on their experiences, many people have a dim view of plans. Top managers often require a plan, but then no one tracks whether the plan was followed. For example, one project manager said he would meet with each project team leader within two months to review their project plans, and he even created a detailed schedule for these reviews. He canceled the first meeting due to another business commitment; he rescheduled the next meeting for unexplained personal reasons. Two months later, the project manager had still not met with over half of the project team leaders. Why should project team members feel obligated to follow their own plans when the project manager obviously does not follow his?

SUMMARY OF PLANNING PROCESSES AND OUTPUTS FOR INTEGRATION AND SCOPE

The *PMBOK® Guide – Sixth Edition* lists over 50 documents that project teams can potentially produce as part of project planning. Other experts suggest even more potential planning documents. Every project is unique, so project managers and their teams must determine which planning outputs are needed for their projects and how they should be created.

Figure 4-1 summarizes the project planning processes and outputs for integration and scope management listed in the *PMBOK® Guide – Sixth Edition*. All of these plans and documents, as well as other project-related information, should be available to all team members on a project website. In this scenario, Global Construction has used project websites for several years, and everyone agrees that they significantly facilitate communications.

Knowledge area	Planning process	Outputs
Project integration management	Develop project management plan	Project management plan
Project scope management	Plan scope management	Scope management plan
		Requirements management plan
	Collect requirements	Requirements documentation
		Requirements traceability matrix
	Define scope	Project scope statement
		Project documents updates
	Create WBS	Scope baseline
		Project documents updates

Figure 4-1. Planning processes and outputs for project integration and scope management

The following sections describe these planning processes and outputs and then provide examples of applying them to the Just-In-Time Training project at Global Construction. You can consider many of these planning processes as generally following a chronological order, especially for the scope, schedule, and cost processes. You need to plan the project scope and determine what activities need to be done before you can develop a detailed project schedule. Likewise, you need a detailed project schedule before you can develop a cost baseline. Once a cost baseline is developed there may be additional iterations required as adjustments are made to the project and more information is gathered. As noted earlier, there are many interdependencies between various knowledge areas and process groups.

PROJECT INTEGRATION MANAGEMENT

Project integration management involves coordinating all the project management knowledge areas throughout a project's life span. It is the project manager's job to lead project integration management and keep an overall view of the project to ensure its success.

Project Management Plans

A **project management plan** is a document used to integrate and coordinate all project planning documents and to help guide a project's execution, monitoring and control, and closure. Plans created in the other knowledge areas are subsidiary parts of the overall project management plan. Project management plans facilitate communication among stakeholders and provide a baseline for progress measurement and project control, as discussed in detail in Chapter 9. The main benefit of the process to create a project management plan is a comprehensive document that defines the basis of all project work and how it will be performed.

A **baseline** is a starting point, a measurement, or an observation that is documented so that it can be used for future comparison. Before project teams define the baselines, project management plans can be updated as often as needed. After the project management plan is baselined, however, it can only be changed through the formal integrated change control process.

The project management plan briefly describes the overall scope, schedule, and cost baselines for the project. Specific plans in each of those knowledge areas provide more detailed baseline information. For example, the project management plan might provide a high-level budget baseline for the entire project, whereas the cost baseline prepared as part of the project cost management knowledge area provides detailed cost projections by WBS by month. The project management plan can also include a project life cycle description and development approach, as shown in Figure 4-2. Also notice the many other project documents that project teams can create, as needed, for their projects.

Project Management Plan	Project Documents	
1. Scope management plan 2. Requirements management plan 3. Schedule management plan 4. Cost management plan 5. Quality management plan 6. Resource management plan 7. Communications management plan 8. Risk management plan 9. Procurement management plan 10. Stakeholder engagement plan 11. Change management plan 12. Configuration management plan 13. Scope baseline 14. Schedule baseline 15. Cost baseline 16. Performance measurement baseline 17. Project life cycle description 18. Development approach	1. Activity attributes 2. Activity list 3. Assumption log 4. Basis of estimates 5. Change log 6. Cost estimates 7. Cost forecasts 8. Duration estimates 9. Issue log 10. Lessons learned register 11. Milestone list 12. Physical resource assignments 13. Project calendars 14. Project communications 15. Project schedule 16. Project schedule network diagram 17. Project scope statement 18. Quality control measurements 19. Quality metrics	20. Quality report 21. Requirements documentation 22. Requirements traceability matrix 23. Resource assignments 24. Resource breakdown structure 25. Resource calendars 26. Resource requirements 27. Risk register 28. Risk report 29. Schedule data 30. Schedule forecasts 31. Stakeholder register 32. Team charter 33. Team resource assignments 34. Test and evaluation documents

Figure 4-2. Project management plan and project documents

Source: Project Management Institute, Inc., *A Guide to the Project Management Body of Knowledge (PMBOK® Guide) – Sixth Edition* (2017).

Project management plans should be dynamic, flexible, and receptive to change when the environment or project changes. These plans should greatly assist the project manager in leading the project team and assessing project status. Just as projects are unique, so are project plans. For a small project involving a few people over a couple of months, a project charter, scope statement, and Gantt chart might be the only formal project planning documents needed; there would not be a need for a separate project management plan. A large project involving 100 people over three years would benefit from having a detailed project management plan and separate plans for each knowledge area. Because all project plans should help guide the completion of the particular project, they should be tailored as needed for each project.

There are, however, common elements to most project management plans, as follows:

- Introduction/overview of the project

- Project organization

- Management and technical processes (including project lifecycle description and development approach, as applicable)

- Work to be performed (scope)

- Schedule and budget information

- References to other project planning documents

Sample Project Management Plan

Figure 4-3 provides partial information from the initial project management plan for Global Construction's Just-In-Time Training project. Of course, the actual document would be longer because this is a one-year, $1 million project involving many different stakeholders, including outside suppliers. The document would also be updated as needed. It is important to mark the date and version number on the document to avoid confusion. Also note that project organization varies on projects, so it is helpful to provide a high-level project organizational chart in the project management plan. On some projects, the project sponsor and project champion are the same person, but not always. The champion is often in a higher-level position than the project sponsor. Projects that cross functional boundaries, as the Just-In-Time Training project does, often benefit from having a high-level project champion, such as a vice president, from a key functional area.

Project Management Plan Version 1.0
September 17

Project Name: Just-In-Time Training Project
Introduction/Overview of the Project
Global Construction employs 10,000 full-time employees in ten different counties and fifteen states in the U.S. The company spends, on average, $1,000 per employee for training (not including tuition reimbursement), which is higher than the industry average. By redesigning training, Global Construction can reduce training costs and improve productivity. The main goal of this project is to develop a new training program that provides just-in-time training to employees on key topics, including supplier management, negotiating skills, project management, and software applications.

Project Organization
The basic organization of the project is provided in Figure 1. The project sponsor, Lucy Camerena, will have the final say on major decisions, with consultation from the project steering committee and project champion, Mike Sundby. The project sponsor should have time to thoroughly review important project information and provide timely feedback to the project manager. The project manager in this case reports to the project sponsor, and the team leaders, and supplier project managers report to the project manager.

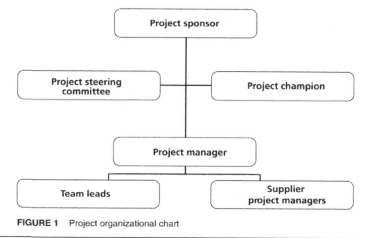

FIGURE 1   Project organizational chart

Management and Technical Processes

Management Processes

1. Management Review Process: The project steering committee will meet at least monthly to provide inputs and review progress on this project.

2. Progress Measurement Process: The project steering committee will review project progress during project review meetings, and they can also review information as needed by viewing reports on the enterprise project management software. Post project progress will also be measured to see if the project met its goals. These goals include reducing the training cost per employee by $100/person/year and receiving positive results from survey participants on the effectiveness of the training.

3. Change Approval Process: See Attachment 1 based on corporate standards.

4. Supplier Management Process: See Attachment 2 based on corporate standards.

Technical Processes

1. Enterprise Project Management Software: All tasks, costs, resources, issues, and risks will be tracked for this project using our enterprise project management software. Data must be entered on a weekly basis, at a minimum, to provide timely information.

2. Supplier Evaluation: The project team will coordinate with the purchasing department to follow our standard procedures for selecting and working with suppliers. See Attachment 2 for corporate standards.

3. Productivity Improvement: The project team will work with the finance and quality assurance departments to develop and implement a system to measure improvements in employee productivity that result from this new training program. The finance department will report on this information annually beginning one year after the first new training course is offered.

Work to be Performed (Scope)

Summary: Research, develop or purchase, and implement a new just-in-time training program covering the topics of supplier management, negotiating skills, project management, and software applications and determine a way to measure the effectiveness of the training and its impact on productivity on an annual basis. See the scope statement, WBS, and other scope documents for further detail.

Schedule Information

The entire project will be completed in one year with a projected completion date of June 30. See the project schedule and other time management documents for further detail.

Budget Information

The total budget for this project is $1,000,000. Approximately half of these costs will be for internal labor, while the other half will be for outsourced labor and training programs. See the cost estimate and cost baseline for further detail.

References to Other Project Planning Documents

All current project plans created for this project are provided in Appendix A. Initial documents and revisions are available on the project website.

Figure 4-3. Sample project management plan (partial)

PROJECT SCOPE MANAGEMENT

Project scope management involves defining and controlling what work is or is not included in a project. Project scope should not be confused with product scope. Projects often produce several products, which have their own product scope to describe their features and functions. For example, in a house construction project, the scope of one particular product, like a driveway, would have its own scope to include items like its dimensions, materials, etc. Project scope includes the scope of all products, services, and results produced plus the work involved in the process of creating them.

The main planning processes performed as part of project scope management include planning scope management, collecting requirements, defining scope, and creating the WBS. The main documents produced are a scope management plan, a requirements management plan, requirements documents, a requirements traceability matrix, and a **scope baseline**, which is composed of an approved project scope statement, a WBS, and a WBS dictionary.

Planning Scope Management

The purpose of the process of planning scope management is to determine how the project scope will be defined, validated, and controlled. Note that the term **validation** means formal acceptance of deliverables by the customer and other identified stakeholders. In contrast, **verification** (done as part of controlling quality) means the deliverable complies with a regulation, requirement, specification, or imposed condition. Project teams usually have several meetings with key stakeholders and experts to help them develop a scope management plan and requirements management plan.

A scope management plan, and all other knowledge area plans (except for integration management, where the project management plan is created), are components of the project management plan. Contents of the scope management plan include descriptions of processes for the following:

- preparing a detailed project scope statement

- creating, maintaining, and approving the WBS

- obtaining acceptance of the completed project deliverables

- controlling how requests for changes to the project scope statement will be processed

The *PMBOK® Guide – Sixth Edition*, defines a **requirement** as "a condition or capability that is necessary to be present in a product, service, or result to satisfy a business need." A **requirements management plan** describes how project requirements will be analyzed, documented, and managed.

Sample Requirements Management Plan

There were many requirements involved in the Just-In-Time Training project. Some requirements, such as the type of training to be provided, are described in the project charter. However, Kristin knew from past experience that it was important to do a good job managing requirements. She worked with her team to develop a requirements management plan. Important contents of this plan include information related to:

- Planning, tracking, and reporting requirements

- Prioritizing requirements

- Using product metrics

- Tracing requirements

- Performing configuration management activities, such as initiating, analyzing, authorizing, tracking, and reporting changes to requirements

Figure 4-4 shows a sample requirements management plan.

Requirements Management Plan Version 1.0
September 30

Project Name: Just-In-Time Training Project

Planning, tracking, and reporting requirements

Information from the Phase I project, the business case, and the project charter will provide valuable information in determining requirements for this project, as will many existing corporate standards and processes. A survey will also be used to gather requirements. All requirements will be documented where appropriate. For example, requirements related to course prerequisites will be documented in course descriptions. Requirements related to facilities, class size, etc. will be documented in the scope statement. Requirements will be tracked by the person in charge of each related deliverable and reported as part of our normal reporting processes (i.e., weekly status reports, monthly review meetings, etc.)

Performing configuration management activities

Requirements can be introduced by several means, such as existing written requirements, suggestions provided from our survey, or direct suggestions from stakeholders. Appropriate project stakeholders will analyze, authorize, track, and report changes to requirements. The project manager must be informed in advance of potential changes to requirements and be involved in the decision process to approve those changes. Any change that will impact the project's cost or schedule significantly must be approved by the project steering committee.

Prioritizing requirements

All requirements will be designated as 1, 2 or 3, for mandatory, desirable, or nice-to-have, respectively. Emphasis will be placed on meeting all mandatory requirements, followed by desirable and then nice-to-have requirements.

Using product metrics

Several product metrics will be used to help in managing requirements. For example, each training class will be compared to similar classes to evaluate its content, length, and quality with similar classes. Course evaluations will be used as the main metric in evaluating the course and instructor.

Tracing requirements

All mandatory requirements will be included in the requirements traceability matrix. Desirable and nice-to-have requirements will be documented in a separate matrix and be addressed only as time and resources allow. The matrix will be created using the company's template file for this document.

Figure 4-4. Sample requirements management plan

WHAT WENT RIGHT?

Requirements management is a challenge on many projects. Mia McCroskey, an IBM Champion (someone recognized for helping others make the best use of IBM software) and project and requirements manager at Emerging Health, described two key challenges they faced. "Deriving meaningful information from the electronic medical record is essential to justifying the cost of those systems. We're piloting the use of predictive analytics—combining statistical methods with the mass of patient data collected every day at our parent medical center—to predict outcomes at the population level. To do it you need a very wide range of data: blood pressure, height, and weight, smoking patterns, history of heart disease, current blood sugar level, and on and on. Just bringing all this data together is the first challenge…Another area of critical concern is patient information. The need to pool patient data for direct care as well as population research is supported by legislature and funding sources. But we are bound, both legally and ethically, to protect patient identity in every circumstance."[1]

Emerging Health started using a tool by IBM called Rational DOORS to help manage requirements. As a result, they saw a 69 percent reduction in the cost of test preparation, testing, and rework in the software development process and a 25 percent reduction in the time it took to customize their Clinical Looking Glass application for unique client requirements. According to McCroskey, "Time to market is always a critical benchmark, but especially so in the fast-paced healthcare industry. Because our industry is so competitive, being able to deliver the product faster enhances our reputation and the confidence our customers have in us. Faster time to market is vital to our success, and we've now achieved that with the more responsive environment Rational DOORS has allowed us to establish."[2]

Collecting Requirements

It is important to document requirements in enough detail so that they can be measured during project execution. After all, meeting scope goals is often based on meeting documented requirements.

The main outputs of collecting requirements include:

- requirements documentation, which can range from a single-page checklist to a room full of notebooks with text, diagrams, images, etc.

- a **requirements traceability matrix (RTM),** which is a table that lists requirements, various attributes of each requirement, and the status of the requirements to ensure that all of them are addressed

There are several ways to collect requirements. Interviewing stakeholders one-on-one is often very effective, although it can be very expensive and time-consuming. Holding focus groups, facilitated workshops, and using group creativity and decision-making techniques to collect requirements are normally faster and less expensive than one-on-one interviews. Questionnaires and surveys can be very efficient ways to collect requirements as long as key stakeholders provide honest and thorough information. Observation can also be a good technique for collecting requirements, especially for projects that involve improving work processes and procedures. Prototyping is a commonly used technique for collecting requirements for software development projects.

The project's type, size, complexity, importance, and other factors will affect how much effort is spent on collecting requirements. For example, a team working on a project to upgrade the entire corporate accounting system for a multibillion dollar company with more than 50 geographic locations should spend a fair amount of time collecting requirements. A project to upgrade the hardware and software for a small accounting firm with only five employees, on the other hand, would need a much smaller effort. In any case, it is important for a project team to decide how they will collect and manage requirements. It is crucial to gather inputs from key stakeholders and align the scope, a key aspect of the entire project, with business strategy, as described in Chapter 2.

Sample Requirements Traceability Matrix

Figure 4-5 provides an example of a few requirements traceability matrix (RTM) entries for the Just-In-Time Training project. Remember that the main purpose of an RTM is to maintain the linkage from the source of each requirement through its decomposition to implementation and verification. For example, the first entry is related to survey questions. The project team knew they had to develop a survey for the project to help assess training needs, and the project steering committee decided in a meeting that they should review and approve the survey questions before the survey went out. They wanted to make sure that there were objective and open-ended questions in the survey, as documented in their project steering committee meeting minutes. The second entry concerns the course evaluations for the new courses that will be developed. The company has documented standards that must be followed for course evaluations.

Require-ment no.	Name	Category	Source	Status
R26	Survey questions	Survey	Project steering committee minutes	Complete. The survey questions were reviewed and approved by the steering committee.
R31	Course evaluations	Assessment	Corporate training standards	In process. The course evaluations have not been created yet.

Figure 4-5. Sample requirements traceability matrix

Defining Scope

Good scope definition is crucial to project success because it helps improve the accuracy of time, cost, and resource estimates; defines a baseline for performance measurement and project control; and aids in communicating clear work responsibilities. A project **scope statement** describes product characteristics and requirements, user acceptance criteria, and deliverables. Work that is not included in the scope statement should not be done, and you can explicitly state what is out of scope for the project under a section called project exclusions. The main techniques used in defining scope include expert judgment, data analysis, decision making, interpersonal and team skills, and product analysis. The main outputs of scope definition are the scope statement and updates to project documents.

The project charter, scope management plan, assumptions log, requirements documentation, risk register, enterprise environmental factors, and organizational process assets (especially past project files and lessons-learned reports from previous, similar projects) are all inputs for creating the initial scope statement. The scope statement should be updated as more information becomes available. Although contents vary, scope statements should include, at a minimum, a product scope description, product user acceptance criteria, and detailed information on all project deliverables. It is also helpful to document project boundaries, constraints, and assumptions. The scope statement should also reference supporting documents, such as product specifications and corporate policies, which often affect how products or services are produced.

Sample Scope Statement

Kristin worked closely with her team to develop the first version of the scope statement, reviewing available information and meeting several times with key stakeholders to develop a thorough document. Part of the scope statement is shown in Figure 4-6. Kristin knew that this document would change as they finalized more details of the project scope. Note that some details have been added and changes have been made since the project charter was completed. For example, class size has been added, more information on the needs assessment and survey has been provided, and the success criteria were changed slightly.

Scope Statement, Version 1.0
August 1

Project Title: Just-In-Time Training Project
Product Characteristics and Requirements
This project will produce three levels of courses, executive, introductory, and advanced, in the following subject areas: supplier management, negotiating skills, project management, and software applications (spreadsheets and Web development). Details on each course are provided below:

1. Supplier management training: The Supplier Management Director estimates the need to train at least 200 employees each year. There should be three levels of courses: an executive course, an introductory course, and an advanced course. Course materials should be developed as a joint effort with internal experts, outside training experts, if needed, and key suppliers.

A partnership might be developed to maximize the effectiveness of the training and minimize development costs. Different delivery methods should be explored, including instructor-led, CD/ROM, and Web-based training. About half of employees would prefer an instructor-led approach, and about half would prefer a self-paced course they could take at their convenience.

Product User Acceptance Criteria
The courses produced as part of this project will be considered successful if they are all available within one year and the average course evaluations for each course are at least 3.0 on a 5.0 scale.

Project Exclusions
Training related to Six Sigma is not part of this project.
Providing new facilities is not part of this project.

Deliverables
Project Management-Related Deliverables
Project charter, project management plan, scope statement, WBS, etc.
Product-Related Deliverables:
1. Supplier management training:

1.1. Needs assessment: A survey will be conducted to determine the learning objectives for the executive, introductory, and advanced courses. The corporate online survey software will be used and coordinated with IT and HR. Results will be documented in a detailed report (8-10 pages) and presentation (15-20 minutes long).

1.2 Research of existing training: A study will be done to identify current training courses and materials available. Results will be documented in a detailed report and presentation.

1.3. Partnerships: Partnership agreements will be explored to get outside training organizations and suppliers to work on developing and providing training.

1.4. Course development: Appropriate materials will be developed for each course. Materials could take various formats, including written, video, CD/ROM, or Web-based. Materials should include interactivity to keep learners engaged.

1.5. Pilot course: A pilot course will be provided for the introductory supplier management course. Feedback from the pilot course will be incorporated into following courses.

Figure 4-6. Sample scope statement

As more information becomes available and decisions are made related to project scope—such as specific products that will be purchased or changes that have been approved—the project team should update the project scope statement. Different iterations of the scope statement should be named by a unique identifier, such as Version 1.0, Version 2.0, and so on. These updates might also require changes to the project management plan. For example, if the team decides to purchase products or services for the project from a supplier with whom it has never worked, the project management plan should include information on working with that new supplier.

An up-to-date project scope statement is an important document for developing and confirming a common understanding of the project scope. Deliverables should be described in more than a few words. For example, it is helpful to estimate the length of a report or presentation so the person responsible for that work has a good understanding of what is expected. The scope statement describes in detail the work to be accomplished on the project and is an important tool for ensuring customer satisfaction and preventing **scope creep**, which is the tendency for project scope to continually increase.

Figure 4-7 shows a humorous example of scope creep no surgeon wants to encounter. The initial estimate of the work did not include a buzzing noise!

Figure 4-7. Scope creep during surgery (www.xkcd.com)

Creating the Work Breakdown Structure

A **work breakdown structure (WBS)** is a deliverable-oriented grouping of the work involved in a project that defines the total scope of the project. In other words, the WBS is a document that breaks *all* the work required for the project into discrete deliverables, and groups them into a logical hierarchy. Because most projects involve many people and many different deliverables, it is important to organize and divide the work into logical parts based on how the work will be performed.

A deliverable at the lowest level of the WBS, where it can be appropriately assigned to and managed by a single accountable person, is called a **work package.** Each work package should be defined in enough detail to estimate what it would cost and how long it would take to create. If you try to assign it to a group or person, and they tell you that they will have to work with another group to complete this work, then you should consider splitting that sub-deliverable down into two or more sub-deliverables so that you can assign them to the areas that will do the work. This practice allows you to hold one person, or group, accountable for the work completion. Each work package is part of a **control account**, a management control point for performance measurement where scope, budget, and schedule are integrated and compared to the earned value. See Chapter 8 for more details on earned value.

The WBS is a foundation document in project management because it provides the basis for planning and managing project schedules, costs, resources, and changes. Because the WBS defines the total scope of the project, work should not be done on a project if it is not included in the WBS. This is a critical point in the definition of the WBS: The WBS contains 100% of the deliverables (often called "work") of the project—not 95%, not 102%, but 100%. The WBS puts the project team, and its stakeholders, on the same page as it is the first time that everyone can look at the work that will be completed. If something is missing, it should be apparent. If something is added in error, it should be apparent. Therefore, it is crucial to develop a good WBS.

A WBS is often depicted in a graphical format, similar to an organizational chart. The name of the entire project is the top box, called level 1, and the main groupings for the work are listed in the second tier of boxes, called level 2. This level numbering is based on PMI's *Practice Standard for Work Breakdown Structure, Second Edition (2006)*. Note that some organizations call the entire project level 0. Each of those boxes can be broken down or decomposed into subsequent tiers of boxes to show the hierarchy of the work. Project teams often organize the WBS around project products, project phases, system modules, geographical regions, or other logical groupings. People often like to create a WBS in a graphical format first to help them visualize the whole project and all of its main parts. You can also show a WBS in tabular form as an indented list of elements.

Example WBSs

Understanding how to create a WBS is difficult. Many people learn by example, so this section includes several of them. The first involves a very simple demonstration of the basic reason for a WBS—to breakdown major project deliverables into smaller ones. Figure 4-8 is a WBS designed to represent a project to bake a Birthday Cake. The cake is decomposed into the cake itself, the frosting, toppings added to the top of the cake, and candles. Note that there is no oven, no pan, and no mixer in the WBS. Furthermore, it does not indicate how to mix the ingredients, the amount of the ingredients, the order of the construction, the baking temperature or time, or any other steps required to actually make this cake. Why? Because the WBS should represent the project deliverables, not the tools, techniques, or actions required to create those deliverables.

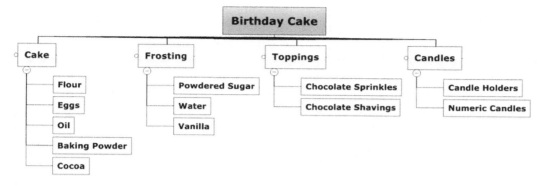

Figure 4-8. WBS for a birthday cake

Of course no one would create a WBS for a birthday cake, but many of us have created documents that are very similar in construction to a WBS, such as a shopping list for a birthday party. You begin with your party's concept and then define the things that you must have in order to make the party happen (food, drinks, decorations, etc.). A WBS is not unlike that shopping list, except you are defining the things that your project must deliver to be successful. It is important to understand that the project does not have to create each of the deliverables (the boxes on the WBS), but it must create, purchase, or in some other way provide those items.

One basic method to verify that your WBS is complete is to look at the lowest level of deliverables and ask yourself, "If I have these deliverables will they, in combination, give me everything I need to create the higher level deliverable?" In the Birthday Cake example, consider the Cake deliverable. The Cake deliverable is decomposed into five smaller deliverables: flour, eggs, oil, baking powder, and cocoa. The question you would then ask the team is, "If I have flour, eggs, oil, baking powder, and cocoa, will I have everything I need to create a cake?" Of course the answer is no, as you forgot about the salt and water! You would then correct the WBS by adding salt and water as two other sub-deliverables under the Cake deliverable. Every box on the WBS is referred to as a deliverable in context of itself, but it is called a sub-deliverable when talking about it in reference to the larger deliverable above it.

Because project managers rarely create Birthday Cakes as projects (with the popular Great British Baking Show or similar television shows as possible exceptions), the following examples are more representative of projects that most project managers can understand. For example, building a house is a common project, but there are many ways to create a WBS for it.

Figure 4-9 and 4-10 show two different WBSs for building a house from examples provided by two companies that design software to help manage projects—MatchWare and Microsoft. MatchWare creates a software product called MindView, mentioned in Chapter 2. You can use this software to create a mind map for many different purposes, including creating a WBS. Microsoft creates Project 2016, mentioned in Chapter 1 and described in detail in Appendix A. Notice that the second tier, or level 2, WBS items in Figure 4-9 includes *six* major deliverables: the foundation, external construction, internal construction, roof, services, and yard & access. (For this example, only the internal construction and services categories are broken down further, but for a real house project they would all be broken down several more levels.) However, in Figure 4-10, there are *ten* different categories for the level 2 items: general conditions, site work, foundation, framing, dry in, exterior finishes, utility rough-ins and complete concrete, interior finishes, landscaping and grounds work, and final acceptance. Some categories are similar, while others are not. Notice that *nouns* are used to describe the deliverables, not verbs.

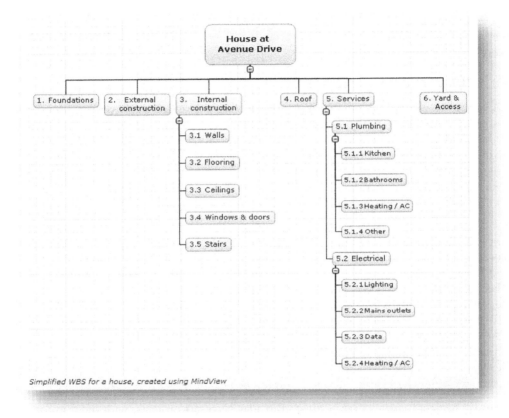

Simplified WBS for a house, created using MindView

4-9. WBS for a house showing 6 main deliverables (www.matchware.com)

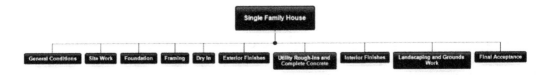

4-10. WBS for a house showing 10 main deliverables (Microsoft Project)

The main thing to understand is that you are organizing the main deliverables based on *what* work needs to be done and *not how* the work will be done. Neither of these examples for building a house includes obtaining financing or moving items from a former residence to the new house. If this work is in the scope of the project, then you could include WBS level 2 deliverables called "financing" and "relocation." If it was important to you to include outdoor recreational items in the scope of the project, you might also include a level 2 category called "outdoor recreation" with level 3 sub-deliverables called "swimming pool," "tennis court," and "hot tub." The key concept is that the WBS includes 100% of the work required to complete the project. If your project will create something, it should be shown in the WBS. Nothing should be created that is not in the WBS. This concept is also true for interim deliverables that will not end up in the hands of the customer. For example, when a firm built a patient walkway that connected two buildings separated by wetlands, the project team had to first build a temporary wooden causeway that stood above the marsh, protecting it from equipment and giving the workers a platform from which to work. When the project was completed, they removed the temporary causeway. This temporary causeway would be included in the WBS as it was required for the project, even though it was not the final deliverable.

These three examples, the birthday cake and two different house projects, show a WBS in a graphical or tree view, resembling the format of an organizational chart. You can also create or display a WBS in a tabular or list view that is text-based. Figure 4-11, described in the next example, shows both a graphical and tabular view of a WBS. When do you use one format versus the other? It depends upon the audience, the complexity of the WBS, and the medium that you are using to represent the WBS. The graphical format is often preferred but can be hard to follow once you get past several hundred deliverables and sub-deliverables, and it often requires a large format printer (36" wide or wider) to be able print in its entirety. The tabular format can be printed on regular letter sized paper (often many pages), but may not show the relationship between the deliverables as clearly.

Figure 4-11 shows a WBS in both graphical and tabular views for a project to create a new patient sign-in kiosk for a small physician practice. The title of the project is Kiosk Project, shown in the top box or level 1 of the WBS, and the level 2 deliverables are location, patient kiosk, staff training, and marketing. Level 3 deliverables are also included.

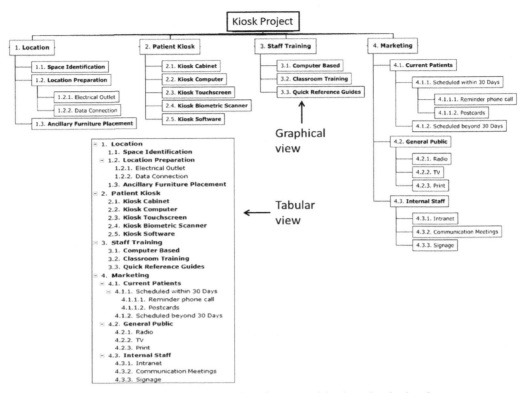

Figure 4-11. WBS for a kiosk project showing graphical and tabular formats

Notice that both of these formats in Figure 4-11 show the same information. Many documents, such as contracts, use the tabular format. Project scheduling software also uses this format, although there often are options to provide graphical formatting, if desired. Also note that work packages exist on different levels, depending on which deliverable thread you follow downward. For example, under the "2. Patient Kiosk" deliverable, the work packages are all listed at the next level as 2.1, 2.2, 2.3, 2.4, and 2.5. However, Marketing is decomposed down to a fourth level for "Current Patients" that are "Scheduled within 30 Days." For this thread the work packages are numbered 4.1.1.1 and 4.1.1.2. Remember, work packages are the lowest level deliverable or sub-deliverable for a given thread, and each deliverable thread can decompose to the level required to manage the project work without regard for how deep the other deliverables are decomposed. The depth at which you decompose a deliverable is based upon the complexity of the work, the uniqueness of the work, the experience of the team, and whether or not you are outsourcing the work.

BEST PRACTICE

If you look closely at the WBS examples shown you will notice that there are no verbs, as verbs represent action, and a WBS is not about action, but rather about deliverables. According to PMI, a WBS only contains deliverables, as it is a deliverables-based representation of the work required. As the definition of a WBS has fluctuated over the decades, sometimes you may still come across a definition that shows activities on the WBS.

However, it is incorrect to show activities on the WBS, according to PMI, so try to consistently use deliverables on your WBS. *After* creating the WBS you then define activities that are required to create those work packages. These activities should be shown on the schedule and not on the WBS itself. Several project management software packages use the WBS to create the activities, which may also cause some confusion.

When PMI refers to project work, it is not talking about activities. Work refers to what the project must complete—deliverables. Think of it as the result, not the effort, required of the project. Merriam-Webster's online dictionary (2015) includes a similar definition of the noun, work, as follows: "Something produced or accomplished by effort, exertion, or exercise of skill <this book is the work of many hands>."

Sometimes teams struggle with finding a way to state something as a deliverable. If you have trouble defining deliverables, consider the activity or action required to create the deliverable, and then swap the verb-noun order, and it becomes a deliverable. For example, if you must clear the site for a house, and your team wants to call it "Clear Site" (an activity), your deliverable can be listed instead as "Site Clearing" or "Site Work," which are both nouns.

Again, every project is unique, as is every organization. Use your judgment to decide the best way to create a WBS and the wording on it.

Recall that a work package represents the level of work that the project manager monitors and controls. You can think of work packages in terms of accountability and reporting. If a project has a relatively short time frame and requires weekly progress reports, a work package might represent work completed in one week or less. On the other hand, if a project has a very long time frame and requires quarterly progress reports, a work package might represent work completed in one month or more. A work package might also be the procurement of a specific product or products, such as an item or items purchased from an outside source. If you can manage a deliverable, which means you are able to estimate the time and resources required to complete it, without more detail, and you can assign that deliverable to one person, you most likely are already at the work package level.

The WBS provides the structure and contents for the Task Name column in tools like Microsoft Project and MindView, and the hierarchy is shown by indenting and numbering items within the software. Note that PMI's *Practice Standard for Work Breakdown Structures, Second Edition*, numbers all WBS items starting with the number 1. For example, the Kiosk Project would be numbered as follows:

1 Kiosk Project
  1.1 Location
      1.1.1 Space Identification
      1.1.2 Location Preparation
         1.1.2.1 Electrical Outlet
         1.1.2.2 Data Connection
      1.1.3 Ancillary Furniture Placement
  1.2 Patient Kiosk
  1.3 Staff Training
  1.4 Marketing

Be sure to check with your organization to see what numbering scheme it prefers to use for work breakdown structures.

The sample WBSs shown here seems somewhat easy to construct and understand. *Nevertheless, it is very difficult to create a good WBS.* To create a good WBS, you must understand both the project and its scope, and incorporate the needs and knowledge of the stakeholders. The project manager and the project team must decide as a group how to organize the work and how many levels to include in the WBS. Many project managers have found that it is better to focus on getting the top levels done well to avoid being distracted by too much detail.

Many people confuse deliverables on a WBS with specifications. Items on a WBS represent work that needs to be completed to finish the project, but do not include detailed characteristics of those deliverables. For example, for the Kiosk Project, the WBS did not include the color or material of the cabinet, the type of CPU in the computer, the size of the monitor, etc. That information would be part of the *product* requirements found in the scope statement and, if you created one, within the WBS dictionary.

A **WBS dictionary** is a document that describes the deliverables on the WBS in more detail. Any attribute, characteristic, or quality that better defines the deliverable should be in the WBS dictionary. It may also include who owns the work package, estimated cost and schedule information, contract information if outsourced, specific quality requirements, technical and performance requirements, etc. Recall that the project scope statement, WBS, and WBS dictionary join together to create the project scope baseline, as all three are required to paint the complete project picture.

Another frequent concern when creating a WBS is how to organize it so that it provides the basis for the project schedule. You should focus on *what* work needs to be delivered, not *when* or exactly *how* it will be done. In other words, the WBS items do not have to be developed as a sequential list of deliverables, and although they may be started that way, they do not typically follow that method beyond the second level.

If you do want some time-based flow for the work, you can create a WBS using the project management process groups of initiating, planning, executing, monitoring and controlling, and closing as level 2 in the WBS, as shown in Appendix A using Project 2016. By using this approach, not only does the project team follow good project management practice, but the WBS tasks can be mapped more easily against time. The executing deliverables are what vary most from project to project. In teaching an introductory project management class, this approach seems to work well, even though it is not that common in practice.

You can also create a WBS that is somewhat time-based in that the deliverables listed follow a required chronological order or work flow, as shown below in Figure 4-12. Construction projects will also sometimes follow a chronological order for the second level, moving from site work to foundation work to framing to exterior work to landscaping. Cautionary note: In most cases, and certainly in both of these examples, a deliverable from the far right side of level 2, such as Testing in Figure 4-12, may have work that needs to be completed during earlier parts in the project, such as System Design. For example, the testing plan may be developed when the system is being designed, as testing should be performed against design and not against the final software that is developed. Some organizations have a standard project life cycle for their type of work, called an Application Area Process (AAP). An AAP is based on the type of product the organization creates. If a project life cycle template exists, align the WBS with it to show a general chronology of the work.

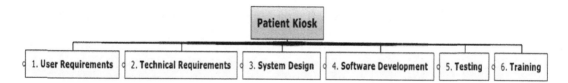

Figure 4-12. WBS showing work flow or chronological order (somewhat)

MEDIA SNAPSHOT

Few events get more media attention than the Olympic Games. Imagine all the work involved in planning and executing an event that involves thousands of athletes from around the world with millions of spectators. The 2002 Olympic Winter Games and Paralympics took five years to plan and cost more than $1.9 billion. PMI awarded the Salt Lake Organizing Committee (SLOC) the Project of the Year award for delivering world-class games that, according to the International Olympic Committee, "made a profound impact upon the people of the world."[3]

Four years before the Games began, the SLOC used a Primavera software-based system with a cascading color-coded WBS to integrate planning. A year before the Games, they added a Venue Integrated Planning Schedule to help the team integrate resource needs, budgets, and plans. For example, this software helped the team coordinate different areas involved in controlling access into and around a venue, such as roads, pedestrian pathways, seating and safety provisions, and hospitality areas, saving nearly $10 million.[4]

Approaches to Developing Work Breakdown Structures

Because it is so important to create a good WBS, this section describes several approaches you can use to develop them. These approaches include:

- Using guidelines or templates
- The analogy approach
- The top-down approach
- The bottom-up approach
- The mind-mapping approach

Using Guidelines or Templates

If organizational, industry, or professional guidelines for developing a WBS exist, it is very important to follow them. Some organizations—for example, the U.S. Department of Defense (DOD)—prescribe the form and content for WBSs for particular projects, such as aircraft. Some industries have guidelines or standards that are commonly used to drive project deliverables, and some professions (engineering fields, especially) have their own guidelines that suggest certain deliverables for all projects. If there are guidelines, there are also often templates available that can be used as the WBS starting point, with project specific deliverables added as required. Templates are especially useful for common or repeatable types of work, such as installing PCs in office areas launching marketing campaigns. Some software products, like Microsoft Project 2016, include templates for WBSs for various types of projects that can be used as a starting point for creating a new WBS, such as building a house, as shown earlier. Remember, a template is a starting point, not a destination! Adapt the template to the project, not vice-versa.

The Analogy Approach

Another approach for constructing a WBS is the analogy approach, where you use a similar project's WBS as a starting point. For example, many organizations have WBSs from past, successful projects and make them available for other project managers to use. While starting with a WBS from a similar project can save a lot of time, it is important that project managers and their teams address their unique project needs and understand how work will be done when creating their own WBS. The project manager must also understand the constraints and assumptions that the previous project worked under, as that may have impacted how they constructed their WBS. There are no two projects that are exactly the same, and using a WBS from another project without understanding how it differs from your project can be risky. One advantage to using this approach, at least as a starting point, is that it is less likely that you will accidently leave deliverables off the WBS because you are copying the WBS of a successful project.

The Top-down Approach

Most project managers consider the top-down approach of WBS construction to be the conventional approach to building a WBS. To use the top-down approach, start with the largest items or deliverables of the project and break them into their subordinate items. This process involves refining the work into greater and greater levels of detail. After breaking down or decomposing the top-level items, resources should then be assigned at the work-package level. The top-down approach is best suited to project managers and teams who have the technical and business insight required (expert judgment) and a big-picture perspective.

The Bottom-up Approach

In the bottom-up approach, team members first identify as many specific activities related to completing the project as possible. They then aggregate the specific activities and organize them into groups based on what they are creating (the work package). Next, they take groups of work packages and determine what they, as a group, will create (the next higher level in the WBS), and so forth. This method is often easier when team members understand the detailed work but are not necessarily thinking of the project from the deliverables perspective.

For example, a group of people might be responsible for creating a WBS to open a new office for an organization. They could begin by listing detailed activities required in order to open the office (get building permits, hire contractors, design the building, pick color schemes, etc.). They may list these activities in the order they believe they will be performed, or they may suggest them based on their limited knowledge of opening a new office. They would then start grouping the activities into what that group of activities, when completed, would create. For example, picking paint colors, choosing furniture fabrics, choosing carpet style, etc., may be grouped into a deliverable called, "Interior Design."

Some people have found that writing all possible activities down on sticky notes and then placing them on a wall helps them see all the work required for the project and develop logical groupings for performing the work. The bottom-up approach can be very time consuming compared to the top-down or analogous approaches, but it can also be a very effective way to create a WBS. Project teams often use the bottom-up approach for projects that represent entirely new products or approaches to doing a job, or to help create buy-in and synergy with a project team.

Mind Mapping

Some project managers like to use mind mapping to help develop a WBS. As described in Chapter 2, mind mapping is a technique that uses branches radiating out from a core idea to structure thoughts and ideas. This more visual, less structured approach to defining and then grouping activities can unlock creativity among individuals and increase participation and morale among teams. You can create mind maps by hand, by using sticky notes, using presentation software like PowerPoint, or by using mind-mapping software.

Figure 4-13 shows a mind-mapping diagram for the Kiosk Project described earlier. This diagram's radiating arms were created as team members identified required deliverables. The facilitator added it to the map, in no particular order. Note there are no numbers associated on the deliverables yet, as they have not yet been organized into a WBS.

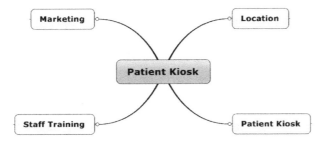

Figure 4-13. Patient kiosk WBS initial mind map

Once the major deliverables, which will comprise level 2 of the WBS, are identified, the team creates sub-deliverables for each of them, as shown in Figure 4-14. They can keep them in the above format or move them into the more common graphical WBS format. The value of leaving the WBS in the mind-map format is that it implies there is no order to the deliverables, which often encourages out-of-the-box thinking by the team. The detailed mind map requires more brainstorming. The threads may be focused on one at a time, or they can be assigned to sub groups within the group based on who best knows the deliverables required for that thread. Remember that the people creating the WBS should include the project team along with other stakeholders, so you may have someone from facilities, marketing, training, and IT involved. Let those identify the work who know the work the best.

At this point the team may decide that the WBS is 100% complete, and with the click of a button they can change the format to the tabular format (shown previously), and with another click they can add numbering to each WBS element. Some tools, such as MindView, also let you easily change the WBS mind map into a Gantt chart, as described in the Video Highlights. There are several good mind-mapping applications available. Some are open source such as X-Mind and FreeMind, while some are purchased such as MatchWare MindView or MindJet MindManager.

Figure 4-14. Patient kiosk WBS detailed mind map

VIDEO HIGHLIGHTS

MindView software allows you to create a WBS with a mind map. You can access a 30-day trial of their software at www.matchware.com. You can also watch several videos about creating a WBS using a mind map from Matchware's site or others. For example, Jim Franklin shows how to use Mindview to create a WBS for a solar panel project. Jim has also created a site called pmmapping.com with more information on using mind maps in project management.

Andy Kaufman, host of PeopleAndProjectsPodcast.com, demonstrates how to engage people in creating a WBS for a vacation by using sticky notes. Jennifer Bridges of projectmanager.com explains how to plan projects with your team and provides tips to perfect the project planning process by using a simple white board. See the companion site for this text at www.intropm.com for links to these and other video highlights.

Sample WBS

The Just-In-Time Training project team decided to use the project management process groups for the level 2 categories in its WBS, following a top-down approach. They also reviewed WBSs of similar projects as they created theirs. (Remember that the process groups include initiating, planning, executing, monitoring and controlling, and closing.) The level 3 activities under "Executing" (where the products and services of the project are produced) included course design and development, course administration, course evaluation, and stakeholder communications. The project team knew that they had to have strong communications to make the project a success, so they created a separate WBS level 3 category for communications under "Executing." They focused on the product deliverables they had to produce in breaking down the course design and development task by having level 4 categories based on the types of courses: supplier management, negotiating skills, project management, and software applications.

Figure 4-15 shows part of the initial WBS Kristin and her team created. You will see this same information later in this chapter as the Task names in the Gantt chart. Some deliverables have been broken down into more detail while others have not. Notice that the numbering scheme is slightly different from the PMI standard. For example, the first item is labeled 1. instead of 1.1. Remember that the WBS creates the structure or hierarchy for the work, and the Gantt chart includes the detailed activities required to produce a schedule for the project. To define the scope of the project accurately, it is very important to ensure consistency between the project charter, scope statement, WBS, Gantt chart, and related documents. It is also very important to involve the entire project team and other stakeholders in creating and reviewing the WBS. *People who will do the work should help to plan the work* by creating the WBS. It is important to let workers be creative and know that they have a say in how their work is done. Having group meetings to develop a WBS helps everyone understand *what* work must be done for the entire project and *how* it should be done, given the people involved. It also helps to identify where coordination between different work packages will be required.

**Work Breakdown Structure (WBS) for the
Just-In-Time Training Project, August 1**

1. Initiating
   1.1. Stakeholder register
   1.2. Project charter
   1.3. Assumption log
   1.4. Project kickoff meeting
2. Planning
   2.1. Project integration management
       2.1.1. Project management plan
   2.2. Project scope management
       2.2.1. Scope management plan
       2.2.2. Requirements management plan
       2.2.3. Requirements documentation
       2.2.4. Requirements traceability matrix
       2.2.5. Project scope statement
       2.2.6. Scope baseline
   2.3. Project schedule management
   2.4. Project cost management
   2.5. Project quality management
   2.6. Project resource management
   2.7. Project communications management
   2.8. Project risk management
   2.9. Project procurement management
   2.10. Project stakeholder management
3. Executing
   3.1. Course design and development
       3.1.1. Supplier management training
           3.1.1.1. Needs assessment
               3.1.1.1.1. Survey development
               3.1.1.1.2. Survey administration
               3.1.1.1.3. Survey results analysis
           3.1.1.2. Research of existing training
           3.1.1.3. Partnerships
               3.1.1.3.1. Research on potential partners for providing training
               3.1.1.3.2. Meetings with potential partners
               3.1.1.3.3. Partnership agreements
           3.1.1.4. Course development
               3.1.1.4.1. Executive course
               3.1.1.4.2. Introductory course
               3.1.1.4.3. Advanced course
           3.1.1.5. Pilot course evaluation
               3.1.1.5.1. Plans for pilot course
               3.1.1.5.2. Pilot course
               3.1.1.5.3. Report on pilot course

> 3.1.1.5.4. Presentation on pilot course
>
> 3.1.2. Negotiating skills training
>
> 3.1.3. Project management training
>
> 3.1.4. Software applications training
>
> 3.2. Course administration
>
> 3.3. Course evaluation
>
> 3.4. Stakeholder communications
>
> > 3.4.1. Communications regarding project and changes to training
> >
> > > 3.4.1.1. Documents (Emails, posters, memos, etc.)
> > >
> > > 3.4.1.2. Meetings
> > >
> > > 3.4.1.3. Information for the corporate intranet
> >
> > 3.4.2. Communications regarding productivity improvements
>
> 4. Monitoring and controlling
>
> 5. Closing

Figure 4-15. Sample WBS

Creating the WBS Dictionary

Many of the activities listed on a WBS can be rather vague. What exactly does WBS item 3.1.1.1.2, "Survey administration" mean, for example? The person responsible for this activity for the Just-In-Time Training project might think that it does not need to be broken down any further, which could be fine. However, the WBS item should be described in more detail so that everyone has the same understanding of what it involves. What if someone else has to perform the work? What would you tell him or her to do? What will it cost to complete the work? How many resources are required? How long will it take to complete? Information that is more detailed is needed to answer these and other questions. Of course you must use common sense in deciding how much documentation is needed. For a simple activity, verbal instructions might be sufficient.

As mentioned previously, a WBS dictionary is a document that describes the deliverables on the WBS in more detail. The format of the WBS dictionary can vary based on project needs. It might be appropriate to have just a short paragraph describing each work package. For a more complex project, an entire page or more might be needed for the work-package descriptions. Hyperlinks to other documents can be helpful if the deliverable must meet quality standards, organization policy and procedures, or external regulations. Such documents should be referenced with a hyperlink to ensure that the latest version is accessed when the deliverable is being produced.

You will most likely maintain your WBS dictionary in your project management software or another tool. Depending on your project and your organization, the WBS dictionary can include some or all of the following elements: WBS item number (e.g., 3.1.1.1.2), WBS item name, requirement trace, responsible person, estimated cost, estimated duration, resource requirements, and description. Of course you are free to add others as you deem fit. Some of these elements may not be known now, but they will be filled in as they become known at a later date:

Sample WBS Dictionary Entry

Project managers should work with their teams and sponsors to determine the level of detail needed in the WBS dictionary. Project teams often review WBS dictionary entries from similar activities to get a better idea of how to create these entries. They should also decide where this information will be entered and how it will be updated. For the Just-In-Time Training project, Kristin and her team will enter all of the WBS dictionary information into their enterprise project management system. Figure 4-16 provides an example of one of the entries.

WBS Dictionary Entry
August 1

WBS Item Number: 3.1.1.1.2
WBS Item Name: Survey administration
Requirement Trace: R12 – Follow corporate policies on surveys
Responsible person: TBD
Estimated Cost: TBD
Estimated duration: TBD
Resource requirements: Mike Sundby, department heads, survey expert
Description: The purpose of the survey for the supplier management training is to determine the learning objectives for the executive, introductory, and advanced supplier management courses (see WBS item 3.1.1.1.1 for additional information on the survey itself). The survey will be administered online using the standard corporate survey software. After the project steering committee approves the survey, the IT department will send it to all employees of grade level 52 or higher in the purchasing, accounting, engineering, information technology, sales, marketing, manufacturing, and human resource departments. The project champion, Mike Sundby, VP of Human Resources, will write an introductory paragraph for the survey. Department heads will mention the importance of responding to this survey in their department meetings and will send an e-mail to all affected employees to encourage their inputs. If the response rate is less than 30% one week after the survey is sent out, additional work may be required.

Figure 4-16. Sample WBS dictionary entry

The approved project scope statement and its associated WBS and WBS dictionary form the scope baseline, as mentioned earlier. Performance in meeting project scope goals is based on the scope baseline.

CASE WRAP-UP

Kristin learned a lot by leading her team during the planning phase of the Just-In-Time Training project. She did her best to get key stakeholders involved, including those who had little experience in planning. She could see that some people jumped to the planning details right away while others wanted to do as little planning as possible. She continued to consult members of the project steering committee for their advice, especially in helping everyone see how crucial it was to understand and document the scope of the project to provide a good baseline for measuring progress in providing all of the required deliverables for the project.

CHAPTER SUMMARY

Successful project managers know how important it is to develop, refine, and follow plans to meet project goals. It is important to remember that the main purpose of project plans is to guide project execution. Planning is done in all ten project management knowledge areas. This chapter summarizes the planning processes and outputs for project integration and scope management.

Planning for integration management includes developing a project management plan. Plans in the other knowledge areas are considered to be subsidiary parts of the project management plan.

Planning processes for scope management include planning scope management, collecting requirements, defining scope, and creating a WBS. A project scope statement describes product scope, product user acceptance criteria, project boundaries, constraints, assumptions, and detailed information on all project deliverables. A WBS is a very important document in project management because it provides the basis for planning and managing project schedules, costs, resources, and changes.

Approaches for developing a WBS include using guidelines, an analogy approach, a top-down approach, a bottom-up approach, and mind mapping. Several examples are provided. A WBS dictionary provides more detail on WBS items.

Samples of several planning documents are provided for the Just-In-Time Training project.

QUICK QUIZ

Note that you can find additional, interactive quizzes at www.intropm.com.

1.   Which of the following is not an output of planning for project integration and scope management?

    A.   a project website

    B.   a project management plan

    C.   a scope management plan

    D.   a WBS

2.   The main purpose of project planning is to:

    A.   obtain funding for the project

    B.   guide project execution

    C.   clarify roles and responsibilities

    D.   keep senior managers informed

3.   Project teams develop a _____ to coordinate all other project plans.

    A.   strategic plan

    B.   project management plan

    C.   master plan

    D.   project website

4.   A requirements _____ _____ is a table that lists requirements, various attributes of each requirement, and the status of the requirements to ensure that all of them are addressed.

    A.   traceability matrix

    B.   management plan

    C.   management matrix

    D.   tracking tool

5.   A _____ is a deliverable-oriented grouping of the work involved in a project that defines the total scope of the project.

    A.   contract

    B.   Gantt chart

    C.   WBS

    D.   network diagram

6.   A _____ is a deliverable at the lowest level of the WBS, where it can be appropriately assigned to and managed by a single accountable person.

   A.   WBS dictionary

   B.   budget item

   C.   control account

   D.   work package

7.   The entire project is considered to be level ___ in the WBS.

   A.   0

   B.   1

   C.   2

   D.   3

8.   A WBS is often depicted in a _____ format, similar to an organizational chart

   A.   tabular

   B.   mind-map

   C.   block

   D.   graphical

9.   According to PMI, which of the following would not be good wording for a WBS item?

   A.   install software

   B.   software

   C.   software installation

   D.   software training

10.   A WBS _____ is a document that describes the deliverables on the WBS in more detail.

   A.   glossary

   B.   statement

   C.   dictionary

   D.   appendix

Quick Quiz Answers

1. A; 2. B; 3. B; 4. A; 5. C; 6. D; 7. B; 8. D; 9. A; 10. C

DISCUSSION QUESTIONS

1. Why does having good plans help project teams during project execution? Why is it difficult to develop good plans?

2. What is the main planning process performed as part of project integration management? What is the main document created, and what are some of its contents?

3. What are the main planning processes performed as part of project scope management?

4. What are some approaches for creating a WBS? Why is it important to develop a good WBS?

5. What do you think about the scope planning documents prepared by the Just-In-Time Training project team? Do they seem too broad or too detailed in certain areas? Be specific in suggesting possible improvements.

EXERCISES

Note: These exercises can be done individually or in teams, in-class, as homework, or in a virtual environment. Learners can either write their results in a paper or prepare a short presentation or video to show their results.

1. Find an example of a large project that took more than a year to complete. Describe some of the planning work completed for the project as part of project integration and scope management. Summarize your findings.

2. Review the sample scope statement in this chapter. Assume you are responsible for planning and then managing the deliverable called "survey development." What additional information would you want to know to develop a good schedule and cost estimate for this deliverable?

3. Create a partial requirements traceability matrix for a project to build a house. Assume you or one of your classmates would use this information to plan his or her dream home. Include at least ten requirements.

4. Go to www.intropm.com and watch the first two Video Highlights related to creating a WBS. Find a similar video on another site, and summarize similarities and differences. Also document any questions you have about creating a WBS.

5. Create your own WBS for a project by using the mind-mapping approach. Break at least two level 2 items down to level 4. Try to use MindView software from www.matchware.com, if possible. You can also create the mind map by using similar mind-mapping software or a tool like PowerPoint.

6.   Find at least four samples of WBSs different from the ones in this chapter. Microsoft Project, MindView, and other project management software tools include templates that you can use as examples. Analyze the similarities and differences between the WBSs. Also review them for completeness. Do they seem to include all the work required for the project? Does the hierarchy make sense? Summarize your findings, and be sure to cite references.

TEAM PROJECTS

Note: These team projects can be done in-class, as homework, or in a virtual environment. Learners can either write their results in a paper or prepare a short presentation or video to show their results.

1.   Your organization initiated a project to raise money for an important charity. Assume that there are 1,000 people in your organization. Also assume that you have six months to raise as much money as possible, with a goal of $100,000. Develop a scope statement, WBS, and partial WBS dictionary for the project. Be creative in deciding how you will raise the money and the deliverables and sub-deliverables required to complete the project.

2.   You are part of a team in charge of a project to help people in your company (500 people) lose weight. This project is part of a competition, and the top "losers" will be featured in a popular television show. Assume that you have six months to complete the project and a budget of $10,000. Develop a scope statement, WBS, and partial WBS dictionary for the project. Be creative in deciding how you will raise the money and the deliverables and sub-deliverables required to complete the project.

3.   Using the information you developed in Project 1 or 2 above, role-play a meeting to review one of these planning documents with key stakeholders. Determine who will play what role (project manager, team member from a certain department, employees, senior managers, and so on). Be creative in displaying different personalities (i.e., a senior manager who questions the importance of the project to the organization, a team member who is very shy or obnoxious, etc.).

4.   Perform the planning tasks (only for the knowledge areas covered in this chapter) for one of the case studies provided in Appendix C. Remember to be thorough in your planning so that your execution goes smoothly.

5.   As a team, find at least four examples of WBSs for various types of projects (different from the examples in this chapter). Discuss the similarities and differences between how the WBSs are structured. Also discuss the quality of the examples you find and if the organization used specific software or provided guidelines for its creation. Include screen shots of the examples and citations.

KEY TERMS

baseline — A starting point, a measurement, or an observation that is documented so that it can be used for future comparison; also defined as the original project plans plus approved changes.

control account — A management control point for performance measurement where scope, budget, and schedule are integrated and compared to the earned value.

organizational process assets — Policies and procedures related to project management, past project files, and lessons-learned reports from previous, similar projects.

project management plan — A document used to coordinate all project planning documents and to help guide a project's execution and control.

requirement — A condition or capability that is necessary to be present in a product, service, or result to satisfy a business need.

requirements management plan — A plan that describes how project requirements will be analyzed, documented and managed.

requirements traceability matrix (RTM) — A table that lists requirements, various attributes of each requirement, and the status of the requirements to ensure that all of them are addressed.

scope baseline — The approved project scope statement and its associated WBS and WBS dictionary.

scope creep — The tendency for project scope to continually increase.

scope statement — Document that describes product characteristics and requirements, user acceptance criteria, and deliverables.

validation — formal acceptance of deliverables by the customer and other identified stakeholders.

verification —evaluating if a deliverable complies with a regulation, requirement, specification, or imposed condition.

work breakdown structure (WBS) — A deliverable-oriented grouping of the work involved in a project that defines the total scope of the project.

work breakdown structure (WBS) dictionary — A document that describes detailed information about WBS deliverables, sub-deliverables, and work packages.

work package — A deliverable at the lowest level of the WBS, where it can be appropriately assigned to and managed by a single accountable person.

END NOTES

[1]IBM, "Emerging Health IT achieves fast ROI with IBM Rational DOORS," IBM Case Studies (March 31, 2011).

[2]Vijay Sankar, "Meet our new IBM Champion Mia McCroskey," IBM Requirements Management Blog (Mar 27, 2013).

[3]Ross Foti, "The Best Winter Olympics, Period," *PM Network* (January 2004) p. 23.

[4]Ibid, p. 23.

Chapter 5

Planning Projects, Part 2
(Project Schedule and Cost Management)

LEARNING OBJECTIVES

After reading this chapter, you will be able to:

- List several planning processes and outputs for project schedule and cost management
- Describe the project schedule management planning processes and understand contents of a schedule management plan, activity list, activity attributes, milestone list, project schedule network diagram, duration estimates, basis of estimates, schedule baseline, project schedule, schedule data, and project calendars
- Understand how to find the critical path and its implications on timely project completion
- Explain the concept of critical chain scheduling and how it can be used in organizations
- Discuss the three project cost management planning processes
- Create a cost management plan, cost estimate, basis of estimates, cost baseline, and project funding requirements

---

OPENING CASE

Kristin and her team continued developing the Just-In-Time Training project plans. Although she always tried to engage those doing the actual work in the planning, she felt it was especially critical when estimating time and cost because it was difficult to hold people accountable if they had no input on the estimates.

Kristin had experience estimating costs and activity durations on past projects in her former department, but she soon realized that her new team members and stakeholders were not familiar with some of the techniques she planned to use, especially the project schedule network diagrams. She also found that none of her team members were familiar with the cost and scheduling features of their company's project management software. She again worked with the steering committee to get their guidance, and they agreed to provide customized training for some of her team members.

INTRODUCTION

In the previous chapter you read about the importance of doing a good job in planning for project integration and scope management. This chapter focuses on planning the next two knowledge areas—schedule and cost—which are also important, as are the others described in the next chapter. Recall that doing a thorough job in planning all applicable knowledge areas is fundamental to guiding project execution.

SUMMARY OF PLANNING PROCESSES AND OUTPUTS

Figure 5-1 summarizes the project planning processes and outputs for project schedule and cost management listed in the *PMBOK® Guide – Sixth Edition*. The following sections describe these processes and outputs further and then provide examples of applying them to the Just-In-Time Training project. After planning the project scope and determining what deliverables need to be produced you can start developing a detailed schedule and cost baseline. Of course, quality and human resource planning affect the scope, schedule, and cost planning, as do the other knowledge areas. As noted earlier, there are many interdependencies between various knowledge areas and process groups, and planning for project integration management is needed to coordinate all of these plans.

Knowledge area	Planning process	Outputs
Project schedule management	Plan schedule management	Schedule management plan
	Define activities	Activity list
		Activity attributes
		Milestone list
		Change requests
		Project management plan updates
	Sequence activities	Project schedule network diagrams
		Project documents updates
	Estimate activity durations	Activity duration estimates
		Basis of estimates
		Project documents updates
	Develop schedule	Schedule baseline
		Project schedule
		Schedule data
		Project calendars
		Project management plan updates
		Project documents updates
Project cost management	Plan cost management	Cost management plan
	Estimate costs	Cost estimates
		Basis of estimates
		Project documents updates
	Determine budget	Cost baseline
		Project funding requirements
		Project documents updates

Figure 5-1. Planning processes and outputs for project time and cost management

PROJECT SCHEDULE MANAGEMENT

Project schedule management involves the processes required to ensure timely completion of a project. The main planning processes performed as part of project schedule management are planning schedule management, defining activities, sequencing activities, estimating activity durations, and developing the project schedule. The main documents produced are a schedule management plan, an activity list and attributes, a milestone list, a project schedule network diagram, activity duration estimates, a schedule baseline, a project schedule, and project calendars. Samples of several of these documents are provided later in this section.

Planning Schedule Management

The purpose of this process is to determine the policies, procedures, and documentation for planning, developing, managing, executing, and controlling the project schedule. The project team holds meetings, consults with experts, and analyzes data to help produce a schedule management plan, which becomes a component of the project management plan.

Contents of the schedule management plan can include the following:
- scheduling methodology and tools used to create a schedule model, if required
- release and iteration length, or time-boxed periods
- level of accuracy required for activity duration estimates
- units of measure, such as staff hours, days, or weeks
- organizational procedure links
- project schedule model maintenance
- control thresholds for monitoring schedule performance, such as a percentage deviation from the baseline plan
- rules of performance measurement, especially if earned value management is used (see Chapter 8, Monitoring and Controlling, for more information on earned value management)
- formats and frequency for schedule reports

VIDEO HIGHLIGHTS

When using agile techniques like Scrum, planning the schedule is based on sprints, as described in Chapter 3. The project team creates a sprint backlog listing the work they plan to accomplish during a specific sprint (usually 2-4 weeks). They plot the planned work against their timeline using a burndown chart and chart progress against the plan.

Several videos describe how to plan and track schedules using Scrums. For example, Harvard Business Review provides a short video and article called "Embracing Scrum." The Agile Alliance provides several videos on this topic. Many software companies explain how to use their tools to help plan agile projects, including burndown charts. See the companion website for links to several videos to help you understand these concepts and tools.

Defining Activities

Project schedules grow out of the basic documents that initiate a project. The project charter often mentions planned project start and end dates, which serve as the starting points for a more detailed schedule. The project manager starts with the project charter and then develops a project scope statement and WBS, as discussed in the previous chapter. Using this information with the scope statement, WBS, WBS dictionary, project management plan, and other related information, the project team begins to develop a schedule by first clearly defining all the activities it needs to perform. As defined in the *PMBOK® Guide – Sixth Edition*, an **activity** is a distinct, scheduled portion of work performed during the course of a project.

Creating the Activity List and Attributes

The **activity list** is a tabulation of activities to be included on a project schedule. The list should include the activity name, an activity identifier or number, and a brief description of the activity. The **activity attributes** provide schedule-related information about each activity, such as predecessors, successors, logical relationships, leads and lags, resource requirements, constraints, imposed dates, and assumptions related to the activity. The activity list is created by identifying the activities required to create each work package on the WBS, and any activity and its attributes must be in alignment with the WBS and WBS dictionary.

Why are activities only created for the work packages, and not for all deliverables on the WBS? Recall from Chapter 4 that a work package is the lowest level item of work in a WBS, and that a WBS includes all project work. Further, when a deliverable is decomposed into smaller deliverables (and eventually the work packages), all work required for a deliverable is included in its sub-deliverables, known as the WBS 100% rule. Therefore, if you complete all activities required to complete all work packages, then you complete all work required for the project. Figure 5-2, a small section of the Kiosk Project WBS from the previous chapter, demonstrates this principle. In this example, if the kiosk cabinet, kiosk computer, kiosk touchscreen, kiosk biometric scanner, and kiosk software are all completed, then the patient kiosk will be completed. Remember, only the work packages (2.1, 2.2, 2.3, 2.4, and 2.5 in this example) have activities assigned to them.

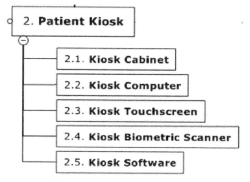

Figure 5-2: WBS 100% rule

The goal of the activity definition process is to ensure that project team members have a *complete* understanding of all the work they must do so that they can start scheduling the work. For example, one of the work packages in the WBS for the Just-In-Time Training project is "Pilot course." The project team would have to understand who will be getting the training, the format of the training (i.e., face-to-face, self-paced, synchronous online, etc.), the length of time that participants will be available for training, the training budget, printing capabilities within the organization (assuming some manuals had to be printed), and so on before they could determine the activities required to complete the training manuals as well as other activities related to delivering the Pilot course. By better understanding the work package, the team can better define what activities are required to create that specific deliverable.

The WBS is often expanded during the activity definition process as the project team members may identify other deliverables required to complete the project. This is especially true of interim deliverables, which are those deliverables required to create the final product, but are then discarded once the project is completed. For example, a project team may decide that they need a temporary data staging server for internal team testing, with the server being repurposed for another project once theirs is completed. This text has repeatedly stated that the WBS is deliverables based, and that is true. However, once you define the activities required to create each work package, those activities essentially hang off the end of the work packages, and therefore off the bottom of the WBS. With so many great software tools that allow you to connect the work packages to the activities, it is tempting to include them on the WBS proper, but they should *not* be if you are following PMI's standards. It is fine to include *all* the activity data in one place, but you should be consistent in how you represent the WBS. You should also present the information at whatever level of detail is required for the audience. Clearly defining the work and having a realistic schedule for all activities is crucial to project success.

Sample Activity List and Attributes

Kristin and her team developed dozens of activities that would be used later for creating the project schedule. Figure 5-3 provides an example of how they reviewed a work package, "3.1.1.5.3 Report on pilot course," and developed a list of activities required to build that work package. Note that unlike the deliverables described within the WBS, which are listed as nouns, activities are all listed using a verb and then a noun, using verbs such as *review, create, develop, interview, write, distribute,* and *analyze*.

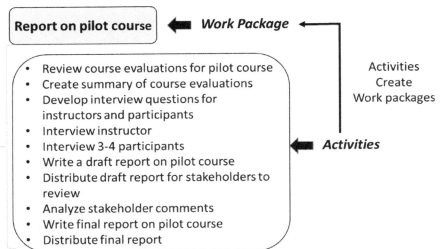

Figure 5-3. Report on pilot course activity list

After the project team creates the activities for each work package, they can begin to fill in the attributes. Not all attributes will be known at this point, but the team will record what is known and update information as it becomes available. For example, the team may know what activities must be completed before this activity, but they may only know this for activities within this single work package. They may later find out that there are activities for other work packages that also must be completed before this activity can start, or vice-versa.

Figure 5-4 shows an example of activity attributes for WBS item "3.1.1.1.2 Survey administration" under 3.1.1 Supplier management training. Notice the detailed information provided, such as the predecessors, successors, resource requirements, and assumptions. As you can see from this sample, Kristin and her team would have to work closely with other stakeholders to define this information. These are just a few of the many activity attributes that you may decide to collect for your project. As with all project management tools, techniques, and processes, you must tailor it to your needs. For example, you may decide to include who is assigned this activity, how it will be tested or verified, whether or not it requires sign off upon completion, etc. It is also important to document the assumptions for activities, as shown in Figure 5-4. These detailed assumptions provide key information for the person who will do the work.

Activity List and Attributes
August 1

Project Name: Just-In-Time Training Project
WBS Item Number: 3.1.1.1.2
WBS Item Name: Survey administration
Predecessors: 3.1.1.1.1 Survey development
Successors: 3.1.1.1.3 Survey results analysis
Logical Relationships: finish-to-start
Leads and Lags: None
Resource Requirements: IT personnel, corporate survey software, corporate Intranet
Constraints: None
Imposed dates: None
Assumptions: The survey for the supplier management training will be administered online using the standard corporate survey software. It should include questions measured on a Likert scale. For example, a question might be as follows: I learned a lot from this course. Respondents would enter 1 for Strongly Agree, 2 for Agree, 3 for Undecided, 4 for Disagree, or 5 for Strongly Disagree. There also should be several open-ended questions, such as "What did you like most about the pilot course? What did you like least about the pilot course?" After the project steering committee approves the survey, the IT department will send it to all employees of grade level 52 or higher in the purchasing, accounting, engineering, information technology, sales, marketing, manufacturing, and human resource departments. The project champion, Mike Sundby, VP of Human Resources, will write an introductory paragraph for the survey. Department heads will mention the importance of responding to this survey in their department meetings and will send an e-mail to all affected employees to encourage their inputs. If the response rate is less than 30% one week after the survey is sent out, additional work may be required, such as a reminder e-mail to follow-up with people who have not responded to the survey.

Figure 5-4. Sample activity list and attributes

Creating a Milestone List

To ensure that all major activities are accounted for, project teams often create a milestone list. A **milestone** is a significant point or event in a project. It usually includes many activities, and therefore a lot of work, to complete a milestone. Unlike a deliverable, which is the output of activities, and unlike an activity, which is the actual project work, a milestone is simply a marker to help in identifying necessary activities. *There is usually no cost or duration associated with a milestone.* Milestones are like the mile markers on a highway. Either you pass them or you do not. It is good practice to have enough milestones to keep the project team on track, similar to mile markers providing motivation and feedback for runners in a long race.

Milestones are useful tools for setting schedule goals and monitoring progress, and project sponsors and senior managers often focus on major milestones when reviewing projects. For example, milestones for many projects include sign-off of key documents, completion of specific products, or completion of important process-related work, such as awarding a contract to a supplier. *Milestone names are generally written in past tense*, such as "Contract awarded" and are indicated on a Gantt chart as diamond shapes with no cost, duration, or resources.

Sample Milestone List

Kristin and her team reviewed the draft WBS and activity list to develop an initial milestone list. They reviewed the list with their sponsor and other key stakeholders. Project teams often estimate completion dates for milestones early in the scheduling process and adjust them after going through additional schedule management planning steps such as activity sequencing, activity resource estimating, duration estimating, and schedule development. Figure 5-5 shows part of the milestone list for the Just-In-Time Training project. This section focuses on the milestones related to the needs assessment for supplier management training (WBS item 3.1.1.1). Kristin knew her team had to complete this survey early in the project and that the results would affect many of the other tasks required for the project. Her team might need to see all the milestones provided in Figure 5-5, but the steering committee might only need to see the last milestone, "Survey results reported to steering committee." The steering committee might focus on other milestones, including the project kick-off meeting, results of the pilot course, dates for each training class provided as part of the project, results of the course evaluations, and the projected end date for the project. Using project management software, such as Project 2016, makes it easy to filter information and create reports so that different people can focus on their own work and milestones. See Appendix A for more details on using Project 2016.

Milestone List August 1	
Project Name: Just-In-Time Training Project	
Milestone	**Initial Estimated Completion Date***
Draft survey completed	8/3
Survey comments submitted	8/8
Survey sent out by IT	8/10
Percentage of survey respondents reviewed	8/17
Survey report completed	8/22
Survey results reported to steering committee	8/24
*Note: Dates are in U.S. format. 8/3 means August 3.	

Figure 5-5. Sample milestone list

BEST PRACTICE

Many people use the SMART criteria to help define milestones. The SMART criteria are guidelines suggesting that milestones should be:

- **Specific** – anyone with a basic knowledge of the project should understand the milestone
- **Measureable** – the milestone must be something you can measure (objective)
- **Attainable** – the milestone and the due date must be attainable
- **Relevant** – the milestone must be relevant to the project and the organization
- **Time-framed** – it must be date driven

For example, completing the online reports, as listed in Figure 5-5, is specific (understandable, clear), measurable (are the reports completed or not?), attainable (the timeline appears to be accurate), relevant (the project will not be successful without the reporting aspects of it), and time-framed (date based).

You can also use milestones to reduce schedule risk by following these best practices:

- Define milestones early in the project and include them in the Gantt chart to provide a visual guide.
- Create milestones of manageable size and duration. If they are too large in size they will not help you manage the project effectively.
- The set of milestones must be all-encompassing.
- Each milestone must be binary, meaning it is either complete or incomplete.
- Carefully monitor the milestones on the critical path (described later in this chapter).[1]

SEQUENCING ACTIVITIES

After defining project activities, the next step in project schedule management is activity sequencing. Activity sequencing involves reviewing the activity list and attributes, project scope statement, and milestone list to determine the relationships or dependencies between activities. It also involves evaluating the reasons for dependencies and the different types of dependencies.

A **dependency**, or **relationship**, relates to the sequencing of project activities. For example, does a certain activity have to be finished before another one can start? Can the project team do several activities in parallel? Can some overlap? Determining these relationships or dependencies between activities has a significant impact on developing and managing a project schedule.

There are four basic attributes of dependencies among project activities:

- **Mandatory dependencies** are inherent in the nature of the work being performed on a project. They are sometimes referred to as hard logic because their relationships are unavoidable. For example, you cannot hold training classes until the training materials are ready, and the training materials cannot be created until the objectives of the course are determined.

- **Discretionary dependencies** are defined by the project team. For example, a project team might follow good practice and not start detailed design work until key stakeholders sign off on all the analysis work. Discretionary dependencies are sometimes referred to as soft logic and should be used with care because they might limit later scheduling options.

- **External dependencies** involve relationships between project and non-project activities. The installation of new software might depend on delivery of new hardware from an external supplier. Even though the delivery of the new hardware might not be in the scope of the project, it should have an external dependency added to it because late delivery will affect the project schedule. External dependencies can be either mandatory or discretionary.

- **Internal dependencies** are within the project team's control, such as testing a machine that must be first assembled, where all the work is done inside the team.

Note that an activity can have two of these attributes, such as an internal mandatory dependency or an external discretionary dependency. As with activity definition, it is important that project stakeholders work together to define the activity dependencies that exist on their project. If you do not define the sequence of activities and estimate their durations, you cannot use some of the most powerful schedule tools available to project managers: project schedule network diagrams and critical path analysis.

Project Schedule Network Diagrams

Project schedule network diagrams are the preferred technique for showing activity sequencing for projects. A project schedule network diagram or simply **network diagram** is a schematic display of the logical relationships among, or sequencing of, project activities. Some people refer to network diagrams as PERT charts. PERT is described later in this section. Figure 5-6 shows a sample network diagram for Project X, which is shown using the arrow diagramming method (ADM), or activity-on-arrow (AOA) approach. (Note: This approach is shown first because the diagrams are often easier to understand and create. Its main limitations are that it can only show finish-to-start dependencies, as described later in this section, and that no major project management software supports it.)

Note the main elements on the network diagram in Figure 5-6. The letters A through I represent activities with dependencies that are required to complete the project. These activities come from the activity definition process described earlier. The arrows represent the activity sequencing, or relationships between activities. For example, Activity A must be done before Activity D, and Activity D must be done before Activity F.

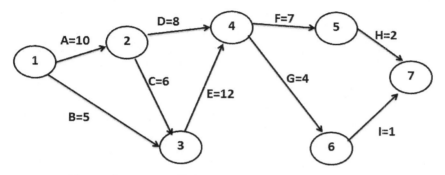

Note: Assume all durations are in days;
A=10 means Activity A has a duration of 10 days.

Figure 5-6. Activity-on-arrow (AOA) network diagram for Project X

The format of this network diagram uses the **activity-on-arrow (AOA)** approach, or the **arrow diagramming method (ADM)**—a network diagramming technique in which activities are represented by arrows and connected at points called nodes to illustrate the sequence of activities. In AOA, a **node** is simply the starting and ending point of an activity. The first node signifies the start of a project, and the last node represents the end of a project. If you are in a meeting and using a whiteboard to sequence a subset of project activities, AOA is frequently used due to its simplicity.

Keep in mind that the network diagram represents activities that must be done to complete the project. It is not a race to get from the first node to the last node. *Every activity on the network diagram must be completed for the project to finish.* It is also important to note that not every single activity needs to be on the network diagram; only activities with dependencies need to be shown on the network diagram. However, some people like to have start and end milestones and to list every activity. It is a matter of preference. For projects with hundreds of activities, it might be simpler to include only activities with dependencies on a network diagram.

Assuming you have a list of the project activities and their start and finish nodes, follow these steps to create an AOA network diagram:

1. Remember that the circles only represent activity boundaries, or connection points, and that the activities themselves are represented by the lines.

2. Draw a circle to represent the start of the project. Refer to this as Node 1.

3. Find all of the activities that have no predecessor, and draw a node for each of these activities to the right of Node 1. Draw arrows connecting Node 1 to each of these new nodes, and put the activity name on each line that connects the node pairs. If you have a duration estimate, write that next to the activity letter or name, as shown in Figure 5-6. For example, A = 10 means that the duration of Activity A is ten days, weeks, or other standard unit of time. Although AOA diagrams always reads left to right, be sure to put arrowheads on all arrows to signify the direction of the relationships.

4. Continue drawing the network diagram, working from left to right. Look for bursts and merges. A **burst** occurs when two or more activities follow a single node. A **merge** occurs when two or more nodes precede a single node. For example, in Figure 5-6, Node 1 is a burst because it goes into Nodes 2 and 3. Node 4 is a merge preceded by Nodes 2 and 3.

5. Continue drawing the AOA network diagram until all activities are included.

6. As a rule of thumb, all arrowheads should face toward the right, and no arrows should cross on an AOA network diagram. You might need to redraw the diagram to make it look presentable.

Even though AOA network diagrams are generally easy to understand and create, a different method is more commonly used: the precedence diagramming method. The **precedence diagramming method (PDM)** (also called activity on node, or AON) is a network diagramming technique in which boxes represent activities. It is particularly useful for visualizing different types of time dependencies, as the AOA diagram can only show the most common type of dependency—finish-to-start (FS), described later in this section. If presented with a network diagram created by someone else, there are a few ways to distinguish an AOA from an AON network diagram, shown below in Figure 5-7.

Distinguishing Factor	Activity on Arrow	Activity on Node
Line information	Represents activities & precedence	Represents precedence
Node shape	Circle shape	Box shape
Activity information	Only duration typically shown	Often includes duration, start date, end date, and assigned resource
Line shape	Straight	Uses right angles
Line direction	Always moves rightward	Can move backwards, depending upon relationship (FF, FS, SF, SS)

Figure 5-7. Activity on arrow vs. activity on node

Figure 5-8 illustrates the four types of dependencies that can occur among project activities, based on a Help screen from Microsoft Project. This screen shows that activity A is the predecessor or "from" activity and B is the successor or "to" activity. After you determine the reason for a dependency between activities (mandatory, discretionary, or external), you must determine the type of dependency. *Note that the terms "activity" and "task" are used interchangeably, as are "relationship" and "dependency."* The four types of dependencies, or relationships, between activities include the finish-to-start (FS) start-to-start (SS), finish-to-finish (FF), and start-to-finish (SF), as described in Figure 5-8.

Finish-to-Start link (fs)   **Start-to-Start link (ss)**

Task B can't start until Task A is done. This is the default link type in Project, and the most commonly used.

Example: *Dig foundation* (Task A) must be complete before your team can start *Pour concrete* (Task B).

Task B can't start until Task A starts. They don't have to start at the same time: Task B can begin any time after Task A begins.

Example: To save time, you want to level concrete at one end of the foundation while it is still being poured at the other end. But *Level concrete* (Task B) can't start until *Pour concrete* (Task A) has also started.

Finish-to-Finish link (ff)   **Start-to-Finish link (sf)**

Task B can't finish until Task A is done. They don't have to end at the same time: Task B can end any time after Task A ends.

Example: Your team is adding the wiring to the building and inspecting it at the same time. Until *Add wiring* (Task A) gets done, you won't be able to finish *Inspect electrical* (Task B).

Task B can't finish until Task A begins. Task B can finish any time after Task A begins. This type of link is rarely used.

Example: The roof trusses for your building are built off-site. You can't finish *Assemble roof* (Task B) until *Truss delivery* (Task A) begins.

Figure 5-8. Activity dependency types

Figure 5-9 illustrates Project X (shown originally in Figure 5-6) using the precedence diagramming method. Notice the activities are placed inside boxes, which represent the nodes on this diagram. Arrows show the relationships between activities. For example, Activity D has a relationship of dependency with Activity A. This figure was created using Microsoft Project, which automatically places additional information inside each node. Each activity box includes the start and finish date, labeled "Start" and "Finish"; the activity ID number, labeled "ID"; the activity's duration, labeled "Dur"; and the names of resources, if any, assigned to the activity, labeled "Res." The border of the boxes for activities on the critical path (discussed later in this section) appears automatically in red in the Microsoft Project network diagram view. In Figure 5-9, the boxes for critical activities (A, C, E, F, and H) are shown in black. See Appendix A for detailed information on using Project 2016.

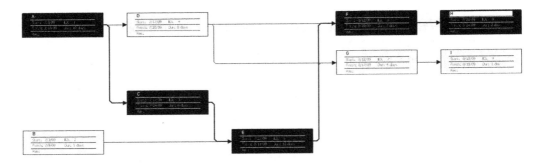

Figure 5-9. Precedence diagramming method network diagram for Project X

Although the AOA diagram might seem easier to understand, the precedence diagramming method is more commonly used than AOA network diagrams. One primary advantage is that PDM allows you to show different types of dependencies among activities, whereas AOA network diagrams use only finish-to-start dependencies. However, because 90% or more of relationships are defined as finish-to-start (FS), you may wonder why everyone does not just use AOA. The answer is simple: The best reason for using PDM is that it is the *only* diagramming method used by the major project management software packages.

Kristin and her team reviewed all the project activities and determined which ones had dependencies. They also determined which activities had **lag** time or required a gap in time and which ones had **lead** time or could be overlapped. For example, you might want to wait a certain period of time, perhaps thirty days, after holding the first training class before holding the second one (a lag of 30 days). Or you might want to get started on writing a long research report 5 days before all reference materials are gathered (a lead of -5 days). See Appendix A for examples of using lags and leads in Project 2016.

Estimating Activity Duration

After working with key stakeholders to define activities, determine their dependencies, and estimate their resources, the next process in project schedule management is to estimate the duration of activities. It is important to note that **duration** includes the actual amount of time spent working on an activity *plus* elapsed time. For example, even though it might take one workweek or five workdays to do the actual work, the duration estimate might be two weeks to allow extra time needed to obtain outside information or to allow for resource availability. Do not confuse duration with **effort**, which is the number of workdays or work hours required to complete an activity. A duration estimate of one day could be based on eight hours of work. Duration is used to determine the schedule, like how long it will take to before you finish reading a particular book. Effort is used to determine labor costs, like how many hours you will spend reading that book. Of course, the two are related, so project team members must document their assumptions when creating duration estimates and update them as the project progresses.

The outputs of activity duration estimating include duration estimates for each activity and the basis of estimates. Estimating techniques are similar to those for preparing cost estimates (i.e., analogous, parametric, etc.). Duration estimates are provided as a discrete number, such as four weeks; as a range, such as three to five weeks; or as a three-point estimate. A **three-point estimate** is an estimate that includes an optimistic, most likely, and pessimistic estimate, such as three weeks, four weeks, and five weeks, respectively. The optimistic estimate is based on a best-case scenario, whereas the pessimistic estimate is based on a worst-case scenario. The most likely estimate, as it sounds, is an estimate based on a most likely or expected scenario.

Program Evaluation Review Technique (PERT) is a network analysis technique used to estimate project duration when there is a high degree of uncertainty about the individual activity duration estimates. A three-point estimate is required for performing PERT estimates. By using the PERT weighted average for each activity duration estimate, the total project duration estimate accounts for the risk or uncertainty in the individual activity estimates.

To use PERT, you calculate a weighted average for the duration estimate of each project activity using the following formula:

PERT weighted
   average =   **optimistic time + 4 x most likely time + pessimistic time**
                                                      6

Sample Activity Duration Estimates

Many project teams use one discrete estimate—the most likely estimate—to estimate activity durations. For example, Kristin's team could enter these discrete estimates into their enterprise project management system. If Kristin's project team used PERT to determine the schedule for the Just-In-Time Training project, they would have to collect numbers for the optimistic, most likely, and pessimistic duration estimates for each project activity. For example, suppose the person assigned to administer the survey for the supplier management training estimated that it would take two workdays to do this activity. Without using PERT, the duration estimate for that activity would be two workdays. Suppose an optimistic time estimate for this activity is one workday, and a pessimistic time estimate is nine workdays. Applying the PERT formula, you get the following:

PERT weighted average   = **1** workday + 4 x **2** workdays + **9** workdays
                                                      6
                                           = (1 + 8 + 9 workdays)/6 (Multiply 4 x 2 before adding)
                                           = 18 workdays/6
                                           = 3 workdays

Instead of using the most likely duration estimate of two workdays, the project team would use three workdays. The main advantage of PERT is that it attempts to address the risk associated with duration estimates. Because many projects exceed schedule estimates, PERT might help in developing schedules that are more realistic. PERT also has disadvantages. It involves more work because it requires several duration estimates, and there are better probabilistic (based on probability) methods for assessing schedule risk, such as Monte Carlo simulations.

A **Monte Carlo simulation** is a quantitative risk analysis technique that provides a probability distribution for outcome values for the whole project. To perform a Monte Carlo simulation for the project time estimate, in addition to the three-point estimate, you also collect probabilistic information for each activity duration estimate. For example, Kristin would ask the person assigned to administer the survey for the supplier management training for an optimistic, pessimistic, and most likely estimate and also for the probability of completing that activity between the optimistic and most likely time estimates. She would need similar information for all of the activity duration estimates. She could then run a computer simulation where the duration estimate values would change randomly based on the collected data. There are several software products that can assist in performing Monte Carlo simulations. As this can be a complex process, be sure to consult with experts before using it.

For this project, Kristin and her team decided to enter realistic discrete estimates for each activity instead of using PERT or a Monte Carlo simulation. She stressed that people who would do the work should provide the estimate, and they should have 50 percent confidence in meeting each estimate. If some tasks took longer, some took less time, and some were exactly on target, they should still meet their overall schedule.

Figure 5-10 illustrates problems people have in providing good duration estimates!

Figure 5-10: Estimating can be difficult! (www.xkcd.com)

Developing the Project Schedule

Schedule development uses the results of all the preceding project schedule management processes to determine the start and end dates of project activities and of the entire project. There are often several iterations of all the project schedule management processes before a project schedule is finalized. The ultimate goal of schedule development is to create a realistic project schedule that provides a basis for monitoring project progress for the time dimension of the project. Project managers must lead their teams in creating realistic schedules and then monitoring and controlling them during project execution.

The main output of the schedule development process is the project schedule, which is often displayed in the form of a Gantt chart. **Gantt charts** provide a standard format for displaying project schedule information by listing project activities and their corresponding start and finish dates in a calendar format. Gantt charts are very useful as they show when activities will be started and completed relative not only to dates, but to each other. Remember that the schedule network diagram only shows precedence (which activity depends upon which activities), so the team must refer to the Gantt chart to get that high level view of when work will be performed.

Figure 5-11 shows a simple Gantt chart for Project X, described earlier, created with Microsoft Project. Recall that this example only uses finish-to-start dependencies and no lead or lag time. Notice the column heading where the activities are listed reads, "Task Name" instead of "Activity Name." This naming convention is from Microsoft Project, but recall that PMI prefers the term activity. See Appendix A for examples and instructions for using other types of dependencies with Project 2016.

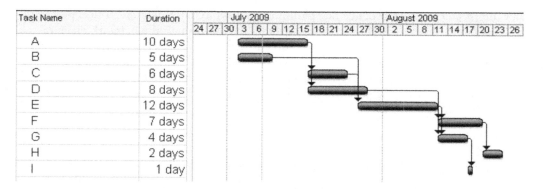

Figure 5-11. Gantt chart for Project X

Recall that the activities on the Gantt chart are those required to build the deliverables at the work package level on the WBS. These activities were previously defined, along with their attributes, and entered into the activity list. Remember also that although only activities have durations and costs, work packages will often appear in the Gantt chart as they serve as summaries for the activities required to build it. Before showing a Gantt chart for the Just-In-Time Training project, it is important to explain a fundamental concept that assists project teams in developing and meeting project schedules: critical path analysis.

Critical Path Analysis

Many projects fail to meet schedule expectations. **Critical path method (CPM)**—also called **critical path analysis**—is a network diagramming technique used to predict total project duration and show the amount of schedule flexibility on the network paths within the schedule model. This important tool will help you combat project schedule overruns. A **critical path** for a project is the series of activities that determine the *earliest* time by which the project can be completed. It may also be defined as the *longest* path through the network diagram that has the least amount of slack or float. **Slack** or **float** is the amount of time an activity may be delayed without delaying a succeeding activity or the project finish date. There are normally several activities conducted in parallel on projects, and most projects have multiple paths through a network diagram. The longest path in terms of total duration (not the number of activities), is what is driving the completion date for the project. Remember that you are not finished with the project until you have finished *all* activities.

Calculating the Critical Path

To find the critical path for a project, you must first develop a good network diagram as described earlier, which requires a good activity list based on the WBS. To create a network diagram, you must determine the dependencies of activities and also estimate their durations. Calculating the critical path involves adding the durations for all activities on each path through the network diagram. The longest path is the critical path and is also the shortest duration in which the entire project can be completed.

Figure 5-12 shows the AOA network diagram for Project X again. Note that you can use either the AOA or the precedence diagramming method to determine the critical path on projects. This figure also shows all the paths—a total of six—through the network diagram. Note that each path starts at the first node (1) and ends at the last node (7) on the AOA network diagram. This figure also shows the total duration of each path, sometimes referred to as its length, through the network diagram. These lengths are computed by adding the durations of each activity on the path. Because path A-C-E-F-H at 37 days has the longest duration, it is the critical path for the project.

What does the critical path really mean? *The critical path shows the shortest time in which a project can be completed.* If one or more of the activities on the critical path takes longer than planned, the whole project schedule will slip *unless* the project manager takes corrective action.

Project teams can be creative in managing the critical path. For example, Joan Knutson, a well-known author and speaker in the project management field, often describes how a gorilla helped Apple computer complete a project on time. Team members worked in an area with cubicles, and whoever was in charge of an activity currently on the critical path had a big, stuffed gorilla on top of his or her cubicle. Everyone knew that this person was under the most time pressure, so they tried not to distract him or her. When a critical activity was completed, the person in charge of the next critical activity received the gorilla.

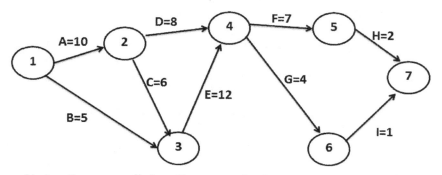

Note: Assume all durations are in days.

Path 1: A-D-F-H   Length = 10+8+7+2 =27
Path 2: A-D-G-I   Length = 10+8+4+1=23
Path 3: A-C-E-F-H   Length = 10+6+12+7+2=37
Path 4: A-C-E-G-I   Length = 10+6+12+4+1 = 33
Path 5: B-E-F-H   Length = 5+12+7+2=26
Path 6: B-E-G-I   Length = 5+12+4+1=22

Figure 5-12. Critical path calculation for Project X

Growing Grass Can Be on the Critical Path

People are often confused about what the critical path is for a project or what it really means. Some people think the critical path includes the most critical activities. However, the critical path focuses on the time dimension of a project. The fact that its name includes the word "critical" does *not* mean that it includes all critical activities in terms of scope, quality, resources, or other areas. For example, Frank Addeman, executive project director at Walt Disney Imagineering, explained in a keynote address at the May 2000 PMI-ISSIG Professional Development Seminar that growing grass was on the critical path for building Disney's Animal Kingdom theme park. This 500-acre park required special grass for its animal inhabitants, and some of the grass took years to grow. The project manager did not assign his top people to watching grass grow! He did use this information, however, to delay the start of other more expensive activities to make effective use of resources. Another misconception is that the critical path is the longest path, in terms of the discrete number of activities, through the network diagram. For a project, however, each activity must be done to complete the project, and as such, every path, and every activity, is important. The critical path is simply the activity path, or thread, that requires the closest attention in order to not delay the project's completion date.

Other aspects of critical path analysis may cause confusion. Can there be more than one critical path on a project? Does the critical path ever change? In the Project X example, suppose that Activity G has a duration estimate of eight days instead of four days. This new duration estimate would make the length of Path 4 equal to 37 days. Now the project has two paths (paths 3 and 4) with equal, longest durations, so there are two critical paths. Therefore, there *can* be more than one critical path on a project, and for complex projects there may be many critical paths identified. Project managers should closely monitor performance of activities on the critical path to avoid late project completion. If there is more than one critical path, project managers must keep their eyes on all of them.

The critical path on a project can change as the project progresses. For example, suppose Activity B from Figure 5-12 has problems and ends up taking 17 days instead of 5 to finish. Assuming no other activity durations change, path 5, B-E-F-H, becomes the new critical path with a duration of 38 days. Therefore, the critical path can, and often does, change on a project. One of the most common reasons for critical paths changing is that the project manager closely manages those activities on the critical path and in doing so may neglect activities not on the critical path. Once the float is used up on the non-critical activities, they can end up on the critical path as well.

Using Critical Path Analysis to Make Schedule Trade-Offs

It is important to know what the critical path is throughout the life of a project so that the project manager can make trade-offs. If project managers know that one of the activities on the critical path is behind schedule, they need to decide what to do about it. Should the schedule be renegotiated with stakeholders? Should more resources be allocated to other items on the critical path to make up for that time? Is it okay if the project finishes behind schedule? By keeping track of the critical path, project managers and their team take a proactive role in managing the project schedule.

It is common for stakeholders to want to shorten a project schedule estimate. Your team may have done its best to develop a project schedule by defining activities, determining sequencing, and estimating resources and durations for each activity. The results of this work may have shown that your team needs 10 months to complete the project. Your sponsor might ask if the project can be done in eight or nine months. Rarely do people ask you to take longer than you suggested, but it can happen in cases where project work must be slowed to meet available funding, for example. By knowing the critical path, you can use several schedule compression techniques to shorten the project schedule. Each technique focuses on shortening the critical path.

Crashing is a technique for making cost and schedule trade-offs to obtain the greatest amount of schedule compression for the least incremental cost. For example, suppose one of the items on the critical path for the Just-In-Time Training project was to design and develop an advanced course for supplier management. If this task is yet to be done and was originally estimated to take four weeks based on key people working 25 percent of their time on this task, Kristin could suggest that people work 50 percent of their time to finish the task faster. This change might cost some additional money if people had to work paid overtime, but it could shorten the project end date by two weeks. By focusing on tasks on the critical path that could be finished more quickly for either no extra cost or a small cost, the project schedule could be shortened. The main advantage of crashing is shortening the time it takes to finish a project.

The main disadvantage of crashing is that it often increases total project costs. If used too often, however, crashing can affect staff negatively by lowering morale or causing burnout.

Another technique for shortening a project schedule is fast tracking. **Fast tracking** involves doing activities in parallel that you would normally do in sequence. For example, Kristin's project team may have planned not to start any of the work on the negotiating skills training until they finished most of the work on the supplier management training. Instead, they could consider performing several of these tasks in parallel to shorten the schedule. As with crashing, the main advantage of fast tracking is that it can shorten the time it takes to finish a project. The main disadvantage of fast tracking is that it can end up lengthening the project schedule, because starting some tasks too soon often increases project risk and results in rework.

Importance of Updating Critical Path Data

In addition to finding the critical path at the beginning of a project, it is important to update the schedule with actual activity data so that the project manager will know which activities are most critical to manage going forward. After the project team completes activities, they should document their actual durations. They should also document revised estimates for activities in progress or yet to be started, if needed. These revisions often cause a project's critical path to change, resulting in a new estimated completion date for the project. Again, proactive project managers and their teams stay on top of changes so that they can make informed decisions and keep stakeholders informed of, and involved in, major project decisions.

Critical Chain Scheduling

Another advanced scheduling technique that addresses the challenge of meeting or beating project finish dates is an application of the Theory of Constraints called critical chain scheduling. The **Theory of Constraints (TOC)** is a management philosophy developed by Eliyahu M. Goldratt and discussed in his books *The Goal* and *Critical Chain*.[2] The Theory of Constraints is based on the fact that, like a chain with its weakest link, any complex system at any point in time often has only one aspect or constraint that limits its ability to achieve more of its goal. For the system to attain any significant improvements, that constraint must be identified, and the whole system must be managed with it in mind. **Critical chain scheduling** is a method of scheduling that considers limited resources when creating a project schedule and includes buffers to protect the project completion date.

An important concept in critical chain scheduling is the availability of scarce resources. Some projects cannot be completed unless a particular resource is available to work on one or several activities. For example, if a television station wants to produce a show centered on a certain celebrity, it must first check the availability of that celebrity. As another example, if a specific piece of equipment is needed full time to complete each of two activities that were originally planned to occur simultaneously, critical chain scheduling acknowledges that you must either delay one of those activities until the equipment is available or find another piece of equipment to meet the schedule.

Other important concepts related to critical chain scheduling include multitasking and time buffers. **Multitasking** occurs when a resource works on more than one activity at a time. This situation occurs frequently on projects. People are assigned to multiple activities within the same project or different activities on multiple projects. For example, suppose someone is working on three different activities, Activity 1, Activity 2, and Activity 3, for three different projects, and each activity takes 10 days to complete. If the person did not multitask, and instead completed each activity sequentially, starting with Activity 1, then Activity 1 would be completed after day 10, Activity 2 would be completed after day 20, and Activity 3 would be completed after day 30, as shown in Figure 5-13.

However, because many people in this situation try to please all three people who need their activities completed, they often work on the first activities for some time, then the second, then the third, then go back to finish the first activities, then the second, and then the third, as shown in Figure 5-14. In this example, the activities were all half-done one at a time, then completed one at a time. Activity 1 is now completed at the end of day 20 instead of day 10, Activity 2 is completed at the end of day 25 instead of day 20, and Activity 3 is still completed on day 30. This example illustrates how multitasking can delay activity completions. Note that this delay only matters if someone else is depending upon Activity 1 or Activity 2 to be completed before they can begin their work, however, it is rare where a resource is working on an activity that does not serve as a predecessor to someone else's activity.

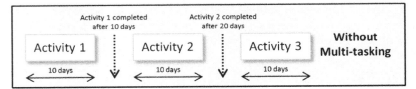

Figure 5-13. Three activities without multitasking (Schwalbe, Information Technology Project Management, Sixth Edition, 2010)

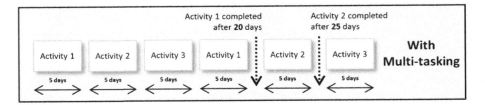

Figure 5-14. Three activities with multitasking (Schwalbe, Information Technology Project Management, Sixth Edition, 2010)

MEDIA SNAPSHOT

Forbes got readers' attention by running an article entitled, "Multitasking Damages Your Brain and Career, New Studies Suggest." The article summarizes three different studies as follows:

1. *Multitasking is less productive than doing a single thing at a time*. Stanford University researchers found that people who are regularly bombarded with several streams of electronic information cannot pay attention, recall information, or switch from one job to another as well as those who complete one task at a time.

2. *Multitasking lowers your IQ*. University of London released a study showing that IQ scores declined in participants who multitasked during cognitive tasks. The IQ drops (about 15 points for multitasking men) were similar to those experienced by people who had smoked marijuana or stayed up all night.

3. *Cognitive impairment from multitasking may be permanent*. "Researchers at the University of Sussex in the UK compared the amount of time people spend on multiple devices (such as texting while watching TV) to MRI scans of their brains. They found that high multitaskers had less brain density in the anterior cingulate cortex, a region responsible for empathy as well as cognitive and emotional control."[3]

An essential concept to improving project finish dates with critical chain scheduling is to change the way people make activity estimates. Many people add a safety or **buffer**— additional time to complete an activity— to an estimate to account for various and sometimes unknown factors. These factors include the negative effects of multitasking, distractions and interruptions, fear that estimates will be reduced, Murphy's Law, etc. **Murphy's Law** states that if something can go wrong, it will. Critical chain scheduling removes buffers from individual activities and instead creates a **project buffer**, which is additional time added before the project's due date. Critical chain scheduling also protects activities on the critical chain from being delayed by using **feeding buffers**, which are additional time added before activities on the critical path that are preceded by non-critical-path activities.

Figure 5-15 provides an example of a network diagram constructed using critical chain scheduling. Note that the critical chain accounts for a limited resource, X, and the schedule includes use of feeding buffers and a project buffer in the network diagram. The activities marked with an X are part of the critical chain, which can be interpreted as being the critical path using this technique. The activity estimates in critical chain scheduling should be shorter than traditional estimates because they do not include their own buffers. Not having activity buffers should mean less occurrence of **Parkinson's Law**, which states that work expands to fill the time allowed. In other words, if you included a buffer in an activity estimate and you did not need it, you would still use it. The feeding and project buffers protect the date that really needs to be met—the project completion date.

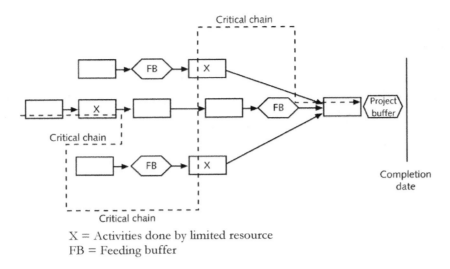

X = Activities done by limited resource
FB = Feeding buffer

Figure 5-15. Example of critical chain scheduling[4]

As you can see, critical chain scheduling is a fairly complicated yet powerful tool that involves critical path analysis, resource constraints, and changes in how activity estimates are made in terms of buffers. Several organizations have reported successes with this approach. Some consider critical chain scheduling one of the most important new concepts in the field of project management.

Sample Project Schedule

Kristin worked with her team to define project activities, determine activity sequencing, estimate activity durations, and make schedule trade-offs to perform all the work required for the project within one year, as desired by the project sponsor.

Figure 5-16 provides part of the resulting Gantt chart the team will use to guide their project schedule, created using Project 2016. Notice that the items in the Task Name column come from the WBS from Chapter 4, Figure 4-15 (and activity list, once broken down in more detail), and duration estimates are entered in the "Duration" column. Also, notice the flow between the initiating, planning, executing, monitoring and controlling, and closing activities. Dependencies between activities are shown by the entries in the "Predecessors" column and the arrows connecting symbols on the Gantt chart. You can learn how to use Project 2016 by reading the section of Appendix A.

Figure 5-16. Sample project schedule

Figure 5-17 shows another view of the Gantt chart for the Just-In-Time Training project, showing all of the summary tasks (represented by thick black lines) and milestones (represented by black diamonds). Note that the milestones include the schedule items that the project manager and the project steering committee would be most interested in monitoring and controlling to make sure the project stays on schedule. You will learn more about monitoring and controlling projects in Chapter 8.

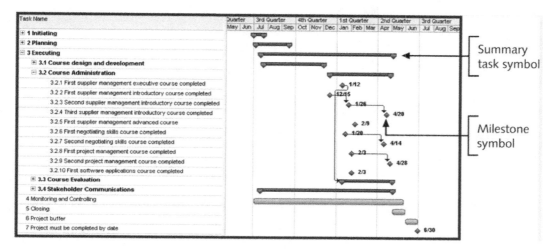

Figure 5-17. Sample Gantt chart showing summary tasks and milestones

By using project management software like Project 2016, you can easily see different levels of detail in the schedule information. Also note that Kristin decided to include a project buffer to account for unexpected factors. This buffer (shown as the second to last item in the Task Name column in Figure 5-17) will help ensure that the project is completed on time. Kristin has learned from past projects that no matter how well you try to schedule everything, it can still be a challenge to finish on time without a mad rush at the end. For this reason, she decided to include a 20-day project buffer, which the project steering committee thought was an excellent idea.

Sample Project Calendar

A project calendar shows work days and shifts available for scheduled activities. Scheduling software makes it easy to set up project calendars. Figures 5-18 shows the standard project calendar for Microsoft Project 2016. Notice that working times are 8:00 AM to 12:00 PM and 1:00 PM to 5:00 PM on Mondays through Fridays. You can set up different calendars for different resources as needed.

Figure 5-17. Sample project calendar

PROJECT COST MANAGEMENT

Project cost management includes the processes required to ensure that a project team completes a project within an approved budget. The main planning processes performed as part of project cost management are planning cost management, estimating costs, and determining the budget. Estimating costs involves developing an approximation or estimate of the costs of the resources needed to complete a project. Cost budgeting involves allocating the overall cost estimate to individual activities over time to establish a baseline for measuring performance. The main documents produced include a cost management plan, cost estimates, basis of estimates, a cost baseline, and project funding requirements.

Planning Cost Management

The purpose of this process is to determine the policies, procedures, and documentation for planning, managing, executing, and controlling project costs. The project team holds meetings, consults with experts, and analyzes data to help produce a cost management plan, which becomes a component of the project management plan.

Contents of the cost management plan can include the following:

- units of measure, such as staff hours or days or a lump sum amount, currency to be used, inflation assumptions, etc.
- level of precision for cost estimates, such as how to round numbers
- level of accuracy, such as +/-10%
- organizational procedure links
- control thresholds for monitoring cost performance, such as a percentage deviation from the baseline plan
- rules of performance measurement, especially if earned value management is used
- reporting formats and frequency for cost reports
- additional details about cost activities, such as strategic funding choices, procedures to account for currency fluctuations, and procedures for recording costs

WHAT WENT RIGHT?

Crowdsourcing provides an interesting approach to funding projects, especially those involving new products. Instead of obtaining funding from traditional sources, you can solicit funds from a large group of people online. For example, the three co-founders of Inspiration Medical, a Minneapolis-based start-up firm, used crowdsourcing to finance the research and development work they need to develop a product to help people with bleeding problems. Their product is called AllaQuix, a nonprescription pad that quickly stops nuisance bleeding (i.e., bleeding that won't stop from small cuts) for people on blood thinners. The founders estimate that up to one in three adults is incapable, for a variety of reasons, of clotting in the typical two to five minutes. They used social media to introduce their product to potential customers and get feedback before spending hundreds of thousands of dollars on marketing.

Stephen Miller from Inspiration explained, "This is why we haven't put it on a retail shelf yet. Some people first said, "Is this a scam or a joke? So, we changed the title from 'Stop nuisance bleeding' to 'Help us launch AllaQuix.' That may have saved us $500,000 in marketing costs."[5]

Estimating Costs

Project teams normally prepare cost estimates at various stages of a project, and these estimates should be fine-tuned as time progresses. Before management approves a project, someone must develop a rough estimate of what it will cost to complete the project. Then, after the project manager and team are assigned to a project, they prepare a more detailed cost estimate. If this estimate is substantially different from the initial budgeted amount, the project manager should negotiate with the project sponsor to increase or decrease the budget, or to make changes to the scope or time goals to meet cost constraints. As more detailed information becomes available, the project team should update the cost estimates and continue negotiating with the sponsor to meet project goals.

In addition to creating cost estimates, it is also important to provide supporting details in the basis of estimates. Topics addressed include any assumptions used in creating the estimate, constraints, risks, ranges, and confidence level of estimates. The basis of estimates should make it easier to prepare an updated estimate or similar estimate as needed.

A large percentage of total project costs are often labor costs, whether internal or external. Many organizations estimate the number of people or hours they need for major parts of a project over the life cycle of the project. They also determine the labor rate to apply based on the category of labor. It is important to work with people in the organization's human resources, payroll, or accounting departments to determine these labor rates and apply the appropriate amounts for benefits and overhead so that total labor costs are included in the estimate. For external labor rates, you may refer to current contracts for other external labor, recent vendor bids, or rate information provided by reputable organizations such as Gartner.

Cost Estimation Tools and Techniques

As you can imagine, developing good cost estimates is difficult. Fortunately, several tools and techniques are available to assist in creating them. Three commonly used techniques for creating estimates include the following:

- **Analogous estimates**, also called **top-down estimates**, use the actual cost of a previous, similar project as the basis for estimating the cost of the current project. This technique requires a good deal of expert judgment and is generally less costly than others are, but it can also be less accurate. Analogous estimates are most reliable when the previous projects are similar in fact, not just in appearance.

- **Bottom-up estimates** involve estimating individual activities and summing them to get a project total. The size of the individual activities and the experience of the estimators drive the accuracy of the estimates. If a detailed WBS is available for a project, the project manager could have people responsible for work packages develop cost estimates for them. The project manager would then add all of the cost estimates to create cost estimates for each higher-level WBS item and finally for the entire project. This approach can increase the accuracy of the cost estimate, but it can also be time intensive and, therefore, expensive to develop.

- **Parametric modeling** uses project characteristics (parameters) in a mathematical model to estimate project costs. A parametric model might provide an estimate of $870 per desktop computer, for example, based on the type of PC required and the location of the installation. Parametric models are most reliable when the historical information used to create the model is accurate, the parameters are readily quantifiable, and the model is flexible in terms of the size of the project. The project manager must be sure that the single-unit estimate, $870 per PC in this case, includes all costs. For example, does this cost include the required cables and wiring? Does it include the monitor, keyboard, and mouse? Does it include any cost allowance for the labor to install the PCs?

Sometimes it makes sense to use more than one approach for creating a cost estimate, and sometimes more than one approach is used on different parts of a project. For example, a project team might develop an analogous estimate for one part of the project, a parametric model for another part, and a bottom-up estimate for the more complex portions (such as software development). Or, they may use parametric or bottom-up estimates for the entire project and then try to identify a similar, analogous project to compare to their new cost estimate. If the estimates were far apart, the team would need to collect more information to develop a better estimate.

Sample Cost Estimate

Every cost estimate is unique, just as every project is unique. This section includes a step-by-step approach for developing the major parts of the cost estimate for the Just-In-Time Training project. Of course, this example is much shorter and simpler than a real cost estimate would be, but it illustrates an easy-to-follow process and uses several of the tools and techniques described earlier.

It is important to first clarify and document ground rules and assumptions for the estimate. For the Just-In-Time Training project cost estimate, these include the following, which should be included in the project cost management document:

- This project was preceded by a project that provided valuable information, such as the training taken in the last two years by all internal employees, the cost of all training, the process for approving/assigning training, the evaluation of the training by participants, what training employees would need in the next two years, how they would like to deliver the training (that is, instructor-led in-house; instructor-led through a local college, university, or training company; or online).

- There is a WBS for the project, as described earlier. The level 2 and some of the level 3 categories are shown as follows:

    1. Initiating

    2. Planning

    3. Executing

        3.1 Course design and development

        3.2 Course administration

        3.3 Course evaluation

        3.4 Stakeholder communications

    4. Monitoring and controlling

    5. Closing

- Costs must be estimated by WBS and by month. The project manager will report progress on the project using earned value analysis, which requires this type of estimate.

- Costs will be provided in U.S. dollars. Because the project length is one year, discounted cash flows are not needed.

- There will be a project manager who spends three-quarters of her time on the project, and three core team members assigned to the project half-time. Two of the team members will be from the training department and one will be from the supplier management department. Additional internal resources from various departments will support the project as needed and charge their time to the project.

- The project steering committee members' time is not directly charged to the project. Internal labor costs include a 40 percent overhead charge as well as a 30 percent benefits charge. For example, if the direct labor rate is $30/hour, the burdened rate, or the rate including benefits and overhead, is $30*1.3*1.4=$55 (rounded to the nearest whole-dollar amount).

- The project cost estimate does not include any hardware, software, or facilities that will be used to develop and administer the courses.

- The project team should purchase training materials and related products and services from qualified suppliers to take advantage of their expertise and to reduce internal costs. Estimates are based on analogous projects and will be updated as contracts are awarded.

- Labor costs for employees to cover their salaries while they attend training classes are not included in this estimate.

- Because several risks are related to this project, the estimate includes 10 percent of the total estimate as reserves.

- A computer model of the project estimate will be developed to facilitate the changing of inputs, such as labor rates or the number of labor hours for various activities.

Fortunately, the project team can easily access cost estimates and actual information from similar projects. A great deal of information is available from the Phase I project, and the team can talk to supplier personnel from the past project to help them develop the estimate.

Because the estimate must be provided by WBS monthly, Kristin and her team reviewed the draft of the project schedule and made further assumptions. They decided first to estimate the cost of each activity and then determine when the work would be performed, even though costs might be incurred at times other than when the work was actually performed. Their budget expert had approved this approach for the estimate. Further assumptions and information for estimating the costs for each WBS category are as follows:

1. *Initiating*: The team used the actual labor costs charged to the project for project initiation activities.

2. *Planning*: The team used actual labor costs to date and added the projected hours and costs per hour to develop this part of the estimate.

3. *Executing*:

   3.1 *Course design and development*: The team used labor hour and rate estimates for internal and external staff, plus estimates for purchasing existing course materials for each course (that is, supplier management, negotiating skills, project management, and software applications). Some of the purchased costs were based on the number of students using the materials each year. The majority of project costs should be applied to this category.

    3.2 *Course administration:* Estimates were made based on the number of courses and number of people expected to take each course using various delivery methods (that is, instructor-led, CD-ROM, Web-based).

    3.3 *Course evaluation:* The team estimated labor hours and rates.

    3.4 *Stakeholder communications:* The team estimated labor hours and rates.

4.   *Monitoring and controlling:* The team estimated labor hours and rates.

5.   *Closing:* The team estimated labor hours and rates.

6.   *Reserves:* As directed, contingency reserves were estimated at 10 percent of the total estimate. Contingency reserves are used for known risks. (See Chapter 6 for more information on reserves).

The project team developed a cost model using the preceding information. Figure 5-19 shows a spreadsheet summarizing costs by WBS based on that information. There are columns for entering the number of labor hours and the costs per hour. Several tasks are estimated using this approach. There are also some short comments within the estimate, such as reserves being 10 percent of the subtotal for the estimate. With this computerized model, you can easily change input variables, such as number of hours or cost per hour, to revise the estimate.

WBS Categories	Internal Labor	$/hour	Internal $ Total	External Labor	$/hour	External $ Total	Total Labor	Non-labor $	Total Cost
1. Initiating	200	$ 65	$ 13,000			$ -	$ 13,000		$ 13,000
2. Planning	600	$ 60	$ 36,000			$ -	$ 36,000		$ 36,000
3. Executing			$ -			$ -	$ -		$ -
3.1 Course design and development			$ -			$ -	$ -		$ -
3.1.1 Supplier management training	600	$ 60	$ 36,000	600	$ 150	$ 90,000	$ 126,000	$ 100,000	$ 226,000
3.1.2 Negotiating skills training	300	$ 55	$ 16,500	300	$ 150	$ 45,000	$ 61,500	$ 50,000	$ 111,500
3.1.3 Project management training	400	$ 60	$ 24,000	400	$ 150	$ 60,000	$ 84,000	$ 50,000	$ 134,000
3.1.4 Software applications training	400	$ 60	$ 24,000	400	$ 150	$ 60,000	$ 84,000	$ 50,000	$ 134,000
3.2 Course administration	400	$ 55	$ 22,000	300	$ 250	$ 75,000	$ 97,000	$ 80,000	$ 177,000
3.3.Course evaluation	300	$ 55	$ 16,500			$ -	$ 16,500		$ 16,500
3.4 Stakeholder communications	300	$ 55	$ 16,500			$ -	$ 16,500		$ 16,500
4. Monitoring and Controlling	500	$ 55	$ 27,500			$ -	$ 27,500		$ 27,500
5. Closing	200	$ 55	$ 11,000			$ -	$ 11,000		$ 11,000
Subtotal									$ 903,000
Reserves			$ -			$ -	$ -		90,300.0
Total	4,200		243,000	2,000	850	330,000	573,000	330,000	$ 993,300

Assumptions:

- Internal labor rates include benefits and overhead. Average hourly rates based on skill levels and departments.

- External labor rates are based on historical average; may change as contracts are awarded.

- Non-labor costs include purchasing licenses for using training materials, books, CD/ROMs, travel expenses, etc.; may change as contracts are awarded.

- Reserves are calculated by taking 10% of the subtotal for the estimate. These contingency reserves are based on known risks.

Figure 5-19. Sample cost estimate

It is very important to have several people review the project cost estimate, including the ground rules and assumptions. It is also helpful to analyze the total dollar value as well as the percentage of the total amount for each major WBS category. For example, a senior executive could quickly look at the Just-In-Time Training project cost estimate and decide whether the costs are reasonable and whether the assumptions are well documented. In this case, Global Construction had budgeted $1 million for the project, so the estimate was right in line with that amount. The WBS level 2 and 3 items also seem to be at appropriate percentages of the total cost based on similar past projects. In some cases, a project team might also be asked to provide a range estimate for each item instead of one discrete amount.

After the total cost estimate is approved, Kristin's team can then allocate costs for each month based on the project schedule and when costs will be incurred. Many organizations also require that the estimated costs be allocated into certain budget categories, such as compensation or travel.

Cost Budgeting

Project cost budgeting involves allocating the project cost estimate to activities over time. These activities are based on the work breakdown structure for the project. The WBS, therefore, is a required input to the cost budgeting process. Likewise, the project scope statement, WBS dictionary, activity cost estimates and supporting detail, project schedule, and other plans provide useful information for cost budgeting.

The main goal of the cost budgeting process is to produce a cost baseline and project budget. A **cost baseline** is a time-phased budget that project managers use to measure and monitor cost performance. Estimating costs for each major project activity over time provides project managers and top management with a foundation for project cost control using earned value management, as described in Chapter 8. The project budget is the cost baseline plus management reserve. Management reserve is money set aside to address unidentified risks, as discussed further in Chapter 6.

Figure 5-20 illustrates the various components of a project budget. Cost estimates from the various activities along with any contingency reserves associated with them create the work package cost estimates. The work package cost estimates plus any contingency reserves associated with them create the control accounts. The summation of all control accounts equals the cost baseline. Management reserve plus the cost baseline equals the project budget.

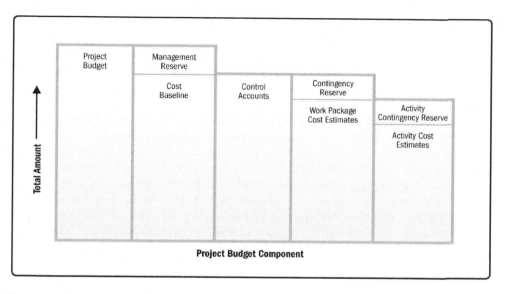

Figure 5-20. Project budget components
Source: Project Management Institute, Inc., *A Guide to the Project Management Body of Knowledge (PMBOK® Guide) – Sixth Edition* (2017).

Figure 5-21 shows the relationship between the cost baseline, expenditures, and funding requirements. The cost baseline is often represented as an S-curve. Notice the uneven, step-like pattern for the funding requirements. This is due to the fact that many projects are funded in incremental amounts that may not be equally distributed.

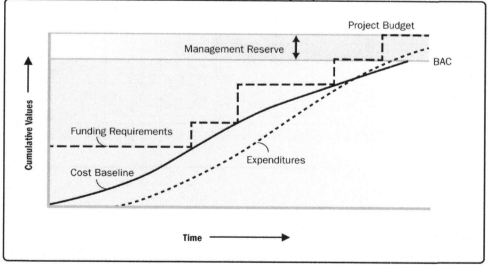

Figure 5-21. Cost baseline, expenditures, and funding requirements
Source: Project Management Institute, Inc., *A Guide to the Project Management Body of Knowledge (PMBOK® Guide) – Sixth Edition* (2017).

WHAT WENT WRONG?

The United Kingdom's National Health Services (NHS) IT modernization program has been called "the greatest IT disaster in history" by one London columnist. This 10-year program, which started in 2002, was created to provide an electronic patient records system, appointment booking, and a prescription drug system in England and Wales. Britain's Labor government estimated that the program eventually cost more than $55 billion, a $26 billion overrun. Problems included incompatible system features, arguments among contractors about who's responsible for what, and lack of inputs by physicians. On September 22, 2012, government officials announced that they were scrapping the program. Health Secretary Andre Lansley said that the program "let down the NHS and wasted taxpayer's money."[6] Poor planning, poor execution, and poor monitoring and controlling were all evident in this project disaster.

Unfortunately, there is no shortage of examples of cost overruns in many countries and industries. The Los Angeles Times in 2017 reported a projected multi-billion dollar overrun on the California bullet train.[7] An Oxford study found a $1.4 billion overrun for the RIO 2016 summer Olympic games.[8] There is a definite need to improve project cost management.

Sample Cost Baseline

The Just-In-Time Training project team used the cost estimate from Figure 5-19 along with the project schedule and other information to allocate costs for each month. Figure 5-21 provides an example of a cost baseline for this project. Again, it is important for the team to document the assumptions they made when developing the cost baseline and have several experts review it. The cost baseline should also be updated as more information becomes available.

WBS Categories	1	2	3	4	5	6	7	8	9	10	11	12	Total Cost
1. Initiating	13,000												$ 13,000
2. Planning	6,000	16,000	8,000	1,000	1,000	1,000	1,000	1,000	1,000				$ 36,000
3. Executing			-			-	-						$ -
3.1 Course design and development			-			-	-						$ -
3.1.1 Supplier management training			5,000	73,667	73,667	73,667							$ 226,000
3.1.2 Negotiating skills training			5,000	35,500	35,500	35,500							$ 111,500
3.1.3 Project management training			5,000	43,000	43,000	43,000							$ 134,000
3.1.4 Software applications training			5,000	43,000	43,000	43,000							$ 134,000
3.2 Course administration						17,000	53,333	53,333	53,333				$ 177,000
3.3.Course evaluation							3,000	3,000	3,000	7,500			$ 16,500
3.4 Stakeholder communications		1,500	1,500	1,500	1,500	1,500	1,500	1,500	1,500	1,500	1,500	1,500	$ 16,500
4. Monitoring and Controlling	1,000	2,000	2,000	2,000	3,000	3,500	3,000	3,000	2,000	3,000	2,000	1,000	$ 27,500
5. Closing											8,000	3,000	$ 11,000
Subtotal													$ 903,000
Reserves*			-			-	-					90,300	$ 90,300
Total	20,000	19,500	31,500	199,667	200,667	218,167	61,833	61,833	60,833	12,000	11,500	95,800	993,300

*Reserves are all entered in month 12

Figure 5-21. Sample cost baseline

CASE WRAP-UP

Kristin learned a lot by leading her team in planning the time and cost aspects of the Just-In-Time Training project. She did her best to get key stakeholders involved, including those who had little experience in estimating. She continued to consult members of the project steering committee for their advice, especially in helping everyone see how crucial it was to understand and document estimates to provide a good baseline for measuring progress.

CHAPTER SUMMARY

Successful project managers know how important it is to develop, refine, and follow plans to meet project goals. This chapter summarizes the planning processes and outputs for project time and cost management.

Planning processes for schedule management include planning schedule management, defining activities, sequencing activities, estimating activity durations, and developing a project schedule. A project network diagram shows the sequencing of project activities, and a Gantt chart is a standard format for displaying project schedule information by listing activities and their corresponding start and finish dates in a calendar format.

It is also important to understand critical path analysis to make schedule trade-off decisions. Critical chain scheduling can also help in scheduling when there are scarce resources involved in a project.

Planning processes for cost management include planning cost management, estimating costs, and determining the project budget. There are several methods for creating cost estimates, such as analogous, bottom-up, and parametric. A cost baseline is a time-phased budget that project managers use to measure and monitor cost performance.

Samples of several planning documents for time and cost management are provided for the Just-In-Time Training project.

QUICK QUIZ

Note that you can find additional, interactive quizzes at www.intropm.com.

1.   What is the first step in planning a project schedule?

    A.   creating a schedule management plan

    B.   developing an activity list

    C.   assigning resources to the project

    D.   determining activity sequencing

2.   The _____ rule is that all work required for a deliverable is included in its sub-deliverables when defining activities.

    A.   golden

    B.   hierarchy

    C.   roll-up

    D.   WBS 100%

3.   A(n) _____ normally does not have any cost or duration.

    A.   activity

    B.   milestone

    C.   critical task

    D.   baseline

4.   What is the most common type of dependency between activities?

    A.   finish-to-start

    B.   start-to-finish

    C.   start-to-start

    D.   finish-to-finish

5.   The _____ method is a network diagramming technique used to predict total project duration.

    A.   PERT

    B.   Gantt chart

    C.   critical path

    D.   crashing

6. _____ is a technique for making cost and schedule trade-offs to obtain the greatest amount of schedule compression for the least incremental cost.

    A. Crashing

    B. Fast tracking

    C. De-scoping

    D. Parametric modeling

7. Critical chain scheduling considers limited resources when creating a project schedule and includes _____ to protect the project completion date.

    A. reserves

    B. multitasking

    C. buffers

    D. outsourcing

8. Using a(n) _____ approach to developing cost estimates requires a good deal of expert judgment and is generally less costly than others are, but it can also be less accurate.

    A. bottom-up

    B. parametric

    C. expert judgment

    D. analogous

9. The _____ must be the basis for a project cost estimate if you plan to create a cost baseline and use earned value management as part of monitoring and controlling costs.

    A. project schedule

    B. cost model

    C. Gantt chart

    D. WBS

10. A _____ is a time-phased budget that project managers use to measure and monitor cost performance.

    A. cost baseline

    B. cost estimate

    C. life-cycle budget

    D. project budget

Quick Quiz Answers

1. A; 2. D; 3. B; 4. A; 5. C; 6. A; 7. C; 8. D; 9. D; 10. A

DISCUSSION QUESTIONS

1. Why does having good plans for the project schedule and costs help project teams during project execution? Why is it difficult to develop good plans in these areas?

2. What are the main planning processes performed as part of project schedule management? What are some of the most common outputs created, and how are they used?

3. What is critical path analysis? Should you know the critical path for all projects? Why or why not?

4. What is critical chain scheduling, and how is it different from critical path analysis? Give an example of its use.

5. What are the main planning processes performed as part of project cost management? What are some of the most common outputs created, and how are they used?

6. What are some approaches for creating a cost estimate? Why is it important to develop a good cost estimate?

7. What is a cost baseline? How is it prepared, and how is it used?

EXERCISES

Note: These exercises can be done individually or in teams, in-class, as homework, or in a virtual environment. Learners can either write their results in a paper or prepare a short presentation or video to show their results.

1. Find an example of a large project that took more than a year to complete, preferably one near where you live. Describe some of the planning work completed for the project as part of project time and cost management. Summarize your findings.

2. Review the features boxes in this chapter with examples of What Went Right, What Went Wrong, Best Practice, and the Media Snapshot. Discuss some of the information presented, and find additional references related to topics discussed in two of these examples. Summarize your findings.

3. Consider Figure 5-22. All duration estimates are in days, and the network proceeds from Node 1 to Node 9.

Activity	Initial node	Final node	Duration estimate
A	1	2	2
B	2	3	2
C	2	4	3
D	2	5	4
E	3	6	2
F	4	6	3
G	5	7	6
H	6	8	2
I	6	7	5
J	7	8	1
K	8	9	2

Figure 5-22. Network diagram data for a small project

   a. Draw an AOA network diagram representing the project. Put the node numbers in circles and draw arrows from node to node, labeling each arrow with the activity letter and estimated duration.

   b. Identify all the paths on the network diagram and note how long they are.

   c. What is the critical path for this project, and how long is it?

   d. What is the shortest possible time it will take to complete this project?

   e. Enter the information into Project 2016. See the *Brief Guide to Microsoft Project Professional 2016* in Appendix A for detailed instructions on using this software. View the network diagram and activity schedule table to see the critical path and float or slack for each activity. Provide screen shots of the Gantt chart and network diagram views and the activity schedule table. Interpret this information for someone unfamiliar with project schedule management.

4. Create a cost estimate/model for redecorating a room using spreadsheet software. Assume you have one month and $5,000 to spend. Develop a WBS for the project and create a cost model based on your WBS. Document the assumptions you made in preparing the estimate and provide explanations for key numbers. (Note: Feel free to pick a different scenario you are familiar with for this exercise.)

5.   Watch the Video Highlight in this chapter. Find at least two other references related to this topic and discuss how it relates to project schedule management. Summarize your findings and opinions in a short paper, presentation, or video.

6.   Read the examples of cost overruns in What Went Wrong? feature in this chapter. Find at least two articles related to cost overruns for hosting Olympic games. Summarize the reasons for the overruns. Document your findings and opinions in a short paper, presentation, or video.

TEAM PROJECTS

Note: These team projects can be done in-class, as homework, or in a virtual environment. Learners can either write their results in a paper or prepare a short presentation or video to show their results.

1.   Your organization initiated a project to raise money for an important charity. Assume that there are 1,000 people in your organization. Also, assume that you have six months to raise as much money as possible, with a goal of $100,000. Using the scope statement and WBS you created in the previous chapter, create a Gantt chart and cost estimate for the project.

2.   You are part of a team in charge of a project to help people in your company (500 people) lose weight. This project is part of a competition, and the top "losers" will be featured in a popular television show. Assume that you have six months to complete the project and a budget of $10,000. Using the scope statement and WBS you created in the previous chapter, create a Gantt chart and cost estimate for the project.

3.   Using the information you developed in Project 1 or 2, role-play a meeting to review one of these planning documents with key stakeholders. Determine who will play what role (project manager, team member from a certain department, senior managers, and so on). Be creative in displaying different personalities (a senior manager who questions the importance of the project to the organization, a team member who is very shy or obnoxious).

4.   Perform the planning tasks (only for the knowledge areas covered in this chapter) for one of the case studies provided in Appendix C. Remember to be thorough in your planning so that your execution goes smoothly.

5.   As a team, find at least six examples of Gantt charts for various types of projects. Discuss the similarities and differences between how the activities are defined, how durations and dependencies are entered, etc. Also discuss the quality of these examples. Include screen shots of the files and citations. Remember that many software products, like MindView and Microsoft Project, include sample or template files.

KEY TERMS

activity – A distinct, scheduled portion of work performed during the course of a project.

activity attributes — Information that provides schedule-related information about each activity, such as predecessors, successors, logical relationships, leads and lags, resource requirements, constraints, imposed dates, and assumptions related to the activity.

activity list — A tabulation of activities to be included on a project schedule.

activity-on-arrow (AOA) approach, or the **arrow diagramming method (ADM)** — A network diagramming technique in which activities are represented by arrows and connected at points called nodes to illustrate the sequence of activities.

analogous estimates, or **top-down estimates** — The estimates that use the actual cost of a previous, similar project as the basis for estimating the cost of the current project.

bottom-up estimates — Cost estimates created by estimating individual activities and summing them to get a project total.

buffer — Additional time to complete a activity, added to an estimate to account for various factors.

burst — An occurrence when two or more activities follow a single node on a network diagram.

cost baseline — A time-phased budget that project managers use to measure and monitor cost performance.

crashing — A technique for making cost and schedule trade-offs to obtain the greatest amount of schedule compression for the least incremental cost.

critical chain scheduling — A method of scheduling that takes limited resources into account when creating a project schedule and includes buffers to protect the project completion date.

critical path — The series of activities that determine the *earliest* time by which the project can be completed; it is the *longest* path through the network diagram and has the least amount of slack or float.

critical path method (CPM), or **critical path analysis** — A network diagramming technique used to predict total project duration and show the amount of schedule flexibility on the network paths within the schedule model.

dependency, or **relationship** — The sequencing of project activities.

discretionary dependencies — The dependencies that are defined by the project team.

duration — The actual amount of time spent working on an activity *plus* elapsed time.

effort — The number of workdays or work hours required to complete an activity.

external dependencies — The dependencies that involve relationships between project and non-project activities.

fast tracking — A schedule compression technique where you do activities in parallel that you would normally do in sequence.

feeding buffers — Additional time added before activities on the critical path that are preceded by non-critical-path activities.

Gantt charts — A standard format for displaying project schedule information by listing project activities and their corresponding start and finish dates in a calendar format.

lag — when an activity requires a gap in time before it can start.

lead — when an activity can overlap a preceding one.

mandatory dependencies — The dependencies that are inherent in the nature of the work being performed on a project.

merge — A situation when two or more nodes precede a single node on a network diagram.

milestone — A significant point or event in a project.

Monte Carlo simulation — quantitative risk analysis technique that provides a probability distribution for outcome values for the whole project.

multitasking — When a resource works on more than one activity at a time.

Murphy's Law — If something can go wrong, it will.

network diagram — A schematic display of the logical relationships among, or sequencing of, project activities.

node — The starting and ending point of an activity on an activity-on-arrow network diagram.

parametric modeling — A technique that uses project characteristics (parameters) in a mathematical model to estimate project costs.

Parkinson's Law — Work expands to fill the time allowed.

precedence diagramming method (PDM) — A network diagramming technique in which boxes represent activities.

Program Evaluation and Review Technique (PERT) — A network analysis technique used to estimate project duration when there is a high degree of uncertainty about the individual activity duration estimates.

project buffer — The additional time added before a project's due date to account for unexpected factors.

slack or **float** — The amount of time an activity may be delayed without delaying a succeeding activity or the project finish date.

task – Work that is done in support of operational, functional, or project performance. Tasks are not part of the schedule (activities are shown on the schedule). Tasks include many management functions such as things done to manage the team, run a production line, or build relationships.

Theory of Constraints (TOC) — A management philosophy that states that any complex system at any point in time often has only one aspect or constraint that is limiting its ability to achieve more of its goal.

three-point estimate — An estimate that includes an optimistic, most likely, and pessimistic estimate.

END NOTES

[1] Luc K. Richard, "Reducing Schedule Risk, Parts 1 and 2," (www.Gantthead.com) (November 10, 2003 and January 31, 2005).

[2] Eliyahu Goldratt, *Critical Chain and The Goal.* Great Barrington, MA: The North River Press (1997 and 2004).

[3] Travis Bradberry, "Multitasking Damages Your Brain And Career, New Studies Suggest," Forbes (Oct. 8, 2014).

[4] Eliyahu Goldratt, *Critical Chain.* p. 218.

[5] Neal St. Anthony, "Crowdsourcing gets valuable R&D cash," Minneapolis Star Tribune (May 6, 2013).

[6] Press Association, "U.K. Health Service To Dismantle National Health IT Program," iHealthBeat (September 23, 2011).

[7] Ralph Vartabedian, "California's bullet train is hurtling toward a multibillion-dollar overrun, a confidential federal report warns," Los Angeles Times (April 24, 2017).

[8] Blake Schmidt, "Rio Olympic Cost Overruns Reach $1.6 Billion: Oxford Study," Bloomberg (July 6, 2016).

Chapter 6
Planning Projects, Part 3
(Project Quality, Resource, Communications, Stakeholder, Risk, and Procurement Management)

LEARNING OBJECTIVES
After reading this chapter, you will be able to:

- List several planning processes and outputs for project quality, resource, communications, stakeholder, risk, and procurement management
- Discuss the project quality management planning process, and explain the purpose and contents of a quality management plan and quality metrics
- Explain the project resource management planning and estimate activity resources processes, and create a resource management plan, team charter, resource requirements, and a resource breakdown structure
- Describe the project communications management planning process, and describe the importance of using a project communications management plan
- Understand the importance of planning stakeholder engagement, and describe the contents of a stakeholder engagement plan
- Discuss the five project risk management planning processes, and explain how a risk management plan, a risk register, and change requests are used in risk management planning
- Discuss the project procurement management planning process, and describe several outputs including a procurement management plan, source selection criteria, and make-or-buy decisions

OPENING CASE

Kristin and her team continued to plan various aspects of the Just-In-Time Training project. About half of her project's budget was allocated for external labor and outsourced training programs, but Kristin and her team were still unsure about what sources to use for most of the training. Kristin had worked with many construction suppliers before, but she had never had to select or negotiate contracts with educational consultants or training companies. She knew that developing and providing quality training courses was very important to this project; however, she also knew that successfully planning the human resource, communications, risk, and procurement management dimensions were also important—especially because the project involved so many different stakeholders. Because some of the plans in these areas might affect the initial scope, time, and cost plans, Kristin knew that she had to focus on project integration management to pull all these plans together and effectively lead the team in preparing and then executing these plans.

Fortunately, Global Construction had well-defined processes for planning all aspects of projects, and the project steering committee provided helpful advice, especially in the areas in which Kristin had little experience. She also relied heavily on her team members and other stakeholders to help create all the initial plans for the project. Because they knew that many of the plans would require updates, they built in as much flexibility as possible.

INTRODUCTION

Most managers know that it is important to effectively plan the scope, schedule, and cost dimensions of a project and to develop the overall project management plan as part of integration management. However, some project managers neglect planning in the other knowledge areas—quality, resource, communications, risk, procurement, and stakeholder management. It is important to skillfully plan *all* of these additional areas because they are also crucial to project success. This chapter summarizes key information on planning in these knowledge areas and specific actions that Kristin and her team took. The next chapter shows how these plans provide the basis for project execution.

SUMMARY OF PLANNING PROCESSES AND OUTPUTS

Figure 6-1 shows the project planning processes and outputs for quality, resource, communications, risk, procurement, and stakeholder management based on the *PMBOK® Guide – Sixth Edition*. As mentioned earlier, these planning documents, as well as other project-related information, will be available to all team members for the Just-In-Time Training Project. This chapter provides samples of some of these outputs, as well as a few additional ones, such as a project dashboard and website.

Knowledge area	Planning process	Outputs
Project quality management	Plan quality management	Quality management plan Quality metrics Project management plan updates Project documents updates
Project resource management	Plan resource management Estimate activity resources	Resource management plan Team charter Project document updates Resource requirements Basis of estimates Resource breakdown structure Project documents updates
Project communications management	Plan communications management	Communications management plan Project management plan updates Project documents updates
Project risk management	Plan risk management Identify risks Perform qualitative risk analysis Perform quantitative risk analysis Plan risk responses	Risk management plan Risk register Risk report Project documents updates Project documents updates Change requests Project management plan updates Project documents updates
Project procurement management	Plan procurement management	Procurement management plan Procurement strategy Bid documents Procurement statement of work Source selection criteria Make or buy decisions Independent cost estimates Change requests Project documents updates Organizational process assets updates
Project stakeholder management	Plan stakeholder engagement	Stakeholder engagement plan

Figure 6-1. Planning processes and outputs for project quality, resource, communications, stakeholder, risk, and procurement management

The following sections describe planning processes in the quality, human resource, communications, stakeholder, risk, and procurement management knowledge areas, and then provide examples of applying them to the Just-In-Time Training project at Global Construction. Although stakeholder management is listed as the last, or tenth, knowledge area in the *PMBOK® Guide – Sixth Edition*, it is presented in this text after communications management because the two are closely related. Templates for creating several of these planning documents are available on the companion website for this text.

PROJECT QUALITY MANAGEMENT

Project quality management ensures that the project will satisfy the stated or implied needs for which it was undertaken. Key outputs produced as part of project quality management planning include a quality management plan and quality metrics. Before describing these outputs, it is important to understand what quality is and why it is an important part of project management.

The International Organization for Standardization (ISO) defines **quality** as "the degree to which a set of inherent characteristics fulfill requirements" (ISO9000:2000). Other experts define quality based on conformance to requirements and fitness for use. **Conformance to requirements** means that the project's processes and products meet written specifications. For example, Kristin's project team might write specifications stating that a course must cover certain topics and be written in English, Chinese, and Japanese. As part of quality management, Kristin's team would verify that the training vendors meet those written requirements. **Fitness for use**, on the other hand, means that a product can be used as it was intended. For example, a training vendor might develop a course in English and then translate it into Chinese and Japanese, but the translations might be faulty, causing confusion to learners. These translated courses, then, would not be fit for use, even though they might have met the written specifications.

Recall that project management involves meeting or exceeding stakeholder needs and expectations. To understand what quality means to the stakeholders, the project team must develop good relationships with them—especially the main customer for the project. *After all, the customer ultimately decides if the quality level is acceptable.* Many projects fail because the project team focuses only on meeting the written requirements for the main products being produced and ignores other stakeholder needs and expectations for the project.

Quality, therefore, must be considered on an equal level of importance with project scope, schedule, and cost. If a project's stakeholders are not satisfied with the quality of the project management or the resulting products or services, the project team will need to adjust scope, schedule, and cost to satisfy stakeholder needs and expectations. Meeting only written requirements is not sufficient.

Planning Quality Management

Quality planning includes identifying which quality standards are relevant to the project and how best to satisfy those standards. It also involves designing quality into the products and services of the project as well as the processes involved in managing the project. It is important to describe important factors that directly contribute to meeting customer requirements. The project charter, project management plan, project documents, enterprise environmental factors, and organizational process assets (i.e., policies and templates related to quality and related standards and regulations, first discussed in Chapter 3) are all important inputs to the quality planning process.

The quality management plan describes how the project management team will implement quality policies. Like other project plans, its format and contents vary based on the particular project and organizational needs. It can be a long, formal document or short and informal. It should be created and reviewed early in the project life cycle to ensure that decisions are made based on accurate information.

Sample Quality Management Plan

Kristin and her team worked together to create a quality management plan for the Just-In-Time Training project (see Figure 6-2). The primary purpose of the plan was to ensure that all the products and services produced as part of the project are of known quality and sufficient quantity to meet customer expectations.

Quality Management Plan

August 20

Project Name: Just-In-Time Training Project

Introduction

The main goal of this project is to develop a new training program that provides just-in-time training to employees on key topics, including supplier management, negotiating skills, project management, and software applications.

Quality Standards

The standards that apply to this project are summarized as follows:

1. Survey standards: See Attachment 1 for corporate standards for developing and administering surveys to employees. Quantitative and qualitative information will be collected. Quantitative data will use a 5-point Likert scale. A corporate expert on surveys will review the survey before it is administered.

2. Supplier selection standards: See Attachment 2 for corporate standards regarding supplier selection. Past performance and developing partnerships will be key issues for this project.

3. Training standards: See Attachment 3 for corporate standards regarding training. The training provided as part of this project will be available in several formats, including instructor-led, CD/ROM, and Web-based. Employees will have access to CD/ROM and Web-based training at any time to meet individual and business needs on a just-in-time manner.

Metrics

Metrics measure quality performance. Several metrics apply to this project, and more may be developed as the project progresses. The project team will use a few key metrics as follows:

1. Survey response rate: For the survey to be successful, a response rate of at least 30% must be achieved.

2. Course evaluations: All course participants must complete a course evaluation for their training to be tracked in our corporate professional development system. In addition to evaluations on more detailed topics, there will be an overall course rating. The average course rating should be at 3.0 or better on a 5.0 scale.

Roles and Responsibilities

Project team members and suppliers are responsible for meeting quality standards when creating the deliverables assigned to them. Instructors of specific courses are responsible for quality in course delivery. The project manager is responsible for overseeing overall quality of the project and meeting stakeholder expectations.

Tools

The project team will use whatever tools are best suited to meeting specific needs. A list of a descriptions of several tools are provided in Attachment 3.

Problem Reporting and Corrective Action Processes

Project plans will include clear roles and responsibilities for all stakeholders. The person responsible for an individual activity should report issues to appropriate managers (see the project organizational chart) and work with them to determine and implement corrective actions. Major issues should be brought to the attention of the project manager, who should escalate issues that might affect project success, including meeting scope, time, cost, and quality goals, to the project steering committee and then the project sponsor. It is crucial to address issues as early as possible and develop several alternative solutions, including timelines for implementation.

Supplier Quality and Control

The project manager will closely monitor work performed by suppliers, with assistance from our supplier management department. All contracts must clearly state quality standards, metrics, etc.

Figure 6-2. Sample quality management plan

Quality Metrics

A **metric** is a standard of measurement. Metrics allow organizations to measure their performance in certain areas and to compare them over time or with other organizations. Examples of common metrics used by organizations include failure rates of products produced, availability of goods and services, and customer satisfaction ratings.

Individual projects also have metrics. Before deciding on the metrics to use for a particular project, it is important to clarify the project goals, business case for the project, and success criteria. Knowing this information, you can then decide what data will give you the information you need, and how to collect it.

For example, the Just-In-Time Training project's success criteria, as documented in the project charter, included metrics based on:

- *Time*: Completing the project within one year

- *Customer satisfaction*: Achieving an average course evaluation of at least 3.0 on a 5.0 scale

- *Cost reduction*: Recouping the cost of the project in reduced training costs within two years after project completion

Global Construction's senior management, therefore, should collect and analyze data to ensure these metrics, as well as other metrics related to the project, are being met, such as how well they are meeting general scope, schedule, and cost goals. Many organizations use charts to keep track of metrics, such as a **project dashboard**—a graphical screen summarizing key project metrics.

BEST PRACTICE

Dragan Milosevic, author of the Project Management Toolbox, has done several studies to investigate what companies that excel in project delivery capability do differently from others. After analyzing data from hundreds of companies, he found four key practices these best-performing companies follow:

1. They build an integrated project management toolbox. In other words, they use several standard and advanced project management tools. They tailor these tools to their organizations and provide employees with lots of templates.
2. They grow competent project leaders, emphasizing business and soft skills. These organizations identify good project leaders and provide training, mentoring, and a career path for them.
3. They develop streamlined, consistent project delivery processes. Project management methodologies are well defined and followed.
4. And probably the hardest of all, they install a sound but comprehensive set of project performance metrics. It is difficult defining, measuring, and tracking metrics across an organization, but in order to improve project delivery capability, these metrics are crucial.[1]

Sample Project Dashboard and Quality Metrics Description

Figure 6-3 provides a sample project dashboard that could be used on the Just-In-Time Training Project. Figure 6-4 shows other examples of project dashboards from www.projectmanager.com. Most dashboards use red, yellow, and green to indicate the status of each metric, where green indicates the metric is on target, yellow means it is slightly off target/caution, and red indicates the metric is off target/problem area. (These examples use different shades of gray because color is not available.) The Just-In-Time Training Project dashboard also describes how each metric is measured and explains the reason for the status rating. You will learn more about earned value charts, a tool for measuring overall scope, time, and cost goals, in Chapter 8.

Just-In-Time Training Project Dashboard
As of January 20

Metric Name	Description	Status	How measured	Explanation
Scope	Meeting project scope goals	◕	Earned value chart	On target
Time	Completing the project within one year	◕	Earned value chart	On target
Cost	Staying within budget – under $1 million	○	Earned value chart	A little over budget
Survey response	Must be at least 30%	◕	Surveys received/sent	Got 33% response
Customer satisfaction	Average course rating of at least 3.0/5.0	○	Course evaluations	Goal part of success criteria
	–Number of course evaluations received	38	Feed from online system	All course participants must complete
	–Average course rating	2.7	Feed from online system	CD/ROM course had low ratings
Cost reduction	Recoup investment within two years	N/A	Cost/employee for training	Can't measure until project is completed
Courses developed	Meeting milestones for development	◕	Milestone dates	Course development on target
Number of people trained	Meeting goals of people trained	○	Filling scheduled classes	Last minute cancellations

◕ = on target
○ = slightly off target/caution
● = off target/problem area

Figure 6-3. Sample project dashboard for Just-In-Time Training Project

Projectmanager.com Sample Dashboards

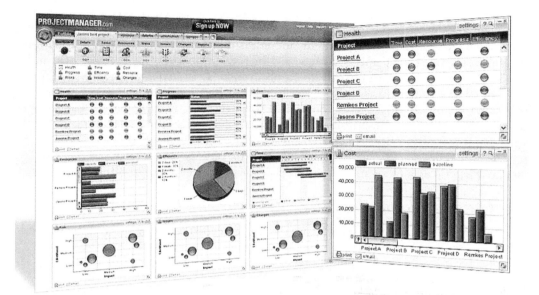

Figure 6-4. Sample project dashboards

As mentioned in the sample quality management plan, two important metrics related to the Just-In-Time Training project include the survey response rate and course evaluation ratings. Figure 6-5 provides more information on these metrics.

Quality Metrics

August 20

Project Name: Just-In-Time Training Project

The following quality metrics apply to this project:

1. Survey response rate: For the survey to be successful, a response rate of at least 30% must be achieved. Most surveys will be administered online using the standard corporate survey software, which can track the response rate automatically. If the response rate is less than 30% one week after the survey is sent out, the project manager will alert the project steering committee to determine corrective action.

2. Course evaluations: All course participants must complete a course evaluation so that their training can be tracked in our corporate professional development system. In addition to evaluations on more detailed topics, there will be an overall course rating. The average course rating should be at least 3.0, with 5 being the highest score. Surveys should include questions measured on a Likert scale. For example, a question might be as follows: "My overall evaluation of this course is ......" Respondents would select 1 for Poor, 2 for Fair, 3 for Average, 4 for Good, or 5 for Excellent.

Figure 6-5. Sample quality metrics description

PROJECT RESOURCE MANAGEMENT

Many corporate executives have said, "People are our most important asset." People determine the success and failure of organizations and projects. Project resource management is concerned with making effective use of the people involved with a project as well as physical resources, like materials, facilities, equipment, and infrastructure. The main outputs produced as part of project resource management planning are the project resource management plan and a team charter. The project resource management plan can be separated into a team management plan and a physical resource management plan. In the Just-in-Time Training project example, Kristin's team took this approach. Key components of their team management plan included a project organizational chart, a responsibility assignment matrix, a resource histogram, and a staffing management plan. They also created a team charter to provide guidance on how the project team would operate. Regardless of whether or not physical and human resources are separated, it is a good idea to include these components in project resource planning.

Project Organizational Charts

After identifying the important skills and types of people needed to staff a project, the project manager should work with top management and project team members to create an organizational chart for the project. Similar to a company's organizational chart, a **project organizational chart** is a graphical representation of how authority and responsibility is distributed within the project. The size and complexity of the project determines how simple or complex the organizational chart is.

Sample Project Organizational Chart

Figure 6-6 shows a project organizational chart that Kristin put together. After supplier project managers and other personnel were assigned, Kristin would fill in more of the chart. Notice that Kristin has a direct reporting line to the project sponsor, and the project team leaders and supplier project managers would report to her. Also note that the project steering committee and project sponsor have a strong role on the project. Sometimes, dotted lines are used to represent indirect reporting relationships.

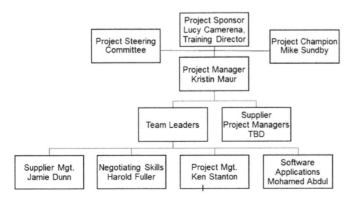

Figure 6-6. Sample project organizational chart

Responsibility Assignment Matrices

A **responsibility assignment matrix (RAM)** is a matrix that maps the work of the project as described in the work breakdown structure (WBS) to the people responsible for performing the work. A RAM allocates work to responsible and performing organizations, teams, or individuals, depending on the desired level of detail. For smaller projects, it is best to assign WBS deliverables to individuals. For larger projects, it is more effective to assign the work to organizational units or teams. In addition to using a RAM to assign detailed work activities, you can use a RAM to define general roles and responsibilities on projects. This type of RAM can include the stakeholders in the project. The project team should decide what to use as categories in the RAM and include a key to explain those categories. For example, a RAM can show whether stakeholders are accountable for (A) or just participants (P) in part of a project, and whether they are required to provide input (I), review (R), or sign off (S) on parts of a project. This simple tool enables the project manager to efficiently communicate the roles of project team members and expectations of important project stakeholders.

Sample Responsibility Assignment Matrix

Some organizations, including Global Construction, use **RACI charts**—a type of responsibility assignment matrix that shows **R**esponsibility (who does the work), **A**ccountability (who signs off on the work or has authority for it), **C**onsultation (who has information necessary to complete the work), and **I**nformed (who needs to be notified of work status/results) roles for project stakeholders. Figure 6-7 shows a RACI chart that Kristin developed for the supplier management training part of the project. Jamie and Mohamed were early members of the project team, and Supplier A represents the supplier who would be selected to provide the supplier management training courses.

Notice that the RACI chart lists the work (usually deliverables or activities) vertically and individuals or groups horizontally, and each intersecting cell contains at least one of the letters R, A, C, or I. For the first deliverable in this example, needs assessment, Kristin is accountable for getting it done, Jamie is responsible for doing the work, Mohamed is providing information in a consultative role, and Supplier A will be informed about it. Each item may have multiple R, C, or I entries, but there can only be one A entry to clarify which specific individual or group has accountability for each deliverable (only one A in a matrix row). One person can also have multiple roles for each deliverable, such as being responsible and accountable.

Just-In-Time Training Project RACI Chart
August 20

Deliverables	Kristin	Jamie	Mohamed	Supplier A
Needs assessment	A	R	C	I
Research of existing training	I	R, A	C	I
Partnerships	R, A	I		C
Course development	A	C	C	R
Course administration	I	A	R	
Course evaluation	I	A	R	I
Stakeholder communications	R, A	C	C	C

R: Responsible   A: Accountable   C: Consulted   I: Informed

Figure 6-7. Sample RACI chart

Resource Histograms

A **resource histogram** is a column chart that shows the number of resources required for or assigned to a project over time. In planning project staffing needs, senior managers often create a resource histogram in which columns represent the number of people (or person hours, if preferred) needed in each skill category, such as managers, IT specialists, and HR specialists. By stacking the columns, you can see the total number of people needed each month. After resources are assigned to a project, you can view a resource histogram for each person to see how his or her time has been allocated. You can create resource histograms using spreadsheets or project management software.

Sample Resource Histogram

Kristin worked with other managers to estimate how many internal resources they would need for the Just-In-Time Training project over time. They decided that in addition to herself (the project manager, or PM), they would require people from human resources (HR), supplier management (SM), information technology (IT), the project management office (PMO), and the contracting department. After contracts were written, Kristin could request a similar resource histogram from each supplier to review overall staffing for the project. Figure 6-8 is the resulting resource histogram for internal resources, showing the total number of people, or head count, by month. For example, it shows the need for a project manager (PM) .75 time for all 12 months, 1 HR person (or several HR people part-time, adding up to 1 total person) for all 12 months, etc. If needed, Kristin could also develop a similar chart showing the estimated number of hours per month. She could also use resource histograms to see where people might be overallocated, as described in Chapter 8.

Type of Resource	Meaning	1	2	3	4	5	6	7	8	9	10	11	12
							Month						
PM	Project Manager	0.75	0.75	0.75	0.75	0.75	0.75	0.75	0.75	0.75	0.75	0.75	0.75
HR	Human Resources	1	1	1	1	1	1	1	1	1	1	1	1
SM	Supplier Management	0.5	0.5	0.5	0.5	0.5	0.5	0.5	0.5	0.5	0.5	0.5	0.5
IT	Information Technology	0.25	0.5	0.5	0.5	0.25	0.25	0.25	0.25	0.25	0.25	0.25	0.25
Contracting	Contracting	0	0	0.25	0.25	0.25	0.25	0.25	0.25	0.25	0.25	0.25	0.25
PMO	Project Management Office	0	0.5	0.5	0.5	0.5	0	0	0	0	0	0	0
Miscellaneous	Miscellaneous	0.25	0.25	0.25	0.25	0.25	0.5	0.5	0.5	0.5	0.25	0.25	0.25

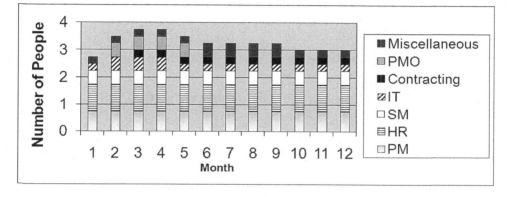

Figure 6-8. Sample resource histogram

Staffing Management Plans

A **staffing management plan** describes when and how people will be added to and removed from a project. The level of detail can vary based on the type of project. The staffing management plan describes the number of and types of people needed to work on the project. It also describes how these resources will be acquired, trained, rewarded, and reassigned after their work on the project is completed. All these considerations are important to meeting the needs of the project, the employees, and the organization. See Chapter 7 for more information on the importance of motivating people and managing teams.

Sample Staffing Management Plan

Figure 6-9 provides part of a staffing management plan that Kristin created for the Just-In-Time Training project.

Staffing Management Plan
August 20

Project Name: Just-In-Time Training Project

Introduction

The main goal of this project is to develop a new training program that provides Just-In-Time training to employees on key topics, including supplier management, negotiating skills, project management, and software applications.

Staffing Requirements

This project will require the following internal staff:

- Project manager (PM) (Kristin was assigned 3/4 time)

- Project team members from the HR department (two people assigned half-time) to help with all the project training

- Project team member from the supplier management (SM) department (assigned half-time) to assist with the supplier management training

- Information technology (IT) department staff to help with technical support and the software applications training

- Project management (PMO) staff to help with the project management training

- Contracting department staff to assist in administering the project contracts. See the resource histogram in Attachment A for projected staffing needs over time.

Staff Assignments

The project manager will work through functional managers to assign individuals to the project. The project manager will interview potential candidates to determine suitability. If particular expertise is required for part of the project, the functional managers will plan to make experts available. Employees will be paid overtime if needed.

Training, Rewards, and Reassignment

Ideally, people assigned to this project will have appropriate experience or be willing to learn quickly on-the-job. The project manager will do his or her best to provide a challenging and enjoyable work environment. Assignment to the project will not affect an individual's salary, but the project manager will write a performance appraisal and recommend appropriate rewards. If an individual is not performing as expected, the project manager will work with him or her and the appropriate functional manager to determine whether corrections can be made or if reassignment is necessary.

Attachment A: Resource histogram

Figure 6-9. Sample staffing management plan

Team Charter

Many companies believe in using **team charters** to help promote teamwork and clarify team communications. (Note that some organizations and previous editions of this text use the term team contract instead of team charter. PMI just added team charters to the *PMBOK® Guide* in 2017.) After core project team members have been selected, they meet to prepare a team charter to guide how the team will function. The process normally includes reviewing a template and then working in small groups of three to four people to prepare inputs for the team charter. Creating smaller groups makes it easier for everyone to contribute ideas. Each group then shares their ideas on what the charter should contain, and then they work together to form one project team charter. Ideally, the charter should be finished in a one- to two-hour meeting. The project manager should attend the meeting and act as a coach or facilitator, observing the different personalities of team members and seeing how well they work together. It is crucial to emphasize the importance of the project team throughout the project's life cycle, and the team charter should be updated as needed.

Sample Team Charter

Figure 6-10 shows a sample team charter, with sections for a code of conduct/values, participation, communication, problem solving, and meeting guidelines. Everyone involved in creating the team charter should sign it, and it should be updated as needed.

Team Charter

Project Name: Just-In-Time Training Project

Project Team Members Names and Sign-off:

Name	Date
Kristin Maur	*July 9*
Other team members	

Code of Conduct/Values: As a project team, we will:
- Work proactively, anticipating potential problems and preventing their occurrence.
- Keep other team members informed of information related to the project.
- Focus on what is best for the entire project team.

Participation: We will:
- Be honest and open during all project activities.
- Provide the opportunity for equal participation.
- Be open to new approaches and consider new ideas.
- Let the project manager know well in advance if a team member has to miss a meeting or may have trouble meeting a deadline for a given activity.

Communication: We will:
- Keep discussions on track and have one discussion at a time.
- Use the telephone, e-mail, a project website, instant messaging, texts, and other media to assist in communicating.
- Have the project manager or designated person facilitate all meetings and arrange for phone and videoconferences, as needed.
- Work together to create the project schedule and related information and enter actuals, issues, risks, and other information into our enterprise project management system by 4 p.m. every Friday.

Problem Solving: We will:

- Only use constructive criticism and focus on solving problems, not blaming people.
- Strive to build on each other's ideas.
- Bring in outside experts when necessary.

Meeting Guidelines: We will:

- Plan to have a face-to-face meeting of the entire project team every Tuesday morning.
- Arrange for telephone or videoconferencing for participants as needed.
- Hold other meetings as needed.
- Develop and follow an agenda for all meetings.
- Record meeting minutes and send out an e-mail within 24 hours stating that the minutes are posted on the project website. Minutes will focus on decisions made and action items and issues from each meeting.

Figure 6-10 Sample team charter

Estimating Activity Resources

Estimating activity resources involves estimating the type, quantity and characteristics of team resources and physical resources (i.e., materials, equipment, and supplies) required to complete the project. This process is closely related to estimating activity durations and costs. It is important that the people who help determine what resources are necessary include people who have experience and expertise in similar projects and with the organization performing the project. Resource estimates should be updated as needed during the project.

Important questions to answer in activity resource estimating include:

- How difficult will it be to perform specific activities on this project?

- Is there anything unique in the project's scope statement that will affect resources?

- Are there specific resources better suited to perform the activities?

- What is the organization's history in doing similar activities? Have they done similar activities before? What level of personnel did the work?

- Does the organization have appropriate people, equipment, and materials available for performing the work? Are there any organizational policies that might affect the availability of resources?

- Does the organization need to acquire more resources to accomplish the work? Would it make sense to outsource some of the work? Will outsourcing increase or decrease the amount of resources needed and their availability?

- What assumptions have been made or need to be made?

It is important to thoroughly brainstorm and evaluate alternatives related to resources, especially on projects that involve multiple disciplines and companies. Because most projects involve many human resources and the majority of costs are for salaries and benefits, it is most effective to solicit ideas from a variety of people and to address human resource-related issues early in a project and then update them as needed. The people who will do the work should be involved in estimating resource requirements. It is also important to document the basis for the estimates, and in some cases, it is helpful to create a resource breakdown structure.

Sample Activity Resource Requirements

A key output of the resource estimating process is documentation of activity resource requirements. This list can take various formats. For the Just-In-Time Training project, Kristin met with her team, her sponsor, and the project steering committee, as needed, to discuss resource requirements for the project. They also discussed which training might be best to outsource, which would be best to perform with internal resources, and which should use both internal and external resources. They entered important resource information for each activity in their enterprise project management software.

Figure 6-11 provides an example of the resource requirements for "Survey administration." In this case, the resource requirements are at the work package level because the team decided not to break it down further. In other words, the WBS deliverable is the same as the activity required to do the work, and it could be named "Administer survey," depending on the team's preference.

Activity Resource Requirements
August 1

Project Name: Just-In-Time Training Project
WBS Item Number: 3.1.1.1.2
WBS Item Name: Survey administration
Resource Source: Internal staffing, hardware, and software from the IT department
Description: The individuals must be knowledgeable in using our online survey software so they can enter the actual survey into this software. They must also know how to run a query to find the e-mail addresses of employees of grade level 52 or higher in the purchasing, accounting, engineering, information technology, sales, marketing, manufacturing, and human resource departments.

Figure 6-11: Sample activity resource requirements information
The team should also document the basis of estimates, similar to doing so for estimating duration. For example, if the person assigned to perform the survey administration activity is known and has done similar work several times in the recent past, it would influence the estimate to be lower than if an inexperienced person was assigned to do the work for the first time.

Sample Resource Breakdown Structure

For some projects, it can be helpful to create a resource breakdown structure. Just like a work breakdown structure in format, this document visually shows a hierarchy of resources by category and type. Figure 6-12 provides a sample resource breakdown structure Kristin and her team started creating to help estimate resources. Level 1 and Level 2 refer to skill levels for internal personnel.

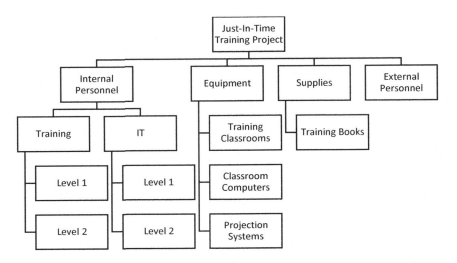

Figure 6-12: Sample resource breakdown structure

PROJECT COMMUNICATIONS MANAGEMENT

Many experts agree that the greatest threat to the success of any project is a failure to communicate. It is often said that project managers spend 90% of time communicating. Yet many project managers fail to take the time to plan for it. Even though having a communications management plan does not guarantee that all project communications will flow smoothly, it certainly helps.

Figure 6-13 provides a humorous example of miscommunication based on selfishness and bad timing. (It's a take-off from O. Henry's "The Gift of the Magi" story about the woman who cuts her long hair to buy her husband a chain for his watch while he sells his watch to buy a comb for her hair.) In the comic, a Roomba is an automatic vacuum cleaner, and Left 4 dead is an Xbox video game.

Figure 6-13. Poor communications (www.xkcd.com)

Project communications management involves generating, collecting, disseminating, and storing project information. Key outputs produced for many projects, including the Just-In-Time Training project, include a communications management plan and a project website.

Communications Management Plans

Because project communication is so important, every project should include a **communications management plan**—a document that guides project communications. The communications management plan will vary with the needs of the project, but some type of written plan should always be prepared and updated as needed. The plan should describe who will provide and receive data, when, and how the information will be presented. Stakeholders may change depending on the project phase, so the plan must be updated as needed.

The communications management plan should address the following items:

- Stakeholder communications requirements

- Information to be communicated, format, content, and level of detail

- Identification of who will receive the information and who will produce it

- Suggested methods or guidelines for conveying the information

- Description of the frequency of communication

- Escalation procedures for resolving issues

- Revision procedures for updating the communications management plan

- A glossary of common terminology used on the project

The plan might also include flow charts of the information flow for the project as well as communications constraints based on legislation, regulation, technology, or organizational policies. The communications management plan may also provide guidelines and templates for creating various project documents and discuss use of a project website and/or project management software.

Sample Communications Management Plan

Kristin and her team drafted a communications management plan for the Just-In-Time Training project as shown in Figure 6-14. The project steering committee reviewed it and provided suggestions on how to keep communication lines open. They advised Kristin to stress the importance of communications with *all* project stakeholders. They also mentioned the fact that people communicate in different ways and recommended that her team not be afraid of over-communicating by providing the same information in multiple formats. The steering committee noted that it is not enough to provide formal documents; Kristin and her team should use face-to-face communications, e-mails, phone calls, and other communications media to ensure optimal communications. Recall that the WBS for this project included an item called stakeholder communications to ensure good project communications.

Communication Management Plan Version 1.0
August 28

Project Name: Just-In-Time Training Project

1.   Stakeholder Communications Requirements

Because this project involves many people from all over the company as well as outside suppliers, the project team will use surveys, interviews, checklists, and other tools and techniques to determine the communications requirements for various stakeholders. Employees will have specific communications needs in that several training programs are being totally changed, and they will likely be uncomfortable with those changes. Suppliers will have communications needs to ensure that they are developing courses that will meet our organization's requirements. Internal experts providing content will have communications needs related to providing useful information and products.

2.   Communications Summary

The following table summarizes various stakeholders, communications required, the delivery method or format of the communications, who will produce the communications, and when it will be distributed or the frequency of distribution. All communications produced will be archived and available on the project website. As more communications items are defined, they will be added to this list. The project team will use various templates and checklists to enhance communications. The team will also be careful to use the appropriate medium (that is, face-to-face meeting, phone, e-mail, website, and so on) and follow corporate guidelines for effective communications. Note the comments/guidelines as well.

Stakeholders	Communications Name	Delivery Method/Format	Producer	Due Date/ Frequency
Project steering committee	Weekly status report	Hard copy and short meeting	Kristin Maur	Wed. mornings at 9 AM
Sponsor and champion	Monthly status report	Hard copy and short meeting	Kristin Maur	First Thursday of month at 10 AM
Affected employees	Project announcement	Memo, e-mail, intranet site, and announcement at department meetings	Lucy C. and Mike S.	July 1
Project team	Weekly status report	Short meeting	All team	Tues. at 2 PM.
Project team	Daily report to PM	Verbal – 1-5 minutes	All team	Each morning by 10:00

3.   Guidelines

- Make sure people understand your communications. Use common sense techniques to check comprehension, such as having them explain what you mean in their own words. Don't overuse/misuse e-mail or other technologies. Short meetings or phone calls can be very effective.

- Use templates as much as possible for written project communications. The project website includes a link to all project-related templates.

- Use the titles and dates of documents in e-mail headings and have recipients acknowledge receipt.

- Prepare and post meeting minutes within 24 hours of a meeting.

- Use checklists where appropriate, such as reviewing product requirements and conducting interviews.

- Use corporate facilitators for important meetings, such as kickoff meetings and supplier negotiations.

---

4. Escalation Procedures for Resolving Issues

Issues should be resolved at the lowest level possible. When they cannot be resolved, affected parties should alert their immediate supervisors of the issues. If it is critical to the project or extremely time-sensitive, the issue should be brought directly to the project manager. If the project manager cannot resolve an issue, he or she should bring it to the project steering committee or appropriate senior management, as required.

5. Revision Procedures for this Document

Revisions to this plan will be approved by the project manager. The revision number and date will be clearly marked at the top of the document.

6. Glossary of Common Terminology

actual cost — the total direct and indirect costs incurred in accomplishing work on an activity during a given period.

baseline — the original project plan plus approved changes.

Etc.

Figure 6-14. Sample communications management plan

Project Websites

In the past few years, more and more project teams have started posting all or part of their project information to project websites. Project websites provide a centralized way of delivering project documents and other communications. Note that some organizations use a different type of repository to store information, such as a SharePoint site. Some teams also create **blogs**—easy-to-use journals on the Web that allow users to write entries, create links, and upload pictures, while allowing readers to post comments to particular journal entries. Project teams can develop project websites using tools such as Wix, Google sites, or WordPress; project management software, if available; or a combination of the two approaches. Part of the website might be open to outside users, whereas other parts might be accessible only by certain stakeholders. Different levels of access would also be provided using the CRUD code: The user can Create, Read, Update, and/or Delete. It is important to decide if and how to use a project website to help meet project communications requirements. Some organizations also create quad charts as part of their project websites where the four quadrants show a project summary, financials, schedules, and issues.

Sample Project Website

Kristin and her team entered detailed project information into the company's enterprise project management software. From within that system, Kristin could control who could and could not see various types of information. In addition, she worked with her team and the IT department to create a simple project website that would be available on the corporate intranet. Kristin's team felt it was important to let all stakeholders access basic information about the project. Figure 6-15 shows the home page of the website for the Just-In-Time Training project. It includes summary information, such as project objectives, new information, and key milestones. It also includes links to information on team members, the project schedule, the project archive, a search feature, a discussions feature, and contact information.

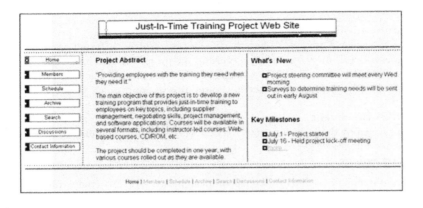

Figure 6-15. Sample project website

Many college courses include a team project. A quick and free way to create a team project website is to use Google sites There are several Google site templates (including a project wiki and project tracking template) that you can use to start your site. You can also create your site with a blank template to control the contents more. You can link to shared Google docs so all team members can collaborate when creating documents, logging hours, etc. See the companion website for instructions for creating a Google site and links to several sites that students created in project management classes. Of course you can use other free or paid sites, such as Basecamp or even Workplace by Facebook, to create a project website as well.

PROJECT STAKEHOLDER MANAGEMENT

Project stakeholder engagement planning involves determining strategies to effectively engage stakeholders in project decisions and activities based on their needs, interests, and potential impact. The main output of this process is a stakeholder engagement plan. Stakeholders change as the project progresses, and stakeholder engagement planning should be updated based on those changes. The staffing management plan shows when project team members join or leave the project. The stakeholder engagement plan, the communications management plan, and the resource management plan are tightly bound and should be in agreement.

Stakeholder Engagement Plans

After identifying and analyzing stakeholders, the project manager and team should develop a stakeholder engagement plan to guide them in effectively engaging stakeholders to make sure good decisions are made throughout the life of the project. This plan may be formal or informal, based on the needs of the project.

A stakeholder engagement plan can include the following:

- Current and desired engagement levels of key stakeholders

- Scope and impact of change to stakeholders

- Identified interrelationships between stakeholders and potential overlap

- Potential management strategies for each stakeholder classification

- Methods for updating the stakeholder management plan

Because a stakeholder engagement plan often includes sensitive information, it should *not* be part of the official project documents that are normally available for all stakeholders to review. Often only project managers and a few other team members prepare the stakeholder engagement plan. In many cases, parts of the plan are not even written down, and if they are, distribution is strictly limited.

Figure 6-16 provides an example of part of a stakeholder engagement plan that Kristin Maur could use to help her engage stakeholders of the Just-In-Time Training project. It is important for project managers to take the time to develop this plan to help them meet stakeholder needs and expectations. In addition, as new stakeholders are added to the project and more information is provided, the plan should be updated. Early in this project, for example, all the stakeholders are internal to the company; later on, however, there will be external stakeholders as well. For example, potential suppliers would be stakeholders, and they could often be grouped together or handled collectively.

Name	Power/ Interest	Current/desired engagement	Potential Management Strategies
Mike Sundby	High/high	Supportive/ Supportive	Mike is very outgoing and visionary. Great traits for a project champion. He is concerned about financials and has an MBA. Manage closely and ask for his advice as needed. Schedule short face-to-face meetings as needed.
Lucy Camerena	High/high	Leading/ Leading	Lucy has a Ph.D. in education and knows training at this company. She is very professional and easy to work with, but she can stretch out conversations. Make sure she reviews important work before showing it to other managers.
Ron Ryan	Low/ medium	Resistant/ Supportive	Ron led the Phase I project and is upset that he was not asked to lead this Phase II project. He's been with the company over 20 years and can be a good resource, but he could also sabotage the project. Ask Lucy to talk to him to avoid problems. Perhaps give him a small consulting role on the project.

Figure 6-16. Sample stakeholder engagement plan

PROJECT RISK MANAGEMENT

Although it is a frequently overlooked aspect of project management, good risk management can often result in significant improvements in the chance of a project succeeding. What is risk as it relates to a project? PMI defines a project **risk** as an uncertainty that can have a *negative or positive* effect on meeting project objectives. Note that some people only view risks as negative (threats) and call positive risks opportunities. The main planning processes performed as part of project risk management are planning risk management, identifying risks, performing qualitative risk analysis, performing quantitative risk analysis, and planning risk responses. You can also plan to reduce procurement-related risks by making risk-related contract decisions.

Risks are always in the future, and some can only occur at specific times in the schedule. As the project progresses, risks occur or they don't. Risks that are in the past as the project progresses are noted as being closed. Risk management planning is repeated at a scheduled frequency such as at the end of a phase or a milestone.

Planning Risk Management

The first process in planning for risk management is called plan risk management, and its main output is a risk management plan. A risk management plan documents the procedures for managing risk *throughout the life of a project*. Project teams should hold several planning meetings early in the project's life cycle to help develop the risk management plan. The project team should review project documents as well as corporate risk management policies, risk categories, lessons learned from past projects, and templates for creating a risk management plan. It is also important to review the risk tolerances of various stakeholders. For example, if the project sponsor is risk-averse, the project might require a different approach to risk management than if the project sponsor were a risk seeker.

A risk management plan outlines how risk management will be performed on a particular project. Like other specific knowledge area plans, it becomes a subset of the project management plan. The general topics that a risk management plan should address include the methodology for risk management, roles and responsibilities, funding and timing, risk categories, risk probability and impact, stakeholder risk appetite, and risk documentation. The level of detail included in the risk management plan will vary with the needs of the project.

In addition to a risk management plan, many projects also include contingency plans, fallback plans, and reserves.

- **Contingency plans** are predefined actions that the project team will take if an identified risk event occurs. For example, if the project team knows that the new version of a product they need might not be available in time, they might have a contingency plan to use the existing, older version of the product.

- **Fallback plans** are developed for risks that have a high impact on meeting project objectives, and are put into effect if attempts to reduce the risk are not effective. For example, a new college graduate might have a main plan and several contingency plans on where to live after graduation, but if none of those plans work out, a fallback plan might be to live at home for a while. Some people view fallback plans as contingency plans of last resort.

- **Contingency reserves** or **contingency allowances** are funds included in the cost baseline that can be used to mitigate cost or schedule overruns if known risks occur. For example, if a project appears to be off course because the staff is not experienced with a new technology and the team had identified that as a risk, the contingency reserves could be used to hire an outside consultant to train and advise the project staff in using the new technology.

- **Management reserves** are funds held for unknown risks that are used for management control purposes. They are not part of the cost baseline, but they are part of the project budget and funding requirements. If the management reserves are used for unforeseen work, they are added to the cost baseline after the change is approved. Contingency plans, fallback plans, and reserves show the importance of taking a proactive approach to managing project risks.

Sample Risk Management Plan

Kristin knew that it was important to plan effectively for risk management. There were several uncertainties, both negative and positive, associated with this project. Kristin asked Ron Ryan, the project manager of the Phase I project, to assist her in drafting the first version of the risk management plan. She also received input from the project steering committee, and as her team and suppliers were identified, they would work together to update the plan as needed. Figure 6-17 shows the initial risk management plan.

Risk Management Plan
September 3

1. Methodology
The project team will review data available from the Phase I project and past training programs within Global Construction. They will also review information related to external projects similar to this one. The team will use several tools and techniques, including brainstorming, surveys, and risk-related checklists to assist in risk management.

2. Roles and Responsibilities
The project manager will be responsible for leading the team and other stakeholders in performing risk-related activities. As detailed risk-related activities and deliverables are determined, the project manager will delegate those activities to others as appropriate.

3. Funding and Timing
As specific risk-related activities and deliverables are determined, budget and schedule information will be provided. Protocols for the application of contingency and management reserves will be reviewed with the project sponsor.

---

4. Risk Categories

General categories and subcategories for risk on this project include business risks (suppliers and cash flow), technical risks (course content, hardware, software, and network), organizational risks (executive support, user support, supplier support, and team support), and project management risks (estimates, communication, and resources).

5. Risk Probability and Impact

Risk probability and impact will initially be estimated as high, medium, or low based on expert judgment. High means a 75% -100% probability or impact, low means 0%-25%, and medium is in between. If more advanced scoring is needed, the project team will determine an appropriate approach.

6. Stakeholder Risk Appetite

Measureable risk thresholds for each project objective will be documented for key stakeholders. These thresholds determine the acceptable overall project risk exposure and influence the probability and impact ratings.

7. Risk Documentation

All risk-related information will be summarized in a risk register. Detailed documentation will be available in a secure area on the project website.

Figure 6-17. Sample risk management plan

Identifying Risks

You cannot manage risks until you identify them. Identifying risks involves determining which risks are likely to affect a project and documenting the characteristics of each. The main outputs of this process are a risk register (described later in this chapter) and a risk report. Teams often hold several brainstorming sessions with various stakeholders and experts to help identify project risks. They also review documents, gather information, analyze assumptions, and use other tools and techniques to identify risks. It is important to consider risks in various categories, such as market risks, financial risks, technical risks, people risks, risks related to specific knowledge areas, and so on. Identified risks are included in a risk register, as described later in this section.

Risk events refer to specific, uncertain events that may occur to the detriment or enhancement of the project. For example, negative risk events might include the performance failure of a product produced as part of a project, delays in completing work as scheduled, increases in estimated costs, supply shortages, litigation against the company, and labor strikes. Examples of positive risk events include completing work sooner than planned or at an unexpectedly reduced cost, collaborating with suppliers to produce better products, and obtaining good publicity from the project.

Overall project risk is the effect of uncertainty on the project as a whole. Contents of a risk report include sources of overall project risk and summary information on risk events, such as number of risks, distribution across risk categories, metrics, and trends. The risk report is developed progressively during the entire risk planning processes.

WHAT WENT WRONG?

Not identifying risks or taking the time to perform adequate risk planning can lead to disaster. In April 2017, several headlines reported how Fyre—what was supposed to be a luxury vacation/concert in the Bahamas— was being called #DumpsterFyre. "A $100 million proposed class-action lawsuit was filed Sunday (May 1, 2017) in California against the organizers of the now infamous Fyre Festival on the grounds of fraud, claiming a 'lack of adequate food, water, shelter, and medical care created a dangerous and panicked situation among attendees — suddenly finding themselves stranded on a remote island without basic provisions — that was closer to 'The Hunger Games' or 'Lord of the Flies' than Coachella,' ABC News reported…The festival, organized by entrepreneur Billy McFarland and Ja Rule, was promoted (with the help of supermodels like Kendall Jenner and Bella Hadid) as a luxury music experience on a "remote and private" island in the Bahamas with the promise of posh accommodations and adventure for a cost between $5,000 and $250,000. Alas, when attendees arrived, they realized the reality of #DumpsterFyre was a stark contrast from the advertisements.[2]

Fyre's failure was nothing compared to the infamous Woodstock music festival in 1969. Then New York Governor Nelson Rockefeller declared it a disaster area after the site was overrun by over 400,000 people (twice the number expected) due to lack of fencing and ticket booths. Roads were impassable, and the Army had to airlift in food and water. "Two people died: one of a drug overdose, the other run over by a tractor. There were 5,162 medical incidents reported, including eight miscarriages."[3]

Performing Qualitative Risk Analysis

After identifying risks, it is important to evaluate risks to determine which ones need the most attention. Qualitative risk analysis often results in prioritizing risks as high, medium, or low. A probability/impact matrix, as described in the following section, is a good technique to help decide which risks are most important on a project.

There are two important dimensions of risk events: *probability* of the risk event occurring and the *impact* or consequence if the risk does occur. People often describe a risk event probability or impact as being high, medium, or low. (High can be defined to mean a 75%-100% probability or impact, low 0%-25%, and medium in between.) For example, a meteorologist might predict that there is a high probability of severe rain showers on a certain day. If that happens to be your wedding day and you are planning a large outdoor wedding, the impact or consequences of severe showers would also be high.

A project manager can chart the probability and impact of risk events on a probability/impact matrix or chart. One side (axis) of a probability/impact matrix or chart lists the relative *probability* of a risk event occurring, and the other side (axis) of the chart shows the relative *impact* of the risk event occurring. To use this approach, project stakeholders identify and list the risk events related to their projects. They then label each risk event as being high, medium, or low in terms of its probability of occurrence and level of impact. The project manager then summarizes the results in a probability/impact matrix. Project teams should initially focus on risk events that fall in the high sections of the probability/impact matrix and develop strategies for minimizing negative risk events and maximizing positive ones.

Sample Probability/Impact Matrix

On the Just-In-Time Training project, Kristin worked with several project stakeholders early in the project to begin identifying several negative and positive risk events related to the project. She held a brainstorming session in which over 100 risk events were identified. To differentiate between the two, she asked participants to identify negative risk events and then positive ones. After people identified a risk event and wrote it down on a sticky note, Kristin asked them to mark each one as having a high, medium, or low probability of occurrence and impact. Kristin had posted on the whiteboard large probability/impact matrices—one for negative risk events and another for positive risk events. Everyone put their sticky notes in the appropriate sections of the appropriate matrix. They then examined the results to combine and reword risk events to improve collaboration and avoid duplicates.

Figure 6-18 shows part of the resulting probability/impact matrix. For example, risks 1 and 2 are listed as high in both categories of probability and impact. Risks 9 and 10 are high in the probability category but low in the impact category. Risk 5 is high in the probability category and medium in the impact category. The team then discussed in detail how they planned to respond to risks, especially those in the medium and high categories, and documented the results in the risk register, as described in the following section.

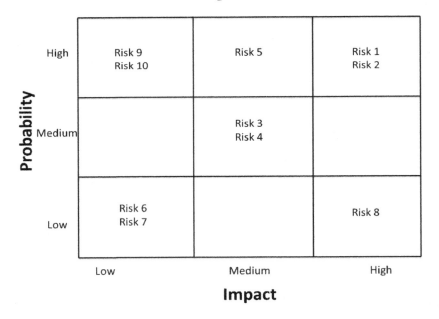

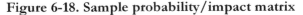

Figure 6-18. Sample probability/impact matrix

Performing Quantitative Risk Analysis

On many projects, the team may only perform qualitative risk analysis. The nature of the project and availability of time and money affect the type of risk analysis techniques used (as documented in the risk management plan). Large, complex projects involving leading-edge technologies often require extensive quantitative risk analysis. Data gathering often involves interviewing experts and collecting probability distribution information. Quantitative risk analysis and modeling techniques include decision tree analysis, simulation, influence diagrams, and sensitivity analysis. The most commonly used simulation tool is Monte Carlo analysis, as described briefly in Chapter 4. See tools and techniques under the Links section of the companion website (www.intropm.com) for more detailed information on these techniques.

Planning Risk Responses

There are several strategies that teams can plan for responding to risks. These responses vary depending on whether or not the risk will have a negative or positive potential impact on meeting project objectives and the severity. The same response strategies can be used to address overall project risks as individual risks.

The five basic response strategies for negative risks or threats are:

1. *Escalation of the risk.* If the risk is outside of the scope of the project or the proposed response is outside of the project manager's authority, it would make sense to escalate the risk to a higher-level manager within the organization.

2. *Risk avoidance* or eliminating a specific threat, usually by eliminating its causes. Of course, not all risks can be eliminated, but specific risk events can be. For example, Kristin's team might decide in their plans that they would not use a new survey tool and instead use the one they have used in the past.

3. *Risk acceptance* or accepting the consequences should a risk occur. For example, Kristin's team might decide to use the new survey tool and suffer the consequences if there are problems.

4. *Risk transference* or shifting the consequence of a risk and responsibility for its management to a third party. For example, many organizations hold golf tournaments to raise money or improve employee morale. They often have a large financial prize if anyone gets a hole-in-one. They can purchase insurance from another company who will then pay the prize should someone be lucky enough to get a hole-in-one. Automobile insurance is another example of risk transference.

5. *Risk mitigation* or reducing the impact of a risk event by reducing the probability of its occurrence. For example, Kristin's team might suggest a strategy to hire a well-known consultant for one of the high risk items to mitigate or reduce the possibility of poor performance.

The five basic response strategies for positive risks or opportunities are:

1. *Escalation of the risk.* If the risk is outside of the scope of the project or the proposed response is outside of the project manager's authority, it would make sense to escalate the risk to a higher level manager within the organization.

2. *Risk exploitation* or doing whatever you can to make sure the positive risk happens. For example, suppose Kristin's company decided to work on a project that included running a golf tournament to raise funds for building a new school in their community. They might select one of their top public relations people to organize news coverage of

the event, write a press release, or hold some other public event to ensure the project produces good public relations for the company, which could lead to more business.

3. *Risk sharing* or allocating ownership of the risk to another party. Using the same example of building a new school, the project manager could form a partnership with the school's principal, school board, or parent-teacher organization to share responsibility for achieving good public relations for the project.

4. *Risk enhancement* or increasing the probability/impact of the opportunity. For example, you could increase the probability of getting good public relations for the school building project by getting the students, parents, and teachers aware of and excited about the project.

5. *Risk acceptance* also applies to positive risks when the project team cannot or chooses not to take any actions toward a risk. For example, the school building project manager might just assume the project will result in good public relations for their company without doing anything extra.

VIDEO HIGHLIGHTS

The story of the Titanic is known throughout the world, and on April 15, 2012, people acknowledged the 100th anniversary of the Titanic's sinking. Many people saw James Cameron's 1997 version of the movie starring Kate Winslet and Leonardo DiCaprio and its 3-D re-release in 2012. You can watch the entire movie or view clips from several Internet sites. You can also read an article explaining how to avoid "the Titanic factor" in your projects by analyzing the interdependence of risks. For example, the probability of one risk event occurring might change if another one materializes, and the response to one risk event might affect another. The author addresses the question of how intra-project risks interact and how project teams can take those interactions into consideration. Some of the interdependent risk events on the Titanic included:

- The design of the bulkheads, rudder, and engines were related. As six of the sixteen watertight compartments were breached and began flooding, the weight of the water in the bow pulled the ship under until the bulkheads overtopped. The design for the rudder was considered adequate for use on the open seas; but it was undersized for the tight maneuvers required that fateful night. The central propeller had a steam turbine as its power source, and this engine could not be reversed and was stopped during the run up to the iceberg. This stopped the water flow past the rudder and became a critical factor in its effectiveness.

- Several procedures were not followed, which caused big problems when combined. Iceberg reports from two other ships were not passed on to the bridge. The wireless radio was inoperable most of the day, so another critical iceberg warning failed to reach the Titanic's captain. The ship was traveling too fast for the amount of ice in the area. Visibility was terrible that night due to ill-equipped lookouts not having binoculars, combined with calm seas, and no moon.

- Unknown risk events also contributed to the sinking of the Titanic. For example, the steel in the hull could not withstand the cold temperatures, causing it to break without bending. Iron rivet heads also burst due to the cold.[3]

Risk Registers

A **risk register** is a document that contains results of various risk management processes, often displayed in a table or spreadsheet format. It is a tool for documenting potential risk events and related information and tracking the risks through the life of the project. The risk register often includes the following main headings:

- *An identification number for each risk event:* The project team might want to sort or quickly search for specific risk events, so they need to identify each risk with some type of unique descriptor, such as an identification number.

- *A rank for each risk event:* The rank can be indicated as high, medium, or low, or it can be a number, with 1 being the highest-ranked risk. The project team would have to determine these rankings. Note that a simple method for ranking is to multiply the probability of risk by the impact of the risk for each risk event.

- *The name of the risk event:* For example, defective product, poor survey results, reduced consulting costs, or good publicity.

- *A description of the risk event:* Because the name of a risk event is often abbreviated, it helps to provide a detailed description in the risk register. For example, reduced consulting costs might be expanded in the description to say that the organization might be able to negotiate lower-than-average costs for a particular consultant because the consultant enjoys working for the company in that particular location.

- *The category under which the risk event falls:* For example, a defective product might fall under the broader category of technology.

- *The root cause of the risk event:* It is important to find the **root cause** of a problem—the real or underlying reason a problem occurs. By finding the root cause, you can deal with it directly rather than dealing with the symptoms of the problem. You can help identify the root cause of problems by creating a cause-and-effect or fishbone diagram (see Chapters 6 and 7), or continually asking why until you find a root cause. For example, the root cause of a defective product, like a defective computer, might be a defective hard drive. Instead of purchasing a brand-new computer or wasting time on other potential causes of the defect, knowing that you need to replace the hard drive provides valuable information that you can act on to fix the problem.

- *Triggers for each risk event:* **Triggers** are indicators or symptoms of actual risk events. For example, a clicking noise or increasing number of bad sectors would be triggers of a bad hard drive. Documenting potential risk triggers also helps the project team identify more potential risk events.

- *Potential responses to each risk event:* There can be one or more potential responses to each risk event. The previous sections described various response strategies.

- *The risk owner, or person who will own or take responsibility for the risk event:* One person should be responsible for monitoring each risk event.

- *The probability of the risk event occurring:* The chance of the risk event becoming a reality is rated as high, medium, or low.

- *The impact to the project if the risk event occurs:* The impact to project success if the risk event actually occurs can be rated as high, medium, or low.

- *The status of the risk event:* Did the risk event occur? Was the response strategy completed? Is the risk event no longer relevant to the project? Is the risk potential increasing or decreasing? For example, a clause may have been written into a contract to address the risk event of a defective product so that the supplier would have to replace the item at no additional cost. If a risk event does not occur, it should be marked as closed.

Sample Risk Register

Kristin began developing a risk register after she and the other stakeholders had prepared the probability/impact matrix. Figure 6-19 shows the format of the risk register and one of the entries. Note that the risk event identification (ID) number is shown in the first column, followed by the rank of the risk event. The risk events are sorted by rank order. As information is added, deleted, or changed, the risk register will be updated on the website.

Risk Register September 3											
Project Name: Just-In-Time Training Project											
No.	Rank	Risk	Description	Category	Root Cause	Triggers	Potential Responses	Risk Owner	Probability	Impact	Status
R15	1										
R21	2										
R7	3										

To understand the risk register more fully, imagine that the following data is entered for the first risk in the register.
- No.: R15
- Rank: 1
- Risk: Poor survey response
- Description: Many people dislike surveys and avoid filling them out, or if they do, they don't offer good or honest feedback
- Category: Organizational/user support risk
- Root cause: People don't want to take the time and think their inputs aren't important
- Triggers: Low survey response rate the first few days, incomplete surveys.

> - Risk Responses: Make sure senior management emphasizes the importance of this project and the survey for designing good courses. Have the functional managers personally mention the survey to their people and stress its importance. Offer a reward like gift certificates to the department with the most responses. Ensure that the survey instructions say it will take ten minutes or fewer to complete. Extend the deadline for survey responses.
> - Risk owner: Mike Sundby, Project champion
> - Probability: Medium
> - Impact: High
> - Status: PM will set up the meeting within the week with the project steering committee to decide which response strategies to implement.

Figure 6-19. Sample risk register

Risk-Related Contract Decisions

Many projects, including the Just-In-Time Training project, involve outside suppliers. Work done by outside suppliers or sellers should be well documented in **contracts**, which are mutually binding agreements that obligate the seller to provide the specified products or services, and obligate the buyer to pay for them. Project managers should include clauses in contracts to help manage project risks. For example, sellers can agree to be responsible for certain negative risks and incur the costs themselves if they occur. Or there can be incentive or liquidated damage clauses in contracts based on seller performance to encourage positive risks and discourage negative risks. You can also use certain types of contracts, such as fixed-price contracts, to reduce the risk of incurring higher costs. Competition for supplying goods and services can also help reduce negative risks and enhance positive risks on projects.

Sample Risk-Related Contract Decisions

Kristin's team had not yet prepared any contractual documents for the Just-In-Time Training project, but they did have access to several other contracts that Global Construction had used in the past. Kristin had come from the supplier management area of the company, so she had personal experience working with suppliers and contracts. She also knew several people who could advise her on writing risk-related contractual agreements. Figure 6-20 provides a list of a few risk-related contract decisions or agreements that Kristin's team would consider for this project. Kristin received these guidelines from the project team's representative from the contracting department. These agreements can take the form of contracts or clauses within contracts that can help prevent negative risk events and promote positive ones related to the project. Kristin also knew that the company's legal professionals would have to review all contracts because they were legally binding.

Guidelines for Risk-Related Contract Decisions/Agreements

The following guidelines are provided for your consideration as you make decisions to develop contracts/agreements between Global Construction (the buyer) and its suppliers (the sellers). Be sure to work with a member of the contracting department to write your specific contracts. All contracts must be reviewed and signed by the legal department, as well.

- Contract termination clauses: These clauses list circumstances under which the buyer and/or seller can terminate a contract and how final payment will be settled. All the contracts must include a termination clause.

- Incentive clauses: These clauses provide incentives for the seller to provide goods or services at certain times, of certain quality, and so on. Incentive clauses can include extra payments or profit sharing, if appropriate.

- Liquidated damage clauses: These clauses specify actions that will be taken when the seller does not provide goods or services as specified in the contract. For example, if a product is delivered late, the seller might be required to pay a certain dollar amount for each day the product is late.

- Fixed price contracts: To minimize the negative risk of paying more than planned for specific goods or services, Global Construction issues fixed priced contracts, which specify that the seller agrees to a fixed price and bears the risk if it costs more to provide the goods or services than originally estimated.

- Competitive contracts: In addition to reviewing bids from several sellers, a good strategy may be to award two small contracts and then award the following larger contract to the seller that does the best job on the first contract.

Figure 6-20. Sample guidelines for risk-related contractual agreements

The example in the following What Went Right? passage shows another contractual approach for managing positive risk on a large project. By having suppliers visibly compete against each other, the buyers reduced their risks and benefited from competition.

WHAT WENT RIGHT?

The Petronas Twin Towers in Malaysia are famous landmarks in Kuala Lumpur. They were the tallest buildings constructed at the time, and the first large construction project to use GPS (Global Positioning System). Over 7000 people were working on the site during the peak of construction. The project management team decided to use competition to help keep the project on time and on budget. The Japanese firm Hazama Corporation led the construction of Tower 1, and the Korean firm Samsung Engineering Co. led the construction of Tower 2. Because the towers were constructed simultaneously, everyone could see the progress of the two competitors as the 88-story towers rose into the sky. "Construction of the towers was fast paced, thanks in part to the decision to grant two contracts, one for each tower, to two separate contractors. This naturally created a competitive environment, to the benefit of the building."[5]

As you can see, risk management planning addresses procurement-related topics, such as preparing risk-related contractual agreements. The following section addresses planning project procurement management.

PROJECT PROCUREMENT MANAGEMENT

Project procurement management includes acquiring or procuring goods and services for a project from outside the organization. As the business world continues to become more competitive and global, more and more projects include procurement. Many project managers realize the advantages of buying goods and services required for their projects, especially as sellers with better goods and services continue to become increasingly available. They also realize that they can find qualified sellers throughout the world. Remember that project managers strive to do what is best for the project and the organization, and that often means acquiring goods and services from the outside. Good procurement management often provides a win-win situation for both buyers and sellers.

Planning project procurement management involves documenting procurement decisions, specifying the procurement approach, and identifying potential sellers. Key outputs include procurement management plans, procurement strategies, bid documents, procurement statements of work, source selection criteria, make-or-buy decisions, independent cost estimates, change requests, project documents updates, and organizational process assets updates. Several of these outputs are described in this section.

Make-or-Buy Decisions

With a make-or-buy decision, an organization decides if it would benefit more by making a product or performing a service itself, or by buying the product or service from a supplier. If there is no need to buy products or services from outside the organization, the organization can avoid the costs involved in managing procurement management processes. **Make-or-buy analysis** involves estimating the internal costs of providing a product or service, and comparing that estimate to the cost of outsourcing.

Many organizations also use a lease-or-buy analysis to decide if they should purchase or lease items for a particular project. For example, suppose you need a piece of equipment for a project that has a purchase price of $12,000. Assume it also has a daily operational cost of $400. Suppose you can lease the same piece of equipment for $800 per day, including the operational costs. You can set up an equation that shows the amount of time it will take for the purchase cost to equal the lease cost. In this way, you can determine when it makes sense financially to buy rather than lease the equipment. In the equation that follows, d = the number of days you need the piece of equipment.

$$\$12{,}000 + \$400d = \$800d$$

Subtracting $400d from both sides, you get:

$$\$12{,}000 = \$400d$$

Dividing both sides by $400, you get:

$$d = 30,$$

which means that the purchase cost equals the lease cost in 30 days. Therefore, if you need the equipment for fewer than 30 days, it would be more economical to lease it. If you need the equipment for more than 30 days, you should purchase it. Note that this simple example assumes there is no disposal value for the purchased item and does not include any tax considerations.

Figure 6-21 graphically shows the costs each day to lease or buy the equipment in the preceding example. Notice that the lines cross at Day 30, showing that the costs are the same to lease or buy the equipment that day. Before Day 30, the lease line is lower than the buy line, meaning it is less expensive to lease the item if it is needed for fewer than 30 days. After Day 30, the buy line is lower, meaning it is less expensive to buy the item after Day 30.

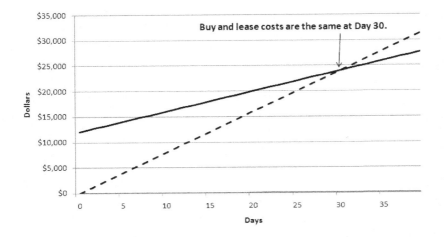

Figure 6-21. Comparing the cost of leasing versus buying

Sample Make-or-Buy Decision

Kristin and her team needed to make several make-or-buy decisions for the Just-In-Time Training project. They knew that they wanted to outsource most of the development and delivery for much of the new training, but because internal expertise existed, it might make sense to do some of the work in-house.

For example, based on information collected in the Phase I project, it was suggested that Global Construction could probably identify internal people to conduct some of the face-to-face training or provide online advice for several courses. Internal resources would be much less expensive than external contractors. In particular, one of the requirements for the Just-In-Time Training project was to provide instructor-led basic project management training and facilitation for online materials. To train 100 employees, there would be five, two-day instructor-led classes with 20 participants in each class in the first year. There would also be 500 hours of online facilitation.

One suggestion was to have current employees conduct the basic project management training—the "make" option—instead of having an outside firm provide the training—the "buy" option. There were a couple of project management professionals in the training department with experience in teaching face-to-face and online courses. They had taken college courses in basic project management and knew of excellent books with online materials. They also knew of several companies that conducted their own in-house courses for basic project management training and then brought in an outside expert, often a qualified college professor, who would conduct advanced courses. They found that college professors or other independent consultants provided high-quality training for much less than most training firms.

Figure 6-22 summarizes the make-or-buy analysis for the basic project management training. In this case, Kristin's team recommended doing the training in-house; for much of the other training, however, they did not have internal experts or training materials available.

Make-Or-Buy Analysis
September 1

Project Name: Just-In-Time Training Project

Background: Global Construction wants to train 100 employees and will consider having the employees sent to an outside course (Buy option) or provide the education using internal employees (Make option). Assuming 20 participants/class and 2 days average course length, 10 total days of training will be needed. Assume 500 hours of online facilitation will be needed as well (5 hours per participant).

Decision Being Analyzed: Project management training

Option 1: (Make): Use in-house instructors for the instructor-led basic project management training and facilitation for online materials (includes purchasing course materials)

Estimated cost per hour for in-house trainer (excludes participant time): $60

Estimated training hours: 80 (10 total days of training X 8 hours per day)

Subtotal: $4,800 (80 hours X $60 per hour)

Materials cost: $7500 ($75/participant/course, 100 participants total)

Estimated cost per hour for online facilitation (excludes employee time): $60

Estimated hours: 500

Subtotal: $30,000 (500 hours X $60 per hour)

   Total: $42,300 ($4,800 + $7,500 + $30,000)

Option 2: (Buy): Outsource instructor-led basic project management training and facilitation for online materials (includes course materials)

Estimated cost for class per participant = (Estimated Cost X Number of Days) = $500 X 2 days = $1,000

Cost of instructor-led classes ($1,000 X 100 participants)

Subtotal: $100,000

Estimated cost per hour for online facilitation (excludes student time): $100

Estimated hours: 500

Subtotal: $50,000 (500 hours X $100 per hour)

   Total $150,000 ($100,000 + $50,000)

Cost Difference: $150,000 - $42,300 = $107,700

Recommendation: Because we have qualified internal staff and can purchase suitable materials, we recommend Option 1, in which we conduct the basic project management training in-house.

Figure 6-22. Sample make-or-buy analysis

Procurement Management Plans

A procurement management plan is a document that describes how the procurement processes will be managed, from developing documentation for making outside purchases or acquisitions to contract closure. Like other project plans, the contents of procurement management plans vary with project needs. Some projects must follow government directives, such as the **Federal Acquisition Regulation (FAR)**, which provides uniform policies for acquisition of supplies and services by executive agencies in the U.S. Topics that can be included in a procurement management plan are as follows:

- Guidelines on types of contracts to be used in different situations

- Standard procurement documents or templates to be used, if applicable

- Guidelines for creating contract work breakdown structures, statements of work, and other procurement documents

- Roles and responsibilities of the project team and related departments, such as the purchasing or legal department

- Guidelines on using independent estimates for evaluating sellers' cost proposals

- Suggestions on managing multiple providers

- Processes for coordinating procurement decisions, such as make-or-buy decisions, with other project areas

- Constraints and assumptions related to purchases and acquisitions

- Lead times for purchases and acquisitions

- Risk-mitigation strategies for purchases and acquisitions, such as insurance contracts and bonds

- Guidelines for identifying prequalified sellers and organizational lists of preferred sellers

- Procurement metrics to assist in evaluating sellers and managing contracts

Types of Contracts

Contract type is a key consideration in a procurement management plan. Different types of contracts can be used in different situations. Three broad categories of contracts are fixed price, or lump sum; cost reimbursable; and time and material. A single contract can include all three of these categories, if it makes sense for that particular procurement. For example, you could have a contract with a seller that includes purchasing specific products for a fixed price or lump sum, some services that are provided on a cost-reimbursable basis, and other services that are provided on a time-and-material basis. It is important to understand and decide which approaches to use to meet particular project needs.

- **Fixed-price contracts** or **lump-sum contracts** involve a fixed total price for a well-defined product or service. The buyer incurs little risk or uncertainty in this situation because the price is predetermined. Sellers often pad their estimates somewhat to reduce their risk, while keeping in mind that their price must still be competitive. For example, using a two-week, fixed-price contract, Global Construction could hire a consultant to develop a survey to determine requirements for its new supplier management training courses under the Just-In-Time Training project. Fixed-price contracts generally have well-defined deliverables and deadlines, and may include incentives for meeting or exceeding selected project objectives. For example, the contract could include an incentive fee that would be paid for early delivery of the survey. A firm-fixed price (FFP) contract has the least amount of risk for the buyer, followed by a fixed-price incentive fee (FPIF) contract.

- **Cost-reimbursable contracts** involve payment to the seller for direct and indirect actual costs. For example, the salaries for people working directly on a project and materials purchased for a specific project are direct costs, whereas the cost of providing a work space for those workers, office furniture, electricity, a cafeteria, and so on, are indirect costs. Indirect costs are often calculated as a percentage of direct costs. Cost-reimbursable contracts often include fees such as a profit percentage, and they can also include incentives for meeting or exceeding selected project objectives. For example, many contracts to build homes are cost-reimbursable contracts. The buyer might expect the home to cost a certain amount, but the total cost could vary if any of the costs of individual goods or services increase or decrease. The buyer reimburses the contractor for allowable costs incurred, and pays a fee or profit percentage as well. Buyers absorb more of the risk with cost-reimbursable contracts than they do with fixed-price contracts. For example, if the cost of wood doubles, the buyer would have to absorb the additional cost. See the Media Snapshot for a great example of using incentives to build a bridge more quickly.

- **Time-and-material contracts** are a hybrid of both fixed-price and cost-reimbursable contracts. For example, an independent consultant might have a contract with a company based on a fee of $100 per hour for his or her services plus a fixed price of $10,000 for providing specific materials for the project. The materials fee might also be based on approved receipts for purchasing items, with a ceiling of $10,000. The consultant would send an invoice to the company each week or month, listing the materials fee, the number of hours worked, and a description of the work produced. This type of contract is often used for services that are needed when the work cannot be clearly specified and total costs cannot be estimated in a contract, such as research projects. Many consultants prefer time-and-material contracts.

Unit pricing can also be used in various types of contracts to require the buyer to pay the supplier a predetermined amount per unit of service. The total value of the contract is a function of the quantities needed to complete the work. For example, many companies use unit price contracts for purchasing computer hardware. If the company purchases only one unit, the cost is $1,000. If it purchases 10 units, the cost is $10,000 if there were no volume discounts involved, but this type of pricing often does involve volume discounts. For example, if the company purchases between 5 and 50 units, the contracted cost is $900 per unit. If it purchases over 50 units, the cost reduces to $800 per unit. This flexible pricing strategy is often advantageous to both the buyer and the seller.

MEDIA SNAPSHOT

Contract type and incentives can be extremely effective. On August 1, 2007, tragedy struck Minneapolis, Minnesota when a bridge on I-35W crossing the Mississippi River suddenly collapsed, killing 13 motorists, injuring 150 other people, and leaving a mass of concrete and steel in the river and on its banks. The Minnesota Department of Transportation (MnDOT) acted quickly to find a contractor to rebuild the bridge. They also provided a strong incentive to finish the bridge as quickly as possible, ensuring quality and safety along the way.

Peter Sanderson, project manager for the joint venture of Flatiron-Manson, hired to build the bridge, led his team in completing the project three months ahead of schedule, and the new bridge opened on September 18, 2008. The contractors earned $25 million in incentive fees on top of their $234 million contract for completing the bridge ahead of schedule. The financial incentive motivated the project team to coordinate their work using around the clock shifts and to develop innovative ways to pour concrete in the dead of winter.

Why did MnDOT offer such a large incentive fee to finish the project early? "I-35W in Minneapolis is a major transportation artery for the Twin Cities and entire state. Each day this bridge has been closed, it has cost road users more than $400,000," MnDOT Commissioner Tom Sorel remarked. "Area residents, business owners, motorists, workers and others have been affected by this corridor's closure. The opening of this bridge reconnects our community." [6]

Sample Procurement Management Plan

Figure 6-23 displays a section of a procurement management plan for the Just-In-Time Training project.

Procurement Management Plan
September 17

Project Name: Just-In-Time Training Project

Guidelines on Types of Contracts: To reduce Global Construction's risk, contracts for the Just-In-Time Training project should be fixed price as often as possible. When goods or services cannot be well defined, cost-reimbursable or time and material contracts may be used. The representative from the contracting department assigned to this project will work with the project manager to determine the appropriate contract type for each contract developed.

Standard procurement documents or templates: Global Construction's intranet site includes many sample documents and templates for project procurement. The project team will review these documents and templates and use them when appropriate.

Guidelines for creating procurement documents: Global Construction's intranet site provides guidelines for creating many procurement documents. The Just-In-Time Training project team should review their current work breakdown structure and scope statement to provide the basis for contract work breakdown structures and statements of work.

Roles and responsibilities: The project manager is the main contact for all procurement matters directly related to the Just-In-Time Training project. The representative from the contracting department assigned to this project will coordinate with other staff in the contracting and legal departments, as needed.
Etc.

Figure 6-23. Sample procurement management plan

Bid Documents: Requests for Information, Proposals, or Quotes

When organizations decide to procure goods or services, they often create bid documents to describe what they plan to procure and how potential sellers should respond. Common examples of procurement documents include:

- A **Request for Information (RFI)** is used when more information about the goods or services is needed. Potential suppliers are asked to provide the information before sending out an RFP or RFQ.

- A **Request for Proposal (RFP)** is a document used to solicit proposals from prospective suppliers. A **proposal** is a document in which sellers describe what they will do to meet the requirements of a buyer. It may or may not include pricing information. It can be expensive and time-consuming to prepare a good RFP or proposal for a large contract, such as building a new bridge or designing a complex information system. For smaller contracts, it would take less time and money. For example, there are several different ways to meet many of Global Construction's training needs. Kristin and her team can write and issue an RFP that outlines training needs so that suppliers can respond with their unique proposals describing how they would meet those needs.

- A **Request for Quote (RFQ)** is a document used to solicit quotes or bids from prospective suppliers. A **bid** (also called a quote) is a document prepared by sellers providing pricing for standard items that have been clearly defined by the buyer. For example, if Kristin's team decided to use a specific book for training courses, they could ask for bids from different sellers for those books. Creating and responding to RFQs is usually a much quicker process than the process of responding to RFPs. Selections are often made based on the lowest bid.

RFPs and RFQs can be issued in several ways. The organization might contact one or several preferred sellers directly and send the RFP or RFQ only to them. To reach more sellers, the organization might post the information on its website, or advertise on other sites or in newspapers. Project managers must carefully consider which approaches are most appropriate in various situations.

Topics addressed in an RFP usually include the following:

- Purpose of the RFP

- Background information, describing the organization issuing the RFP and the project itself

- Basic requirements for the products and/or services being proposed

- Hardware and software environment (for technology-related proposals)

- RFP process, describing how sellers should prepare and submit their proposals

- Statement of work and schedule information

- Appendices providing more detailed information, as appropriate

A simple RFP might be three- to five-pages long, whereas an RFP for a larger, more complicated procurement might be hundreds of pages long.

Sample Requests for Proposal

Kristin knew that the project would require several RFPs and RFQs, but it was still very early in the project. Kristin asked the project steering committee for advice because she knew how important it was to develop good procurement documents. They suggested that Kristin's team work with the contracting department to issue an RFP for expert advice to help make major procurement decisions related to the project. The RFP would be for a fixed-price contract to hire an expert to help develop a list of qualified sellers for developing the courses for the Just-In-Time Training project. Figure 6-24 shows the RFP. Lucy, the project sponsor and training director for Global Construction, suggested that they send the RFP to several preferred vendors. They estimated that the work required to develop this qualified-sellers list should take no more than a couple weeks and cost no more than $5,000.

Request for Proposal
August 1

Project Name: Just-In-Time Training Project
RFP Name: Qualified Sellers List for Just-In-Time Training Project

Purpose of RFP

Global Construction wants to improve training in supplier management, negotiating skills, project management, and software for its employees. In the fast-paced, ever-changing construction market, effectively training employees across a globally dispersed company with different populations is a challenge. By redesigning our current training, Global Construction can reduce training costs and improve productivity. In addition to traditional instructor-led courses provided on-site, we also want to allow our employees to learn about specific topics on a just-in-time basis by having quick access to materials and expert advice. The purpose of this RFP is to hire experts to help us find qualified sellers to develop and deliver these new training courses.

Background Information

Global Construction employs 10,000 full-time employees in ten different counties and fifteen states in the U.S. We want to increase the productivity of our employees, especially in the sales, purchasing, engineering, and information technology departments. The Just-In-Time Training Project, a one-year project, began on July 2. A key part of this project is working with outside firms to develop and provide just-in-time training in supplier management, negotiating skills, project management, and software applications. See Appendix A for detailed information on the project and specific training needs.

Basic Requirements

The basic requirements for this work include the following:
1. Develop a list of qualified sellers to develop and provide the training as described in Appendix A.
2. Provide a summary description and detailed evaluation of each seller. Provide company brochures, websites, annual reports, and other appropriate information.
3. Work with Global Construction to develop an evaluation system to evaluate each seller.
4. Provide an objective evaluation of each seller using this evaluation system.
5. Develop a list of the top five sellers for each course.
6. Provide recommendations for developing partnerships/relationships with each of the top five sellers.
7. Complete the above work no later than September 9.

RFP Process

Prospective sellers will send written proposals to Global Construction no later than August 10. To prepare your proposal, use the outline in Appendix B, and examine Appendix C for our evaluation criteria. We expect to award the contract no later than August 20.

Statement of Work and Schedule Information

See Appendix D for a statement of work. The work must be completed no later than September 9.

Appendices

Figure 6-24. Sample RFP

Procurement Statements of Work

Another important procurement document is a **procurement statement of work (SOW)**, a document that describes the goods or services to be purchased. The SOW should be included with the RFP to clarify the work that needs to be performed. It is a type of scope statement that describes the work in sufficient detail to allow prospective suppliers to both determine if they are capable of providing the goods and services required and to determine an appropriate price for the work. A procurement SOW should be clear, concise, and as complete as possible. It should describe all services required and include performance information, such as the location and timing of the work. It is important to use appropriate words in a procurement SOW—for example, *must or shall* instead of *may*. *Must or shall* implies that something has to be done; *may* implies that there is a choice involved. The procurement SOW should specify the products and services required for the project, use industry terms, and refer to industry standards. Note that a SOW is a contractual document, and as such it could have legal ramifications.

Sample Procurement Statement of Work

Figure 6-25 shows the procurement statement of work for the qualified-sellers list described in the RFP.

Procurement Statement of Work
August 1

Project Name: Just-in-Time Training Project
Contract Name: Qualified Sellers List
Scope of Work:
1. Develop a list of qualified sellers to develop and provide the training as described in Appendix A.
2. Provide a summary description and detailed evaluation of each seller. Provide company brochures, websites, annual reports, and other appropriate information.
3. Work with Global Construction to develop an evaluation system to evaluate each seller.
4. Provide an objective evaluation of each seller using this evaluation system.
5. Develop a list of the top five sellers for each course.
6. Provide recommendations for developing partnerships/relationships with each of the top five sellers.
7. Complete the above work no later than September 9.

Location of Work:
The seller can perform the work at any location. The seller must physically meet with representatives from Global Construction in our corporate office at least twice during the term of the contract.

Period of Performance:
Work is expected to start on or around August 20 and end no later than September 9. The seller will prepare a detailed schedule for all work required, including dates for deliverables and meetings. After meeting with representatives from Global Construction to review and update the schedule, the seller will agree to the schedule for this work.

Deliverables Schedule:
The seller will prepare a detailed schedule for all required work, including dates for all deliverables and meetings. After meeting with representatives from Global Construction to review and update the schedule, the seller will agree to the schedule for this work.
Applicable Standards:
The seller will use standard software to produce the required documentation for this project. Draft and final documents will be sent via e-mail.
Acceptance Criteria:
The seller will work closely with the project manager, Kristin Maur, to clarify expectations and avoid problems in providing acceptable work. Kristin will provide written acceptance/non-acceptance of all deliverables.
Special Requirements:
The seller's staff assigned to work on this contract must verify appropriate education and experience. The seller will work with Global Construction to make all travel arrangements and minimize travel costs.

Figure 6-25. Sample procurement statement of work

Source Selection Criteria and Supplier Evaluation Matrices

It is highly recommended that buyers use formal supplier evaluation procedures to help select sellers. In addition to reviewing their proposals or quotes, buyers should also review sellers' past performance, talk to recent customers, interview management teams, and request sample products or demos, if applicable. After doing a thorough evaluation, many organizations summarize criteria and evaluations using a **supplier evaluation matrix**—a type of weighted scoring model. Recall from Chapter 2 that a weighted scoring model provides a systematic process for selection based on numerous criteria. For example, suppliers are often evaluated on criteria related to cost, quality, technology, past performance, and management. The weights for all of the criteria must add up to 100%.

Sample Supplier Evaluation Matrix

Kristin knew her team would have to evaluate suppliers for various goods and services as part of the Just-In-Time Training project. Kristin and her team reviewed Global Construction's previously used supplier evaluation matrices, and then prepared a simple matrix to evaluate the suppliers for the qualified-sellers list, as shown in Figure 6-26. This figure was created using the supplier evaluation matrix template from the companion website, and it shows results based on three suppliers. In this example, Supplier 2 has the highest weighted score, so that supplier would be selected.

Just-In-Time Training Project Supplier Evaluation Matrix
September 9

Criteria	Weight	Supplier 1	Supplier 2	Supplier 3
Past performance	30%	70	90	70
Cost	25%	80	75	70
Educational background	25%	70	75	70
Management Approach	20%	85	80	70
Weighted Scores		**75.5**	**80.5**	**70**

Figure 6-26. Sample supplier evaluation matrix

CASE WRAP-UP

Kristin was pleased with the progress on planning for the Just-In-Time Training project. Several members of her project team and the project steering committee had complimented Kristin on her ability to get key stakeholders involved. They also liked the way she admitted her own areas of weakness and sought out expert advice. Kristin was grateful for the steering committee's suggestion to hire an outside firm early in the project to help find qualified suppliers for the training courses. Everyone felt confident that the project team had a handle on risk management. Kristin felt ready to tackle the challenges she would face in leading her team during project execution.

CHAPTER SUMMARY

Successful project managers know how important it is to develop, refine, and follow plans to meet project goals. This chapter summarizes the planning processes and outputs for quality, resource, communications, stakeholder, risk, and procurement management.

Planning outputs related to quality management include a quality management plan and quality metrics.

Planning outputs related to resource management include a resource plan, which includes a project organizational chart, responsibility assignment matrix, resource histogram, and staffing management plan. Other outputs include a team charter, resource requirements, basis of estimates, and resource breakdown structures.

Planning outputs related to communications management include a communications management plan and project website.

Planning outputs related to stakeholder management include a stakeholder engagement plan.

Risk management includes several planning processes: plan risk management, identify risks, perform qualitative risk analysis, perform quantitative risk analysis, and plan risk responses. Planning outputs related to risk management include developing a risk management plan, risk report, risk response strategies, a risk register, and risk-related contract decisions.

Planning outputs related to procurement management include procurement management plans, procurement strategies, bid documents, procurement statements of work, source selection criteria, make-or-buy decisions, independent cost estimates, and change requests.

Samples of several planning documents are provided for the Just-In-Time Training project.

QUICK QUIZ

Note that you can find additional, interactive quizzes at www.intropm.com.

1. _____ is defined as the degree to which a set of inherent characteristics fulfill requirements.

    A. Fitness for use

    B. Conformance to requirements

    C. Metrics

    D. Quality

2. _____ allow organizations to measure their performance in certain areas—such as failure rates, availability, and reliability—and compare them over time or with other organizations.

    A. Ratings

    B. Metrics

    C. Quality-control charts

    D. Checklists

3. A RACI chart is a type of _____.

    A. project organizational chart

    B. resource histogram

    C. responsibility assignment matrix

    D. project dashboard

4. A _____ describes when and how people will be added to and taken off of a project.

    A. project organizational chart

    B. resource histogram

    C. responsibility assignment matrix

    D. staffing management plan

5.   Topics such as who will receive project information and who will produce it, suggested methods or guidelines for conveying the information, frequency of communication, and escalation procedures for resolving issues should be described in a

_____.

A.   communications management plan

B.   staffing management plan

C.   team charter

D.   scope statement

6.   Suppose you are a member of Kristin's team and you are having difficulties communicating with one of the supplier management experts who is providing important content for a class you are developing. What strategy might you use to help improve communications?

A.   put all communications in writing

B.   put all communications on your project website

C.   use several different methods to communicate with this person

D.   ask Kristin to find a better person to provide the technical content

7.   What two dimensions should you use when evaluating project risks?

A.   probability and impact

B.   cost and schedule

C.   negative and positive

D.   source and responsibility

8.   A _____is a document that contains results of various risk management processes, often displayed in a table or spreadsheet format.

A.   risk event

B.   trigger

C.   risk register

D.   risk management plan

9.   You can purchase an item you need for a project for $10,000 and it has daily operating costs of $500, or you can lease the item for $700 per day. On which day will the purchase cost be the same as the lease cost?

   A.   day 5

   B.   day 10

   C.   day 50

   D.   day 100

10.   You want to have the least risk possible in setting up a contract to purchase goods and services from an outside firm. As the buyer, what type of contract should you use?

   A.   fixed price

   B.   unit price

   C.   cost reimbursable

   D.   time and materials

Quick Quiz Answers

1. D; 2. B; 3. C; 4. D; 5. A; 6. C; 7. A; 8. C; 9. C; 10. A

DISCUSSION QUESTIONS

1.   What is the main purpose of a project quality management plan? What are two metrics besides those provided in this chapter that Kristin and her team could use on the Just-In-Time Training project?

2.   What is the main purpose of a staffing management plan? What tool should you use to graphically show total staffing needs for a project? What tool should you use to clarify roles and responsibilities for work?

3.   Why is it so difficult to ensure good communication on projects? What strategies can any project team use to improve communications?

4.   Why is it important to plan for stakeholder engagement? Why is some of the information sensitive when planning how to work with stakeholders? Give examples of how you can plan in advance how to work with difficult stakeholders.

5.   Why is risk management often neglected on projects? Why is it important to take the time to identify and rank risks throughout the project's life?

6.   What is the difference between an RFP and an RFQ? Give an example of the appropriate use of each. How does procurement planning differ for government projects versus those in private industry?

EXERCISES

1. Find an example of a large project that took more than a year to complete. You can ask people at your college, university, or work about a recent project, such as a major fundraising campaign, information systems installation, or building project. Describe some of the tasks performed in planning the quality, human resource, communications, stakeholders, risk, and procurement aspects of the project. Write a one-page paper or prepare a short presentation summarizing your findings.

2. Search the Internet for "project dashboard." Find at least three different charts or examples that can be used on a project dashboard. Document your findings in a two-page paper or short presentation, including screen shots of the charts you find and your assessment of their value.

3. Your company is planning to launch an important project starting January 1, which will last one year. You estimate that you will need one half-time project manager; two full-time business analysts for the first six months; two full-time marketing analysts for the whole year; four full-time business interns for the months of June, July, and August; and one full-time salesperson for the last three months. Use spreadsheet software such as Microsoft Excel to create a stacked-column chart showing a resource histogram for this project, similar to the one shown in Figure 6-8. Be sure to include a legend to label the types of resources needed, and use appropriate titles and axis labels. You can use the resource histogram template on the companion website to make this exercise easier.

4. List three negative risk events and three positive risk events for the Just-In-Time Training project. Briefly describe each risk, and then rate each one as high, medium, or low in terms of probability and impact. Plot the results on a probability/impact matrix. Also, prepare an entry for one of the risks for the risk register.

5. Assume the source selection criteria for evaluating proposals for a project is as follows:

    *   Management approach 15%

    *   Technical approach 15%

    *   Past performance 20%

    *   Price 20%

    *   Interview results and samples 30%

Use Figure 6-26 as a guide and the supplier evaluation matrix template from the companion website to calculate the total weighted scores for three proposals. Enter scores for Proposal 1 as 80, 90, 70, 90, and 80, respectively. Enter scores for Proposal 2 as 90, 50, 95, 80, and 95. Enter scores for Proposal 3 as 60, 90, 90, 80, and 65. Add a paragraph summarizing the results and your recommendation on the spreadsheet. Print your results on one page.

6. Find at least two video clips and one article that show some of the risks involved in building and sailing the Titanic. Document your findings in a short paper, video, or presentation.

TEAM PROJECTS

1. Your organization initiated a project to raise money for an important charity. Assume that there are 1,000 people in your organization. Also, assume that you have six months to raise as much money as possible, with a goal of $100,000. Create a checklist to use in soliciting sponsors for the fundraiser, a responsibility assignment matrix for various stakeholders, a project website (just the home page), a probability/impact matrix with six potential negative risks, and a request for quote for obtaining items your team will need. Be creative in your responses. Remember that this project is entirely run by volunteers.

2. You are part of a team in charge of a project to help people in your company (500 people) lose weight. This project is part of a competition, and the top "losers" will be featured in a popular television show. Assume that you have six months to complete the project and a budget of $10,000. Develop metrics for the project, a project organizational chart, a communications management plan, and a risk register with at least three entries for the project.

3. Using the information you developed in Team Project 1 or 2, role-play a meeting to review one of these planning documents with key stakeholders. Determine who will play what role (project manager, team member from a certain department, senior managers, and so on). Be creative in displaying different personalities (a senior manager who questions the importance of the project to the organization, a team member who is very shy or obnoxious).

4. Develop a project dashboard for your team project, using Figure 6-3 as an example. Be sure to include at least eight different metrics. Document your results in a one-page paper or short presentation, showing the actual dashboard you created.

5. Perform the planning tasks (only for the knowledge areas covered in this chapter) for one of the case studies provided in Appendix C. Remember to be thorough in your planning so that your execution goes smoothly. Be sure to have your sponsor and other stakeholders provide inputs on your plans.

6. Find at least two video clips and two articles that show some of the risks involved in the Fyre Festival from April 2017, Woodstock from 1969, or another large music festival. Describe what risk planning should have been done before this event and for future events. Document your findings in a short paper, video, or presentation.

KEY TERMS

bid — A document prepared by sellers providing pricing for standard items that have been clearly defined by the buyer.

blogs — Easy-to-use journals on the Web that allow users to write entries, create links, and upload pictures, while allowing readers to post comments to particular journal entries.

communications management plan — A document that guides project communications.

conformance to requirements — The process of ensuring that the project's processes and products meet written specifications.

contingency plans — The predefined actions that the project team will take if an identified risk event occurs.

contingency reserves or **contingency allowances** — The funds held by the project sponsor that can be used to mitigate cost or schedule overruns if known risks occur.

contracts — The mutually binding agreements that obligate the seller to provide the specified products or services, and obligate the buyer to pay for them.

cost-reimbursable contract — A contract that involves payment to the seller for direct and indirect actual costs.

fallback plans — The plans that are developed for risks that have a high impact on meeting project objectives, and are put into effect if attempts to reduce the risk are not effective.

Federal Acquisition Regulation (FAR) — Regulation that provides uniform policies for acquisition of supplies and services by executive agencies in the U.S.

fitness for use — The ability of a product to be used as it was intended.

fixed-price or **lump-sum contract** — A type of contract that involves a fixed price for a well-defined product or service.

make-or-buy analysis — The process of estimating the internal costs of providing a product or service and comparing that estimate to the cost of outsourcing.

management reserves — Funds held for unknown risks that are used for management control purposes.

metric — A standard of measurement.

procurement statement of work (SOW) — A document that describes the goods or services to be purchased.

project dashboard — A graphic screen summarizing key project metrics.

project organizational chart — A graphical representation of how authority and responsibility is distributed within the project.

proposal — A document in which sellers describe what they will do to meet the requirements of a buyer.

quality — The degree to which a set of inherent characteristics fulfill requirements.

RACI charts — A type of responsibility assignment matrix that shows **R**esponsibility, **A**ccountability, **C**onsultation, and **I**nformed roles for project stakeholders.

Request for Proposal (RFP) — A document used to solicit proposals from prospective suppliers.

Request for Quote (RFQ) — A document used to solicit quotes or bids from prospective suppliers.

resource histogram — A column chart that shows the number of resources required for or assigned to a project over time.

responsibility assignment matrix (RAM) — A matrix that maps the work of the project as described in the WBS to the people responsible for performing the work.

risk — An uncertainty that can have a negative or positive effect on meeting project objectives.

risk events — The specific, uncertain events that may occur to the detriment or enhancement of the project.

risk register — A document that contains results of various risk management processes, often displayed in a table or spreadsheet format.

root cause — The real or underlying reason a problem occurs.

staffing management plan — A plan that describes when and how people will be added to and taken off of a project.

team charter — A document created to help promote teamwork and clarify team communications

time-and-material contract — A type of contract that is a hybrid of both a fixed-price and cost-reimbursable contract.

triggers — The indicators or symptoms of actual risk events.

END NOTES

[1] Dragan Milosevic, Portland State University, "Delivering Projects: What the Winners Do," PMI Conference Proceedings (November 2001).

[2] Cavan Sieczkowski, "Fyre Festival Organizers Hit With $100 Million Lawsuit," HuffPost (May 1, 2017).

[3] Kevin Lui, "Fyre Festival Was Awful, But It Had Nothing on Woodstock: A Brief History of Music Festivals Gone Wrong," Time (May 2, 2017).

[4] Weeks, J. Bruce, "Risk Determination in Highly Interactive Environments: How to Avoid the Titanic Factor in Your Project," PMI Virtual Library (2010).

[5] Cesar Pelli and Michael J. Crosbie, "Building Petronas Towers," *Architecture Week* (February 19, 2003).

[6] Rohland, Dick, "I-35W Bridge Completion Brings Closure to Minneapolis," ConstructionEquipmentGuide.com (October 4, 2008).

Chapter 7
Executing Projects

LEARNING OBJECTIVES

After reading this chapter, you will be able to:

- List the processes and outputs of project execution
- Discuss what is involved in directing and managing project work and managing project knowledge as part of project integration management, including the importance of producing promised deliverables, implementing solutions to issues, evaluating work performance data, preparing issue logs, requesting changes to a project, and managing lessons learned
- Explain the importance of creating quality reports, test and evaluation documents, and change requests as part of quality assurance
- Describe the executing processes performed as part of resource management— acquiring resources, developing the team, and managing the team
- Discuss important communications concepts, and describe the process of managing communications
- Describe the process of managing stakeholder engagement
- Understand the process of implementing risk responses
- Explain the process of conducting procurements and the need to effectively select sellers and create agreements

---

OPENING CASE

Kristin reviewed initial project plans with the steering committee for the Just-In-Time Training project. Committee members felt that everything was going well so far and that it was time to commit more resources to the project. At later steering committee meetings, Kristin brought up several challenges she was facing in executing the project plans. For example, Jamie, the supplier management expert assigned to her team half-time, was not working out. In addition, there were several conflicts between various stakeholders on how to perform certain tasks, and several people complained about a lack of communication about the project. The IT people supporting the project were overallocated, yet some of their activities were on the critical path for the project. The prototype for the supplier management introductory course was not as well received as the team had hoped, and Kristin was afraid that the seller might demand more money to make major changes to the course. Kristin would need to use her experience—especially her soft (interpersonal) skills—as well as advice from the project steering committee to deal with these and other challenges.

INTRODUCTION

Whereas project planning is considered to be the most unappreciated project management process group, project execution is the most noticed. Of course, good plans are important, but it is even more important to execute them well. In fact, *Fortune* magazine summarized research showing that without a doubt, the main reason chief executive officers (CEOs) failed was poor execution. Failed CEOs simply did not get things done, were indecisive, and did not deliver on commitments. The same is true for project managers and all leaders. Stakeholders expect to see results from their projects through effective execution.

Recall that, in general, the majority of a project's time and budget is spent on project execution. Many of the deliverables and outputs created in the other process groups are fairly similar from project to project, but no two projects are ever executed in the exact same way. Why? Because projects involve uncertainty or risk. No one can ever predict the challenges that project teams will face in trying to meet project goals. This chapter summarizes the main processes involved in executing projects and discusses some challenges that Kristin faced in managing the execution of the Just-In-Time Training project.

SUMMARY OF EXECUTING PROCESSES AND OUTPUTS

Figure 7-1 summarizes processes and outputs of project execution by knowledge area, based on the *PMBOK® Guide – Sixth Edition*. Notice that not every knowledge area is included, and change requests and updates to the project management plan, project documents, and organizational process assets are outputs of several of these knowledge areas. Although there are many planning processes related to scope, schedule, cost, and risk management, these knowledge areas do not have processes directly related to project execution. Changes to the triple constraint and risk management are addressed in the next chapter on monitoring and controlling projects. This chapter focuses on processes and outputs that project teams perform to execute projects and provides specific examples for Global Construction's Just-In-Time Training project.

Knowledge area	Executing process	Outputs
Project integration management	Direct and manage project work	Deliverables
		Work performance data
		Issue log
		Change requests
		Project management plan updates
		Project documents updates
		Organizational process assets updates
	Manage project knowledge	Lessons learned register
		Project management plan updates
		Organizational process assets updates
Project quality management	Manage quality	Quality report
		Test and evaluation documents
		Change requests
		Project management plan updates
		Project documents updates
Project resource management	Acquire resources	Physical resource assignments
		Project team assignments
		Resource calendars
		Change requests
		Project management plan updates
		Project documents updates
		Enterprise environmental factors updates
		Organizational process assets updates
		Team performance assessments
	Develop team	Change requests
		Project management plan updates
		Project documents updates
		Enterprise environmental factors updates
		Organizational process assets updates
	Manage team	Change requests
		Project management plan updates
		Project documents updates
		Enterprise environmental factors updates
Project communications management	Manage communications	Project communications
		Project management plan updates
		Project documents updates
		Organizational process assets updates
Project risk management	Implement risk responses	Change requests
		Project documents updates

Project procurement management	Conduct procurements	Selected sellers
		Agreements
		Change requests
		Project management plan updates
		Project documents updates
		Organizational process assets updates
Project stakeholder management	Manage stakeholder engagement	Change requests
		Project management plan updates
		Project documents updates
		Organizational process assets updates

Figure 7-1. Executing processes and outputs

PROJECT INTEGRATION MANAGEMENT

During project execution, the project manager must direct and manage stakeholders to complete the project. Project managers can follow several important practices to help accomplish this challenging job:

- *Coordinate planning and execution:* As mentioned earlier, the main purpose of project planning is to guide execution. If the project manager and team did a good job planning, the plans will be easier to execute. As things change, team members need to update the plans to keep everyone working on the same page.

- *Develop and use soft skills:* Several studies of project managers suggest that soft skills (for example, strong leadership, effective team building, strong communication, motivation, negotiation, conflict management, and problem solving) are crucial to the success of project managers, especially during project execution. Project managers must lead by example in demonstrating the importance of creating good project plans and then following them in project execution. Project managers often create plans for things they need to do themselves, such as meeting with key stakeholders, reviewing important information, and so on. If project managers follow through on their own plans, their team members are more likely to do the same.

- *Provide a supportive organizational culture:* Good project execution requires a supportive organizational culture. For example, organizational procedures can help or hinder project execution. If an organization has useful guidelines and templates for project management that everyone in the organization follows, it will be easier for project managers and their teams to plan and do their work. If the organization uses the project plans as the basis for performing and monitoring progress during execution, the culture will promote the relationship between good planning and execution. Even if the organizational culture is not supportive, project managers can create a supportive culture within their own project and work on improving the culture in other parts of the organization.

- *Break the rules when needed:* Even with a supportive organizational culture, project managers might sometimes find it necessary to break the rules to produce project results in a timely manner. When project managers break the rules, politics will play a role in the results. For example, if a particular project requires use of nonstandard software, the project manager must use his or her political skills to convince concerned stakeholders of the need to break the rules.

- *Capitalize on product, business, and application area knowledge:* The application area of the project directly affects project execution because the products of the project are produced during project execution. For example, if a project involves constructing a new building, the project manager and other stakeholders would need to use their expertise in architecture, engineering, and construction to produce the product successfully. Project managers should use their expertise to guide their team and make important decisions.

- *Use project execution tools and techniques:* For example, following a project management methodology and using a project management information system can help project execution go more smoothly. The project management methodology should include guidelines on how to communicate project status, handle conflicts, work with suppliers and other stakeholders, and perform other important tasks.

As listed in Figure 7-1, the main outputs of directing and managing project work are deliverables, work performance data, issue logs, change requests, project management plan updates, project documents updates, and organizational process assets updates. Performing updates is self-explanatory. These other outputs will be described in more detail, along with a discussion of how to implement solutions to problems that often occur during execution.

Deliverables

Most project sponsors would say that the most important output of any project is its deliverables. Recall that deliverables are products or services produced or provided as part of a project. They include product and process-related items. For the Just-In-Time Training project at Global Construction, key product-related deliverables include the training materials and courses (instructor-led, Web-based, and CD-ROM). Process-related deliverables related to developing and delivering those training materials and courses include researching existing training and meeting with potential partners.

Sample Deliverables

Because the Just-In-Time Training project is fictitious, it is impossible to show the actual training materials, courses, and other deliverables produced during execution. Because you are probably reading this book as part of a course and have taken other courses in both an instructor-led or online fashion, you have some feel for what training materials and courses are like. Recall that several of the training courses for this project must be available on a just-in-time basis (that is, they must be available whenever the employee wants to learn), so deliverables must be created to provide effective Web-based and/or CD-ROM instruction.

Note the word *effective*. The main objective of this training is to provide employees with the knowledge and skills they need to do their jobs when they need it. Just because training is available around the clock does not mean that it is effective. The section on quality assurance later in this chapter describes the importance of ensuring quality during project execution.

Work Performance Data

One of a project manager's main jobs during project execution was collecting, assessing, and communicating work performance data. This data includes key performance indicators, technical performance measures, actuals (for start and end dates, durations, and costs), etc. In addition to reviewing this data, sometimes project managers use the "management by wandering around" (MBWA) approach, meaning they informally observe and talk to project team members and other stakeholders as much as possible. Kristin used this approach because she wanted to know firsthand how project activities were progressing, and she wanted to offer suggestions as often as possible. Of course, she also used more formal communications, such as status reports, the project dashboard (which summarized key project metrics, as described in Chapter 6), survey results, and course evaluations, to address work performance on the project.

Sample Work Performance Data

A common way to summarize work performance data is by using a milestone report. Recall that a milestone is a significant point or event in a project, such as completing a major deliverable or awarding a major contract. Figure 7-2 provides part of a milestone report for the Just-In-Time Training project. Notice that in addition to listing the milestones, the report lists the planned date for completion (in month/day format), the status, the person responsible for the milestone, and issues/comments. The format and content of the milestone report (and all other reports) are defined in the communications management plan. Project 2016 also includes a standard milestone report, as described in Appendix A.

Just-In-Time Training Project Milestone Report
September 1

Milestone	Date	Status	Responsible	Issues/Comments
Researched existing training	8/13	Complete	Jamie (replaced by Abner)	Many basic courses available, but not much advanced/tailored training. (Note: Replaced Jamie with better candidate for project after Jamie completed this task)
Presented supplier management training survey results to steering committee	8/24	Complete	Kristin	Great feedback. Many people stressed the need to have instructor-led training and mentors for soft skills development
Meetings with potential partners	9/21	In progress	Kristin/ Contracting	May need more time for meetings

Figure 7-2. Sample milestone report for reporting work performance data

Issue Logs

Many project managers keep an **issue log** to document, monitor, and track issues that need to be resolved for effective work to take place. An **issue** is a matter under question or dispute that could impede project success. Issues could include situations in which people disagree, situations that need more clarification or investigation, or general concerns that need to be addressed. It is important to acknowledge issues that can hurt team performance and take action to resolve them. A critical issue is anything that prevents progress on scheduled activities. If the activity is on the critical path, resolution is urgent. There should be an issue escalation process that ensures issue resolution action. For critical activities, resolution time limits and responsible roles must be defined. For some issues, the steering committee may be the final resolution authority.

Sample Issue Log

Figure 7-3 shows part of an early issue log that Kristin and her team used to help document and manage the resolution of issues on their project. The issue log includes columns for the issue number, the issue description, the impact of the issue on the project, the date the issue was reported, who reported the issue, who the issue resolution was assigned to, the priority of the issue (High, Medium, or Low), the due date to report back on the issue, the status of the issue, and comments related to the issue. Project managers can tailor the format of issue logs as needed. The project management software that Kristin's team used included an online issue log that could be sorted and filtered various ways. For example, Kristin always sorted issues by priority so that she could focus on high priorities. She also sorted them by who reported the issue and who was assigned to each issue to make sure that the appropriate people were making progress.

Issue Log as of October 1

Issue #	Issue Description	Impact on Project	Date Reported	Reported By	Assigned To	Priority (H/M/L)	Due Date	Status	Comments/ Follow-up
1	Key project team member is not working out	Can severely hurt project because Jamie is our supplier management expert	Aug 2	Kristin	Kristin	H	Sep 2	Open	Working with Jamie and appropriate managers to find a replacement
2	IT staff that is performing survey is over allocated	Delaying the survey will delay the entire project because it is a critical task	Sep 26	Mohamed	Kristin	H	Aug 5	Closed	Paid overtime was approved
Etc.									

Figure 7-3. Sample issue log

Change Requests

Often, several change requests emerge during project execution. Recall that a process for handling changes should be defined during project planning as part of the project management plan. Chapter 8, which covers monitoring and controlling projects, provides detailed information on handling changes. It is important during project execution to formally and informally request appropriate changes. Project managers, team members, suppliers, and other stakeholders can make change requests, so it is important to have a good process in place for handling them.

Sample Change Request

Successful project teams use well-defined processes and standard forms for requesting project changes. Some changes are requested using other established change processes. For example, when Kristin requested that Jamie be replaced with Abner as the project team member from the supplier management department, she used Global Construction's personnel transfer process. Jamie's department head and the human resources department handled necessary paperwork for the reassignment. For other change requests—especially those that may impact achieving scope, time, or cost goals of the project—a formal change request form should be submitted according to the project's change management plan.

Figure 7-4 provides a sample of a completed change request form for the Just-In-Time Training project. It is important to have a good justification for the requested change and address the benefits of incurring any additional costs. In this case, if the additional $550 is not provided, the entire project will be delayed.

Just-In-Time Training Project Change Request

Project Name: Just-In-Time Training Project
Date Request Submitted: September 22
Title of Change Request: Provide overtime to get survey results in time
Change Order Number: A200-17
Submitted by: Kristin Maur

Change Category:__Scope   __Schedule   **X** Cost   __Technology   __Other
Description of change requested:
In order to avoid a schedule slip and have appropriate internal resources available, we are requesting the approval of paid overtime for creating and distributing the survey for the supplier management course.
Events that made this change necessary or desirable:
The IT person assigned to our project has several other important projects on-hand. If these scheduled activities are delayed, the entire project will be delayed as they are on the critical path.
Justification for the change/why it is needed/desired to continue/complete the project:
We must send out and analyze the survey in a timely manner since we need the information to develop the first supplier management course and select an appropriate supplier.
Impact of the proposed change on:
Scope: None   **Schedule:** None   **Cost:** $550

Staffing: One IT person will work 10 hours of paid overtime basis over a period of several weeks.

Risk: Low. This person suggested the paid overtime and has successfully worked overtime in the past.

Other: None

Suggested implementation if the change request is approved: Include the overtime pay in the normal paycheck.

Required approvals:

Name/Title	Date	Approve/Reject
Evan George/Affected Employee		
Stella Jacobs/Employee's Supervisor		
Julia Portman, VP of IT		

Figure 7-4. Sample change request

Implemented Solutions to Problems

Of course, all project teams face numerous problems. Some surface early during project initiation or planning, but some do not occur until project execution, when many things are happening at once. Many problems can be avoided by doing a good job of initiating, planning, or monitoring and controlling the project, but other problems cannot be avoided. Some common problems encountered during project execution include the following:

1. The project sponsor and/or other senior managers are not very supportive of the project.

2. Project stakeholders, such as people who would use the products and services the project is attempting to create, are not sufficiently involved in project decision-making.

3. The project manager is inexperienced in managing people, working in a particular organization, or understanding the application area of the project.

4. The project objectives/scope are unclear.

5. Estimates for time and cost goals are unreliable or unrealistic.

6. Business needs/technology changes have impacted the project.

7. People working on the project are incompetent or unmotivated.

8. There are poor conflict-management procedures.

9. Communications are poor.

10. Suppliers are not delivering as promised.

The first five problems should have been addressed during project initiation or planning (and were addressed in previous chapters), but they can also cause difficulties during execution. Addressing business and technology changes are discussed in the next chapter on monitoring and controlling. The last four problems are discussed in this chapter and presented in the context of the Just-In-Time Training project.

Sample Implemented Solutions to Problems

Kristin Maur had been working hard to direct and manage project execution, but she encountered several problems. The following sections discuss the problems of incompetent or unmotivated people working on the project and poor conflict-management procedures. Later sections discuss strategies for improving communications and supplier delivery.

Issues with Competence and Motivation

Jamie, the project team member assigned to work half-time from the supplier management department, was not contributing much to the project. Jamie's main role was to provide expertise in developing the supplier management courses. She was well qualified for this assignment, having over 10 years of experience with Global Construction managing major accounts with suppliers. (Recall that supplier management was the most important training topic for the project.) Kristin knew that Jamie was very good at negotiating with and managing suppliers, but Jamie felt that she was assigned to the project primarily because she was available, having recently finished another large project. Although Jamie was assigned to work on this project from its start, she was on vacation for most of the first month and seemed uninterested in the project when she was around. Kristin tried her best to motivate her, but she could see that Jamie was simply not the right person for the project. (See a later section in this chapter on motivation.) Kristin talked to Jamie directly, and she admitted that she would much rather deal directly with suppliers than work on this training project. Just two months into the project, Kristin used her experience and contacts within the company to find a suitable replacement. She worked through the project steering committee and other managers to quickly approve the personnel change.

Poor Conflict Management

Most large projects are high-stake endeavors that are highly visible within organizations. They require tremendous effort from team members, are expensive, require significant resources, and can have an extensive impact on the way work is done in an organization. When the stakes are high, conflict is never far away, and even small projects with low budgets have conflicts—it is a natural part of work and life in general. Project managers should lead their teams in developing norms for dealing with various types of conflicts that might arise. For example, team members should know that disrespectful behavior toward any project stakeholder is inappropriate, and that team members are expected to try to work out small conflicts themselves before elevating them to higher levels. The team charter, created during project planning, should address team conduct and conflict management.

Blake and Mouton (1964) delineated five basic modes for handling conflicts. Each strategy can be considered as being high, medium, or low on two dimensions: importance of the task or goal, and importance of the relationship between the people having the conflict.

1. *Confrontation/problem-solving*: When using the **confrontation mode**, project managers directly face a conflict using a problem-solving approach that allows affected parties to work through their disagreements. This approach is also called the problem-solving mode. It is best used when *both the task and the relationship are of high importance*. For example, Kristin confronted Jamie when she was not working well on the project. They discussed the problem and decided it was best for both parties for Jamie to leave the project team. They also discussed who could take her place. This mode reflects a win/win approach.

2. *Compromise/reconcile*: With the **compromise mode**, project managers use a give-and-take approach to resolve conflicts, bargaining and searching for solutions that will bring some degree of satisfaction to all the parties in a dispute. This give-and-take approach works best when both the task and the relationship are of medium importance. For example, suppose one of Kristin's stakeholders wanted to add a new topic to one of the courses for no extra cost, and the supplier wanted payment for it, as agreed to in their contract. They could compromise and add the new topic at a discounted cost. This mode reflects a lose/lose approach, since both parties are giving up something.

3. *Smooth/accommodate:* When using the **smoothing mode**, the project manager de-emphasizes or avoids areas of differences and emphasizes areas of agreement. This method, sometimes called the accommodating mode, is best used when the *relationship is of high importance and the task is of low importance*. For example, two members of the project steering committee might totally disagree on whether they should provide incentive bonuses to suppliers for achieving outstanding ratings on courses. Kristin could use the smoothing mode to ensure that the relationship between the steering committee members remains harmonious by discussing with these team members the areas in which they agree and by downplaying the topic of bonuses during meetings.

4. *Force/direct*: The **forcing mode** can be viewed as the win-lose approach to conflict resolution. People exert their viewpoints even though they contradict the viewpoints of others. This approach is appropriate when *the task is of high importance and the relationship is of low importance*. For example, if you are competing against another firm for a contract, it may be appropriate to use the forcing mode.

5. *Withdraw/avoid*: When using the **withdrawal mode**, project managers retreat or withdraw from an actual or potential disagreement. This approach, sometimes called the avoidance mode, is the least desirable conflict-handling mode. It may be appropriate when *both the task and the relationship are of low importance*.

Note that the *PMBOK® Guide – Sixth Edition* uses the term collaboration instead of confrontation as being synonymous with problem-solving. Other sources list collaborating as a sixth conflict-handling mode. Using the **collaborating mode**, decision makers incorporate different viewpoints and insights to develop consensus and commitment. *It can also be effective when both the task and relationship are of high importance.*

Figure 7-5 summarizes information about these conflict-handling modes.

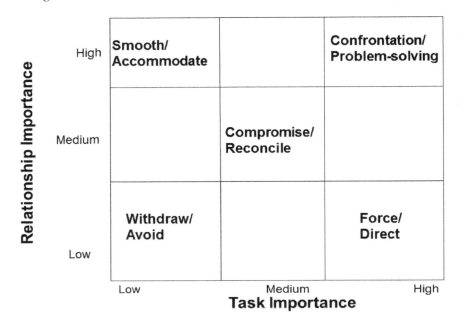

Figure 7-5. Conflict-handling modes

Effective project managers often use confrontation or collaborating for conflict resolution instead of the other modes. The term *confrontation* may be misleading. This mode focuses on a win-win problem-solving approach, in which all parties work together to find the best way to solve the conflict.

Project managers must also realize that not all conflict is bad. In fact, conflict can often be good. Conflict often produces important results, such as new ideas, better alternatives, and motivation to work harder and more collaboratively. Project team members might become stagnant or develop **groupthink**—conformance to the values or ethical standards of a group— if there are no conflicting viewpoints on various aspects of a project. Research suggests that task-related conflict, which is derived from differences over team objectives and how to achieve them, often improves team performance. Emotional conflict, however, which stems from personality clashes and misunderstandings, often depresses team performance. Project managers should create an environment that encourages and maintains the positive and productive aspects of conflict.

WHAT WENT WRONG?

Groupthink can definitely cause problems on projects. Forbes Coaches Council provided a list of ten negative effects of groupthink:

1. Common responses to threat, such as everyone becoming more risk averse under pressure
2. Limits and inclusion, where people feel safe yet closed-minded by not having diverse ideas.
3. Focusing only on what is known, which can cause critical information to be uncovered
4. The "corporate nod," preventing transparent and truthful conversions
5. Extinction, where the entire project is dissolved for not being able to address changing dynamics
6. Blind commitments to best practices, which can prevent taking new approaches when needed
7. Lack of engagement, causing some workers to feel unheard and underappreciated
8. Disasters, like the financial crisis caused by blind trust in financial institutions
9. Drowned-out voices, caused by the most vocal people drowning out potentially great ideas
10. Over confidence in your decision, because everyone supports it, even though they shouldn't. [1]

Managing Project Knowledge

PMI added this new process to the PMBOK® Guide in 2017 to highlight the importance of managing project knowledge. There are two basic types of knowledge:

1. **Explicit knowledge**: This type of knowledge can be easily explained using words, pictures, or numbers and is easy to communicate, store, and distribute. Examples include information found in text books and encyclopedias as well as project documents and plans.
2. **Tacit knowledge**: Unlike explicit knowledge, tacit knowledge, sometimes called informal knowledge, is difficult to express and is highly personal. Examples include beliefs, insight, and experience. It is often shared through conversations and interactions between people. Many organizations set up programs like mentorships, communities of practice, or workshops to assist in passing on tacit knowledge.

Knowledge management should be done before, during, and after projects are completed. It is often very difficult to accomplish. Organizations can provide explicit knowledge in writing or other formats, including audio, pictures, and videos. They can also build a culture of trust and sharing so people work together to pass on tacit knowledge. One of the main outputs of managing project knowledge is a lessons learned register.

Lessons Learned Register

A lessons learned register should document challenges, problems, realized risks and opportunities, and other content to assist in knowledge management on current and future projects. It is best if project team members document lessons learned throughout the life of the project. At the end of the project, all lessons learned should be both discussed with the team and archived in a lessons learned repository, a key organizational process asset.

Sample Lessons Learned Register

Throughout the project, Kristin and her team documented lessons learned in a simple register. Instead of asking each member of the Just-In-Time Training project team and the project managers from the major supplier organizations to create entries individually, Kristin decided to use a technique in which key stakeholders attended a sticky-note party to document lessons learned. Instead of writing lessons learned in a traditional way, people met, enjoyed refreshments, wrote down all the lessons they had learned on sticky notes, and then posted them to the wall. It was an enjoyable way for everyone to get together and share what they had learned from the project. After they finished, Kristin summarized the inputs in a list, as shown in Figure 7-6, that everyone could access on the project website.

ID	Date identified	Owner	Name	Category	Situation	Recommendation
01	9/22	Kristin	Overtime	Cost	IT person was overbooked. Decided to pay overtime to finish survey work in time and not delay project end date.	Don't be afraid to suggest paid overtime, even though it's not used often at our organization.
02	10/1	Kim	Curriculum blog	Tech-nology	Kim was having trouble getting inputs on specific requirements for curriculum, so she set up a blog and provided incentives for inputs.	Encourage people to be creative. Allow use of some of the budget for incentives related to producing that deliverable.

Figure 7-6. Sample lessons learned register

MANAGING QUALITY

It is one thing to develop a plan for ensuring quality on a project; it is another to ensure delivery of quality products and services. The term **quality assurance** is often used to describe the activities related to satisfying the relevant quality standards for a project. It addresses the following question: Are we doing what we said we would do, when we said we would do it, and in the way we said we would do it? For example, it was important for the Just-In-Time Training project that the course materials included content that would meet participants' needs. Kristin made sure that the people developing those materials reviewed results of the needs assessment, were experts in the field, and reviewed the content with Global Construction, Inc. managers in those areas (supplier management, negotiating skills, project management, and software applications). Another goal of managing quality is continual quality improvement. Many companies understand the importance of quality and have entire departments dedicated to this discipline. These companies have detailed processes in place to make sure that their products and services conform to various quality requirements. They also know they must produce products and services at competitive prices. To be successful in today's global business environment, successful companies develop their own best practices and evaluate other organizations' best practices to continuously improve the way they do business.

Key outputs of managing quality include a quality report, test and evaluation documents, change requests, project management plan updates, and project documents updates. There are several tools and techniques involved in managing quality, as described in the next section.

Quality Improvement Tools and Techniques

It is important for organizations to use common techniques to identify areas in which they would benefit from taking actions to improve quality. While there are many tools and techniques, several common ones include benchmarking, quality audits, and process analysis.

- **Benchmarking** generates ideas for quality improvements by comparing specific project practices or product characteristics to those of other projects or products within or outside of the organization itself. For example, one reason that Global Construction initiated the Just-In-Time Training project was because it discovered that its cost of training per employee was higher than that of similar firms. The amount of money that organizations spend on training is a benchmark. As another example, many organizations have overall course ratings using a Likert scale, with 1 being the lowest rating and 5 being the highest. A benchmark for a good rating might be an average rating of 3.0 or higher. If training participants rated the prototype supplier management course lower than 3.0 on average, then Kristin's team would need to take corrective actions to improve the quality of the course. Note that benchmarking can also be used during quality planning.

- A **quality audit** is a structured review of specific quality management activities that helps identify lessons learned, which could improve performance on current or future projects. In-house auditors or third parties with expertise in specific areas can perform quality audits, which can be either scheduled or random. Recall that several of the main goals of the Just-In-Time Training project were to reduce training costs at Global Construction, provide training when it was needed, and improve employee productivity. By establishing measurement techniques for monitoring these goals and performing an audit to see how well they are being met, Kristin's team can see how well they are doing in meeting specific goals. For example, they could send out a monthly survey asking employees if they are getting training when they need it and if it is helping improve their productivity. A quality audit could be done periodically to review the survey results. If there is a sudden decrease in ratings, Kristin's team would need to take corrective actions.

- **Process analysis** involves analyzing how a process operates and determining improvements. Many organizations use **lean**, a system based on the Toyota Production System to help improve results and efficiency by eliminating waste and reducing idle time and non-value added activities. As mentioned in Chapter 3, kanban is a visual technique used to improve workflow. Root cause analysis is also often part of process analysis. **Cause-and-effect diagrams**—also called fishbone diagrams (because their structure resembles a fishbone) or Ishikawa diagrams (named after their creator)—can assist in ensuring and improving quality by finding the root causes of quality problems. Recall from Chapter 6 that a root cause is the real or underlying reason a problem occurs. The following sections provide examples of kanban boards and cause-and-effect diagrams.

BEST PRACTICE

In the late 1940s, Toyota engineers noticed that grocery store clerks restocked items by their store's inventory instead of their vendor's supply. Their "just-in-time" approach of ordering more items only when they were near sellout sparked the engineers to pioneer a new approach to engineering using a kanban system by matching inventory with demand to achieve better throughput. (The word kanban is Japanese for sign.) In 2005 David J. Anderson, a founder of the agile movement and author of several books, visited Japan. While visiting Tokyo's Imperial Palace gardens, he realized that kanban was used at the gardens to manage the flow of visitors and that it could be applied to many processes, including software development.

Kanban uses five core properties:
1. Visual workflow
2. Limit work-in-process
3. Measure and manage flow
4. Make process policies explicit
5. Use models to recognize improvement opportunities

In his book called *Kanban*, Anderson explains that the application of kanban is different for every team. Visitors to his company saw that no set of kanban boards were alike, and all their teams used a different process to develop software. Anderson explains that kanban requires some type of process to already be in place, and it is used to incrementally improve the process. It gives teams permission to be different. "Each team's situation is different. They evolve their process to fit their context…The simple act of limiting work-in-progress with kanban encourages higher quality and greater performance."[2]

Sample Kanban Board

An important topic covered in the Just-In-Time Training project course materials was how to streamline several processes involved in supplier management and project management. Several stakeholders wanted the training to include the use of kanban boards. As explained in the Best Practice feature, kanban boards are tailored for every team using them. The purpose of the boards is to help the team visualize and improve their workflow. Figure 7-7 provides a very simple example of using kanban boards. Notice that the main categories where tasks are placed include To Do, In Progress, and Done. Team members work together to complete all of the tasks, clearly showing which ones need to be done (in the To Do section), which ones are being worked on (in the In Progress section), and which ones are completed (in the Done section). People using kanban boards can tailor the concept to meet their needs. For example, they could create a physical board or use a wall in their office environment, write the names of tasks on sticky notes, and physically move the sticky notes along the board. Or, a team could use an online tool to enter and track their workflow. They could add people's names to each task, color code tasks, include a calendar, or use whatever approach helps the team improve their performance.

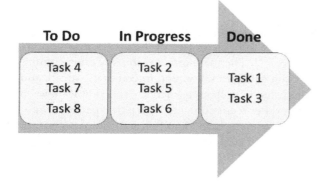

Figure 7-7. Sample kanban board

Figure 7-8 provides an amusing example showing how people spend their time trying to streamline the wrong tasks. Remember to focus on improving workflow and performance in getting work done!

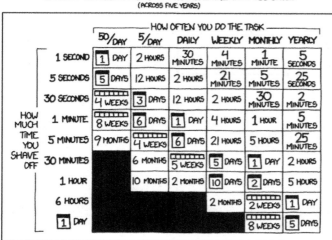

Figure 7-8. Is it worth the time? (www.xkcd.com)

Sample Cause and Effect Diagram

After participants rated the prototype supplier management course less than 3.0 on average, Kristin's team knew they had to recommend corrective actions. They first decided to determine the root cause of the problem. The prototype course was available in three formats: instructor-led, Web-based, and CD-ROM. The Web-based and CD-ROM courses were virtually identical, except participants in the Web-based course could also access interactive discussion boards and chat rooms as they accessed the course via the Internet. The evaluations for the instructor-led course were actually above average; however, the Web-based and CD-ROM courses were rated below average.

The student evaluation forms provided some open-ended feedback, so Kristin and her team decided to use that information plus other possible causes of the low ratings to prepare a cause-and-effect diagram, as shown in Figure 7-9. The main effect is the low course ratings, and potential causes are grouped into several main categories: content, interactivity, speed, and graphics/fonts. Potential subcategories are listed in each area, such as "too simple" and "not enough examples" under content. Kristin and her team contacted the participants in the prototype courses to get more specific information to help identify the root cause(s) of the low ratings. When they discovered that the majority of respondents rated the CD-ROM course poorly because it lacked interactivity, they discussed the option of supplementing the course with the Web-based interactivity features, such as the discussion board and chat room. Respondents were enthusiastic about the Web-based course, except for those who did not always have an Internet connection or had a very slow connection. A simple solution would be to have them use the CD-ROM for most of the course and use the Internet for the discussion board and chat room. Because the other potential causes were not the main reasons for the low ratings, they were not addressed.

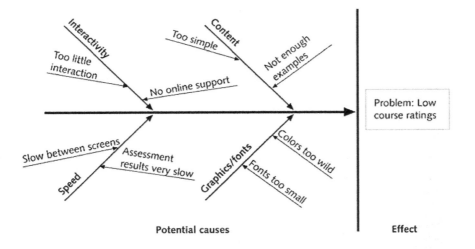

Figure 7-9. Sample cause-and-effect diagram

Kristin and her team recommended that the discussion board and chat room features of the Web-based course be integrated into the CD-ROM course. The supplier who developed both courses said it would be a very simple change and would not affect time or cost estimates.

PROJECT RESOURCE MANAGEMENT

Effective use of resources is crucial to project execution. The main processes project managers perform include acquiring resources, developing the team, and managing the team. Key outputs include physical resource assignments, project team assignments, resource calendars, team performance assessment, change requests, and updates to the project management plan, enterprise environmental factors, and organizational process assets.

Resource calendars are simply calendars for each resource showing work assignment dates. Before discussing resource assignments and team performance assessment, it is important to understand basic concepts related to dealing with people in a work setting. Key concepts include motivation, influence, and effectiveness.

Motivation

Psychologists, managers, coworkers, teachers, parents, and most people in general still struggle to understand what motivates people, or why they do what they do. **Intrinsic motivation** causes people to participate in an activity for their own enjoyment. For example, some people love to read, write, or play an instrument because it makes them feel good. **Extrinsic motivation** causes people to do something for a reward or to avoid a penalty. For example, some young children would prefer *not* to play an instrument, but do so to receive a reward or avoid a punishment. Why do some people require no external motivation whatsoever to produce high-quality work while others require significant external motivation to perform routine tasks? Why can't you get someone who is extremely productive at work to do simple tasks at home? Mankind will continue to try to answer these overarching questions, but a basic understanding of motivational theory will help all of us as we have to work or live with other people.

Maslow's Hierarchy of Needs

Abraham Maslow, a highly respected psychologist who rejected the dehumanizing negativism of psychology in the 1950s, is best known for developing a hierarchy of needs. In the 1950s, proponents of Sigmund Freud's psychoanalytic theory were promoting the idea that human beings were not the masters of their destiny and that their actions were governed by unconscious processes dominated by primitive sexual urges. During the same period, behavioral psychologists saw human beings as controlled by the environment. Maslow argued that both schools of thought failed to recognize unique qualities of human behavior: love, self-esteem, belonging, self-expression, and creativity. He argued that these unique qualities enable people to make independent choices, which give them full control over their destiny.

Figure 7-10 shows the basic pyramid structure of **Maslow's hierarchy of needs**, which states that people's behaviors are guided or motivated by a *sequence* of needs. At the bottom of the hierarchy are physiological needs, such as air, water, and food. After physiological needs are satisfied, safety needs—such as shelter from bad weather, lack of physical or mental abuse, and a low-crime environment—guide behavior. After safety needs are satisfied, social needs—such as having friends, belonging to groups, and having a sense of community—come to the forefront, and so on up the hierarchy. Examples of esteem needs include personal achievement, recognition, and respect, whereas self-actualization needs include a sense of fulfillment and belief that one is working to his or her potential. The order of these needs in the pyramid is significant. Maslow suggests that each level of the hierarchy is a prerequisite for the level above. For example, it is not possible for people to consider self-actualization if they have not addressed basic needs concerning security and safety. People in an emergency situation, such as a flood or hurricane, cannot be concerned with personal growth but will be motivated solely by the requirements of personal survival. After a particular need is satisfied, however, it no longer serves as a potent motivator of behavior.

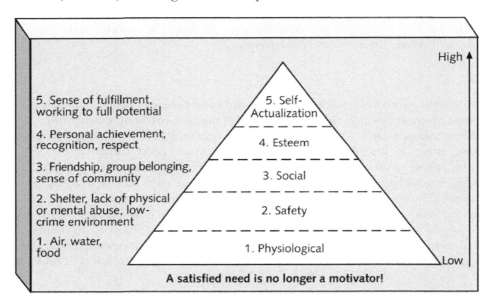

Figure 7-10. Maslow's hierarchy of needs (Schwalbe, Information Technology Project Management, Sixth Edition, 2010)

The bottom four needs in Maslow's hierarchy—physiological, safety, social, and esteem needs—are referred to as deficiency needs, and the highest level, self-actualization, is considered a growth need. Only after meeting deficiency needs can individuals act on growth needs. Self-actualized people are problem-focused, have an appreciation for life, are concerned about personal growth, and can have peak experiences.

Most people working on corporate projects probably have their basic physiological and safety needs met. If someone has a sudden medical emergency or is laid off from work, however, physiological and safety needs move to the forefront. To motivate project team members, the project manager needs to understand each person's motivation, especially with regard to social, esteem, and self-actualization needs. For example, team members new to a company and city might be motivated by social needs. To address social needs, a project manager could organize gatherings and social events for new workers. If a project manager knew a team member was interested in pursuing an advanced degree, he or she could offer suggestions on graduate programs, provide information on tuition reimbursement policies, and allow the team member some scheduling flexibility to balance work and school.

Maslow's hierarchy conveys a message of hope and growth. People can work to control their own destinies and naturally strive to achieve higher and higher needs. Some cultures disagree with Maslow's philosophy and have other beliefs on motivation. Recent brain research also suggests that there are physiological reasons for certain behaviors. In any case, successful project managers know that to provide appropriate motivation and maximize team performance, they must both meet project goals and understand team members' personal goals and needs.

Herzberg's Motivation-Hygiene Theory

Frederick Herzberg, a psychologist and professor, is best known for distinguishing between motivational factors and hygiene factors when considering motivation in work settings. He called factors that cause job satisfaction motivators, and factors that cause dissatisfaction hygiene factors. A hygiene factor is a basic necessity, such as proper heating or cooling during extreme weather. Heating or air-conditioning do not in themselves provide team satisfaction, but without it you might have disgruntled staff on very cold or hot workdays.

Head of Case Western University's psychology department, Herzberg wrote the book *Work and the Nature of Man* in 1966 and the famous *Harvard Business Review* article "One More Time: How Do You Motivate Employees?" in 1968. Herzberg analyzed the factors that affected productivity among a sample of 1,685 employees. Popular beliefs at that time were that work output was most improved through larger salaries, more supervision, or a more attractive work environment. According to Herzberg, these hygiene factors would cause dissatisfaction if not present but would not motivate workers to do more if present. Herzberg found that people were motivated to work mainly by feelings of personal achievement and recognition. Motivators, Herzberg concluded, included achievement, recognition, the work itself, responsibility, advancement, and growth.

In his books and articles, Herzberg explained why attempts to use positive factors such as reducing time spent at work, implementing upward-spiraling wages, offering fringe benefits, providing human relations and sensitivity training, and so on did not instill motivation. He argued that people want to actualize themselves; they need stimuli for their growth and advancement needs in accordance with Maslow's hierarchy of needs. Factors such as achievement, recognition, responsibility, advancement, and growth produce job satisfaction and are work motivators.

McClelland's Acquired-Needs Theory

David McClelland proposed that an individual's specific needs are acquired or learned over time and shaped by life experiences. The main categories of acquired needs include achievement, affiliation, and power. Normally, one or two of these needs is dominant in individuals.

- *Achievement*: People with a high need for achievement (nAch) seek to excel and tend to avoid both low-risk and high-risk situations to improve their chances of achieving something worthwhile. Achievers need regular feedback and often prefer to work alone or with other high achievers. Managers should give high achievers challenging projects with achievable goals. Achievers should receive frequent performance feedback, and although money is not an important motivator to them, it is an effective form of feedback as a way to keep score.

- *Affiliation*: People with a high need for affiliation (nAff) desire harmonious relationships with other people and need to feel accepted by others. They tend to conform to the norms of their work group and prefer work that involves significant personal interaction. Managers should try to create a cooperative work environment to meet the desires of people with a high need for affiliation.

- *Power*: People with a need for power (nPow) desire either personal power or institutional power. People who need personal power want to direct others and can be seen as bossy. People who need institutional, or social, power want to organize others to further the goals of the organization. Management should provide those seeking institutional power with the opportunity to manage others, emphasizing the importance of meeting organizational goals.

The Thematic Apperception Test (TAT) is a tool to measure the individual needs of different people using McClelland's categories. The TAT presents subjects with a series of ambiguous pictures and asks them to develop a spontaneous story for each picture, assuming they will project their own needs into the story.

McGregor's Theory X and Theory Y

Douglas McGregor was one of the great popularizers of a human relations approach to management, and he is best known for developing Theory X and Theory Y. In his research, documented in his 1960 book *The Human Side of Enterprise*, McGregor found that although many managers spouted the right ideas, they actually followed a set of assumptions about worker motivation that he called Theory X (sometimes referred to as classical systems theory). People who believe in Theory X assume that workers dislike and avoid work if possible, so managers must use coercion, threats, and various control schemes to get workers to make adequate efforts to meet objectives. Theory X managers assume that the average worker wants to be directed and prefers to avoid responsibility, has little ambition, and wants security above all else. When research seemed to demonstrate that these assumptions were not valid, McGregor suggested a different series of assumptions about human behavior that he called Theory Y (sometimes referred to as human relations theory). Managers who believe in Theory Y assume that individuals do not inherently dislike work but consider it as natural as play or rest. The most significant rewards are the satisfaction of esteem and self-actualization needs, as described by Maslow. McGregor urged managers to motivate people based on these more valid Theory Y notions.

Thamhain and Wilemon's Influence Bases

Many people working on a project do not report directly to project managers, and project managers often do not have control over project staff that report to them. For example, people are free to change jobs. If they are given work assignments they do not like, many workers will simply quit or transfer to other departments or projects. H. J. Thamhain and D. L. Wilemon investigated the approaches project managers use to deal with workers and how those approaches relate to project success. They identified nine influence bases available to project managers:

1. *Authority:* The legitimate hierarchical right to issue orders

2. *Assignment:* The project manager's perceived ability to influence a worker's assignment to future projects

3. *Budget:* The project manager's perceived ability to authorize the use of discretionary funds

4. *Promotion:* The ability to improve a worker's position

5. *Money:* The ability to increase a worker's pay and benefits

6. *Penalty:* The project manager's perceived ability to dispense or cause punishment

7. *Work challenge:* The ability to assign work that capitalizes on a worker's enjoyment of doing a particular task, which taps an intrinsic motivational factor

8. *Expertise:* The project manager's perceived specialized knowledge that others deem important

9. *Friendship:* The ability to establish friendly personal relationships between the project manager and others

Top management grants authority to the project manager, but not necessarily the power to control personnel assignments, budgets, promotions, and penalties. Team members, however, may misperceive their project manager's sphere of influence and expect him to have the power, for example, to grant promotions and transfers. If project managers' power is limited, they can still influence workers by providing challenging work, and they can increase the power of their influence by using expertise and friendship.

Thamhain and Wilemon found that projects were more likely to fail when project managers relied too heavily on using *authority, money, or penalty* to influence people. When project managers used *work challenge and expertise* to influence people, projects were more likely to succeed. The effectiveness of work challenge in influencing people is consistent with Maslow's and Herzberg's research on motivation. The importance of expertise as a means of influencing people makes sense on projects that involve special knowledge. For example, people working on a project to build a spaceship would expect the project manager to have appropriate education and experience in that area. They would also be impressed if he or she had actually worked on other space projects or traveled into space.

VIDEO HIGHLIGHTS

Books and articles are written every year on the topic of human motivation. Many videos are also available on this subject. One humorous example is Jimmy Kimmel's popular video on the Handsome Men's Club, illustrating Jimmy's Theory X approach to management.

Another popular, more educational video is by Daniel Pink. RSA Animate used its whiteboard drawing technique to summarize key points from Pink's book in a YouTube video called "Drive: The surprising truth about what motivates us." Pink narrates the video, summarizing several studies about how money often causes people to perform worse on tasks that involve cognitive skills. He suggests that organizations pay people enough to take money off the table and stop using the carrot and stick approach to motivation.

Pink suggests that managers focus on the following three motivators:

- *Autonomy:* People like to be self-directed and have freedom in their work. Maslow, Herzberg, and other researchers also found that people are motivated by autonomy. Pink gives an example of how a software company in Australia, Atlassian, lets people decide what they want to work on and with whom for one day every quarter. Workers show the results of their work that day in a fun meeting. This one day of total autonomy has produced many new products and fixes to problems.

- *Mastery:* People like to get better at things, such as playing an instrument, participating in a sport, writing software, and other work-related activities. Pink states that several products like Unix, Apache, and Wikipedia were created because people enjoyed the challenge and mastery involved.

- *Purpose:* People want to work for a good purpose. When the profit motive is separated from the purpose motive, people notice and do not perform as well. Many great products were created for a purpose. For example, the founder of Skype wanted to make the world a better place, and Steve Jobs wanted to put a ding in the universe.

Covey's Effectiveness Research

Stephen Covey, author of *The 7 Habits of Highly Effective People* and several other books, expanded on the work done by Maslow, Herzberg, and others to develop an approach for helping people and teams become more effective. Covey's first three habits of effective people—be proactive, begin with the end in mind, and put first things first—help people achieve a private victory by becoming independent. After achieving independence, people can then strive for interdependence by developing the next three habits—think win/win; seek first to understand, then to be understood; and synergize. (**Synergy** is the concept that the whole is equal to more than the sum of its parts.) Finally, everyone can work on Covey's seventh habit—sharpen the saw—to develop and renew their physical, spiritual, mental, and social/emotional selves.

Project managers can apply Covey's seven habits to improve effectiveness on projects, as follows:

1. *Be proactive:* Covey, like Maslow, believes that people can be proactive and choose their responses to different situations. Project managers must be proactive, anticipate, and plan for problems and inevitable changes on projects. They can also encourage team members to be proactive in their work.

2. *Begin with the end in mind:* Covey suggests that people focus on their values, what they really want to accomplish, and how they really want to be remembered in their lives. He suggests writing a mission statement to help achieve this habit. Many organizations and projects have mission statements that help them focus on their main purpose. The project manager must have and share the vision of the final outcome of the project.

3. *Put first things first:* Covey developed a time-management system and matrix to help people prioritize their time. He suggests that most people need to spend more time doing things that are *important but not urgent.* Important but not urgent activities include planning, reading, and exercising. Project managers should focus on important and not urgent activities, such as developing various project plans, building relationships with major project stakeholders, and mentoring project team members. They also need to avoid focusing only on important and urgent activities—that is, putting out fires.

4. *Think win/win:* Covey presents several paradigms of interdependence, with "think win/win" being the best choice in most situations. When you use a win/win paradigm, parties in potential conflict work together to develop new solutions that make them all winners. Project managers should strive to use a win/win approach in making decisions, but sometimes, especially in competitive situations, they must use a win/lose paradigm.

5. *Seek first to understand, then to be understood:* **Empathic listening** is listening with the intent to understand by putting yourself in the shoes of the other person. You forget your personal interests and focus on truly understanding the other person and feeling what he or she is feeling. To truly understand other people, you must learn to focus on others first. When you practice empathic listening, you can begin two-way communication. Making empathic listening a habit enables project managers to fully understand their stakeholders' needs and expectations.

6. *Synergize:* In projects, a project team can synergize by creating collaborative products that are much better than a collection of individual efforts. For example, engineers helped the crew of the *Apollo 13* return to Earth safely by working together to develop a solution to their potentially deadly technical problems. One person came up with an idea, which prompted another person to have an idea, and so on. The team devised a solution that no one person could have discovered. Covey also emphasizes the importance of valuing differences in others to achieve synergy. Synergy is essential to many complex projects; in fact, several major

breakthroughs in technology, such as manned flight, drug development, and various computer technologies, occurred because of synergy.

7. *Sharpen the saw:* When you practice sharpening the saw, you take time to renew yourself physically, spiritually, mentally, and socially. The practice of self-renewal helps people avoid burnout. Project managers must make sure that they themselves and their project team have time to retrain, reenergize, and occasionally even relax to avoid burnout.

Several experts suggest that empathic listening is a powerful skill for project managers and their teams to possess. Understanding what motivates key stakeholders and customers can mean the difference between project success and project failure. After project managers and team members begin to practice empathic listening, they can communicate and work together to tackle problems more effectively.

Before you can practice empathic listening, you first have to get people to talk to you. In many cases, you must work on developing a rapport with other people before they will really open up to you. **Rapport** is a relationship of harmony, conformity, accord, or affinity. Without rapport, people cannot begin to communicate, or the strong person might dominate the weaker one. For example, if you meet someone for the first time and find that you cannot communicate, you need to focus on developing rapport.

One technique for establishing rapport is using a process called mirroring. **Mirroring** is the matching of certain behaviors of the other person. Although establishing rapport involves a number of complex human interactions, the simple technique of mirroring can sometimes help. You can mirror someone's voice tone and/or tempo, breathing, movements, or body postures. For example, when Kristin was negotiating with suppliers, she found that some of them were very abrupt, while she was fairly laid back. Kristin would use mirroring by matching the supplier's posture or voice tone to develop rapport and a strong negotiating position. In fact, mirroring was one of the skills emphasized in the negotiations course the Just-In-Time Training project team was developing.

You can see from the material covered in this chapter so far that many important topics related to motivation, influence, and effectiveness are relevant to project management. Projects are done by and for people, so it is important for project managers and team members to understand and practice key concepts related to these topics. Kristin must keep these topics in mind and use her knowledge and skills to successfully execute the project.

WHAT WENT RIGHT?

A young business consultant who worked in the IT department of a major aerospace firm met with a senior project manager and his core team. The project involved providing updated electronic kits for a major aircraft program. The company was losing money on the project because the upgrade kits were not being delivered on time. Most buyers had written severe late-penalty fees into their contracts, and other customers were threatening to take their business elsewhere. The project manager blamed it all on the IT department for not letting his staff access the information system directly to track the status of kit development and delivery. The tracking system was old and difficult to use.

The consultant was warned that this project manager was very difficult to work with. When he entered the meeting room with three of his staff, all older men, he threw his books on the table and started yelling at the young consultant and her even younger assistant. Instead of backing down, the consultant mirrored the project manager's behavior and started yelling right back at him. He stood back, paused, and said, "You're the first person who's had the guts to stand up to me. I like that!" After that brief introduction, rapport was established, and everyone began communicating and working together as a team to solve the problem at hand.

You should, of course, take this message with a grain of salt. Few circumstances merit or benefit from yelling matches, but occasionally they cut through the tangle of human complexities. (The story is completely true; the author of this book, who very rarely yells at anyone, was the business consultant and had just completed a weeklong course on communications skills.)

Acquiring Resources

As described earlier, project resources include both physical and human resources. Physical resources include equipment, supplies, and materials. Human resources include the people required to perform the project work. There's a saying that the project manager who is the smartest person on the team has done a poor job of recruiting! After developing a staffing management plan during project planning, project managers must work with other managers in their organizations to assign personnel to their project or to acquire additional human resources needed to staff their project. Project managers with strong influencing and negotiating skills are often good at getting internal people to work on their project. However, the organization must ensure that people assigned to the project best fit the project's requirements, and that these people are motivated to remain on the project. (See the previous section on motivation.)

Problems that often occur when assigning resources are availability and overallocation. You can use resource loading and leveling to help address these problems.

Resource Loading and Leveling

Resource loading refers to the number of individual resources an existing schedule requires during specific time periods. Resource loading helps project managers develop a general understanding of the demands a project will make on the organization's resources (physical and human), as well as on individual people's schedules. Project managers often use resource histograms, as described in Chapter 6, to depict period-by-period variations in resource loading.

A histogram can be very helpful in determining staffing needs or in identifying staffing problems.

A resource histogram can also show when work is being overallocated to a certain resource or group. **Overallocation** means more resources than are available are assigned to perform work at a given time. For example, Figure 7-11 provides a sample resource histogram created in Microsoft Project. (The data was actually from one of the template files Microsoft used to provide with the software.) This histogram illustrates how much one individual, Joe Franklin, is assigned to work on the project each week. The percentage numbers on the vertical axis represent the percentage of Joe's available time that is allocated for him to work on the project. The top horizontal axis represents time in weeks. Note that Joe Franklin is overallocated most of the time. For example, for most of March and April and part of May, Joe's work allocation is 300 percent of his available time. If Joe is normally available eight hours per day, this means he would have to work 24 hours a day to meet this staffing projection! Many people don't use the resource assignment features of project management software properly.

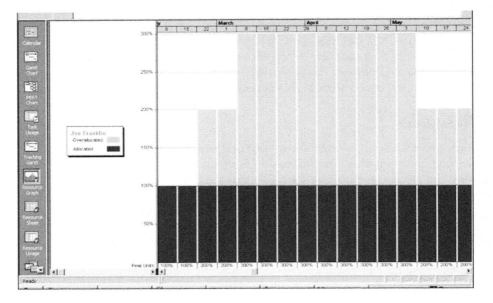

Figure 7-11. Sample resource histogram showing an overallocated individual

Resource leveling is a technique for resolving resource conflicts by delaying tasks. It is a form of network analysis in which resource management concerns drive scheduling decisions (start and finish dates). The main purpose of resource leveling is to create a smoother distribution of resource usage. Project managers examine the network diagram for areas of slack or float, and to identify resource conflicts. For example, you can sometimes remove overallocations by delaying noncritical tasks, which does not result in an overall schedule delay. Other times you will need to delay the project completion date to reduce or remove overallocations. See Appendix A for information on using Project 2016 to level resources using both of these approaches. Overallocation is one type of resource conflict. If a certain resource is overallocated, the project manager can change the schedule to remove resource overallocation. If a certain resource is underallocated, the project manager can change the schedule to try to improve the use of the resource. Resource leveling, therefore, aims to minimize period-by-period variations in resource loading by shifting tasks within their slack or float allowances.

Figure 7-12 illustrates a simple example of resource leveling. The network diagram at the top of this figure shows that Activities A, B, and C can all start at the same time. Activity A has a duration of two days and will take two people to complete; Activity B has a duration of five days and will take four people to complete; and Activity C has a duration of three days and will take two people to complete. The histogram on the lower-left of this figure shows the resource usage if all activities start on day one. The histogram on the lower right of Figure 7-12 shows the resource usage if Activity C is delayed two days, its total slack allowance. Notice that the lower-right histogram is flat or leveled; that is, its pieces (activities) are arranged to take up the least space (lowering the highest number of workers needed). You may recognize this strategy from the computer game Tetris, in which you earn points for keeping the falling shapes as level as possible. The player with the most points (most level shape allocation) wins.

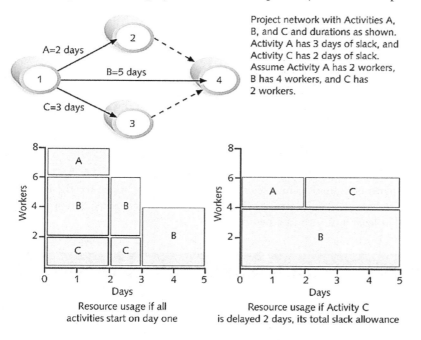

Figure 7-12. Resource leveling example (Schwalbe, Information Technology Project Management, Sixth Edition, 2010)

Resource leveling has several benefits:

- When resources are used on a more constant basis, they require less management. For example, it is much easier to manage a part-time project member who is scheduled to work 20 hours per week on a project for the next three months than it is to manage the same person who is scheduled to work 10 hours one week, 40 the next, 5 the next, and so on.

- Resource leveling may enable project managers to use a just-in-time inventory type of policy for using subcontractors or other expensive resources. For example, a project manager might want to level resources related to work that must be done by specific subcontractors such as testing consultants. This leveling might allow the project to use four outside consultants full-time to do testing for four months instead of spreading the work out over more time or needing to use more than four people. The latter approach is usually more expensive.

- Resource leveling results in fewer problems for project personnel and accounting departments. Increasing and decreasing labor levels and human resources often produce additional work and confusion. For example, if a person with expertise in a particular area is only assigned to a project two days a week and another person they need to work with is not assigned to the project those same days, they cannot work well together. The Accounting department might complain when subcontractors charge a higher rate for billing fewer than 20 hours a week on a project. The accountants will remind project managers to strive for getting the lowest rates possible.

- Resource leveling often improves morale. People like to have some stability in their jobs. It is very stressful for people not to know from week to week or even day to day what projects they will be working on and with whom they will be working.

Sample Physical Resource Assignments

Kristin worked with her team to create physical resource assignments. Figure 7-13 shows an example of the resource assignments made when searching for classroom space for the many instructor-led classes delivered as part of the project. Many organizations require that spaces like classrooms be reserved at least a month in advance.

Physical Resource	Date(s) Reserved	Description
Classroom 1	1/12	Need this room for executive course
Classroom 2	12/15, 1/20, 1/26, 2/3, 2/9	Need this room or Classroom 4
Classroom 3	2/3	Need this room for software applications course – has required student computers

Figure 7-13. Sample physical resource assignments

Sample Project Team Assignments

Kristin worked with managers in the human resource department and other managers to staff the internal project team members for the Just-In-Time Training project. She also made staffing changes, such as replacing Jamie, the supplier management expert assigned to the team. Although Jamie had great qualifications, she was not a good fit for the project. Jamie needed a break after coming off a big project, and she did not feel that she would personally enjoy working on the Just-In-Time Training project. Kristin updated the project staff by replacing Jamie with Abner. Kristin was also involved with other staffing updates as people joined and left the project team.

To keep everyone up to date on current project team assignments, Kristin provided a current team roster on the project website, including team member names, roles, and contact information. As suppliers were added to the project, she included supplier staff information as well. Figure 7-14 provides a sample of part of the team roster for the project.

Team Roster
September 1

Project Name: Just-In-Time Training Project

Name	Role on Project	Position	Email	Phone	Location
Mike Sundby	Project Champion	VP of HR	msundby@ globalconstruction.com		
Lucy Camerena	Project Sponsor	Training Director	lcamerena@ globalconstruction.com		
Kristin Maur	Project Manager	Project Manager	kmaur@ globalconstruction.com		
Mohamed Abdul	Team Member	Senior programmer/ analyst	mabdul@ globalconstruction.com		
Kim Johnson	Team Member	Curriculum designer	kjohnson@ global construction.com		
Abner Tomas	Team Member	Supplier management expert	atomas@ globalconstruction.com		

Figure 7-14. Sample team roster

Developing the Project Team

Even if a project manager has successfully recruited enough skilled people to work on a project, he or she must ensure that people can work together as a team to achieve project goals. Many failed projects have been staffed by highly talented individuals; however, it takes teamwork to complete projects successfully. The main goals of team development are to help people work together more effectively, improve interpersonal skills, increase motivation, reduce attrition, and improve overall project performance.

Dr. Bruce Tuckman published his four-stage model of team development in 1965 and modified it to include an additional stage in the 1970s. The **Tuckman model** describes five stages of team development:

1. *Forming* involves the introduction of team members, either at the initiation of the team or as new members are introduced. This stage is necessary, but little work is actually achieved.

2. *Storming* occurs as team members have different opinions as to how the team should operate. People test each other, and there is often conflict within the team.

3. *Norming* is achieved when team members have developed a common working method, and cooperation and collaboration replace the conflict and mistrust of the previous phase.

4. *Performing* occurs when the emphasis shifts to reaching the team goals rather than working on team process. Relationships are settled, and team members are likely to build loyalty toward each other. At this stage, the team can manage tasks that are more complex and cope with greater change. Note that not all teams are able to progress through the team development stages to reach the performing level.

5. *Adjourning* involves the breakup of the team after they successfully reach their goals and complete the work. Teams might also adjourn due to poor performance or project cancellation.

There is an extensive body of literature on team development. This section highlights a few important tools and techniques for team development, including training, team-building activities, and reward and recognition systems. Keep in mind that having teams focus on completing specific tasks is often the most effective way to help teams be productive.

Training

In addition to traditional, instructor-led training, many organizations provide e-learning opportunities for their employees so that they can learn specific skills at any time and any place, similar to several of the courses being developed for the Just-In-Time Training project. It is important to make sure that the timing and delivery methods for the training are appropriate for specific situations and individuals. Project managers often recommend that people take specific training courses to improve individual and team development. For example, Kristin recommended that Mohamed, the IT member of her project team, take training courses in designing e-learning courses so that he could contribute even more to this project. Early in the project, Kristin also organized a special team-building session for her internal project team.

Team-Building Activities

Many organizations provide in-house team-building training activities, and many also use specialized services provided by external companies that specialize in this area. Two common approaches to team-building activities include using physical challenges and psychological preference indicator tools.

Sometimes, organizations have teams of people go through certain physically challenging activities to help them develop as a team. Military basic training or boot camps provide one example. Men and women who want to join the military must first make it through basic training, which often involves several strenuous physical activities such as rappelling off towers, running and marching in full military gear, going through obstacle courses, passing marksmanship training, and mastering survival training. Many non-military organizations use a similar approach by sending teams of people to special locations, where they work as a team to navigate white-water rapids, climb mountains or rocks, participate in ropes courses, and so on.

More often, organizations have teams participate in mental team-building activities in which they learn about themselves, about each other, and how to work as a group most effectively. It is important for people to understand and value each other's differences to work effectively as a team. Two common tools used in mental team building include the Myers-Briggs Type Indicator and the Wilson Learning Social Styles Profile. Effective teams include a variety of personalities. The main purpose of these tools is to help people understand each other and learn to adjust their personal communication styles to work well as a team.

The **Myers-Briggs Type Indicator (MBTI)** is a popular tool for determining personality preferences. During World War II, Isabel B. Myers and Katherine C. Briggs developed the first version of the MBTI based on psychologist Carl Jung's theory of psychological type. The four dimensions of psychological type in the MBTI are as follows:

1. *Extrovert/Introvert (E/I):* This first dimension determines if you are generally extroverted or introverted. The dimension also signifies whether people draw their energy from other people (extroverts) or from inside themselves (introverts). About 75 percent of people in the general population are extroverts.

2. *Sensation/Intuition (S/N):* This second dimension relates to the way you gather information. Sensation (or Sensing) type people take in facts, details, and reality and describe themselves as practical. Intuitive type people are imaginative, ingenious, and attentive to hunches or intuition. They describe themselves as innovative and conceptual. About 75 percent of people in the general population have a preference for sensation.

3. *Thinking/Feeling (T/F):* This third dimension represents thinking judgment and feeling judgment. Thinking judgment is objective and logical, and feeling judgment is subjective and personal. The general population is generally split evenly between these two preferences.

4. *Judgment/Perception (J/P):* This fourth dimension concerns people's attitude toward structure. Judgment type people like closure and task completion. They tend to establish deadlines and take them seriously, expecting others to do the same. Perceiving types prefer to keep things open and flexible. They regard deadlines more as a signal to start rather than complete a project and do not feel that work must be done before play or rest begins. People are generally split evenly between these two preferences.

There are 16 MBTI categories based on combinations of the four dimensions. For example, one MBTI category is ESTJ, another is INFP, and another is ENTP. Project managers can often benefit from knowing their team members' MBTI profiles by adjusting their management styles for each individual. For example, if the project manager is a strong N and one of the team members is a strong S, the project manager should take the time to provide more concrete, detailed explanations when discussing that person's task assignments. Project managers might also want to make sure that they have a variety of personality types on their team. For example, if all team members are strong introverts, it might be difficult for them to work well with other stakeholders who are often extroverts.

Many organizations use Wilson Learning's Social Styles Profile in team-building activities. Psychologist David Merril, who helped develop the Social Skills Profile, categorizes four approximate behavioral profiles, or zones. People are perceived as behaving primarily in one of four zones, based on their assertiveness and responsiveness:

- "Drivers" are proactive and task oriented. They are firmly rooted in the present, and they strive for action. Adjectives to describe drivers include pushy, severe, tough, dominating, harsh, strong-willed, independent, practical, decisive, and efficient.

- "Expressives" are proactive and people oriented. They are future oriented and use their intuition to look for fresh perspectives on the world around them. Adjectives to describe expressives include manipulating, excitable, undisciplined, reacting, egotistical, ambitious, stimulating, wacky, enthusiastic, dramatic, and friendly.

- "Analyticals" are reactive and task oriented. They are past oriented and strong thinkers. Adjectives to describe analyticals include critical, indecisive, stuffy, picky, moralistic, industrious, persistent, serious, expecting, and orderly.

- "Amiables" are reactive and people oriented. Their time orientation varies depending on whom they are with at the time, and they strongly value relationships. Adjectives to describe amiables include conforming, unsure, ingratiating, dependent, awkward, supportive, respectful, willing, dependable, and agreeable.

Figure 7-15 shows these four social styles and how they relate to assertiveness and responsiveness. Note that the main determinants of the social style are levels of assertiveness— if you are more likely to tell people what to do or ask what should be done—and how you respond to tasks—by focusing on the task itself or on the people involved in performing the task. For example, a driver is assertive in telling other people what to do and focuses on completing tasks. An amiable prefers to ask others what to do and focuses on pleasing people versus completing tasks.

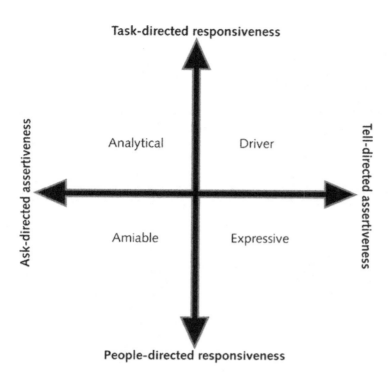

Figure 7-15. Social styles of Wilson Learning (Schwalbe, Information Technology Project Management, Sixth Edition, 2010)

Knowing the social styles of project stakeholders can help project managers understand why certain people may have problems working together. For example, drivers are often very impatient working with amiables, and analyticals often have difficulties understanding expressives. Project managers can use their facilitation skills to help all types of people communicate better with each other and focus on meeting project goals.

Reward and Recognition Systems

Another important tool for promoting team development is the use of team-based reward and recognition systems. If management rewards teamwork, it promotes or reinforces people to work more effectively in teams. Some organizations offer bonuses, trips, or other rewards to workers who meet or exceed company or project goals. In a project setting, project managers can recognize and reward people who willingly work overtime to meet an aggressive schedule objective or go out of their way to help a teammate. If teamwork is the essential goal, project managers should not reward people who work overtime just to get extra pay or because of their own poor work or planning. They should, however, recognize individuals who volunteer to put in additional time to meet a deadline or show other exemplary behavior.

Project managers must continually assess their team's performance. When they identify weaknesses in individuals or in the entire team, it's their job to find the best way to develop their people and improve performance.

Sample Team Performance Assessment

Project managers assess team performance in several different ways. Note that the term performance assessment is used for project teams while performance appraisal is for individuals. As mentioned earlier, Kristin believed in management by wandering around, and she liked to have many short, informal discussions with various stakeholders, especially her project team members. She also observed them working alone and as a team, and assessed the quality of deliverables they produced. Kristin and other project managers at Global Construction also filled out performance appraisals for each team member once a year or when a project was completed. These performance appraisals can be addressed in the team charter during project planning or discussed in early team meetings.

Kristin also felt that it was important for people to assess their own performance and the performance of their teammates. She talked to each team member individually and the team as a group about this assessment because she knew that some people felt uncomfortable evaluating themselves or other people. She stressed that she had successfully used this approach in the past, and she would keep the information confidential. Her main goal was to help everyone work well together on the project. Figure 7-16 is a sample of an informal questionnaire that Kristin periodically asked her project team members to fill out to assist in performance assessment. Kristin would discuss each person's assessment and take corrective actions as needed.

Team Performance Assessment

August 1

Project Name: Just-In-Time Training Project

Individual's Name: _____   **Project Manager:** <u>Kristin Maur</u>

Date: _____

1. Using a scale of 0-100, assess how you think **the project team** is performing: ___
2. Explain the rationale behind the above score.
3. Using a scale of 0-100, assess how **you** are performing on this project: _____
4. Explain the rationale behind the above score. What are your roles and responsibilities, and how well have you performed them?
5. Briefly assess each team member's performance. If you had to give each person a score between 0-100, what would it be?
6. To compare individual contributions, if you had 100 points to allocate to your team, how would you allocate them?
7. What suggestions do you have for improving team performance?

Figure 7-16. Sample team performance assessment

Managing the Project Team

Another project resource management process performed as part of executing a project is managing the project team, which, of course, is no small task. After assessing team performance and related information, the project manager must decide if changes to the project should be requested or if updates need to be made to enterprise environmental factors, organizational process assets, or the project management plan. Project managers also must use their interpersonal and team skills to find the best way to motivate and manage each team member, as described earlier in this chapter.

Examples of important interpersonal and team skills include leadership, influence, effective decision making, empathy, creativity, and group facilitation. A few approaches to help manage the project team include:

- *Observation and conversation:* It is hard to assess how your team members are performing or how they are feeling about their work if you seldom watch and evaluate their performance or discuss these issues with them. Many project managers, like Kristin, like to physically see and hear their team members at work. Informal or formal conversations about how a project is going can provide crucial information. For virtual workers, project managers can still observe and discuss work and personal issues via e-mail, telephone, video chat, or other communications media.

- *Feedback:* People expect and appreciate timely performance feedback. Project managers should recognize good performance often. Likewise, if a team member hands in sloppy or late work, the project manager should determine the reason for this behavior and take appropriate action. Perhaps the team member had a death in the family and could not concentrate. Perhaps the team member was planning to leave the project. The reasons for the behavior would have a strong impact on the action the project manager would take.

- *Conflict management:* Few projects are completed without any conflict. Some types of conflict are actually desirable on projects, but many are not. As described previously in this chapter, there are several ways to handle conflicts. It's important for project managers to understand strategies for handling conflicts and to proactively manage them.

Project management information systems are another useful tool to help manage project teams. After entering and assigning people to specific activities in the system, the project manager can run reports to check the progress on their work. Knowing this information in a timely manner makes it easier to take corrective action quickly, if needed.

General Advice on Managing Teams

Effective project managers must be good team leaders. Suggestions for ensuring that teams are productive include the following:

- Be patient and kind with your team. Assume the best about people; do not assume that your team members are lazy and careless.

- Fix the problem instead of blaming people. Help people work out problems by focusing on behaviors.

- Establish regular, effective meetings. Focus on meeting project objectives and producing positive results.

- Allow time for teams to go through the basic team-building stages of forming, storming, norming, performing, and adjourning, as described previously in this chapter. Do not expect teams to work at the highest performance level from the start; moreover, not all teams will even reach the performing level.

- Limit the size of work teams to three to seven members to enhance communications.

- Plan some social activities to help project team members and other stakeholders become acquainted. Make the social events fun and not mandatory.

- Stress team identity. Create traditions that team members enjoy.

- Nurture team members and encourage them to help each other. Identify and provide training that will help individuals and the team as a whole become more effective.

- Acknowledge individual and group accomplishments.

- Take the additional actions necessary to work with virtual team members. If possible, have a face-to-face or phone meeting at the start of a virtual project or when introducing a virtual team member. Screen people carefully to make sure they can work effectively in a virtual environment. Clarify how virtual team members will communicate.

PROJECT COMMUNICATIONS MANAGEMENT

Good communications management is also crucial to project execution. The process of managing communications involves gathering information to create, distribute, store, retrieve, and dispose of project communications in accordance with the communications management plan. Disposal does not mean discarding. It means putting documents in a defined place, and document retention regulations may determine document disposal policies. The main outputs of the manage communications process are project communications and updates to project documents, the project management plan, and organizational process assets.

Important Project Communications Concepts

Because communications are a crucial part of executing projects, it is important to address important concepts related to improving project communications. Key concepts include formal and informal communications, nonverbal communications, using the appropriate communications medium, understanding individual and group communication needs, and the impact of team size on project communications.

Formal and Informal Communications

It is not enough for project team members to submit formal status reports to their project managers and other stakeholders and assume that everyone who needs to know that information will read the reports. In fact, many people may prefer to have a two-way conversation about project information rather than reading detailed reports, e-mails, or Web pages to try to find pertinent information. These people may want to know the people working on their projects and develop a trusting relationship with them, and so they use informal discussions about the project to develop these relationships. Therefore, project managers must be good at nurturing relationships through good communication. Many experts believe that the difference between good project managers and excellent project managers is their ability to nurture relationships and use empathic listening skills, as described earlier.

Nonverbal Communications

People make or break projects, and people like to interact with each other to get a true feeling for how a project is going. Research poses the theory that in a face-to-face interaction, 58 percent of communication is through body language, 35 percent through how the words are said, and a mere 7 percent through the content or words that are spoken. The author of this information (see *Silent Messages* by Albert Mehrabian, 1980) was careful to note that these percentages were specific findings for a specific set of variables. Even if the actual percentages are different in verbal project communications today, it is safe to say that it is important to pay attention to more than just the actual words someone is saying. Nonverbal communications, such as a person's tone of voice and body language, are often more important than the words being used.

Using the Appropriate Communications Medium

Different types of media—such as hard copy, phone calls, voice mail, e-mail, texts, face-to-face meetings, blogs, websites, videos, and various forms of social media (Facebook, Twitter, LinkedIn, YouTube, Instagram, etc.)—are suited to different communication needs. For example, if you were trying to assess commitment of project stakeholders, a meeting would be the most appropriate medium to use. A phone call would be adequate, but the other media would not be appropriate. Project managers must assess the needs of the organization, the project, and stakeholders in determining which communication medium to use, and when. The media choices are detailed in the communications management plan and stakeholder engagement plan.

Although social media and mobile devices can be great tools, they can also cause problems, as discussed in the following Media Snapshot.

MEDIA SNAPSHOT

Some companies encourage workers to use social media tools to get to know their colleagues better, especially for global work teams. A 2011 survey, however, shows that companies have changed their tune after realizing that worker productivity often suffers due to social media and other distractions. According to harmon.ie, nearly 60% of work interruptions involved either using tools like social networks, text messaging, and IM. The survey found that 45% of employees work only 15 minutes or less without getting interrupted, and 53% waste at least one hour a day due to distractions. Based on an average salary of $30 per hour, that wasted hour a day translates into $10,375 of lost productivity per worker each year. 68% of survey respondents said their employers use corporate policies and/or technologies to minimize distractions at work, with the most popular policy of blocking access to Facebook and other websites unrelated to work.[3]

Psychologists have even created a term—Internet addiction disorder (IAD)—for the increasingly common addiction to Web-based activity. Many children suffer from this disorder, especially in Asian countries like China, Taiwan, and South Korea. "Earlier research has found some changes in the brain of people who are hooked on the Web, and a new study shows reductions in volume of certain areas of the brain and in its white matter – the highways of connection between brain cells – of young people who are addicted to the Internet. What's interesting is that these brain changes mirror the ones in people who are addicted to other kinds of things, like heroin, for example."[4]

Although the U.S. has not officially recognized Internet addiction as a disorder, a recent study found that 59 percent of parents thought their teens were addicted to mobile devices, and 50 percent of the teens felt the same way. Several rehabilitation centers have been created to help deal with IAD, such as those run by the reSTART program.[5]

Understanding Individual and Group Communication Needs

Many top managers think they can remediate project delays simply by adding people to a project. Unfortunately, this approach often causes setbacks because of the increased complexity of communications. In his popular book *The Mythical Man-Month*, Frederick Brooks illustrates this concept very clearly. People are not interchangeable parts. You cannot assume that an activity originally scheduled to take two months of one person's time can be done in one month by two people. A popular analogy is that you cannot take nine women and produce a baby in one month![6]

In addition to understanding that people are not interchangeable, it is also important to understand individuals' personal preferences for communications. People have different personality traits, which often affect their communication preferences. For example, if you want to praise a project team member for doing a good job, an introvert might be more comfortable receiving that praise in private, whereas an extrovert might like everyone to hear about his or her good work. An intuitive person might want to understand how something fits into the big picture, whereas a sensing person might prefer more focused, step-by-step details. A strong thinker might want to know the logic behind information, whereas a feeling person might want to know how the information affects him or her personally, as well as other people. Someone who is a judging person might be very driven to meet deadlines with few reminders, whereas a perceiving person might need more assistance in developing and following plans.

Geographic location and cultural backgrounds also add to the complexity of project communications. For example, if project stakeholders are in different countries, it is often difficult or impossible to schedule times for two-way communication during normal working hours. Language barriers can also cause communication problems—for example, the same word may have very different meanings in different languages. Times, dates, and other units of measure are also interpreted differently. People from some cultures also prefer to communicate in ways that may be uncomfortable to others. For example, managers in some countries still do not allow workers of lower ranks or women to give formal presentations.

The Impact of Team Size on Project Communications

Another important aspect of information distribution is the number of people involved in a project. As the number of people involved increases, the complexity of communications increases because there are more communications channels, or pathways, through which people can communicate. The number of communications channels in relation to the number of people involved can be calculated as follows:

number of communications channels = n(n-1)/2

where *n* is the number of people involved.

For example, two people have one communications channel: (2(2–1))/2 = 1. Three people have three channels: 3(3–1))/2 = 3. Four people have six channels, five people have 10, and so on. You can see that as the number of people communicating increases, the number of communications channels increases rapidly. A soccer team with eleven people on the field have people have 55 channels! The lesson is a simple one: If you want to enhance communications, you must consider the interactions among different project team members and stakeholders.

It is often helpful to form several smaller teams within a large project team to help improve project communications. Amazon founder and CEO Jeff Bezos has a "two pizza rule" to help communications. He says you should never have a meeting where two pizzas cannot feed he entire group!

As you can see, information distribution involves more than creating and sending status reports or holding periodic meetings. Many good project managers know their personal strengths and weaknesses in this area and surround themselves with people who complement their skills. It is good practice to share the responsibility for project communications management with the entire project team.

Project Communications and Updating Business Processes

Getting project information to the right people at the right time and in a useful format is just as important as developing the information in the first place. The communications management plan prepared during project planning serves as a good starting point for project communications. During execution, project teams must address important considerations for creating and distributing project communication, as described previously. One of the outputs of managing communications is organizational process assets updates, such as improving business processes. Chapter 8, Controlling, provides examples of work performance information, such as progress and status reports.

Sample Updates to Business Processes

Organizations have many different assets to help them improve business processes. Examples of these assets include various policies and procedures, guidelines, information systems, financial systems, management systems, lessons learned, and historical documents that help people understand, follow, and improve business processes.

As part of the Just-In-Time Training project, Kristin's team followed several existing business processes and provided new information to update some of them. For example, they used several communications media already well-established at Global Construction, such as e-mail and project websites. Kristin's team also used several new technologies to enhance project communications and processes. Examples of these updated business processes include the following:

- Kristin and her team used instant messaging and texting on a regular basis both within their team and with suppliers. Several of the people working on the project were in various parts of the world, so they found it very useful to use instant messaging and texting. Their project management information system also included a team messaging feature that they found extremely useful.

- Several suppliers used Webcasts to communicate information in a more dynamic way without incurring travel expenses. The Webcasts included visuals, such as PowerPoint slides, along with audio and animation to point to and write in key information. There were several other interactive features available in the Webcasts, such as polling the audience and letting other people add their audio input.

- The Web-based courses that suppliers were developing for the project included discussion threads and an "Ask the Expert" feature, in which learners could ask specific questions of the instructor or experts within the company on various topics related to the course. The questions and their answers were automatically added to a database that future learners could access. They also created several short videos to include in the system to address the most frequently asked questions.

- Kristin kept her own personal project blog to document important events and lessons she was learning while managing the project. She had used blogs for personal communications in the past, such as documenting her last trip to Europe, but she had never used one in a work setting before. She found it very useful for personal reflection and knew it would help her write her final lessons-learned document for the project.

The project steering committee—pleased and fascinated with the success of these new communications media—asked Kristin to prepare guidelines on using them that employees could access on the corporate intranet after the project was completed. Kristin was glad to do so.

PROJECT STAKEHOLDER MANAGEMENT

After identifying stakeholders and planning stakeholder engagement, project managers must manage stakeholder engagement during project execution. This process involves working with various project stakeholders to meet their needs and expectations, addressing stakeholder issues as they occur, and fostering engagement in project decisions and activities. The key benefit of managing stakeholder engagement, if done well, is that it allows the project manager to increase support and minimize resistance from stakeholders, significantly increasing the chances to achieve project success.

Managing Stakeholder Engagement

Many teachers are familiar with the term engagement as schools have emphasized the importance of engaging students to help them learn. Most teachers, especially in elementary and high schools, have their students in a room for most of the day, so they can easily see if students are engaged or not. If students are not coming to class, sleeping during class, chatting with classmates about unrelated subjects, texting or using technology for unrelated activities, or just looking bored or confused, teachers know the students are not engaged. Teacher training includes many ideas and hands-on experiences in engagement. Most classes start with some kind of ice-breaker activity so students and teachers can get to know each other. Several activities and exercises are built into lesson plans to engage students.

Likewise, it is important for project managers to engage their stakeholders to help their projects succeed. Although project managers do not have project stakeholders in a room in front of them for a large portion of the day like teachers often do, they can take actions to manage stakeholder engagement. The stakeholder management plan should identify key stakeholders and describe strategies for managing relationships with them. It is easy to say that all project managers have to do is follow their plans. Managing stakeholder engagement, like managing student engagement, can be extremely difficult. It is important to set the stage early that stakeholder engagement is expected and welcomed. A project manager's leadership and interpersonal skills are crucial in making that happen.

Inputs to managing stakeholder engagement include the project management plan, (especially the sections regarding stakeholder engagement, communications, and risk), project documents (i.e., change log, issue log, lessons learned register, and stakeholder register), enterprise environmental factors, and organizational process assets. Tools and techniques include expert judgment, inspection, communication skills, interpersonal and team skills, ground rules, and meetings. Many of the outputs are similar to other knowledge areas, such as change requests and updates to the project management plan and project documents.

PROJECT RISK MANAGEMENT

The main executing process performed as part of project risk management is implementing risk responses as defined in the process to plan risk responses. Key outputs include change requests and project documents updates (i.e., issue log, lessons learned register, project team assignments, risk register, and risk report).

Implementing Risk Responses

It is important to plan risk responses, and it is even more important to implement them well. For example, Kristin's team had identified the risk event of a poor survey response in their risk register. During execution, they would implement the planned response if the risk event occurred. Note that for this particular risk response, several items were listed, such as having functional managers personally mention the survey to their people and ensuring the survey instructions said it would take ten minutes or fewer to complete. This work would be done before the survey was sent out to help minimize the risk of a poor response If these risk responses did not work, there were additional ones already planned, such as offering a reward to the department with the most responses and extending the deadline If none of the planned responses worked, they would have to work together to think of new ones. As you can see, the project manager and team must be on top of risk responses throughout project execution.

PROJECT PROCUREMENT MANAGEMENT

Many projects include work performed by outside sources. The main executing process performed as part of project procurement is conducting procurements. Many larger organizations have procurement departments that project managers work with for procurement activities. Key outputs of conducting procurements include selected sellers, agreements or contract awards, resource calendars, change requests, and updates to the project management plan and project documents.

Conducting Procurements

After planning for procurements, the next procurement management process involves conducting procurements, which involves obtaining seller responses to requests for proposals or bids, selecting sellers, and making agreements, often by awarding contracts. Prospective sellers do most of the work in this process by preparing their proposals and bids, normally at no cost to the buyer. The buying organization is responsible for deciding how to approach sellers and providing required procurement documents. Important documents created as a result of conducting procurements include contracts.

Organizations can use several different methods to approach and select qualified sellers or suppliers:

- *Approaching a preferred supplier:* Sometimes, a specific supplier might be the number-one choice for the buyer. In this case, the buyer gives procurement information to just that company. If the preferred supplier responds favorably, the organizations proceed to work together. Many organizations have formed good working relationships with certain suppliers, so they want to continue working with them.

- *Approaching several qualified suppliers:* In many cases, several suppliers could meet an organization's procurement needs. The buying organization can send procurement information to those potential sellers and then evaluate the responses. If it does not get the desired response, the buyer can either expand its list of potential sellers until it gets the desired response or revise its procurement plans.

- *Advertising to many potential suppliers:* In many cases, several suppliers may be qualified to provide the goods and services, and the buyer may not know who they are in advance. Advertising the procurement (on a website, in a trade journal, or by other means) and receiving proposals and bids from multiple sources often takes advantage of the competitive business environment. Increased globalization and virtual project teams have increased tremendously as organizations find suitable sellers around the globe. As a result of pursuing a competitive bidding strategy, the buyer can receive better goods and services than expected at a lower price or with faster delivery.

Sample Qualified Seller List

The Just-In-Time Training project required goods and services from several different suppliers. Recall that the project involved training in four different areas: supplier management, negotiating skills, project management, and software application. The training also had to be provided in various delivery formats—instructor-led, Web-based, and CD-ROM. Kristin and her team used their knowledge of current training suppliers and researched additional ones. They were not sure if they should have different suppliers for each course or have a different supplier based on each delivery method.

As described in Chapter 6, because Global Construction was new to the concept of just-in-time training, the company decided to hire a consulting firm that both specialized in just-in-time training and worked with all types of training suppliers. The consulting firm then developed a qualified sellers list containing 30 potential sellers, as provided in Figure 7-17. In addition to the list, the firm also provided a report with information on each seller, such as relevant products and services, backgrounds of senior management, and current customers. It also provided recommendations for developing partnerships with each seller. See Chapter 6 for the RFP and contract statement of work for this procurement.

Qualified Sellers List
September 9

Project Name: Just-In-Time Training Project

Seller Name/ Website	Areas of Expertise	Full-Time Staff	Reputation
Company A www.coA.com	Construction industry, supplier management, project management	40	One of few training firms that specializes in training for the construction industry
Company B www.coB.com	E-learning, custom course development	100	Has many partnerships with other companies, reasonable prices
Company C www.coC.com	Project management, negotiating skills	10	Small firm but well respected, does instructor-led and e-learning
Etc.			

Figure 7-17. Sample qualified sellers list

After buyers receive proposals or bids, they can select a supplier or decide to cancel the procurement. Selecting suppliers or sellers, often called source selection, involves evaluating proposals or bids from sellers, choosing the best one, negotiating the contract, and awarding the contract. Several stakeholders in the procurement process should be involved in selecting the best suppliers for the project. Often, teams of people are responsible for evaluating various sections of the proposals. There might be a technical team, a management team, and a cost team to focus on each of those major areas. Often, buyers develop a **short list** of the top three to five suppliers to reduce the work involved in selecting a source. Reviewers often follow a more detailed proposal evaluation process for sellers who make the short list, often checking their references, requesting special presentations, or having them provide sample products. Recall from Chapter 5 that a weighted scoring model is often used to help select sellers.

It is customary to conduct contract negotiations during the source selection process. Sellers on the short list are often asked to prepare a best and final offer (BAFO). Expert negotiators often conduct these negotiations, especially for contracts involving large amounts of money. In addition, senior managers from both buying and selling organizations often meet before making final decisions.

Sample Agreement or Contract

As mentioned in Chapter 6, a contract is a mutually binding agreement that obligates the seller to provide the specified products or services, and obligates the buyer to pay for them. Chapter 6 also described the different types of contracts and provided sample clauses that can be included to address risks. The Just-In-Time Training project would include contracts with several different suppliers. Some might be short, fixed-price contracts, such as one for the consulting firm to develop a list of qualified sellers. Others might be much longer and involve fixed-price, cost-reimbursable, and unit-pricing aspects, such as a contract to develop and deliver several training courses in different formats.

Figure 7-18 provides a sample of part of a contract or service agreement, as some contracts are called, that could be used to produce a qualified sellers list. Note the reference to exhibit A, the statement of work. (A sample procurement statement of work was provided in Chapter 6 and sent out to prospective sellers as part of the procurement package.) This document should be modified based on the selected seller's proposal. There is also a reference to a schedule for the work, which the seller also prepared as part of the proposal. It is good practice to include a detailed statement of work and schedule as part of the contract to clarify exactly what work the seller will perform and when.

Global Construction, Inc.

Service Agreement

August 10

Title of Work: Qualified Sellers List and Report

This is an Agreement made as of _____ by ABC Training Consultants, 2255 River Road, Boston, MA (the "Seller"), and Global Construction, Inc., 5000 Industrial Drive, Minneapolis, MN (the "Buyer").

THE SELLER AND THE BUYER AGREE THAT:

1. The Work: The Seller will create the Work as set forth in Exhibit A hereto. The Buyer will provide the Seller with the format and specifications in which each element of the Work is to be submitted. The Seller agrees to conform to such format and specifications.

2. Delivery of the Work: The Seller agrees to deliver to the Buyer the Work in form and content acceptable to the Buyer on or before the dates outlined in Exhibit B of this Agreement, time being of the essence to the Buyer.

3. Right to Terminate: If the Seller materially departs from the agreed-upon schedule or if the Work is not satisfactory to the Buyer (based on reviews of drafts, market conditions, and/or other criteria as determined by the Buyer), the Buyer may at its option:

    A.   Allow the Seller to finish, correct, or improve the Work by a date specified by the Buyer;

    B.   Terminate this Agreement by giving written notice to the Seller.

4. Payments: The Buyer will pay the Seller a fixed price of $5,000 upon accepted completion of the Work.

5. Exhibit: The following Exhibit is hereby incorporated by reference into this Agreement:

    Exhibit A: Statement of Work

    Exhibit B: Schedule

IN WITNESS WHEREOF, THE PARTIES HERETO HAVE EXECUTED THIS
Agreement as a sealed instrument as of the date first above written.

      Global Construction, Inc.   ABC Training Consultants

By: _____

Date   _____

Figure 7-18. Sample agreement or contract

CASE WRAP-UP

Kristin did her best to lead the team in executing the Just-In-Time Training project. Like most project managers, however, she faced several challenges. It was hard for Kristin to confront Jamie, a key project team member, about her poor performance. Kristin knew that it was best to address problems head on and come up with the best possible solution. Kristin and her team also had to determine how to address poor ratings for the prototype supplier management course. She was proud of the way they worked together to find the root cause of problems and take corrective actions. Understanding important quality, motivation, and communications concepts and using several tools and techniques helped ensure successful project execution.

CHAPTER SUMMARY

Good execution is crucial to project success. Without it, the products, services, and results planned from the project cannot materialize. This chapter summarizes the executing processes and key outputs for project integration, quality, resource, communications, stakeholder, risk, and procurement management. It also discusses important concepts and tools and techniques to help improve project execution.

Common outputs to these knowledge areas include change requests and updates to the project management plan, project documents, and organizational process assets. Unique ones are listed below.

- Integration management: deliverables, work performance data, issue log, and lessons learned register

- Quality management: Quality report, test and evaluation

- Resource management: Physical resource assignments, project team assignments, resource calendars, and team performance assessments

- Communications management: Project communications

- Procurement management: selected sellers and agreements

Samples of several outputs are provided for the Just-In-Time Training project.

QUICK QUIZ

Note that you can find additional, interactive quizzes at www.intropm.com.

1.   *Fortune* magazine summarized research showing that the main reason CEOs failed was due to _____.

    A. poor planning

    B. poor execution

    C. global competition

    D. low stock prices

2.   Which of the following is not an executing process?

    A. validate scope

    B. manage project knowledge

    C. acquire resources

    D. implement risk responses

3.   Most project sponsors would say that the most important output of any project is _____.

    A. a satisfied customer/sponsor

    B. good financial results

    C. its deliverables

    D. good plans

4.   Which of the following conflict handling modes do successful project managers use most often?

    A. confrontation/problem-solving

    B. compromise/reconcile

    C. smoothing/accommodating

    D. forcing/directing

5.   _____ includes all of the activities related to satisfying the relevant quality standards for a project.

    A. Quality assurance

    B. Quality control

    C. Customer satisfaction

    D. ISO certification

6. _____ can assist in ensuring and improving quality by improving work flow.

    A. Pareto

    B. Mind map

    C. Fishbone or Ishikawa

    D. Kanban

7. Which of the following statements is false?

    A. The highest need in Maslow's pyramid is called self-actualization.

    B. Most people today prefer managers who follow Theory X versus Theory Y.

    C. Herzberg distinguished between motivating and hygiene factors.

    D. Projects are more likely to succeed when project managers influence team members by using work challenge and expertise.

8. Some project managers like to assess team performance by using a technique known as MBWA, which stands for _____.

    A. management by wondering aloud

    B. management by wandering around

    C. measuring by work areas

    D. measuring by watching alertly

9. If a project team goes from three people to six, how many more communications channels are there?

    A. 3

    B. 6

    C. 9

    D. 12

10. Buyers often develop a _____ of the top three to five suppliers to reduce the work involved in selecting a source.

    A. short list

    B. weighted decision matrix

    C. qualified sellers list

    D. BAFO

Quick Quiz Answers

1. B; 2. A; 3. C; 4. A; 5. A; 6. D; 7. B; 8. B; 9. D; 10. A

DISCUSSION QUESTIONS

1.   Describe practices that should be followed in directing and managing project execution. Why are deliverables such an important output of project execution? What are some of the typical problems that project teams face during project execution?

2.   Why is it important to manage project knowledge during execution? Provide one example of how this can be done.

3.   What is involved in managing quality, and how does it affect project execution? What are tools and techniques used in performing quality assurance? How did Kristin's team use one of these tools to find the root cause of a quality problem?

4.   Why is resource management so important during project execution? Briefly discuss the following aspects of managing people.

   a.   How does Maslow's hierarchy of needs affect motivation?

   b.   What are some examples of motivators and hygiene factors, according to Herzberg?

   c.   What are the three main categories in McClelland's acquired-needs theory?

   d.   What is the difference between Theory X and Theory Y?

   e.   What are the five steps in Tuckman's team-building model?

5.   What are the advantages of resource leveling?

6.   Why is communications management so important during project execution? What is the difference between formal and informal communications? Why are nonverbal communications so important?

7.   Why do communications become more complicated when team size increases?

8.   What is stakeholder engagement? What can project managers do to engage stakeholders? Can they use any techniques that your teachers have used to engage students in classes? Why or why not?

9.   What risk management process is done during project execution? Provide an example.

10.   What is involved in conducting procurements? How do project teams develop a list of qualified sellers? What are some of the main topics addressed in a contract or agreement?

EXERCISES

1.   Find an example of a large project that took more than a year to complete, such as a major construction project. You can ask people at your college, university, or work

about a recent project, such as a major fundraising campaign, information systems installation, or building project. You can also find information about projects online such as the Big Dig in Boston (www.masspike.com/bigdig), the Patronas Twin Towers in Malaysia, and many other building projects (www.greatbuildings.com). Describe some of the activities performed to execute the integration, quality, resource, communications, stakeholder, risk, and procurement aspects of the project. Write a one-page paper or prepare a short presentation summarizing your findings.

2. Assume that you are working on a one-year project that involves about 20 team members and many different stakeholders working across the globe. Even though your team created a communications management plan and you have all types of communication technologies available, everyone knows that communications is a problem. Create a cause and effect diagram to identify potential root causes of the communications problems. You can use the cause and effect diagram template or create the diagram by hand or using other software. Be creative in your response.

3. Research online tools for creating kanban boards and examples of how project teams use them to improve work flow. Summarize your findings in a short paper or presentation.

4. Take the Myers-Briggs Type Indicator (MBTI) test and research information on this tool. There are several websites that have different versions of the test available free, such as *www.humanmetrics.com*, *www.personalitytype.com*, and *www.keirsey.com*. Write a short paper describing your MBTI type and what you think about this test as a team-building tool. Be sure to summarize and cite references related to using it in team-building on projects.

5. Review the following scenarios, and then write a paragraph for each one describing what media you think would be most appropriate to use, and why.

    a. Many of the technical workers on the project come in between 9:30 and 10:00 a.m., while the business users always come in before 9:00 a.m. The business users have been making comments. The project manager wants the technical staff to come in by 9:00 a.m., although many of them leave late.

    b. Your company is bidding on a project for the entertainment industry. You know that you need new ideas on how to put together the proposal and communicate your approach in a way that will impress the customer.

    c. Your business has been growing successfully, but you are becoming inundated with phone calls and e-mails asking similar types of questions.

    d. You need to make a general announcement to a large group of people and want to make sure they get the information.

6. Develop your own scenarios for when it would be appropriate to use each of the six conflict-handling modes discussed in this chapter (confrontation, compromise, smoothing, forcing, withdrawal, and collaborating). Document your ideas in a one- to two-page paper.

7.   Watch the YouTube video by RSA Animate about Daniel Pink's views on motivation. (See the link on www.intropm.com or search for it on youtube.com.) Discuss the video with at least two of your classmates. Document your observations and opinions in a short paper or presentation.

8.   Find at least three videos and/or articles related to engaging people in a work setting. What are some of the common challenges managers face in engaging workers and other stakeholders? What techniques can be useful in improving stakeholder engagement on projects? Document your findings in a short paper or presentation.

TEAM PROJECTS

1.   Your organization initiated a project to raise money for an important charity. Assume that there are 1,000 people in your organization. Also, assume that you have six months to raise as much money as possible, with a goal of $100,000. List three problems that could arise while executing the project. Describe each problem in detail, and then develop realistic approaches to solving them in a two- to three-page paper or a 15-minute presentation. Be creative in your responses, and reference ideas discussed in this chapter. Remember that this project is run solely by volunteers.

2.   You are part of a team in charge of a project to help people in your company (500 people) lose weight. This project is part of a competition, and the top "losers" will be featured in a popular television show. Assume that you have six months to complete the project and a budget of $10,000. You are halfway through the project, and morale is very low. People are also complaining about a lack of communication and support on the project. Although many people have been participating and have lost weight, many have plateaued or started gaining weight back. Identify four strategies you can implement to improve morale and communications, referencing some of the theories discussed in this chapter. Document your responses in a two- to three-page paper or a 15-minute presentation.

3.   Using the information you developed in Team Project 1 or 2, role-play a meeting to brainstorm and develop strategies for solving problems with key stakeholders. Determine who will play what role (project manager, team member from a certain department, senior managers, and so on). Be creative in displaying different personalities (a senior manager who questions the importance of the project to the organization, a team member who is very shy or obnoxious).

4.   Perform the executing tasks for one of the case studies provided in Appendix C. (Note: Your instructor might select just a few of these tasks as they can be very time-consuming.) If you are working on a real team project, perform the applicable executing tasks for that project. Remember to address common problems, focus on deliverables, and practice good soft skills.

5.   As you are executing your team project, document the top three problems you have experienced and how you are dealing with them. Document your results in a one- to two-page paper or short presentation.

KEY TERMS

benchmarking — The process of generating ideas for quality improvements by comparing specific project practices or product characteristics to those of other projects or products within or outside of the performing organization.

cause-and-effect diagrams — Also called fishbone or Ishikawa diagrams, these diagrams can assist in ensuring and improving quality by finding the root causes of quality problems.

collaborating mode — The conflict-handling mode where decision makers incorporate different viewpoints and insights to develop consensus and commitment.

compromise mode — The conflict-handling mode that uses a give-and-take approach to resolve conflicts.

confrontation mode — The conflict-handling mode that involves directly facing a conflict using a problem-solving approach that allows affected parties to work through their disagreements.

empathic listening — The process of listening with the intent to understand by putting yourself in the shoes of the other person.

explicit knowledg— Knowledge that can be easily explained using words, pictures, or numbers and is easy to communicate, store, and distribute.

extrinsic motivation — A motivation that causes people to do something for a reward or to avoid a penalty.

forcing mode — The conflict-handling mode that involves exerting one's viewpoint at the potential expense of another viewpoint.

groupthink — The conformance to the values or ethical standards of a group.

intrinsic motivation — A motivation that causes people to participate in an activity for their own enjoyment.

issue — a matter under question or dispute that could impede project success.

issue log — a tool used to document, monitor, and track issues that need to be resolved for effective work to take place.

lean — a system based on the Toyota Production System to help improve results and efficiency by eliminating waste and reducing idle time and non-value added activities.

Maslow's hierarchy of needs — A hierarchy that states that people's behaviors are guided or motivated by a sequence of needs (physiological, safety, social, esteem, and self-actualization).

mirroring — The matching of certain behaviors of the other person.

Myers-Briggs Type Indicator (MBTI) — A popular tool for determining personality preferences.

overallocation — When more resources than are available are assigned to perform work at a given time.

process analysis — Analyzing how a process operates and determining improvements.

quality assurance — The activities related to satisfying the relevant quality standards for a project.

quality audit — A structured review of specific quality management activities that helps identify lessons learned, which could improve performance on current or future projects.

rapport — A relationship of harmony, conformity, accord, or affinity.

resource leveling — A technique for resolving resource conflicts by delaying tasks.

resource loading — The amount of individual resources an existing schedule requires during specific time periods.

short list — A list of the top three to five suppliers created to reduce the work involved in selecting a source.

smoothing mode — The conflict-handling mode that de-emphasizes or avoids areas of differences and emphasizes areas of agreement.

synergy — The concept that the whole is equal to more than the sum of its parts.

tacit knowledge — Sometimes called informal knowledge, this type of knowledge is difficult to express and is highly personal.

Tuckman model — A model that describes five stages of team development (forming, storming, norming, performing, and adjourning).

withdrawal mode — The conflict-handling mode that involves retreating or withdrawing from an actual or potential disagreement.

END NOTES

[1]Forbes Coaches Council, "10 Effects Of Groupthink And How To Avoid Them," Forbes (November 4, 2016).

[2]David J. Anderson, Kanban, Blue Hole Press Inc. (November 12, 2013).

[3]Nerny, Chris, "Survey: Facebook and Twitter hurt work productivity," IT World (May 20, 2011).

[4]Walton, Alice G. "Internet Addiction Shows Up in the Brain," Forbes (January 17, 2012).

[5]Hayley Tsukayama "This dark side of the Internet is costing young people their jobs and social lives," The Washington Post (May 20, 2016).

[6]Frederick Brooks, *The Mythical Man-Month*, Addison-Wesley Professional (1995).

Chapter 8
Monitoring and Controlling Projects

LEARNING OBJECTIVES

After reading this chapter, you will be able to:

- List several processes and outputs of project monitoring and controlling, and describe outputs common to all knowledge areas
- Discuss monitoring and controlling project work and performing integrated change control as part of project integration management and how to use earned value management
- Explain the importance of validating and controlling scope
- Describe the schedule control process and schedule performance measurement tools, such as tracking Gantt charts
- Discuss tools and techniques to assist in cost control
- List the Seven Basic Tools of Quality, and provide examples of how they assist in performing quality control
- Explain the process of controlling resources
- Summarize methods for monitoring communications
- Discuss different approaches to monitoring stakeholder engagement
- Describe the process of monitoring risks
- Explain how to control procurements

OPENING CASE

Kristin worked closely with the project steering committee to monitor and control the Just-In-Time Training project. She knew that they were keeping a watchful eye on this project to ensure that it met its objectives and also addressed changing business needs. For example, since the project started, Global Construction had won several major construction projects and increased hiring by 10%. Therefore, there were more people than ever who needed the training the Just-In-Time Training project would provide. At their weekly meetings, Kristin, her team, and suppliers provided performance information and discussed changes that were required. The steering committee decided to have major suppliers report their progress directly to them as often as needed. They knew from past projects that to get the best results, it was important to develop a close relationship with suppliers and to monitor them as closely as internal employees. They also hoped to continue their partnerships with several suppliers to expand the training into other areas after this project was completed.

INTRODUCTION

Monitoring and controlling involves regularly measuring progress to ensure that the project is meeting its objectives and addressing current business needs. The project manager and other staff monitor progress against plans and take corrective action when necessary. This chapter summarizes the main processes involved in monitoring and controlling projects and provides examples of key outputs from this process group for the Just-In-Time Training project.

SUMMARY OF MONITORING AND CONTROLLING PROCESSES AND OUTPUTS

Figure 8-1 summarizes processes and outputs of project monitoring and controlling by knowledge area, based on the *PMBOK® Guide – Sixth Edition*. Notice that every knowledge area is included. Also note that several knowledge areas include similar outputs that have been discussed in earlier chapters, such as change requests and updates to the project management plan, project documents, and organizational process assets.

Knowledge area	Monitoring and controlling process	Outputs	
Project integration management	Monitor and control project work	Work performance reports Change requests Project management plan updates Project documents updates	
	Perform integrated change control	Approved change requests Project management plan updates Project documents updates	
Project scope management	Validate scope	Accepted deliverables Work performance information Change requests Project documents updates	
	Control scope	Work performance information Change requests Project management plan updates Project documents updates	
Project time management	Control schedule	Work performance information Schedule forecasts Change requests Project management plan updates Project documents updates	
Project cost management	Control cost	Work performance information Cost forecasts Change requests Project management plan updates Project documents updates	
Project quality management	Control quality	Quality control measurements Verified deliverables Work performance information Change requests Project management plan updates Project documents updates	
Project resource management	Control resources	Work performance information Change requests Project management plan updates Project documents updates	

Knowledge area	Monitoring and controlling process	Outputs
Project communications management	Monitor communications	Work performance information Change requests Project management plan updates Project documents updates
Project stakeholder management	Monitor stakeholder engagement	Work performance information Change requests Project management plan updates Project documents updates
Project risk management	Monitor risks	Work performance information Change requests Project management plan updates Project documents updates Organizational process assets updates
Project procurement management	Control procurements	Closed procurements Work performance information Procurement documentation updates Change requests Project management plan updates Project documents updates Organizational process assets updates

Figure 8-1. Monitoring and controlling processes and outputs

PROJECT INTEGRATION MANAGEMENT

The main monitoring and controlling processes performed as part of project integration management include monitoring and controlling project work and performing integrated change control. These are crucial processes that must be done well to ensure project success.

Monitoring and Controlling Project Work

Project changes are inevitable, so it is important to develop and follow a process to monitor and control them. Monitoring and controlling project work includes collecting, measuring, and disseminating performance information. It also involves assessing measurements and analyzing trends to determine what process improvements can be made. The project team should continuously monitor project performance to assess the overall health of the project and identify areas that require special attention.

The project management plan, project documents, work performance reports (including earned value management and performance reports), agreements, enterprise environmental factors, and organizational process assets are all important inputs for monitoring and controlling project work. The main tools and techniques for monitoring and controlling project work are expert judgment, data analysis, decision making, and meetings. Earned value management reports are a powerful tool for monitoring and controlling overall project performance.

Forecasting with Earned Value Management

Earned value management (EVM) is a project performance measurement technique that integrates scope, time, and cost data. Given a baseline, project managers and their teams can determine how well the project is meeting scope, time, and cost goals by entering actual information and then comparing it to the baseline. As defined in Chapter 4, a baseline is a starting point, a measurement, or an observation that is documented so that it can be used for future comparison.

In earned value management, a baseline includes the following:

- Scope (WBS deliverables)

- Time (start and finish estimates for each activity)

- Cost information (cost estimates for each activity)

Actual information includes whether or not a WBS deliverable was completed or approximately how much of the work was completed; when the work actually started and ended; and how much it actually cost to do the completed work. Some project teams do not define work using a WBS or have cost estimates for each activity. Some project teams do not periodically enter actuals for scope, time, and cost information. If you do not have a good baseline or actual information, you cannot use earned value management. Also, you must periodically update the actuals to use EVM throughout your project.

In the past, earned value management was primarily used on large government projects. Today, however, more and more companies are realizing the value of using this tool to help control projects. Larger companies use EVM to quickly analyze different projects across their organization, even with varying sizes. Most project management software products, including Microsoft Project, provide tables and reports for entering and viewing earned value information. See Appendix A for detailed instructions on using this software for earned value management.

Earned value management involves determining three values for each deliverable or summary deliverable from a project's WBS.

1. The **planned value (PV)** is the authorized budget assigned to scheduled work. The cost baseline for the Just-In-Time Training project included $5,000 to be spent on course development for supplier management training. If the activity involved delivering a detailed course outline to be finished in one week for $5,000, then the planned value (PV) for that activity that week would be $5,000.

2. The **actual cost (AC)** is the realized cost incurred for the work performed on an activity during a specific time period. For example, suppose it actually took one week and cost $6,000 to create the detailed course outline because the hourly rate

for the person doing the work was higher than planned. The actual cost (AC) for the activity would therefore be $6,000.

3. The **earned value (EV)** is the measure of work performed expressed in terms of the budget authorized for that work. It cannot be greater than the authorized PV budget for a component as it is calculated as the sum of the PV of the completed work. For this example, the EV is $5,000.

Figures 8-2 a. and b. summarize the general formulas used in earned value management and provide a chart to help visualize the information. Note that the formulas for variances and indexes start with EV, the earned value. Variances are calculated by subtracting the actual cost or planned value from EV, and indexes are calculated by dividing EV by the actual cost or planned value. You can use the indexes to forecast what the project will cost when completed (the Estimate at Completion or EAC) and when the project will finish. Figure 8-2.b. shows the earned value, planned value, and actual cost for a project about halfway through its life. Notice that this project is over budget and behind schedule because the earned value line is below both the planned value and actual cost lines. The estimate at completion, therefore, is higher than the budget at completion, and the end date of the project is later than planned. This chart also shows that management reserve can be used to provide some of the funds required to complete the project. In this case, the EAC is even more than the project budget, so additional funds would be required unless changes are made to reduce costs.

The projected end date in this example is calculated by dividing the original time estimate by the SPI. This calculation should be used with care. As a project nears completion, the EV will approach PV, and as such the SPI will approach 1. This means the projected end date will not provide an accurate estimate of the revised duration. Also, since the EV value includes critical and non-critical activities, this could over or under state the impact on the project duration. For a more accurate estimate of the project duration, the project schedule should be reviewed and updated by the project team.

Term	Formula
Planned Value (PV)	PV = authorized budget assigned to scheduled work
Earned Value (EV)	EV = PV of all completed work
Cost Variance (CV)	CV = EV – AC
Schedule Variance (SV)	SV = EV – PV
Cost Performance Index (CPI)	CPI = EV/AC
Schedule Performance Index (SPI)	SPI = EV/PV
Estimate at Completion (EAC)	EAC = Budget at Completion (BAC)/CPI
Estimate To Complete (ETC)	EAC-AC

Figure 8-2.a. Earned value formulas

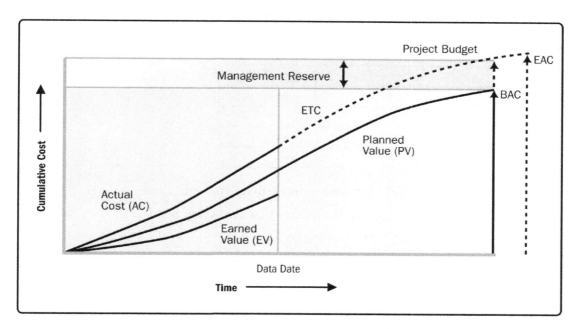

Figure 8-2.b. Earned value, planned value, and actual cost
Source: Project Management Institute, Inc., *A Guide to the Project Management Body of Knowledge (PMBOK® Guide) – Sixth Edition* (2017).

Note: In general, negative numbers for cost and schedule variance indicate problems in those areas. Negative numbers mean the project is costing more than planned (over budget) or taking longer than planned (behind schedule). Likewise, CPI and SPI less than one or less than 100% indicate problems.

You can use earned value management at either a detailed or a summary level. In other words, you can use a detailed WBS and its associated time and cost data (using level four, five, or whatever is the most detailed), or you can apply earned value at a higher WBS level, such as level two or three.

Figure 8-3 summarizes the earned value information and also computes the cost and schedule variance and the cost and schedule performance indexes for the Just-In-Time Training project activities for course development for supplier management training discussed earlier.

Term or Calculation	Amount
Earned Value (EV)	$5,000
Planned Value (PV)	$5,000
Actual Cost (AC)	$6,000
Cost Variance (CV)	–$1,000
Schedule Variance (SV)	0
Cost Performance Index (CPI)	83.33%
Schedule Performance Index (SPI)	100%

Figure 8-3. Earned value calculations for one activity after one week

The earned value calculations in Figure 8-3 are carried out as follows:

$$EV = \$5,000 \times 100\% = \$5,000$$

$$CV = \$5,000 - \$6,000 = -\$1,000$$

$$SV = \$5,000 - \$5,000 = 0$$

$$CPI = \$5,000/\$6,000 = 83.33\%$$

$$SPI = \$5,000/\$5,000 = 100\%$$

Earned value calculations for all project activities (or summary level activities) are required to estimate the earned value for the entire project. Some activities may be over budget or behind schedule, whereas others may be under budget and ahead of schedule. By adding all the earned values for all project activities, you can determine how the project as a whole is performing and forecast both when it will be completed and how much it will cost at completion. You can also use this same methodology for program level EVM.

The **budget at completion (BAC)**, or the approved total budget for the project, can be divided by the cost performance index to calculate the **estimate at completion (EAC)**, which is a forecast of how much the project will cost upon completion. This calculation assumes you will be spending at the same rate as your current level of spending. Likewise, the approved time estimate for the project can be divided by the schedule performance index to calculate when the project will be completed. Earned value, therefore, provides an excellent way to monitor project performance and provide forecasts based on performance to date.

PMI conducted a study in 2011 to help understand and gauge the current level of EVM practice. The researchers surveyed more than 600 project management practitioners in 61 countries. Figure 8-4 shows the percentage or organizations that reported using EVM. Key findings include the following:

- EVM is used worldwide, and it is popular in the Middle East, South Asia, Canada, and Europe.
- Most countries require EVM for large defense or government projects.
- Project budget size appears to be the most important factor in deciding whether or not to use EVM.

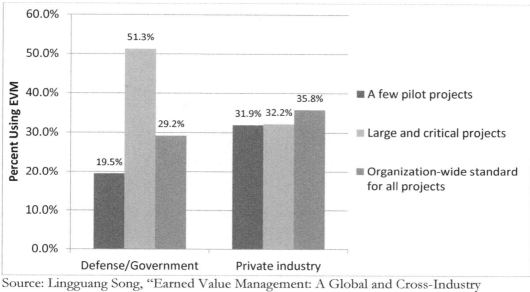

Source: Lingguang Song, "Earned Value Management: A Global and Cross-Industry Perspective on Current EVM Practice," PMI (2011).

Figure 8-4. Percentage of organizations using EVM

Sample Forecast Using an Earned Value Chart

You can graph earned value information to track project performance and to forecast when a project will be completed and for how much. Figure 8-5 shows an earned value chart for a project that has larger and simpler variances than the Just-In-Time Training project to make the chart easier to read. The budget at completion is $1.2 million for this one-year project. The BAC point on the chart, therefore, is at 12 months and $1.2 million. Based on data for months one through six, an earned value chart was created. In this example, the planned value is $100,000 for each month, so the cumulative planned value at month 6 is $600,000. The earned value is $150,000 each month, with the cumulative earned value at month 6 of $900,000. The actual cost is $200,000 each month, with the cumulative actual cost at month 6 of $1,200,000. Note that most projects do not have a linear progression for data, but this is a simplified example.

You can also forecast when the project will be completed and what its final cost will be based on this information.

$$CPI = EV/AC = \$900,000/\$1,200,000 = .75$$

$$SPI = EV/PV = \$900,000/\$600,000 = 1.5$$

$$EAC = BAC/CPI = \$1,200,000/.75 = \$1,600,000$$

New completion date estimate   = Original time estimate / SPI

= 12 months/1.5 = 8 months

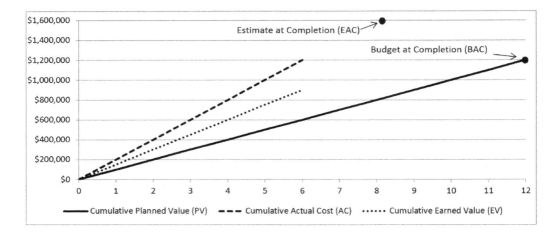

Figure 8-5. Sample earned value chart

Notice that the EAC point is provided on the chart in Figure 8-5 at 8 months and at the cost of $1,600,000. Viewing earned value information in chart form helps you visualize how the project has been performing and forecasts both the end date and the total cost. For example, you can see the planned performance by looking at the planned value line. If the project goes exactly as planned, it will finish in 12 months and cost $1,200,000, as represented by the BAC point. Notice in the example that the actual cost line is always above the earned value line. When the actual cost line is above the earned value line, costs are more than planned. That situation is usually not good. The planned value line in this example is always below the earned value line. This relationship means that the project has been ahead of schedule the first six months. That situation is normally good, but it may not be. The forecasted completion date, therefore, is earlier than planned while the forecasted total cost is higher than planned. As this trend started at month one and continued each month, you can assume that the project sponsor did want the project completed early and was willing to pay the extra cost. If this was not the case and the sponsor was not willing to pay more for an early completion, the project manager would have to scramble to try to complete the project within the approved time and budget constraints.

If there are serious cost and schedule performance problems, management may decide to terminate projects or take other corrective action. The estimate at completion (EAC) is an important input to budget decisions, especially if total funds are limited. Earned value management is an important technique because when used effectively, it helps in evaluating progress and making sound management decisions.

Performance Reports

Performance reports keeps stakeholders informed about how resources are being used to achieve project objectives. Performance reports are normally provided as status reports or progress reports. Many people use the two terms interchangeably, but some people distinguish between them as follows. A third type of report often used is a forecast. Types of reports include:

- **Status reports** describe where the project stands at a specific point in time. Recall the importance of the triple constraint. Status reports address where the project stands in terms of meeting scope, time, and cost goals. Is work being accomplished as planned? How long did it take to do certain activities? How much money has been spent to date? Status reports can take various formats depending on the stakeholders' needs.

- **Progress reports** describe what the project team has accomplished during a certain period. In many projects, each team member prepares a weekly or monthly progress report. Team leaders often create consolidated progress reports based on the information received from team members.

- **Forecasts** predict future project status and progress based on past information and trends. How long will it take to finish the project based on how things are going? How much more money will be needed to complete the project? Project managers can also use earned value management, as described in the previous section, to answer these questions by estimating the budget at completion and the projected completion date based on how the project is progressing.

Stakeholders often review project performance reports at status review meetings, such as the ones Kristin has with the project steering committee. Status review meetings are a good way to highlight important information, empower people to be accountable for their work, and have face-to-face discussions about key project issues. Many project managers also hold periodic status review meetings with their own team members to exchange important project information and motivate people to make progress on their parts of the project. Likewise, many senior managers, who are often part of a review board or oversight committee, hold status review meetings. At these meetings, several program and project managers must report overall status information to keep everyone abreast of important events and to learn from each other as well.

Sample Performance Report

Figure 8-6 provides a sample progress report that Kristin gave at a performance review meeting with the Just-In-Time Training project steering committee. Notice that the report references an earned value chart. Make special note of metrics that are of key interest to senior managers, such as the number of people trained to date and registered for courses. Also note the issues and suggestions and the project changes sections of the report. Performance review meetings should focus on addressing these items to ensure that projects succeed.

Progress Report

Project Name: Just-In-Time Training Project

Project Manager Name: Kristin Maur

Date: February 3

Reporting Period: January 1 – February 1

Work completed this reporting period:

- Held first negotiating skills course (instructor-led) with 20 participants

- Held first supplier management executive course (instructor-led) with 17 participants

- Held second supplier management introductory course (instructor-led) with 20 participants

- Had 32 people begin the Web-based introductory supplier management course

- Continued developing other Web-based courses

- Prepared evaluations of all courses held to date

Work to complete next reporting period:

- Hold first advanced supplier management course

- Hold first project management course

- Hold first software applications course

What's going well and why:

- Participation in all courses is good. Every instructor-led course was full, except the supplier management executive course. All the courses were advertised well, and we had more than enough people sign-up for the classes. We put several people on the list for later courses after courses were filled in the registration system.

- The average course ratings were above 3.8 on a 5.0 scale. Comments were generally very positive.

- More people than expected started the first Web-based course. Development of new Web-based courses is going well.

What's not going well and why:

- We did not fill the supplier management executive course as planned. Three people could not attend at the last minute, and it was too late to get replacements. We will work on a policy to help prevent this problem in the future for all instructor-led classes.

- We were surprised that so many people started the Web-based introductory supplier management course. We can handle the numbers, but we could have done a better job at forecasting demand.

Suggestions/Issues:

- Develop a policy to handle people not being able to attend instructor-led courses at the last minute.

- Try to do a better job at forecasting demand for Web-based courses.

Project changes:

No major changes to report. The earned value chart in Attachment 1 shows planned value, actual cost, and earned value information to date. We are very close to our plans, running slightly ahead of schedule and a bit over budget.

Figure 8-6. Sample performance report

Integrated Change Control

Integrated change control involves identifying, evaluating, and managing changes throughout the project's life cycle. The three main objectives of integrated change control are as follows:

1. *Influencing the factors that cause changes to ensure that changes are beneficial:* Changes can often be good for a project, so it is important to let everyone know that and focus on promoting changes that are beneficial. For example, changes that improve quality, reduce costs, save time, or improve stakeholder relationships are beneficial.

2. *Determining that a change has occurred:* To determine that a change has occurred, project managers must know the status of key project areas at all times. In addition, they must communicate significant changes to senior management and key stakeholders, who normally do not like surprises—especially unpleasant ones. The types of changes that might occur could be an alteration or variation to the scope of work, a deviation or departure in a work product or deliverable from established requirements, or a trend or non-random variance of actual project performance from the plan.

3. *Managing actual changes as they occur:* Managing change is a key role of project managers and their teams. It is important that project managers exercise discipline in managing the project to help control the number of changes that occur. Managers should focus on achieving project goals rather than putting out fires.

The project management plan provides the baseline for identifying and controlling project changes as follows:

- A section of the plan describes the work to be performed on a project, including key deliverables for the project and quality requirements.

- The schedule section of the plan lists the planned dates for completing key deliverables.

- The budget section provides the planned cost for these deliverables.

The project team must focus on delivering the work as planned. If the project team or someone else causes significant changes during project execution, project managers must formally revise the project management plan and have it approved by the project sponsor.

WHAT WENT RIGHT?

Chicago's Museum of Contemporary Art (MCA) provides a great example of tracking key project performance information to ensure project success. In September 2014 MCA became the first U.S. venue to stage the "David Bowie Is" exhibit. The $2 million project took thirteen months to complete. The MCA team knew they had to sell a lot of tickets for the four-month run of the exhibit—about 150,000, which was more than half if its annual average. They put metrics in place to track several key items, including ticket sales. Their online ticket sales dashboard allowed the team to compare sales each day with projections so they could adjust the marketing strategy as needed.

For example, dashboard metrics helped the team decide to provide student discounts to lure more students to the exhibit, especially on Friday nights. "It's the ability to adjust in real time that is the hardest part of project management, because you have to be willing to say, 'I'm not going to make all the decisions now. I'm going to be nimble and adjust on the fly,'" said Susan Chun, the MCA chief content officer.[1]

PROJECT SCOPE MANAGEMENT

The main monitoring and controlling processes performed as part of project scope management are validating scope and controlling scope. Key outputs are accepted deliverables and work performance information. It is difficult to create a good project scope statement and WBS. It is often even more difficult to validate the project scope and minimize scope changes. Some project teams know from the start that the scope is very unclear and that they must work closely with the project customer to design and produce various deliverables. Some project teams use an agile approach in this type of environment, as described in Chapter 3. For all types of projects and approaches to managing them, it is important to develop and follow a process for scope validation that meets unique project needs. Careful procedures must be developed to ensure that customers are getting what they want and that the project team has enough time and money to produce the desired products and services.

Even when the project scope is fairly well defined, many projects suffer from scope creep, as discussed in Chapter 4. Even for somewhat simple projects, people tend to want more. How many people do you know, for example, who said they wanted a simple wedding or a basic new house constructed, only to end up with many more extras than they initially planned? In contrast, some projects also suffer from *not* delivering the minimum scope due to time or cost issues. A couple may have planned to go on a luxurious honeymoon until they saw how much the wedding cost, or a new homeowner may have settled for an unfinished basement in order to move in on time. These scenarios are similar to those faced by a project manager who must constantly cope with the triple constraint of balancing scope, time, and cost.

Validating Scope

Scope validation involves formal acceptance of the completed project deliverables by the project customer or designated stakeholders. This acceptance is often achieved through customer inspection and then sign-off on key deliverables. To receive formal acceptance of the project scope, the project team must develop clear documentation of the project's products and procedures, which the appropriate stakeholders can then evaluate for completion and their satisfaction with the results. For example, part of the scope of Kristin's project was to develop a deliverable of a survey to help assess training needs. As part of scope validation, the project steering committee would need to approve the survey before it could be sent out. Scope planning documents, such as the WBS dictionary for that activity would define the scope validation required.

The project management plan, project documents, verified deliverables, and work performance data are the main inputs for scope validation. Recall from Chapter 4 that a verified deliverable has been completed and checked for correctness as part of quality control, while validation means acceptance by the customer or identified stakeholders. The main tools for performing scope validation are inspection and decision-making. The customer inspects the work after it is delivered to decide if it is acceptable. The customer is often more than one person, so group decision-making is often required for the inspection and acceptance.

Sample of Accepted and Unaccepted Deliverables

The Just-In-Time Training project included many deliverables. Kristin, the project sponsor, the project steering committee, and other stakeholders—including employees taking the training courses—were all involved in accepting deliverables. Kristin worked closely with her project team and suppliers to make sure that deliverables were being developed correctly along the way. She knew that working closely with key stakeholders and reviewing progress was often the best way to ensure that final deliverables would be acceptable. Kristin knew from experience that foregoing draft reviews and delaying consultation with stakeholders until the final deliverable was ready often resulted in disaster.

Because Global Construction often worked with suppliers on projects, they had a formal process for accepting deliverables produced by suppliers. The project manager was responsible for signing off on their acceptance, as was the project sponsor. Figure 8-7 provides a sample deliverable acceptance form. In this example, Kristin and Lucy, the project sponsor, document the fact that they do *not* accept the deliverable and provide feedback on what must be done to make it acceptable. Kristin did talk to the supplier about the changes required before accepting this specific deliverable—the course materials for the introductory supplier management course—but the supplier still did not deliver what was expected. The deliverable acceptance form provides formal documentation to ensure that deliverables meet project needs. In this case, because the particular deliverable was part of a contract, the supplier would not be paid until the deliverable was accepted.

Deliverable Acceptance Form			
Project Name:	Just-In-Time Training Project		
Deliverable Name:	Course materials for introductory supplier management course		
Project Manager:	Kristin Maur		
Project Sponsor:	Lucy Camerena		
Date:	November 12		

(We), the undersigned, acknowledge and accept delivery of the work completed for this deliverable on behalf of our organization. My (Our) signature(s) attest(s) to agreement that this deliverable has been completed. No further work should be done on this deliverable. If the deliverable is not acceptable, reasons are stated and corrective actions are described.

Name	Title	Signature	Date

1. Was this deliverable completed to your satisfaction? Yes_____No _X_

2. Please provide the main reasons for your satisfaction or dissatisfaction with this deliverable.

As stated in the contract statement of work, the course materials are not completed until all constructive feedback from the prototype course has been incorporated or the supplier has provided strong rationale as to why the feedback should not be incorporated. We requested that a new section be added to the course to cover issues related to working with suppliers in virtual settings. The final materials delivered did not include this new section or discuss why it was not added. We believe it was an oversight that can be corrected with a minimal amount of additional work.

3. If the deliverable is not acceptable, describe in detail what additional work must be done to complete it.

The supplier will add a new section to the course on working with suppliers in a virtual setting. This section should take about thirty minutes of class time in a face-to-face or e-learning setting. This new section will follow the format and review process used for other topics in the course. We request delivery of the draft of this new section within one week and the final delivery within two weeks.

Contact's signature for resubmission of deliverable if found unacceptable:

Kristin Maur

Figure 8-7. Sample deliverable acceptance form

Controlling Scope

You cannot control the scope of a project unless you have first clearly defined the scope and set a scope validation process in place. You also need to develop a process for soliciting and monitoring changes to project scope. Stakeholders should be encouraged to suggest beneficial changes and discouraged from suggesting unnecessary changes.

BEST PRACTICE

An example of successfully controlling scope comes from Northwest Airlines (based on a cases study written by the author several years ago). The company developed a new reservation system in the late 1990s that took several years and millions of dollars to develop. They knew that users would request changes and enhancements to the system, so they built in a special function key for submitting change requests. They also allocated resources for specifically handling change requests by assigning three full-time programmers to work exclusively on them. Users made over 11,000 enhancement requests the first year the system was in use, which was much more than the three programmers could handle. The managers who sponsored the four main software applications had to prioritize the software enhancement requests and decide as a group what changes to approve. Given the time they had, the three programmers then implemented as many items as they could, in priority order. Although they only implemented 38% of the requested enhancements, these were the most important, and users were very satisfied with the system and process. You can read the full ResNet case study from www.intropm.com under Resources.

Another example of scope control is a practice some parents follow when their children get married. The parents provide a fixed budget for the wedding and honeymoon and let the young couple decide how to spend it. If the couple minimizes and controls the scope of the wedding, they can have extra money to pay off other debts or save for a down payment on a home. If they suffer from scope creep, they may not have any money for a honeymoon or become further in debt. This practice can be adapted to most business projects by providing incentives for workers to deliver the work as planned within time and budget constraints.

PROJECT SCHEDULE MANAGEMENT

The main monitoring and controlling process performed as part of project schedule management is controlling the schedule or schedule control. Project managers often cite delivering projects on time (schedule control) as one of their biggest challenges, because schedule problems often cause more conflict than other issues. During project initiation, priorities and procedures are often most important, but as the project proceeds, especially during the middle and latter stages of a project, schedule issues become the predominant source of conflict.

Perhaps part of the reason schedule problems are so common is that time is easily and simply measured. After a project schedule is set, anyone can quickly estimate schedule performance by subtracting the original time estimate from the time actually expended. People often compare planned and actual project-completion times without considering the approved project changes. Time is also the variable with the least amount of flexibility. Time passes no matter what happens on a project.

Individual work styles and cultural differences may also cause schedule conflicts. For example, one dimension of the Myers-Briggs team-building tool that was described in Chapter 6 (Judgment/Perception, or J/P) deals with peoples' attitudes toward structure and deadlines. Some people (J's) prefer detailed schedules and focus on task completion. Others (P's) prefer to keep things open and flexible. Different cultures and even entire countries have different attitudes about schedules. For example, in some countries, businesses close for several hours every afternoon so workers can take naps. Others observe religious or secular holidays during which little work is accomplished. Cultures may also have different perceptions of work ethic—some may value hard work and strict schedules, whereas others may value the ability to remain relaxed and flexible.

MEDIA SNAPSHOT

In contrast to the 2002 Olympic Winter Games in Salt Lake City (see the Media Snapshot of Chapter 4), planning and scheduling for the 2004 Olympic Summer Games in Athens, Greece and the 2014 Sochi Winter Olympic Games did not go so well. Many articles were written before the opening ceremonies of the Athens Games predicting that the facilities would not be ready in time. "With just 162 days to go to the opening of the Athens Olympics, the Greek capital is still not ready for the expected onslaught…. By now 22 of the 30 Olympic projects were supposed to be finished. This week the Athens Olympic Committee proudly announced 19 venues would be finished by the end of next month. That's a long way off target."[2] However, many people were pleasantly surprised by the amazing opening ceremonies, beautiful new buildings, and state-of-the-art security and transportation systems in Athens. One spectator at the Games commented on the prediction that the facilities would not be ready in time: "Athens proved them all wrong…. It has never looked better."[3] The Greeks even made fun of critics by having construction workers pretend to still be working on the stage as the ceremonies began. Unfortunately, the Greek government suffered a huge financial deficit because the games cost more than twice the planned budget.

The 2014 Winter Olympic Games in Sochi, Russia suffered even more financial losses. Originally budgeted at US$12 billion, final costs reached over US$51 billion, making it the most expensive games in history. Unlike the humorous response to challenges at the Athens games, Russian citizens were much more serious. In 2006, 86 percent of Sochi residents supported the games, 57 percent supported it in 2010, and only 40 percent supported it 2013. Russian citizens, especially those in Sochi, understood the negative impacts of hosting the games when they heard about the poor planning and huge cost overruns. "…the Sochi Olympics will continue to be a burden for the Russian state, with expenses for operation, maintenance and foregone interest and tax revenue in the order of USD$1.2 billion per year. The event also did not manage to improve the image of Russia in the world and among the domestic population support dropped over the seven years of its implementation, most notably among the local population."[4]

The goal of schedule control is to know the status of the schedule, influence the factors that cause schedule changes, determine whether the schedule has changed, and manage changes when they occur. Key output of schedule control include schedule forecasts and work performance information. There are several tools and techniques for schedule control, including data analysis (such as earned value management, as described earlier in this chapter), project management information systems, resource optimization, and several tools discussed in Chapter 5 (such as critical path method, leads and lags, and schedule compression).

Sample Work Performance Information

The project steering committee for the Just-In-Time Training project held weekly meetings to make sure the project was meeting schedule and other goals. Project managers often illustrate schedule progress at these meetings with a **tracking Gantt chart**—a Gantt chart that compares planned and actual project schedule information. Many project managers believe that tracking

Gantt charts are an excellent tool for tracking project schedule performance and reporting that information to stakeholders. Figure 8-8 provides a sample tracking Gantt chart created in Appendix A. The tracking Gantt chart shows bars for both planned and actual start and finish dates for each task as well as the percent of work completed. See the *Brief Guide to Microsoft Project Professional 2016* in Appendix A for information on creating a tracking Gantt chart and other types of performance reports.

Figure 8-8. Sample schedule performance measurement using a tracking Gantt chart in Microsoft Project

To serve as a schedule performance measurement tool, a tracking Gantt chart uses a few additional symbols not found on a normal Gantt chart:

- Notice that the tracking Gantt chart in Figure 8-8 often shows two horizontal bars for tasks. The top horizontal bar represents the planned or baseline duration for each task. The bar below it represents the actual duration. If the top and bottom bars are the same length and start and end on the same date, the actual schedule was the same as the planned schedule for that task. If the bars do not start and end on the same date, the actual schedule differed from the planned or baseline schedule. If the top horizontal bar is shorter than the bottom one, the task took longer than planned. If the top horizontal bar is longer than the bottom one, the task took less time than planned. A striped horizontal bar represents the planned duration for summary tasks. Recall from Chapter 4 that summary tasks are tasks that are decomposed into smaller tasks. The black bar adjoining the striped horizontal bar shows the progress for summary tasks.

- A white diamond on the tracking Gantt chart represents a slipped milestone. A **slipped milestone** refers to a milestone activity that was completed later than originally planned.

- Percentages to the right of the horizontal bars display the percentage of work completed for each task. For example, 100% indicates that the task is finished, whereas 50% indicates that the task is still in progress and is 50% completed.

- In the columns to the left of the tracking Gantt chart, you can display baseline and actual start and finish dates. See Appendix A for more information on tracking Gantt charts.

Kristin also believed in reviewing worker morale and using discipline to help control the schedule. She knew from experience that if project team members are always working extra hours, the schedule might not be realistic. She might need to negotiate a new schedule or request more resources. On the other hand, if workers are coming in late and leaving early while still producing quality work on time, the schedule might not be challenging enough. Kristin believed that project managers must empower team members to be responsible for completing work on time, yet they often have to use discipline to keep things on track and do what is in the best interest of the organization.

Project sponsors hate surprises, so the project manager must be clear and honest in communicating project status. By no means should project managers create the illusion that the project is going fine when, in fact, serious problems have emerged. When conflicts arise that could affect the project schedule, the project manager must alert the project sponsor and other stakeholders and work with them to resolve the conflicts. The communications management plan should describe escalation procedures for resolving issues.

PROJECT COST MANAGEMENT

Cost control includes monitoring cost performance, ensuring that only appropriate project changes are included in a revised cost baseline, and informing project stakeholders of authorized changes to the project that will affect costs. The project management plan, project documents, project funding requirements, work performance data, and organizational process assets are inputs to the cost-control process. Outputs of cost control include work performance information, cost forecasts, change requests, project management plan updates, and project documents updates.

Several tools and techniques assist in project cost control, including expert judgment, data analysis, project management information systems, and the **To-complete performance index (TCPI)**, which is a measure of the cost performance that must be achieved on the remaining work in order to meet a specified goal, such as the BAC or EAC. Some project leaders blame quality problems on poor cost control, as described in the following passage.

WHAT WENT WRONG?

Many people have heard about the problems with Boston's Big Dig project. Newspapers and websites showed the many leaks in the eight- to 10-lane underground expressway that took over 14 years and $14 billion to build. Did the project overseers cut corners to save time and money?

Representative Stephen F. Lynch believes the answer to that question is yes, and that at some point, pressure to get the project done distracted Bechtel/Parsons Brinckerhoff from getting the project done right. "Under the pressure and scrutiny of a lot of people, they went back to look at areas where they could reduce cost in areas of material and time," said Lynch, a South Boston Democrat, in the aftermath of the Big Dig congressional hearing he brought to Boston on April 22, 2005. Pressure to finally speed up the costly, long-running project may explain why the new Artery tunnel is plagued by leaks. "As a casual observer, I am forced to conclude that the focus on the cost overrun and the schedule distracted attention from quality control issues on the Central Artery project," declared George J. Tamaro in written testimony to the Congressional Committee on Government Reform.[5]

PROJECT QUALITY MANAGEMENT

The main project quality management process for monitoring and controlling is quality control. Key outputs include quality-control measurements, verified deliverables, work performance information, change requests, project management plan updates, and project documents updates. Although one of the main goals of quality control is to ensure and improve quality, the main outcomes of this process are acceptance decisions, rework, and process adjustments.

- *Acceptance decisions* determine if the products or services produced as part of the project will be accepted or rejected. If they are accepted, they are considered to be verified deliverables. If project stakeholders reject some of the products or services produced as part of the project, there must be rework.

- *Rework* is action taken to bring rejected items into compliance with product requirements or specifications or other stakeholder expectations. Rework can be very expensive, so the project manager who excels at quality planning and quality assurance can reduce the need for rework.

- *Process adjustments* correct or prevent further quality problems. Based on the implementation of quality-control measurements, process adjustments often result in updates to the quality baseline, organizational process assets, and the project management plan.

Sample Quality-Control Tools

Many different tools and techniques are available for performing quality control. The *PMBOK® Guide – Sixth Edition*, lists the following:

- Data gathering: Checklists, check sheets, statistical sampling, questionnaires, and surveys

- Data analysis: Performance reviews and root cause analysis

- Inspection

- Testing/product evaluations

- Data representation: cause-and-effect diagrams, control charts, histograms, and scatter diagrams

- Meetings

The following seven tools are known as the Seven Basic Tools of Quality, as defined by the American Society for Quality (ASQ), a knowledge-based global community of quality professionals founded in 1946.

1. *Cause-and-effect diagram*: Cause-and-effect diagrams help you find the root cause of quality problems. Figure 8-9 provides the same cause-and-effect diagram from Chapter 6 that can be used to find the root cause of low course ratings for the Just-In-Time Training project.

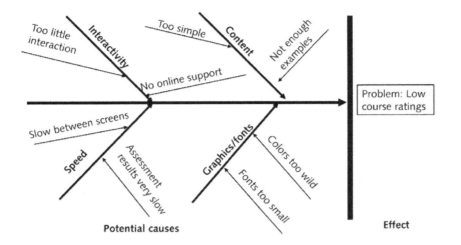

Figure 8-9. Sample cause-and-effect diagram

2. *Check sheet:* A **check sheet**, also called a tally sheet, is a structured form for collecting and analyzing data. Check sheets are often used during inspections to log the frequencies of defects. Figure 8-10 shows a sample check sheet that the Just-In-Time Training project team could use for inspecting the web-based courses for their new training courses.

Defect	Day 1	Day 2	Day 3	Day 4	Total
Broken link	5	3	2	4	14
Spelling error	2	1	2	2	7
Wrong format	3	2	4	1	10

Figure 8-10. Sample check sheet

3. *Control chart:* A **control chart** is a graphical display of data that illustrates the results of a process over time. Control charts allow you to determine whether a process is in control or out of control. When a process is in control, any variations in the results of the process are created by random events. Processes that are in control do not need to be adjusted. When a process is out of control, variations in the results of the process are caused by nonrandom events. When a process is out of control, you need to identify the causes of those nonrandom events and adjust the process to correct or eliminate them. Figure 8-11 provides an example of a control chart for a process that manufactures 12-inch rulers. Assume that these are wooden rulers created by machines on an assembly line. Each point on the chart represents a length measurement for a ruler that comes off the assembly line. The scale on the vertical axis goes from 11.90 to 12.10. These numbers represent the lower and upper specification limits for the ruler. In this case, this would mean that the customer has specified that all rulers purchased must be between 11.90 and 12.10 inches long, or 12 inches plus or minus 0.10 inches. The lower and upper control limits on the control chart are 11.91 and 12.09 inches, respectively. This means the manufacturing process is designed to produce rulers between 11.91 and 12.09 inches long. Looking for and analyzing patterns

in process data is an important part of quality control. You can use control charts and the seven run rule to look for patterns in data. The *seven run rule* states that if seven data points in a row are all below the mean, above the mean, increasing, or decreasing, then the process needs to be examined for nonrandom problems. In Figure 8-11, data points that violate the seven run rule are starred. The first starred point has seven data points in a row that are all below the mean. The second one has seven data points in a row that are all decreasing. Note that you include the first point in a series of points that are all increasing or decreasing. In the ruler-manufacturing process, these data points may indicate that a calibration device may need adjustment. For example, the machine that cuts the wood for the rulers might need to be adjusted, or the blade on the machine might need to be replaced.

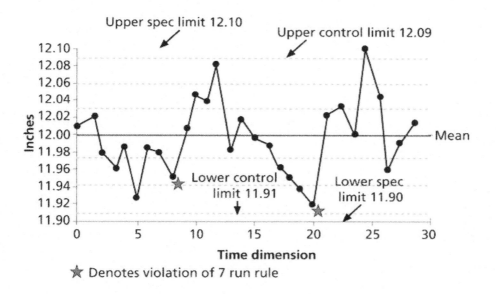

Figure 8-11. Sample control chart (Schwalbe, Information Technology Project Management, Sixth Edition, 2010)

4. *Histograms:* A **histogram** is a bar graph of a distribution of variables. Each bar represents an attribute or a characteristic of a problem or situation, and the height of the bar represents its frequency. Chapter 5 provides a sample resource histogram, showing the number of people required for a project over time. The Just-In-Time Training project team created a histogram to show how many total complaints they received each month related to the project. Figure 8-12 shows the sample histogram.

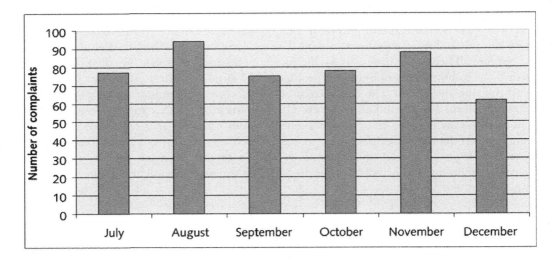

Figure 8-12. Sample histogram

5. *Pareto charts:* A **Pareto chart** is a histogram that can help you identify and prioritize problem areas. The variables described by the histogram are ordered by frequency of occurrence in a column chart, and a line chart is added to show cumulative percentage on the right of the chart. Pareto charts help you identify the vital few contributors that account for most quality problems in a system. Pareto analysis is sometimes referred to as the 80/20 rule, meaning that 80% of problems are often due to 20% of the causes. Figure 8-13 is a sample Pareto chart that the Just-In-Time Training project team developed. They used it to help improve the quality of the information they provided about training courses on the corporate intranet. It shows the number of times people complained about the information on the intranet by category of complaint. Notice that the first two complaints account for a large percentage of the problems, so the team should focus on improving those areas to improve quality. The solid line represents the cumulative amount of problems. Note that Pareto charts work best when the problem areas are of equal importance. For example, if a life-threatening problem was reported, it should be considered before less important problems.

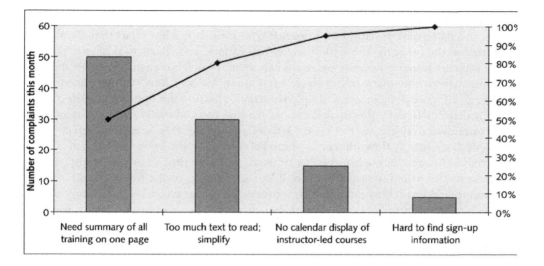

Figure 8-13. Sample Pareto chart

6. *Scatter diagram:* A **scatter diagram** helps show if there is a relationship between two variables. The closer data points are to a diagonal line, the more closely the two variables are related. Figure 8-14 provides a sample scatter diagram that Kristin's project team might create to compare training participants' course evaluation ratings with their ages to see if there is a relationship between those two variables. They might find that younger workers prefer the Web-based courses, for example, and make decisions based on that finding.

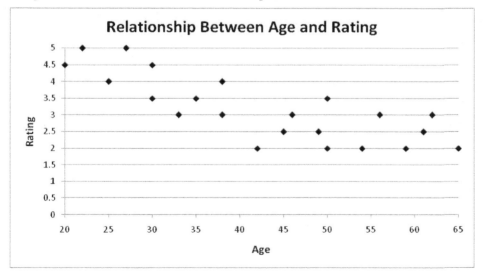

Figure 8-14. Sample scatter diagram

7. *Stratification:* **Stratification** is a technique used to separate data to see patterns in data. Some sources use run charts or flow charts in place of stratification. A **run chart** displays the history and pattern of variation of a process over time. It is a line chart that shows data points plotted in the order in which they occur. You can use run charts to perform trend analysis to forecast future outcomes based on historical results. For example, trend analysis can help you analyze how many defects have been identified over time to determine if there are trends. Figure 8-15 shows a sample run chart, charting the number of defects each day for three different types of defects. Notice that you can easily see the patterns of Defect 1 continuing to decrease over time, Defect 2 increasing over time, and Defect 3 fluctuating each month. A **flow chart** is a graphical display of the logic and flow of processes that help you analyze how problems occur and how processes can be improved. They show activities (using the square symbol), decision points (using the diamond symbol), and the order of how information is processed (using arrow symbols). Figure 8-16 provides a simple example of a flowchart that shows the process Kristin's team used for accepting or rejecting deliverables.

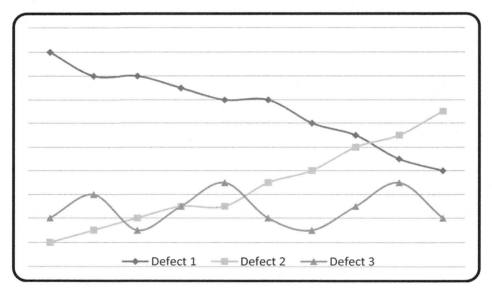

Figure 8-15. Sample run chart

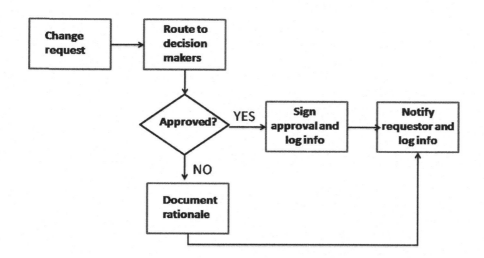

Figure 8-16. Sample flowchart

Figure 8-17 provides a humorous example of auto-correct, a common tool to supposedly control quality of spelling.

Figure 8-17. Lunch order (www.xkcd.com)

PROJECT RESOURCE MANAGEMENT

Controlling resources involves ensuring that the *physical* resources assigned to the project are available as planned and monitoring the planned versus actual resources utilization, taking corrective actions as needed. Making effective use of team members is addressed under the Manage Team process. Tools and techniques include data analysis, problem solving, interpersonal and team skills, and project management information systems. Key outputs include work performance information, change requests, project management plan updates, and project documents updates.

PROJECT COMMUNICATIONS MANAGEMENT

Monitoring communications involves monitoring communications throughout the project life cycle to ensure that stakeholder information needs are met. Key outputs include work performance information, change requests, project management plan updates, and project documents updates. Work performance information focuses on how well project communication is performed compared to what was planned. Examples include survey results on the effectiveness of project communication.

PROJECT STAKEHOLDER MANAGEMENT

You cannot control stakeholders, but you can monitor their level of engagement. Monitoring stakeholder engagement involves monitoring overall project stakeholder relationships and adjusting strategies and plans for engaging stakeholders as needed. If project managers perform this process well, they can maintain or increase the efficiency of stakeholder engagement activities as the project evolves and the environment changes. The project management plan, project documents, work performance data, enterprise environmental factors, and organizational process assets are important inputs to this process. The project team uses data analysis, decision making, data representation, communication skills, interpersonal and team skills, and meetings as the main tools and techniques. The outputs of monitoring stakeholder engagement are work performance information, change requests, project management plan updates, and project documents updates.

On some projects, stakeholder engagement is monitored by making them key members of the project team. Review the first Best Practice example earlier in this chapter describing how Northwest Airlines (now part of Delta) used innovative ideas to control project scope on a large software development project called ResNet. The project manager interviewed reservation agents for positions as programmers on the project team. There were many people excited about the opportunity, so the project manager had great candidates to choose from. Northwest Airlines made sure that user needs were understood by having them develop the user interface for the new reservation system. See the companion website for a detailed case study on ResNet.

If you cannot have key stakeholders on the project team, you can monitor their engagement by planning for it and then following and adjusting those plans as needed. For example, if you plan for several senior managers to attend a kick-off meeting, meet with them ahead of time to develop a relationship with them. Put them on the agenda and give them a specific role in the meeting. Encourage open dialog and participation of key stakeholders in review meetings. For example, the ResNet project manager required all progress reports to include issues, primarily as a means to engage stakeholders in discussing and resolving issues.

VIDEO HIGHLIGHTS

Many governments have had difficulties controlling large projects, especially those involving advanced technologies and many different users. For example, the state government of Victoria, Australia has a website for its public transportation system smart card at www.myki.com.au. In describing the card, their site includes the following information: "Many cities around the world have public transport smart cards. Myki has been designed to fit our State's unique needs. myki users enjoy an integrated ticketing system that works across the state on trains, trams and buses."[6]

Unfortunately, there were many problems in developing and implementing the smart cards. One 2009 YouTube video shows a news story called "Myki embarrasses the Government." A 2011 video is called "Not So Smart," and a 2012 video is called "Police could be called in to control myki barriers." Obviously, key stakeholders, the users of the smart card, have not been happy.

The $1.35 billion system became valid on all forms of Melbourne public transportation in July 2010, three years and five months after it was meant to replace the Metcard. Users' initial reactions to the myki smart card were mixed, with several reports of myki readers on trams not working. Many skeptics said they would wait until problems were fixed before trying the new system.[7] Many articles described the problems with the myki card, revealing obvious problems in validating the scope and involving key stakeholders in this high-visibility project. The Public Transport Users Association (PTUA) compiled a long list of problems with the new card and suggested that people stick to the old card for a while. Obviously, the new system did not meet user requirements and had major flaws. In January 2012, over 18 months later, 70% of users still used the old Metcard. The Government decided to keep the troubled myki system in June 2011 after estimating that it would cost taxpayers more than $1 billion to scrap it. myki continued to make headlines in 2015, but not in a good way. "Two years after myki became the only ticket in town, frustrated commuters say the system is still riddled with issues."[8]

PROJECT RISK MANAGEMENT

Monitoring risks involves tracking identified risks events and implementing the risk response plans, while continuing to identify and analyze new risks and evaluate risk process effectiveness. Recall from Chapter 6 that a risk event is a specific, uncertain event that may occur to the detriment or enhancement of the project. Following the risk management processes means ensuring that risk awareness is an ongoing activity performed by the entire project team throughout the project. Project risk management does not stop with the initial risk analysis. Identified risk events may not materialize, or their probabilities of occurrence or impact may diminish or increase. Similarly, new risk events are normally identified as the project progresses. Newly identified risk events need to go through the same process of analysis and monitoring as those identified during the initial risk assessment. A redistribution of resources devoted to risk management may be necessary because of relative changes in risk exposure.

Carrying out individual risk management plans involves monitoring risks based on defined milestones and making decisions regarding risks and their response strategies. It might be necessary to alter a strategy if it becomes ineffective, implement planned contingency activities, or eliminate a risk event from the list of potential risks. Project teams sometimes use **workarounds**—unplanned responses to risk events—when they do not have contingency plans in place.

Data analysis (i.e., technical performance measurement and reserve analysis), audits, and meetings are all tools and techniques for performing risk monitoring. Outputs of this process include work performance information, change requests, project management plan updates, project documents updates (especially updating the risk register), and organizational process assets updates.

Sample Risk Register Updates

Recall from Chapter 6 that the number one risk event in the risk register for the Just-In-Time Training project at that time was a poor survey response. Because the project was now halfway completed, the risk register would have to change significantly. New risks would be identified and potential responses would change based on the current situation. Status of all risks would also be updated.

For example, six months into the project, senior management informed Kristin that the company was growing faster than expected, and they thought the number of people needing training would be higher than expected. This information resulted in the identification of several new risks related to the difficulty of accommodating this growth in trainees. For example, although the Web-based courses were the most popular and adding participants to them would be less expensive than adding to any other type of course, there was a risk that the discussion board would become unmanageable. People might waste time reading through hundreds of messages or just ignore this part of the course altogether. Kristin and her team, including suppliers for the Web-based courses, would need to develop potential responses to this risk and take action if it did occur. Another risk related to employee growth might be the need to offer more instructor-led classes, which would result in increased costs to the project. As you can see, the risk register must be constantly updated as part of project monitoring and controlling.

PROJECT PROCUREMENT MANAGEMENT

Controlling procurements involves managing procurement relationships, monitoring contract performance, making changes and taking corrective actions as needed, and closing out contracts. Recall that the contractual relationship is a legal relationship and, as such, is subject to state and federal contract laws. Someone from the procurement or legal department in organizations usually closes out contracts.

Several tools and techniques can help in contract administration, including expert judgment, claims administration, data analysis, inspection, and audits. In addition to work performance information, change requests, project management plan updates, project documents updates, and organizational process asset updates, key outputs of controlling procurements include closed procurements and procurement documentation updates. Procurement documentation would include the contract itself along with requested unapproved contract changes and approved change requests. It is very important to document all changes to the contract and communicate those changes to all affected stakeholders. For example, if a supplier developing a course for the Just-In-Time Training project agreed to add a topic to the course at no extra cost, that agreement must be added to the contract to make it legal. Likewise, if Global Construction decided to add more than the agreed on number of instructor-led courses, it would need to update that information in the contract as well. Updates are often made by having both parties—the buyer and the seller—sign an addendum to the contract.

Project team members must be aware of the potential legal problems of their not understanding a contract. Changes must be handled properly for items under contract. Without understanding the provisions of the contract, a project manager might not realize that she is authorizing the contractor to do additional work at additional cost. Therefore, change control is an important part of the contract administration process. Professionals in procurement management should be consulted as needed.

It is critical that project managers and team members watch for constructive change orders. **Constructive change orders** are oral or written acts or omissions by someone with actual or apparent authority that can be construed to have the same effect as a written change order. For example, if a member of Kristin's project team has met with a supplier or contractor on a weekly basis for three months to provide guidelines for performing work, he can be viewed as an apparent authority. If he tells the contractor to redo part of a report that has already been delivered and accepted by the project manager, that action can be viewed as a constructive change order and the contractor can legally bill the buyer for the additional work. Likewise, if this apparent authority tells the contractor to skip parts of a critical review meeting in the interests of time, it would not be the contractor's fault if he missed important information.

Sample Written Notice of a Closed Contract

Figure 8-18 provides an example of a formal letter that Global Construction sent to one of its sellers, ABC Training Consultants, to formally close out their contract. The contract, a service agreement in this case, included a clause stating that written notice would be provided to formally close the contract. The seller in this particular example also requested that the buyer provide a short performance assessment as part of the closure letter. (See Chapter 7 to review the service agreement and Chapter 6 for the contract statement of work. Recall that the work had to be completed by September 9 for this contract.)

Global Construction, Inc. Contract Closure Notice

September 16

As described in our service agreement, this letter provides formal notice that the work you were contracted to perform for Global Construction has been completed. ABC Training developed a qualified sellers list containing thirty potential sellers and a report with one-page of key information on each seller. Payment is being processed based on the invoice provided by ABC Training.

Kristin Maur, the project manager, has provided the following performance assessment for the work provided:

> "We were very pleased with the work of ABC Training. Members of the firm were professional, knowledgeable, and easy to work with. Global Construction depended on ABC Training to develop a qualified sellers list for this important project, and we were extremely happy with the results. On a scale of 1 to 10, you earned a 10!"

Lawrence Scheller

By: Lawrence Scheller, Contract Specialist

Date   September 16

Figure 8-18. Sample contract closure notice

CASE WRAP-UP

The project steering committee kept a watchful eye on the Just-In-Time Training project. They were impressed with Kristin's leadership abilities and the way she handled inevitable changes on the project. They especially liked the detailed, honest progress reports Kristin provided to them. They enjoyed brainstorming ideas on solving some of the issues presented to them at review meetings, and Kristin was always very open to their suggestions. Everyone was confident the project could be completed successfully.

CHAPTER SUMMARY

Monitoring and controlling involves regularly measuring progress to ensure that the project is meeting its objectives and addressing current business needs. The project manager and other staff monitor progress against plans and take corrective action when necessary.

Every knowledge area includes processes and outputs to help monitor and control projects. Outputs common to several knowledge areas include change requests, work performance information, organizational process assets updates, project management plan updates, and project document updates.

As part of integration management, project managers must monitor and control project work and perform integrated change control. Earned value management is a project performance measurement technique that integrates scope, time, and cost data. You can use it to forecast when a project will be completed and how much it will cost given past performance data.

Monitoring and controlling processes related to scope management include validating scope and controlling scope. Scope validation means the customer or designated stakeholders have formally accepted the completed project deliverables.

Controlling costs and schedules are common challenges for project managers. Earned value management can aid in creating cost and schedule forecasts.

Unique outputs of controlling quality include quality control measurements and verified deliverables. Verified deliverables have been completed and checked for correctness as part of quality control. There are many tools and techniques for controlling quality, including the seven basic tools of quality.

Controlling resources involves ensuring that the *physical* resources assigned to the project are available as planned and monitoring the planned versus actual resources utilization, taking corrective actions as needed.

Monitoring communications involves monitoring communications throughout the project life cycle to ensure that stakeholder information needs are met.

Monitoring stakeholder engagement involves monitoring overall project stakeholder relationships and adjusting strategies and plans for engaging stakeholders as needed.

It is important to reassess risks, and an important output of controlling risks is updating the risk register.

Controlling procurements involves managing procurement relationships, monitoring contract performance, making changes and taking corrective actions as needed, and closing out contracts.

Samples of several monitoring and controlling outputs are provided for the Just-In-Time Training project.

QUICK QUIZ

Note that you can find additional, interactive quizzes at www.intropm.com.

1.   Which knowledge areas include processes related to monitoring and controlling?

    A. project scope, schedule, cost, and quality management

    B. project integration, scope, schedule, cost, and quality management

    C. project human resource, communications, risk, and procurement management

    D. all ten knowledge areas

2.   _____ is a project performance measurement technique that integrates scope, time, and cost data.

    A. Integrated change control

    B. Flowcharting

    C. Earned value management

    D. Forecasting

3.   _____ involves formal acceptance of the completed project scope by the stakeholders.

    A. Verification

    B. Scope validation

    C. Deliverable acceptance

    D. Customer sign-off

4.   _____ issues cause the most conflict over the life of projects.

    A. Change control

    B. Scope creep

    C. Cost

    D. Schedule

5.   A _____ chart is a histogram that can help you identify and prioritize problem areas.

    A. Pareto

    B. control

    C. run

    D. scatter

6.   When a process is out of control, variations in the results of the process are caused by _____ events.

    A. random

    B. nonrandom

    C. planned

    D. unplanned

7.   Controlling resources involves _____ resources.

    A. human

    B. physical

    C. material

    D. all

8.   _____ predict future project status and progress based on past information and trends.

    A. Forecasts

    B. Status reports

    C. Progress reports

    D. Histograms

9.   _____ are unplanned responses to risk events.

    A. Contingencies

    B. Reserves

    C. Workarounds

    D. Overallocations

10.   Which of the following is not part of controlling procurements?

    A. Selecting sellers

    B. Monitoring contract performance

    C. Managing procurement relationships

    D. Closing out contracts

Quick Quiz Answers

1. D; 2. C; 3. B; 4. D; 5. A; 6. B; 7. B; 8. A; 9. C; 10. A

DISCUSSION QUESTIONS

1.   What is involved in monitoring and controlling projects? What outputs of monitoring and controlling are common to all knowledge areas?

2.   Explain how earned value management helps you monitor project performance and forecast future cost and schedule information. What do you need to do to use earned value management?

3.   What are the three main objectives of integrated change control?

4.   What is the difference between scope validation and verification? Why are both important to project success?

5.   What are the Seven Basic Tools of Quality? If applicable, describe how you have you used these tools in the workplace.

6.   What is involved in monitoring stakeholder engagement?

7.   Why is it important to keep the risk register up to date?

8.   Why is it important to document contract changes? Why should project teams be watchful for constructive change orders?

EXERCISES

1.   Find an example of a large project that took more than one year to complete, such as a major construction project. You can ask people at your college, university, or work about a recent project, such as a major fundraising campaign, information systems installation, or building project. You can also find information about projects online such as the Big Dig in Boston (*www.masspike.com/bigdig*), the Patronas Twin Towers in Malaysia, and many other building projects (*www.greatbuildings.com*). Describe some of the tasks performed to monitor and control the project. Write a one-page paper or prepare a short presentation summarizing your findings.

2.   Given the following information for a one-year project, answer the following questions. Assume you have actual and earned value data at the end of the second month. Recall that PV is the planned value, EV is the earned value, AC is the actual cost, and BAC is the budget at completion.

$$PV = \$23,000$$

$$EV = \$20,000$$

$$AC = \$25,000$$

$$BAC = \$120,000$$

a. What is the cost variance, schedule variance, cost performance index (CPI), and schedule performance index (SPI) for the project?

b. How is the project progressing? Is it ahead of schedule or behind schedule? Is it under budget or over budget?

c. Use the CPI to calculate the estimate at completion (EAC) for this project.

d. Use the SPI to estimate how long it will take to finish this project.

e. Sketch the earned value chart for this project, using Figure 8-5 as a guide. Assume the data for month 1 is half of the values given for PV, EV, and AC at the end of month 2.

3. Follow the steps for using Microsoft Project 2016 provided in the *Brief Guide to Microsoft Project Professional 2016* in Appendix A through the section on earned value management. Open the data files as directed and then establish a baseline plan, create a tracking Gantt chart, and implement earned value management using this software.

4. Assume you are working on a project to improve customer service. Create a Pareto chart based on the information in the following table. Use the Pareto chart template from the companion website or sketch the chart by hand so that your resulting chart looks similar to Figure 8-13.

Customer complaints	Frequency/week
Customer is on hold too long	90
Customer gets transferred to wrong area or cut off	20
Service rep cannot answer customer's questions	120
Service rep does not follow through as promised	40

5. Watch the three YouTube videos mentioned in the Video Highlights feature of this chapter about Australia's myki transportation smart card. Also find a more recent video or article about myki. Describe what went wrong in monitoring and controlling this project and what lessons can be learned on similar projects in the future. Document your findings and opinions in a short paper, presentation, or video.

TEAM PROJECTS

1.   Your organization initiated a project to raise money for an important charity. Assume that there are 1,000 people in your organization. Also, assume that you have six months to raise as much money as possible, with a goal of $100,000. List three problems that could arise while monitoring and controlling the project. Describe each problem in detail, and then develop realistic approaches to solving them in a two- to three-page paper or a 15-minute presentation. Be creative in your responses, and use at least one quality-control tool in your analysis. Remember that this project is run solely by volunteers.

2.   You are part of a team in charge of a project to help people in your company (500 people) lose weight. This project is part of a competition, and the top "losers" will be featured in a popular television show. Assume that you have six months to complete the project and a budget of $10,000. You are halfway through the project, and morale is very low. People are also complaining about a lack of communication and support on the project. Although many people have been participating and have lost weight, many have plateaued or started gaining weight back. Discuss strategies for addressing these problems, and create two new entries for the risk register for this project. Document your responses in a two- to three-page paper or a 15-minute presentation.

3.   Using the information you developed in Team Project 1 or 2, role-play a meeting to brainstorm and develop strategies for solving problems with key stakeholders. Determine who will play what role (project manager, team member from a certain department, senior managers, and so on). Be creative in displaying different personalities (a senior manager who questions the importance of the project to the organization, a team member who is very shy or obnoxious).

4.   Brainstorm two different quality related problems that you are aware of at your college or organization. Then review the charts found in the section of this chapter on the seven basic tools of quality and create two charts to help analyze the quality problems. Prepare a one- to two-page paper or short presentation describing the problems and how the charts help to visualize them.

5.   Perform the monitoring and controlling tasks for one of the case studies provided in Appendix C. If you are working on a real team project, create relevant monitoring and controlling documents, such as performance reports or quality assurance-related charts using the templates and samples in this chapter as guides. Present your results to the class.

KEY TERMS

actual cost (AC) — The realized cost incurred for the work performed on an activity during a specific time period.

budget at completion (BAC) — The approved total budget for the project.

constructive change orders — Oral or written acts or omissions by someone with actual or apparent authority that can be construed to have the same effect as a written change order.

control chart — A graphical display of data that illustrates the results of a process over time.

earned value (EV) — The measure of work performed expressed in terms of the budget authorized for that work.

earned value management (EVM) — A project performance measurement technique that integrates scope, time, and cost data.

estimate at completion (EAC) — A forecast of how much the project will cost upon completion.

flowcharts — The graphic displays of the logic and flow of processes that help you analyze how problems occur and how processes can be improved.

forecasts — Reports that predict future project status and progress based on past information and trends.

histogram — A bar graph of a distribution of variables.

integrated change control — The process of identifying, evaluating, and managing changes throughout the project's life cycle.

Pareto chart — A histogram that can help you identify and prioritize problem areas.

planned value (PV) — The authorized budget assigned to scheduled work.

progress reports — Reports that describe what the project team has accomplished during a certain period.

run chart — A chart that displays the history and pattern of variation of a process over time.

scatter diagram — A diagram that helps show if there is a relationship between two variables.

scope validation — The formal acceptance of the completed project deliverables by the customer or designated stakeholders.

slipped milestone — A milestone activity that was completed later than originally planned.

status reports — Reports that describe where the project stands at a specific point in time.

stratification — A technique used to separate data to see patterns in data.

to-complete performance index (TCPI) — The measure of the cost performance that must be achieved on the remaining work in order to meet a specified goal, such as the BAC or EAC

tracking Gantt chart — A Gantt chart that compares planned and actual project schedule information.

verified deliverable — A deliverable that has been completed and checked for correctness as part of quality control.

workarounds — The unplanned responses to risk events.

END NOTES

[1]Novid Parsi, "'David Bowie Is' a Project," PM Network (April 2015).

[2]Fran Kelly, "The World Today—Olympic Planning Schedule behind Time," *ABC Online* (March 4, 2004).

[3]Jay Weiner and Rachel Blount, "Olympics Are Safe but Crowds Are Sparse," *Minneapolis Star Tribune* (August 22, 2004).

[4]Martin Muller, "After Sochi 2014: Costs and Impacts of Russia's Olympic Games", Social Science Research Network (February 2015).

[5]Joan Vennochi, "Time, Money, and the Big Dig," *Boston Globe* (April 26, 2005).

[6]http://www.myki.com.au/About-myki/What-is-myki-(accessed March 1, 2012).

[7]Levy, Megan, "Peak-hour test for myki smartcard system," The Age (July 26, 2010)

[8]Alex White, "The $1.5 Billion myki Debacle Labor Doesn't Want to Know About," Herald Sun (January 3, 2015).

Chapter 9
Closing Projects

OPENING CASE

The Just-In-Time Training project was almost finished. Twenty instructor-led courses had been conducted over the past year, and a majority of Global Construction's employees took at least one Just-In-Time course, most using the Web-based delivery option. Some senior managers were surprised at how quickly workers took to the Web-based courses and were also pleased that many employees took the courses on their own time. Participants liked the interactive feedback and started networking more internally to improve productivity and collaboration. Employees provided excellent feedback on the new approach to training and suggested several new topics to be added to the list of training subjects. The project steering committee was looking forward to Kristin's final report and presentation on the project.

INTRODUCTION

Closing projects or phases involves finalizing all activities and bringing the project or phase to an orderly end. It includes archiving project information, ensuring the planned work is complete, and releasing organizational resources. It often includes a final presentation and report. For both projects that are completed and those that are canceled before completion, it is important to formally close the project and reflect on what can be learned to improve future projects. As philosopher George Santayana said, "Those who cannot remember the past are condemned to repeat it."

There are four common ways to close or terminate a project:

1.   *Integration:* A project is completed, and products and services created are integrated into operations, as was done in the Just-In-Time Training project. This is the most common approach. Project staff and other resources are released and distributed into the organization.

2.   *Addition:* A project creates a new product or service that results in a new unit in the organization, such as a department, division, or company. Project staff and other resources move into the new unit.

3.   *Extinction:* A project may end because it was successful and achieved its goals, and there is no need for further work. Another form of extinction is when a project is stopped because it was unsuccessful or superseded. A special case of termination by extinction is called termination by murder, when there is a sudden end to a project.

4.   *Starvation:* A project can also be terminated by decreasing its budget or suddenly ending funding. This approach is also known as withdrawal of life support. The reason for starving a project is generally to shadow the failure of non-accomplishment of the goals. Management sometimes uses this approach to avoid embarrassment.

Many companies terminated projects by extinction or starvation due to poor economic conditions. Even Google, the "number one" company to work for in America for several years, canceled several projects. They evaluated how popular development projects were with customers and employees, how big a problem they addressed, and whether they were meeting internal performance targets. If they didn't meet those criteria, they were closed. "There's no single equation that describes us, but we try to use data wherever possible," said Jeff Huber, Google's senior vice president of engineering. "What products have found an audience? Which ones are growing?"[1]

It is also important to plan for and execute a smooth transition of the project into the normal operations of the company if it is completed. Most projects produce results that are integrated into the existing organizational structure. For example, Global Construction's Just-In-Time Training project will require staff to coordinate future training after the project is completed. Recall from the business case in Chapter 3 that the life-cycle cost estimate for the project included $400,000 each year for three years for work to be done after the project was completed. Before ending the project, Kristin and her team created a transition plan as part of the final report to integrate the new training into the firm's standard operations.

SUMMARY OF CLOSING OUTPUTS

Figure 9-1 summarizes key outputs of project closing by knowledge area, based on the *PMBOK® Guide – Sixth Edition*. Procedures for administrative and contract closure are part of organizational process assets. For example, many organizations require some type of customer acceptance or project completion form. Every project should have procedures to guide closure. Samples of closing procedures and other outputs produced in closing the Just-In-Time Training project are provided in this chapter, such as a close-out meeting, project celebration, final project report, and lessons learned report.

Knowledge area	Closing process	Outputs	
Project integration management	Close project or phase	Project documents updates	
		Final product, service, or result transition	
		Final report	
		Organizational process assets updates	

Figure 9-1. Closing processes and outputs

PROJECT INTEGRATION MANAGEMENT

The last process in project integration management is closing the phase or project. To close a project or phase of a project, you must finish all activities and transfer the completed or canceled work to the appropriate people. The main outputs of closing a project or phase are as follows:

- *Project documents updates:* All project documents should be reviewed and marked as final versions. For example, the lessons learned register should be updated to include information learned during the closing process.

- *Final product, service, or result transition:* Project sponsors are usually most interested in making sure that the final products, services, or results are delivered and transitioned to the appropriate part of the organization.

- *Final report:* A final project report and presentation are also commonly used during project closing. The *PMBOK® Guide – Sixth Edition* suggests the final report include the following topic:

  o	Summary level description of the project or phase

  o	Scope objectives, the criteria used to evaluate the scope, and evidence that the completion criteria were met

  o	Quality objectives, the criteria used to evaluate the project and product quality, and the verification and validation information

  o	Schedule objectives including planned and actual milestone delivery dates and reasons for variances

  o	Cost objectives, including the acceptable cost range, actual costs, and reasons for variances

  o	Summary of how the final project, service, or result achieved the benefits that the project was undertaken to address.

  o	Summary of how the final project, service, or result achieved the business needs identified in the business plan.

  o	Summary of any risks or issues encountered on the project and how they were addressed

- *Updates to organizational process assets:* Recall that organizational process assets help people understand, follow, and improve business processes. Examples of organizational process assets include plans, processes, policies, procedures, and knowledge bases, such as templates and lessons-learned reports. During closing, the project team should update appropriate process assets, especially the lessons learned repository. At the end of the Just-In-Time Training project, Kristin's team prepared a lessons-learned report, which will serve as a tremendous asset for future projects.

VIDEO HIGHLIGHTS

Some of the most useful lessons learned come from project failures. One very visible, painful project failure occurred in 1986 when the Space Shuttle Challenger exploded only 73 seconds after liftoff, killing all seven astronauts onboard. You can watch CNN's live video of the disaster on YouTube by searching for "Challenger disaster live on CNN." This 25th Space Shuttle mission altered the history of manned space exploration. In 2011, the Associated Press released a video called "Challenger's Lessons Still Echo 25 Years Later." President Ronald Reagan formed a presidential committee which grounded the program, and senior management reconsidered what some people thought was a "gung ho" launch culture. Some of the narrative in this video includes the following:

Roger Laune's, Senior Curate at the Air and Space Museum, stated, "What had failed was the communication process where people at a lower level thought there was a problem, but that did not get to the higher level. So communication is the key thing to change."

Mark Hamrick of the Associated Press said that "Challenger's legacy is still debated today…NASA learned quickly that a launch was anything but routine…Ironically, the legacy of Challenger may be that tragedy produced results that made space travel safer for those who followed."[2]

The Challenger was the 25th space shuttle launch. The final (135th) shuttle launch was on July 8, 2011.

In addition to these outputs, it is also good practice to hold a close-out meeting and celebrate completion of the project or phase. In closing the Just-In-Time Training project, Kristin and her team prepared a customer acceptance/project completion form, a final report and presentation, a transition plan (provided as part of the final report), and a lessons-learned report. They also held a project close-out meeting to help transfer knowledge to other people in the organization. Kristin also organized a project closure luncheon for the project team right after the final project presentation. She and her team used the luncheon to celebrate a job well done.

Sample Customer Acceptance/Project Completion Form

As part of project closing, Global Construction had the project sponsor complete a customer acceptance/project completion form. Even if the project had been terminated, the sponsor would still have completed the form to signify the end of the project. Figure 9-2 shows the form that was filled out for the Just-In-Time Training project. Note that this form refers to completion of the entire project, not just a specific phase. It should be completed and signed by the project sponsor.

Customer Acceptance/Project Completion Form

June 30

Project Name: **Just-In-Time Training Project**

Project Manager: **Kristin Maur**

I (We), the undersigned, acknowledge and accept delivery of the work completed for this project on behalf of our organization. My (Our) signature(s) attest(s) to my (our) agreement that this project has been completed. No further work should be done on this project.

Signature area (use company standard for signatures)

1. Was this project completed to your satisfaction?   **X**   Yes   _____ No
2. Please rate project performance based on a scale of 1 to 10, with 10 being the best. **9**
3. Please provide the main reasons for your satisfaction or dissatisfaction with this project. The project met and exceeded my expectations. In my 15 years with this company, I have never seen workers so interested in training courses. Kristin effectively coordinated all of the people who worked on this project. We worked with a number of new suppliers, and everything went very smoothly.
4. Please provide suggestions on how our organization could improve its project delivery capability in the future.

One suggestion would be to try to improve our estimating and forecasting abilities. The project costs were slightly over budget, even with some reserve built in. The schedule buffer prevented the project from finishing late. We also need to improve the way we forecast the number of people who want to take courses. The demand for the Web-based courses was much higher than expected. Even though that was a pleasant surprise, it was still poor forecasting and caused extra work for project and support staff.

Thank you for your inputs.

Figure 9-2. Sample customer acceptance/project completion form

Sample Final Report

Figure 9-3 is the table of contents for the final project report for the Just-In-Time Training project (the cover page of the report included the project title, date, and team member names). Notice that the report includes a transition plan and a plan to analyze the benefits of the training each year. Also notice that the final report includes attachments for all the project management and product-related documents. Kristin knew the importance of providing complete final documentation on projects and that the project steering committee would expect a comprehensive final report on such an important project. The project team produced a hard copy of the final documentation for the project sponsor and each steering committee member, and placed an electronic copy on the corporate intranet with the other project archives. Kristin also led the team in giving a final project presentation, which summarized key information in the final project report.

Final Project Report
June 20

Project Name: Just-In-Time Training Project
1. Project Description and Summary of Results
2. Original and Actual Scope
3. Original and Actual Schedule
4. Original and Actual Budget
5. Quality Objectives, Verification, and Validation
6. Risk/Issue Summary
7. Project Assessment
8. Lessons Learned Summary
9. Transition Plan
10. Training Benefits Plan

Attachments:
A. Key Project Management Documentation
   - Business case
   - Project charter
   - Project management plan
   - Performance reports
B. Product-Related Documentation
   - Survey and results
   - Summary of user inputs
   - Report on research of existing training
   - Partnership agreements
   - Course materials
   - Intranet site training information
   - Summary of course evaluations

Figure 9-3. Sample table of contents for a final project report

Sample Transition Plan

As mentioned earlier, the life-cycle cost estimate for Global Construction's Just-In-Time Training project included $400,000 each year for three years for work to be done after the project was completed. The transition plan included information related to what work had to be done, by whom, and when. When developing a transition plan, the project team should work with managers in affected operating departments, and the contents of the plan should be tailored to fit the support needs of the project. Figure 9-4 provides part of the transition plan for the Just-In-Time Training project.

Transition Plan
June 20

Project Name: Just-In-Time Training Project

Introduction

The main goal of this project was to develop a new training program at Global Construction to provide just-in-time training to employees on key topics, including supplier management, negotiating skills, project management, and software applications. New courses were developed and offered in instructor-led, CD-ROM, and Web-based formats. These courses will continue to be offered at Global Construction for the next several years. This transition plan describes the work required to support these courses.

Assumptions

- Support for the just-in-time training will be handled by staff in affected operational departments, including the training, IT, HR, and contract departments.

- Funding for the required support is budgeted at $400,000 per year for three years. These funds will be used to pay staff in the operational departments supporting this project, experts providing information for courses, and suppliers providing training materials and courses.

- New course topics will be developed under a new project and are not part of this transition plan.

Organization

The Training Director, Lucy Camerena, will lead all efforts to support the Just-In-Time Training courses. Staff from the training, IT, HR, and contract departments will provide support as required. See the organizational chart provided in Attachment 1.

Work Required

The main work required to support the training developed from this project includes:

- Maintaining related information on the intranet site

- Handling course registration

- Determining the number of courses offered each year and when they will be offered

- Providing classrooms for the instructor-led training

- Coordinating with suppliers for all training courses

- Planning and managing the internal experts who provide some of the training and expert support for the courses

- Collecting course evaluation information and suggestions for changing the content or format of courses

- Reporting information to senior management on a monthly basis

See Attachment 2 for detailed information on the work required.

Schedule

See Attachment 3 for a draft schedule of work to be performed in the next year. The Training Director is responsible for scheduling and managing the work required to support the Just-In-Time training.

Figure 9-4. Sample transition plan

Kristin also used the corporate template to prepare a short lessons-learned report for inclusion in the final documentation for the project, as shown in Figure 9-5. A short summary was also included in the final project report. Notice the question-and-answer format, which was used for all projects done at Global Construction, Inc. Also notice that the lessons-learned report was finished 10 days before the project ended.

Lessons-Learned Report
June 20

Project Name: Just-In-Time Training Project
Project Sponsor: Lucy Camerena
Project Manager: Kristin Maur
Project Dates: July 1 – June 30
Final Budget: $1,072,000

1. Did the project meet scope, time, and cost goals?

We did meet scope and time goals, but we had to request an additional $72,000, which the sponsor approved. We actually exceeded scope goals by having more people take training courses than planned, primarily the Web-based courses.

2. What was the success criteria listed in the project scope statement?

The following statement outlined the project scope and success criteria:

"Our sponsor has stated that the project will be a success if the new training courses are all available within one year, if the average course evaluations are at least 3.0 on a 1-5 scale, and if the company recoups the cost of the project in reduced training costs within two years after project completion."

3. Reflect on whether or not you met the project success criteria.

All of the new training courses were offered within a year, and the course evaluations averaged 3.4 on a 5-point scale. The number of people who took the Web-based training courses far exceeded our expectations. Because the Web-based training is more cost-effective than the instructor-led training, we are confident that the cost of the project will be recouped in less than two years.

4. In terms of managing the project, what were the main lessons your team learned from this project?

The main lessons we learned include the following:

- Having good communications was instrumental to project success. We had a separate item in the WBS for stakeholder communications, which was very important. Moving from traditional to primarily Web-based training was a big change for Global Construction, so the strong communications was crucial. The intranet site information was excellent, thanks to support from the IT department. It was also very effective to have different departments create project description posters to hang in their work areas. They showed creativity and team spirit.

- Teamwork and supplier partnerships were essential. It was extremely helpful to take time to develop and follow a team charter or contract for the project team and to focus on developing good partnerships with suppliers. Everyone was very supportive of each other.

- Good planning paid off when plans were executed. We spent a fair amount of time developing a good project charter, scope statement, WBS, schedules, and other plans. Everyone worked together to develop these planning documents, and there was strong buy-in. We kept the plans up-to-date and made key project information available for everyone on a secure website.

- Creativity and innovation are infectious: Many creative and innovative ideas were used on this project. After departments had so much fun making their posters in their work areas, people picked up on the idea of being creative and innovative throughout the project. Everyone realized that training and learning could be enjoyable.

- The project steering committee was very effective. It was extremely helpful to meet regularly with the project steering committee. Having members from different departments in the company was very important and helped in promoting the training created as part of this project.

5. Describe one example of what went right on this project.

We were skeptical about hiring an outside consultant to help us develop a short list of potential suppliers for the training courses, but it was well worth the money. We gained useful information very quickly, and the consultant made excellent recommendations and helped us develop partnerships that benefited suppliers and us.

6. Describe one example of what went wrong on this project.

The senior supplier management specialist assigned to the team at the beginning of the project was not a good fit. The project manager should have more involvement in selecting project team members.

7. What will you do differently on the next project based on your experience working on this project?

For future training projects, it would be helpful to line up experts and mentors further in advance. We underestimated the number of people who would take the Web-based courses, and participants liked the interactive features, such as getting expert advice and having a list of people willing to mentor them on various topics. We were scrambling to get people and had to figure out how to organize them in an effective manner.

Figure 9-5. Sample lessons-learned report

WHAT WENT WRONG?

Everyone seems to agree that it is important to document and share project lessons learned, yet a survey of 961 experienced project managers found that although 62 percent had formal procedures for learning lessons from projects, only 12 percent adhered closely to them.

The Project Management (PM) Perspective research team wanted to discover how organizations capture lessons learned and apply them to new projects. Their findings were very discouraging. Although many tools and processes were in place for capturing lessons-learned information at the end of a project, few organizations bothered to use them.

"End-of-project post-mortems were infrequently and inadequately performed. Project managers cited the usual problems: a lack of time, key people not available, a culture of blame. And, as one interviewee noted, 'Most projects don't have enough budget to support any good closure.'"[3]

Another format for preparing a lessons-learned report is available from Microsoft. Figure 9-6 on the following two pages shows this Word template, available from www.microsoft.com by searching for "project lessons learned template."

[Project Name]

Project Lessons Learned

Department: **Document Owner:**

Focus Area: **Project or Organization Role:**

Product or Process:

Version	Date	Author	Change Description

LESSONS LEARNED PURPOSE AND OBJECTIVES

Throughout each project phase, lessons are learned and opportunities for improvement are discovered. As part of a continuous improvement process, documenting lessons learned helps the project team discover the root causes of problems that occurred and avoid those problems in later project stages or future projects. Data for this report was gathered by using Project Lessons Learned Record sheets and is summarized in the table.

The objective of this report is gathering all relevant information for better planning of later project stages and future projects, improving implementation of new projects, and preventing or minimizing risks for future projects.

Lessons learned questions

- What worked well—or didn't work well—either for this project or for the project team?
- What needs to be done over or differently?
- What surprises did the team have to deal with?
- What project circumstances were not anticipated?
- Were the project goals attained? If not, what changes need to be made to meet goals in the future?

Project Highlights

Top 3 Significant Project Successes

Project Success	Factors That Supported Success

Other Notable Project Successes

Project Success	Factors That Supported Success

Project Shortcomings and Solutions

Project Shortcoming	Recommended Solutions

Approvals

Prepared by:_____
                Project Manager

Approved by: _____
                Project Sponsor

                _____
                Executive Sponsor

                _____
                Client Sponsor

Figure 9-6. Microsoft lessons-learned template

Media Snapshot

Many readers of this book grew up using social media sites like Facebook and Twitter, but you may not have learned your lesson on what you should not be posting! You may be surprised to learn that 93% of recruiters check out social media profiles of prospective hires. A recent article in Money Magazine provides a list of "10 Social Media Blunders That Cost a Millennial a Job — or Worse," as follows:

1. Posting something embarrassing on the corporate Twitter feed
2. Sexual oversharing
3. Revealing company secrets
4. Blowing your own cover
5. Talking smack about a job before you've even accepted it
6. Making fun of clients or donors
7. Making fun of your boss / team.
8. Posting while you're supposed to be working
9. Complaining about your job
10. Drinking in a photo—even if you're over 21[4]

Project Close-Out Meeting and Knowledge Transfer

It is good practice to hold a close-out meeting as a project nears completion or termination. At this meeting, like the kick-off meeting, you should invite key project stakeholders. Some people call this close-out meeting a **post-mortem** since it is normally held after the project has died or been put to rest. The project champion should start off the meeting, and the project manager and his/her team should review information such as:

- The scope, time, and cost goals and outcomes

- The success criteria and results in achieving them

- Main changes that occurred during the project and how they were addressed

- The main lessons learned on the project

- A summary of the transition plan

The project team should also ask for comments and questions from stakeholders. It's important to get other perspectives on how things went. If there are still any issues that need to be addressed, the project manager should follow through on them to successfully close them out.

It is also important to take time to transfer knowledge learned while working on the project. **Knowledge transfer** is the process of communicating knowledge that was developed by one person or in one part of an organization to another person or other parts of an organization. In particular, people who will take over products or results produced as part of the project would need to spend time with project team members so they understand what is involved in detail. In this example, people from the training, IT, HR, and contract departments would gain from knowledge transfer from the Just-In-Time Training project.

Of course, these people could read the final report, transition plan, and lessons learned, but most people also want face-to-face interaction to really benefit from knowledge transfer. For example, since Kristin would move on to another project after completing this one, she should meet with the person from the training department who would handle many of the management tasks involved in planning and implementing future training courses. She should offer to mentor this person and be available as needed to answer questions. Likewise, the IT person who developed the intranet materials related to the project should also meet with whoever will take over that work and share his/her expertise as well. If it makes sense to provide further documentation, the person who knows the most about the work should take the time to write it.

Many organizations are working hard to improve the knowledge transfer process, since employee knowledge or human capital is one of their key assets. It is crucial, therefore, to make project knowledge transfer a priority, especially if the benefits of a project are not achieved immediately. For example, one of the success criteria for the Just-In-Time Training project was to recoup the cost of the project in reduced training costs within two years after project completion. The business case stated that a goal was to reduce training costs per employee by 10 percent each year or about $100 per employee per year. Kristin should work with the people taking over the training to ensure that they measure training costs and work to achieve their goals.

BEST PRACTICE

Kent Greenes is an expert and consultant on knowledge management. Blogger Dale Arseneault captured the following useful ideas from one of Kent's presentations on best practices in knowledge transfer:

1. "Best" or "better" practices are not adopted; they're adapted.
2. As Jack Welch said, "You don't have a better or best practice until someone else is using it."
3. The learner is important, and making learning easy is critical or people will recreate "good enough."
4. Focus on general, broadly applicable practices first, rather than choosing highly specialized practices.
5. Do something, see what works, then broaden the scope.
6. Peer assistance is a critical tool to begin, and even conclude, the process.
7. Uncover success stories, communicate the stories, and assist the learning and adaption processes.
8. Facilitation is critical to the process - both the role and the capability.
9. Documentation/video/audio artifacts are the starting point for discovery and productive conversation; it is vital to put the people with the learning needs and the people who have the experience together to enable transfer.
10. To facilitate discovery of best practices, leverage communities wherever possible.[5]

ADVICE ON CLOSING PROJECTS

Although project teams do not typically spend much time on closing projects, it is important to do it well. Below are a few words of advice on quickly and successfully closing projects, whether they were successful or not:

- It is important to plan for project closing. There should be deliverables in the WBS and resources allocated to perform project closing. For example, someone should be assigned the activity of reviewing lessons learned and creating one final lessons-learned report. Resources should be assigned to prepare the final project report, presentation, and some type of celebration.

- It will be much easier to close a project if the project team captures lessons learned and other important information required for closing as soon as possible. For example, the project team should have a lessons-learned repository where everyone can document lessons learned as they occur. A simple blog would work well for this purpose, or team members could document lessons learned as part of progress reports.

- Project managers should take time to thank their team and other project stakeholders and have some type of closing celebration. Just having a team lunch or informal gathering with refreshments might be appropriate. If it was a big, highly successful project, a more formal celebration and rewards would be appropriate. See the examples in the following What Went Right? passage.

WHAT WENT RIGHT?

Many project teams go all out to celebrate the closing of their projects, especially when the project went well. A quick search on www.youtube.com and similar sites shows many videos of project closing celebrations. Below are a few examples:

- Popular television shows likes American Idol and The Voice have great closing shows. For example, in 2016, several famous celebrities (Kelly Clarkson, Jennifer Hudson, etc.) performed before ending the fifteenth season of American Idol and announcing the new winner, Trent Harmon. You can find several video clips of this and other final talent-related shows on the Internet.

- Many viewers got tears in their eyes watching the last few minutes of Extreme Home Makeover episodes. Ty Pennington and his team of designers, builders, volunteers, friends, family, and neighbors gathered to see the new home built quickly for a family in need. Everyone enjoyed the tradition of shouting, "Move that bus!"

- On a smaller scale, Allegheny College put together a five minute video of their senior project celebration. Many colleges require senior projects, so why not have a formal celebration when the projects are completed and document the event in a video?

Of course this chapter would not be complete without a cartoon about closing projects (Figure 9-7). May you never have nightmares from not finishing your projects!

Figure 9-7. Bad dreams about not finishing projects (www.xkcd.com)

CASE WRAP-UP

Kristin Maur stood in front of the project steering committee. She invited her entire team to give the final presentation as a group effort. Of course they had several challenges along the way, but overall, the project was a success. All the new training courses were offered within a year, and the course evaluations averaged 3.4 on a 5.0 scale, which exceeded the committee's goal of 3.0. More people took training courses than planned, primarily the Web-based courses. Because the Web-based training was more cost-effective than the instructor-led training, the team was confident that the costs of the Just-In-Time Training project would be recouped in less than two years, as projected. Kristin watched each team member summarize key project results, and she sensed the pride that everyone felt in a job well done. She also felt good knowing that she helped her team members get assigned to even more challenging projects, and she was ready to start her next project as well.

CHAPTER SUMMARY

Closing projects or phases involves finalizing all activities and bringing the project or phase to an orderly end. It includes archiving project information, ensuring the planned work is complete, and releasing organizational resources. This chapter summarizes the closing processes and key outputs for project integration management.

Closing outputs related to integration management include project documents updates, final products, services, or result transition, a final report, and updates to organizational process assets. Sample closing documents for the Just-In-Time Training project include a final project report, lessons-learned report, and customer acceptance/project completion form. It is also good practice to hold a close-out meeting and hold some type of celebration when a project ends.

Helpful advice for closing projects includes planning for closure, documenting lessons learned and other important information as soon as possible, and celebrating project closure.

QUICK QUIZ

Note that you can find additional, interactive quizzes at www.intropm.com.

1.   Which knowledge areas include processes related to closing?

   A.   project scope, schedule, cost, and quality management

   B.   project integration, scope, schedule, cost, and quality management

   C.   project integration and procurement management

   D.   project integration management

2.   Which of the following statements is false?

   A.   Even though many projects are canceled before completion, it is still important to formally close any project.

   B.   Closing includes releasing organizational resources.

   C.   Closing often includes a final presentation and report.

   D.   Closing does not include developing a transition plan.

3.   Updating processes, policies, procedures, and knowledge bases is part of _____.

   A.   updating organizational process assets

   B.   archival

   C.   updating project documents

   D.   lessons learned

4.   Answering questions such as, "What will you do differently on the next project based on your experience working on this project?" is part of a _____.

   A.   lessons-learned report

   B.   customer acceptance/project completion form

   C.   written notice of contract closure

   D.   transition plan

5.   What is the most common reason for closing or terminating a project?

A. addition

B. integration

C. extinction

D. starvation

6.   This approach to project termination occurs when a project is ended by decreasing its budget or suddenly ending funding.

A. addition

B. integration

C. extinction

D. starvation

7.   A _____ is another name for a project close-out meeting

A. celebration

B. post project

C. final review

D. post mortem

8.   _____ is the process of communicating knowledge that was developed by one person or in one part of an organization to another person or other parts of an organization.

A. Cross training

B. Lessons learned transfer

C. Knowledge transfer

D. Transitional planning

9.   Which of the following was not a lesson learned from the Just-In-Time Training project?

A. good communications was instrumental to project success

B. supplier partnerships were not very effective

C. good planning paid off in execution

D. the project steering committee was very helpful

10.   Which of the following is not advice for closing projects or phases?

    A. You don't need to celebrate completing a project, especially if it did not go well.

    B. You should capture lessons learned as soon as possible, not just at the end of a project

    C. You should include tasks in the WBS for project closing

    D. You should assign resources to specific project closing tasks

Quick Quiz Answers

1. D; 2. D; 3. A; 4. A; 5. B; 6. D; 7. D; 8. C; 9. B; 10. A

DISCUSSION QUESTIONS

1.   What is involved in closing projects? Why should all projects be formally closed?

2.   What are the main closing outputs created as part of integration management?

3.   Why is it important to create a final project report, presentation, and lessons-learned report?

4.   What are the main topics included in a lessons-learned report?

5.   What is a post-mortem?

6.   What advice about project closing is most useful to you? What other advice would you add?

EXERCISES

1.   Find an example of a large project that took more than a year to complete, such as a major construction project. You can ask people at your college, university, or work about a recent project, such as a major fundraising campaign, information systems installation, or building project. You can also find information about projects online such as the Big Dig in Boston (*www.masspike.com/bigdig*), the Patronas Twin Towers in Malaysia, and many other building projects (*www.greatbuildings.com*). Describe some of the tasks performed to close the project. Write a one-page paper or prepare a short presentation summarizing your findings.

2.   Using the lessons-learned template on the companion website or the one available from Microsoft as shown in Figure 8-6, write a lessons-learned report for a project you worked on. If you cannot think of one, interview someone who recently completed a project and write a lessons-learned report on that project.

3.   Compare the lessons-learned template on the companion website and the one available from Microsoft as shown in Figure 8-6. Search for at least one other

example of lessons-learned report or template. Summarize their similarities and differences in a one-page paper, citing your references.

4. Find an article or video that provides a good example of closing a project. See the What Went Right? passage for ideas, but find your own unique example. Document your findings in a one-page paper, citing your references.

5. Watch the videos mentioned in the Video Highlights for this chapter about the Space Shuttle Challenger disaster and lessons learned from it. (See www.intropm.com for the direct links.) Research other articles and videos about the lessons learned from the Challenger and space travel since then. Document your findings and opinions in a short presentation, paper, or video.

TEAM PROJECTS

1. Your organization is about to complete a project to raise money for an important charity. Assume that there are 1,000 people in your organization. Also, assume that you had six months to raise as much money as possible, with a goal of $100,000. With just one week to go, you have raised $92,000. You did experience several problems with the project, which you described in Chapter 8. Using that information and information you prepared in other chapters related to this project, prepare a two- to three-page paper or 15-minute final presentation for the project. Be creative in your responses.

2. You are part of a team in charge of a project to help people in your company (500 people) lose weight. This project is part of a competition, and the top "losers" will be featured in a popular television show. Assume that you had six months to complete the project and a budget of $10,000. The project will end in one week, so you and your team are busy closing out the project. Prepare a lessons-learned report for the project, using information from your responses to this exercise in previous chapters as well as your creativity to determine what the final outcome was for the project.

3. Using the information you developed in Team Project 1 or 2, role-play the final project meeting, at which you present the final project presentation to key stakeholders. Determine who will play what role (project manager, team member from a certain department, senior managers, and so on). Be creative in displaying different personalities (a senior manager who questions the importance of the project to the organization, a team member who is very shy or obnoxious).

4. Perform the closing tasks for one of the case studies provided in Appendix C. If you are working on a real team project, create relevant closing documents, such as a final project report and lessons-learned report, using the templates and samples in this chapter as guides. Present your results to the class.

KEY TERMS

knowledge transfer — The process of communicating knowledge that was developed by one person or in one part of an organization to another person or other parts of an organization.

post-mortem — A term sometimes used for a project close-out meeting since it is held after the project has died or been put to rest.

END NOTES

[1]Vindu Goel, "How Google Decides to Pull the Plug," The New York Times (February 14, 2009).

[2]Associated Press, "Challengers Lessons Still Echo 25 Years Later," www.youtube.com (January 27, 2011).

[3]Blaize Reich, "Lessons Not Learned," Projects @ Work, (October 9, 2008).

[4]Susie Poppick, "10 Social Media Blunders That Cost a Millennial a Job — or Worse," Money Magazine (Sept. 5, 2014).

[5]Dale Arseneault, "Best Practice Knowledge Transfer – Practical Ideas," Reflections on Knowledge Management and Organizational Innovation (January 15, 2008).

Chapter 10
Best Practices in Project Management

LEARNING OBJECTIVES

After reading this chapter, you will be able to:

- Define best practices in general and best practices in project management for organizations
- Summarize best practices in project management for individuals
- Explain how improving project management maturity can improve project and organizational performance
- Describe research on project management maturity
- Discuss best practices described in this text
- Read final advice about project management

OPENING CASE

After completing the Just-In-Time Training project, Kristin was asked to join a special task force to work with the company's Program Management Office (PMO). Their purpose was to create a repository of best practice information and make recommendations on specific best practices most useful for Global Construction. The PMO Director, Marie Scott, led the task force. Other members included representatives from each department in the company as well as three other members of the PMO. They were expected to complete their work within two months, and Kristin was asked to spend about ten hours per week on this task force. She had a good experience as project manager on the Just-In-Time Training project, but she knew that she had a lot to learn about improving her skills. She was excited to be a part of this team and looked forward to improving the company's project management capabilities.

INTRODUCTION

Many organizations understand the value of project management, yet they struggle to implement it well. There is great value to learning about best practices in project management on a case by case basis, but you can also learn a lot by looking at larger studies of best practices. This chapter defines project management best practices and provides information on best practices for organizations and individuals. It also describes how increasing an organization's project management maturity level can improve project and organizational performance.

WHAT WENT RIGHT?

It may seem surprising to know that many famous corporations still do not follow very basic project management processes or have just recently adopted them. Below are a few examples of how organizations have benefited from following best practices in project management:

- One of the world's largest rental-car companies, Hertz, established project management offices in 2007 and developed standard processes for their organization. For example, in order to optimize bus service for customers at Heathrow Airport in London, bus drivers defined project goals and outcomes, analyzed information, established simple milestones, and performed measurements of the scope, time, cost, and customer satisfaction goals of the project. This simple process helped Hertz to greatly improve bus services. "Project management is changing the face of Hertz. It's the toolbox the company has never had before, and it's changing who we are."[1]

- The board of Siemens launched a worldwide initiative to improve its project management. The German electronics group had worked out that half its turnover came from project-like work, and it calculated that if it could complete all of these projects on time and to budget, it would add $3.7 billion U.S. dollars to its bottom line over three years. A key element of the scheme was the introduction of project managers to the company's sales teams to try and temper their more extravagant promises, a move that requires a careful balance between reining them in and killing the deal. [2]

- Some companies have changed their whole business philosophy to become more project-oriented. Project management has become an important competitive tool or core competence. For example, "Nike now manages footwear projects instead of just making and selling shoes. Coca-Cola has people called "orchestrators" who manage a collection of projects since most of the company's bottling and marketing of its drinks is outsourced to others. Germany's BMW treats each new car platform as a separate project. BP converted its exploration division, BPX, into a portfolio of projects, and profits soared after project managers were given more autonomy and had to build their own self-sufficient teams."[3]

DEFINING PROJECT MANAGEMENT BEST PRACTICES

To benefit from best practices in project management, it is important to first define what best practices are. Below are three general definitions of best practices:

- Webster's Dictionary (2017) defines a **best practice** as "a procedure that has been shown by research and experience to produce optimal results and that is established or proposed as a standard suitable for widespread adoption."
- Wikipedia (2009) defines a best practice as "the most efficient (least amount of effort) and effective (best results) way of accomplishing a task, based on repeatable procedures that have proven themselves over time for large numbers of people…The idea is that with proper processes, checks, and testing, a desired outcome can be delivered with fewer problems and unforeseen complications."
- Wikipedia (2017)) defines a best practice as "a method or technique that has been generally accepted as superior to any alternatives because it produces results that are superior to those achieved by other means or because it has become a standard way of doing things, e.g., a standard way of complying with legal or ethical requirements."

Perhaps you do not think it is a best practice to use a dictionary or Wikipedia definition in a textbook! The point is that there is more than one definition of a best practice, and the concept itself is complex and evolving. A best practice for one industry or region may not work in a different one, as you will see later in this chapter.

For example, if you are reading this text as part of a course, you should know about best practices for studying and getting good grades in college. There are general best practices that most people might agree on, such as showing up for and paying attention in class, doing homework on time, setting aside time to study and get a good night's rest before exams, and so on. For individual students, however, there might be other best practices that are more effective, and those practices might vary based on the subject and course. Perhaps you need to be part of study group to do well on homework assignments and exams in a particular subject. Perhaps for another class or student you need to study alone in a very quiet location. Perhaps a particular course requires a lot of online participation to get a good grade. In another course, you might be able to earn an outstanding grade with a minimal amount of work. Some general best practices might apply, but there are also some that are unique to each person or course.

VIDEO HIGHLIGHTS

Many people enjoying watching experts speak on various topics as part of the TED Talks series. In December 2016 Ling Wong published a list called "11 TED Talks Every Project Manager Should Watch." Below are titles and lengths of the talks:
1. Daniel Levitin: How to stay calm when you know you'll be stressed [12:20]
2. Dan Pink: The puzzle of motivation [18:32]
3. Itay Talgam: Lead Like the Great Conductors [20:44]
4. Kelly McGonigal: How to make stress your friend [14:25]
5. Yves Morieux: As work gets more complex, 6 rules to simplify [11:58]
6. David Allen: The Art of Stress-Free Productivity [22:15]
7. Navi Radjou: Creative problem-solving in the face of extreme limits [16:25]
8. David Grady: How to save the world (or at least yourself) from bad meetings [6:40]
9. Tom Wujec: Build a tower, build a team [6:44]
10. Roselinde Torres: What It Takes to Be a Great Leader [9:15]
11. Julia Galef: Why you think you're right — even if you're wrong [11:37]

The following sections describe PMI's view of best practices in project management as well as information from a popular business text on the subject.

The Project Management Institute's Definition of Best Practices

The Project Management Institute (PMI) Standards Development Program published the first version of the Organizational Project Management Maturity Model (OPM3®) in December 2003 to address the need to bridge the gap between organizational strategy and successful projects. (Maturity models are described in more detail later in this chapter.) OPM3® is a standard developed to provide a way for organizations to measure their organizational project management maturity against a comprehensive set of best practices. The third edition of this document was published in 2013.

OPM3® defines best practices as "methods, currently recognized within a given industry or discipline, to achieve a stated goal or objective."[4] It lists hundreds of best practices, which PMI says are achieved through developing and consistently demonstrating their supporting capabilities, as observed through measurable outcomes. **Capabilities** are incremental steps leading up to one or more best practices, and **outcomes** are the tangible or intangible results of applying capabilities. A **key performance indicator (KPI)** is a criterion used to determine the degree to which an outcome is achieved.

The first edition of OPM3® provides the following example to illustrate a best practice, capability, outcome, and key performance indicator:

- *Best practice:* Establish internal project management communities

- *Capability (one of four for this best practice):* Facilitate project management activities

- *Outcome:* Local initiatives, meaning the organization develops pockets of consensus around areas of special interest

- *Key performance indicator:* Community addresses local issues

Best practices are organized into three levels: project, program, and portfolio. Within each of those categories, best practices are categorized by four stages of process improvement: standardize, measure, control, and improve. For example, the list that follows contains several best practices listed in OPM3®:

- Project best practices:

  o *Project initiation process standardization*—Project initiation process standards are established.

  o *Project plan development process measurement*—Project plan development process measures are established, assembled, and analyzed.

  o *Project scope planning process control*—Project scope planning process controls are established and executed to control the stability of the process.

- Program best practices:

  o *Program activity definition process standardization*—Program activity definition process standards are established.

  o *Program activity sequencing process measurement*—Program activity sequencing process measures are established, assembled, and analyzed.

  o *Program activity duration estimating process control*—Program activity duration estimating process controls are established and executed to control the stability of the process.

- Portfolio best practices:

  o *Portfolio resource planning process standardization*—Portfolio resource planning process standards are established.

  o *Portfolio cost estimating process measurement*—Portfolio cost estimating process measures are established, assembled, and analyzed.

  o *Portfolio cost budgeting process control*—Portfolio cost budgeting process controls are established and executed to control the stability of the process.

MEDIA SNAPSHOT

The Project Management Institute published a list of twenty-four organizations from around the world that are considered to be outstanding in project management. These organizations apply project management best practices that are fully supported by the entire organizations and have a significant impact on the bottom line. Project management is a core component of their business. Below is an alphabetical list of these organizations and their countries:

- AgênciaClick (Brazil)
- Airports Company South Africa (South Africa)
- Beijing Organizing Committee for the Olympic Games (China)
- Central Federal Lands Highway Division (United States)
- Commonwealth Scientific and Industrial Research Organisation (Australia)
- Fluor Corp. (United States)
- IBM (United States)
- Indra Sistemas S.A. (Spain)
- Infosys Technologies (India)
- Intel Corp. (United States)
- MD Anderson Cancer Center (United States)
- Memphis Managed Care Corp. (United States)
- Missouri State Government (United States)
- Mutual of Omaha (United States)
- National Aeronautics and Space Administration (United States)
- Petrobras (Brazil)
- Saudi Aramco (Saudi Arabia)
- Serasa (Brazil)
- Shell (Netherlands)
- Stork NV (Netherlands)
- Suncorp (Australia)
- TV Guide Interactive (United States)
- Wipro Technologies (India)Workplace Technology Services (Canada)[5]

Ultimate Business Library Best Practices

The Ultimate Business Library published a book called *Best Practice: Ideas and Insights from the World's Foremost Business Thinkers*. This book includes articles by well-known business leaders such as Warren Bennis (author of over 30 books on leadership, including *On Becoming a Leader*), Daniel Goleman (author of *Emotional Intelligence* and other popular books), and Thomas Stewart (editor of the *Harvard Business Review* and author of *Intellectual Capital: The New Wealth of Organizations*).

In the book's introduction, Rosabeth Moss Kanter, a professor at Harvard Business School and a well-known author and consultant, says that visionary leaders know "the best practice secret: Stretching to learn from the best of the best in any sector can make a big vision more likely to succeed."[6] Kanter also emphasizes the need to have measurable standards for best practices. Organizations can measure performance against their own past; against peers; and, even better, against potential. Kanter suggests that organizations need to continue to reach for higher standards. She suggests the following exercise regimen for business leaders who want to intelligently adapt best practices to help their own organizations:

- Reach high. Stretch. Raise standards and aspirations. Find the best of the best and then use it as inspiration for reaching full potential.

- Help everyone in your organization become a professional. Empower people to manage themselves through benchmarks and standards based on best practice exchange.

- Look everywhere. Go far afield. Think of the whole world as your laboratory for learning.[7]

In addition, Robert Butrick, author of *The Project Workout*, wrote an article on best practices in project management for the Ultimate Business Library book. He suggests that organizations need to follow these basic principles of project management:

- Make sure your projects are driven by your strategy. Be able to demonstrate how each project you undertake fits your business strategy, and screen out unwanted projects as soon as possible.

- Use a staged approach. You can rarely plan a project in its entirety. Use progressive steps or stages to project planning, and use the same generic stages for all types of projects. Have gate reviews before starting each stage to revalidate a project and before committing more resources and funding for the project. Place high emphasis on the early stages of a project to reduce risks and decrease time to market.

- Engage your stakeholders. Ignoring stakeholders often leads to project failure. Be sure to engage stakeholders at all stages of a project, and encourage teamwork and commitment at all times.

- Ensure success by planning for it. To help projects succeed, the balance of power often needs to be tipped toward the project and away from line management.

- Monitor against the plan. Everyone working on projects must have guidance, training, and support in creating plans and making project-related decisions. Organizations must develop and follow control techniques for managing risks, issues, scope changes, schedule, costs, and project reviews. Monitoring and forecasting against a plan ensure that everyone is on the same page and prevent unwanted surprises.

- Manage the project control cycle. Monitoring should focus more on the future than on the past. Project managers must continuously check that the project plan is still fit for the purpose of the project and likely to deliver the business benefits on time. Project changes must be managed to ensure that only those enabling project benefits to be realized are accepted. Avoid the dangers of scope creep, and let stakeholders know that project benefits drive the scope.

- Formally close the project: Every project should be closed to make sure that all work ceases, that lessons are learned, and that remaining resources are released for other purposes.[8]

BEST PRACTICES OF INDIVIDUAL PROJECT MANAGERS

Andy Crowe, founder and CEO of Velociteach, wrote a book called *Alpha Project Managers: What the Top 2% Know That Everyone Else Does Not*. As the title suggests, an alpha project manager is defined as one who falls in the top two percent of project managers in terms of performance. Project managers were rated by their customers, senior managers, and team members based on their performance in the following areas:

- Setting expectations

- Communicating efficiently and effectively

- Managing issues

- Identifying and managing risks

- Leading the project team

- Meeting the scope, quality, time, and budget baselines for the project

- Managing the procurement process

- Managing changes to the project

- Balancing competing stakeholder needs

- Delivering a product, service, or result that met expectations

For this study, Crowe surveyed 860 project managers who had all been clients/students at Velociteach. Although this was not a scientific study, the aggregate results provide interesting information that can help define best practices for project managers. The 860 project managers, their senior managers, customers, and project team members all answered numerous survey questions. The general format of the questions was as follows: Mark the degree with which you agree with the following statement: Strongly disagree (0%), Somewhat disagree (20%), Neutral (50%), Somewhat agree (75%), Strongly agree (100%). For some questions, the scale was based on the degree of importance, with 100% being the most important.

The 18 people identified as alpha project managers varied most from the other project managers in the following ways:

- *They enjoy their work more than their counterparts.* When asked to mark the degree to which they agreed with the statement: "On the whole, I generally love my job," the alpha average response was 67% while the non-alpha average was only 32%. They also view their jobs more as a career and took 19% more job-related training than the non-alphas (45.1 hours vs. 38.0 hours in the past three years).

- *They believe they have more authority than their counterparts.* When asked to mark the degree to which they agreed with the statement: "I have adequate authority to manage the projects for which I am responsible," the alpha average response was 89% while the non-alpha average was only 47%. It is interesting to note that from senior management's point of view, the alphas and non-alphas had about the same level of organizational authority at about 87%.

- *They believe they can have a personal impact on project success.* When asked to mark the degree to which they agreed with the statement: "What is the importance of your role on your current project," the alpha average response was 96% while the non-alpha average was only 70%. It is interesting to note that the senior managers' response to this question was very close to the project managers for both groups.

- *They are more efficient and effective communicators.* When project managers' customers, senior managers, and team members were asked, "How would you rank this project manager's overall responsiveness to your project-related requests?" (from very ineffective to very effective) the alphas' stakeholders' average response was 88% while the non-alpha average was only 49%. It is also interesting to note that alpha project managers send *fewer* e-mails per day and spend *less* time in meetings than the non-alphas. They know how to prioritize work and focus on what is most important. When the alphas were probed in interviews to understand more about their communication best practices, key traits emerged:

- o *They talk to stakeholders very early in the project and tailor communication to meet their needs.*

- o *They create a communication schedule and stick to it.*

- o *They communicate their messages quickly in a clear and concise manner.*

- o *They create an open communication channel and talk with stakeholders regularly about the topic of communication itself.*

- o *They know that on many projects, communication is the only deliverable stakeholders will receive until the product or service is completed.*

- *They allocate about twice as much time toward project planning.* Alpha project managers spend more time in every process group than their counterparts except for execution, as follows:

  - o *Initiating:* 2% vs. 1%

  - o *Planning:* 21% vs. 11%

  - o *Executing:* 69% vs. 82%

  - o *Controlling:* 5% vs. 4%

  - o *Closing:* 3% vs. 2%

- *They think it is important for the project manager to be a hands-on manager and a domain expert.* When asked to "Rank the importance of the project manager being a domain expert as a contributor to overall project success," the average alpha response was 94% vs. 68% for the non-alphas.

- *They can get consensus and handle conflicts.* When senior managers and customers were asked "How would you rate this project manager's ability to identify, understand, and satisfy your individual goals for the project," the average alpha response was 92% vs. 64%. When asked a similar question about conflict resolution, the alpha average was 61% vs. 46%.

- *They are managing more strategic projects and understand strategic goals.* When asked "Is your primary project considered highly strategic to your organization," the average alpha response was 60% vs. 41%. When asked, "Can you state your organization's top (three) strategic goals," the average alpha response was 60% vs. 23%.

The results of this study can be interpreted in several ways, especially if you analyze the interview responses, as Crowe does in his book. Some of the areas where alpha project managers are different from non-alpha project managers are based on their attitudes and beliefs, such as enjoying their work, believing they have authority, and believing they can have a personal impact on a project. Most of the other areas, however, are based on best practices which *can be learned*, such as being a good communicator, spending more time on project planning, being a hands-on project manager and a domain expert, being able to get consensus and handle conflict, and understanding and supporting strategic goals.[9]

WHAT WENT WRONG?

Many people are "thrown" into the role of project manager. For example, Nick Carson (his name is disguised) was an outstanding technical specialist on a large biotech project. He was working on a crucial project for his small company when the project manager quit. Senior management asked Nick to take over. Nick had never led a project, and he made the mistake of trying to still do his old job while also managing the project.

Nick worked lots of overtime and did actually complete the project, but his senior managers were not happy. Nick never gave them a detailed schedule or understandable status reports. Whenever he talked to them, they could not understand all of the technical detail he focused on. Nick thought he did a great job, so he was amazed when he was offered a severance package to leave the company. He decided he never wanted to manage a project again.

This true story illustrates the fact that many organizations do not do a good job of selecting, training, or mentoring their project managers.

PROJECT MANAGEMENT MATURITY

In addition to following best practices, organizations can improve project management performance by using **maturity models**, which are frameworks for helping organizations improve their processes and systems. Maturity models describe an evolutionary path of increasingly organized and systematically more mature processes. Many maturity models have four to six levels, with the first level describing characteristics of the least organized or least mature organizations, and the highest level describing the characteristics of the most organized and mature organizations.

Capability Maturity Model Integration

A popular maturity model is in continuous development at the Software Engineering Institute at Carnegie Mellon University. The Software Engineering Institute (SEI) is a federally funded research and development center established in 1984 by the U.S. Department of Defense with a broad mandate to address the transition of software engineering technology. The **Capability Maturity Model Integration** (CMMI) is "a process improvement approach that provides organizations with the essential elements of effective processes. It can be used to guide process improvement across a project, a division, or an entire organization. CMMI helps integrate traditionally separate organizational functions, set process improvement goals and priorities, provide guidance for quality processes, and provide a point of reference for appraising current processes."[10]

Many companies that want to work in the government market have realized that they will not get many opportunities even to bid on projects unless they have a CMMI Level 3.

The capability levels of the CMMI, numbered zero through five, are:

0.   *Incomplete*: At this level, a process is either not performed or partially performed. No generic goals exist for this level, and one or more of the specific goals of the process area are not satisfied.

1.   *Performed*: A performed process satisfies the specific goals of the process area and supports and enables the work needed to produce work products. Although this capability level can result in improvements, those improvements can be lost over time if they are not institutionalized.

2.   *Managed*: At this level, a process has the basic infrastructure in place to support it. The process is planned and executed based on policies and employs skilled people who have adequate resources to produce controlled outputs. The process discipline reflected by this level ensures that existing practices are retained during times of stress.

3.   *Defined*: At this maturity level, a process is rigorously defined and the standards, process descriptions, and procedures for a project are tailored from the organization's set of standard processes to suit that particular project.

4.   *Quantitatively Managed*: At this level, a process is controlled using statistical and other quantitative techniques. The organization establishes quantitative objectives for quality and process performance that are used as criteria in managing the process.

5.   *Optimizing*: An optimizing process is improved based on an understanding of the common causes of variation inherent in the process. The focus is on continually improving the range of process performance through incremental and innovative improvements.[11]

Project Management Maturity Models

In the late 1990s, several organizations began developing project management maturity models based on the Capability Maturity Model (CMM), an earlier version of CMMI. Just as organizations realized the need to improve their software development processes and systems, they also realized the need to enhance their project management processes and systems for all types of projects. A few of these maturity models include:

- PMI's OPM3®, as mentioned earlier, which includes four process improvement stages or levels:

    1. Standardize

    2. Measure

    3. Control

    4. Continuously improve

- The International Institute for Learning, Inc. uses Kerzner's model, with five levels of project management maturity:

  1. Common language

  2. Common processes

  3. Singular methodology

  4. Benchmarking

  5. Continuous improvement

- ESI International's ProjectFRAMEWORK™ is a five-level model:

  1. Ad-hoc

  2. Consistent

  3. Integrated

  4. Comprehensive

  5. Optimizing

- Berkeley's Project Management Process Maturity (PM) model includes these five levels:

  1. Ad-hoc: No project management processes or practices are consistently available, and data is not consistently collected or analyzed

  2. Planned: Project management processes, problem areas, and data are informally defined, identified, collected

  3. Managed: Formal project planning and control systems and data are managed

  4. Integrated: Program management is used, and project management data and processes are integrated and quantitatively analyzed, measured, and stored

  5. Sustained: Project management processes are continuously improved and are fully understood, and data is optimized and sustained

Figure 10-1 provides an illustration of the Berkeley model. Each project management maturity model shows a progression from the least mature to most mature level, although the number and title of levels vary somewhat.

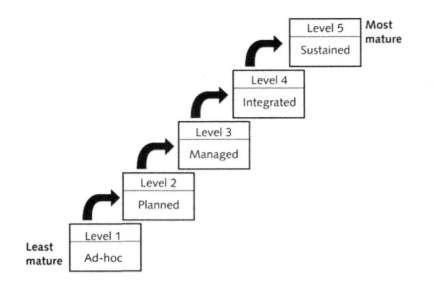

Figure 10-1. Berkeley project management process maturity model

Research on Project Management Maturity

Regardless of the project management maturity model followed, the goal is clear: organizations want to improve their ability to manage projects. Many organizations are assessing where they stand in terms of project management maturity, just as they did for software development maturity with the CMMI maturity model. Organizations are recognizing that they must make a commitment to the discipline of project management to improve project quality and organizational performance. Several studies have proven the value of improving project management maturity to organizations.

PMI's Pulse of the Profession® Reports

PMI has released several reports under this title since 2006. As stated on their website in May 2017:

> Project success rates are rising. Organizations today are wasting an average of US$97 million for every US$1 billion invested — that's a significant 20 percent decline from last year's findings.
>
> What Pulse has shown in the past still holds true: when proven practices are implemented, projects are more successful. At the same time, the definition of success is evolving. Traditional measures of scope, time, and cost are no longer sufficient, and the ability of projects to deliver what they set out to do — the expected benefits — is just as important. So, for the first time, when determining project success, we looked at levels of benefits realization maturity in addition to the traditional measures.[12]

You can read the 2017 and previous Pulse of the Profession® reports from PMI's website.

PM Solutions Research

PM Solutions, a project management services firm, produced their first study on project management maturity in 2001. The purpose of their research is to help understand current project management practices and trends that will lead to improved project management success. Their 2014 study defined high performing organizations as those that were more mature in their project management practices and showed greater value in project performance measures than low performers. The average level of maturity for high performers was 3.4 vs. 1.7 (with 5 being the highest), and the percentage of cost savings per project was 26% vs. 6%. Key findings of the 2014 survey of 293 different organizations in several countries include the following:

- A majority of firms (91%) have project management processes in place.

- There is a direct and strong correlation between the project management maturity of a firm and its overall performance.

- High-performing firms are much more mature in their project management practices than low performers.

- There is a correlation between the length of time project management has been in place in a firm and its project management maturity and overall performance.

- Organizations have seen considerable value by increasing the level of their project management maturity.

- Most organizations (76%) have improved in PM maturity over the past five years with 33% moving from Level 1 to Level 2.

- Firms have steadily and consistently moved up in levels of project management maturity between 2001 and 2014.[13]

Ibbs' The Value of Project Management Research

William Ibbs, a Professor at the University of California at Berkeley, led a PMI-sponsored research study published in 2002 called "The Value of Project Management." After assessing project management maturity using Berkeley's model and reviewing data from 52 companies in the U.S., the researchers made the following conclusions:

- *Companies with more mature project management practices have better project performance.* They deliver projects on time and on budget more often. Less mature companies often miss their schedule targets by 40 percent and their cost targets by 20 percent.

- *Project management maturity is strongly correlated with more predictable project schedule and cost performance.* More mature companies have a schedule performance index (SPI) variation of 0.08 and a cost performance index (CPI) variation of 0.11. Less mature companies have indexes of 0.16 for SPI and CPI. For a $10 million project, this translates into a $1.6 million cost variation.

- *High project management maturity results in lower direct costs of project management.* Companies with a high maturity level spend 6–7 percent of total project costs on project management. Companies with low maturity spent about 11 percent.[14]

Thomas and Mullaly Research on Project Management Value

PMI sponsored a study entitled "Researching the Value of Project Management," which was published in 2008. This 400+-page report summarizes research on 65 organizations. In general, most of the organizations did see value in project management. The researchers stated that they were "extremely comfortable stating unequivocally that project management delivers value to organizations."[15]

It is interesting to note that in this study, unlike the earlier one led by Ibbs, the researchers found that most organizations did not try to quantify the value of project management. They said that measuring ROI "proved extremely elusive."[16] In this study, value focused on measuring project management and satisfaction, alignment, process outcomes, and business outcomes. The authors of this study also found that project management value appears to increase in proportion to the maturity level of the organization. Organizations with a higher level of maturity reported greater levels of intangible value.

Crawford and Cook-Davies Study on Best Industry Outcomes

In 2012 PMI published another study by Lynn Crawford and Terry Cook-Davies called "Best Industry Outcomes." One purpose of this research was to find best practices and organizational project management outcomes (OPMs) common to different industries by project type, not to specific companies or organizations. The researchers addressed questions related to finding the strategic drivers that are characteristic of specific project types and industries, including utilities, IT/telecommunications, engineering/construction, government, financial and business systems, automotive, aerospace/defense, fast moving consumer goods, and pharmaceutical. These industry sectors are listed in order of the mean OPM capabilities found in this study. The researchers also examined outcomes that are most valued based on strategic drivers as well as project management systems and practices associated with strategic drivers and goals.

In the conclusions section of their 152-page report, the authors state, "The presence of patterns between industries…is proven beyond any reasonable doubt…while each industry has evolved its own systems and capabilities in light of its own strategic intentions and drivers, no industry has yet fully developed a suite of systems and capabilities that are sufficiently rounded and robust to produce the OPM outcomes that are necessary to achieve the business success criteria. No industry is without room for improvement." [17]

Customer focus was an important strategic driver across all industries, and execution performance was clearly valued as a success criterion in all sectors. Delivery of a product or service was the most common type of project across all sectors, and meeting time, cost, and resource constraints was a shared challenge. Program management was most ubiquitous across all industries, and quality was also commonly used. The most underrepresented project management concepts or tools included stakeholder management, value management, and organizational change management. All industries were better at achieving cost and schedule outcomes than they were at managing scope and quality, achieving positive trends in productivity, and in implementing strategy.

One interesting finding in this study, among many, was that although the aerospace and defense industry had the highest overall percentage of project management systems in place (followed by IT/telecommunications), they did not use them as frequently or as well as the IT and telecommunications sector. Organizational capabilities were among the lowest of all industry sectors for the aerospace and defense industry, explained by one manager by the desire for engineers to do things their own way. The automotive industry came in last place in terms of overall percentage of project management systems in place, followed by the pharmaceutical industry.

Members of PMI can read this and other PMI-sponsored studies for free from www.pmi.org. Note there are extensions to the *PMBOK® Guide* for the construction industry and for government.

PriceWaterhouseCoopers' Study on Boosting Business Performance

As mentioned in Chapter 1, PriceWaterhouseCoopers surveyed 200 companies from 30 different countries about their project management maturity and found that *over half of all projects fail.* They also found that only 2.5% of corporations consistently meet their targets for scope, time, and cost goals for all types of projects. The survey's main objective, however, was to investigate whether a higher maturity level would provide a higher project performance level. The following conclusions were made by the survey authors:

- *A higher maturity level for an organization enhances overall project performance, not in just one project, but in the overall portfolio of projects. It makes sense for organizations to develop policies and processes that apply for all types of projects, programs, and project portfolios.*

- *Most organizations are not satisfied with their current maturity level.* The total average for survey participants was 2.5 on a 5.0 scale, meaning the organizations use informal processes that are not yet institutionalized. This low maturity level contributes to the high project failure rate.

- *Project failures are often a consequence of organizational aspects over which project managers have little influence.* The top reasons cited for project failure included bad estimates, missed deadlines, scope changes, change in environment, insufficient resources, and change in strategy. Poor quality of deliverables and not adequately defining stakeholders were the least prevalent reasons for project failure.

- *Organizational structure has a big impact on overall project performance.* The higher the alignment between structure and business requirements, the higher the overall project performance. The optimal structure should be based on industry, location, and business objectives. The highest performing companies in terms of project results had a project-oriented or strong matrix structure, giving project managers the most authority and control over resources.

- *Staff development and professional certification enhance overall project performance.* However, more than 60% of the companies surveyed do not regularly offer a development program to their project managers. Investments in project management certification do pay off, and the organizational benefits exceed the costs.

- *A systematic approach to change management is fundamental for superior project performance.* The majority of the best performing and most mature organizations always or frequently apply change management to their projects.

- *Staffing projects with a majority of internal resources as opposed to external resources is a better guarantee of success.* External resources add value when employed in moderation. The highest performance was achieved by using 25% external resources and 75% internal resources.

- *The extent to which project management software is used is correlated to maturity levels. The* lower the maturity level, the more difficulties the organization will have in implementing software. Processes must be established for the software to provide benefits.[18]

BEST PRACTICE

Wrike, an online project management software provider, created a short list and creative infographic to help you remember ten project management best practices. They suggest that you review these tips every time you start a new project to help achieve greater success.

1. Communicate with all project stakeholders from day 1: team members, managers, project sponsors, clients, valued users, etc.
2. Create a risk response team as the first line of defense when problems occur.
3. Always hold a project kick-off meeting and include everyone.
4. Start your project with a detailed work definition document, and make all stakeholders sign in agreement.
5. Create a detailed work plan and model it off of previous, similar projects (if possible.).
6. Document everything: steps, bottlenecks, changes in scope, etc.
7. Ask the team for feedback on your management methods and what you can do better to help them.
8. When stakeholders come to you with new requests, show them how the change will affect your project timeline or budget.
9. If scope changes due to new requests, have everyone sign a new agreement document.
10. Hold a wrap-up meeting after the project ends to discuss lessons learned and ways to improve for next time.[19]

SUMMARY OF BEST PRACTICES MENTIONED IN THIS TEXT

As you can see, understanding and applying best practices can help improve the management of projects, programs, portfolios, and entire companies. Several best practices were described throughout this text. Following is a brief summary of some of them:

- Determine how project, program, and portfolio management will work best in your own organization.

- Involve key stakeholders—including shareholders, customers, and employees—in making major decisions.

- Develop and follow a formal project selection process to ensure projects support business needs.

- Lay the groundwork for projects before they officially start.

- Separate projects by phases when it makes sense to do so.

- Designate a project champion to provide high-level support and participate in key meetings.

- Assign a project manager from operations to lead projects that affect operations.

- Form a steering committee with key managers from various departments for projects that will cause major organizational change.

- Provide mentoring and training for project managers and other stakeholders.

- Document action items at meetings, and set the next meeting time.

- Document meeting with minutes, focusing on key decisions and action items, and send them out quickly.

- Use more than one approach for creating cost estimates.

- Use formal supplier evaluation procedures to help select sellers.

- Include a detailed statement of work and schedule in contracts.

- Develop and follow a formal change-control process.

- Work with suppliers to ensure that deliverables are produced properly.

- Follow a deliverable acceptance process to verify project scope.

- Be clear and honest in communicating project status information, and share the responsibility for project communications with the entire project team.

- Formally close projects and share lessons learned.

FINAL ADVICE ON PROJECT MANAGEMENT

Now that you have read this text and discussed project management with others, I hope that you have matured to see project management as a valuable skill for you as an individual and for all types of organizations. The number of projects and their complexity will continue to increase, so it is important to understand, apply, and improve the state of project management.

The knowledge and experience I have gained working on and managing projects continues to help me in my career and my personal life. I was fortunate to step into a project management role very early in my career as a U.S. Air Force officer. My first real job at the age of 22 was as a project manager, and we followed a very disciplined approach to project, program, and portfolio management. I have held several job titles at different organizations since then—systems analyst, senior engineer, technical specialist, information technology management consultant, independent consultant, college professor, and now author and publisher. All of these jobs included working on or managing projects. As a wife and mother of three, I can also attest to the fact that project management skills help in planning and executing personal activities (weddings, birthday parties, vacations, moves, fundraisers, and so on) and in dealing with the joys and challenges of everyday life. When people ask me how I can do so much and still seem so relaxed, I have to say that using good project management definitely helps.

This book would not be complete without one final cartoon, as shown in Figure 10-2. In project management and life in general, it helps to follow best practices and also keep a sense of humor.

Figure 10-2. Use best practices! (www.xkcd.com)

CASE WRAP-UP

Kristin Maur learned a lot about her company and best practices in project, program, and portfolio management working on the best practices task force. She loved being paid to read books and articles on the subject, and the whole team worked well together. They developed a new section on the corporate Intranet with project management best practice information. As more workers and customers were using smart phones, they also developed a free application people could download to their phones to access key information.

Marie Scott encouraged Kristin to share some of the task force's findings as well as lessons learned on the Just-In-Time Training project in an article and presentation at a large, international conference. Marie even offered to pay for Kristin's trip to the conference out of the PMO's budget. Kristin was honored and excited for this new challenge since she had never done anything like it before.

CHAPTER SUMMARY

Many organizations study and apply best practices to improve their ability to manage projects, programs, and portfolios. PMI developed the Organizational Project Management Maturity Model (OPM3®) to help organizations assess and improve their project management maturity. It lists hundreds of best practices organized by project, program, and portfolio management. The Ultimate Business Library published *Best Practices*, which provides advice on best practices to follow for managing projects and organizations in general.

Individual project managers can also use best practices to improve their performance. Andy Crowe did a study to help understand best practices of alpha project managers, or the top 2%. A few findings include the fact that alpha project managers spend much more time on planning and enjoy their jobs more than other project managers.

A maturity model is a framework for helping organizations improve their processes and systems. Several organizations are using project management maturity models to help improve their project management processes and systems. Several studies, including those by PMI, PM Solutions, Ibbs, Thomas and Mullaly, Crawford and Cook-Davies, and PriceWaterhouseCoopers, show the benefits of improving project management maturity.

This text also describes several best practices in managing projects, programs, and portfolios. A summary list is provided in this chapter.

Project management is a valuable skill for individuals and organizations. As the number of projects and their complexity continue to increase, it is important to understand, apply, and improve the discipline of project management.

QUICK QUIZ

Note that you can find additional, interactive quizzes at www.intropm.com.

1.   A _____ is a procedure that has been shown by research and experience to produce optimal results and that is established or proposed as a standard suitable for widespread adoption.

   A. benchmark

   B. key performance indicator

   C. capability

   D. best practice

2.   The Project Management Institute initially published the _____ to address the need to bridge the gap between organizational strategy and successful projects.

   A. Organizational Project Management Maturity Model (OPM3®)

   B. Best Practices Report

   C. Alpha Project Managers Guide

   D. Project Management Process Maturity (PM)² model

3.   The Project Management Institute defines best practices in each of the following areas except _____.

   A. projects

   B. programs

   C. project personnel

   D. portfolios

4.   Organizations can measure performance against their own past; against peers; and, even better, against _____.

   A. profits

   B. potential

   C. revenues

   D. the future

5.   Alpha project managers represent the top _____.of project managers based on performance.

    A.   1%

    B.   2%

    C.   5%

    D.   10%

6.   Which of the following is a trait of alpha project managers?

    A.   They spend more time on execution than other project managers.

    B.   They spend more time in meetings than other project managers.

    C.   They send fewer emails than other project managers.

    D.   They make more money than other project managers.

7.   Which of the following is true regarding studies on the value of project management and project management maturity?

    A.   The PMI-sponsored study by Ibbs found that companies with a high maturity level spend less money on project management than companies with a low maturity.

    B.   The PMI-sponsored study by Thomas and Mullaly found that companies focus even more on measuring the ROI or tangible benefits of project management.

    C.   The PMI-sponsored study by Crawford and Cook-Davies found that several industries have reached an optimal level of organizational project management maturity.

    D.   The PriceWaterhouseCoopers study found that the higher the maturity level, the more difficulties the organization will have in implementing software.

8.   What was the average maturity level (with a high of 5) reported by survey participants for high performing organizations and low performing ones in the 2014 study by PM Solutions?

    A.   3.4 and 1.7

    B.   4.4 and 2.7

    C.   4.4 and 1.7

    D.   4.7 and 2.4

9. Which of the following is not a best practice listed in this text?

    A. Determine how project, program, and portfolio management will work best in your own organization.

    B. Involve key stakeholders—including shareholders, customers, and employees—in making major decisions.

    C. Develop and follow a formal project selection process to ensure projects support business needs.

    D. Don't spend time or money on projects before they officially start.

10. What is the main message of the final cartoon in this chapter in the section on final advice on project management?

    A. Follow best practices, and keep a sense of humor.

    B. Don't invest too much in the stock market.

    C. Always back up your computer files.

    D. Don't fall asleep in class!

Quick Quiz Answers

1. D; 2. A; 3. C; 4. B; 5. B; 6. C; 7. A; 8. A; 9. D; 10. A

DISCUSSION QUESTIONS

1. What is a best practice in general? Give examples of best practices in an area unrelated to project management, such as nutrition, exercise, or child rearing.

2. Why should organizations identify and use best practices? What are the main categories of best practices developed as part of OPM3®?

3. What are some of the things that alpha project managers do differently from other project managers?

4. What is a project management maturity model? What is CMMI? What benefits have studies shown from increasing project management maturity levels in organizations?

5. Do you believe that developing and applying project management skills can help most individuals and organizations? Justify your response.

EXERCISES

1. Review the project management best practices presented in this chapter or describe several used in an organization you are familiar with. Select any two of them and write a short paper describing how each practice could help improve project

management. Develop examples of how they could be applied to real project situations.

2.   Read information from one of the studies referenced in this chapter on project management maturity models or best practices. Summarize your findings in short paper or presentation.

3.   Skim PMI's latest version of OPM3®. Summarize key information in this document and your opinion of it in a one-to-two-page paper.

4.   Interview an experienced project manager about best practices he or she has used on an individual and organizational level. Document your findings in a short paper, presentation, or video.

5.   Search for articles and research done in the past three years regarding best practices in project management. What do you think about the quality of what you found? Summarize the findings of least two articles and one research study in a short paper or presentation.

6.   Watch at least three of the eleven Ted Talks listed in the Video Highlights feature. Summarize the key points and your opinion of each video in a short paper or presentation.

TEAM PROJECTS

1.   Read one of the reports or books listed in the Endnotes. Summarize key information in this document and your opinions of it in a two-to-three-page paper. Also prepare a short (10-15 minute presentation) on the topic.

2.   Research two or three different project management maturity models in more detail, such as those described in this chapter. Several include a sample or free assessment you can take to determine your organization's maturity level. Summarize the results as well as other information about the maturity models in short paper and presentation.

3.   Based on your team's experiences on your class project and your work experiences, prepare a short paper, presentation, or video describing what you believe are the most useful best practices for project management. Be sure to include specific examples that describe the best practices you include.

KEY TERMS

best practice — A procedure that has been shown by research and experience to produce optimal results and that is established or proposed as a standard suitable for widespread adoption.

capabilities — The incremental steps leading up to one or more best practices.

key performance indicator (KPI) — A criterion used to determine the degree to which an outcome is achieved.

maturity model — A framework for helping organizations improve their processes and systems.

outcomes — The tangible or intangible results of applying capabilities.

END NOTES

[1]Boyd. L. Switching Gears, PM Network (June, 2008).

[2]Mary Evans, "Overdue and Over Budget, Over and Over Again," Economist.com (June 9, 2005).

[3]Ibid.

[4]Project Management Institute, Inc., Organizational Project Management Maturity Model (OPM3®) Knowledge Foundation, Third Edition (2013), p 283.

[5]Sarah Fister Gale, "Outstanding Organizations 2007," PM Network (October 2007).

[6]Ultimate Business Library, *Best Practice: Ideas and Insights from the World's Foremost Business Thinkers*. Cambridge, MA: Perseus Publishing (2003), p. 1.

[7]Ibid., p. 8.

[8]Ibid.

[9]Andy Crowe. Alpha Project Managers: What the Top 2% Know That Everyone Else Does Not, Velociteach press, Atlanta, GA (2006).

[10]Software Engineering Institute, "What is CMMI," Carnegie Mellon (*http://www.sei.cmu.edu/cmmi/general/general.html*) (January 2007).

[11]CMMI Product Team, "CMMI® for Development, Version 1.2," CMU/SEI-2006-TR-008ESC-TR-2006-008 (August 2006).

[12]Project Management Institute, http://www.pmi.org/learning/thought-leadership/pulse (accessed May 15, 2017).

[13]PM Solutions, "Project Management Maturity and Values Benchmark 2014," (2014), p. 3.

[14]William Ibbs, and Justin Reginato, "Quantifying the Value of Project Management," Project Management Institute (2002).

[15]Janice Thomas and Mark Mullaly, "Researching the Value of Project Management," PMI, (2008), p. 349.

[16]Ibid., p. 246.

[17]Crawford, Lynn and Terry Cook-Davies, "Best Industry Outcomes," Project Management Institute (2012).

[18]PriceWaterhouseCoopers, "Boosting Business Performance through Programme and Project Management," (June 2004).

[19]Ashley Coolman , "Don't Forget These 10 Project Management Best Practices (Infographic)," Wrike Blog (May 3, 2017).

Appendix A:
Brief Guide to Microsoft Project Professional 2016

Note: This guide was written using the free trial of Microsoft Project Professional 2016 and Windows 10. Your screens may appear slightly different. You can download a free trial from Microsoft's website. Windows 7 or later is required to install Project Professional 2016. You can access updated information on the companion website at www.intropm.com.

Also, note that Microsoft offers several different products for managing projects, as described in this Appendix. The purpose of this guide is to provide current or future project managers hands-on experience in using a popular and powerful project management software tool.

I want to thank two special people for reviewing this text: Betty Boushey, PMP®, Adjunct Instructor at Pierce College, and David Klempke, PMP® Manager, PMO at IWCO Direct and Adjunct Instructor of Project Management at Augsburg College.

July 2017 update: Check with your instructor about using Project 2016. Microsoft changes what free trials are available. Your school might have a remote access option. If you cannot get access to a copy (it is very expensive to purchase), consider using one of the many other tools available to perform some of the tasks shown in this appendix.

Detailed Table of Contents

INTRODUCTION

There are hundreds of project management software products on the market today. "The Project Portfolio Management (PPM) market size is expected to grow from USD 2.52 Billion in 2015 to USD 4.63 Billion by 2020, at a Compound Annual Growth Rate (CAGR) of 12.9%."[1] Leading vendors include Microsoft, CA Technologies, HP, Oracle (who acquired Primavera), Planview, and SAP. Many smaller companies also provide their own products. Unfortunately, many people who own this type of software have little idea how to use it. It is important to understand basic concepts of project management, such as creating a work breakdown structure, determining task dependencies, assigning resources, setting up project portfolios, and so on before making effective use of PPM software. Many project teams still use spreadsheets or other familiar software to help manage projects. However, if you can master a good project management software tool, it can really help in managing projects. This appendix summarizes basic information on project management software in general. It also provides a brief guide to using Microsoft Project Professional 2016, the latest version of this popular software.

PROJECT MANAGEMENT SOFTWARE

As described at the end of Chapter 1, there are three basic categories of project management software based on their capabilities: low-end, midrange, and high-end tools. The market size mentioned by Gartner is for Project Portfolio Management (PPM) software, or the high-end category. It is often used across large organizations to manage thousands of projects while also providing portfolio management features. Low-end tools today are often free or very inexpensive, and most are available online. For example, popular tools include Basecamp, Trello, Zoho Projects, and Wrike, to name a few. Several low-end tools focus on project team collaboration and coordination and may not have features like critical path analysis, resource allocation, and status reporting, like mid-range and high-end tools do.

Microsoft Project Professional 2016 is considered to be a midrange tool. It is only one of Microsoft's offerings in the project management realm as of 2016. Figure A-1 provides a summary of the "plans" or options for project management software available just from Microsoft. Notice that the options focus on who will be using the software and what type of features are needed. Often an organization needs a combination of tools. For example, project managers might focus on using Project Professional synced with Project Online, team members might use Project Lite, and PMO staff and executives might use Project Online. Now more than ever, deciding what project management software to use is a project in itself!

Because this text focuses on work done by project managers and the software is available as a free 60-day trial, this Appendix provides a guide for using Project Professional 2016.

Select a plan

	Project managers			Team members	PMO & Executives	
	Project Pro for Office 365	Project Professional	Project Standard	Project Lite	Project Online	Project Server
	Desktop client w/ Cloud subscription	Desktop client	Desktop client	Add-on module ⓘ	Cloud subscription	Server on premises
	$25.00 user/month	$1159.99	$589.99	$7.00 user/month	$33.00 user/month	Find a Partner →
	Buy now	Buy now	Buy now	Buy now	Buy now	
	Learn more →	Learn more →	Learn more →	Learn more →	Learn more →	Learn more →
Fully Installed Project Application	✓ On up to 5 PCs	✓ On 1 PC only	✓ 1 PC only			
Project scheduling & costing	✓	✓	✓			
Manage tasks	✓	✓	✓	✓	✓	✓
Reporting & business intelligence	✓	✓	✓		✓	✓
Share documents				✓	✓	✓
Collaborate with Skype for Business presence	✓	✓		✓	✓	✓
Resource management	✓	✓			✓	✓
SharePoint task sync	✓	✓		✓	✓	✓
Project Online & Project Server Sync	✓	✓				
Click to run deployment	✓					
Version upgrades	✓				✓	
Submit timesheets				✓	✓	✓
Demand management					✓	✓
Portfolio selection & optimization					✓	✓

Figure A-1. Microsoft Project Options, Source: Microsoft, April 2016

(https://products.office.com/en-us/project/compare-microsoft-project-management-software)

BASIC FEATURES OF PROJECT MANAGEMENT SOFTWARE

What makes project management software different from other software tools? Why not just use a spreadsheet to help manage projects?

You can do a lot of project management planning and tracking using non-project management software. You could use a simple word processor to list tasks, resources, dates, and so on. If you put that information into a spreadsheet, you can easily sort it, graph it, and perform other functions. A relational database tool (such as Microsoft Access) could provide even more manipulation of data. You can also use email, social media, and other tools to collaborate with others.

However, project management software is designed specifically for managing projects, so it normally includes several distinct and important features not found in other software products:

- *Creating work breakdown structures, Gantt charts, and network diagrams*: As mentioned in this text, a fundamental concept of project management is breaking down the scope of the project into a work breakdown structure (WBS). The WBS is the basis for creating the project schedule, normally shown as a Gantt chant. The Gantt chart shows start and end dates of tasks as well as dependencies between tasks, which are more clearly shown in a network diagram. Project management software makes it easy to create a WBS, Gantt chart, and network diagram. These features help the project manager and team visualize the project at various levels of detail.

- *Integrating scope, time, and cost data*: The WBS is a key tool for summarizing the scope of a project, and the Gantt chart summarizes the time or schedule for a project. Project management software allows you to assign cost and other resources to activities on the WBS, which are tied to the schedule. This allows you to create a cost baseline and use earned value management to track project performance in terms of scope, time, and cost in an integrated fashion.

- *Setting a baseline and tracking progress*: Another important concept of project management is preparing a plan and measuring progress against the plan. Project management software lets you track progress for each activity. The tracking Gantt chart is a nice tool for easily seeing the planned and actual schedule, and other views and reports show progress in other areas.

- *Providing other advanced project management features*: Project management software often provides other advanced features, such as setting up different types of scheduling dependencies, determining the critical path and slack for activities, working with multiple projects, and leveling resources. For example, you can easily set up an activity to start when its predecessor is halfway finished. After entering dependencies, the software should easily show you the critical path and slack for each activity. You can also set up multiple projects in a program and perform portfolio management analysis with some products. Many project management software products also allow you to easily adjust resources within their slack allowances to create a smoother resource distribution. These advanced features unique to project management are rarely found in other software tools.

As you can see, there are several important features that are unique to project management software that make them worth using. Next you'll learn what's new in Project Professional 2016 and how to use basic features.

WHAT'S NEW IN PROJECT PROFESSIONAL 2016

If you are familiar with Project Professional 2013 or earlier versions, it may be helpful to review some of the new features in Project Professional 2016. An easy way to do this is by using one of the new features – a tab on the ribbon called "Tell me what you want to do." Figure A-2 shows the results after typing in "What's new" and then selecting "Get started." Figure A-3 summarizes the results after selecting "What's new in Project 2016."

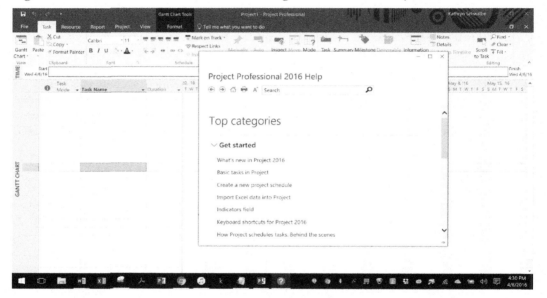

Figure A-2. Finding what's new with the Tell me what you want to do feature

More flexible timelines

With Project 2016, not only can you leverage **multiple timelines** to illustrate different phases or categories of work, but you can also **set the start and end dates for each timeline** separately, to paint a clearer overall picture of the work involved.

Better control over resource scheduling

Some resources have limited availability, and may have their time scheduled by a resource manager. With Project Professional 2016 and Project Online, project managers and resource managers can negotiate an agreement, called a **resource engagement**, to make sure that resources are being used appropriately and effectively throughout your organization.

Do things quickly with Tell Me

You'll notice a text box on the ribbon in Project 2016 that says **Tell me what you want to do**. This is a text field where you can enter words and phrases related to what you want to do next and quickly get to features you want to use or actions you want to perform. You can also choose to get help related to what you're looking for.

New themes for Project

There are now three Office themes that you can apply to Project 2016: Colorful, Dark Gray, and White.

Figure A-3. What's New in Project 2016

Next, you will learn some basic information about Project Professional 2016 and explore the main screen elements and Help facility.

USING PROJECT PROFESSIONAL 2016

Before you can use any project management software effectively, you must understand the fundamental concepts of project management, such as creating a work breakdown structure (WBS), establishing dependencies between activities, entering duration estimates, assigning resources, and so on. This Appendix is included with several project management text books by the author. Make sure you review these concepts before using Project Professional 2016 so you understand what you are doing.

Before You Begin

This appendix assumes you are using Microsoft Project Professional 2016 with Windows 10 and are familiar with other Windows-based applications. Check your work by reviewing the many screen shots included in the steps, or by using the solution files that are available for download from the companion website for this text or from your instructor.

> **NOTE**: *You need to be running* **Windows 7 or later** *to use Project Professional 2016 and an up-to-date browser. Certain features require internet connectivity.* You can **read more detailed system requirements** and download a free trial from Microsoft. This powerful software is very expensive. Microsoft sells Project Professional 2016 on its website for $1,159.99 as of April 2016. Many colleges and universities provide the software to students either on campus or through remote access. If you can use remote access, the main requirement is high speed internet connectivity. Check with your instructor for details or for alternatives if you do not have easy access to the software.

This appendix uses several template files and a fictitious project to illustrate how to use the software. The WBS for the fictitious file uses the five project management process groups as level 2 items (initiating, planning, executing, monitoring and controlling, and closing). Standard deliverables under each of those process groups are included. Each section of the appendix includes hands-on activities for you to perform.

> **NOTE:** To complete some of the hands-on activities in the appendix, you will need to download files from www.intropm.com to your computer. When you begin each set of steps, make sure you are using the correct file. Save the files you create yourself in a different folder so you do not write over the ones you download.

In addition, you will create the following files from scratch as you work through the steps:

- 2016wbs.mpp

- 2016schedule.mpp

- 2016actuals.mpp

You will also use the following file to create a hyperlink:

- stakeholder register.doc

Using the 60-day Trial of Project Professional 2016:

If you plan to download the free trial, perform the following steps:
1. Go to Microsoft's website for free trials (https://www.microsoft.com/en-us/evalcenter/evaluate-project-professional-2016 as of April 2016) and click on the **Try** button under Project Professional 2016. If that link does not work, check for updates on www.intropm.com. Also be sure to read the preinstall information, including the FAQs.

2. Enter your account information. You do need a Microsoft account. It used to be called a Windows Live account, so you may already have one if you set it up for Xbox, SkyDrive, Office 2013, Office 365 or other items. If you do not have a Microsoft account, set one up for free.

3. Install Project Professional 2016. Try the 32-bit option first. After downloading the exe file, run it and enter the product key Microsoft provides when prompted. If you have problems, contact your instructor or Microsoft support.

Next you will learn how to start Microsoft Project Professional 2016 and open a Blank Project.

Overview of Project Professional 2016

The first step to mastering Project Professional 2016 is to become familiar with the major screen elements and the Help facility. This section describes each of these features.

Getting Started and Finding Help

To start Project Professional 2016:

1. *Open Project Professional 2016.* There are slightly different methods for opening Project Professional 2016 depending on your operating system. For example, in Windows 10, click the **Start** button on the taskbar, All Apps, and then click **Project 2016 or type it in the search bar.** Alternatively, a shortcut or icon might be available on the desktop; in this case, double-click the icon to start the software.

2. *Start a Blank Project.* Click on **Blank Project**, the first option as shown in Figure A-4. The left part of the screen shows recent files (if you have any) and allows you to open other projects as well. The current date is the default project start date.

Figure A-4. Project Professional 2016 initial options – access Blank Project

3. *Learn about basic tasks in Project.* Click the **Tell me what you want to do** tab, type **Help,** click **Get started**, and then click **Basic tasks in Project**, as shown in Figure A-5.

NOTE: The term "tasks" is used in Project Professional 2016, while PMI prefers to use the terms deliverables and activities. Also, the name of the software is often referred to as just Project or Project 2016.

Figure A-5. Help on basic tasks in Project

4. *Explore the basic tasks information.* Click on **Add tasks**. Scroll down to read about the other options. You can also type in the search bar to explore other Help topics. When you are finished, **close** the Help window.

Understanding the Main Screen Elements

Review the main screen elements, as shown in Figure A-6. Look at some of the elements of the screen.

- The Ribbon, tabs, and Quick Access toolbar are similar to other Office applications.

- The timeline view is displayed below the ribbon. It shows a high-level view of the project schedule. You can easily copy the timeline into other software, as most of your stakeholders may want to see it and not the detailed schedule.

- The default manual scheduling for new tasks is on the lower left of the screen. You can click that option to switch to automatic scheduling.

- The default view is the Gantt chart view, which shows tasks and other information in a calendar display. (Recall from the note on the previous page that Microsoft uses the term tasks instead of deliverables or activities.) You can access other views by clicking the View icon on the far left side of the ribbon.

- The areas where you enter information in a spreadsheet-like table are part of the Entry table. For example, you can see entry areas for Task Name, Duration, Start, Finish, and Predecessors.

- You can make the Entry table more or less wide by using the Split bar. When you move the mouse over the split bar, your cursor changes to the resize pointer. Clicking and dragging the split bar to the right reveals columns for Resource Names and Add New columns.

- The first column in the Entry table is the Indicators column. The Indicators column displays indicators or symbols related to items associated with each task, such as task notes or hyperlinks to other files.

- The file name displays centered at the top of the screen. When you open a Blank Project after starting Project 2016, it opens a new file named Project1, which is shown in the title bar. If you open a second Blank Project, the name will be Project2, and so on, until you save and rename the file.

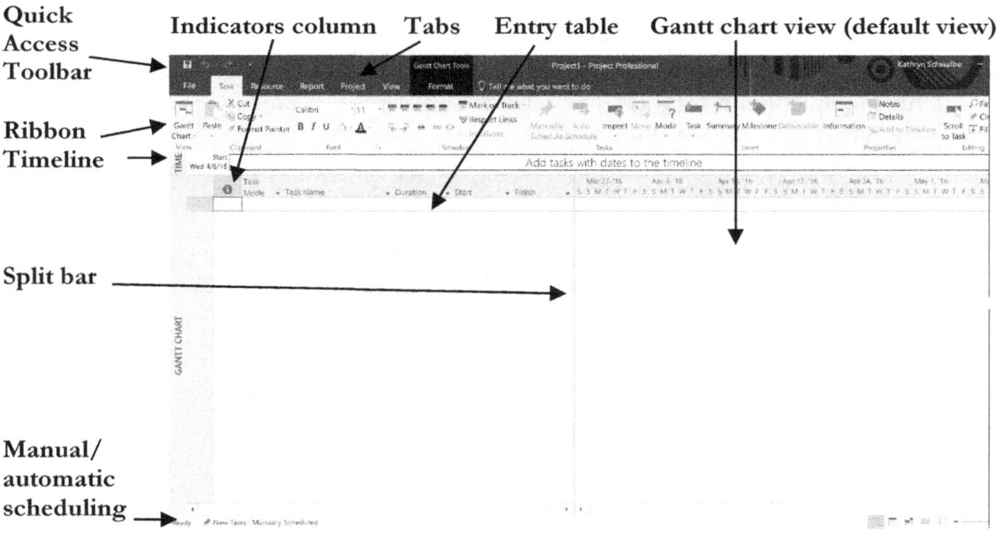

Figure A-6. Project Professional 2016 main screen

Many features in Project Professional 2016 are similar to ones in other Windows programs. For example, to collapse or expand tasks, click the appropriate symbols to the left of the task name. To access shortcut items, right-click in either the Entry table area or the Gantt chart. Many of the Entry table operations are very similar to operations in Excel. For example, to adjust a column width, click and drag between the column heading titles.

Next, you will get some hands-on experience by opening an existing file to explore various screen elements. Project Professional 2016 comes with several template files, and you can also access templates from various websites.

EXPLORING PROJECT PROFESSIONAL 2016 USING A TEMPLATE FILE

To open a template file and adjust screen elements:

1. *Open a template file.* Click the **File tab,** select **New, click Market Research Schedule, and then click Create. These screen shots were taken on April 7, 2016, so you can enter that date if you like or leave the default as "Today" or the current date. Your screen should resemble Figure A-7. (Note: If you cannot find the template, you can download it from www.intropm.com and open it. To open an existing file, c**lick the **File tab, then select Open, and** browse to find the file.)

2. *Move the Split Bar.* Move the **Split Bar** to the right so the Task Name and Duration columns are visible.

3. *Expand a WBS item.* Click on the **arrow to the left of Initiation Phase** in the Task Name column to reveal the activities under that WBS item.

4. *View the second Note:* Move your mouse over the yellow **Notes** symbol in the Indicators column for Task 7 to read it. You can insert notes for any task by using the Notes icon on the ribbon.

Figure A-7. Market research schedule template file

To show different WBS levels and adjust the timescale:

1. *Select Outline Level 1 to display WBS level 2 tasks.* Click the **View** tab and then the **Outline** button's list arrow, and then click **Outline Level 1**. Notice that only the level 2 WBS items display in the Entry table. The black bars on the Gantt chart represent the summary tasks. Recall that the entire project is normally referred to as WBS level 1, and the next highest level is called level 2.

2. *Adjust the timescale.* Click the **Zoom out** button (minus sign) on the left side of the Zoom slider on the lower left of the screen, as shown in Figure A-8, until you see all of the symbols on the Gantt chart (click it three times). Notice the timescale is now showing quarters instead of weeks. It is often easier to read the schedule when all of the symbols are visible. You can also Zoom in when more details are needed.

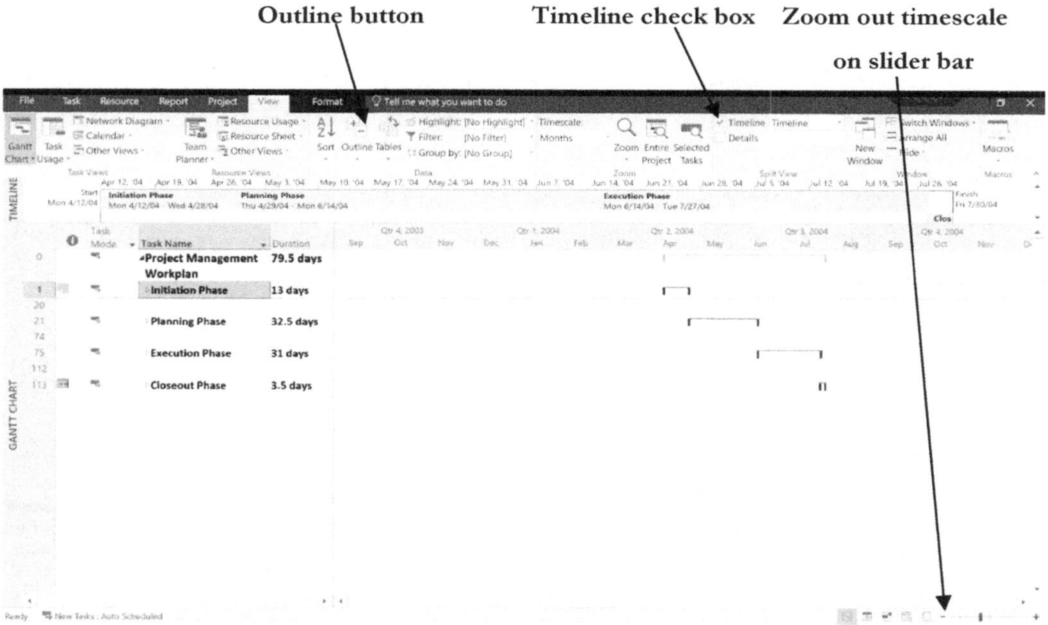

Figure A-8. Showing level 1 of the WBS and adjusted timescale

3. *View all tasks.* Click the Outline button and select All Subtasks to see all of the items in the Task Name column again. Remember that you can expand or collapse tasks as desired.

To adjust, add multiple timelines, share, and print the timeline:

1. *Remove the timeline and display it again.* Click the Timeline checkbox on the Ribbon to unselect it. Click it again to display it. The timeline is different than the time scale as it shows a high-level schedule on one line while the timescale adjusts the time units for symbols on the Gantt chart.

2. *Add a new timeline:* Click anywhere on the current timeline (toward the left side of the screen), click the Format tab, and then click Timeline Bar button under the Timeline Tools. Drag the line between the Timeline and Gantt Chart to reveal the second timeline. Your screen should resemble Figure A-9.

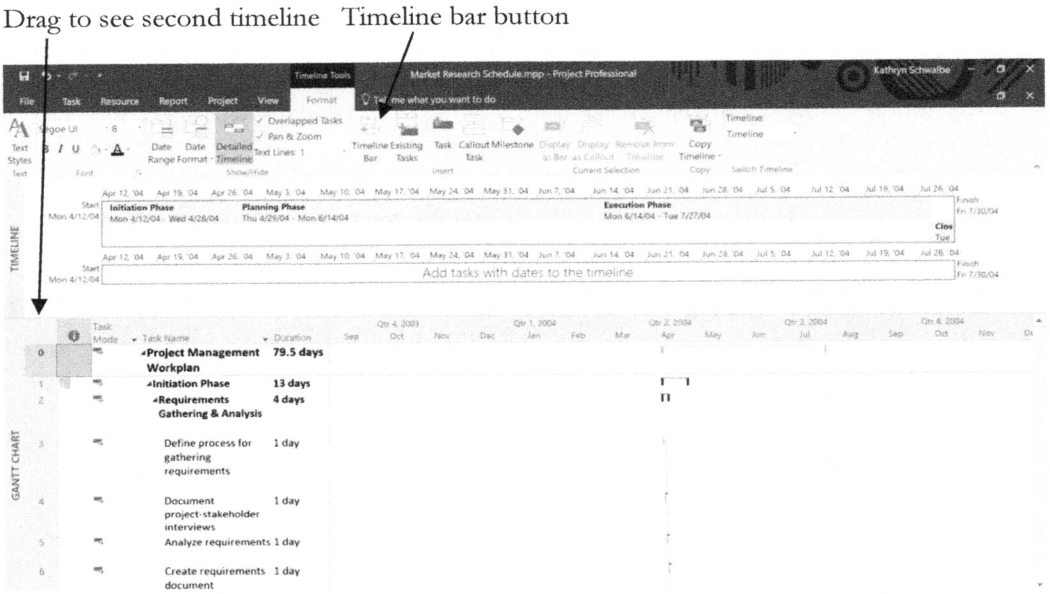

Drag to see second timeline   Timeline bar button

Figure A-9. Adding a second timeline.

3. *Add tasks to the new timeline.* Right-click on Task 2, Requirements Gathering & Analysis, then click Add to Timeline. Scroll down to also right-click on Task 7, Project Charter Development, and then click Add to Timeline to add it as well.

4. *Adjust the dates and format of the new timeline.* Right-click anywhere in the second timeline, click Date Range, and then click Set custom dates. Enter 4/1/04 for the Start date and 5/1/04 for the finish dates. (Remember that this is a template file from Microsoft, and it had the dates entered as 2004).

5. *Display a task as a callout on the timeline.* Right-click on Project Charter Development in the second timeline, and then click Display as callout. Click and drag on the callout to move it down and to the right, as shown in Figure A-10. You can also right-click on a task to change its color or font, if desired.

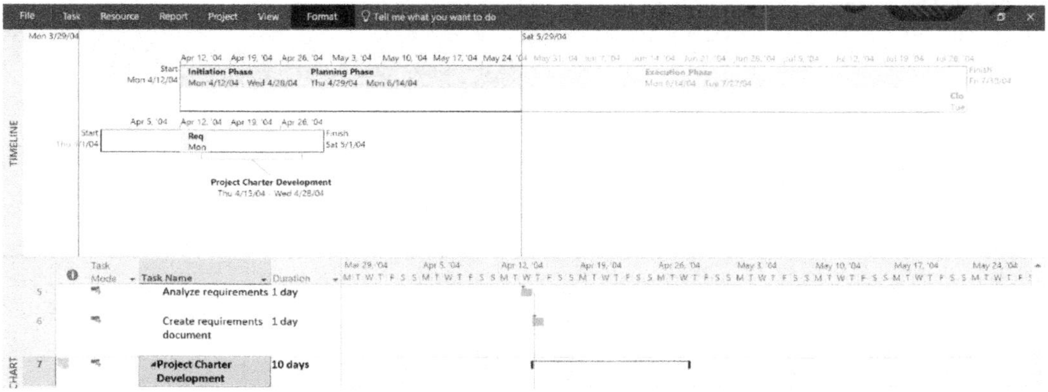

Figure A-10. Second timeline with callout.

6. *Close the file without saving.* Click the Close icon in the upper right of the window, and select No when prompted to save the file.

Project Professional 2016 Views

Project Professional 2016 provides many ways to display or view project information. In addition to the default Gantt chart, you can view the network diagram, calendar, and task usage views, to name a few. These views allow you to analyze project information in different ways. The View tab also provides access to different tables that display information in various ways. In addition to the default Entry table view, you can access tables that focus on data related to areas such as the Schedule, Cost, Tracking, Variance, and Earned Value tables.

To access and explore different views:

1. *Explore the Network Diagram for the Market Research Schedule file. Open the **Market Research Schedule** file again.* Click the **View** tab, the **Outline** button, and **All Subtasks** again. Click the **Network Diagram button**, and then move the **Zoom slider** on the lower right of the screen all the way to the left. Your screen should resemble Figure A-11. Critical tasks automatically display in red in the Network Diagram view.

2. *Explore the Calendar view.* Click the **Calendar** button (under the Network Diagram button). Notice that the screen lists tasks each day in a calendar format.

3. *Change the table view.* Click the **Gantt Chart** button on the ribbon, click the **Tables** button, and then click **Schedule**. Figure A-12 shows the tables view options.

Network Diagram

Figure A-11. Network diagram view

Figure A-12. Tables view options

4. Examine the Schedule table and other views. Move the **Split bar** to the right to review the Total Slack column. Notice that the columns in the table to the left of the Gantt chart, as shown in Figure A-13, now display more detailed schedule information, such as Late Start, Late Finish, Free Slack, and Total Slack. Remember that you can widen columns by double-clicking the resize pointer to the right of that column. You must do this for the Start, Finish, and Late Start columns to remove the #### symbols. You can also move the split bar to reveal more or fewer columns. Experiment with other table views, then return to the **Entry** table view.

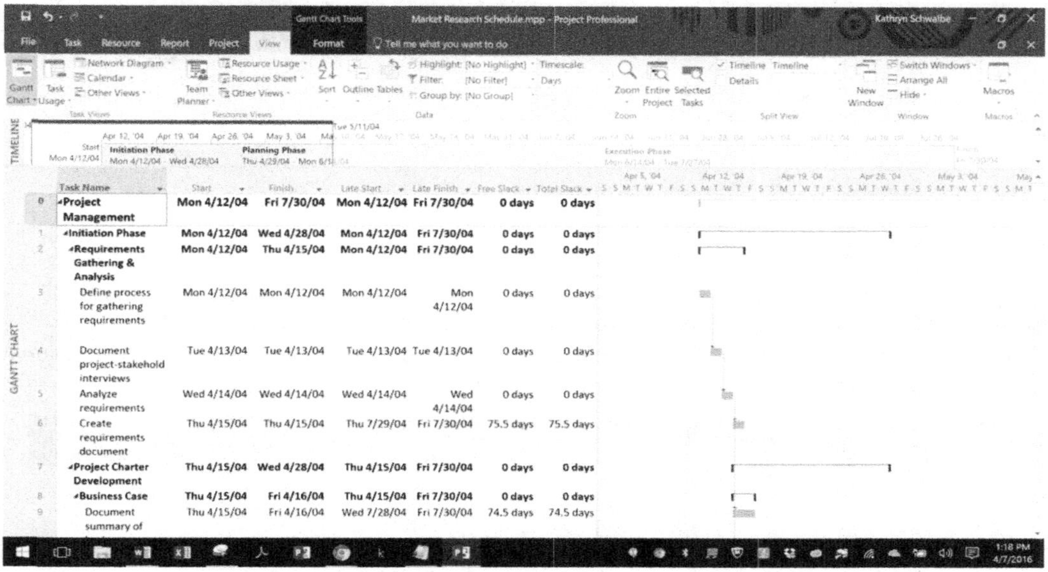

Figure A-13. Schedule table view

5. *Close the file without saving.* Click the **Close icon** in the upper right of the window, and select **No** when prompted to save the file. You can also close Project Professional 2016 if you want to take a break.

Project Professional 2016 Reports

Project Professional 2016 provides many ways to report project information as well. In addition to traditional reports, you can also prepare visual reports, with both available under the Report tab. Note that the visual reports often require that you have other Microsoft application software, such as Excel and Visio. Project Professional 2016 automatically formats reports for ease of printing.

To access and explore different reports:

1. *Open another template file.* With Project 2016 open, click on the **File tab,** click **New**, then double-click on the template called **Earned value**. Read the information on the initial screen to learn more about the concept of earned value. Click on the **View tab**, then click the **Gantt chart** icon.

2. *Explore the reports feature.* Click the **Report tab to see the variety of reports available in Project 2016**, as shown in Figure A-14.

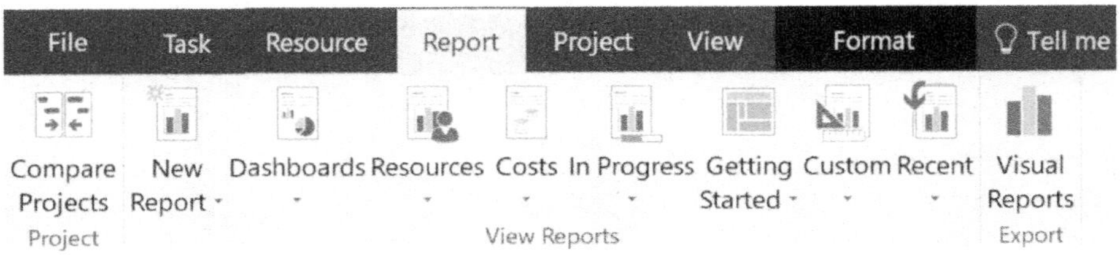

Figure A-14. Report options

    3.   View the Project Overview report. Click **Dashboards**, and then double-click **Project Overview**. Review the report, noting that the project is 17% complete. You must have entered some actual information and cost data to take advantage of this report. Also notice the new options on the ribbon, as shown in Figure A-15.

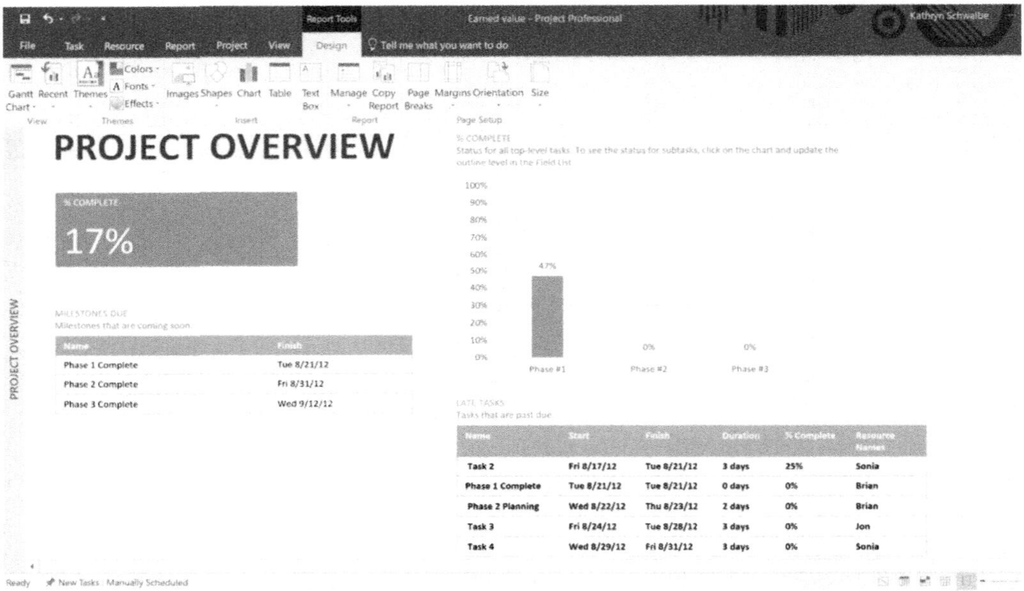

Figure A-15. Project Overview report

    4.   Open the Resource Overview report. Click the **Report tab again**, click **Resources**, and then click **Resource Overview**. Review the report, as shown in Figure A-16.

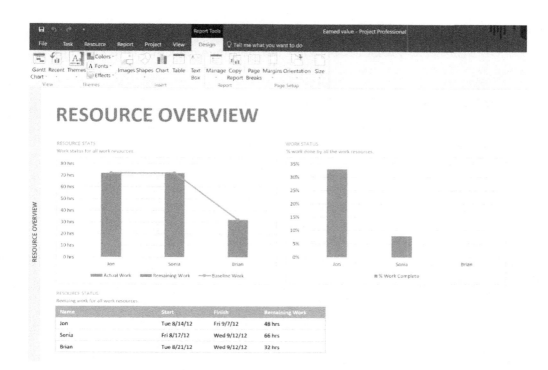

RESOURCE OVERVIEW

Figure A-16. Resource Overview report

5. *Examine other reports.* Click on the **Report tab**, click **In Progress**, and then click **Critical Tasks** to display the Critical Tasks report, as shown in Figure A-17. Examine other reports.

CRITICAL TASKS

A task is critical if there is no room in the schedule for it to slip.
Learn more about managing your project's critical path.

Name	Start	Finish	% Complete	Remaining Work	Resource Names
Task 2	Fri 8/17/12	Tue 8/21/12	25%	18 hrs	Sonia
Phase 1 Complete	Tue 8/21/12	Tue 8/21/12	0%	0 hrs	Brian
Phase 2 Planning	Wed 8/22/12	Thu 8/23/12	0%	16 hrs	Brian
Task 3	Fri 8/24/12	Tue 8/28/12	0%	24 hrs	Jon
Task 4	Wed 8/29/12	Fri 8/31/12	0%	24 hrs	Sonia
Phase 2 Complete	Fri 8/31/12	Fri 8/31/12	0%	0 hrs	Brian
Phase 3 Planning	Mon 9/3/12	Tue 9/4/12	0%	16 hrs	Brian
Task 5	Wed 9/5/12	Fri 9/7/12	0%	24 hrs	Jon
Task 6	Mon 9/10/12	Wed 9/12/12	0%	24 hrs	Sonia
Phase 3 Complete	Wed 9/12/12	Wed 9/12/12	0%	0 hrs	Brian

Figure A-17. Critical tasks report

> 6. *Return to the Gantt chart.* Click the **View tab, and then click on Gantt Chart** to return to the Gantt chart view. Next, you will use this same file to explore filters.

Project Professional 2016 Filters

Project Professional 2016 uses a relational database to filter, sort, store, and display information. Filtering project information is very useful. For example, if a project includes thousands of tasks, you might want to view only summary or milestone tasks to get a high-level view of the project by using the Milestones or Summary Tasks filter from the Filter list. You can select a filter that shows only tasks on the critical path if that is what you want to see. Other filters include Completed Tasks, Late Tasks, and Date Range, which displays tasks based on dates you provide. As shown earlier, you can also click the Outline button on the toolbar to display different levels in the WBS quickly.

To explore Project Professional 2016 filters:

> 1. *Access filters.* Click the **Filter list arrow**, as shown in Figure A-18. The default filter is No Filter, which shows all tasks.

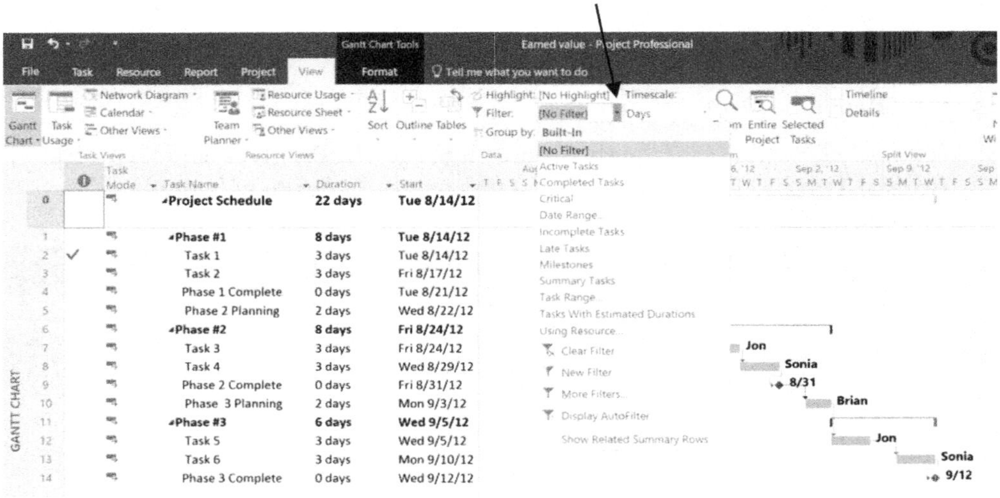

Figure A-18. Using a filter

> 2. *Filter to show milestones.* Click **Milestones** in the list of filters. Notice that the Gantt chart only shows the summary tasks and milestones for the project. Your screen should resemble Figure A-19. Recall that milestones are significant events.

> 3. *View other filters.* Click the **Filter** list arrow, and then click **Critical**. Now only the critical tasks appear in the WBS (which happens to be all of the tasks in this file). Experiment with other filters.

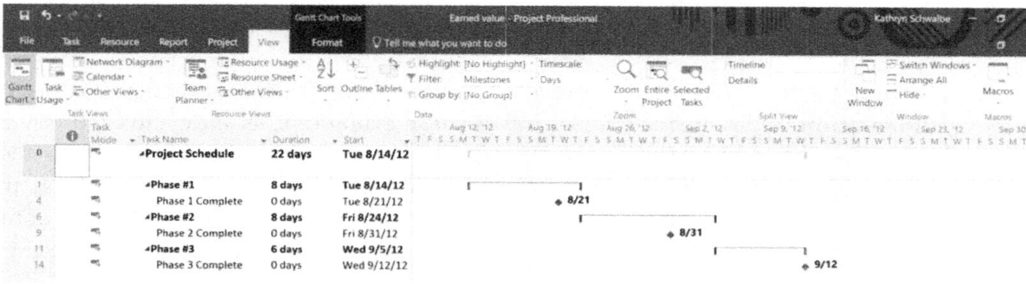

Figure A-19. Milestones filter applied

4.   *Close the file without saving.* When you are finished reviewing the Earned value file, click the **Close icon** for the window, and select **No** when prompted to save the file.

5.   *Exit Project 2016.* Review other template files, if desired. When you are finished, click the **Close icon** for Project 2016.

Now that you are familiar with the main screen elements, views, reports, and filters, you will learn how to use Project Professional 2016 to create a new file.

CREATING A NEW FILE AND ENTERING TASKS IN A WORK BREAKDOWN STRUCTURE

To create a new Project Professional 2016 file, you must first enter the start date, and then enter the tasks. The list of tasks, if entered properly, show the deliverables for the project in a work breakdown structure (WBS) format. Deliverables can be broken down into activities to show more specific actions required to complete the work. The file you create in the following steps could be used for a class project which lasts approximately three months. It uses the project management process groups to reinforce use of several project management deliverables described in this text.

NOTE: In this section, you will go through several steps to create a new Project Professional 2016 file named 2016wbs.mpp. If you want to download the completed file to check your work or continue to the next section, a copy is available on the companion website for this text at www.intropm.com. Try to complete an entire section of this appendix (entering tasks in a work breakdown structure, developing the schedule, and so on) in one sitting to create the complete file.

Creating a New Project File

To create a new project file:

1.   *Create a blank project.* Open Project 2016 and click on **Blank Project**. A blank project file opens with a default filename of Project1, Project2, and so on. (If Project

2016 is already open and you want to open a new file, click the **File tab,** select **New,** and then **Blank Project**.)

2.   *Open the Project Information dialog box.* Click the **Project** tab, and then click **Project Information** to display the Project Information dialog box, as shown in Figure A-20. This dialog box enables you to set dates for the project, select the calendar to use, and view project statistics. The project start date will default to the current date. Note that in Figure A-20 the file was created on 4/11/16 and a Start date of 5/2/16 was entered.

NOTE: All dates are entered in month/day/year or American format. You can change the date format by selecting Options from the File tab. Click the date format you want to use in the Date Format box under the General settings. You can also customize the Ribbon, change default currencies in the display, and so on under Project Options.

---

3.   *Enter the project start date.* In the Start date text box, enter **8/1/16**. Setting your project start date to 8/1/16 will ensure that your work matches the results that appear in this appendix. Change the Current date to **8/1/16** as well. Click **OK or press Enter.**

Start date text box   **Current date text box**

Project Information for 'Project1'			×
Start date:	Mon 8/1/16	Current date:	Mon 8/1/16
Finish date:	Mon 8/1/16	Status date:	NA
Schedule from:	Project Start Date	Calendar:	Standard
	All tasks begin as soon as possible.	Priority:	500

Enterprise Custom Fields

Department:

Custom Field Name	Value

Help   Statistics...   OK   Cancel

Figure A-20. Project information dialog box

Creating a Work Breakdown Structure Hierarchy

A work breakdown structure (WBS) is a fundamental part of project management. Developing a good WBS takes time, and it will make entering tasks into the Entry table easier if you develop the WBS first. For this example, you will use the project management process groups as the main WBS categories and add some key deliverables, activities, and milestones under each one. You will use the information in Figure A-21 to enter tasks. For the first task, enter **your name**, not the text "enter your name." Note that Microsoft Project uses the term tasks instead of deliverables or activities or milestones, so it is also used in this appendix.

1. Initiating – enter **your name**	16. Activity D1
2. Stakeholder identification	17. Activity D2
3. Stakeholder register completed	18. Deliverable 1 completed
4. Stakeholder management strategy completed	19. Deliverable 2
5. Project charter	20. Deliverable 3
6. Project charter completed	21. Monitoring and Controlling
7. Kickoff meeting	22. Actual hours tracking
8. Kickoff meeting completed	23. Project documents updates
9. Planning	24. Progress report 1
10. Schedule	25. Progress report 2
11. Gantt chart completed	26. Team review meetings
12. Scope statement	27. Closing
13. Initial scope statement completed	28. Final project report
14. Executing	29. Final project presentation
15. Deliverable 1	30. Project completed

Figure A-21. Task list for 2016wbs file

1. *Enter task names.* Enter the 30 items in Figure A-21 into the Task Name column in the order shown. To not have the text wrap, click on the **Format** Tab,

click **Column Settings**, and then click **Wrap Text** to turn it off. Do not worry about durations or any other information at this time. Type the name of each item into the Task Name column of the Entry table, beginning with the first row. Press **Enter** or the **down arrow** key on your keyboard to move to the next row.

HELP: If you accidentally skip a row, highlight the task row, right-click, and select Insert Task. To edit a task entry, click the text for that task, and either type over the old text or edit the existing text. Entering tasks into Project Professional 2016 and editing the information is similar to entering and editing data in an Excel spreadsheet. You can also easily copy and paste text from Excel or Word into Project, such as the list of tasks.

---

2. *Adjust the Task Name column width as needed.* To make all the text display in the Task Name column, move the mouse over the right-column gridline in the **Task Name** column heading until you see the resize pointer , and then click the **left mouse** button and drag the line to the right to make the column wider, or simply double-click to adjust the column width automatically.

This WBS separates tasks according to the project management process groups of initiating, planning, executing, monitoring and controlling, and closing. These categories will be the level 2 items in the WBS for this project. (Remember the whole project is level 1.) It is a good idea to include all of these process groups because there are important deliverables that must be done under each of them. Recall that the WBS should include *all* of the work required for the project. In this example, the WBS will be purposefully left at a high level (level 3). You will create these levels, or the WBS hierarchy, next when you create summary tasks. For a real project, you would usually break the WBS into even more levels and then enter activities to provide more details to describe all the work involved in the project. For example, each deliverable would probably have several levels, activities, and milestones under it. You can review other texts, template files, or other WBSs for more information. This appendix focuses on the mechanics of using Project Professional 2016.

Creating Summary Tasks

After entering the items listed in Figure A-21 into the Entry table, the next step is to show the WBS levels by creating summary tasks. The summary tasks in this example are Tasks 1 (initiating), 9 (planning), 14 (executing), 21 (monitoring and controlling), and 27 (closing). Task 15 (Deliverable 1) under executing is also a summary task with Activity D1 and Activity D2 under it. You create summary tasks by highlighting and indenting their respective subtasks.

To create the summary tasks:

1. *Select lower level or subtasks.* Click on the **Task** tab. Highlight **Tasks 2** through **8** by clicking the cell for Task 2 and dragging the mouse through the cells to Task 8.

2.   Indent subtasks. Click the **Indent Tasks** button on the ribbon (or press Alt + Shift + right arrow) so your screen resembles Figure A-22. After the subtasks (Tasks 2 through 8) are indented, notice that Task 1 automatically becomes boldface, which indicates that it is a summary task. A collapse symbol appears to the left of the new summary task name. Clicking the collapse symbol (filled triangle sign) will collapse the summary task and hide the subtasks beneath it. When subtasks are hidden, an expand symbol (unfilled triangle sign) appears to the left of the summary task name. Clicking the expand symbol will expand the summary task. Also, notice that the symbol for the summary task on the Gantt chart has changed from a blue to a black line with arrows indicating the start and end dates. The Task Mode has also changed to make this task automatically scheduled. You'll learn more about this feature later. For now, focus on entering and indenting the tasks to create the WBS.

**Expand or collapse symbols by
Summary tasks**   **Indent Task   Summary task symbol**

Figure A-22. Indenting tasks to create the WBS hierarchy

3.   Create other summary tasks and subtasks. Create subtasks and summary tasks for the other process groups by following the same steps. Indent **Tasks 10** through **13** to make Task 9 a summary task. Indent **Tasks 15** through **20** to make Task 14 a summary task. Indent **Tasks 22** through **26** to make Task 21 a summary task. Indent **Tasks 28** through **30** to make Task 27 a summary task. Widen the Task Name column to see all of your text, as needed.

4.   Create another level in the WBS. Indent **Tasks 16 and 17** to make Task 15 a summary task. Notice that Task 15 is indented even further. On a real project, you would also break down the activities for other deliverables.

TIP: To change a task from a subtask to a summary task or to change its level in the WBS, you can "outdent" the task. To outdent the task, click the cell of the task or tasks you want to change, and then click the Outdent Task button (the button just to the left of the Indent Task button). You can also press Alt + Shift + Right Arrow to indent tasks and Alt + Shift + Left Arrow to outdent tasks.

Numbering Tasks

To display automatic numbering of tasks using the standard tabular numbering system for a WBS:

1. *Show outline numbers.* Click **the Format tab**, and then click the **Outline Number checkbox** on the right side of the ribbon. Project Professional 2016 adds the appropriate WBS numbering to the task names. Note that you can customize the numbering format as desired.

2. *Show project summary task.* Click the **Project Summary checkbox** just below the Outline Number checkbox. Scroll to the top of the file to see that a new task, Project 1, the name of the file, has been added under row 0. Your file should resemble Figure A-23.

Outline Numbers   **Outline Number and Project Summary Task check boxes**

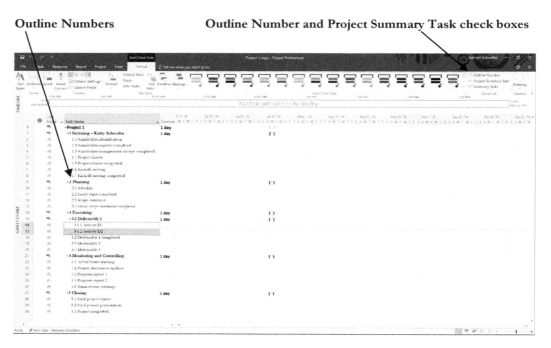

Figure A-23. Adding automatic outline numbers and a project summary task

Saving Project Files without a Baseline

An important part of project management is tracking performance against a baseline, or approved plan. It is important to wait until you are ready to save your file with a baseline because Project Professional 2016 will show changes against a baseline. Since you are still developing your project file for this project, you want to save the file without a baseline, which is the default way to save a file. Later in this appendix, you will save the file with a baseline. You will then enter actual information to compare planned and actual performance data.

To save a file without a baseline:

1. *Save your file.* Click the **File** tab and then click **Save**, or click the **Save** button on the Quick Access toolbar.

2. *Enter a filename.* In the Save dialog box, type **2016wbs** in the File name text box. Browse to the location in which you want to save the file, and then click **Save**.

3. *Close Project Professional 2016.* Click the **Close icon** to exit.

HELP: If you want to download the file 2016wbs.mpp to check your work or continue to the next section, a copy is available on the companion Website for this text, the author's Website, or from your instructor.

DEVELOPING THE SCHEDULE

Many people use Project Professional 2016 for its scheduling features. The first step in using these features, after inputting the tasks for the project, is to change calendars, if needed, and then enter durations for tasks or specific dates when tasks will occur. You must also enter task dependencies in order for schedules to adjust automatically and to do critical path analysis. After entering durations and task dependencies, you can view the network diagram, critical path, and slack information.

Calendars

The standard Project Professional 2016 calendar assumes that working hours are Monday through Friday, from 8:00 a.m. to 5:00 p.m., with an hour for lunch from noon until 1:00 p.m. In addition to the standard calendar, Project also includes a 24 Hours calendar and Night Shift calendar. The 24 Hours calendar assumes resources can work any hour and any day of the week. The Night Shift calendar assumes working hours are Monday through Saturday, from 12:00 a.m. to 3:00 a.m., 4:00 a.m. 8 a.m., and 11 p.m. to 12 a.m. You can create a different base calendar to meet your unique project requirements.

To create a new base calendar:

1. *Open a new file and access the Change Working Time dialog box.* With Project Professional 2016 open, click the **Project** tab, and then click the **Change Working Time** button under the Properties group. The Change Working Time dialog box opens, as shown in Figure A-24.

2. *Name the new base calendar.* In the Change Working Time dialog box, click **Create New Calendar**. The Create New Base Calendar dialog box opens. Click the **Create**

new base calendar radio button, type **Fiscal** as the name of the new calendar in the **Name** text box, and then click **OK**.

3. *Change the fiscal year start.* In the Change Working Time dialog box, click **Options** at the bottom of the screen. Change the **fiscal year** to start in **October** instead of January. Review other options in this screen, and then click **OK twice**.

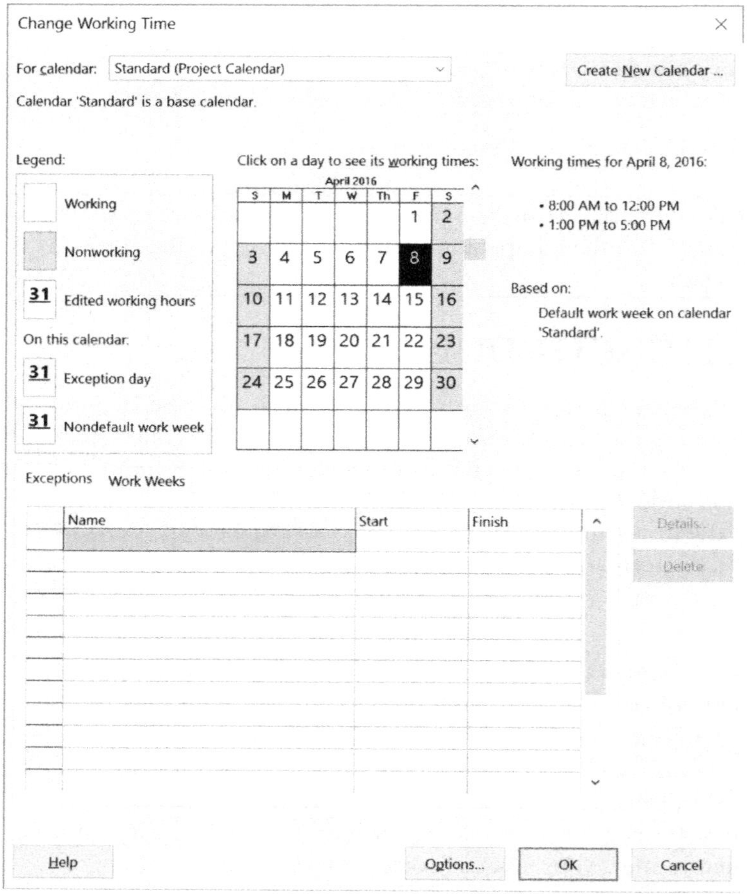

Figure A-24. Change Working Time dialog box

You can use this new calendar for the whole project, or you can assign it to specific resources on the project.

To assign the new calendar to the whole project:

1. *Open the Project Information dialog box.* Click the **Project** tab, and then click the **Change Working Time** button.

2.   *Select a new calendar.* Click the **For calendar** list arrow to display a list of available calendars. Select your new calendar named **Fiscal** from this list, and then click **OK**.

To assign a specific calendar to a specific resource:

1.   *Assign a new calendar.* Click the **View** tab, and then click the **Resource Sheet** button under the Resource Views group. Type **Adam** in the Resource Name column, and then press **Enter**.

2.   *Select the calendar.* Click the cell under the **Base** column that says **Standard** on the right part of the screen for Adam. Click the list arrow to display the options, and then select **Fiscal** as shown in Figure A-25.

Resource Name	Type	Material	Initials	Group	Max.	Std. Rate	Ovt. Rate	Cost/Use	Accrue	Base
Adam	Work		A		100%	$0.00/hr	$0.00/hr	$0.00	Prorated	Fiscal

Figure A-25. Changing calendars for specific resources

3.   *Block off vacation time.* Double-click the resource name **Adam** to display the Resource Information dialog box, and then click the **Change Working Time** button, located on the General tab in the Resource Information dialog box. You can block off vacation time for people by selecting the appropriate days on the calendar and marking them as nonworking days. Click **OK** to accept your changes, and then click **OK** to close the Resource Information dialog box.

4.   *Close the file without saving it.* Click the **Close** box, and then click **No** when you are prompted to save the file.

Entering Task Durations

Recall that duration includes the actual amount of time spent working on an activity plus elapsed time. Duration does not equal effort. For example, you might have an activity that you estimate will take one person 40 hours of effort to complete, but you allow two weeks on a calendar for its duration. You can simply enter 2w (for two weeks) in the Duration column for that activity (called a task in Project Professional 2016).

Manual and Automatic Scheduling

If you have used older versions of Project, you may have noticed that when you entered an item in the Task Name column, it was automatically assigned a duration of one day, and Start and Finish dates were also automatically entered. This is still the case in Project 2016 (and Project 2013) *if* you use automatic scheduling for a task. If you use manual scheduling, no durations or dates are automatically entered. The other big change with manual scheduling is that summary task durations are not automatically calculated based on their subtasks when they are set up as manually scheduled tasks. Figure A-26 illustrates these differences. Notice that the Manual subtask 1 had no information entered for its duration, start, or finish dates. Also note that the duration for Manual summary task 1's duration is not dependent on the durations of its subtasks. For the automatic summary task, its duration is dependent on its summary tasks, and information is entered for all of the durations, start, and end dates. You can switch between automatic and manual scheduling for tasks in the same file, as desired, by changing the Task Mode.

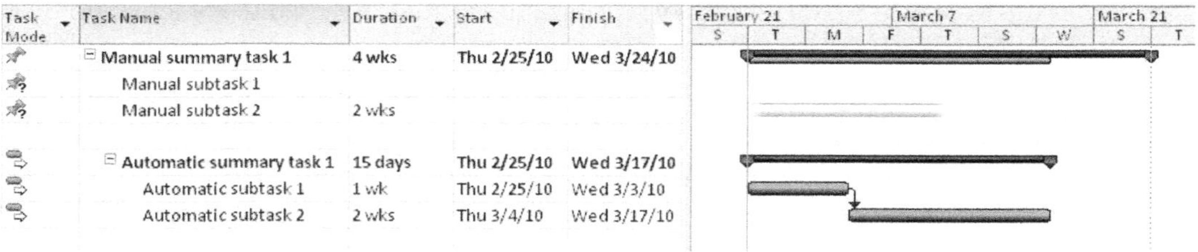

Figure A-26. Manual versus automatic scheduling

When you move your mouse over the Task Mode column (shown in the far left in Figure A-26) Project Professional 2016 displays the following information:

- A task can be either Manually Scheduled or Automatically Scheduled.
- Manually Scheduled tasks have user-defined Start, Finish and Duration values. Project will never change their dates, but may warn you if there are potential issues with the entered values.
- Automatically Scheduled tasks have Start, Finish and Duration values calculated by Project based on dependencies, constraints, calendars, and other factors.

Project Help provides the following example of using both manual and automatic scheduling. You set up a preliminary project plan that's still in the proposal stage. You have a vague idea of major milestone dates but not much detail on other dates in various phases of the project. You build tasks and milestones using the Manually Scheduled task mode. The proposal is accepted and the tasks and deliverable dates become more defined. You continue to manually schedule those tasks and dates for a while, but as certain phases become well-defined, you decide to switch the tasks in those phases to the Automatically Scheduled task mode. By letting the software handle the complexities of scheduling, you can focus your attention on those phases that are still under development.

Duration Units and Guidelines for Entering Durations

To indicate the length of a task's duration, you normally type both a number and an appropriate duration symbol. If you type only a number, Project Professional 2016 automatically enters days as the duration unit. Duration unit symbols include:

- d = days (default)
- w = weeks
- m = minutes

- h = hours

- mo or mon = months

- ed = elapsed days

- ew = elapsed weeks

For example, to enter two weeks for a task's duration, type 2w in the Duration column. (You can also type wk, wks, week, or weeks, instead of just w.) To enter four days for a task's duration, type 4 or 4d in the Duration column. You can also enter elapsed times in the Duration column. For example, 3ed means three elapsed days, and 2ew means two elapsed weeks.

You would use an elapsed duration for a task like "Allow cement to dry." The cement will dry in exactly the same amount of time regardless of whether it is a workday, a weekend, or a holiday. Project's default calendar does not assume that work is done on weekends. You will learn to change the calendar later in this appendix.

It is important to follow a few important rules when entering durations:

- To mark a task as a milestone, enter 0 for the duration. You can also mark tasks that have a non-zero duration as milestones by checking the "Mark task as milestone" option in the Task Information dialog box on the Advanced tab. You simply double-click a task to access this dialog box. The milestone symbol for those tasks will appear at their start date.

- You can enter the exact start and finish dates for activities instead of entering durations in the automatic scheduling mode. To enter start and finish dates, move the split bar to the right to reveal the Start and Finish columns. You normally only enter start and finish dates in this mode when those dates are certain.

- If you want task dates to adjust according to any other task dates, do not enter exact start and finish dates. Instead, enter durations and then establish dependencies to related tasks.

- To enter recurring tasks, such as weekly meetings, select Recurring Task from the Task button under the Task tab, Insert group. Enter the task name, the duration, and when the task occurs. Project Professional 2016 will automatically insert appropriate subtasks based on the length of the project and the number of tasks required for the recurring task.

- Remember to change the default calendar if needed, as shown earlier.

Next, you will set task durations in the file that you created and saved in the previous section. If you did not create the file named 2016wbs.mpp, you can download it from the companion Website for this text.

Use the information in Figure A-27 to enter durations. The Project Professional 2016 row number is shown to the left of each task name in the table.

Task Row	Task Name	Duration
2	Stakeholder identification	1w
3	Stakeholder register completed	0
4	Stakeholder management strategy completed	0
5	Project charter	1w
6	Project charter completed	0
7	Kickoff meeting	3d
8	Kickoff meeting completed	0
10	Schedule	5d
11	Gantt chart completed	0
12	Scope statement	8d
13	Initial scope statement completed	0
16	Activity D1	4w
17	Activity D2	6w
18	Deliverable 1 completed	0
19	Deliverable 2	3w
20	Deliverable 3	5w
24	Progress report 1	0
25	Progress report 2	0
28	Final project report	4d
29	Final presentation	4d
30	Project completed	0

Figure A-27. Task durations

Entering Task Durations

To enter task durations:

1. *Enter the duration for Task 2.* Open the **2016wbs** file, and move the split bar to the right, if needed, to reveal the Duration, Start, and Finish columns. Click the **Duration** column for row 2, Stakeholder identification, type **1w**, and then press **Enter**. Notice that the duration for the first task, Initiating, also changed since it is a summary task and is an Automatically scheduled task, as shown in the **Task Mode** column. When you created summary tasks earlier, the software changed their scheduling mode to Automatic. Also notice that the Start and Finish date for Task 2 remain blank, since that task is a Manually scheduled task.

2. *Enter the duration for Task 3.* In the **Duration** column for row 3, Stakeholder register completed, type **0**, and then press **Enter**. Remember that a task with zero duration is a milestone. Notice the milestone or diamond symbol next to the date 8/1 that appears on the Gantt chart, as shown in Figure A-28. Remember that you can adjust the Task Name column width to see all of the text and use the Zoom slider to change the length of the Gantt chart bars.

Task Mode column

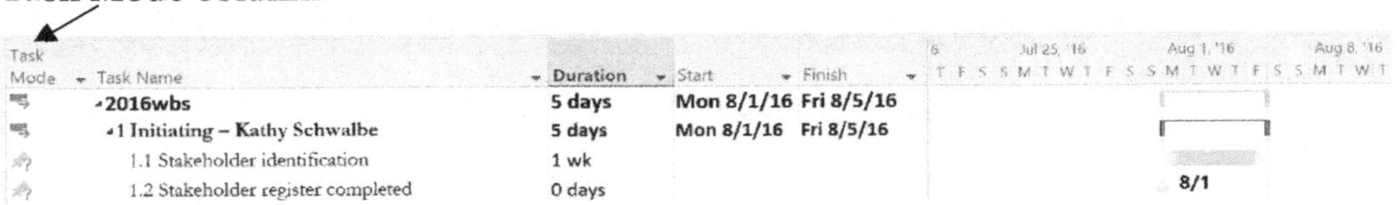

Figure A-28. Entering task durations

3. *Make all tasks automatically scheduled tasks.* To save time because you do want most of the tasks to be automatically scheduled, select all of the tasks by clicking the **Task Name** column heading, and then click the **Auto Schedule** button under the **Task** tab, as shown in Figure A-29. Most of the durations change to 1.

4. *Enter remaining task durations.* Continue to enter the durations using the information in Figure A-27 or Figure A-30. Do not enter durations for tasks not listed in the figure. Notice that the Planning Wizard dialog box displays when you make the same entry several times in a row, such as after task 20. Click OK to close the dialog box. You can adjust the column widths and Zoom, if desired.

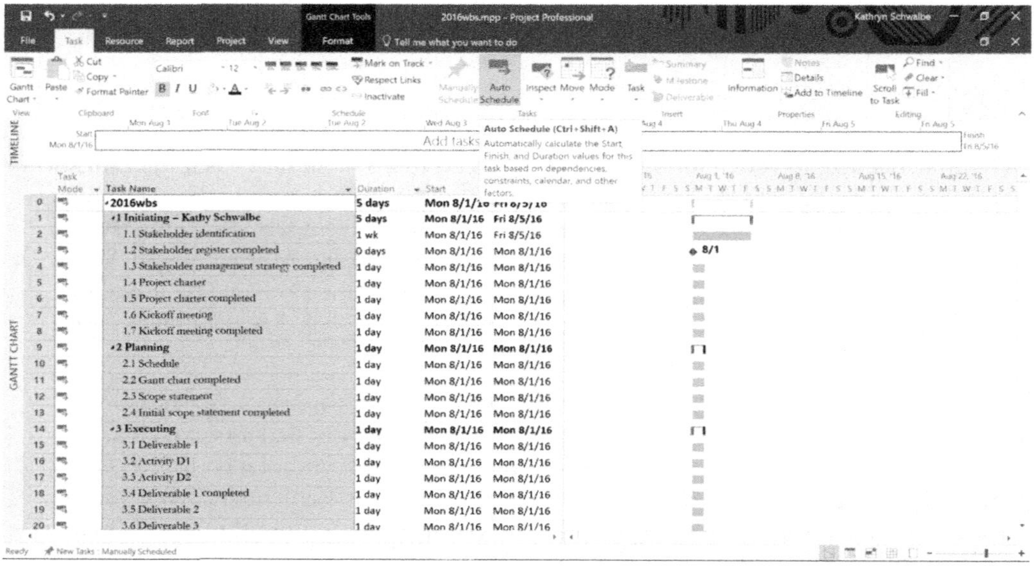

Figure A-29. Auto scheduling tasks

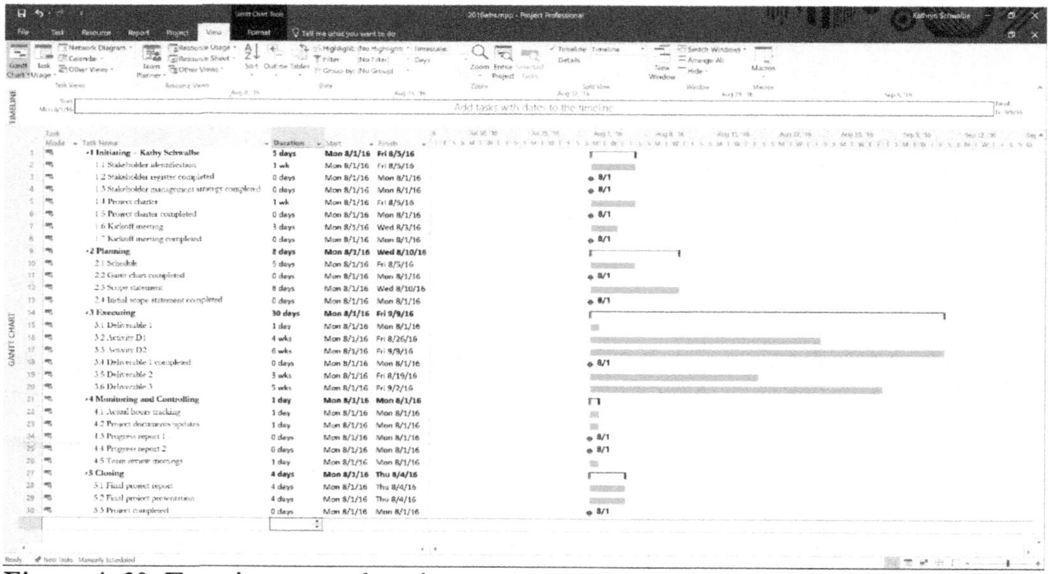

Figure A-30. Entering more durations

  5. *Insert a recurring task above Task 26, Team meetings.* Click **Team review meetings**
(Task 26) in the Task Name column to select that task. Click **the Task tab, and click
the Task button** drop-down box, and then click **Recurring Task**. The Recurring Task
Information dialog box opens.

6. *Enter task and duration information for the recurring task.* Type **Team review meetings** as the task title in the Task Name text box. Type **15min** in the Duration text box. Select the **Weekly** radio button under Recurrence pattern. Make sure that **1** is entered in the **Recur every** list box. Select the **Thursday** check box. In the Range of recurrence section, click the **End after** radio button, and then type **12** in the occurrences text box, as shown in Figure A-31. The new recurring tasks will appear indented below Task 26 when you are finished.

7. *Delete row 39 to avoid redundancy.* Right-click on row **39**, then click **Delete Task**.

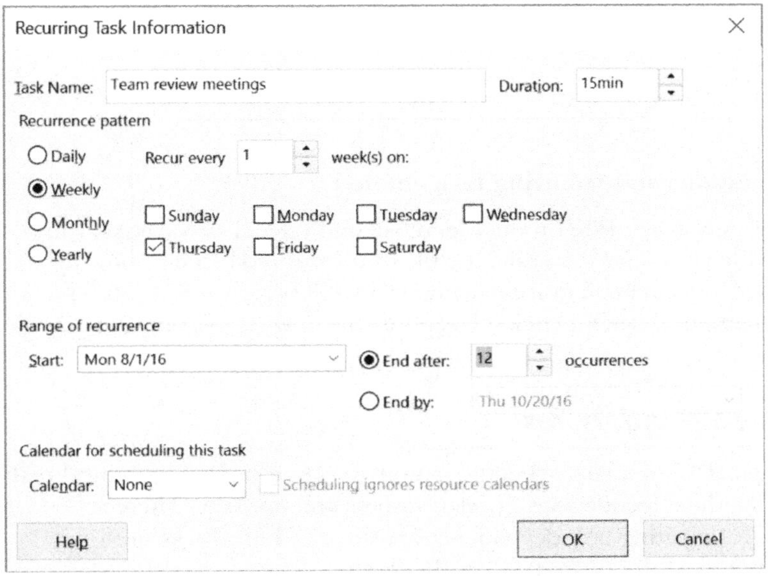

Recurring Task Information   ✕

Task Name: Team review meetings   Duration: 15min

Recurrence pattern
○ Daily   Recur every 1   week(s) on:
◉ Weekly
○ Monthly   ☐ Sunday   ☐ Monday   ☐ Tuesday   ☐ Wednesday
○ Yearly   ☑ Thursday ☐ Friday   ☐ Saturday

Range of recurrence
Start: Mon 8/1/16   ◉ End after: 12   occurrences
                            ○ End by: Thu 10/20/16

Calendar for scheduling this task
Calendar: None   ☐ Scheduling ignores resource calendars

Help   OK   Cancel

Figure A-31. Recurring task information dialog box

> **TIP:** You can also enter End by date for a recurring task instead of a number of occurrences. You might need to adjust the entry after you enter all of your task durations and dependencies.

8. *View the new summary task and its subtasks.* Click **OK**. Project Professional 2016 inserts 12 team review meetings subtask in the Task Name column. Notice that the recurring tasks appears on the appropriate dates on the Gantt chart.

9. *Adjust the columns displayed and the timescale.* Move the **split bar** so that only the Task Name and Duration columns are visible, if needed. Click the **Zoom Out** button on the Zoom slider in the lower left of the screen to display all of the symbols in the Gantt chart. Your screen should resemble Figure A-32.

		Task Mode	Task Name	Duration
19			3.3 Deliverable 2	3 wks
20			3.4 Deliverable 3	5 wks
21			⊿4 Monitoring and Controlling	58.03 days
22			4.1 Actual hours tracking	1 day
23			4.2 Project documents updates	1 day
24			4.3 Progress report 1	0 days
25			4.4 Progress report 2	0 days
26	○		⊿4.5 Team review meetings	55.03 days
27			4.5.1 Team review meetings 1	15 mins
28			4.5.2 Team review meetings 2	15 mins
29			4.5.3 Team review meetings 3	15 mins
30			4.5.4 Team review meetings 4	15 mins
31			4.5.5 Team review meetings 5	15 mins
32			4.5.6 Team review meetings 6	15 mins
33			4.5.7 Team review meetings 7	15 mins
34			4.5.8 Team review meetings 8	15 mins
35			4.5.9 Team review meetings 9	15 mins
36			4.5.10 Team review meetings 10	15 mins
37			4.5.11 Team review meetings 11	15 mins
38			4.5.12 Team review meetings 12	15 mins
39			⊿5 Closing	4 days
40			5.1 Final project report	4 days
41			5.2 Final project presentation	4 days
42			5.3 Project completed	0 days

Figure A-32. All task durations and recurring task entered

10. *Save your file and name it.* Click **File** on the Menu bar, and then click **Save As**. Enter **2016schedule** as the filename, and then save the file to the desired location on your computer or network. Notice that all non-recurring tasks still begin on 8/1/16. This will change when you add task dependencies. Keep this file open for the next set of steps.

Establishing Task Dependencies

To use Project Professional 2016 to adjust schedules automatically and perform critical path analysis, you *must* determine the dependencies or relationships among tasks. There are several different methods for creating task dependencies: using the Link Tasks button, using the Predecessors column of the Entry table or the Predecessors tab in the Task Information dialog box, or clicking and dragging the Gantt chart symbols for tasks with dependencies. You will use the first two methods in the following steps.

To create dependencies using the Link Tasks button, highlight tasks that are related and then click the Link Tasks button under the Task tab, Schedule group. For example, to create a finish-to-start (FS) dependency between Task 1 and Task 2, click any cell in row 1, drag down to row 2, and then click the Link Tasks button. The default type of link is finish-to-start. In the following steps, you will also set up some other types of dependencies and use the lag option to set up overlaps between dependent tasks.

TIP: To select adjacent tasks, click and drag the mouse to highlight them. You can also click the first task, hold down the Shift key, and then click the last task. To select nonadjacent tasks, hold down the Control (Ctrl) key as you click tasks in order of their dependencies.

When you use the Predecessors column of the Entry table to create dependencies, you must manually enter the information. To create dependencies manually, type the task row number of the preceding task in the Predecessors column of the Entry table. For example, Task 3 has Task 2 as a predecessor, which can be entered in the Predecessors column, meaning that Task 3 cannot start until Task 2 is finished. To see the Predecessors column of the Entry table, move the split bar to the right. You can also double-click on the task, click the Predecessors tab in the Task Information dialog box, and enter the predecessors there.

Next, you will enter the predecessors for tasks as indicated. You will create some dependencies by manually typing the predecessors in the Predecessors column, some by using the Link Tasks button, and the remaining dependencies by using whichever method you prefer.

To link tasks or establish dependencies:

1. *Display the Predecessors column in the Entry table.* Move the split bar to the right to reveal the full Predecessors column in the 2016schedule.mpp file you saved in the previous section. Widen the Task Name or other columns, if needed.

2. *Highlight the cell where you want to enter a predecessor, and then type the task number for its predecessor task.* Click the **Predecessors cell for Task 3**, Stakeholder register completed, type **2**, and press **Enter**. Notice that as you enter task dependencies, the Gantt chart changes to reflect the new schedule. Also notice that several cells become highlighted, showing *the Visual Change Highlights feature of Project 2016.*

3. *Enter predecessors for Task 4 and view the Task Path.* Click the **Predecessors cell for Task 4**, type **2**, and press **Enter**. Click the **Format** tab, and then click the **Task Path** button under the Bar Styles group. Experiment with the options to highlight Predecessor, Driving Predecessors, Successors, and Driven Successors, and then click **Remove Highlighting**. Click the **Tasks** tab.

4. *Establish dependencies using the Link Tasks button.* To link Tasks 5 and 6, click the **task name for Task 5** in the Task Name column and drag down through **Task 6**. Then, in the **Task** tab, click the **Link Tasks** button **(looks like a chain link)** under the Schedule group. Notice that the result is the same as typing 5 in the Predecessors column for Task 6, as shown in Figure A-33.

Figure A-33. Entering predecessors

  5. Enter dependencies and lag time using the Task Information dialog box. Double-click on the **Task Name** *for* **Task 5***, Project charter, and then click on the* **Predecessors tab** *in the Task Information dialog box. Click in the cell under Task Name, and then click the* **Task Name** *down arrow and select* **Stakeholder identification***. Click the* **Type** *drop down arrow to see the various types of dependencies. For this task, you will keep the default type of finish-to-start. Click the* **cell under the Lag column***, then* **type -50%** *and press* **Enter***. (Lag means there is a gap between tasks, and lead or negative lag means there is an overlap). Your screen should resemble Figure A-34. Click* **OK** *to close the dialog box. Notice that the Predecessor column for task 5 displays 2FS-50%, meaning there is a finish-to-start relationship with task 2 and a lag of -50%, meaning the task can start when task 2 is 50% completed.*

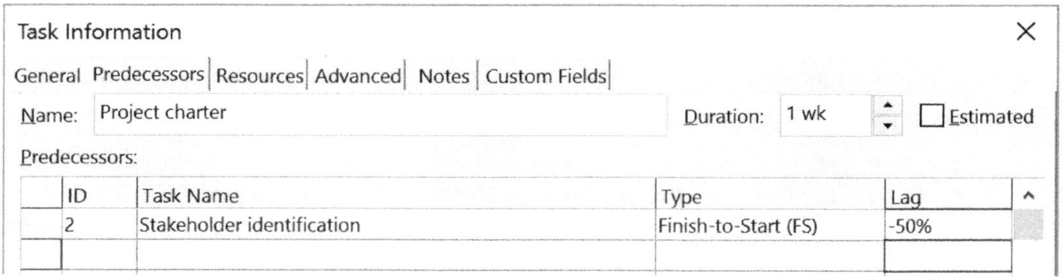

Task Information				✕
General Predecessors Resources Advanced Notes Custom Fields				
Name: Project charter			Duration: 1 wk ▲▼	☐ Estimated
Predecessors:				

	ID	Task Name	Type	Lag	^
	2	Stakeholder identification	Finish-to-Start (FS)	-50%	

Figure A-34. Entering predecessor information using the task information dialog box

  6. Enter remaining dependencies. **Link the other tasks** by either manually entering the predecessors into the Predecessors column, by using the Link Tasks button, or using the Task Information dialog box. Use the information in Figure A-35 to make your entries, being careful to leave some of the predecessors blank, as shown. If you have entered all data correctly, the project should end on 11/11, or November 11, 2016.

Task Row	Task Name	Predecessors
3	Stakeholder register completed	2
4	Stakeholder management strategy completed	2
5	Project charter	2FS-50%
6	Project charter completed	5
7	Kickoff meeting	2,6
8	Kickoff meeting completed	6,7
9	Planning	
10	Schedule	5,12FS-50%
11	Gantt chart completed	10
12	Scope statement	5
13	Initial scope statement completed	12
14	Executing	
15	Deliverable 1	
16	Activity D1	12
17	Activity D2	12
18	Deliverable 1 completed	16, 17
19	Deliverable 2	18
20	Deliverable 3	18
21	Monitoring and Controlling	
22	Actual hours tracking	2
23	Project documents updates	3
24-39	Progress Report 1 through Closing	
40	Final project report	20
41	Final presentation	20
42	Project completed	40, 41

Figure A-35. Predecessor information

7. *Adjust several dates.* You know that you have to deliver the two progress reports on specific dates. Click on the **Start dates for Tasks 24 and 25** and change those dates to September 2 and October 7. Also change the **Finish dates for tasks 22 and 23** to November 10 to be more realistic. Project 2016 will display a yellow warning symbol to remind you that you are changing default dates, which is fine in these examples.

8. *Review the file.* If needed, click the **Zoom Out** button on the Zoom slider to adjust the timescale so all of the information shows on your screen. Collapse the recurring tasks for the Team review meetings. When you finish, your screen should resemble Figure A-36. Double-check your screen to make sure you entered the dependencies correctly.

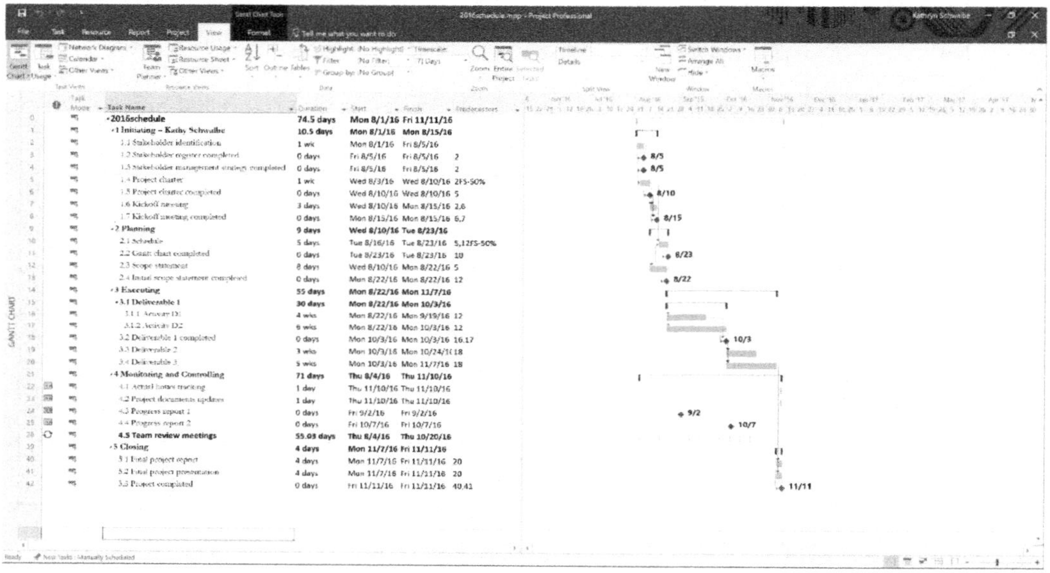

Figure A-36. File with durations and dependencies entered

9. *Preview and save your file.* Click the **File** tab, and then select **Print to preview and print your file. Click Page Setup, and then click the option to Fit to 1 so it will print on one page, as shown in Figure A-37.** Be careful before printing any Project 2016 files so you do not waste a lot of paper. When you are finished, click **Save** to save your file again. Keep the file open for the next set of steps.

Figure A-37. File set up to print on one page

Gantt Charts, Network Diagrams, and Critical Path Analysis

Project Professional 2016 shows a Gantt chart as the default view to the right of the Entry table. As described earlier in this text, network diagrams are often used to show task dependencies. This section explains important information about Gantt charts and network diagrams and describes how to make critical path information more visible in the Gantt Chart view.

Because you have already created task dependencies, you can now find the critical path. You can view the critical tasks by changing the color of those items in the Gantt Chart view. Tasks on the critical path will automatically be red in the Network Diagram view. You can also view critical path information in the Schedule table or by using the Critical Tasks report.

To make the text for the critical path tasks appear in red on the Gantt chart:

1.   Change the critical tasks format. Using the 2016schedule.mpp file you previously saved, click the **Format** *tab, and then click the* **Critical Tasks check box** *in the Bar Styles group, as shown in Figure A-38. Notice that the critical tasks display in red in the Gantt chart. You can also quickly change the Gantt Chart Style by clicking one of those options.*

Figure A-38. Formatting critical tasks

2. *View the network diagram.* Click the View tab, and then click the **Network Diagram** button under the Task Views group. Click the **Zoom Out** button on the Zoom slider several times and watch the view change. Figure A-39 shows all of the tasks in the network diagram. Note that milestone tasks, such as Stakeholder management strategy completed, the fourth box on the top, appear as pointed rectangular boxes, while other tasks appear as rectangles. Move your mouse over that box to see it in a larger view. Notice that tasks on the critical path automatically appear in red. A dashed line on a network diagram represents a page break. You often need to change some of the default settings for the Network Diagram view before printing it. As you can see, network diagrams can be messy, so you might prefer to highlight critical tasks on the Gantt chart as you did earlier for easier viewing.

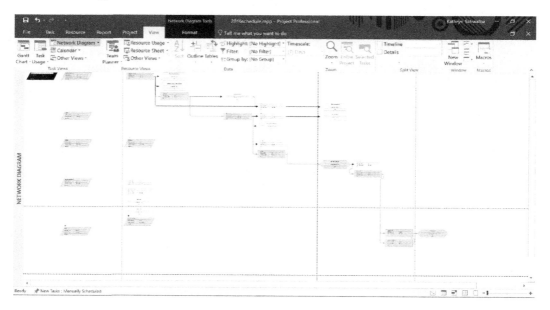

Figure A-39. Network diagram view

3. *View the schedule table.* Click the **Gantt Chart** button under the **View** tab to return to Gantt Chart view. Right-click the **Select All** button to the left of the Task Mode column heading and select **Schedule**. Alternatively, you can click the **View**

tab and click the **Tables** button under the Data group and then select **Schedule**. The Schedule table replaces the Entry table to the left of the Gantt Chart. Your screen should resemble Figure A-40. This view shows the start and finish (meaning the early start and early finish) and late start and late finish dates for each task, as well as free and total slack. Right-click the **Select All** button and select **Entry** to return to the Entry table view.

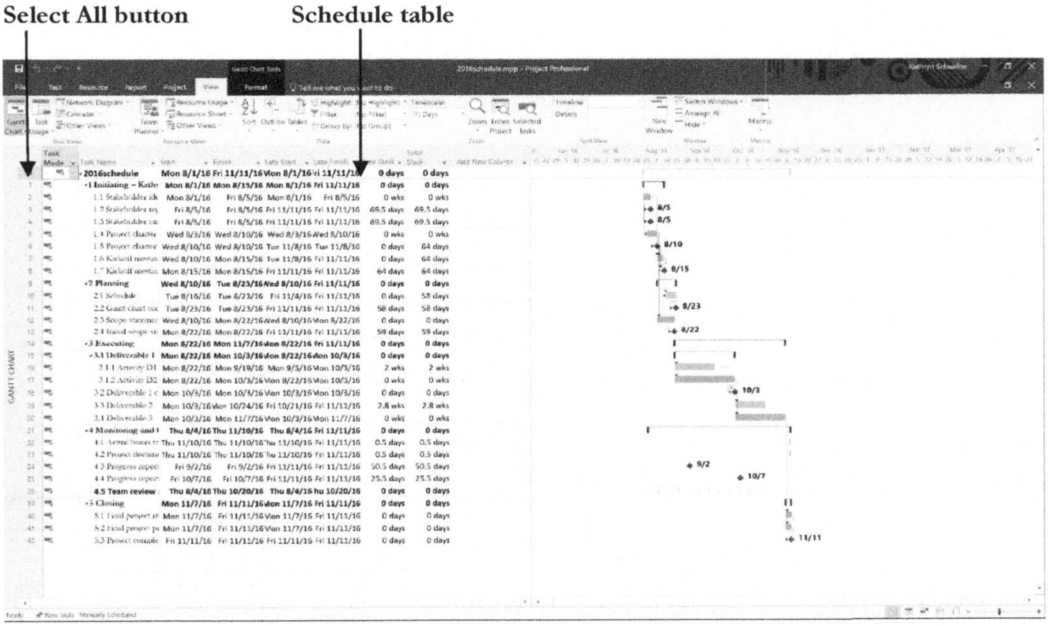

Select All button   **Schedule table**

Figure A-40. Schedule table view

4.   *Open the Project Overview report.* Click the **Report** tab, and click the **Dashboards button under the View Reports group, and then click Project Overview** to open the Overview Reports, as shown in Figure A-41. Note that the report shows the milestones due and % complete. Examine other reports, as desired.

5.   *Close the report and save your file.* When you are finished examining the reports, return to the Gantt chart view, and then click the **Save** button on the Quick Access toolbar to save your final 2016schedule.mpp file, showing the Entry table and Gantt chart view. Close Project 2016 if you are not continuing to the next section.

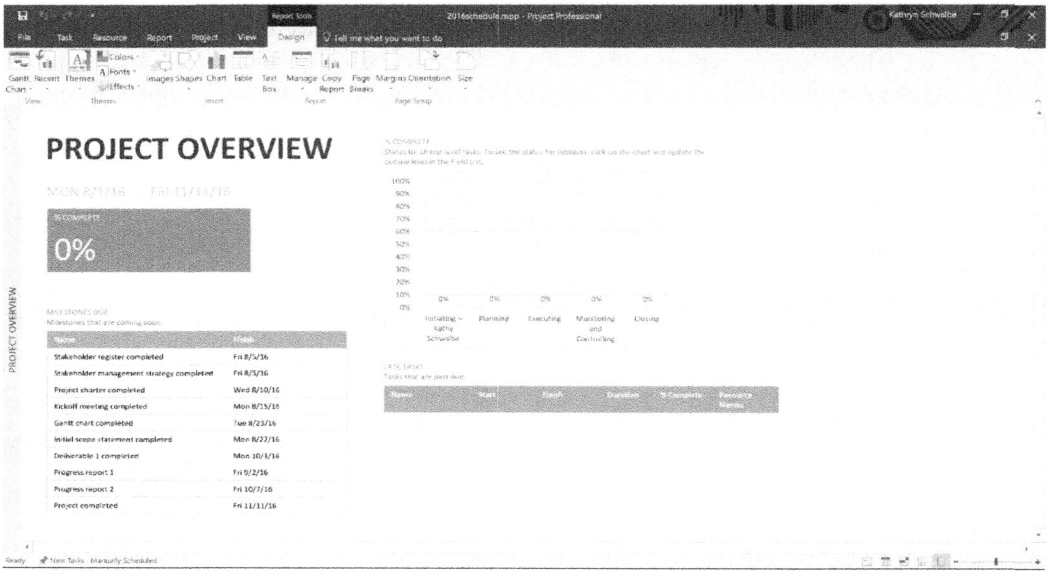

Figure A-41. Project Overview report

> **HELP:** If you want to download the file 2016schedule.mpp to check your work or continue to the next section, a copy is available on the companion Website for this text at www.intropm.com.

Next you will explore some of the cost and resource management features of Project Professional 2016.

PROJECT COST AND RESOURCE MANAGEMENT

Many people do not use Project Professional 2016 for cost or resource management. Some organizations have more established cost management software products and procedures in place, and many people simply do not know how to use the cost or resource management features. However, these features make it possible to integrate total project information more easily. This section offers brief instructions for entering fixed and variable cost estimates, assigning resources to tasks, viewing resource histograms, and entering actual cost and schedule information after establishing a baseline plan. It also explains how to use Project Professional 2016 for earned value management. More details on these features are available in Project Help, online tutorials, or other texts. See other chapters of this text for information on some of these concepts.

Entering Fixed and Variable Cost Estimates

You can enter costs as fixed or variable. Fixed costs include costs like a specific quantity of materials or costs for consultants hired at a fixed cost. Variable costs vary based on the amount of materials or hours people work. On many projects, human resource costs are the largest percentage of total project costs.

Entering Fixed Costs in the Cost Table

The Cost table allows you to easily enter fixed costs related to each task. You will enter a fixed cost of $200 related to Task 15, Deliverable 1.

To enter a fixed cost:

1. *Display the Cost Table view.* Open the file 2016schedule.mpp, if necessary. Right-click the **Select All** button to the left of the Task Mode column heading and select **Cost**. The Cost table replaces the Entry table to the left of the Gantt chart. **Widen** the Task Name column and then move the **Split bar** to the right, as needed, until you see the entire Cost table.

2. *Enter a fixed cost.* In the **Fixed Cost column for Task 16**, Activity D1, type **200**, and press **Enter**. Notice that the Total Cost and Remaining Cost columns reflect this entry, and changes are made to several summary tasks and the entire project as well. Your screen should resemble Figure A-42.

Select All button   Fixed Cost column of cost table

Task Name	Fixed Cost	Fixed Cost Accrual	Total Cost	Baseline	Variance	Actual	Remaining
0 ⁴2016schedule	$0.00	Prorated	$200.00	$0.00	$200.00	$0.00	$200.00
1 ⁴1 Initiating – Kathy Schwalbe	$0.00	Prorated	$0.00	$0.00	$0.00	$0.00	$0.00
2 1.1 Stakeholder identification	$0.00	Prorated	$0.00	$0.00	$0.00	$0.00	$0.00
3 1.2 Stakeholder register completed	$0.00	Prorated	$0.00	$0.00	$0.00	$0.00	$0.00
4 1.3 Stakeholder management strategy completed	$0.00	Prorated	$0.00	$0.00	$0.00	$0.00	$0.00
5 1.4 Project charter	$0.00	Prorated	$0.00	$0.00	$0.00	$0.00	$0.00
6 1.5 Project charter completed	$0.00	Prorated	$0.00	$0.00	$0.00	$0.00	$0.00
7 1.6 Kickoff meeting	$0.00	Prorated	$0.00	$0.00	$0.00	$0.00	$0.00
8 1.7 Kickoff meeting completed	$0.00	Prorated	$0.00	$0.00	$0.00	$0.00	$0.00
9 ⁴2 Planning	$0.00	Prorated	$0.00	$0.00	$0.00	$0.00	$0.00
10 2.1 Schedule	$0.00	Prorated	$0.00	$0.00	$0.00	$0.00	$0.00
11 2.2 Gantt chart completed	$0.00	Prorated	$0.00	$0.00	$0.00	$0.00	$0.00
12 2.3 Scope statement	$0.00	Prorated	$0.00	$0.00	$0.00	$0.00	$0.00
13 2.4 Initial scope statement completed	$0.00	Prorated	$0.00	$0.00	$0.00	$0.00	$0.00
14 ⁴3 Executing	$0.00	Prorated	$200.00	$0.00	$200.00	$0.00	$200.00
15 ⁴3.1 Deliverable 1	$0.00	Prorated	$200.00	$0.00	$200.00	$0.00	$200.00
16 3.1.1 Activity D1	$200.00	Prorated	$200.00	$0.00	$200.00	$0.00	$200.00
17 3.1.2 Activity D2	$0.00	Prorated	$0.00	$0.00	$0.00	$0.00	$0.00
18 3.2 Deliverable 1 completed	$0.00	Prorated	$0.00	$0.00	$0.00	$0.00	$0.00
19 3.3 Deliverable 2	$0.00	Prorated	$0.00	$0.00	$0.00	$0.00	$0.00
20 3.4 Deliverable 3	$0.00	Prorated	$0.00	$0.00	$0.00	$0.00	$0.00

Figure A-42. Entering a fixed cost

Entering Resource Information and Cost Estimates

Several methods are available for entering resource information in Project Professional 2016. The Resource Sheet allows you to enter the resource name, initials, resource group, maximum units, standard rate, overtime rate, cost/use, accrual method, base calendar, and code. Once you have established resources in the Resource Sheet, you can assign those resources to tasks in the Entry table with the list arrow that appears when you click a cell in the Resource Names column. The Resource Names column is the last column of the Entry table. You can also use other methods for assigning resources, such as using the Assign Resources button or using the split window, which is the recommended approach to have the most control over how resources are assigned because Project Professional 2016 makes several assumptions about resources assignments that might mess up your schedule or costs. Next, you will enter information for three people and assign them to a few tasks using various methods.

To enter basic information about each person into the Resource Sheet and assign them to tasks using the Entry table and toolbar:

1. *Display the Resource Sheet view.* Click the **View** tab, and then click the **Resource Sheet** button under the Resource Views group.

2. *Enter resource information.* Enter the information from Figure A-44 into the Resource Sheet. The three resources names are **Kathy, Dan, and Scott**. The Std. Rate and Ovt. Rate for Kathy is **40**, and the Std. and Ovt. Rates for Dan and Scott are **30**. Type the information as shown and press the **Tab** key to move to the next field. When you type the standard and overtime rates, you can just type the number, such as 40, and Project Professional 2016 will automatically enter $40.00/hr. The standard and overtime rates entered are based on hourly rates. You can also enter annual salaries by typing the annual salary number followed by /y for "per year." Your screen should resemble Figure A-43 when you are finished entering the resource data.

Resource Name	Type	Material	Initials	Group	Max.	Std. Rate	Ovt. Rate	Cost/Use	Accrue	Base
Kathy	Work		K		100%	$40.00/hr	$40.00/hr	$0.00	Prorated	Standard
Dan	Work		D		100%	$30.00/hr	$30.00/hr	$0.00	Prorated	Standard
Scott	Work		S		100%	$30.00/hr	$30.00/hr	$0.00	Prorated	Standard

Figure A-43. Resource sheet view with resource data entered

TIP: If you know that some people will be available for a project only part time, enter their percentage of availability in the Max Units column of the Resource Sheet. Project Professional 2016 will then automatically assign those people based on their maximum units. For example, if someone can work only 50% of his or her time on a project throughout most of the project, enter 50% in the Max Units column for that person. When you enter that person as a resource for a task, his or her default number of hours will be 50% of a standard eight-hour workday, or four hours per day. You can also enter the number of hours each person is scheduled to work, as shown later.

3.   *Assign resources to tasks.* From the **View** tab, select the **Gantt Chart** button under the Task Views group, and then click the **Select All** button and switch back to the **Entry** table. Move the Split bar to reveal the Resource Names column, if needed.

4.   *Assign Kathy to task 2, Stakeholder identification.* Click in the **Resource Names** cell for **row 2**. Click the list arrow, click on the **checkbox** by **Kathy**, and then press **Enter** or click on another cell. Notice that the resource choices are the names you just entered in the Resource Sheet. Also notice that after you select a resource by checking the appropriate checkbox, his or her name appears on the Gantt chart, as shown in Figure A-44. To assign more than one resource to a task using the list arrow, simply select another checkbox. Note that Project Professional 2016 will assume that each resource is assigned full-time to tasks using this method since the task is in automatically schedule mode. Also note that you can use filter by Resource Names to only show tasks assigned to specific resources after you enter the resources.

Filter Resource Names

	Task Mode	Task Name	Duration	Start	Finish	Predecessors	Resource Names	Aug '16 / Sep '16
0		⁴2016schedule	74.5 days	Mon 8/1/16	Fri 11/11/16			
1		⁴1 Initiating – Kathy Schwalbe	10.5 days	Mon 8/1/16	Mon 8/15/16			
2		1.1 Stakeholder identification	1 wk	Mon 8/1/16	Fri 8/5/16		Kathy	Kathy
3		1.2 Stakeholder register completed	0 days	Fri 8/5/16	Fri 8/5/16	2		8/5
4		1.3 Stakeholder management strategy completed	0 days	Fri 8/5/16	Fri 8/5/16	2		8/5

Figure A-44. Resource assigned using the entry table

5.   *Assign two resources to a task.* Click in the **Resource Names** cell for **row 5 (Project charter)**. Click the **list arrow**, then click on the **checkbox by Dan and Kathy,** and then press **Enter**. Notice that both resource names appear in the Resource Names column and on the Gantt chart for this task, and the task duration remains at 1 week.

6.   *Change the resource assignments.* Click in the **Resource Names** cell for **Task 2**, Stakeholder identification, click the **list arrow**, and add **Dan** as another resource. Notice that when you change an original resource assignment, Project prompts you for how you want to handle the change, as shown in Figure A-45. Click the **Exclamation point** symbol to read your options. In past versions of Project Professional, resource additions would change schedules automatically unless the user entered them a certain way. Now you have much more control of what happens to your schedule and costs. In this case, we do want to accept the default of keeping the duration constant.

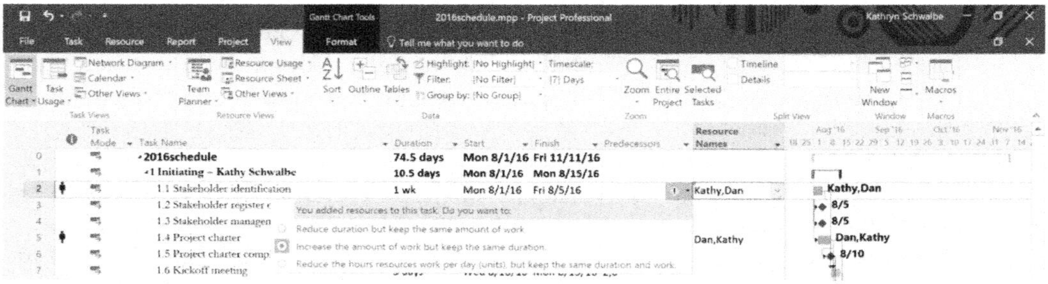

Figure A-45. Options when additional resources are added to tasks

7.   *Review the cost table.* Right-click the **Select All** button to the left of the Indicators column heading and select **Cost**. Notice that costs have been added to the tasks where you added resources. Project assumes that people are assigned full-time to tasks. It is showing a cost of $2,800 each for Task 2 and Task 5. In the next section, you will see how to control resources entries even more. First, right-click the **Select All** button and select **Entry** to return to the Entry table.

To control resource and work assignments using the Resource details window:

1.   *Open the Resource Form.* Notice the **red symbols in the Indicator columns** for rows/tasks 2 and 5. Move your mouse over the symbol to read the message about resources being overallocated. Click the Task Name for row 2, Stakeholder identification, click the **Resource tab, and then click on the Details button under the Properties group.** A Resource Form is displayed at the bottom of the screen, as shown in Figure A-46. Project Professional 2016 assumes every task is assigned full-time, so since Kathy is scheduled on two tasks on the same day, it says she is overallocated.

> **TIP:** You can right-click on the lower screen to see additional forms/views. You can click the Select All button at the top right of the screen to view different tables at the top of the screen. You want to make sure that resource and work hour assignments do not adjust your schedules in ways you did not intend.

2.   *Make tasks 2 and 5 manually scheduled.* Click the drop-down in the **Task Mode** column for Tasks 2 and 5 to make them **manually scheduled**. When you assigned resources, Project Professional 2016 assumed they were working full-time or 40 hours per week on each task. Because these two tasks have days that overlap, there is an overallocation. You do not expect each resource to work that many hours, so you can change them by using the Resource Form.

3.   *Change the number of Work hours.* Select Task 2, **Stakeholder identification** in the top window, and then click the **Work** column in the Resource Form window for **Kathy** in the lower part of your screen. Type **10h**, press **Enter**, and again type **10h** and press **Enter** for the next task, Task 5, Project charter, and then click the **OK** button. Click **Next** to see Dan's Resource Form.

Task mode indicator   Change # work hours

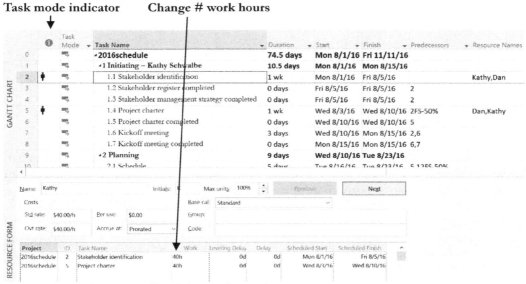

Figure A-46. Changing Work hours for tasks

4.   *Enter additional work hours and review the Gantt chart.* Change Dan's work hours to **10h for Tasks 2 and 5** as well. Notice in the Gantt chart that the duration for Tasks 2 and 5 are still one week. The overallocation indicator should now disappear because the number of hours has been reduced from the default of 8 hours per day, or 40 hours for a 5-day task. To remove the Resource Form, click **Details** on the Ribbon under the Resource tab.

5.   Examine the new cost information. Click the Select All button, and then click **Cost** to view the Cost table. Tasks 2 and 5 each show only $700 for Total Cost.

6.   *Close the file without saving it.* Close the file, but do not save the changes you made.

Using the Team Planner Feature

Another way to assign resources and reduce overallocations is by using the Team Planner feature. Assume you have two people assigned to work on a project, Brian and Cindy, as shown in Figure A-47. Notice that Brian is assigned to work on both Task 1 and Task 2 full-time the first week. Therefore, Brian is overallocated. Cindy is scheduled to work on Task 3 full-time the second week, and Task 4, also scheduled for the second week, is not assigned yet.

Overallocation indicator

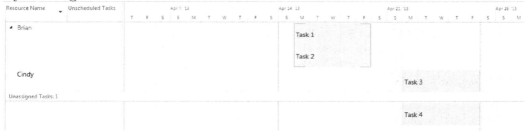

Figure A-47. Overallocated resource

You can click on the Team Planner view under the View tab to see a screen similar to the top section of Figure A-48. Notice that Brian has both Tasks 1 and 2 assigned to him at the same time. These tasks and Brian's name display in red to show the overallocation. Cindy is assigned Task 3 the following week, and Task 4 is unassigned. By simply clicking and dragging Task 4 straight up so it is under Brian in Week 2 and Task 2 straight down so it is under Cindy in Week 1, you can reassign those tasks and remove Brian's overallocation, as shown in the bottom section of Figure A-48. Many people will appreciate the simplicity of this feature, first introduced in Project 2010!

Before moving tasks in the Team Planner View:

Resource Name	Unscheduled Tasks	Apr 7, 13							Apr 14, 13							Apr 21, 13							Apr 28, 13		
		T	F	S	S	M	T	W	T	F	S	S	M	T	W	T	F	S	S	M	T	W	T	F	S	S	M
⊿ Brian											Task 1															
											Task 2															
Cindy																	Task 3					
Unassigned Tasks: 1																					
																	Task 4				

After moving tasks in the Team Planner View:

Resource Name	Unscheduled Tasks	Apr 7, 13							Apr 14, 13							Apr 21, 13							Apr 28, 13		
		T	F	S	S	M	T	W	T	F	S	S	M	T	W	T	F	S	S	M	T	W	T	F	S	S	M
Brian											Task 1						Task 4				
Cindy											Task 2						Task 3				
Unassigned Tasks: 0																					

Figure A-48. Adjusting resource assignments using the Team Planner feature

Using the New Resource Engagement Feature

If you are using Project Professional 2016 with Project Online, then you can take advantage of the new resource engagement feature. Figure A-49 shows the Help screen explaining how it works.

Better control over resource scheduling

Some resources have limited availability, and may have their time scheduled by a resource manager. With Project Professional 2016 and Project Online, project managers and resource managers can negotiate an agreement, called a **resource engagement**, to make sure that resources are being used appropriately and effectively throughout your organization.

IMPORTANT: Resource engagements only work if you're using Project Professional 2016 or Project Pro for Office 365, connected to Project Online. If you are not connected to Project Online, the resource engagements functionality will be hidden from view. Project Standard 2016 does not include resource engagements.

How does it work? When a resource manager sets up the enterprise resource pool in Project Online, he or she can identify some resources as requiring approval to be assigned to projects.

When a project manager decides to use one of these resources on a project, he or she submits an engagement request with the date range for when the resource is needed, and either a certain percentage of that resource's time during that date range, or a set number of hours during that date range.

The resource manager reviews this request, and can accept it, suggest changes, or reject it. The project manager refreshes the engagement status in the **new Resource Plan view** in Project Professional 2016 to see the resource manager's response.

Once the engagement is finalized, the project manager has the go-ahead to assign that resource to tasks in the project.

Figure A-49. Using the resource engagement feature

Entering Baseline Plans, Actual Costs, and Actual Times

After entering information in the Task Name column, establishing task durations and dependencies, and assigning costs and resources, you are ready to establish a baseline plan. By comparing the information in your baseline plan to actual progress during the course of the project, you can identify and solve problems. After the project ends, you can use the baseline and actual information to plan similar, future projects more accurately. To use Project Professional 2016 to help control projects and view earned value information, you must establish a baseline plan, enter actual costs, and enter actual durations. In the next series of steps you will use a new file called 2016actuals.mpp that you downloaded from the companion Website for this text (www.intropm.com).

To save a file as a baseline and enter actual information:

1. *Open the file called 2016actuals.mpp.* The file should be showing the Cost table view. Notice that this short project was planned to start on January 7, 2013 and end on February 13 of the same year, have three resources assigned to it, and cost $11,200. Click the **Project** tab, click the **Set Baseline** button under the Schedule group, and click **Set Baseline**. Your screen should resemble Figure A-50.

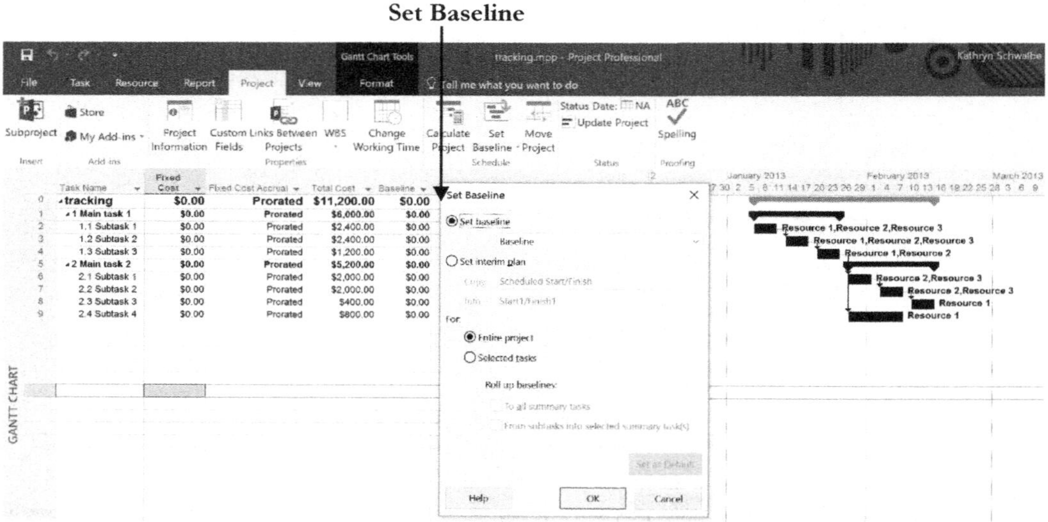

Set Baseline

Figure A-50. Saving a baseline

2. *Save the file as a baseline.* Examine the **Set Baseline** dialog box. Click the drop-down arrow to see that you can set up to ten baselines. Accept the default to save the entire project. Click **OK**. Notice that the Baseline column changes to have a light blue background color.

3. *Display the Tracking table.* Click the **Task** tab, right-click the **Select All button** and then click **Tracking to view the tracking table**. Move your mouse over each

tracking button in the Ribbon to see what it does. Your screen should resemble Figure A-51.

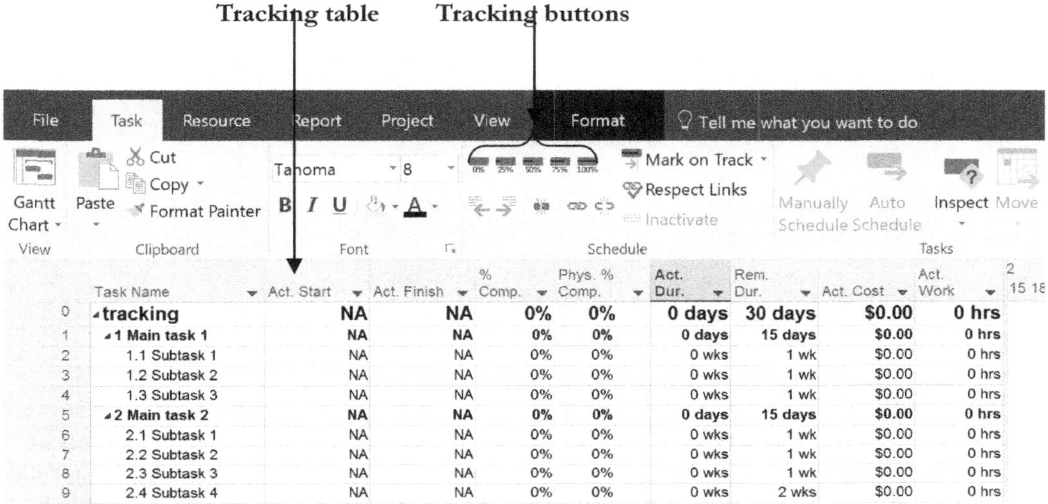

Figure A-51. Using the tracking table and tracking buttons

4.   *Mark Tasks 2 through 4 as 100% complete.* Click the Task Name for Task 2, **Subtask 1 under Main task 1**, and drag down through Task 4 to highlight those tasks. Click the **100% Complete** button on the Ribbon. The columns with dates, durations, and cost information should now contain data instead of the default values, such as NA or 0%. The % Comp. column should display 100%. Adjust column widths if needed. Your screen should resemble Figure A-52. Notice that the Gantt chart bars for those three tasks now have a black line through them.

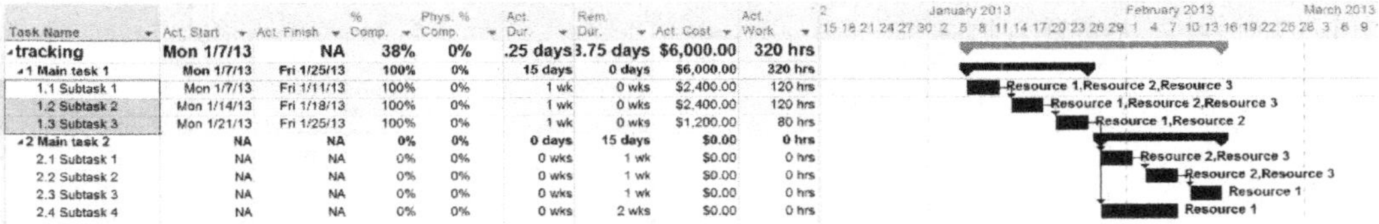

Figure A-52. Tracking table information

5.   *Enter actual completion dates for Task 6.* Click the Task Name for Task 6, **Subtask 1 under Main task 2**, click the **Mark on Track drop-down**, and then click **Update Tasks.** The Update Tasks dialog box opens. For Task 6, enter the Actual Start date as **1/28/13 (the same as the Current Start date)** and the Actual Finish date as **2/11/13 (ten days later than the Current Finish date)**, as shown in Figure A-53. Click **OK**. Notice how the information in the tracking sheet has changed.

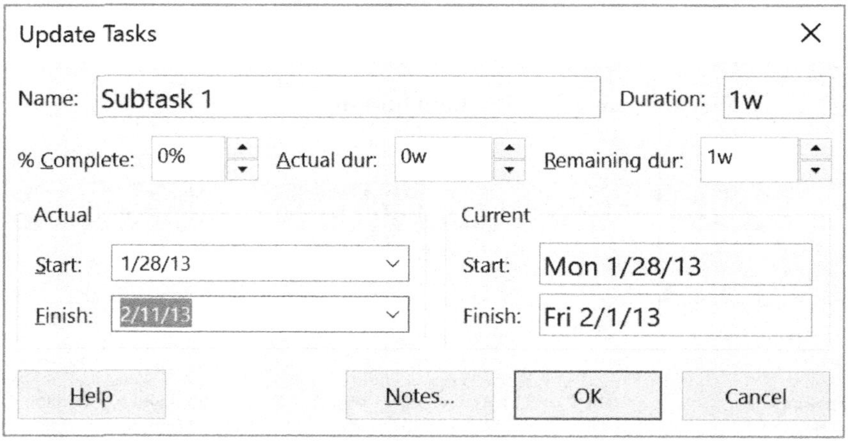

Figure A-53. Update Tasks dialog box

6.   *View the Tracking Gantt chart.* Click the drop-down arrow on the far left of the screen where it says Gantt chart, and then click **Tracking Gantt** to quickly switch to that view. Move the **split bar** and adjust column widths as needed. Use the **horizontal scroll bar** in the Gantt chart window to the right (move the slider to the left) to see symbols on the Tracking Gantt chart. Use the **Zoom slider** on the lower right of the screen to adjust the timescale so you can see all of the symbols. Your screen should resemble Figure A-54. The blue bar for task 6 shows the actual time you just entered. Notice that the delay in this one task on the critical path has caused the planned completion date for the entire project to slip (now Feb 25 versus Feb 13). Also notice the Indicator column to the far left. The check marks show that tasks are completed.

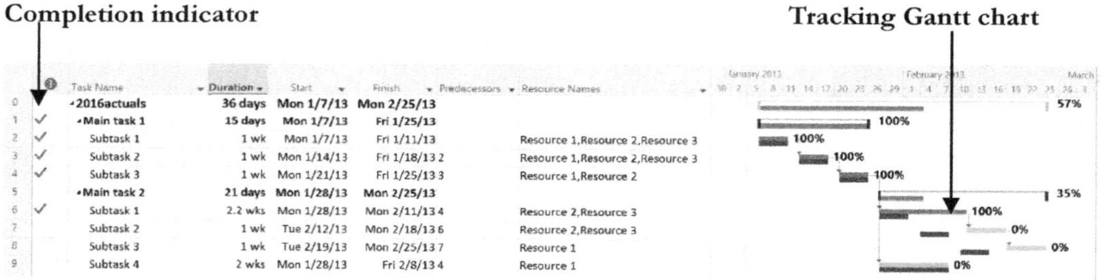

Completion indicator   **Tracking Gantt chart**

Figure A-54. Tracking Gantt chart view

7.   *Save your file as a new file named 2016actuals.mpp.* Click **File** on the Menu bar, and then click **Save As**. Name the file **2016actuals**, and then click **Save**.

Notice the additional information available on the Tracking Gantt chart. Completed tasks have 100% by their symbols on the Tracking Gantt chart. Tasks that have not started yet display 0%. Tasks in progress, such as Task 5, show the percentage of the work completed (35% in this example). The project summary task bar indicates that the entire project is 57% complete. Viewing the Tracking Gantt chart allows you to easily see your schedule progress against the baseline plan. After you have entered some actuals, you can review earned value information for the initiating tasks of this project. Of course you should continue this process of entering actuals on a real project until it is completed and include the final earned value data in a final project report.

VIEWING EARNED VALUE MANAGEMENT DATA

Earned value management is an important project management technique for measuring project performance. Because you have entered actual information, you can now view earned value information in Project Professional 2016. You can also view an earned value report using the visual reports feature.

To view earned value information:

1. *View the Earned Value table.* Using the 2016actuals file you just saved (or downloaded from the companion Website), click the **Select All** button, select **More Tables, and d**ouble-click **Earned Value**. Move the split bar to the right to reveal all of the columns, as shown in Figure A-55. Note that the Earned Value table includes columns for each earned value acronym, such as PV, EV, AC, SV, CV, etc. Also note that the EAC (Estimate at Completion) is higher than the BAC (Budget at Completion) for Task 6, where the task took longer than planned to complete. Task 0 shows a VAC (Variance at Completion) of ($3,360.00), meaning the project is projected to cost $3,360 more than planned at completion. Remember that not all of the actual information has been entered yet. Also note that the date on your computer must be set later than the date of a completed task for the data to calculate properly.

Select All button

Task Name	Planned Value PV (BCWS)	Earned Value EV (BCWP)	AC (ACWP)	SV	CV	EAC	BAC	VAC
0	2016actuals	$11,200.00	$8,000.00	$10,400.00	($3,200.00)	($2,400.00)	$14,560.00	$11,200.00	($3,360.00)
1	Main task 1	$6,000.00	$6,000.00	$6,000.00	$0.00	$0.00	$6,000.00	$6,000.00	$0.00
2	Subtask 1	$2,400.00	$2,400.00	$2,400.00	$0.00	$0.00	$2,400.00	$2,400.00	$0.00
3	Subtask 2	$2,400.00	$2,400.00	$2,400.00	$0.00	$0.00	$2,400.00	$2,400.00	$0.00
4	Subtask 3	$1,200.00	$1,200.00	$1,200.00	$0.00	$0.00	$1,200.00	$1,200.00	$0.00
5	Main task 2	$5,200.00	$2,000.00	$4,400.00	($3,200.00)	($2,400.00)	$11,440.08	$5,200.00	($6,240.08)
6	Subtask 1	$2,000.00	$2,000.00	$4,400.00	$0.00	($2,400.00)	$4,400.00	$2,000.00	($2,400.00)
7	Subtask 2	$2,000.00	$0.00	$0.00	($2,000.00)	$0.00	$2,000.00	$2,000.00	$0.00
8	Subtask 3	$400.00	$0.00	$0.00	($400.00)	$0.00	$400.00	$400.00	$0.00
9	Subtask 4	$800.00	$0.00	$0.00	($800.00)	$0.00	$800.00	$800.00	$0.00

Figure A-55. Earned value table

2. *View the earned value chart.* Click the **Report** tab, and then click **Costs** under the View Reports group, and then click **Earned Value Report**, as shown in Figure A-56. You can experiment with different report options or click the link to Learn more about earned value, as desired.

EARNED VALUE

Earned value management helps you quantify the performance of a project. It compares costs and schedules to a baseline to determine if the project is on track.

If the charts don't look right, make sure you have set a baseline, assigned costs to tasks or resources, and entered progress.

EAC	ACWP	BCWP
$14,560.00	$10,400.00	$8,000.00

EARNED VALUE OVER TIME
The project's earned value based on the status date. If actual cost (ACWP) is higher than earned value (BCWP), then the project is over budget. If planned value (BCWS) is higher than earned value, then the project is behind schedule.

Learn more about earned value.

VARIANCE OVER TIME
Cost and schedule variances for the project based on status date. If CV is negative then, the project is over budget. If SV is positive then the project is behind schedule.

INDICES OVER TIME
Cost and schedule performance indices for the project based on status date. The greater the performance index, the more on schedule and cost saving the project.

Figure A-56. Earned value report

3.   *Close without saving the file.* Click the **File** tab, click **Close**, and select **No** when prompted to save the file. You can also exit Project Professional 2016 and take a break, if desired.

Next you will use a few more features to help tie your project to other applications.

INTEGRATING PROJECT PROFESSIONAL 2016 WITH OTHER APPLICATIONS AND APPS FOR OFFICE

Project Professional 2016 provides several features to make it easy to integrate with other applications. For example, you can copy data between Project Professional 2016 and other applications (including the timeline), or you might want to create hyperlinks to project documents created in Word, Excel, PowerPoint, or other applications from within your project files. You can also purchase and add new apps to Project 2016 from Microsoft's Office Store.

Copying Information between Applications

Most people are familiar with copying information between Office applications. For example, you can highlight a column of data in Excel, select copy, and then select Paste in Project Professional 2016 or other applications. You can also create a new Project Professional 2016 file from an existing Excel file by select New from Excel Workbook. It is also easy to copy a timeline into another application.

To copy a timeline:

1. *Open another Project Professional 2016 template file.* Start Project Professional 2016, and open a template file, such as **Residential Construction**, as shown in Figure A-57. Notice the timeline near the top of the screen.

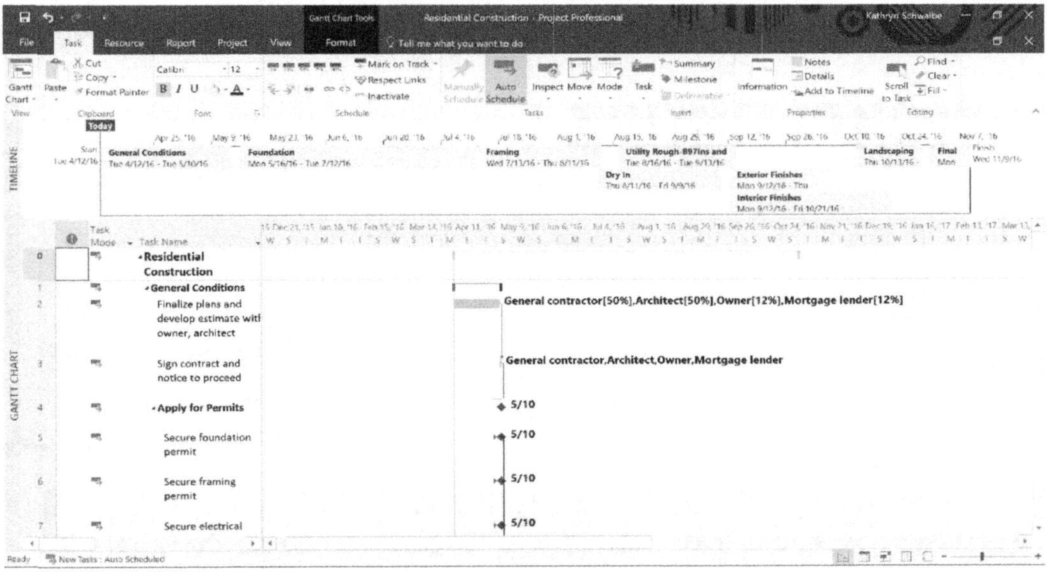

Figure A-57. Residential construction template

2. *Copy the Timeline.* Click anywhere on the Timeline, and then click the **Copy Timeline button** in the Copy group on the Ribbon, as shown in Figure A-57, and select **For Presentation**.

3. *Paste the Timeline into PowerPoint.* Open **PowerPoint**, change the slide layout to Title and Contents, type "**Project Timeline**" as the title for the slide, and change the theme, as desired (Main Event is selected here), and then **right-click** in the contents section and select **Paste picture**. Your screen should resemble Figure A-

58, showing the Project Professional 2016 Timeline in your presentation. You can also paste the timeline into other presentation software, as desired.

4.   *Close the file without saving it.* Click the **File** tab, click **Close**, and select **No** when prompted to save the file.

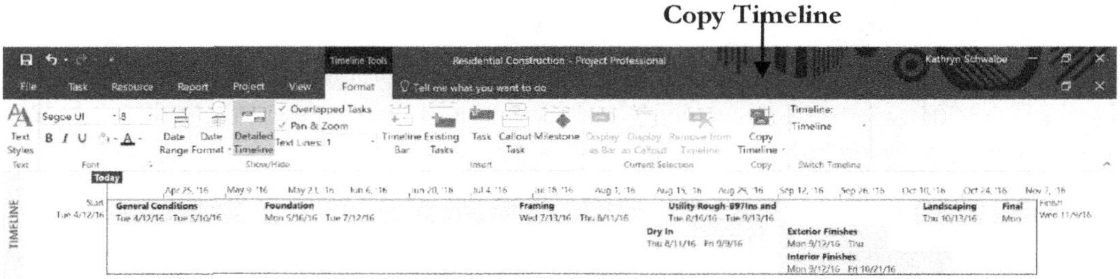

Figure A-58. Copy Timeline

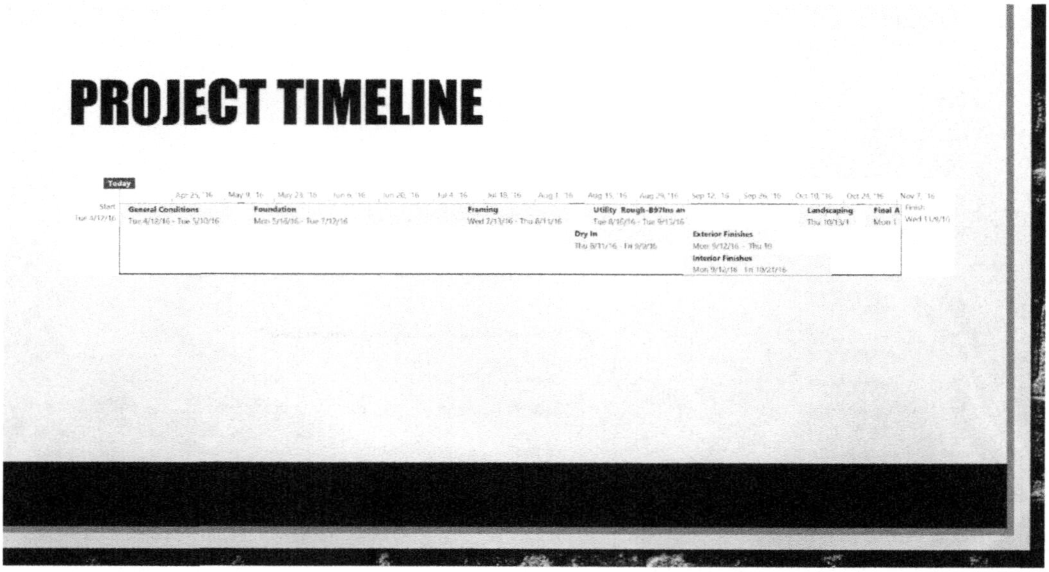

Figure A-59. Timeline picture pasted into PowerPoint

Creating Hyperlinks to Other Files

Some people like to use their Project Professional 2016 file as a main source of information for many different project documents. To do this, you can simply insert a hyperlink to other document files. For example, you can create a hyperlink to the file with the stakeholder register you listed as a milestone in your Task Name column earlier.

To insert a hyperlink within a file:

*1.   Open the **2016schedule.mpp** file.* Use the file you saved earlier or download it from the companion Website for this text. The Entry table and Gantt Chart view should display.

2.   Select the task in which you want to insert a hyperlink. Click the Task Name **for Task 3**, **Stakeholder register completed.**

3.   Open the Insert Hyperlink dialog box. Right-click in that cell, then click **Hyperlink**. The Insert Hyperlink dialog box opens, as shown in Figure A-60. You will have different folders visible based on your computer's directory structure.

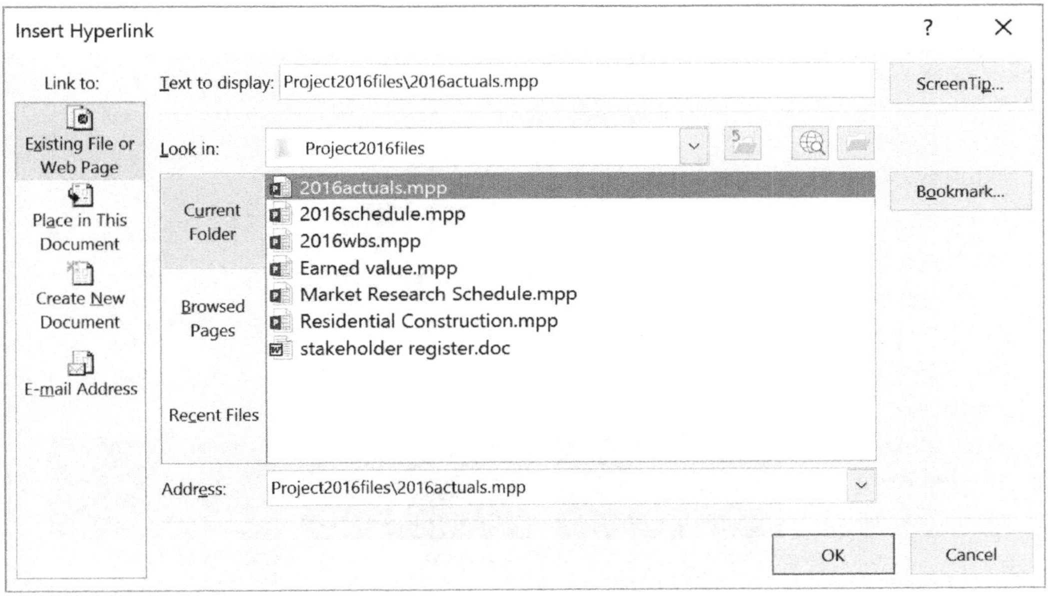

Figure A-60. Insert hyperlink dialog box

4.   Double-click the filename of the hyperlink file. Change the **Look in:** information until you find where you have saved the files you downloaded for this appendix. Double-click the Word file named **stakeholder register**, and then click **OK**. A Hyperlink button appears in the Indicators column to the left of the Task Name for Task 3. (Note: If that column does not display, click the **Format** tab, **Insert Column**, and select **Indicators**). Move your mouse over the hyperlink button until the mouse pointer changes to the Hand symbol to reveal the name of the hyperlinked file. If you click on it, the file will open.

Using Project Professional 2016 Apps

Microsoft has an Office Store where you can download special apps for Project Professional 2016. New apps are added often.

To explore Project Professional 2016 apps:

1. *Access the Office Store.* With Project Professional 2016 open, click the **Project** tab, then click **Store button** on the left of the Ribbon under the Add-ins group. The Office Add-ins dialog box opens, as shown in Figure A-61.

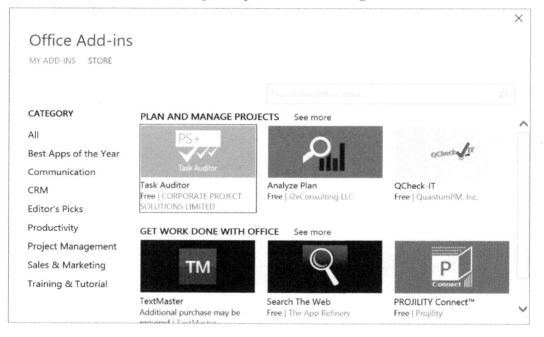

Figure A-61. Apps for Office dialog box (as of April 2016)

2. *Explore the Add-ins.* Read information about various apps, as desired.

3. *Close Project Professional 2016.* Click the **Close icon** in the upper right of the window to close the application. Select **No** when prompted to save the file.

Synching with Project Server and Project Online

Recall from Figure A-1 that Project Professional 2016 is one of six different versions of Project 2016. One of its features is that it can be synched with Project Server and Project Online to allow collaboration with team members, PMO staff, and senior executives. Remember that individual projects are often part of programs and portfolios created to support organizational strategy.

You have really just touched the surface of Project Professional 2016's powerful features, but you probably know more than most people who have this software! Consult other books, online resources, and experts for more detailed information to learn even more about Project Professional 2016 and other versions of Project 2016.

DISCUSSION QUESTIONS

1.   What are the six different versions of project management software offered by Microsoft as of April 2016? Briefly describe how they differ and who uses them.

2.   What are some unique features of project management software in general?

3.   What are the new features of Project Professional 2016?

4.   How do you create a WBS in Project 2016?

5.   How do you enter task durations and establish dependencies between tasks?

6.   How do you establish a baseline in Project 2016 and enter actual information?

7.   What type of information do you see in the Earned Value table?

8.   What are some of the reports built-in to Project 2016? Which ones do you think are commonly used?

9.   How can you access other application files from within Project 2016?

EXERCISES

1.   To make sure you understand the information in this appendix, perform the steps yourself. Print out the following screen shots or send them to your instructor, as directed. Remember that you can download required files from www.intropm.com.
     a.   Figure A-11. Network diagram view
     b.   Figure A-16. Resource Overview report
     c.   Figure A-23. Adding automatic outline numbers and a project summary task
     d.   Create a new Project Professional 2016 file called general-wbs. Make the main categories survey phase, design phase, and implementation phase. Include at least two deliverables with at least two activities and one milestone under each of the phases. Use meaningful, fictitious names for them. For example, you might have a deliverable under survey phase called survey with activities called create survey and administer survey and a deliverable called survey completed. Enter 0 for the duration of the milestones, but do not enter any durations for the other tasks. Be sure to indent tasks and show the outline numbers before printing or submitting the file.

2.   Continue performing the steps in this appendix, starting with the section called Developing the Schedule. Print out the following screens or send them to your instructor, as directed:

   a.   Figure A-32. All task durations and recurring task entered
   b.   Figure A-39. Network diagram view
   c.   Figure A-46. Changing Work hours for tasks
   d.   Figure A-56. Earned value report
   e.   Continue performing the steps, or at least read them. Write a one-to-two page paper describing the capabilities of Project Professional 2016 and your opinion of this software. What do you like and dislike about it?

3.   If you are doing a team project as part of your class or for a project at work, use Project Professional 2016 to create a detailed file describing the work you plan to do for the project.

   a.   Create a detailed WBS, including several deliverables, activities, and milestones. Also estimate task durations, link tasks, add tasks to the timeline, and enter resources and costs, assign resources, and so on. Save your file as a baseline and print it out or send it to your instructor, as directed.

   b.   Track your progress on your team project by entering actual cost and schedule information. Create a new baseline file if there have been a lot of changes. View earned value information when you are halfway through the project or course. Continue tracking your progress until the project or course is finished. Print or submit your Gantt chart, Project Summary report, Earned Value table, and relevant information to your instructor.

   c.   Write a two- to three-page report describing your experience. What did you learn about Project Professional 2016 from this exercise? How do you think the software helps in managing a project? You may also want to interview people who use project management software for their experiences and suggestions.

END NOTES

[1]Marketsandmarkets.com, "Project Portfolio Management (PPM) Market by Platform Type (Software and Services), Deployment Type (On-Premises and Cloud), End User, Business Solutions, Industry Vertical, and Region - Global Forecast and Analysis to 2020," February 2016). Note: USD means U.S. dollars.

Appendix B:
Resources

Detailed Table of Contents

INTRODUCTION

This appendix summarizes resources you can use to expand your understanding of project management. It describes information related to the following: the companion Websites for students and instructors, template files, MindView software, and Basecamp project management software.

COMPANION WEBSITES

For Students (www.intropm.com or www.pmtexts.com)

The student companion Website for this text is not password-protected. Anyone can access it, and it is updated regularly. The site includes the following:

- Interactive, multiple-choice quizzes for each chapter where you can test your understanding of key concepts

- Jeopardy-like games for each chapter, another method for testing your understanding of materials

- Template files, as described in the following section

- Microsoft Project 2016 data files for performing steps in Appendix A

- Links to several valuable sites under the Resources tab, including project management simulation software tools, as described later in this appendix

- Additional resources related to project management, including advice for certifications, more resources on Agile, and links to other useful sites.

For Instructors

The instructor companion Website for this text is password-protected. Contact the author at schwalbe@augsburg.edu to verify that you are an instructor using this text to gain access. In addition to the information on the student site, the instructor site includes the following:

- Lecture slides for each chapter, created in PowerPoint. Note: These slides are copyrighted and must remain on a secure site. Instructors can copy them onto their own school's secure network and make changes as desired.

- An instructor manual for the text

- A solution manual for the text

- Several test banks and sample tests

- Teaching ideas, including information on using real projects in classes and using other cases, and inputs from other instructors.

TEMPLATE FILES

As mentioned throughout this text, using templates can help you prepare various project management documents, spreadsheets, charts, and other files. Figure B-1 lists the template name, the chapter where it is used in the text, and the application software used to create it. Be careful to enter information into the templates carefully, and feel free to modify the templates to meet your particular project needs. You can download the files in one compressed file from the companion Website. The files are saved in Office 2013 format.

Template name	Chapter	Application software
Payback period chart	2	Excel
Weighted scoring model	2	Excel
Stakeholder register	3	Word
Stakeholder management strategy	3	Word
Business case	3	Word
Business case financials	3	Excel
Charter	3	Word
Kick-off meeting agenda	3	Word
Team contract (team charter)	4	Word
Project management plan	4	Word
Project organizational chart	4	Word
Requirements management plan	4	Word
Requirements traceability matrix	4	Word
Scope statement	4	Word
WBS	4	Word
WBS dictionary entry	4	Word
Activity list and attributes	5	Word
Milestone list	5	Word
Activity resource requirements	5	Word
Project schedule	5	Project
Cost estimate	5	Excel
Cost baseline	5	Excel
Quality management plan	6	Word
Quality metrics	6	Word
Quality checklist	6	Word
Project organizational chart	6	PowerPoint
RACI chart	6	Excel
Resource histogram	6	Excel

Human resource plan	6	Word
Communications management plan	6	Word
Project Website	6	FrontPage
Risk management plan	6	Word
Probability/impact matrix	6	PowerPoint
Risk register	6	Excel
Make-or-buy analysis	6	Word
Procurement management plan	6	Word
Request for proposal	6	Word
Contract statement of work	6	Word
Supplier evaluation matrix	6	Excel
Milestone report	7	Word
Change request	7	Word
Cause-and-effect diagram	7 and 8	PowerPoint
Team roster	7	Word
Team performance assessment	7	Word
Issue log	7	Excel
Qualified sellers list	7	Word
Contract	7	Word
Earned value chart	8	Excel
Performance report (progress report)	8	Word
Deliverable acceptance form	8	Word
Run chart	8	Excel
Scatter diagram	8	Excel
Histogram	8	Excel
Pareto chart	8	Excel
Flow chart	8	PowerPoint
Contract closure notice	8	Word
Customer acceptance-project completion form	9	Word
Final project report table of contents	9	Word
Transition plan	9	Word
Lessons-learned report	9	Word
Potential project	App C	Word
Draft schedule	App C	Excel

Figure B-1. Templates available for download on the companion Website

MINDVIEW SOFTWARE

As mentioned in earlier chapters, you can use mind-mapping software to perform a SWOT analysis, create a WBS, and more. After creating a WBS with MindView software, you can easily view it in a Gantt chart format as well. You can download a 30-day free trial of MindView software by Matchware, Inc. Version 7 of this product was available in 2017 for Windows, and Version 7 for Mac computers. There is also a cloud-based version called MindView Online with limited capabilities. Go to www.matchware.com for more information. Figure B-2 provides sample screen shots from MindView Business 6, the previous version for Windows.

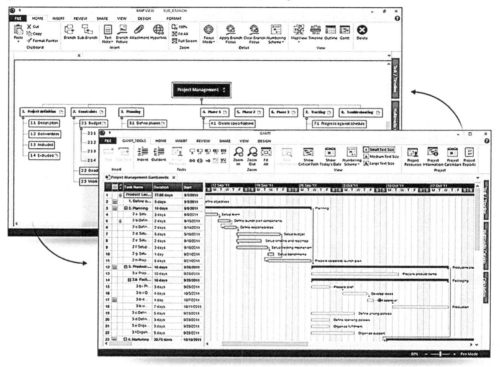

Figure B-2. MindView screenshots

You can find numerous videos on how to use this powerful software under the Support tab from www.matchware.com or on the Matchware Software YouTube channel. The following information on using MindView for project planning is from Matchware's website in July 2017:

> Need a better way to visualize your tasks and work streams? Frustrated by note taking during planning meetings? Looking for a professional Gantt chart tool that is fast and easy to use? Then MindView is the ideal project management software tool for you!

MindView lets you use mind mapping to help every member of your team fully understand the project, contribute to planning, follow the project timeline and clearly visualize all tasks in an organized manner. It lets you take notes "on-the-fly" for criteria or risk management and allows you to attach relevant files to each task in your Mind Map (Excel® files, technical drawings, etc). Task information such as resources, duration and priorities can also easily be applied directly onto your Mind Map.

MindView bridges the gap between Mind Mapping and project planning by integrating a dynamic Gantt chart. This allows you to create most of your project plan in the Mind Map view and then simply switch to the Gantt view for fine-tuning. Your final Gantt chart can then easily be printed or integrated with Microsoft Project.

BASECAMP PROJECT MANAGEMENT SOFTWARE

There are hundreds of project management software tools available. Appendix A provides a brief guide to using Microsoft Project 2016, the most popular tool. However, Microsoft Project may not be the best tool for some situations, especially in teaching courses in project management. Most students want to use an easier, totally web-based tool that works on PCs, Macs, and smart phones at no cost. Instructors want the same, and they also want a tool that they can use for more than 30 or 60 days. At the recommendation of several people, this book now includes a brief guide to a popular tool that meets those desires: Basecamp. Instructors can request a free account with no time limit from Basecamp.

Figure B-3 shows the initial screen a user sees when visiting www.basecamp.com in July 2017. Notice the friendly approach Basecamp takes to explaining its product. The company has been in business since 2004, and the number of users continues to grow, with over 2.5 million accounts created by 2017. Notice that Forbes reported that Basecamp is one of America's top small companies, in 2017, as noted in the top right of the figure.

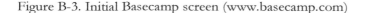

Figure B-3. Initial Basecamp screen (www.basecamp.com)

Students in the author's spring 2015 Project Management course at Augsburg College completed a project to evaluate Basecamp for their team project. The students also used a Google site, Google docs, and Microsoft Project 2013 as part of the class. (The author retired from teaching that spring, so older screen shots are still shown here in this text. Additional features have been added to Basecamp since then.) Figure B-4 shows the initial Basecamp screen from this project. Notice that all of the information related to the project is contained within Basecamp. The team could:

- Have discussions
- Create To-do lists (similar to parts of a WBS)
- Upload, download, and manage files
- Collaborate on Text documents within Basecamp
- Create events (similar to creating milestones)

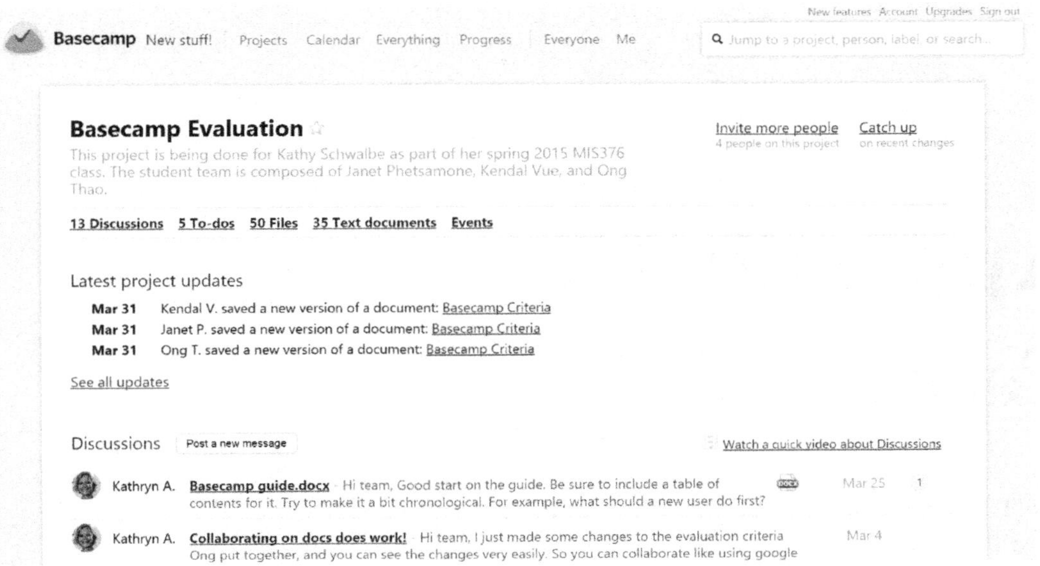

Figure B-4. Class project home page in Basecamp, created by Janet Phetsamone, project manager, and team members Ong Thao and Kendal Vue

Basecamp was found to be much easier to use than Project 2013. Students liked that they could store all of their files in one place and access the information from any device with an Internet connection, especially smart phones. They could not find an easy way to create a comprehensive Gantt chart, but they did use the To-do lists and other features to keep track of their work. Students also found that they could use the templates for this book as Text files within Basecamp to collaborate online, similar to Google Docs.

One of the main deliverables of this project was a Basecamp Guide written specifically for students in a project management class. As Basecamp is a totally online tool, screens and features change often based on user feedback. To learn more, take advantage of the many videos, user guides, and other help features under the Learn and Support tabs from www.basecamp.com.

Appendix C:
Case Studies

NOTE: Instructors can find this whole appendix on the instructor site in Microsoft Word for easy editing.

INTRODUCTION

Each chapter of this text includes Exercises and Team Projects, but some instructors like to assign more detailed case studies. This section provides three running case studies: Real Projects, New Business Venture, and Fixer Upper. You can also find further suggestions for using real projects or other case studies, such as those provided by the Harvard Business Review, on the companion Website for instructors under "Teaching Ideas." There are also samples of completed student projects on www.intropm.com based on an international new business venture (variation of the New Business Venture case) and the Project Management Videos case (formerly in the third edition of this text and now on the instructor site).

The first running case provides two individual homework assignments to solicit real project ideas from each student and to assess the team project. It then provides detailed instructions on what is required for the real projects. The two other running cases include five parts—initiating, planning, executing, monitoring and controlling, and closing—with scenario-based information and several tasks to complete under each part. Students can refer to the sample documents found in the text to help them complete the tasks. Several of the tasks involve using templates provided on the companion Website. Anyone can use these cases as long as they mention the source. Feel free to modify them to meet your class needs, and feel free to share additional case studies on the instructor site.

Case Study 1: Real Projects

Note: My personal preference is to use real projects as part of a project management class. It helps students gain real-world experience and practice working with a "real" sponsor and other stakeholders. Projects often produce very useful results for the college, non-profit organizations, businesses, or the students themselves. The information below is based on my personal experience and syllabi instructions for having students work on real projects in a team setting. I give students the option of doing another case study, but the vast majority of students choose to work on a real project.

An important part of coming up with good project ideas is the following required homework assignment, due very early in the course. Each student must do the homework, so as long as you get about one good idea out of every four, you should have enough real projects to work on. I often propose additional project ideas, mostly from suggestions from colleagues or former students.

Individual Homework: Project Proposal (100 points)

Here's your chance to get some useful work done! Each student will propose a project to be done as part of this class, and hopefully we will do several of them. Even if you want to do a case study instead of a real project, you must still propose a real project. Projects must have a sponsor (can be a student, friend, relative, boss, community leader, etc.), provide a needed service or product, and be a good fit for this class. Each student normally spends between 20-40 hours on the class project. Review my Website and look at some of the past student projects and the information in the syllabus about the projects. Then write a proposal for a potential project, using the **potential project template**. Talk to the sponsor **before** writing the proposal, and try to come up with a good proposal! Think about projects at work, for community groups, etc. that you could do. If you do not do a real project, you will work on a case study. You still need to propose a real project, though, to get experience doing that!

It is also important to explain how grades will be determined for these team projects. Below is another individual homework assignment that allows each student to provide inputs on his/her own team project grade and the grade of each team member. They do this assignment for both the real projects and case studies, and it is due the last day of class.

Individual Homework: Self-Assessment (100 points)

Write a 1-2-page self-assessment based on the team project, answering the following questions:

- If you had to give your team a grade for the project, what would it be? Why?
- What were your roles and responsibilities on the group project? How well do you think you performed on this project?
- Briefly assess each team member's performance. If you had to give each person, including yourself, a grade, what would it be and why? To compare individual contributions, if you had 100 points to allocate to your team, how would you allocate them? If you're an Apprentice fan, what would be the order you would use to fire people from your team?

Syllabus Description of Team Projects

The purpose of the team project is to use a structured approach to project management in a team setting (3-5 students/team). I normally let teams self-select and assign people to teams as needed. One person could take the lead on each task, but other team members should provide inputs and edit the work so it is consistent and of high quality and reflects a team effort. Each team member should plan to spend **20-40 hours** total on the team project, including some time in class. If the project is done for someone outside of Augsburg, students can earn the Augsburg Experience credit. **You must have the sponsor call or email me to approve the project after you propose it if you really want to work on it.** If you do not choose to work on a real project, teams will work on one of the case studies in the text (New Business Venture or Fixer Upper). You can substitute a different business idea for the new business venture case study, if you like, with my approval.

Examples of "real" class projects: One example of a past project called the Tempting Templates Project Website (which I sponsored, and which was all done virtually) is available on my personal Website (www.kathyschwalbe.com) under PM Info. I will show some other student project sites in class. Most of them were done as Google sites starting in 2011. Other examples of recent class projects include the following:

- Organizing and running a fundraising event, like the Hockey Team Fights Cancer project (raised over $5,000 last fall), a benefit for someone with a disease, a game night at Grand Slam, a 5K race for the Make a Wish foundation, or making baby blankets for hurricane victims

- Creating/updating a Website or smart phone/table app for a small business or non-profit organization

- Helping a new store market its products to college students (i.e., Punch Pizza, Edible Arrangements)

- Organizing and running a shark tank type of event to help promote entrepreneurship (Note: We did this twice at Augsburg College with great interest and success.)

- Redesigning/renovating one or more rooms of someone's home or rental property

Team Progress Reports:
If you are working on a case study, I'll provide instructions on which tasks you should have completed by the progress report dates and which ones to present. In general, you should have the initiating tasks done for the first progress report and the planning tasks and some of the executing tasks done for the second one. Below are instructions for what is needed for progress reports for the "real" projects. I will review some of this information before you present as part of an online assignment. I also want to communicate directly with your project sponsor and have access to your team's website at least a week before your first progress report.

Progress Report 1: Assume you, the project manager, are giving a formal progress report to senior managers. You will present and review highlights of the following information:

- a brief introduction of your project and your team, emphasizing why you are doing the project, what your main deliverables will be, and how you will measure success
- a one-page progress report (using the template called performance report)

- a project charter (using template), signed by all stakeholders, including your sponsor (an email confirmation is okay in place of a signature for now)

- a summary of communications so far with your project sponsor and instructor (emails or documented meeting minutes)
- a preliminary scope statement (using template. Note: Describe each product-oriented deliverable using at least two complete sentences)
- a team charter/contract, emphasizing the communications section (using template)
- a draft schedule (using the template in Moodle for this class. I will be most interested in what you have under Executing and your total estimated hours by person. I know this is a rough estimate, but do the best you can for now. Your team can update actual hours using Google docs or other means)
- a brief summary of your team's MBTI types and how they might affect your team dynamics

Be sure all of your documents and your presentation are on your team's website, and also provide me with a hard copy of them all before you present. Put key information from each document in a presentation and make sure it is easy to read. For example, you can paste the information from all of these documents into PowerPoint slides. You can also pull up some of the documents and zoom in so they are easier to read, like the draft schedule. Make sure you have consistent information in each document. For example, if you say in your project charter under the approach that you will prepare a flyer for your project, describe that flyer in more detail as a deliverable in the scope statement and include it in the executing section of the draft schedule. It would probably fall under a summary category called marketing. I will provide written and verbal feedback during the presentation, just as a program manager would.

Progress Report 2: Assume you, a team member, are giving a formal progress report to senior managers. You will present and review highlights of the following information:

- a one-page progress report (using the template called performance report. Be sure to focus on work completed since the first progress report)
- an updated scope statement, including **more detailed** descriptions of key deliverables
- a Gantt chart created in Microsoft Project, based on the draft schedule you created. Be sure to include your detailed WBS under executing, and list at least 4 milestones under executing. Note: You can create the Gantt chart in Basecamp or MindView or other software, if you prefer.
- a probability/impact matrix, including at least 10 potential risks for your project. For at least three of them (most important ones), describe your strategy for managing them
- a summary/sample of completed deliverables under executing

- a comparison and explanation of estimated versus actual hours to date (show your updated draft schedule)
- feedback from your sponsor since the last progress report. I also want your sponsors to email or call me to verify their involvement at least three days before you present the second progress report

Final Project Presentations and Notebooks

By the last day of class, each team will present a **final project presentation** and hand in a **project notebook** (stapled pages or soft cover; no spiral notebooks, please). Assume you are giving a presentation to senior managers and potential employers. If you do a case study, put all of that information together in a notebook. If you do a real project, include the following information. All documentation should also be available on the team's website. Note: Each team member must give part of the 20-30 minute final presentation.

1. Cover page and detailed table of contents. List the project name, team members, and date on the cover page of the notebook. Be sure to number all pages (by hand is fine), which should match the table of contents. You may include tabs or dividers between major sections of the notebook, too.

2. A double-spaced 3-4-page project report. Address the following questions in your report, which should be in the front of your notebook after the table of contents: What did your team produce? Was the project a success or not, and what was your criteria for determining success? (Remember that should be defined in your scope statement early in the project). What project management tools/documents did you use, and did they help? How close was your draft schedule and estimate of hours to the actual schedule and actual hours worked on the project? What went right on the project? What went wrong? What did your team learn by working on this project? How did you select the project manager? Did he/she do a good job at leading your team? Did you work well as a team? What was your project sponsor's final assessment of the project? Include some written feedback from the sponsor in your final report and presentation. See the sample customer acceptance form in your text for an example. **Discuss this information in your final project presentation** and show/summarize the main products produced. **If your project involves some type of event, be sure to show pictures of the event.**

3. Hard copies of all of the products your team produced. Include the project management documents you created (charter, Gantt chart, etc.), communications with your sponsor, and all product-related items.

Note: Part of the grade for the team project will be based on the team's final presentation and progress reports, and part of grade will be based on the quality of the project and its notebook (one notebook per team, due the last day of class). You should also include a project completion form or some method of evaluation for real projects. I will look at the final homework where everyone suggests grades as well. Team project managers will earn a small amount of extra credit for successfully leading their project teams.

Case Study 2: New Business Venture

This case should be interesting to anyone interested in starting a new business. It involves research, marketing, finance, technology, and personal ethics. Feel free to change the type of business, if desired. The main purpose of this and other cases, however, is to help you practice some of the project management skills you are developing as part of your course. Note: If students want to propose a different business idea, let them! You can still use many of the tasks listed below, but modified as needed.

Part 1: Initiating

Background Scenario:

You and several of your friends have been working for corporations for over five years, but several of you have a desire to start your own business. You have decided that you are ready to pursue your idea of starting a music academy for children ages 3-16. You all enjoy creating music, and you saw the advantages that some children had from participating in special music programs beyond those available in schools. In particular, you see the need for music training in your area for children interested in voice, guitar, keyboard, and percussion so they can perform in their own bands.

This New Business Venture Project would primarily involve you and three of your friends, who were all part of your high school band:

1. You are an excellent bass player, and you were the one who organized your band in high school and got the few paid gigs that you had. You can also play keyboard. You continue to play both instruments occasionally, but your full-time job and new spouse take up a lot of your time. Your current full-time job is working as a business analyst for a large retail store. Although your job is going well, you realize that you would be happier working in your own business and with something involving music. Your strengths are your creativity, organization, and analytical skills. Your spouse is employed full-time and supports your idea to start your own business, as long as you have a detailed plan and financial backing.

2. Brian, one of your best friends since sixth grade, played lead guitar in your band. He is a natural musician and has little trouble learning to play very complicated songs. Brian is very quiet, but he would love to work for a successful small business and be able to share his passion for guitar with children. He is also a whiz at music technology, having recorded and edited CDs for several years. He works as a software developer for a large consulting firm. He is married and has one young child, and his spouse works part-time. Brian would not give up his full-time job until he knew he could support his family in this new business venture, but he could do a lot of part-time work.

3. Nicole, also one of your best friends since sixth grade, was the lead singer in your band. She has a great voice and really knows how to work a crowd, too. She is currently working as a part-time telemarketer, but she doesn't like her job at all and is ready for something new. Her spouse has a great job and supports her in pursuing a new business opportunity. Her strengths are her vocal talent, professional voice training, and

sales ability. She also loves working with children and would be willing to work full-time on this new business venture.

4. Andres was the last person to join your band in high school, having replaced your original drummer. He currently works as a music teacher at a local middle school. He has a lot of contacts with local schools and is dying to get this new music academy started. He is single and would want to keep his current job, but he could devote a fair amount of time to the business in the evenings, on weekends, and full-time in the summer. His strengths are his drumming expertise, teaching ability, music technology experience, and contacts with school-age children, parents, and school administrators. He currently gives some private lessons and knows other people who do as well, so he has potential clients and instructors that he could bring into the business.

The main goals of the New Business Venture Project are to prepare a business plan, get financial backing, handle legal issues, develop marketing materials, find a rental space for the music academy, purchase/develop curriculum, hire staff, and open for business by one year from now, September 1, to coincide with the school year. Your team has already analyzed the market, and you know you can make this business succeed. Your goal would be to cover your investment costs after two years in business.

Work with your teammates and instructor to perform all or just some of the following initiating tasks for this project.

Tasks

1. To become more familiar with the children's music instruction market, do some preliminary research to find out how big this market is, who the main companies are in the market, what the best-selling services are, pricing and marketing strategies, etc. If you do not want to focus on your own geographic area, pick one to focus on for this and future tasks. Write a two- to three-page paper (double-spaced) with your findings, citing at least two references. For example, the author's son took lessons and performed in rock bands from Virtuosos Music Academy in Plymouth, Minnesota (*www.virtuososonline.com*). You can also include a paragraph or two with your team's personal experience in this area, if applicable.

2. Prepare a stakeholder register and management strategy for the project. Include all project team members and make up names and information for at least one spouse, one potential financial backer, and one local competitor. Assume that you and your three friends are all team members, and you each invest $10,000 into the business. Your mother, a retired business professor, has decided to provide a substantial loan ($30,000), so she will be the sponsor. You still need to figure out how to get an additional $30,000 for the first-year start-up costs. Use the templates provided on the companion Website, and review the sample stakeholder register and management strategy in the text.

3. Prepare a team charter/contract for this project. Use the template provided on the companion Website, and review the sample in the text.

4. Prepare a project charter for the New Business Venture Project. Assume the project will take one year to complete and cost about $100,000. Recall that the main project objectives are to prepare a business plan, get financial backing, handle legal issues, develop marketing materials, find a rental place for the music academy, purchase/develop curriculum, hire staff, and open for business by one year from now. Your project team will not get paid for the hours they put into this project, but once the business opens, they will be compensated. You will incorporate the business and hire a lawyer to help with this and other legal issues. Use the template provided on the companion Website, and review the sample in the text.

5. An important part of starting any business is preparing financial projections. Although you will prepare a more detailed financial analysis when you create your business plan, you still want to do rough projections at this stage. Prepare a spreadsheet that can be used to determine the profit potential of starting this business. Include inputs for the initial investment cost, number of customers in the first month, customer growth rate/quarter, average monthly fee per customer, fixed and variable monthly operating costs, and variable costs per customer. Use the most likely, optimistic, and pessimistic inputs as shown in Figure C-2 to generate results for all three scenarios. For each month (Month 1-24), calculate your revenues (number of customers that month X monthly fee/customer) and expenses (fixed monthly salaries plus fixed monthly operative costs plus variable costs/customer/month X number of customers that month). Then determine the cumulative income each month. For example, the cumulative income in Month 1 is the Monthly Revenues - Monthly Expenses for Month 1. The cumulative income for Month 2 is the Monthly Revenues - Monthly Expenses for Month 2 plus the Cumulative Income for Month 1. The first month for the most likely scenario is filled in for you to check your formulas. Will you be able to recoup your start-up costs within two years in each scenario? If so, in what month? There is no template for this example, but you can use the format in Figure C-2. Print out a sheet with results for each scenario, clearly labeling if/when you recoup your investment.

Financial Projections for New Business Venture

Assumptions/Inputs:	Most likely	Optimistic	Pessimistic	
Year 0 investment cost:	$100,000	$80,000	$120,000	
Number of customers in month 1	150	200	100	
Quarterly customer growth rate	10%	30%	5%	
Monthly fee/customer	$150	$175	$125	
Fixed monthly salaries	$9,000	$8,000	$10,000	
Fixed monthly operating costs	$5,000	$4,000	$6,000	
Variable costs/customer/month	$80	$70	$100	

	Most likely Solution			
Month	No. Customers	Mo. Income	Mo. Expenses	Cum. Mo. Income
1	150	$22,500	$26,000	($3,500)
2				
3				
4				
...24				

Figure C-2. Financial Projections Format

6.   Prepare a 10–15 minute presentation that you would give to summarize results from the initiating phase of the project. Assume the presentation is for a management review to decide if the project should move on to the next phase.

Part 2: Planning

Work with your teammates and instructor to perform all or just some of the following planning tasks for this project.

Tasks

1.   Develop a requirements traceability matrix and a scope statement for the project. Use the templates provided on the companion Website, and review the samples in the text. Remember that the main project goals are to prepare a business plan, get financial backing, handle legal issues, develop marketing materials, find a rental space for the music academy, purchase/develop curriculum, and hire staff so you can open for business by one year from now. Be as specific as possible in describing product characteristics and requirements, as well as key deliverables. For example, assume that you need to rent a space for your business that is in a desirable part of town near other businesses and schools, has enough room for a reception area, technology lab with five computers, two larger band rooms that have soundproofing or can be sound proofed, and five small rooms for private lessons.

2.   Develop a work breakdown structure (WBS) for the project. Break down the work to what you think is an appropriate level. Use the template provided on the companion Website, and review the samples in the text. Print the WBS in list form as a Word file. Be sure the WBS is based on the project charter, scope statement, and other relevant information.

3.   Create a milestone list for this project, and include at least 10 milestones and estimated completion dates for them.

4.   Use the WBS and milestone list you developed in numbers 2 and 3 above to create a Gantt chart and network diagram in Project 2016 for the project. Estimate task durations and enter dependencies, as appropriate. Remember that your scheduled goal for the project is one year. Print the Gantt chart and network diagram.

5.   Develop a cost estimate for developing just the technology lab for your music academy. Assume that you will purchase five personal computers that can connect to the Internet and run several popular music creation and editing programs. Include the costs of the desks, chairs, microphones, keyboards, soundproofing the room, set-up, testing, etc.

6.   Create a quality checklist for ensuring that the business is ready to open its doors. Also define at least two quality metrics for the project. Use the templates and samples provided.

7.   Create a RACI chart for the main tasks and deliverables for the project. Use the template and sample provided.

8. Develop a communications management plan for the project. Use the template and sample provided.

9. Create a probability/impact matrix and list of prioritized risks for the project. Include at least 10 risks. Use the template and sample provided.

10. Prepare a request for proposal for the technology lab (including purchasing the hardware, software, installation, soundproofing, testing, and maintenance) for your music academy and describe at least two procurement issues you need to consider for the project.

11. Prepare a 10–15 minute presentation that you would give to summarize results from the planning phase of the project. Assume the presentation is for a management review to decide if the project should move on to the next phase.

Part 3: Executing

Remember that the main project goals are to prepare a business plan, get financial backing, handle legal issues, develop marketing materials, find a rental space for the music academy, purchase/develop curriculum, and hire staff so you can open for business by one year from now.

Work with your teammates and instructor to perform all or just some of the following executing tasks for this project.

Tasks

1. Write a business plan for this project. Review sample business plans. For example, *www.bplans.com/*, *www.score.org*, and Microsoft Office online (select File, New, Microsoft Online, Plans from within Microsoft Word) provide templates and/or guidelines for preparing business plans. Decide on a name for this business, as well. Include, at a minimum, the following sections in a five- to eight-page paper:

    *   Executive Summary

    *   Company Description

    *   Products and Services

    *   Marketing Plan

    *   Operational Plan

    *   Management Summary

    *   Financial Plan

2. Research options for getting small business loans. For example, most governments have a small business administration office that offers loans or loan information. (See *www.sba.gov* for U.S. information.) Several colleges provide loans to alumni. You can also go to banks and credit card companies for funds. Develop a list of at least five different, realistic

options for getting financial backing for your new business. Recall that you estimate that you will need $100,000 the first year alone, and you are still short $30,000. Include the source of the funds, interest rates, payment arrangements, etc. Document your results in a two- to three-page paper, including a recommendation on which option to pursue.

3. Create a one-page flier for your new business, a home page for a Website, and a tri-fold brochure listing key services/courses of the business, and any other marketing materials you think you would need for your business.

4. Research options for a rental space for the music academy. Develop at least five alternative sites. Include a picture of the site, if available, square footage, cost, pros and cons, etc. Document the results and make a recommendation for which site to select in a three- to four-page paper.

5. Assume that you decide to have students sign up for weekly individual instruction on a term basis. You will offer a fall, spring, and two summer terms consisting of 12 hours of instruction in each. Half of the hour will be one-on-one with an instructor, and the other half will be in the music technology lab. You will also have several rock band courses with three to five students each that will meet weekly for six weeks, followed by a performance. Research where to purchase curriculum or what is involved in developing it, if needed, for the following courses:

    - Basic, intermediate, and advanced keyboard

    - Basic, intermediate, and advanced bass

    - Basic, intermediate, and advanced guitar

    - Basic, intermediate, and advanced percussion/drums

    - Basic, intermediate, and advanced voice

    - Basic, intermediate, and advanced rock band

6. Include a one-page curriculum sheet for each course and a one-page schedule for all of the courses, including times for performances for the rock band. Also include a performance each term for students taking the individual lessons.

7. Create a plan for hiring staff for your new business. Assume that you will work full-time as the main manager, providing some front-desk coverage, giving some lessons, and managing most of the business. Assume that Nicole will also work full-time, heading up the vocal lessons area, marketing, and providing some front-desk coverage. Brian will lead the music technology lab development, outsourcing a fair amount of the work. He will also teach some of the rock band ensembles in the evenings or on weekends. Andres will help with marketing and give percussion instructions as his schedule allows. You will also need to hire a part-time receptionist to always have front-desk and phone coverage. You also need to hire several part-time instructors for all of the classes provided. Include job descriptions for all of the positions, salary/pay information, and a work schedule. Document your results in a four- to six-page paper.

8. Assume that the following has occurred since the project started: As usual, you ended up taking lead of this team, but you're starting to get burned out. You are four months into the project. You are still working your full-time job, and your spouse has been complaining that you work too much and aren't delegating enough. Nicole quit her telemarketing job to focus on this new business, and she is getting nervous about the business actually opening. Andres promised to get a big list of potential students and instructors to you for the past two months, but he still hasn't delivered it. Brian thinks that he can set up the whole music technology lab instead of outsourcing it, as you planned. Write a two- to three-page paper describing how you would handle these challenges.

Part 4: Monitoring and Controlling
Background Scenario:

You are six months into the project. You completed the business plan and most of the marketing materials. You had planned to have the location for your business selected and additional start-up funds by now, but you are behind schedule. Brian and Nicole seem to disagree on a lot of key decisions, especially the location. Your mother calls at least three times a week asking how things are going. You are happy that she lives 500 miles away, but you know that she needs assurance that the business will actually open. Andres is in charge of purchasing/developing the curriculum, but he has had very little time to work on it since school is in session. You want him to focus on creating a list of potential students and instructors, so you might hire someone else to help with the curriculum.

Work with your teammates and instructor to perform all or just some of the following monitoring and controlling tasks for this project.

Tasks

1. Create a new Gantt chart based on the revised information above, if needed. Briefly describe other plans you have created so far that you think you should update in a one- to two-page paper.

2. Prepare an agenda for a team meeting to discuss several of the issues you are facing. You definitely want to decide on the location at this meeting, since it is down to two and you have to decide soon. Also write a one- to two-page paper summarizing how you will approach particular people during the meeting.

3. Prepare a 10–15 slide presentation to give to potential funders for your business. Use information from your business plan.

4. Write a two- to three-page statement of work to hire someone to help you purchase/develop the curriculum. Use the template and sample provided.

5. Review the Seven Basic Tools of Quality. Based on the current project scenario, pick one of these tools and create a chart/diagram to help you solve problems you are facing. Use the templates and samples provided.

6.   Update your list of prioritized risks. Create a risk register entry for two of them. Use the template and sample provided.

Part 5: Closing

Background Scenario:

It is one month before you plan to open your new business. You just got into your leased building, and you are busy starting to get it ready to open. You have hired a small construction firm to put in a few walls, do some painting, etc. You also got a lot of help from family and friends. You quit your job, and Nicole is also working every day now on the new business. She did a great job at marketing, and you are getting calls and e-mails from your new Website every day. Brian's friend, Tom, built the site for you at no charge after Brian said he could come in and use the technology lab when it wasn't busy. Eric, the person you hired to help with the curriculum, was a fantastic resource, even though it cost you $10,000 you had not planned on spending. He did help you expand your list of potential students and instructors, as well, since he knew the local market very well. You did meet your schedule goal, but you had to borrow another $10,000 from your mom. She is only charging you 5% interest, starting when your doors open. She is happy with the results and has already booked a flight to visit for your grand opening celebration, where you and your team will be performing. Your mom loves to cook and bake, so she volunteered to handle the food for the opening.

Work with your teammates and instructor to perform all or just some of the following closing tasks for this project.

Tasks

1.   You have scheduled a final project presentation two days before your grand opening. Prepare a 10–15 slide presentation to summarize the results of the project. Describe the initial project goals, planned versus actual scope, time, and cost information, challenges faced, and key products produced.

2.   Prepare a lessons-learned report for the entire project. Include input from all stakeholders in summarizing the lessons learned. Use the template and sample provided, and be creative in your response.

3.   Prepare a final project report, using information from your final project presentation and the template provided. Be sure to include all of the documents you have prepared as appendices.

4.   Document your own list of best practices that you think helped or could have helped you on this project in a two- to three-page paper.

CASE 3: FIXER UPPER

This case should be interesting to anyone interested in purchasing a house that needs some fixing up. It involves research, procurement, finance, technology, and personal ethics. The main purpose of this and other cases, however, is to help you practice some of the project management skills you are developing as part of your course. (Note: Instructors should feel free to modify background information or tasks. This case is based on a true story! If you would like more details and actual photos, please consult the author.)

Part 1: Initiating

Background Scenario:

Many people today cannot afford to buy a home, including you! Your favorite Aunt Julie, however, has some extra money, and she has been disappointed with the low returns she has been getting on her investments. She knows that many houses are priced to sell, and mortgage rates are low to those who qualify. Julie already bought a second home that she uses as a vacation property, and she is interested in owning more real estate as an investment. She would really like to buy a property and act more like a bank than a landlord. Why should a bank get 4% or more in interest for a loan when she can only get a little over 1% on a savings account? You told her that you would love to stay in the area for a very long time and live in a house, but you could not qualify for a loan yourself. You would be happy to find roommates to help pay rent and help your financial situation, too. Julie agrees to go house-hunting with you, and she is willing to pay up to $350,000 for the right property, including any renovations. (Note that this amount may vary by location. The number here is based on northern California, where that would be a low number. Check with your instructor about the amount for your particular case.) Julie suggests you look for a 3 or 4 bedroom house with at least 2 full bathrooms. She also suggests that you try to find a house that is in a nice area but needs some remodeling, but not more than $40,000 of work, including "sweat equity," meaning the two of you plus some family and friends should be willing to help out without pay.

Work with your teammates and instructor to perform all or just some of the following initiating tasks for this project.

Tasks

1. Research the rental market for single-family houses in your area or another area where you would like to live and work for a long time. Find at least three references about investing in rental properties and advice on finding a good fixer upper. Prepare a short paper and presentation summarizing your findings.

2. Determine a location where you would like to live for at least ten years and where you think your aunt would like to buy a property. (Note: Check with your instructor to agree on a location or ask someone you know who would really like to pursue this idea. If you cannot decide, select northern California, within a 20- mile radius of San Jose.) Your aunt wants to make sure it's a good investment, so be realistic in determining a property and a location. For example, research the population trends and rental homes available for the area and what's available given the cost and size requirements. Also assume that you will have to find one to three roommates who will help you pay for rent each month. Document your research and three potential locations in a one- to two-page paper. Try to narrow the locations to a certain part of a city or town, not a whole city. Find five sample houses in each area that meet your aunt's criteria (3 or more bedrooms, 2 or more full baths, good investment potential, under $310,000 before renovations (or your agreed-upon amount). Use a real estate website like www.zillow.com to find information.

3.   Prepare a stakeholder register and management strategy for the project. Include all project team members and make up names and information for the following: a realtor to aid in house-hunting, a bank who will lend Julie money to refinance her current home so she can pay cash to purchase this investment property, a contractor who can do a lot of renovation work at a great price, and friends and family you think could help fix up a house. Assume that your Aunt Julie is very knowledgeable about finances and purchasing and renovating houses but only handy when it comes to painting. She's also very organized and cost-conscious and leads a very busy life. Assume that you have a relative in the area you choose, Nick, who can help with a lot of basic renovations on weekends. Assume you will have some other friends (your classmates in this case) and family who can help with some of the work for free, and you know a few skilled acquaintances (an electrician and a plumber) whom you would need to pay for their services, but you think they'd give you a nice discount. Use the templates provided on the companion Website, and review the sample stakeholder register and management strategy in the text.

4.   Prepare a project charter for the Fixer Upper Project. Assume the project will take six months to complete and cost about $350,000 (or agreed upon price), that you estimate you will spend $40,000 for renovations. The first three months of the project will involve finding and closing on the property, and the last three months will involve fixing up the property, finding renters (preferably two renters), and preparing financial information for you and your aunt. Assume the project starts on October 1 and finishes on April 1. Recall that the main project objectives are to find and renovate a house that your Aunt Julie would own but you would live in and be able to rent out one to three rooms. Julie has also agreed that she will let you earn equity on the house. As she has said to you a few times, "Pretend I'm your banker, and it's your home." You will do all of the renovation planning work, including creating detailed cost estimates for all of the renovations, preparing a detailed schedule for the renovations, overseeing renovations, preparing a rental agreement and a strategy for finding renters, and creating a spreadsheet to analyze your "mortgage" payments and other financial information. Use the project charter template provided on the companion Website, and review the sample in the text.

5.   Prepare an initial scope statement for the project. Assume that your Aunt Julie is doing the work to find and close on the house, which will take three months and be completed by January 1. The main scope of your work is to plan and oversee the renovations of the house, find renters, and prepare a spreadsheet for financial analysis. Your aunt wants you to get at least three bids on all major expenses, like the flooring and windows. Define key deliverables in as much detail as you can, asking your instructor for guidance if needed. Even though you will not actually find and renovate a house, describe the work as if you were. Assume that the main renovations you will need to do include the following: tent the house to get rid of termites and other insects; rent a dumpster to get rid of a lot of junk in the yard and house, like the old carpet and kitchen materials; totally remodel the kitchen (new cabinets, appliances, sink, lights, counter tops, etc.); buy a new furnace, washer and dryer, sump pump, and several electrical outlets; replace all the windows; put in laminate flooring in the entire house (except the bathrooms); paint the entire inside of the house, and spruce up the yard by removing some old shrubs, planting flowers, repairing the wooden fence, and leveling and seeding the lawn. (Note: If you find an actual property, feel free to change the renovation work as desired.)

6. Complete a draft schedule in Excel for your class team to work on this case study. Include all of the tasks in this case study using the main categories of initiating, planning, executing, monitoring and controlling, and closing. Break down the executing work to what you think is an appropriate level. The main executing deliverables should be a renovation cost estimate, renovation schedule, rental strategy, and financial spreadsheet. Be sure the WBS is based on the project charter, scope statement, and other relevant information. Estimate how many hours each of your team members will spend on each task in the Excel file. See the draft schedule template on www.intropm.com.

7. Prepare a 10–15 minute presentation to summarize results from the initiating phase of the project. Assume the presentation is for a management review to decide if the project should move on to the next phase. Be sure that all of your project documents are on a website that you share with your instructor for viewing only.

Part 2: Planning

Background Scenario: Congratulations on finding a property! It has 4 bedrooms and 2 full baths, is one-story, has a nice open family/dining area, and decent yard. It is one of the cheapest houses on the street, and neighbors are happy you are moving in and plan to fix it up! The previous owner kicked out the previous renters and decided to sell it instead of fixing it up. You love the location and are excited to fix it up and move in. Your aunt is taking care of the financing and other paperwork, and you close on the property on January 1. Your main concern is how to redo the whole kitchen without spending a fortune, and you have a good friend/relative who will fly in town to do the total kitchen remodel if you pay him or her $1,000 plus transportation, meals, and a couple of nights on the town. You will make sure you buy the pre-assembled cabinets, appliances, etc. before he/she arrives. You decide to have laminate flooring installed in 1500 feet of the house (everywhere except the two bathrooms) and get three bids for the job from professional companies. All of the interior walls need to be painted, and the yard needs a good clean-up. One section of the fence also needs to be repaired, and you need a new sliding glass door with a doggie door for the family room. Your aunt suggests that you replace all of the windows to make the house more energy efficient. At least they are all standard sizes. You also need a new furnace, sump pump, washer and dryer, and associated electrical work for them. You also want to replace most of the light fixtures and put in a couple of ceiling fans. Your aunt would like you to try to get all of this work done for under $40,000. She will fly out and do a lot of painting and yard clean-up, and you and some friends and relatives will do some of the simpler work (like gutting the kitchen, taking out the old carpeting, fixing the fence, helping with the painting, and cleaning up the yard), but you will hire professionals as needed for the other work. Work with your teammates and instructor to perform all or just some of the following planning tasks for this project.

Tasks

1. Develop a requirements traceability matrix and a more detailed scope statement for the project. Use the templates provided on the companion Website, and review the samples in the text.

2. Create a milestone list for the executing part of the renovation part of this project, and include at least 10 milestones and estimated completion dates for them. Assume that you

close on the house on Jan. 1, you and some friends will tear out the carpeting, gut the kitchen, and prepare the walls for painting the first two weeks in January, and you, your aunt, and three friends will paint the interior walls the third weekend in January. Assume your friend will fly in the first week of February. You will have the flooring and windows put in as soon as possible after the kitchen is done and do other necessary work so that you can move in by Feb. 20 and then start showing some rooms to potential renters. Ideally you would like the house to look like a home and have two renters sign agreements no later than April 1.

3. Use the WBS you created earlier, the milestone list you developed in numbers 2 above, and the new information provided to create an initial Gantt chart and network diagram in Project 2016 for the project. Create one Gantt chart for the actual fixer upper project, assuming a start date of October 1 and end date of April 1. Create a second Gantt chart for your team to do this case study, including all the project management tasks and the dates of your class for them. (You will break down the renovation work in more detail in the Executing part of this project.) Estimate task durations and enter dependencies, as appropriate. Print the Gantt chart and network diagram.

4. Create a quality checklist for ensuring that the remodeling goes well. Also define at least two quality metrics for the project. Use the templates and samples provided.

5. Create a RACI chart for the main tasks and deliverables for the project, focusing on what you and your class mates need to do. Use the template and sample provided.

6. Create a probability/impact matrix and list of prioritized risks for the renovation part of the project. Include at least 10 risks. Use the template and sample provided.

7. Prepare a 10–15 minute presentation that you would give to summarize results from the planning phase of the project. Assume the presentation is for a management review to decide if the project should move on to the next phase.

Part 3: Executing

1. Develop a cost estimate for all of the renovations. Try to get real bids from real contractors and search for actual costs for materials, such as appliances, cabinets, etc. Include photos of potential items as well. Be sure to list all of your major assumptions, and document your results in a spreadsheet format. Make it easy to change inputs, such as cost per foot of flooring, number of windows, cost for appliances, the furnace, etc.

2. Prepare a more detailed Gantt chart for just the renovations part of the project. Be aware of dependencies, such as washing the walls before priming them and priming them before painting them. Document questions you have in preparing this Gantt chart to discuss with your instructor.

3. Prepare a strategy for finding renters, developing a rental agreement, and collecting and making payments. You know what you need to pay your Aunt Julie every month, but you need to figure out what to charge renters and how to manage your personal cash flow. Research methods for finding renters in the area and find good samples of rental agreements. Also research various tax strategies your aunt could use to minimize paying

taxes on this property. (Hint: Look into "gifting.") Document your findings and recommendations in a 2-3 page report, plus references and attachments as needed.

4. Create a spreadsheet to summarize financial information that includes four sheets called Loan, Cash Flow, Investment, and Sell. Name the first sheet Loan and figure out your monthly payments and interest paid on a loan from your Aunt Julie for $350,000 over 30 years, using realistic interest rates. (Hint: Look into loan amortization schedules and current mortgage rates). Add a second sheet call Cash Flow to show your total monthly expenses, including the cost for utilities, taxes (assume $3,500 per year, increasing 3% per year), homeowners insurance, basic maintenance, etc. on top of the payment you make to your aunt. Also include other expenses, such as food, gas, car payments, etc. Add your projected income, including money you would receive from renters. Assume you earn $50,000/year at your job and pay taxes, of course. Determine your monthly cash flow for a year. Add a third sheet called Investment to show your aunt that she is making a good investment, assuming she could have invested the same amount of money ($350,000) in a safe, low-interest investment. Add a fourth sheet called Sell that assumes you sell the house in ten years for $450,000. Suggest options to your aunt for how to handle that situation, including your equity in the house.

Part 4: Monitoring and Controlling

Background Scenario:

You and your friends had fun gutting the kitchen and tearing out the ugly carpets in the house. Painting the walls went well, and the house already looks much better. Your friend flew in to install the kitchen cabinets, appliances, and so on. However, when you try to put the refrigerator in, you realize that the ceiling is 6 inches too low. Your friend says he/she can raise the ceiling, but it will take at least a full day of work, and he/she will not have time to put in the counter tops or skim coat and paint the ceiling. You think your relative, Nick, can do that for you, but he is very busy. You cleaned up the yard pretty well, but now you discover that you have gophers. You don't want to try to level the back yard or plant new grass seed until you can get rid of your gopher problem.

Work with your teammates and instructor to perform all or just some of the following monitoring and controlling tasks for this project.

Tasks

1. Discuss with your team members what you can do to convince your relative, Nick, to install your laminate counter tops and finish the kitchen ceiling. Also get at least two bids for what it would cost to hire someone to do the work. (Hint: Local hardware stores often do this kind of work). Prepare a short paper summarizing the information.

2. Research different approaches for getting rid of gophers and make a recommendation on what to do in a short paper. Include three references.

3. Review the Seven Basic Tools of Quality. Based on the current project scenario, pick one of these tools and create a chart/diagram to help you solve problems you are facing. Use the templates and samples provided.

4. Update your list of prioritized risks. Create a risk register entry for two of them. Use the template and sample provided.

Part 5: Closing

Background Scenario:

It is March 1. You moved into the renovated house on Feb. 20, as planned. Several of your family, friends, and co-workers helped you with furnishing and decorating the house, and it is starting to feel like a home. You tried your first approach to get rid of the gophers, but it has not worked. You decide to wait a few months and deal with the back yard then. A friend of a friend is very interested in renting a room, and you are excited about that. One of your other relatives, a 21-year-old who dropped out of college and is working 20-30 hours a week at a local hardware store, has moved in. He can only contribute $200/month toward rent, but he is very handy, loves your two small dogs, and you like having him around. Your Aunt Julie strongly encouraged you to let him live with you until he decides what to do with his life. You feel very lucky to be living in your own house and want to learn more about doing things like landscaping.

Work with your teammates and instructor to perform all or just some of the following closing tasks for this project.

Tasks

1. Your Aunt Julie is coming to visit March 16-18 as part of her vacation. She has not seen the house since she came to help paint. You've been sending her pictures and getting her advice along the way, but you really want to impress her and thank her for what she's done. Prepare a 10–15 slide presentation to summarize the results of the renovation project. Describe the initial project goals, planned versus actual scope, time, and cost information, challenges faced, and before and after pictures (be creative in finding pictures).

2. Prepare a lessons-learned report for the entire project, focusing on what you and your class mates learned about project management and investing in a fixer upper. Include input from all stakeholders in summarizing the lessons learned. Use the template and sample provided, and be creative in your response.

3. Prepare a final project report, using information from progress reports and your final project presentation and the template provided. Be sure to include all of the documents you have prepared as appendices.

GLOSSARY

activity – A distinct, scheduled portion of work performed during the course of a project.

activity attributes — Information that provides schedule-related information about each activity, such as predecessors, successors, logical relationships, leads and lags, resource requirements, constraints, imposed dates, and assumptions related to the activity.

activity list — A tabulation of activities to be included on a project schedule.

activity-on-arrow (AOA) approach, or the **arrow diagramming method (ADM)** — A network diagramming technique in which activities are represented by arrows and connected at points called nodes to illustrate the sequence of activities.

actual cost (AC) — The realized cost incurred for the work performed on an activity during a specific time period.

agile — able to move quickly and easily.

analogous estimates, or **top-down estimates** — The estimates that use the actual cost of a previous, similar project as the basis for estimating the cost of the current project.

balanced scorecard — A methodology that converts an organization's value drivers to a series of defined metrics.

baseline — A starting point, a measurement, or an observation that is documented so that it can be used for future comparison; also defined as the original project plans plus approved changes.

benchmarking — The process of generating ideas for quality improvements by comparing specific project practices or product characteristics to those of other projects or products within or outside of the performing organization.

best practice — A procedure that has been shown by research and experience to produce optimal results and that is established or proposed as a standard suitable for widespread adoption.

best practice — An optimal way recognized by industry to achieve a stated goal or objective.

bid — A document prepared by sellers providing pricing for standard items that have been clearly defined by the buyer.

blogs — Easy-to-use journals on the Web that allow users to write entries, create links, and upload pictures, while allowing readers to post comments to particular journal entries.

bottom-up estimates — Cost estimates created by estimating individual activities and summing them to get a project total.

budget at completion (BAC) — The approved total budget for the project.

buffer — Additional time to complete a activity, added to an estimate to account for various factors.

burst — An occurrence when two or more activities follow a single node on a network diagram.

capabilities — The incremental steps leading up to one or more best practices.

cash flow — Benefits minus costs, or income minus expenses.

cause-and-effect diagrams — Also called fishbone or Ishikawa diagrams, these diagrams can assist in ensuring and improving quality by finding the root causes of quality problems.

charismatic— These people can inspire others based on their enthusiasm and confidence.

collaborating mode — The conflict-handling mode where decision makers incorporate different viewpoints and insights to develop consensus and commitment.

communications management plan — A document that guides project communications.

compromise mode — The conflict-handling mode that uses a give-and-take approach to resolve conflicts.

conformance to requirements — The process of ensuring that the project's processes and products meet written specifications.

confrontation mode — The conflict-handling mode that involves directly facing a conflict using a problem-solving approach that allows affected parties to work through their disagreements.

constructive change orders — Oral or written acts or omissions by someone with actual or apparent authority that can be construed to have the same effect as a written change order.

contingency plans — The predefined actions that the project team will take if an identified risk event occurs.

contingency reserves or **contingency allowances** — The funds held by the project sponsor that can be used to mitigate cost or schedule overruns if known risks occur.

contracts — The mutually binding agreements that obligate the seller to provide the specified products or services, and obligate the buyer to pay for them.

control account — A management control point for performance measurement where scope, budget, and schedule are integrated and compared to the earned value.

control chart — A graphical display of data that illustrates the results of a process over time.

cost baseline — A time-phased budget that project managers use to measure and monitor cost performance.

cost-reimbursable contract — A contract that involves payment to the seller for direct and indirect actual costs.

crashing — A technique for making cost and schedule trade-offs to obtain the greatest amount of schedule compression for the least incremental cost.

critical chain scheduling — A method of scheduling that takes limited resources into account when creating a project schedule and includes buffers to protect the project completion date.

critical path — The series of activities that determine the *earliest* time by which the project can be completed; it is the *longest* path through the network diagram and has the least amount of slack or float.

critical path method (CPM), or **critical path analysis** — A network diagramming technique used to predict total project duration and show the amount of schedule flexibility on the network paths within the schedule model.

dependency, or **relationship** — The sequencing of project activities.

directives — The new requirements imposed by management, government, or some external influence.

discount factor — A multiplier for each year based on the discount rate and year.

discount rate — The rate used in discounting future cash flows.

discretionary costs — costs that organizations have discretion in deciding whether to fund them

discretionary dependencies — The dependencies that are defined by the project team.

duration — The actual amount of time spent working on an activity *plus* elapsed time.

earned value (EV) — The measure of work performed expressed in terms of the budget authorized for that work.

earned value management (EVM) — A project performance measurement technique that integrates scope, time, and cost data.

effort — The number of workdays or work hours required to complete an activity.

empathic listening — The process of listening with the intent to understand by putting yourself in the shoes of the other person.

estimate at completion (EAC) — A forecast of how much the project will cost upon completion.

ethics — A set of principles that guide our decision making based on personal values of what is "right" and "wrong."

explicit knowledg — Knowledge that can be easily explained using words, pictures, or numbers and is easy to communicate, store, and distribute.

external dependencies — The dependencies that involve relationships between project and non-project activities.

extrinsic motivation — A motivation that causes people to do something for a reward or to avoid a penalty.

fallback plans — The plans that are developed for risks that have a high impact on meeting project objectives, and are put into effect if attempts to reduce the risk are not effective.

fast tracking — A schedule compression technique where you do activities in parallel that you would normally do in sequence.

Federal Acquisition Regulation (FAR) — Regulation that provides uniform policies for acquisition of supplies and services by executive agencies in the U.S.

feeding buffers — Additional time added before activities on the critical path that are preceded by non-critical-path activities.

fitness for use — The ability of a product to be used as it was intended.

fixed-price or **lump-sum contract** — A type of contract that involves a fixed price for a well-defined product or service.

flowcharts — The graphic displays of the logic and flow of processes that help you analyze how problems occur and how processes can be improved.

forcing mode — The conflict-handling mode that involves exerting one's viewpoint at the potential expense of another viewpoint.

forecasts — Reports that predict future project status and progress based on past information and trends.

Gantt charts — A standard format for displaying project schedule information by listing project activities and their corresponding start and finish dates in a calendar format.

groupthink — The conformance to the values or ethical standards of a group.

histogram — A bar graph of a distribution of variables.

integrated change control — The process of identifying, evaluating, and managing changes throughout the project's life cycle.

interactional— This leadership style is a combination of transactional, transformational, and charismatic.

internal rate of return (IRR) — The discount rate that results in an NPV of zero for a project.

intrinsic motivation — A motivation that causes people to participate in an activity for their own enjoyment.

issue — a matter under question or dispute that could impede project success.

issue log — a tool used to document, monitor, and track issues that need to be resolved for effective work to take place.

key performance indicator (KPI) — A criterion used to determine the degree to which an outcome is achieved.

knowledge transfer — The process of communicating knowledge that was developed by one person or in one part of an organization to another person or other parts of an organization.

lag — when an activity requires a gap in time before it can start.

laissez-faire— Meaning "let go," this hands-off approach lets teams determine their own goals and how to achieve them.

lead — when an activity can overlap a preceding one.

leader — A person who focuses on long-term goals and big-picture objectives, while inspiring people to reach those goals.

lean — a system based on the Toyota Production System to help improve results and efficiency by eliminating waste and reducing idle time and non-value added activities.

make-or-buy analysis — The process of estimating the internal costs of providing a product or service and comparing that estimate to the cost of outsourcing.

management reserves — Funds held for unknown risks that are used for management control purposes.

manager — A person who deals with the day-to-day details of meeting specific goals.

mandatory dependencies — The dependencies that are inherent in the nature of the work being performed on a project.

Maslow's hierarchy of needs — A hierarchy that states that people's behaviors are guided or motivated by a sequence of needs (physiological, safety, social, esteem, and self-actualization).

maturity model — A framework for helping organizations improve their processes and systems.

megaproject — A very large project that typically costs over US $1 billion, affects over one million people, and lasts several years.

merge — A situation when two or more nodes precede a single node on a network diagram.

metric — A standard of measurement.

milestone — A significant point or event in a project.

mind mapping — A technique that uses branches radiating out from a core idea to structure thoughts and ideas.

mirroring — The matching of certain behaviors of the other person.

Monte Carlo simulation — quantitative risk analysis technique that provides a probability distribution for outcome values for the whole project.

multitasking — When a resource works on more than one activity at a time.

Murphy's Law — If something can go wrong, it will.

Myers-Briggs Type Indicator (MBTI) — A popular tool for determining personality preferences.

net present value (NPV) analysis — A method of calculating the expected net monetary gain or loss from a project by discounting all expected future cash inflows and outflows to the present point in time.

network diagram — A schematic display of the logical relationships among, or sequencing of, project activities.

node — The starting and ending point of an activity on an activity-on-arrow network diagram.

nondiscretionary costs — costs that organizations must fund to stay in business

opportunity cost of capital — The return available by investing the capital elsewhere.

organizational process assets — Policies and procedures related to project management, past project files, and lessons-learned reports from previous, similar projects.

organizational project management — a framework in which portfolio, program, and project management are integrated with organizational enablers in order to achieve strategic objectives.

outcomes — The tangible or intangible results of applying capabilities.

overallocation — When more resources than are available are assigned to perform work at a given time.

parametric modeling — A technique that uses project characteristics (parameters) in a mathematical model to estimate project costs.

Pareto chart — A histogram that can help you identify and prioritize problem areas.

Parkinson's Law — Work expands to fill the time allowed.

payback period — The amount of time it will take to recoup, in the form of net cash inflows, the total dollars invested in a project.

planned value (PV) — The authorized budget assigned to scheduled work.

portfolio — Projects, programs, subsidiary portfolios, and operations managed as a group to achieve strategic objectives.

post-mortem — A term sometimes used for a project close-out meeting since it is held after the project has died or been put to rest.

precedence diagramming method (PDM) — A network diagramming technique in which boxes represent activities.

process analysis — Analyzing how a process operates and determining improvements.

procurement statement of work (SOW) — A document that describes the goods or services to be purchased.

program — A group of related projects, subsidiary programs, and program activities managed in a coordinated manner to obtain benefits not available from managing them individually.

Program Evaluation and Review Technique (PERT) — A network analysis technique used to estimate project duration when there is a high degree of uncertainty about the individual activity duration estimates.

program manager — A person who provides leadership and direction for the project managers heading the projects within the program.

progress reports — Reports that describe what the project team has accomplished during a certain period.

project — A temporary endeavor undertaken to create a unique product, service, or result.

project buffer — The additional time added before a project's due date to account for unexpected factors.

project dashboard — A graphic screen summarizing key project metrics.

project management — The application of knowledge, skills, tools, and techniques to project activities to meet project requirements.

Project Management Institute (PMI) — International professional society for project managers.

project management knowledge areas — Project integration management, scope, schedule, cost, quality, human resource, communications, risk, and procurement management.

project management plan — A document used to coordinate all project planning documents and to help guide a project's execution and control.

project management process groups — Initiating, planning, executing, monitoring and controlling, and closing.

Project Management Professional (PMP®) — Certification provided by PMI that requires documenting project experience, agreeing to follow the PMI code of ethics, and passing a comprehensive exam.

project management tools and techniques — Methods available to assist project managers and their teams; some popular tools in the time management knowledge area include Gantt charts, network diagrams, critical path analysis, and project management software.

project manager — The person responsible for working with the project sponsor, the project team, and the other people involved in a project to meet project goals.

project organizational chart — A graphical representation of how authority and responsibility is distributed within the project.

project portfolio management — The grouping and managing of projects and programs as a portfolio of investments.

project sponsor — The person who provides the direction and funding for a project.

proposal — A document in which sellers describe what they will do to meet the requirements of a buyer.

quality — The degree to which a set of inherent characteristics fulfill requirements.

quality assurance — The activities related to satisfying the relevant quality standards for a project.

quality audit — A structured review of specific quality management activities that helps identify lessons learned, which could improve performance on current or future projects.

RACI charts — A type of responsibility assignment matrix that shows **R**esponsibility, **A**ccountability, **C**onsultation, and **I**nformed roles for project stakeholders.

rapport — A relationship of harmony, conformity, accord, or affinity.

Request for Proposal (RFP) — A document used to solicit proposals from prospective suppliers.

Request for Quote (RFQ) — A document used to solicit quotes or bids from prospective suppliers.

required rate of return — The minimum acceptable rate of return on an investment.

requirement — A condition or capability that is necessary to be present in a product, service, or result to satisfy a business need.

requirements management plan — A plan that describes how project requirements will be analyzed, documented and managed.

requirements traceability matrix (RTM) — A table that lists requirements, various attributes of each requirement, and the status of the requirements to ensure that all of them are addressed.

resource histogram — A column chart that shows the number of resources required for or assigned to a project over time.

resource leveling — A technique for resolving resource conflicts by delaying tasks.

resource loading — The amount of individual resources an existing schedule requires during specific time periods.

responsibility assignment matrix (RAM) — A matrix that maps the work of the project as described in the WBS to the people responsible for performing the work.

return on investment (ROI) — (Benefits minus costs) divided by costs.

risk — An uncertainty that can have a negative or positive effect on meeting project objectives.

risk events — The specific, uncertain events that may occur to the detriment or enhancement of the project.

risk register — A document that contains results of various risk management processes, often displayed in a table or spreadsheet format.

root cause — The real or underlying reason a problem occurs.

run chart — A chart that displays the history and pattern of variation of a process over time.

scatter diagram — A diagram that helps show if there is a relationship between two variables.

scope baseline — The approved project scope statement and its associated WBS and WBS dictionary.

scope creep — The tendency for project scope to continually increase.

scope statement — Document that describes product characteristics and requirements, user acceptance criteria, and deliverables.

scope validation — The formal acceptance of the completed project deliverables by the customer or designated stakeholders.

servant leader — People using this approach focus on relationships and community first and leadership is secondary.

short list — A list of the top three to five suppliers created to reduce the work involved in selecting a source.

slack or **float** — The amount of time an activity may be delayed without delaying a succeeding activity or the project finish date.

slipped milestone — A milestone activity that was completed later than originally planned.

smoothing mode — The conflict-handling mode that de-emphasizes or avoids areas of differences and emphasizes areas of agreement.

staffing management plan — A plan that describes when and how people will be added to and taken off of a project.

stakeholders — People involved in or affected by project activities.

status reports — Reports that describe where the project stands at a specific point in time.

strategic planning — The process of determining long-term objectives by analyzing the strengths and weaknesses of an organization, studying opportunities and threats in the business environment, predicting future trends, and projecting the need for new products and services.

stratification — A technique used to separate data to see patterns in data.

SWOT analysis — Analyzing **S**trengths, **W**eaknesses, **O**pportunities, and **T**hreats.

synergy — The concept that the whole is equal to more than the sum of its parts.

tacit knowledge— Sometimes called informal knowledge, this type of knowledge is difficult to express and is highly personal.

task – Work that is done in support of operational, functional, or project performance. Tasks are not part of the schedule (activities are shown on the schedule). Tasks include many management functions such as things done to manage the team, run a production line, or build relationships.

team charter — A document created to help promote teamwork and clarify team communications.

Theory of Constraints (TOC) — A management philosophy that states that any complex system at any point in time often has only one aspect or constraint that is limiting its ability to achieve more of its goal.

three-point estimate — An estimate that includes an optimistic, most likely, and pessimistic estimate.

time-and-material contract — A type of contract that is a hybrid of both a fixed-price and cost-reimbursable contract.

to-complete performance index (TCPI) — The measure of the cost performance that must be achieved on the remaining work in order to meet a specified goal, such as the BAC or EAC

tracking Gantt chart — A Gantt chart that compares planned and actual project schedule information.

transactional— This management by exception approach focuses on achieving goals or compliance by offering team members appropriate rewards and punishments.

transformational— By working with others to identify needed changes, these leaders empower others and guide changes through inspiration.

triggers — The indicators or symptoms of actual risk events.

triple constraint — Balancing scope, schedule, and cost goals.

Tuckman model — A model that describes five stages of team development (forming, storming, norming, performing, and adjourning).

validation — formal acceptance of deliverables by the customer and other identified stakeholders.

verification —evaluating if a deliverable complies with a regulation, requirement, specification, or imposed condition.

verified deliverable — A deliverable that has been completed and checked for correctness as part of quality control.

weighted scoring model — A technique that provides a systematic process for basing project selection on numerous criteria.

withdrawal mode — The conflict-handling mode that involves retreating or withdrawing from an actual or potential disagreement.

work breakdown structure (WBS) — A deliverable-oriented grouping of the work involved in a project that defines the total scope of the project.

work breakdown structure (WBS) dictionary — A document that describes detailed information about WBS deliverables, sub-deliverables, and work packages.

work package — A deliverable at the lowest level of the WBS, where it can be appropriately assigned to and managed by a single accountable person.

workarounds — The unplanned responses to risk events.

INDEX

Made in the USA
Columbia, SC
28 November 2021

49711894R00280